Cultural Anthropology & Human Experience

Cultural Anthropology & Human Experience

The Feast of Life

Katherine A. Dettwyler
University of Delaware

WAVELAND
PRESS, INC.
Long Grove, Illinois

For information about this book, contact:
Waveland Press, Inc.
4180 IL Route 83, Suite 101
Long Grove, IL 60047-9580
(847) 634-0081
info@waveland.com
www.waveland.com

10-digit ISBN 1-57766-681-X
13-digit ISBN 978-1-57766-681-3

Printed in the United States of America

7   6   5   4   3   2

To my descendants:

Miranda, Peter, Alexander, and Henry—May your tribe increase!

And in memory of Brett J. Griffin—www.gordie.org

Contents in Brief

Contents

Preface

To the Student

This textbook provides an introduction to the subfield of anthropology known as cultural anthropology. Anthropology is *the study of humans* in all their wild and wonderful diversity. Cultural anthropology focuses specifically on those aspects of human beliefs and practices that are learned (rather than genetically inherited) and that each individual shares with multiple, overlapping groups of other people. Humanity's evolutionary legacy as animals, mammals, and primates underlies and shapes our experiences, and the interactions between culture and biology help us understand human behavior. I have tried to write in a clear, straightforward manner, using an informal style and minimum jargon. In each chapter, the focus is on explaining how the world works, with select ethnographic examples drawn from my own research and experiences, from a handful of ethnographies, and from world events. Each chapter makes explicit how the anthropological perspective can help you understand your own experiences and learn to appreciate cultural diversity.

Students in any introductory course are expected to read extensively, to learn a large body of information (using a fair amount of memorization), to understand terms, concepts, and theories, to remember ethnographic examples from the textbook and lectures, to be able to apply concepts and theories to new data, and to critically analyze data and interpretations of data. This material should challenge you, emotionally as well as intellectually, and motivate you to consciously consider, perhaps for the first time, your own cultural beliefs and practices. You will learn specific information, including different perspectives for looking at the world, that will be of practical use to you for the rest of your life, regardless of your major, or what career you end up pursuing. A course in cultural an-

thropology may not be easy, but it certainly will be rewarding and fun.

A number of specific objectives guided the writing of this text. By the end of the course you should:

- have developed the ability to think logically, objectively, and critically about different cultural beliefs, practices, and social structures (including your own), be able to evaluate them on the basis of Western scientific knowledge and internal logic, and be able to comprehend the consequences—both advantageous and disadvantageous—of alternate cultural belief systems, practices, and social structures to the individual, the group, and the environment;

- understand that humans are "primates with culture"—specifically Great Apes, with a complex overlay of environmental and cultural influences that have consequences for our health and well-being;

- be able to appreciate how *powerful* cultural beliefs and practices can be in shaping human perceptions of the world, and be able to give examples of how culture affects biology and vice versa;

- gain in-depth knowledge of the complexity of culture and realize that "culture" *is not the same thing* as social constructions of "race," "ethnic identity," or "place of geographic origin";

- be mindful of the common underlying structure of political disputes so you can make (at least some) sense of world news;

- understand why/how cultural practices such as female circumcision, honor killings, and breast augmentation surgery make (at least some) sense within the cultures that practice them;

- be able to articulate how an anthropological perspective helps you discern everyday situations and interactions at the local, national, and international levels;

- understand that *anthropology is not just an academic discipline—it is a way of looking at and understanding the world;*
- realize that the emerging concept of *cultural competence* as used in government, health, and business contexts can be both misleading and counterproductive;
- be able to appreciate the variety of ways that cultural beliefs and practices, social structures, and human lifestyles vary around the world and contribute to living a meaningful life.

For success in this course, I recommend the following: (1) read each chapter at least twice: first, prior to the lecture to get the general ideas on those topics, and then again after class, taking careful notes by hand, and thinking about the material and how it relates to the lecture, discussions, and your own life; (2) attend every class meeting, be on time, stay awake, pay attention, take comprehensive notes, participate in discussions, and ask for clarification if you don't understand something; (3) spend three hours outside of class every week for every hour of class time; (4) for studying, put your cell phone on silent and move away from your computer; (5) plan your study time in increments of 45–60 minutes maximum, and then take a short break (this is the most effective way for most people to learn); (6) be aware that *stuff happens*, to everyone— you get sick, your roommate has a romantic crisis, your car gets a flat tire, you have a last-minute opportunity to go to a great concert, you've just fallen in (or out of) love (again), one of your grandparents dies, etc.—therefore, *always keep up with your work*; (7) speak with your professor if you need help—the sooner the better; (8) take advantage of the various academic help resources on campus; there is no need to struggle alone when helpful strategies, support, and advice are readily available; (9) read and know the guidelines for student conduct and academic integrity at your school; and finally (10) be friendly and get to know other students in class so you can study together!

This introductory cultural anthropology textbook focuses on the joy and wonder and awe of the variety of human experience; you are invited to partake of *more than a fraction of the feast* that is life as a human on this planet.

To the Instructor

I have been teaching cultural anthropology since my graduate school days at Indiana University, Bloomington, in the early 1980s, where I was trained as both a biological and a cultural anthropologist. I have taught at the University of Southern Mississippi, Texas A&M University, Millersville University, and the University of Delaware. Most of the time, I used one of the exhaustive and expensive introductory textbooks, even as it got longer and longer, covered more and more topics, and included more and more chapters chock full of ethnographic examples (often of the remote and exotic type), while giving short shrift to the fact that humans are "primates with culture." Eventually, I decided to write my own text, which takes a compelling and original approach to the subject.

This text fits in between an exhaustive (and expensive) introductory text that tries to cover everything, and the shorter, abridged versions that provide just the bare bones of cultural anthropology. It has twelve chapters, which makes it easy to fit into quarter or semester terms, and leaves room for assigning additional readings, exploring your own research, and discussing current events. All the standard topics are covered, but with less emphasis on method and theory and more coverage of a variety of industrial and postindustrial societies. Sex, gender, and sexual orientation are explained clearly, consistently, and in some detail. Chapter 4 includes coverage of medical anthropology, nutritional anthropology, and reproductive anthropology. The chapter on human communication goes beyond spoken language to discuss tactile and visual channels. Two chapters are devoted to human creativity, including music, sports, human modification of the environment and the body, architecture, and the visual and performing arts.

Auxiliary materials—bells and whistles—within the text have been kept to an absolute minimum to reduce distractions and to keep the cost affordable. The photographs have been chosen with great care to illustrate important points. The Instructor's Manual includes summaries of each chapter, student exercises, and a test bank. The exercises can be turned in for homework credit or used as study guides/discussion topics; they can be assigned as is, or modified by you.

Your feedback is welcome and greatly appreciated (kathyd@udel.edu)!

Acknowledgments

Many different people and experiences have contributed to my understanding of anthropology and to the particular approach I take to the teaching of introductory cultural anthropology. Jane Dabaghian of American River Junior College was my very first cultural anthropology professor (1973). She was brilliant, amusing, and a wonderful teacher. From my years as an undergraduate at the University of California, Davis, it was Delbert True who introduced me to Julian Steward, and Richard T. Curley who taught me to think like an anthropologist about religion and kinship. From my graduate school days at Indiana University, I owe the most to my advisor Paul Jamison, who never let me get away with illogical thinking or lack of data to support my ideas. Ivan Karp introduced me to E. E. Evans-Pritchard and Roger M. Keesing, and (most importantly) I met my husband in Ivan's Proseminar in Socio-Cultural Anthropology the first day of graduate school. Emilio Moran taught me about cultural ecology. Although I never took any classes from Harold K. Schneider, and he could never remember who I was—"Are you Steve's girlfriend?"—I still learned economic anthropology from him, through Steven. For that matter, every idea, every thought, every perspective on cultural anthropology that I have is the direct result of almost 34 years of intellectual interaction with my husband and best friend, the cultural anthropologist Steven Dettwyler. My debts to him go far beyond his contributions to this book.

During my years at Texas A&M, I benefited greatly from lively discussions with my colleague Lee Cronk, now at Rutgers University. At the University of Delaware, I have been most influenced by Karen Rosenberg and Ken Ackerman. Feedback from students throughout the years at the University of Southern Mississippi, Texas A&M University, Millersville University, and the University of Delaware has guided and shaped my understanding of what students know, what they know that ain't so, what confuses them, what bores them, and what they find interesting and useful. Many of the chapters in this book are based on lectures developed and tweaked over many years of teaching cultural anthropology, during which I almost always used William Haviland et al.'s excellent introductory textbook.

Steven Dettwyler and Cassady Yoder both read every chapter as it was written and offered numerous helpful suggestions and constructive criticisms. I didn't always follow their advice, and any mistakes remain my own. Alexander Dettwyler read several chapters and found great delight in pointing out problems with his mother's writing.

At Waveland Press, I am extremely grateful to Tom Curtin, my wonderful editor, who has been an enthusiastic supporter of this book from the start, and Jeni Ogilvie, who copyedited and proofread the text with great attention to detail and tracked down the photos I requested for inclusion. Many others at Waveland Press worked on this monumental task as well. I appreciate their faith in me.

To the student who wrote me a note thanking me for teaching him to appreciate more than "a fraction of the feast"—thanks for the great phrase, and I'm sorry I don't remember your name!

Finally, I want to thank the people who have helped keep me more-or-less sane over the years, starting with neuropsychologist Dr. Nancy Leslie of Bryan/College Station, Texas, who provided absolutely critical support following a traumatic brain injury in 1988, as well as "Dr. J" in Delaware, and my friend Karen Rosenberg. My husband Steven, my remarkable children Miranda, Peter, and Alexander, my son-in-law Mark Douglas Hannam, and my grandson Henry Graham Hannam contribute to my life every day.

Cultural Anthropology
& Human Experience

Chefchaouen, Morocco.

1

A FRACTION OF THE FEAST

Introduction to Cultural Anthropology

One of the great things about learning to think like an anthropologist is that you become more aware of how the world works. There are many right ways to live, many fulfilling ways to be a human being.
Life is a feast. *Don't let your assumptions, your fears, or your enculturation during childhood limit you to only* **a fraction of the feast.**

Anthropology literally means "the study of humans." Anthropology as an academic discipline, as a field of study and research, combines aspects of the hard sciences such as chemistry and physics, the social sciences such as history and economics, and the humanities, such as music and literature. Although many other disciplines focus on humans as well, anthropology has three features that distinguish it from other fields of study.

ANTHROPOLOGY'S DISTINCTIVE FEATURES

First, anthropologists study *all humans, everywhere.* Around the planet, wherever you find people living—in big cities, in rural towns and villages, in the tropical rain forest, on steppes, or in mountainous regions—you will find anthropologists studying them. Unlike many other disciplines, anthropology does not limit itself to studying people living in Western industrialized countries, or people who share the basic worldview of the researcher. This is an important hallmark of anthropology—that all people, everywhere, form our knowledge base, and we are interested in both what people have in common as well as how they differ, in every aspect of their lives, and in every corner of the planet.

Second, anthropologists study *all humans, all the time.* Many other fields of study focus exclusively on the present or on the very recent past. Thus, they limit

themselves to people who are currently alive or who were recently alive and left written records of their activities. Anthropologists, on the other hand, are interested in all humans, both living and dead, including those who are recently dead, those who lived 500 or 5,000 or 50,000 years ago, and even those who lived 500,000 to five million years ago, when our distant ancestors had scarcely evolved to the point of being recognizably human. This incredible time depth allows anthropologists to study and test hypotheses about long-term developments in human lifestyles and human biological and cultural evolution. It gives us a perspective on the human species that is unmatched by any other discipline, a viewpoint from which we can discern all sorts of interesting patterns, as well as exceptions to those patterns.

Third, anthropologists study *humans as both biological and cultural beings.* It isn't possible to truly understand humans without acknowledging that we are animals, first and foremost. We must breathe air; drink water; eat food; protect ourselves from predators, accidents, and disease; urinate and defecate; find sexual partners to reproduce with; give birth; raise our children; and, eventually, die. We aren't just any kind of animals, though. We are specifically vertebrates, with internal skeletons; we are placental mammals—warm-blooded, with four-chambered hearts, covered with hair, nourishing our offspring via a placenta before birth and with milk from our mammary glands after birth. We are members of the zoological order Primates. This marks us as a particular type of placental mammal, one that shares many features in common

2

with other primates such as the prosimians, monkeys, and apes. For example, all primates—not just humans—have relatively large brains for their body size and relatively long childhoods, allowing plenty of time to learn the knowledge needed to survive in our physical environments and our complex social worlds.

However, to a greater extent than any other primate, humans modify and shape their biological existence through cultural means—through learned, shared, patterned, and (mostly) adaptive ways of understanding and interacting with the world. We can't fully understand humans without acknowledging the myriad ways that cultural beliefs and practices affect our experiences of life on this planet. Truly, humans are *animals with culture*. And while other primates such as chimpanzees and bonobos may be described as having rudimentary forms of culture, humans have carried the cultural modification of primate life to its most elaborate and diverse extremes, in a vast array of different environmental settings. Humans are endlessly fascinating and incredibly complex, and anthropology provides us with the tools for understanding humans—for understanding ourselves.

Subfields of Anthropology

Traditionally, anthropology has been divided into four subfields, each of which will be described below. These divisions are somewhat arbitrary and have fuzzy, ever-changing borders; much anthropological research draws on two or more of the subfields. However, most college courses focus primarily on one subfield of anthropology, and it is useful to begin our exploration of anthropology with a standard description of the four subfields.

Cultural Anthropology

The first subfield is **cultural anthropology,** also known as social anthropology or socio-cultural anthropology. Cultural anthropologists study living people; they are interested in *what humans do, why they do it*, and what the *consequences* are. The *"what humans do"* part includes all aspects of human behavior and actions, how humans organize themselves, how they conduct and carry out their daily lives and long-term affairs. For example: how do they get their food, how do they organize marriage and reproduction, how do they solve conflicts between individuals and groups,

and what sorts of creative activities do they engage in? The *"why they do it"* part focuses on the reasons underlying human behavior and actions. These reasons can be described using many terms, including: cultural beliefs, ideas, notions, worldviews, assumptions, knowledge, attitudes, perspectives, values, customs, and traditions. The *"consequences"* part includes the impact of different beliefs and practices on the individual, the group, and the environment—including both positive and negative impacts.

Cultural anthropologists focus on the learned aspects of human behavior, while acknowledging that many aspects of our behavior are rooted in our biology and evolutionary history and that much of human life is the result of the complex interaction of our underlying biology and physiology with natural and cultural environments.

Anthropologists may focus on one very narrow aspect of culture, or they may do a broad general study of a group. They may work alone, or as part of an interdisciplinary research team. The results of anthropological fieldwork are then compared to what is already known about this and other groups of people, analyzing both the similarities and differences. The ultimate goals are to understand the wide range of behaviors and actions humans engage in around the world, to understand the underlying belief systems that contribute to these behaviors and actions, and to evaluate the consequences at different levels of analysis.

Archeology

The second subfield of anthropology is **archeology.** Many people think archeology is its own discipline, but it is part of anthropology, just as an apple is a type of fruit or a Jersey is a type of cow. The goals of archeology are exactly the same as those of cultural anthropology—to understand what people do and why, and what the consequences are—but with one significant difference. Archeologists study people who are dead. That is to say, they study people who lived in the past, who are no longer alive, which puts a real crimp in their research methodologies. Archeologists can't live among the people they are studying, because the people are dead. They can't observe the people as they go about their daily lives, because the people are dead. They can't conduct interviews, or have informal chats, or eavesdrop on others' conversations, because the people are dead. They can't participate in daily activities, such as washing clothes or hoeing the corn-field, or become involved in ritual ceremonies or high dramas, because the people are dead. They can't listen to the people's own explanations of why they do what they do, or what it means to them.

In order to obtain the information they need, arche-ologists study **material culture**—the cultural remains that people leave behind. Material culture includes the remains of buildings and other structures such as fences, walls, fortifications, or fish weirs. It includes the garbage tossed out or buried around the settlement, or left be-hind in the houses when the site was abandoned. It in-cludes remains of food items, clothing, jewelry, musical instruments, art objects, and tools. Where burials are present, archeologists examine the objects left in the graves and call in specialized biological anthropologists (also called bioarcheologists or human osteologists) to study the skeletal remains for indications of diet, health, stature, age and sex structure of the population, and for other clues to behavior left behind in the people's physi-cal remains. Archeologists are limited in their acquisi-tion of knowledge and in their interpretations by the na-ture of the research materials—stone tools and pottery last practically forever, while cloth and baskets deterio-rate quickly over time. Beliefs and behaviors don't pre-serve at all—instead, they must be inferred from the pat-terns seen in the material remains.

Historical archeologists study the material re-mains of people who also left behind written records that provide more detailed information about the what, the why, and the various consequences of past patterns of culture.

Biological Anthropology

The third subfield of anthropology is **biological an-thropology,** also known as **physical anthropology.** This is the subfield most directly concerned with humans as physical beings and includes the study of human evolu-tion (paleoanthropology); human genetics; human vari-ation and adaptation at the physical/anatomical and physiological levels; bioarcheology; forensic anthropol-ogy (the analysis of skeletal remains from criminal cases); and the evolution, anatomy, ecology, and behav-ior of the nonhuman primates. Biological anthropolo-gists, like other anthropologists, study all people, every-where, all the time. Thus, they study both living and recently dead populations, as well as our distant ances-tors represented only through the fossil record. They of-ten collaborate with archeologists and cultural anthro-pologists, as well as researchers from other disciplines.

Linguistic Anthropology

The fourth subfield of anthropology is **linguistic anthropology,** which focuses on the use of language and other types of communication in human cultural contexts. Small anthropology departments may not have any linguistic anthropologists, relying on their cultural anthropologists to include these topics in their classes. Larger departments may include historical lin-guists, folklorists, sociolinguists, ethnomusicologists, and experts in the form and structure of various lan-guages. Linguistic anthropologists may study how a new sign language springs up in a population with many members who are deaf, how the members of a group use their language for various purposes, or how languages disappear, or are revived, over time.

Integrated Research

There are a number of areas of anthropological re-search that cross-cut the four traditional subfields, and some involve researchers from other disciplines as well. Many anthropologists turn their research interests and methodological expertise to the study of real-world problems, trying to come up with solutions that are fea-sible, sustainable, and just. This type of anthropology is known as **applied anthropology** and can involve one or more of the four subfields. **Biocultural anthropologists** tackle research questions from an integrated approach, combining the data and methodologies of both biologi-cal and cultural anthropology. Medical, nutritional, and reproductive anthropology are three examples of the biocultural approach. Human behavioral ecologists are biocultural anthropologists who study human be-havior from both evolutionary and cultural perspec-tives. Applied and biocultural anthropology are among the fastest growing sectors of the discipline today.

CULTURAL ANTHROPOLOGY

The Concept of Culture

What exactly do anthropologists mean when they talk about **culture?** There are many different ways to define or explain the term *culture* and not every anthropologist uses the term the same way. Edward Tylor is usually credited with coming up with the first formal definition of culture when he wrote: "Culture is that complex whole which includes knowledge, belief, art, law, morals, custom, and any other capability acquired by man as a member of society" (Tylor 1871[2010]:1).

Culture: What's Inside People's Heads

Cultural anthropologists are generally interested, first and foremost, with what is inside people's minds—their knowledge or information, their beliefs or ideas, and their attitudes or perspectives. These intangible aspects of culture include a group's assumptions about the world, as well as their values. We say that *culture is learned*, meaning that it is acquired after birth, as people grow up in a particular place and time. Culture is not genetic—your parents may pass along genes for height, hair color, personality traits, and musical ability. Your parents gave you the genetic capacity to learn culture, but which specific culture an infant learns will depend entirely on the culture she is born into. From the moment of conception, you are stuck with whatever genetic traits your parents bequeath you, but you continue to learn culture—knowledge, beliefs, and attitudes—throughout your life, and thus your culture is constantly changing.

We say that *culture is shared*, meaning that the members of any group tend to have similar knowledge, beliefs, and attitudes. Each individual belongs to many different groups and will share some aspects of their culture with other members of the various groups to which they belong. We will discuss this in more detail below. For now, it is sufficient to point out that some tidbit of knowledge or belief that only one person has—something that isn't shared with anyone else—could be said to be *idiosyncratic* rather than cultural, in the sense that it is not shared with others.

We say that *culture is patterned*, meaning that we find organized systems of thought and belief, patterns of thinking and systems of knowledge, not just a random hodgepodge of factoids and unrelated ideas. Every person's mind contains plenty of such factoids and unrelated snippets of ideas and beliefs, but when we speak of culture, we are referring to the patterned ways of thinking that guide people in their everyday lives.

Culture: What People Do

Cultural anthropologists are also interested in what people do, how they act, and how they behave, especially in their interactions with other people and with the natural world. Culture as behavior is assumed to be predicated, to a large degree, on what is in people's heads. In other words, anthropologists assume that much of human behavior can be understood with reference to knowledge, beliefs, and attitudes. Much of human behavior is learned, shared, and patterned and is passed along both within and between generations through learning, rather than being limited to genetic inheritance passed from parents to children.

At the same time, anthropologists realize that human behavior is also shaped by our genetic heritage as animals, mammals, and primates, and that some features of human behavior are universal because we all share the same underlying human nature. Donald Brown's book *Human Universals* outlines a number of universal human characteristics that are the same in all populations (Brown 1991). For example, the Universal People, as Brown refers to them, have a sense of humor and laugh at whatever they think is funny. What is considered amusing in any particular culture may vary, but all people think some things are funny and other things are tragic. Passing gas (farting) is considered hysterically funny in some cultural contexts but is hugely embarrassing in others. Facial expressions that indicate happiness, sadness, anger, fear, pain, and disgust are human universals. Religion and language are human universals, but the specific content and form of the religion and the language are determined by local cultural beliefs. All people mourn loved ones who have died, and learn the rules for how to behave in their culture under such circumstances. All people think about and plan for the future.

In addition, every person's behavior is constrained by other people, by access to resources, by laws and traditions, by the threat of punishment or promise of rewards, and many other variables. People are not 100 percent free agents, able to do whatever they please based on their own belief system, even if that system is shared with a number of other people.

Culture: What People Make

Although some cultural anthropologists would exclude *material culture,* in this text we consider all the objects that people use, modify, make, or produce to

 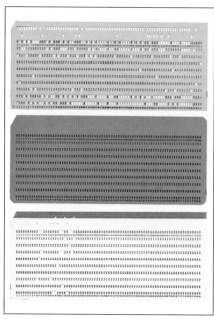 

Material culture refers to the objects that people make, from Northwest Coast Indian masks to IBM punch cards to tall ships.

be a part of their culture. The specific types of objects associated with a group are dependent, in part, on the knowledge and ideas inside people's heads, as well as their behavior. For example, the elaborate carved wooden masks of the Kwakiutl people of the Northwest Coast of North America tell us much about their religious beliefs, their knowledge of wood carving, and their behavior as the masks are danced or displayed. IBM punch cards are now obsolete, but in their heyday, they represented all sorts of knowledge, technology, and beliefs about data processing and scientific research among the people who used them. Clothing and jewelry—even the roast turkey and cranberry sauce at Thanksgiving dinner—are examples of material objects that are used in learned, shared, patterned ways that reflect aspects of culture.

Characteristics of Culture

Culture as Ever-Changing

Culture is not a static entity. Ideas, behaviors, and material objects are constantly changing, shifting, reinventing themselves, and becoming more or less popular. New ideas and ways of doing things are continuously being invented, new objects are produced, or they are used in novel ways or take on different meanings. Ideas, behaviors, and objects also disappear, as they are no longer useful and therefore no longer produced (like IBM punch cards). People may not be 100 percent free agents, but they often challenge the culture they find themselves in, creating new things and deliberately attempting to steer the course of cultural change in particular directions.

Culture as Adaptation

Anthropologists often say that culture is humankind's primary means of adapting to the environment and that, since cultural change is quicker and easier than genetic change, humans have essentially stopped evolving biologically. There are two problems with this view. First, not all cultural beliefs and practices are adaptive. In other words, they don't all function to allow humans to survive and thrive and to overcome challenges posed by the environment. Undoubtedly, many cultural beliefs and practices range from slightly adaptive to extremely adaptive. Knowledge of how to build ice houses allows Inuit populations to survive in the Arctic. Knowledge of how to process acorns allowed pre-European contact California Indian populations to use them as a staple in their diet. Widespread immunization prevents many deaths and episodes of illness.

At the same time, many other cultural beliefs and practices range from slightly maladaptive to extremely maladaptive. Breast implants and female circumcision are examples of maladaptive practices that adversely affect women's health. Cigarette smoking and abuse of alcohol and opiate drugs are likewise maladaptive. In the long run, being able to reproduce at a phenomenal rate and keep most of our children alive will probably turn out to be toxic to the planet. Our very success at adaptation in the short term may turn out to be maladaptive in the long term.

You should not assume that every cultural belief or practice, every idea or behavior, is adaptive. As long as the system works well enough—as long as two or more children survive, across the generations, for every adult couple—the population will endure, and many maladaptive elements may persist. Even when people recognize that such practices are maladaptive, such as cigarette smoking or the use of infant formula, it isn't always easy to purge these elements of culture.

Second, although cultural adaptation has allowed humans to expand into many different environments around the world, and has made many aspects of life easier for us, that doesn't mean that we have stopped evolving biologically. On the contrary, human biological evolution proceeds apace, and some would say even faster than it used to simply because there are more humans alive on the planet than at any other time in our history or prehistory. Natural selection continues to act on the human gene pool, through environmental stresses such as disease and malnutrition. Other evolutionary forces such as mutation and random genetic drift continue to affect human evolution as well.

Cultural Beliefs versus Social Structure

Cultural beliefs and the social structures that are built on them are not always completely in sync. Social structure refers to the institutions, the traditions, and the organization of social life that arise out of cultural beliefs but then take on a somewhat independent existence. New members born into the population

have to deal with the social structure they find in place, whether or not they agree with the underlying cultural beliefs. In addition, the way the society is organized may affect "if and how" cultural beliefs actually turn into observable behaviors.

Domestic violence (one spouse physically abusing the other) and child abuse (parents physically abusing their children) in Mali and the United States will serve as specific examples of how cultural beliefs may or may not be reflected in specific behavior. During my research among the Bambara of Mali (West Africa) in the 1980s, the prevailing sentiment in the community was that a man had the right to physically discipline his wife. If she did something he had forbidden, failed to do something she was supposed to do, or showed disrespect to him, he was allowed to hit her. That was considered perfectly reasonable, a man's right. Likewise, once a child had reached the age of three to four years, he was expected to have some sense, to know right from wrong, to do what his parents told him, and to show them respect. If the child misbehaved, his parents had the right to physically discipline him, including hitting him with their hands or a nearby stick, or throwing rocks at him.

The prevailing sentiment in the United States at the time (and still today) was that domestic violence and child abuse were absolutely wrong, not justifiable under any circumstances, and punishable by the criminal justice system. Any person who beat a spouse and parents who were even suspected of child abuse were viewed with disdain, and every year many people were sent to prison on such charges. The general cultural view on corporal punishment of children changed during the last half of the twentieth century. In the United States in the 1950s and 1960s, many children were routinely paddled by their parents or the school principal, had their knuckles whacked with a ruler by a teacher, or were otherwise physically punished by adults for infractions of the rules. By the end of the century, corporal punishment had come to be seen by most people not only as child abuse, but as counterproductive and violence promoting. Many schools no longer allowed physical discipline of students, and *time out* or threats to take away the video games had replaced a quick swat on the behind in most households.

Given the stated cultural beliefs in these two different contexts, you might expect to find that domestic violence and child abuse were much more common in Mali than in the United States. But you would be wrong. In Mali, although physical punishment was seen as an appropriate and justifiable response to misbehavior, the reality is that life there is very much lived in public. Most adult men live with their parents, their brothers, their own wife (or wives) and children, and their brothers' wives and children. Most daily activities take place outside, in the central courtyard of the compound. If you want to hit your wife, fine, but you have to do it in front of any number of other adults and children, including your own parents and your brothers. Other family members would generally not intervene if a man hit his wife once, or even twice, but they would certainly stop him if there was even a remote possibility that he would seriously hurt the woman. She could appeal to the other adults in the compound for help or simply run outside into the street while his brothers restrained him. More often, a man would control his own behavior, because he didn't want to be seen as someone who flew off the handle and let his emotions get the best of him. Thus, although it was permitted for men to hit their wives, it very seldom happened.

In the United States, although the cultural beliefs say that violence is wrong, the reality is that most married adults live by themselves, with no other adults around to hear or observe or intervene in their violent behavior. People live in separate houses, where the neighbors can't hear, or in apartment buildings where the neighbors are prone to mind their own business and not call the police for fear of turning the man's wrath on whoever reported the violence. Because domestic violence is stigmatized, women are more likely to suffer in silence and not to tell anyone of the abuse, thus perpetuating the cycle. Perpetrators may convince their wives or girlfriends that it is their own fault they are being hit, saying: "It's not OK for a man to hit a woman, but damn, you leave me no choice!" With no one around to witness the violence, to stand up for the woman, or to restrain the man, the woman may suffer serious injury, including black eyes, broken bones, miscarriage, and even death.

The same is true of child abuse. In Mali, people laugh at a small child being pelted with rocks by his mother or father. An adult might find a branch for another to use to chase the child around the compound and out into the street, but serious injuries to children

at the hands of their parents were unknown. If a mother or father was getting angry at a young child, it was much more likely that the adult would hand responsibility for the child off to one of the many other adults in the vicinity, and stalk off. A woman might go to the market, or take some clothes down to the river to wash, or simply say "I need to go cool down." There were always other adults around to share the burden of child care if a parent was sick, or tired, or just at her limit; the care of young children didn't fall only to the parents, or only to the mother. And if a child was being beaten, the other adults and even older children in the compound would make sure that the child was not seriously injured. The child would be rescued and taken elsewhere, or the mother or father would be physically restrained. A smack with a stick was OK, a serious beating with a belt, or burning with hot oil, or locking the child in a closet, even serious emotional abuse, was completely unknown.

In the United States, however, just as with domestic violence, the care and raising of children is often done in privacy, in the confines of one's own home or apartment. A woman may be alone much of the day with one or more young children—a trying experience even for the most loving of mothers. If she loses her temper, even though she believes that violence against children is wrong, she may find herself hitting her child and flying out of control. There are no other adults around to stop her, or to ease the burden in the first place so she doesn't become so frustrated and upset. There is no one there to help the child or to chastise the mother. Many people will do things when unobserved that they wouldn't dream of doing if other adults were watching, including child sexual abuse, rape, and even verbal or emotional abuse.

Thus, even though Malian cultural beliefs allow a man to physically discipline his wife, and parents to physically punish their children, the public nature of domestic life means that there is practically no serious domestic or child abuse—no broken bones, no deaths, no slow starvation, no eroding away of one's sense of self through chronic emotional abuse. Although American beliefs discourage physical discipline, the private nature of domestic life means that men can get away with seriously injuring or even killing their wives, and children can be horribly abused for years by parents, while the neighbors are not aware that anything bad is happening inside the house.

Conscious Beliefs versus Tradition

Cultural beliefs are not always consciously recognized by the people who hold them. Many people assume that the way they do things is simply "how things are done," or is fundamental to human nature. They may never have consciously contemplated why they do things, or why they do things the particular way they do—it hasn't occurred to them that other people might do things differently, or hold different beliefs about how things should be. We can't imagine things being any other way.

Thus, the cultural anthropologist can't just ask people "Why do you do this?" and expect a clear and articulate answer. Many people aren't aware of why they do things. It's just how things are, it's just tradition. They may not be aware of the functions their beliefs and actions serve, and they may not be aware of the particular historical chain of events that led to things being the way they currently are.

Why do people in the United States carve pumpkins at Halloween and send little children in costumes around the neighborhood to knock on strangers' doors and ask for candy? Why do people drive on the right side of the road? Why do we bathe so often? Why do we let teenagers spend time together unsupervised by adults? Why do we stand patiently in line to get on a bus, instead of climbing in through the windows, or pushing and shoving others out of the way? Why do we expect prompt service in a restaurant and not linger over our meals for hours the way many people do in Europe? Why don't we go home for a two-hour nap after lunch every day?

We do things because that's the way they are done. Because "Mother Culture" has been whispering in our ears since birth, telling us that this is the right way to live, and convincing us so thoroughly that we don't even question most of her messages. *Culture* can be like the air around us—ubiquitous and ever-present and taken for granted. It often takes in-depth and detailed data collection and analysis to pry apart the cultural beliefs that underlie behavior and social structure in any context. People may not be able to explain why they do something, or why they hold particular beliefs, and they may not understand all the reasons, or know the historical background, of the social structures they operate within and perpetuate every day.

Thus, the job of the cultural anthropologist can be a difficult one, trying to make sense of what people do and why, when even the people they are studying may not reach the same conclusions. Sometimes, when the underlying cultural beliefs are pulled out into the sunlight for examination, people are horrified by what is revealed.

How Is Cultural Anthropology Different from the Other Social Sciences?

Length of Research

Compared to the other social sciences, cultural anthropologists tend to spend much more time gathering data. The primary means of collecting cultural anthropological data involves living among the group of people one is studying, learning to speak their language, gaining their trust, watching what is going on (making observations), participating in their activities as much as possible, and listening to their explanations of what they are doing and why. Cultural anthropologists watch people; they talk to people; they listen as others are talking; they ask questions. In many ways, they take on the role of a child and learn the rules, sometimes explicitly and sometimes by trial and error, just as children do. By spending significant amounts of time among the subjects of their research, they are able to modify and adapt their research as time goes by.

Most cultural anthropologists spend two years or more during their initial research project, known as **fieldwork,** carried out during graduate school. Fieldwork may involve traveling to a distant land, or not. Cultural anthropologists may return many times to the same area for continued research over the years, or they may conduct research in other locations or with other groups. They may spend their summers in the field, when they aren't teaching classes, or they may take time off from teaching to spend another year or longer conducting research. Many applied anthropologists work for businesses, government agencies, or nonprofit organizations and conduct research on a full-time basis, rather than teach at a college or university.

Language of Research

When anthropologists conduct research among people who speak a different language, they go to great lengths to learn the language themselves. They often make use of translators or field assistants who are fluent in the language to help them learn it or to help them formulate research questions. However, as much as possible, they try to become fluent enough to ask questions themselves, to understand the answers people give, and to recognize when a person doesn't really understand the question or is reluctant to answer. If possible, the researcher studies the language before going to the field. Even if the anthropologist has taken classes in the language, it can often take six months or longer before he feels comfortable enough to do research without a field assistant. It may also take that long for the local people to accept the anthropologist and be willing to talk to him and allow him to participate in daily activities. Making the effort to learn the language, including how to appropriately participate in greetings, and to understand and make jokes, helps the anthropologist be accepted by the community and earn their trust. Even so, it may take years for an anthropologist to gain access to secret or esoteric knowledge.

Research Methodologies

As described above, the main research tool of the cultural anthropologist is **participant-observation.** One lives among the people one is studying, one listens and observes, and one participates as much as possible. One-on-one interviews or focus group interviews may be conducted and tend to be open-ended rather than structured, informal rather than formal, and face-to-face rather than from a distance, such as those conducted through phone interviews, mail surveys, or online questionnaires. During the interview, the anthropologist may refer to a list of topics she wishes to cover but avoids asking specific questions or providing answer choices for the respondents to pick. This approach allows the people being interviewed to steer the conversation in the direction of topics that are most important to them and often opens up avenues of research inquiry that the anthropologist could not have known about ahead of time.

Much important information comes from simply hanging out, which is sometimes called **accidental fieldwork.** In Mali, I did research in a town that Americans often drove through on their way to an American Community Center that served hamburgers and French fries and screened current U.S. movies. These Americans might later tell me that they had seen me just hanging out in the market. I would ex-

plain that I was doing research and they would say, "No, you were just sitting there talking to someone, holding a baby." "Yes, but I was doing research," I would respond. Often the most critical insights would come while I was chatting with one mother, listening while others nearby discussed a sick child, and simultaneously observing still more women interacting with their children in the market setting.

Some anthropologists use life-history approaches, where they interview elderly people about their lives or follow a small group of individuals over a number of years through repeated field research trips. A number of other research methodologies are also employed by cultural anthropologists, depending on where they are conducting research. If participants can read and write, written surveys may provide additional data. If other researchers have already been working in the area, or a nongovernmental organization has a project set up in the village, it may be easier for the anthropologist to come in for a brief visit and elicit important information that will help the larger project with its goals.

Anthropologists analyze their data and write up their results for publication in Ph.D. dissertations, scholarly journal articles, and books. The word **ethnography** refers to such written descriptions of human cultural beliefs and practices.

Ethnology is a nonfieldwork-based research methodology that involves comparing one or more aspects of life in a number of different cultures, based on the ethnographic information collected and published by other anthropologists. The Human Relations Area Files (www.yale.edu/hraf/) are a primary source of such ethnographic descriptions.

Cultural Ideals, Perceptions, and Behavior

Anthropologists are especially attuned to the differences between what people *say is ideal* in their culture, what they *say they actually do,* and then *how they actually behave.* It is impossible for everyone to follow the ideals of their culture all the time. There are many situations where we know what would be best, or what is considered ideal, but circumstances don't allow us to meet those expectations. The ideal may, in fact, be out of reach for most people most of the time. People are often quite up-front about the difference between the cultural ideal and their own descriptions of what they do, and they readily may offer explanations or justifications for deviating from the cultural ideal.

For example, a Malian mother might say, "You shouldn't continue to nurse your baby once you get pregnant again." When I point out that she looks pregnant to me, and her toddler is nursing, she might laugh and say, "Well, but I have some special medicine that allows me to continue." Or, "I haven't decided that I'm pregnant yet." Or, "Oh, she only nurses once or twice a day, that doesn't really count."

In addition, people may report that they act in one way, but it turns out that they don't actually behave that way. During Ramadan, the Muslim month of fasting during daylight hours, I might ask a woman how her health was during the previous month, and she would say she had been perfectly healthy. Later, I would ask if she was fasting for Ramadan, and she would begin coughing and explain that, no, she had been sick. Or she would say that the toddler wasn't nursing very often any more, but then explain that she was not fasting for Ramadan because she still had a child who nursed a lot. Being sick, or breastfeeding a young child, are culturally approved reasons not to fast during Ramadan. This scenario played out many times, during both years of my initial field research. Finally, I realized that hardly any of the women fasted for Ramadan, but most of them felt that they were supposed to, and so would backtrack to justify to me why they were not fasting.

Sometimes, people don't have a very good idea of how often they eat a particular food, or how much money they spend on clothes or medical care. They may be reporting what they believe to be the case, but only careful observation and comparison can show if what people say matches what they really do. And of course, people do mislead anthropologists deliberately, either to hide information they don't want to share or simply to amuse themselves at the anthropologist's expense. That's why it is important to ask questions multiple times, in a variety of ways, and to pay attention not only to what people report is the cultural ideal but also to what they say they actually do and to whether their behavior matches their descriptions. People often recast and reshape prior actions after the fact, as they construct and reconstruct the narratives of their lives. They tell stories, and it isn't always clear how the story might be changed by the context in which it is told, or the point of its telling.

Another problematic situation arises when people say they believe one thing, but their observable behaviors clearly contradict that stated belief. Either they don't really believe what they claim to or they are able to sincerely hold the belief while acting in ways that don't match. Many of my students will say that they are firm believers in "the rule of law"—the notion that people should abide by culturally developed rules and laws, rather than everyone just doing what they please (anarchy). These same students can be seen later in the day jaywalking, or crossing the street at a crosswalk against a red light, or riding their bikes the wrong way down a one-way street or on the sidewalk, or if driving, they may cruise through a stop sign while barely slowing down (the "no cop, no stop" rule of driving). They may drink before they are 21, smoke marijuana, even cheat on a test—all the while firmly believing that people should follow the law, and not viewing themselves as criminals in any sense. They may believe in an abstract notion of the rule of law, especially for everyone else, but not follow it in their daily lives.

Finally, it is important to understand that not everyone conforming to cultural practices in a particular society or group shares the underlying belief system. People may disagree partly or completely with the beliefs that underlie the behavior that is typically seen, yet still behave that way. People may conform because the benefits or rewards of conforming are high and therefore worth it. Or, they may conform because the costs of, or punishment for, nonconformity are high and therefore not worth it. Concrete examples of the former might include: (1) a man works for a company whose corporate policy is that all males wear suits and ties in order to look professional; he thinks this is silly, but he enjoys his interesting and well-paying job, so he wears a suit and tie; and (2) a student completes all her professor's homework assignments and turns them in on time, even though she thinks they are pointless; she wants a good grade in the class. Concrete examples of the latter might include: (1) driving at or below the speed limit in town because you don't want to get a ticket; the speed limit is deliberately set ridiculously low and the fines for speeding are very high to earn money for the local community when outsiders speed through town; and (2) my sister wore pants to high school in 1971, which was strictly forbidden, and she was suspended for three days; she never wore pants again, even though all the students thought the "no pants for girls" rule was stupid.

It may be the case that many people in a group disagree with the belief system and the behaviors that it leads to, but each individual thinks she is the only one who disagrees, and so she keeps her thoughts and feelings to herself. This perpetuates the idea that everyone agrees, so everyone keeps on conforming—they cave in to peer pressure, not realizing that even those advocating conformity don't necessarily agree with the underlying beliefs. It may take some drastic event for people to admit their true feelings, only to discover that a majority of others feel the same way. Once this happens, though, it can lead to very rapid cultural transformations.

Basic Theoretical Orientations in Cultural Anthropology

Anthropology is a very complex and broad-ranging discipline, and many different theoretical perspectives have been adopted by its practitioners over the years and are alive and well in the discipline today. In this section, we will briefly discuss four theoretical orientations that are useful for the introductory student.

Evolution

The insights of evolutionary theory are critical to understanding human culture and experience. Humans are animals, mammals, and primates and, as such, are subject to all the same biological limitations and evolutionary forces as other living creatures. Our biology and physiology constrain where and how we can live successfully.

Environmental stresses, such as differing levels of ultraviolet radiation, hypoxia at high altitude, and malaria in the humid tropics, continue to affect human populations. We have adapted partially through genetic changes at the population level (evolution by natural selection), as well as through developmental changes as a result of growing up in specific environments and through short-term biological changes available to people of all ages, such as tanning in response to sunlight. In addition, a variety of cultural coping mechanisms help people deal with environmental stresses. We can use sun block, clothing, and changes in patterns of activity to protect us from UV radiation; we can carry supplemental oxygen for use at high altitudes; we have mosquito nets, repellents, and medicines to prevent malaria, and other medicines to treat it.

At the same time, cultural beliefs and practices are constrained by the limits of human biological adaptation and can themselves lead to additional problems for vulnerable individuals. In other words, we can create innovative systems of beliefs and ways of doing things, but if we set up cultural systems that contradict our underlying biological nature, there will be negative consequences, ranging from stress to illness and death. Culture effectively **creates new environments**, with additional forces of natural selection to which individuals must adapt.

For example, societies vary in terms of how often most people eat, ranging between one and four regular meals per day. There are no societies where people routinely eat only once a week, or once a month, because such systems are not compatible with human health. Likewise, when societies adopt the routine substitution of artificial infant formula in bottles for breastfeeding, they may gain some small measure of convenience, but they lose much more in terms of infant survival and health. Where diseases are rampant and water supplies contaminated, formula use leads to very high rates of child mortality. In the United States—where diseases are mitigated by immunizations and antibiotics and water supplies are clean—it is estimated that close to 1,000 children die each year because they were not exclusively breastfed for the first six months. Rates of Sudden Infant Death Syndrome (SIDS) are higher when infants are formula-fed, sleep in cribs, are put to sleep on their stomachs, and/or live with adults who smoke. Where people routinely share needles for the injection of drugs, the transmission of HIV is more likely. Many cultural systems have negative consequences for the individuals who participate in them.

One of the most important lessons of a course in cultural anthropology is to learn to recognize both the advantages and the disadvantages of contrasting cultural ways of thinking and behaving, particularly in terms of human physical and emotional health. Culture can buffer us from the physical environment, but it can also create new environments to which humans are not well adapted.

Structural-Functionalism

Human cultural systems almost always have some structure or pattern to them, in terms of beliefs, behavior, and social organization. In addition, they usually serve one or more specific purposes—they help solve universal human problems—they have a function. The structural-functional approach asks "What function does this system serve?" and "How does the structure of this system help it fulfill that function?" and "How well does it work?" Functions include staying alive (food, water, shelter, safety, health), raising children (marriage, child-rearing practices, family and kinship organization), maintaining internal and external social order (criminal justice systems, laws, politics), providing creative outlets, which humans seem to require (art, music, dance, athletics) and answering unanswerable questions (religion).

Historical Particularism

Structural-functionalism can go a long ways toward helping us understand human culture and experience. For more specific questions about exactly how and why a particular system developed the way it did in a particular time and place, we turn to the historical particularist perspective. Historical particularism is not a competing theoretical orientation to structural-functionalism, rather it is a complementary approach. Looking at the specific events and persons who have shaped a cultural system over the years helps us understand more about any one system and helps explain differences between systems. New ideas and technology may arise out of the brain of a creative individual and lead the group along a particular path. Or an individual may spread ideas from one region to another through exploration or trade routes. The Kiowa of Oklahoma now practice a particular form of Christianity as the result of the work of a Baptist missionary who began the Saddle Mountain Mission in 1896 (Lassiter, Ellis, and Kotay 2002). People in the United States drink more coffee than tea as the result of our specific history of rebellion against the tea-drinking and tea-taxing British.

A great example of the historical particularist approach comes from South America:

Outside England, the only culture in the world that still prizes the bowler hat as an essential item of everyday wear are the Aymara women of the Bolivian and Peruvian highlands. The traditional dress of full skirts and woolen tops (voluminous shawls over cardigans) is thought to have been adopted from Spanish settlers of the seventeenth century. But where did the brown felt bowler hat, or *bombín*, come from?

The story has it that, in the 1920s, a Bolivian outfitter accidentally ordered too many derby hats, and decided to market the surplus ones as women's wear. Within a decade, they had caught on so tenaciously that an Italian millinery firm, Borsalino, began mak-

Left: an Aymara woman wearing a bowler hat, which is distinctive from other hat styles around the world.

ing bowlers specifically for export to the Andes. Now they are manufactured locally. Oddly, most wearers appear to favor a size that looks far too small for their heads to the Western eye. The Aymara women believe that hats enhance fertility. (ICONS 2010)

One of the limits of the historical particularist approach is the lack of written documentation in some regions of the world. In these cases, we must rely on people's memories, and on stories passed down through the generations about why things are done a particular way. Even where historical (written) records are available, the local people may no longer refer to them and may not know, or even care, what they say. Arno van Voorst (2006) points out that once a building has been completed, the scaffolding used during the building process is removed. Nothing about the completed building gives any hint to the scaffolding and cranes that were used to erect it. The people who live and work in the building today may not have been around when the building was under construction; they have no idea how it came to be.

The same process may apply to cultural development. According to van Voorst, "small changes in behaviour can lead to stable, self-sustaining collections of behaviours" (2006). Once a stable, self-sustaining system is in place, the original small changes in ideas and behavior that began the process may no longer be apparent. The scaffolding has been taken down, and no one today participating in the system of cultural beliefs and behaviors can provide an historical explanation for how the system was built. We can, however, still analyze its structure and function, which is why the two approaches—structural-functionalism and historical particularism—work hand-in-hand to help us understand human culture and experience.

Symbolic Anthropology and the Power of Meaning

Symbolic anthropology is another important theoretical perspective. Rather than looking at the adaptive functions of culture, or how the structure of a system helps it fulfill its function, or even the history of a particular cultural system, symbolic anthropologists are more interested in the meanings that people assign to their lives. The ability of humans to create symbols and assign meanings to words, objects, motions, places, natural processes, and complex ritual behaviors is much more intricate than anything seen in the rest of the animal world. Some anthropologists have focused their attention specifically on this ability that humans have to create entirely new cultural worlds of meaning.

Anthropologist Claude Lévi-Strauss (1968, 1995) noted that humans everywhere like to think in terms of opposite pairs: culture and nature, raw food and cooked food, light and dark, good and evil, the world of the heavens and the world below, the world of the living and the world of the spirits. Such contrasting characteristics may be elaborated and imbued with deep meaning and power. Following the lead of Victor Turner, anthropologist Mary Douglas (1966, 2003) carried this notion further, pointing out that many people assign particular power and significance to things that fall "betwixt and between"—things that do not clearly belong in one category or the other.

For example, blood holds great power in many cultural contexts. On the one hand, it is necessary for life and is usually contained within the body. When blood is spilled, death often follows. On the other hand, women bleed when they menstruate and after giving birth, both circumstances where blood is outside the body but represents either the potential for life or the birth of a new member of the group. In Jewish dietary laws, the foods that are forbidden are those from animals that do not fall neatly into typical categories. Animals that live in the sea usually have scales, and animals that chew their cud usually have cloven hooves. Animals from the sea that don't have scales, such as shrimp, lobster, and crab, are considered "improper" sea creatures and are not supposed to be eaten. Likewise, animals who have cloven hooves but don't chew their cud, such as pigs and camels, are considered "improper" land animals, and their meat is forbidden as well.

In order to fully understand a people's beliefs and behaviors, one must try to develop a deep understanding of the symbolic meanings that people attribute to them.

ASPECTS OR LEVELS OF CULTURE

Aspects of Culture Based on Geography

People who live near each other tend to be exposed to many of the same ideas and influences. They interact face-to-face on a regular basis. They also cope with similar environmental issues such as climate, natural disasters, regional flora and fauna, and so on. In addition, communications media can help distribute information from person to person or from one person to many others. Trade networks and markets ensure that many people have access to similar goods and services. Thus, we begin our discussion of the different aspects or levels of culture with those based on geographic proximity.

International Culture

Previously, we mentioned the concept of the Universal People—certain attributes of beliefs and behavior that all people share due to our common heritage as humans. Once we get below the level of cultural universals, we find that people share different aspects of their culture with other people depending on the geographic level of focus. The biggest of these would be aspects of what may be called *international culture*, or *global culture*. Access to common media, including books, newspapers, television, radio, and especially the Internet, have erased geographical restrictions to the spread of knowledge, beliefs, and attitudes across much of the planet. Certainly not everyone has access to the Internet, and governments may censor certain information or viewpoints, but the limits to knowledge that were once a function of distance are no longer as relevant in the age of the Internet.

Around the world, many people have access to CNN and al-Jazeera news broadcasts and can watch sports competitions and political demonstrations from distant lands. Information about disasters such as the 9/11 attacks on the United States in 2001, the election of Barack Obama in 2008, and the Haitian earthquake in 2010 are quickly transmitted around the world via computer, TV, and radio. Movies, music, and celebrity gossip travel around the world. Corporations such as IKEA, Coca-Cola, McDonald's, and Microsoft can now be found in many countries. Google lets anybody find anything. Thus, we can identify aspects of international culture—knowledge, beliefs, and attitudes that many people share, regardless of where they live on the planet, through shared access to the same information sources.

Biome

The next geographic level of culture is the biome. A *biome* refers to an area with a characteristic climate, flora, and fauna. Regardless of where they may live, people who live in similar biomes will share many aspects of culture. People who live at high altitudes, whether in the Peruvian Andes, the Himalayas, or the Swiss Alps will share knowledge about the environment, including strategies for dealing with the low levels of oxygen in the air and cold temperatures. Goat herders in Switzerland and the mountains of Pakistan will share knowledge about the behavior and physiology of goats, know the same signs to watch for to tell when the summer pastures are ready, and know when a goat is about to give birth. Likewise, people who live on islands in the South Pacific may differ in many details of their cultures but will share vast stores of knowledge with other people who live on tropical islands around the world, including knowledge about boat building and sailing, weather patterns, the behavior of fish and whales, net making, and so forth. People who live in deserts will share knowledge and beliefs about adapting to a desert environment. This is, perhaps, an obvious thing to note, but it is often a surprise to travelers who discover that others who live in a similar environment on the far side of the world do things in much the same way.

National Culture

The next, smaller level of culture based on geography is *national culture*—beliefs, knowledge, and behaviors that people share as members of a modern nation-state. National identity or citizenship is aided by music, movies, national chains of stores, restaurants and hotels, national television shows and print media, and national-level sports teams, including the Olympics. Nationalism or patriotism may be explicitly taught in the home or in schools, where all children may recite a pledge of allegiance to their flag or sing the national anthem. Children may be encouraged to view themselves as citizens of their country as one of their primary identities and to be proud to be a citizen of that country.

However, not all nation-states have equivalent levels of national identity. Many modern nation-states were created by fiat, at the whim of outsiders, especially European colonial powers such as England, Germany, the Netherlands, France, Belgium, Spain, and Portugal. In many cases, such nation-states have no natural or historical identity, and the people who find themselves living in the country may not particularly identify themselves as citizens of the country. Where multiple ethnic groups, or people who speak different languages, are lumped together in an artificial nation-state, and other people with the same ethnic identity and language are divided up and defined as belonging to several other nation-states, nationalism may not be very important. For example, the modern nation of Iraq was crafted in a hotel in Cairo, Egypt, in 1921, with its boundaries drawn by a British woman named Gertrude Bell. With the agreement of the other participants, mostly British, she consolidated three separate regions of the Ottoman Empire—Kurdish Sunni Muslims in the north, Arab Shia Muslims in the middle, and Arab Sunni Muslims in the south—into a single nation to be known as Iraq. The ethnic group known as the Kurds, in turn, was split up among a number of different countries. Kevin McKiernan writes:

> I didn't realize it at first, but the Kurds are the largest ethnic group in the world without their own state. Like many first-time visitors, I would learn that "Kurdistan" was an ethnic mosaic of shifting tribal alliances that had been divided historically among the Ottoman, Persian, and Russian empires. It had never been a unified nation, but the territory of the Kurds inside the Ottoman empire, a politically and linguistically diverse area, had been carved up after World War I, the land parceled out to Iraq, Turkey, and Syria (at this point, the borders of Kurdish areas in Iran and the Soviet Union already existed). (McKiernan 2006:4; see also Brenneman 2007)

Tribal or Ethnic Identity

One of the most important geography-based levels of culture is that of *tribal* or *ethnic identity*, where people have a long history of residence in the same place for hundreds or even thousands of years. In the early years of anthropological field research, many anthropologists worked among such populations, in relatively remote, isolated settings. In such contexts, people share almost all aspects of their lives in common with all other members of the group. Everyone in the community speaks the same language; holds the same religious beliefs; participates in the same kinship, economic, and political systems; shares the same music and food; and so on. It has become common to speak of such ethnic groups as "a culture" and to talk about "the culture of the _____ people." Still today, many people take their primary sense of self from their ethnic or tribal identity. This is particularly the

case where most members of the group still live on or near their ancestral lands. Examples include the Kurds of the Middle East, the Hopi and Navajo of Arizona, the Dani of highland New Guinea, the Songhay of Niger, the Inupiaq of Alaska, the Tonga in the South Pacific, and literally thousands of other ethnic groups around the world.

At the same time, many people today live in much more complex cultural contexts, where they interact on a regular basis with many different, overlapping circles of people with whom they share some aspects of their culture, but not others. This will become clearer as we continue our discussion of the different aspects of culture based on geography as well as nongeographically based levels, and we will return to this issue later when we talk about "cultural competency," a notion that has become a controversial issue in North American businesses and governmental organizations.

Regional, State, and Local Culture

Even within complex modern nation-states, where people who originally hail from many different regions of the world live side-by-side, regional and local differences in many aspects of culture still exist. Using the United States as an example, we will briefly explore regional, state, and local levels of culture. In the United States, regional differences exist based on climate and topography, the history of the region, and so on. Although the following examples may sound like stereotypes, and certainly don't apply to everyone in a particular region, they do capture the flavor of regional culture.

People in the southern states of the United States, including Texas, tend to be very friendly—some would say overly friendly. People will strike up conversations with complete strangers, stop to help someone whose car has broken down on the road, refer to you as "honey" and "sweetie" the first time they meet you, and just exude friendliness and hospitality. There is an assumption that people are generally nice and trustworthy. Innocent until proven guilty, one might say. In contrast, people along the eastern seaboard tend not to be so openly friendly, and reticence and suspicion of strangers increases the farther north you go, at least as far as New York City. People typically are skeptical of the motives of any stranger who tries to talk to them, or ask for directions, often looking right through the person as though they were invisible. People are more wary, assuming that anyone they don't know is likely to be a bad person, not someone to trust. Not only do many people go out of their way to remain aloof, some treat strangers with rudeness and scorn.

Across the southern states, you can find wood-smoked barbecue restaurants serving amazing, mouth-watering beef and pork BBQ. Grocery stores sell fresh tortillas, and grits come as a side-dish with breakfast, regardless of what you order. "Tea" means iced tea, saturated with sugar. In central Texas, because of all the Czech immigrants in the 1900s, you can still find kolaches at local bakeries and hear Czech spoken at the neighborhood gas station. In the Philadelphia-Delaware-Maryland corridor, you can find crabs, subs, cheese steaks, Tasty-Cakes, "water ice," and even muskrat in season—but you would be hard-pressed to find decent barbecue, fresh tortillas, or grits.

Politically, both coasts tend to be more liberal than the heartland of the Midwest, with California, Oregon, and Washington having the reputations of being the most liberal states of all. In the Pacific Northwest, every city and town has sizeable populations of immigrants from all across Asia, while southern Delaware has many recent immigrants from Guatemala, who come to work in the chicken-processing industry. Arizona and Florida have large populations of transplanted northerners, who retired to the warmer climates, and many amenities that cater to the retired. In Texas, it is taken for granted that all government and school forms are printed in English on one side and Spanish on the other, that Friday nights are devoted to high school football games, and that rodeos are important events. Even the way people speak— the tempo, the grammatical constructions, and the wordiness of their utterances—reflects distinctive local variations across the United States.

The same is true for any large nation-state, where different regions will have their own local cuisines, styles of dress and speech, regional businesses, and other defining characteristics. Each region of Germany is famous for its own particular type and style of sausage. Mexican and Italian cooking varies tremendously by region, and large countries such as Russia and China encompass even more regional variety in all aspects of culture.

In the United States, only a few states have what might be referred to as "state level" culture. Texas is the most obvious, reveling in its historical uniqueness of being the only state in the union that was once an independent country. People are inordinately proud to be Texans, and parents and public schools teach children to think of themselves as Texans first, and U.S. citizens second! The same cannot be said of Iowa, say, or Rhode Island, or Tennessee. Alaskans also view themselves as somewhat separate from the rest of the United States, more independent and adventuresome and, like Texans, have talked about seceding from the union on several occasions.

Below the level of the region and state, there are still smaller geographic levels of culture, where people who live in the area have many beliefs and practices in common. This can be at the city or town level, the neighborhood level, the university campus level, and so on. For example, Arden is a small artists' community in northern Delaware. The houses are unique, many of the residents are professional artists, and they have rules about the types of buildings and activities that can take place in the community. Most of the neighborhood is closed to automobile traffic, and there is a community Gild Hall where people can listen to music or lectures, have community dinners, and swim in the community pool. Texas A&M University claims to have the most distinctive college-campus culture of any institute of higher learning in the country. All the members of the Corps of Cadets (ROTC for all military branches) wear their uniforms to class, and male freshmen in the Corps have their heads shaved when school begins in the fall. There is always a massive turnout for football games, the "yell leaders" are male (rather than female cheerleaders), the students all stand during football games, and they kiss their dates whenever a touchdown is scored. People say "howdy" to everyone they meet as they walk across campus, and most students are overly polite to professors ("Yes ma'am" and "No ma'am," "Yes sir" and "No sir").

All of these levels of learned, shared culture are based on geography, on physical proximity, on where you live and who you live amidst. However, these represent only some of the many different levels of culture each of us belongs to. Next we turn our attention to the aspects of culture that are not based on geography.

Aspects of Culture Not Based on Geography

In addition to cultural features we share with those we live closest to, there are many other arenas of culture that every person participates in. These may be based on many different things that we share in common with other people who may be scattered across the country, or around the world.

Ethnic Identity

Some people view their "ethnicity" as an important part of their personal identity and cultural affiliation. They may, indeed, share some cultural beliefs and practices with other people across the globe who also define themselves as members of the same ethnic group. However, ethnicity or ethnic identity is a complex notion. First, it should be clear that there are *no such things as human races* based on genetic or physical differences between groups of people. All humans belong to the same genus, *Homo*, the same species, *sapiens*, and the same subspecies (race), *sapiens*. Thus, all humans can be classified zoologically as *Homo sapiens sapiens*—there is only one human race.

Ethnicity or ethnic identity, on the other hand, is a cultural construct. In different regions of the world, ethnicity may be based in part on some aspects of physical appearance, presumably based on ancestry, including body size and shape, skin color, facial features, hair type, and so on. Cultural variables such as language and religion may also factor into ethnicity, and categories of ethnicity will vary from one country to another or one region or state to another. Ethnicity is an identity designation that individuals can shape, ignore, or manipulate to further their goals, and one's ethnicity can change over time. It is quite foolhardy for people to assume they can determine another person's ethnicity simply by looking at her and equally foolhardy to assume that all members of one ethnic group share a number of cultural beliefs and practices simply by virtue of membership in that group. A few specific examples will serve to make this issue more concrete.

In the United States, people of European ancestry make up the majority of the population. Whether we call them Caucasian, Euro-Americans, or "white folks," as members of the numerically dominant group, most consider themselves to be "normal"—they are the standard, the unmarked category, the mode, in a statistical sense. Most of them conceive of other people as having an ethnic identity, but they seldom think of their own ethnicity. Go into any Kmart and you'll find a special section for "ethnic hair care products." One aisle at the grocery store may be labeled "ethnic foods," and a party invitation might specify "come dressed in ethnic clothing." Of course, all hair-care products are ethnic, all foods are ethnic, and all clothing is ethnic.

In the early years of European immigration to what is now the United States, white people didn't exist. You might be British, Scottish, Swedish, Dutch, Italian, or Greek, but you weren't simply "white." Employers looking for laborers might post a NINA sign: No Irish Need Apply. The country you came from, your national origin, as indicated by your appearance, your name, your dress, and your accent, distinguished you from people from other countries. As time passed, intermarriage among people from different European countries became more and more common. Their descendants, a mixture of many different ancestries, stopped identifying themselves as "half Irish, one-quarter French, one-quarter German" and became simply *white folks*.

Today, the category of *African American* is usually understood to refer to the descendants of people brought to the New World as slaves from the coastal regions of western Africa. Most African Americans have some European ancestors and some have Native American ancestry as well. Their biological heritage may not be specifically traceable without DNA analysis, but it is a safe assumption that their ancestors came from many different regions of West Africa, with many different tribal/ethnic identities, as well as from various European countries and Native American tribes. Barack Obama, on the other hand, would not be classified as an African American under the traditional definition, since his father was an African, a member of the Luo tribe of Kenya, and his mother, Ann Dunham, was a Euro-American of mostly English ancestry (she was also a cultural anthropologist!).

Is there such a thing as *African American culture?* Certainly, many people identify themselves proudly as African Americans. But is there some specific set of information, beliefs, and practices that everyone who identifies themselves as African American shares in common? Probably not. They may be more likely to share some cultural knowledge and beliefs distinct from their Euro-American counterparts, but there are not any specific beliefs or behavior patterns that apply to every member of this ethnic group. So much depends on other aspects of a person's cultural identity, including the region of the country he lives in, his educational and socioeconomic status, his religion, his occupation, his political leanings, and so forth. It is a mistake to assume that you know very much about a person's *culture* simply by the way he looks or even the ethnicity he claims as his own.

The same is true for the ethnic category *Hispanic* (which may be known variously as Latina/Latino, Chicana/Chicano, or by any number of other names); it is even more nebulous than *African American.* It in-cludes people who have lived in the United States since the 1800s or before, as well as people who are "just off the jet" from Spain, and "just off the bus" from Guatemala. It includes people from Puerto Rico, including those who have lived in New York City for generations and call themselves New Yoricans. Not all Hispanics speak Spanish (though many do), not all are Roman Catholic (though many are), not all know how to make their own tortillas (though their grand-

A Navajo mother and daughter from Arizona (bottom left) represent people with a clear ethnic identity that can be traced back for many generations. The little girl in the photograph below belongs to the Hmong tribe of highland Laos. The little girl (left) is of indeterminate ethnic origin, because her grandparents and parents came from very different populations.

mother might), and not all believe in the "Evil Eye" or the hot/cold theory of illness (though some do). As with the category of *African American*, there is no one set of beliefs and practices shared in common by all Hispanics; there is no such thing as *Hispanic culture*.

Ethnic identity based on one's ancestors from another country or countries is part of everyone's sense of self; it contributes to an individual's culture. But confusing *ethnicity* with *culture* leads to much misunderstanding, and remains a serious problem in North America and parts of Europe. If someone self-identifies as a member of a specific ethnic group, that doesn't mean that she automatically subscribes to a laundry list of cultural attributes shared by all members of that group. Assuming that she does will only lead to trouble. We will return to these issues later when we discuss notions of so-called *cultural competency*.

Religious Affiliation

There is much variation within each named religion, in terms of which beliefs people subscribe to and which practices they regularly participate in. Nevertheless, if you belong to a specific religion, no matter where you live in the world, and if you find other people who belong to the same religion, you can expect to share some of the same beliefs and practices with them. I was raised as a United Methodist (Protestant denomination) and if I attend services at a United Methodist church, I know more or less what to expect. I know the words to the prayers and the songs and the order of service. I know what sort of message to expect from the minister during the sermon. Today, I occasionally attend services at the local Unitarian Universalist (UU) Fellowship. UU is a much less doctrinaire religion, with little in the way of specific beliefs or rules that must be followed. Still, I am familiar enough with a variety of UU congregations that I would feel comfortable attending a service in any city where I might find a UU Fellowship or Church.

The Bahá'í religion developed in Persia (Iran) in the second half of the nineteenth century. In part due to their history of being oppressed and persecuted because of their religious beliefs, one of the main tenets of the Bahá'í religion is to offer hospitality, shelter, and help to any other Bahá'í who shows up on their doorstep. Likewise, if you are an Orthodox Jew, you will automatically share many aspects of religious culture with other Orthodox Jews, no matter where they live.

Some aspects of shared culture, such as religious beliefs, cut across geographic boundaries. These people from Indonesia, Turkey, and Saudi Arabia all identify themselves as Muslims.

And the same is true for most religions, although some relatively recently introduced religions, such as Roman Catholicism in Latin America, will take on various local flavors as they merge with traditional beliefs.

Political Beliefs

One's political beliefs can vary independently of all other aspects of culture. You may be liberal or conservative, or independent, a socialist, a communist, or an anarchist. You may share political beliefs with other people across a wide spectrum of ethnic identities, religious affiliations, socioeconomic statuses, and educational levels. You may have a worldview that includes a variety of political positions on different topics. For example, many people in the U.S. are social liberals but economic conservatives. Some people are ardent antiabortionists yet support the death penalty for serious crimes.

A person may agree with many political stances taken by one party but disagree with its position on one or two issues. In some countries, coalition governments are formed when no one party has a clear majority. In the U.S., whichever party's candidates win an election, that party sets the agenda and policies until the next election.

Some people label themselves as "independents," without affiliation with any organized political group, while others choose not to reveal their stances on political issues at all. Still others openly identify themselves as members of a specific political persuasion through such techniques as yard signs, bumper stickers, lapel buttons, or participation in protest rallies and marches. Even though positions within one political party can vary widely from person to person, you can be sure that you share some beliefs and values with other people who identify themselves the same way.

Social Class

In industrial and postindustrial countries, the amount of income you have determines many other aspects of your life, including where you live, the type of transportation you use, where you shop, how well you eat, where you go on vacation, who your friends and peers are likely to be, and so on. You will share knowledge, beliefs, and practices with others who share similar socioeconomic circumstances. For example, people in the United States with limited incomes living in cities will likely know how to use public transport, where to get groceries that are discounted because they have passed their sell-by date, and where the nearest Goodwill or Salvation Army store can be found (for used clothing, furniture, and appliances). Middle-class people will probably not want to shop at Goodwill, but may shop at Walmart, J.C. Penney's, or Macy's. Those with more income may prefer high-end retail shops such as Neiman Marcus, Saks Fifth Avenue, or Tiffany's.

Likewise, people without health insurance rely more on local emergency rooms for medical care, rather than getting routine checkups and preventive care from a family physician. People with lots of money may make use of concierge medical practices, where one doctor limits the number of patients she sees, and each patient gets undivided attention. A wealthy family may think it entirely appropriate to fly the family to Australia in a private jet for a three-week vacation, while a middle-class family goes camping in the mountains or goes to the beach for a week, and a poor family goes to the local pool.

Anthropologists have written about the *culture of poverty*—shared beliefs and perspectives found among poor people around the world, but *middle-class values* and the *culture of the wealthy and super-wealthy* are also useful concepts. We share similar patterns of thinking and doing with others who have similar levels of income at their disposal. Remember, however, that social class is just one of many different aspects of culture.

Educational Level

People who have completed a certain level of education will share some aspects of their culture with others who have achieved similar levels. One of the functions of a college education is to broaden students' knowledge of the world and how things work and to introduce them to knowledge that all college graduates are expected to share. People who continue on to graduate school and earn a Doctorate of Philosophy (Ph.D.—this includes most of your professors), have gone through similar experiences, including several years of intensive classes in their discipline, written and oral exams, research (data collection and analysis), the writing of a dissertation, and an oral defense of that dissertation. Such a commitment of time and effort means that people with Ph.D.s share a passion for a life of the mind, a passion for learning, and a passion for making new discoveries—whether their field is anthropology, chemical engineering, or music. At the same time, people certainly can be intellectuals, philosophers, and experts in their field without having any formal education.

Subsistence Strategy

Like the notion of shared culture through similar biomes, people who follow one particular subsistence strategy will share certain aspects of their culture with others around the world who follow the same subsistence strategy. For example, dairy farming can be carried out in a variety of different physical environments, but dairy farmers everywhere lead similar lives based on the care, feeding, and milking of their animals. Deep-sea fishermen likewise share much in common with other deep-sea fishermen. Hunters and gatherers are characterized by living in small groups, with generally egalitarian social structures, and in-depth knowledge of the food resources available in

their region. If there were an annual conference of hunters and gatherers, or goat pastoralists, or people who grow paddy rice for subsistence-level consumption, attendees from every region of the world would find much to talk about, much that they share in terms of beliefs, knowledge, attitudes, and behaviors.

Occupation

For people who have jobs that earn money, rather than working directly for their food, occupational culture takes the place of subsistence-strategy culture. One of the most interesting modern ethnographies ever written was based on a study of photocopier repairmen (Orr 1996). Long-distance truck drivers, neurosurgeons, janitorial staff, college professors, lumberjacks, computer animators for Industrial Light & Magic—all members of any occupation—will share aspects of their culture as the result of their similar jobs. Even so, local office culture may vary dramatically from one lo-

Some aspects of culture are based on subsistence strategies. These net fishermen from India (left), Malaysia (bottom left), and Myanmar (Burma) (bottom right) share similar knowledge of fish species, water currents, weather, net making and repair, and other aspects of fishing.

cal region to another, even within the same company. Dress codes for professors in the business school will be much more formal than dress codes for professors in the anthropology department. And an anthropology department at a big research university will have a different flavor than a combined sociology/anthropology department at a small, teaching-oriented college.

Rural/Urban Setting

Whether one lives in a rural area, a medium-sized town, or a big city, one shares certain aspects of one's culture with others who live in similar circumstances. If you live in a rural area, you can't order takeout for delivery for dinner every night. Shopping trips into town must be planned, and you wouldn't be surprised to see cows wandering across the road or to hear roosters crowing at dawn. You might not see films when they are first released, and certainly not the art films or independent films, which likely don't play in the local movie theater.

If you live in a big city, you may be familiar with the subway and bus systems and know that pretty much anything you might want—food, clothes, entertainment—is available within a few minutes. People who live in cities know that dogs must be walked, while people who live in the country may view dogs as outside animals that roam loose. Around the world,

Urban dwellers will have similar knowledge of how to negotiate a postindustrial mega-metropolitan environment and will share many experiences as a result of living in a big city, such as Shanghai (right), London (bottom left), and Kuala Lumpur (bottom right).

big cities have many features in common, and the same is true of rural areas where transportation and communication are less reliable and where many consumer goods are not easily available.

Chronological Age, Historical Age, and Stage of Development in the Life Cycle

In societies that are strictly age graded and segregated, such as the United States, people spend much of their lives hanging out mostly with other people who are the same age. It begins with preschool, or kindergarten, as you must be a certain age to participate. In middle school or junior high, most of your classmates are beginning to go through puberty, just as you are. If you are middle- or upper-class, you may have braces on your teeth. In high school, you share the same experiences with classes, teachers, sports teams, popular music, fashion, and concerns about the future. In college, likewise, you may encounter a broader range of ages in your classes, but most everyone is between the ages of 18 and 22 years. Most are experiencing the freedoms and responsibilities of living away from home and parental control for the first time, exploring academic interests and career possibilities, falling in and out of love, and perhaps losing a grandparent to old age.

Another significant proportion of one's culture comes from living at a specific time in history. Over the course of a lifetime, many aspects of culture will change, but people who were the same age at the same time will have shared thousands of similar experiences. For example, Tom Brokaw has used the phrase "The Greatest Generation" to refer to those people who grew up in the United States during the Depression and served in the military during World War II (and some in Korea as well). Baby Boomers, people born in the United States between 1946 and 1964, are the children of the Greatest Generation, and they grew up watching the same TV shows (*Captain Kangaroo, Bonanza, M*A*S*H*) and Tarzan movies, playing with the first Barbie and Ken dolls, watching as men walked on the moon, and grieving when President John F. Kennedy was assassinated (then Bobby Kennedy and Martin Luther King, Jr.). We witnessed the rise of The Beatles and rock and roll, and many Baby Boomers fought in Vietnam (or protested the war at home).

My daughter Miranda, born in 1980, listened to Raffi songs as a child, watched *Sesame Street,* and played with Transformers and Teenage Mutant Ninja Turtles. During her childhood, the space shuttle *Challenger* blew up, the Branch Davidian compound in Waco burned to the ground, the Murrah Federal Building in Oklahoma City was bombed, and she had just turned 21 when the 9/11 attacks happened. Sharing significant historical events with others of the same age and stage of life binds people together, as much as any other aspect or level of culture.

College students today were children during 9/11, and many readers of this text probably can't remember a time before cell phones, iPods, and the Internet, or a time when *American Idol, Survivor,* and *The Daily Show* weren't staples of prime-time TV. Facebook, MySpace, Twitter, and blogs are all entrenched parts of contemporary life, while the Berlin Wall and the USSR are ancient history.

An additional aspect of the time-dependent nature of culture is sharing experiences with other people going through the same *stage of life*, even if your chronological ages don't exactly match. For example, first-time mothers, ranging in age across their 20s, 30s, and even 40s, will find common ground with other first-time mothers. Likewise, as their friends become engaged and marry, people who are still single will find they have less and less in common with their former friends, and more in common with other singles, regardless of age. You may retire from your career early, at age 50, or late, at age 75, but face many of the same issues that all new retirees face. Thus, one's overlapping circles of shared knowledge, beliefs, attitudes, practices, and behaviors—one's culture—is constantly evolving, shifting, and changing.

Hobbies, Sports, and Leisure Activities, and Special Interest Groups or Voluntary Organizations

In addition to all of the levels or aspects of culture discussed above, people often develop one or more specific interests, and share beliefs and practices with others who have similar interests. It may be a hobby such as model trains, bird watching, gardening, historical reenactments, or a book club. Or it may be philanthropic work such as volunteering at a museum, raising funds for medical research, or raising awareness of the importance of breastfeeding. There are literally thousands of such special interest groups or voluntary organizations that one can choose to belong to, and where one will find other people who share one's passion for the issue.

The development of the Internet has made it possible for people with esoteric interests to find others around the world who feel the same. Alas, my father was born too soon (1918) to be able to use the Internet to find anyone else who shared his passion for collecting mechanical pencils. Today it would be easy to find others.

Final Thoughts

This multi-faceted view of *culture* reveals the complexity of human interactions and experiences in the modern world. It is no longer the case that most people live only among others who share all, or even most, of the same beliefs, attitudes, knowledge, and behaviors. We share different aspects of our culture with different, overlapping groups of people to varying degrees. Culture is much more than simply what country we live in, or where our parents and grandparents came from, and it is much more than ethnic identity. Culture permeates every aspect of our lives and allows us to find common ground with many different types of people from all around the world.

Why Is U.S. Culture So "Weird"?

Everyone Is an Immigrant

Growing up and living in the United States are especially interesting for a variety of reasons. First, and foremost, we are a nation of immigrants. Native Americans came first, in several distinct waves of migration from various regions of north and east Asia, dating back at least 15,000 years, and as recently as

Modern Chinese immigration to the U.S. began in the eighteenth century and peaked following the California Gold Rush of 1849. Every year, thousands of people from all across Asia immigrate to the U.S. The image above shows a modern Chinese American family.

3,000 years. The next major group of immigrants were Western Europeans, who brought with them slaves from along the coast of West Africa ranging from Senegal to Namibia. Chinese immigrants came in great numbers to build the railroads and settle the west. Eastern and southern Europeans immigrated after the turn of the twentieth century, and for the past 50 years

Many European immigrants to the U.S. came through Ellis Island, including a group of children who arrived in 1908 (left). The photograph on the right shows a group of Hungarian immigrants in Cleveland in 1913, celebrating the sunflower harvest.

or longer, people have come from every corner of the globe to live in the United States. Whether our ancestors came over the Bering Land Bridge as hunters and gatherers at the end of the Pleistocene, on the *Mayflower*, in the hold of a slave ship, or by jet from any region of the world, we are all immigrants to this land. This means that literally thousands and thousands of different geographically-based cultural traditions have been brought to these shores.

Assimilation Is a Patchwork Quilt

One finds different rates of assimilation to the developing national culture of the United States. Rates of assimilation vary by area of origin, by how many immigrants came from one place at one time, by why they came (voluntary or forced, looking for educational and economic opportunities, or trying to escape oppression or war at home), and by how persistent different aspects of one's national or tribal/ethnic identity might be. Often, people who immigrate as children or who were born in the United States to immigrant parents try to distance themselves from the culture of the "old country" in which their parents grew up. They may refuse to speak to their grandparents in the grandparents' native tongue, or they may disdain their parents' traditional cuisine, preferring pizza and cheeseburgers instead. Sometimes, in the second or third generation, they may develop an interest in their heritage and seek to learn more about the land their ancestors came from. One of my students who was of Greek ancestry traveled to Greece for a study abroad program, only to discover that the Greece of his grandparents' memories and stories no longer existed. They remembered rural-village Greece of pre–World War II, while he was visiting the Greece of the twenty-first century. The foods, the music, the language, the dress, the lifestyles, had continued to change after his grandparents left.

Democracy, Religious Freedom, and Capitalism

The United States has an unusual political history as a nation-state, originating as a democracy set up in defiance of the inherited ruling system of kings and queens and the rigid socioeconomic class structure of Western Europe in the 1600s and 1700s. We have an unusual religious history, with a constitution guaranteeing the right to freedom of religion, rather than having a state-sponsored religion (or state-sponsored atheism) to which everyone must adhere. We have an unusual economic history, focusing on capitalism. Many Americans have distant or recent ancestors who voluntarily immigrated for economic and educational opportunities—they were willing to leave their home towns, to be adventurous, and to strike out for a new land and the promise of a new life.

Progress Is Good, Resistance Is Futile

Finally, Americans have an underlying deeply embedded and widely shared belief that change equals progress, that progress is always good, and that scientific and technological improvements will continue to make life better. This goes hand-in-hand with a general dissatisfaction with things the way they are, and a constant striving for whatever is perceived to be new and better. Thus, we expect change, we embrace change, we build our hopes and dreams on the future. All of these attributes make the United States a unique place to grow up and reside in, and provide an especially complicated and interesting cultural experience.

Ethnocentrism, Cultural Relativism, and a "Theory of Mind"

How should we think about our own culture, and the culture of others? Traditionally, anthropologists have used the terms **ethnocentrism** and **cultural relativism** to discuss this issue—promoting cultural relativism and urging people to avoid ethnocentrism. However, there has been much misunderstanding of these concepts, especially cultural relativism, both within anthropology and in the broader society. In the sections to follow, we provide clear and detailed explanations of these terms and bring in a most useful concept from psychology, the **Theory of Mind.**

Ethnocentrism

Ethnocentrism, literally "being focused on one's own ethnic group," follows from the view that culture is equivalent to ethnic identity—that one's membership in an ethnic group compromises most, if not all, of one's culture. If you are a Navajo, then you *have* Navajo culture; if you are a Gikuyu, then you *have* Gikuyu culture; if you are a Canadian, then you *have* Canadian culture. Hopefully, the previous sections of this chapter have convinced you that culture is much more complex (and more nebulous) than simply reflecting one's membership in an ethnic group.

Nevertheless, anthropologists often use the term **ethnocentric** to refer to a person's tendency to think that their patterns of thinking and doing—which they have learned, and which they share with others around them—are the best way, the only right way, to think and do things. It is perhaps natural for most people to think that their way is the best; it's what they are familiar with, the system they know how to operate under, and it works for them. It is perhaps natural for people to be initially skeptical when they hear about or observe other ways of thinking and doing. "Their way can't be as good as our way" is a common reaction. We tend to focus on the advantages of our ways, which seem obvious to us, and ignore the disadvantages of our ways, which we never may have recognized or even contemplated. When we encounter others, we spot the disadvantages of their ways immediately; it seems obvious why their ways are inferior to ours, and we fail to look for any advantages that their ways might have over ours.

In his novel of anthropological philosophy, *Ishmael* (1992), author Daniel Quinn divides the world up into two basic cultural divisions, the Takers and the Leavers. He traces the origin of the Takers to the Neolithic Revolution—the domestication of plants and animals and the adoption of a settled way of life. He says that Takers think their way of life, their culture, is the only right way to live. Leavers, on the other hand, represent most of human existence, the people who live a hunting and gathering lifestyle. Quinn says that Leavers believe there are many right ways to live, and they don't particularly care if other people lead different sorts of lives, as long as everyone co-exists more or less peacefully.

According to the main character, Ishmael (a telepathic gorilla), whenever Takers encounter Leavers in the world, they view Leaver ways of life as being inferior, backwards, and primitive. They either destroy the Leavers in order to take their resources or try to convert them to a Taker lifestyle. Ishmael would say that Takers are ethnocentric and Leavers are not. That Leavers observe other people's ways of life, both Takers as well as other Leavers, and think, "Hmm, well, that's a different way to do things," but don't necessarily condemn them out of hand.

Most anthropologists describe some degree of ethnocentrism as being natural and understandable: "Of course we view our way of life as the best, the only right way to live; all people everywhere are ethnocen-tric." Ishmael would disagree, saying that for most of human existence, all people lived as nonethnocentric Leavers. At the same time, most anthropologists view ethnocentrism as a flaw, a problem, something to be overcome, especially by exposure to the cultural anthropological perspective on the world. They would prefer that people give up their ethnocentrism and adopt a stance known as cultural relativism.

Cultural Relativism

The concept of cultural relativism has been horribly misinterpreted and maligned throughout the years. It has nothing to do with such notions as "All cultures are equal," "All values are acceptable," or "Whatever other people do, however they behave, it's hunky-dory, because that's simply *their culture*, and we mustn't pass judgment on other people's culture." Such sentiments are *not* what cultural relativism and cultural anthropology are all about.

Cultural relativism refers to a perspective, an attitude, a viewpoint, an approach to the world. To be a cultural relativist is to attempt to understand the assumptions and beliefs that underlie behavior—the system of logic within which the behavior makes sense. The goal is to reach a point where you can say, "Oh, now I understand why these people act like they do, because I understand their beliefs, their assumptions, their knowledge about the world, their goals, their values, their reasoning." The point of cultural relativism is to understand, not to judge. You absolutely do not have to agree with their beliefs or their assumptions, you do not have to accept their knowledge as "true," and you certainly don't have to think that whatever people do is fine. You are entitled to your own beliefs, assumptions, knowledge, and patterns of behavior, and you are entitled to your own opinions of others' beliefs, assumptions, knowledge, and behaviors. Taking away your rights to your opinions is explicitly *not* the point of cultural relativism and specifically not the point of learning cultural anthropology. To repeat, the point of cultural relativism is to understand, not to judge.

The very first step in adopting the standpoint of cultural relativism is to realize that not everyone shares the same beliefs, assumptions, and knowledge about the world and that not everyone values the same things, or has the same goals. This can be very surprising to people who have grown up in small communities where everyone they have encountered thus far has shared all or most aspects of their culture in common. The first time you encounter a person who doesn't share your values, you may be taken by surprise, as you may not even have realized that there *are* other ways to think about or view something, other ways of doing things. You may think a person is simply rather odd, until you discover that there are entire groups of people who agree with her and disagree with you, and still other groups who have entirely different beliefs and practices. This can be very disconcerting.

The second step in adopting the standpoint of cultural relativism is to realize that most of the time, people's behavior does, in fact, make sense, when viewed from their perspective. "If you believe A, B, and C, and make assumptions D, E, and F, then it is perfectly logical to come to conclusion X, and follow through with actions Y and Z." If another person doesn't share these beliefs and assumptions, then they won't come to the same conclusion, X, and actions Y and Z will not seem reasonable. Two concrete examples may help clarify this point (tables 1.1 and 1.2). Study and think about these examples before continuing to read!

In the example of the geese and swans at Millersville University, federal law is on the side of the Tri-State volunteers. The students at MU are no longer encouraged to harass the geese. Both sides still feel their views are the right way to think.

In the example from the excellent documentary film *Sound and Fury* (Aronson 2001), whether you agree with Peter and Nita or with Chris and Mari, you should be able to *understand* the beliefs and values that underlie their conclusions and their actions. A follow-up film about the Artinian families (Aronson 2006) revealed several interesting points. Heather eventually did get a cochlear implant, as did her mother Nita and her two brothers. They are all still actively involved in deaf culture and do not look down on deaf people without implants. Baby Peter's cochlear implant was a success, and he can hear and speak with other hearing people. He knows about and is involved in deaf culture through his many deaf relatives and communicates fluently with them using American Sign Language. In other words, some of the assumptions on both sides were inaccurate; some of the fears and concerns on both sides were unwarranted. After several years of strained relationships on both sides, the families have reconciled, and each family has accepted the other's viewpoints and decisions.

Theory of Mind

The concept known as *Theory of Mind*, developed by cognitive psychologists, is particularly useful in thinking about ethnocentrism and cultural relativism. By Theory of Mind (TOM), psychologists mean the understanding

Table 1.1   Two groups, each with a shared culture concerning Canada geese, and the contrasting beliefs between the groups

Administrators at Millersville University in Pennsylvania, circa 2004	Volunteers at Tri-State Bird Research & Rescue in Newark, Delaware, circa 2004
Canada geese are ugly and a nuisance.	Canada geese are important and valuable because they are wild, native birds; as migratory waterfowl, they are protected by U.S. federal law.
White swans are beautiful and rare, while Canada geese are everywhere, and not nearly as elegant as swans.	White swans are non-native domesticated birds, introduced to the United States from Europe, who compete with native species such as Canada geese; they are a nuisance.
The white swans on campus have difficulty reproducing because the Canada geese harass them and destroy their eggs.	It's more important to respect and protect Canada geese than to have cute baby swans on campus in the spring.
It would be a good idea to hire MU students to chase away the Canada geese every spring so the swans can reproduce.	It is a violation of federal law for MU students to chase and bother the Canada geese.
The people from Tri-State are kooks.	The people from MU are kooks.
Students stop harassing the geese, but people at MU are annoyed at Tri-State.	Tri-State volunteers educate MU administrators about federal law concerning wild, native, migratory waterfowl.

Table 1.2 Two groups, each with a shared culture concerning children who are deaf, and the contrasting beliefs between the groups*	
Peter and Nita Artinian (both deaf, parents of three deaf children; their siblings and parents are hearing; their daughter Heather is interested in a cochlear implant)	**Chris and Mari Artinian (both hearing, parents of a daughter who can hear and twins sons, one of whom (Baby Peter) is deaf; Chris is the elder Peter's brother; both of Mari's parents are deaf)**
It's not a problem at all to have a child who is deaf; if the parents are deaf, it is better to have children who are also deaf.	It is a huge tragedy to have a child who is deaf, whether the parents are hearing or deaf.
It isn't worth the medical risks to give your child a cochlear implant, especially since it might not work very well, and both deaf and hearing people can learn American Sign Language.	It is worth risking facial paralysis, among other risks of brain surgery, to give your deaf child a chance at normal hearing and speech through a cochlear implant.
Deaf culture is a valuable resource and should be preserved; it is different from, but not inferior to, the culture of the hearing world.	Deaf culture is disappearing, and that is OK; people can learn about it in the history books.
Deafness is not a significant handicap to leading a happy and satisfying life.	Being deaf is a significant handicap to leading a happy and satisfying life.
Deaf culture is rich and meaningful; parents should accept their children for who they are and love them whether they are deaf or hearing (it is child abuse to want to make your child "not deaf").	It is child abuse to withhold a cochlear implant from a deaf child now that the technology is available.
If Heather gets an implant, she will no longer be part of deaf culture and may look down on deaf people.	If Baby Peter gets an implant, he will not be a part of deaf culture but will be taught not to look down on deaf people.
Parents *should not* give their deaf children cochlear implants so they can (maybe) hear.	Parents *should* give their deaf children cochlear implants so they can (maybe) hear.
Chris and Mari are well intentioned, but wrong.	Peter and Nita are well intentioned, but wrong.
Heather does not get a cochlear implant.	Baby Peter does get a cochlear implant.

*Based on the documentary film *Sound and Fury* directed by Josh Aronson (2001)

that most individuals have that other individuals have separate brains, with different thoughts and feelings and different knowledge than their own. It is what allows a person to predict what another might say or do under certain circumstances, given what one knows about the other person. Researchers who study autism spectrum disorders have hypothesized that the lack of a Theory of Mind (or improper development of TOM) is what makes it so difficult for people with these conditions to communicate and interact socially with others—they think that everyone has the same knowledge and feelings that they do, or at the least, they don't realize that other people may have distinct knowledge and feelings.

The classic example demonstrating the TOM is to have two young children in a room with an adult. The adult puts a piece of candy in a box on a table and then leaves the room, taking one of the children with him. The adult then comes back alone and moves the candy from the box to another location. The other child is then returned to the room. The child who remained in the room, and saw the candy being moved, is asked: "Where will the other child look for the candy?" If you have a typical human brain, you will respond that the other child will look in the box on the table. *You* know the candy isn't there anymore, but you also know that the other child still thinks it is—that she has different information in her brain, because she wasn't in the room to see the candy being moved. However, if you don't possess a well-developed Theory of Mind, you might say that the other child will go to the new place to find the candy. Since *you* know where the candy really is, surely the other child must know as well, even though she was out of the room when the candy was moved.

TOM helps explain empathy, when we understand why another person is sad or angry or happy or in pain, even though we aren't experiencing the same emotion or physical response. It is what leads most people to consider the consequences of their actions, both for themselves and for others, before acting, and to care about how others might be affected. It is what encourages us to communicate new information to others—because we know that they haven't yet heard some piece of news. It also allows us to predict how they will react upon hearing the news. It allows us to manipulate people through lying, and to express ourselves in a joking or sarcastic manner. It is what enables us to read others' emotional and intentional states from their facial expressions and body postures and movements.

Evolutionary psychologists view the evolution of conscious awareness and the development of a theory of mind as being critical steps on the path to becoming fully social human beings. Our well-functioning TOM allows us to be successful, to cooperate and work with others, to get along, and to move confidently through our social worlds. Without a theory of mind, it becomes very difficult to know how to behave, how to interact socially with others, and how to communicate clearly. So, what does the Theory of Mind have to do with ethnocentrism and cultural relativism?

All humans share a set of fundamental facial expressions and body postures that reveal our internal emotional states. As mentioned earlier in the discussion of the Universal People, facial expressions that indicate happiness, sadness, anger, fear, pain, and disgust are human universals. Indeed, many characteristic facial expressions and body postures are shared with our primate relatives, especially chimpanzees and bonobos, but also various types of monkeys, and even nonprimate mammals. Comforting behaviors, aggressive threats, and indications of fear or submission can all be accurately interpreted across a wide range of mammalian species.

But of course, in addition to these basic behaviors, postures, and expressions, humans add multiple layers of cultural modification and meaning. A wink may mean a variety of things even within one culture, as well as across cultures. Does nodding your head up and down always mean yes, or can it mean no? Does holding hands with someone of the same sex imply anything about one's sexual orientation? Does the way you walk reveal your gender identity?

As we grow up in a particular set of cultural circumstances, we learn and absorb the beliefs, knowledge, and attitudes of those around us. Much of it is by observation and imitation, and some of it is through explicit teaching and learning from our parents and others we interact with. Finally, some of it is through other people's reactions to what we do. When we do something wrong or express an opinion that isn't popular, we are scolded or corrected, or at least we are ineffective. When we do something right or express an opinion that others share, we are rewarded through praise or by getting whatever it was we wanted. We grow up surrounded by many people who share all or most of our culture and among others who share significant portions of it. We rely on our TOM to move confidently through our social worlds. If we are not exposed, early in life, to people with *different* ideas and opinions and knowledge, then we don't know that such creatures exist.

People may speak of **culture shock,** of feeling disoriented, lost and adrift, when visiting another country or finding themselves in any circumstances outside their normal range of comfort and experience. Culture shock is what happens when we first realize that our TOM, which has served us so well within our usual circles, is of little or no help at all in our present circumstances. We don't know the rules. People don't share our beliefs; they don't know the same things we know (and vice versa); they don't react the way we think they will. We make a joke, and they are offended; we wear shorts, and they assume we are promiscuous; we take some proffered food morsel with our left hand, and they think we are either deliberately being rude or are simply clueless or disgusting. Likewise, they are flummoxed that we don't seem to know the first thing about how a proper human behaves—how can anyone *not know* that taking food with your left hand is forbidden?

When I was doing research in Mali, the only other "white" people that most Malians had interacted with were French. Because the French had been their colonial masters, Malians had had to get used to French views and opinions, including the disdain with which many French people viewed them. Malians knew that most French people looked down on them and would not bother to learn any Bambara (the local language). Thus, Malians tended to be wary of white people and to assume that they were French and held typical French views.

Imagine the scene: I'm walking along the street and some Malian women are giving me annoyed looks. I suspect they think I am French, so I go over to talk to them. They say something to me in French, and I respond, in Bambara, that I don't speak French. I introduce myself as an American, and speak to them in their own language (however bad my accent and grammar might be). They are surprised and delighted that I know some Bambara and relieved that I am not French, as they have more favorable opinions of Americans.

In one extremely remote rural village in northern Mali, I met an *ancient combatant*, an elderly Malian man who had fought in North Africa for the French army during World War II. Proud of his ability to still speak French fluently, he came up to me and offered greetings in French. When I tried to explain to him, in his own native language, that I didn't speak French, he didn't believe me. He could understand my Bambara clearly, but surely I must be kidding that I didn't speak *toubabou-kan* (the Bambara term for French, which literally translates as *the language of white people*). I was white, therefore I had to know toubabou-kan. He was not aware, until meeting me, that there were non-French white people in the world, who spoke non-French languages. When I explained that I came from the United States, he responded indignantly that he'd never heard of such a place and stalked off quite grumpily. So much for globalization!

Thus, our Theory of Mind works for some aspects of predicting thoughts and behavior when we encounter other people, due to our common human heritage. But our theory of mind doesn't function so well for other aspects of predicting thoughts and behavior when we encounter people who don't share our cultural background. Having come to rely on our TOM, we may feel bewildered, even betrayed, by its failure in some cultural contexts.

THINKING LIKE AN ANTHROPOLOGIST

Remember These Things

As you study cultural anthropology, and learn more about your own culture and the cultures of other groups of people, you will realize that not everyone shares the same beliefs and knowledge or the same ways of doing things. You will hopefully learn not to assume *anything* about what's inside the mind of a person you have just met. You can expect to share some things, and to differ in other ways, but you won't know what common ground you share or what differences of opinion you hold until you have interacted with them over at least some period of time and in various circumstances. A list of things to keep in mind as you go out into the world and meet new people might include:

- The world can't be divided into us and them.
- People who share skin color (and body shape and facial features, and so on), may belong to many different cultures.
- People who live in one country or nation-state may belong to many different cultures.
- People who share many aspects of culture may end up living in different regions of the world.
- People who look very different from you may share many aspects of culture with you, especially if they grew up in the same region.
- People who look and act just like you in many ways may, in fact, have very different beliefs and practices concerning some issues.

So, how should you approach new people you meet? Most importantly, *don't make assumptions*. If you meet one person who belongs to a particular identifiable group, and he is a jerk, don't generalize that opinion to all other members of the group. Just because one skateboarder almost mowed you down on the sidewalk doesn't mean all skateboarders are reckless or lack concern for others around them. Don't conclude that you don't like Indian food just because you ate one meal at an Indian restaurant and you didn't care for it. If, as a male anthropologist, you meet men in one Mexican village who don't like you talking to their wives, don't assume that this is a "Mexican" trait and apply it to men in neighboring villages, as they may not object if you interview their wives (Fry 2000).

Don't assume anything. Learn to appreciate all the many fascinating ways there are of being human. Learn to listen and observe, and try to understand where people are coming from, and what their goals are. Try to understand why they do what they do, even if it is very different from what you would do in similar circumstances. Treat everyone with respect, as you would like to be treated.

Evaluating Culture

So . . . does being a cultural relativist, overcoming ethnocentrism, mean that we have to agree with everyone else's ideas and opinions? Are all viewpoints equally valid? Do we have to excuse behavior we find abhorrent since it is based on different beliefs from our own? *Absolutely not.* Nothing in the anthropological perspective says that all cultures are the same, that all values are interchangeable, that all actions have equivalent outcomes. You don't have to agree, you don't have to approve—all you are being asked to do is try to understand.

Once you do understand the cultural beliefs and assumptions underlying people's actions, if you want to move on to the level of comparison and making judgments about them, there are better and worse ways of going about it. The worse way is just to proclaim, "Whatever I think, whatever I do, is right, and everyone else is wrong. So there!" A better way is to look at a particular belief or practice, or set of beliefs or practices, and ask a series of questions about it. The answers to these questions will go a long way toward helping you make a more objective evaluation.

Question #1:
Is the Belief True from a Scientific Perspective?

Some anthropologists (those of a *postmodern* persuasion) might say that we shouldn't even consider privileging the Western scientific perspective, as it is no more valid than any other belief system. However, I remain a positivist, someone who believes there is a reality out there that we can study and learn about.

Even though it is the nature of scientific knowledge to be constantly in flux, ever changing as more data are collected and different analyses are performed, there are many enduring truths that have been established beyond a reasonable doubt through the use of the scientific perspective. In addition, science is not explicitly Western—it is a method of formulating hypotheses, gathering information to test those hypotheses, and either supporting or refuting the hypotheses. It is a way of trying to understand the world through data that we can measure and collect and through forces we can subject to testing (which is why untestable supernatural explanations aren't considered). Scientists throughout the world operate in similar ways—science itself has a culture, if you will.

Whether you live in Japan or Zimbabwe or Canada or the Republic of Georgia, all scientists operate from the same basic set of assumptions, using the same reasoning and the same set of rules. Thus, it seems reasonable to begin our inquiries with the question: Is the belief *true* from a scientific perspective?

At the same time, we must acknowledge that *we may not even know* if a belief is true or false from a scientific perspective. The scientific perspective is not all knowing—there remain many unanswered questions, and many more *unasked* questions. Even if scientists have explored a particular issue, the data may be sketchy and/or inconsistent. And just because some scientist, somewhere, knows a lot about a particular topic, that doesn't mean that the individual anthropologist is even aware of the research. No one person can know everything there is to know about a single topic, let alone all topics! Scientific knowledge is often lost in back issues of dusty journals, and new scholars often reinvent a particular wheel, only to discover later that their new idea was proposed by someone else years before.

One of my favorite examples of why a humble attitude is most appropriate comes from my research in Mali. I was talking with my good friend Ami about her birth experience. She mentioned that her son was born via a Cesarean section. When I asked her why a C-section had been required, she said it was because her husband lived in France. I must have looked at her dumbly; she explained that when a woman goes into labor, someone goes to find her husband. He hurries home and they have sexual intercourse, because sex during labor helps "open the pathway" for the baby and makes the delivery easier. Since her husband was in France, they couldn't have sex, and thus her labor was difficult and she ended up with a C-section.

Of course, I'm thinking, "Who in their right mind wants to have sex when they're in labor?!" I simply dismissed her explanation as some bizarre idea the local people had come up with. Several years later, I discovered that in the United States, doctors may apply commercially produced prostaglandin gel to a laboring woman's cervix, as it relaxes the muscle and helps the cervix dilate fully so the baby can be born. It turns out that male ejaculate is full of natural prostaglandins. In other words, the Malians are right—sex during labor does make the birth easier. Just because I didn't know that when I heard it, doesn't mean that I was right and Ami was wrong. Just the opposite. Therefore, be humble when considering Question #1: Is the belief *true* from a scientific perspective?

Question #2:
Is the Belief System Internally Consistent and Logical?

Given the assumptions and beliefs and knowledge of the people, is their reasoning consistent and logical? Does the cultural logic lead to the conclusion that people draw? Most of the time, within the cultural context, the reasoning is indeed consistent and logical. As stated previously, "If you believe A, B, and C, and make assumptions D, E, and F, then it is perfectly logical to come to conclusion X, and follow through with actions Y and Z." It may be difficult to set aside your objections to, or disagreements with, people's beliefs and assumptions. But if you do, you will usually find that people are acting rationally from their perspective—think about the examples of the geese and the cochlear implants.

Question #3:
What Are the Consequences of This Particular Complex of Cultural Beliefs and Practices for the Individual?

As you answer, include both disadvantages (risks or costs) and advantages (benefits or gains) for the individual. Most behaviors or systems of behaviors have some consequences for the individual who participates. Often, the consequences are neither all good nor all bad but rather a complex mixture. The person may not even be aware of all the costs or all the benefits. Or they may decide that the benefits outweigh the costs.

It is easier to grasp the benefits of something you believe or do yourself, and more difficult to conceptualize what the benefits of something might be that you don't do yourself. For example, think about the possible *benefits* to individuals of living in a culture where marriages are arranged by relatives of the bride and groom and the corresponding *costs* of living in a culture where you have to find your own marriage partner. Think about the possible *benefits* to individual women of living in a culture where they wear modest clothing that disguises their weight and appearance, which therefore cannot be used to judge a woman's value. And think about the corresponding costs of living in a culture where one's physical appearance, especially for women, is considered more important than one's intelligence, kindness, character, or courage.

Question #4:
What Are the Consequences for the Group/Society?

Again, consider both the disadvantages and the advantages for the group as a whole. Apply the same type of analysis as before, but shift your focus to the level of the group. Sometimes a practice may be harmful to the individual but beneficial to the group. Or some individuals may benefit, but the group as a whole suffers. This is a very enlightening exercise to practice, beginning with your own familiar beliefs and practices, before you expand to consider other cultures.

Question #5:
What Are the Consequences for the Environment?

As before, consider both advantages and disadvantages to the natural environment (including plant, animal, and inorganic components). A particular set of beliefs and practices may be generally advantageous to the individual and/or the group, but devastating to the environment. Garrett Hardin's famous example of "The Tragedy of the Commons" (1968) comes readily to mind. In such situations, it is in every individual's best interests to exploit jointly owned environmental resources to their fullest extent, even if that eventually leads to degradation or destruction of the resources for everyone. The commercial fishing industry provides employment and food for many people, but overfishing of the ocean has resulted in the widespread extinction or extirpation (local extinction) of many once-plentiful species.

Industrialized nations are dependent on vast quantities of natural resources obtained through mining, cutting down rain forests, and other extractive technologies. Many of these processes destroy habitats for plants, animals, and people and leave behind high levels of toxic waste. Industrialized nations also require energy from many sources, including solar power, hydroelectric (water) power, coal, nuclear reactors, and oil. With the exception of solar energy, the production of power from these other sources can lead to environmental disasters, including the drying up of the Aral Sea in Central Asia, widespread toxic air pollution from the burning of coal, nuclear disasters such as the meltdown at Chernobyl in 1986, and oil spills such as the Exxon Valdez in Alaska in 1989 and the 2010 British Petroleum oil well explosion and subsequent leak in the Gulf of Mexico.

Time Frames and Cost/Benefit Analyses

Simple and straightforward examples of the previous concepts are easy to come up with. The reality, though, is that most cultural beliefs and practices have complex consequences at all three levels, with both advantages and disadvantages. In addition, one has to consider not only short-term consequences but also medium- and long-term consequences at all three levels. Some behaviors might be advantageous in the short-term but turn out to have long-term consequences that no one foresaw. Or, like any sort of delayed gratification, the behavior might be disadvantageous in the short run but have long-term benefits that make the short-term costs worthwhile—for example, eating peanut butter and jam sandwiches for a month while saving money to buy a new coat, or foregoing a couple of invitations to party so you can go to the library and study for your upcoming anthropology exam instead! Delayed gratification—something you must work hard for, over a period of time—is often sweeter than instant gratification.

In the real world, the costs and benefits don't necessarily accrue to the same individual, or to the same group, or to the local environment. If I can reap the benefits, while someone else pays the cost, I am more likely to choose that course of action. For example: "If I'm paying for my own meal, I'll go to McDonald's, but if my parents are paying, I'll choose somewhere nice and have a steak!" or "If I can tap into my neighbor's wireless connection, why pay for my own?"

Think of all the people in North America who heat their houses with coal. Coal heat is relatively inexpensive and seems to have few drawbacks for the individual consumer. Most of the risks and costs fall on the people who produce the coal—the miners, who are at a much higher risk of death and chronic lung disease. Other costs fall on everyone, as coal mining destroys the landscape, pollutes the air, and contributes to global warming. In the United States, nuclear power plants provide clean, efficient energy for many regions of the country at reasonable rates, but only if you don't have to calculate in the costs of uranium mining in the Four Corners region, where radioactive dunes of mine tailings cover many acres of land and where high levels of radioactivity can be found in sidewalks, houses, and the meat supply (McLeod 1983). When there are safety problems with the nuclear plants themselves, everyone pays.

Remember that the point of asking these questions, and searching for the answers, is to provide a more objective evaluation of a particular set of cultural beliefs and behaviors. You may still conclude that you like your own group's traditional ways of thinking and doing better than any others you know about. But you might also discover that you are paying a much higher price for some of your beliefs and practices than you realized—and you may decide that they are not worth the true price. Or you may discover that others are paying the price while you reap the benefits, and that may not sit well with you.

FINAL THOUGHTS

One of the great things about learning to think like an anthropologist is that you become more aware of how the world works. You become more aware of your own beliefs and assumptions and values. You may discover that you want to discard or modify some of the cultural beliefs you have held to this point, and change how you do some things. Unlike the genes your parents bequeathed to you, you can *change* the ideas in your head and you can *change* your behavior. Culture is not written in stone.

There are many right ways to live, many fulfilling ways to be a human being. *Life is a feast.* Don't let your assumptions, your fears, or your enculturation during childhood limit you to only *a fraction of the feast.*

Key Concepts Review

Anthropology is a complex discipline: part hard science, part social science, and part humanities.

Anthropology is distinguished by three unique characteristics;
- Anthropologists study all humans, everywhere.
- Anthropologists study all humans, all the time.
- Anthropologists study humans as both biological and cultural beings.

Cultural anthropology is one of the traditional four subfields of anthropology; the other three are: archeology, biological anthropology, and linguistic anthropology.

Two approaches that combine elements of the traditional four subfields are applied anthropology and biocultural anthropology.

Cultural anthropologists study what people do, why they do it, and what the consequences are for the individual, for the group, and for the environment.

Culture includes what's inside people's heads (knowledge, beliefs, attitudes) and is therefore learned, shared, and patterned.

Culture includes what people do as a result of what's inside their heads (our biological propensities are modified and given meaning by cultural beliefs).

Culture includes what people make (material culture, the items they produce).

Culture is ever-changing; cultural beliefs and practices may be adaptive, neutral, or maladaptive at the level of the individual, the group, or the environment.

Much of culture is not explicitly known—it is simply *tradition*, the way things are done; cultural beliefs give rise to social structure.

Cultural anthropologists typically spend several years doing research with a particular group. and learn the local language in order to communicate directly with the research subjects; the main research methodology is participant-observation.

Cultural anthropologists examine what people say is ideal in their culture, as well as what they claim they do; they also make observations in order to understand how people behave.

Four main theoretical perspectives are useful in introductory cultural anthropology: evolution, structural-functionalism, historical particularism, and symbolism.

Many aspects of culture are based on geography, including international culture, biome, national culture, tribal or ethnic identity, and regional, state, and local culture.

Many aspects of culture are based on learned, shared, patterned ways of thinking and doing that are not related to geography, including ethnic identity, religious affiliation, political beliefs, social class, educational level, subsistence strategy, occupation, rural/urban setting, chronological age, historical age, stage of development in the life cycle, hobbies, sports, and leisure activities, and special interest groups or voluntary organizations.

Culture in the United States is "weird" for a number of reasons:
- Everyone is an immigrant.
- Assimilation is a patchwork quilt.
- Democracy has always been the major political force.
- Capitalism has always been the major economic force.
- Americans believe in *progress*.

continued

Through anthropology, we try to become less ethnocentric and embrace cultural relativism—understanding people's behavior based on their cultural beliefs, rather than our own.

There are ways to evaluate and compare cultures without being ethnocentric; these include asking a series of questions to help understand what the advantages and disadvantages of any particular set of cultural beliefs might be at various levels and across different time frames.

Humans are endlessly fascinating and it is a grand adventure to explore all the many different ways of being human.

2

BASIC NEEDS

Food, Shelter, & Stuff

*The future of subsistence for the entire world may indeed
be in a return to having each person or family produce
much of their own food supply through direct labor or
by purchasing from local farmers, herders, and fisherfolk.*

In this chapter, we explore issues related to how humans provide for their most basic needs. Like other mammals, humans require water and food to survive. We need shelter from the elements, we must get rid of waste products through urination and defecation, and we have to figure out how to reproduce and care for our children. Being humans, of course, we accomplish these goals, in part, through a vast array of cultural means, and we create elaborate, multilayered systems of meaning surrounding each of these activities.

GETTING FOOD:
MODES OF SUBSISTENCE, PART I

When anthropologists talk about **modes of subsistence,** they are referring to how people get the food they need to survive. To subsist means "to exist" or "to live on." The five basic modes of subsistence that humans rely on are introduced in the first part of the chapter and described in more detail later. It is important to realize that this classification scheme is only a *heuristic device*—a way of simplifying and ordering the complex reality that exists in the world. Most people today combine two or more modes of subsistence in their daily lives.

Anthropologists also use the term **subsistence** as an adjective to mean that people are eating all of the food they hunt, gather, or raise, rather than selling it in the market. Thus, a subsistence farmer grows crops only for his own family's needs. A subsistence fisherman gets much of his diet from the fish he catches and eats himself.

Hunting and Gathering

Hunting and gathering (also known by the term **foraging),** is the original way that all humans met their needs for food. The key feature of a hunting and gathering lifeway is that all of the food consumed is wild—*wild plants, wild animals,* honey from *wild bees,* and so forth. From the time of the earliest bipedal hominids some 5–6 million years ago, until relatively recently, all humans lived as omnivorous hunters and gatherers. Around 10,000 years ago, populations living in several different areas of the world began trying to modify the wild plants and animals in their environments to make them more useful. Over time, some of these plants and animals became *domesticated*, and people began relying more and more on these domesticated sources of food. The transition to a primary reliance on domesticated foods is known as the Neolithic Revolution. The distinction between wild and domesticated will be explored in more detail later.

The hunting and gathering lifestyle was not abandoned at the time of the Neolithic Revolution. It is not a primitive or backward way of obtaining food, and foragers didn't simply "miss the memo" or *forget* to switch to raising their own plants and animals. Today, some people living on every continent (except Antarctica) continue to live as hunters and gatherers. Hunting and gathering is an effective and sustainable lifestyle. Moreover, many people who rely primarily on domesticated food sources combine these foods with wild plants and animals obtained through their own labor or through trade or purchase.

Pastoralism

Pastoralism refers to a mode of subsistence that is based on the raising of *domesticated or semidomesticated animals*. People raise or herd many different types of animals. Domesticated animals can provide food through their meat and other body parts, their milk, their blood, or their eggs. They can also be traded or sold in order to obtain other products.

Horticulture and Agriculture

Horticulture and agriculture are the terms anthropologists use to refer to two slightly different modes of subsistence based on the raising of *domesticated plants*. Humans grow thousands of different types of domesticated plants and use different parts of the plant for food, just as foragers do with wild plants. Domesticated plant products, including nonfood crops (opium poppies, tobacco, cotton, and sisal), can also be traded or sold in order to obtain other products.

In anthropological contexts, **horticulture** refers specifically to the growing of domesticated plants using humans as the only source of power and using a digging stick or a hoe rather than a plow. Most horticulturalists are subsistence farmers, growing crops for their own needs. **Agriculture,** in contrast, refers to the addition of domesticated animals as a power source and the addition of the plow as a tool. A plow completely overturns the surface of the ground prior to planting. Some agriculturalists are subsistence farmers, while others produce crops for their own family's use and trade or sell the surplus. Note that these are the specific, anthropological meanings of these terms, which are used differently by other academic disciplines and by the general public.

Intensive and Industrial Agriculture

The last mode of subsistence refers to the further addition of power sources and more complex technology to the raising of domesticated plants. It is known variously as mechanized or intensive agriculture, factory farming, or industrial agriculture and involves the addition of machine power and extensive modification of the soil and growing conditions (irrigation, fertilizer, terracing of hillsides, etc.). Some people around the world grow food for their own families using these techniques, as well as surplus to trade or sell in the marketplace. In the context of factory farming/industrial agriculture, the crops are grown on a vast scale, with the use of machines powered by oil or electricity for planting, weeding, harvesting, storing, and transport; the use of commercial irrigation systems; and the use of chemical fertilizers, herbicides, and pesticides. Most or all of the harvest is sent to market or to processing plants. In order to access these crops for food, people must pay for them in the marketplace.

WHY DO WE CARE?

Why do anthropologists study subsistence patterns and strategies? At one time, cultural anthropologists were interested mainly in people's ideas—their beliefs about the world. The prevailing attitude in the discipline was, "Yeah, sure, everybody has to eat, and every population has obviously figured out how to get food somehow, or they wouldn't still be around, but subsistence is peripheral to the interesting aspects of culture, like religion and kinship, art, music, and social organization."

Eventually, anthropologists came to appreciate that how people thought and how they organized themselves, even their artistic expression and religious beliefs, had a lot to do with how they got their food. They realized that *subsistence comes first*, in many ways, and that understanding the relationships between human societies and their natural environments explained much of the variation found around the world in other aspects of culture.

Several different theoretical orientations were applied to this new focus on subsistence. An early view, **environmental determinism,** held that the environment *determined*, in a very rigid and narrow way, what sort of subsistence patterns a population would have. A second approach, **environmental possibilism,** suggested that the environment *limited the range of choices* people had for subsistence but did not determine which option people would choose under particular circumstances. People living in similar environments might exploit them in very different ways, within the possible choices available.

Julian Steward and the Concept of the *Culture Core*

Environmental possibilism was most coherently developed by Julian Steward, an American archeologist and ethnohistorian who spent many years studying the Shoshone of the Great Basin in the western United States. His theoretical and methodological approach is today known as **cultural ecology** and requires a careful study of the relevant environmental variables, as well as the way in which specific groups of people adapt to, interact with, and exploit the resources available to them. For Steward and other cultural ecologists, subsistence activities can be considered the **culture core,** the heart of a culture. Steward defined the culture core as: those features of a culture that play a part in the society's way of making its living—the production and distribution of food, and the technology, knowledge, attitudes, and beliefs that affect subsistence.

From its primary position at the center of a population's adaptation, subsistence activities influence other, more peripheral aspects of culture such as property ownership, settlement patterns, kinship and political organization, and the paucity or wealth of material culture. Even many aspects of religion, art, music, language and other expressive realms are influenced by subsistence. Steward allowed for lots of sloppiness and overlap—subsistence activities *do not determine* other aspects of culture, just as the environment *does not determine* the subsistence patterns themselves. As long as the system works *well enough* over time for the population to survive, the population can be considered to have adapted to its environment. If the population overexploits its resources, however, it will eventually have to expand its range, move to another area, or change its subsistence base; otherwise it will become extinct.

Carrying Capacity

The concept of **carrying capacity** is used by plant and animal ecologists to understand the number of individuals of a particular species that can be supported successfully in a given environment in a sustainable fashion. It is also used by cultural ecologists. Although the parameters are difficult to define precisely for humans, the concept of carrying capacity is a useful *heuristic device* for thinking about these topics. In trying to assess the human carrying capacity of a particular environment, or of the planet as a whole, we have to consider many variables.

Natural Resources

Just as for plants and nonhuman animals, the natural resources of a region are paramount in determining how many humans the land can support. By natural resources, we mean many different aspects of the environment, including the physical landscape. How much soil is there (as opposed to barren rocks, sand, or ice), and how deep is the soil? Is the soil barren and fragile, or deep and rich? Does the soil periodically get replenished by flood waters or runoff from nearby hills or mountains? What is the terrain like? How steep are the hills? How broken is the landscape?

How much sunlight is available year-round? Does it vary seasonally (temperate and polar regions) or is it pretty much the same all the time (the tropics). How much of it reaches the ground (more in the desert, less under the tropical rain forest canopy)? What is the weather like in terms of seasonality, temperature extremes and average temperatures, rainfall patterns, humidity, and storm activity? How variable is the

Clean water is a necessity for human health. USAID has sponsored new clean water sources for villagers in Eritrea.

weather on a daily, monthly, seasonal, yearly, and multi-year basis? Are there water sources available other than rainfall, such as springs, wells, creeks, rivers, lakes, or the ocean? What types of natural disasters occur in the area—volcanic activity, earthquakes, tornadoes, hurricanes, flooding, or drought? Are high winds or dust storms ever a problem?

Are the resources distributed evenly across the landscape, or are they patchy? Are there multiple types of resources, such as those found at different altitudes in mountainous regions, or a combination of fresh- and/or salt-water resources as well as land-based resources, such as those found along rivers as they enter the sea?

What sorts of plants grow in the region naturally, and how lush or sparse is the vegetation? What sorts of insects live there—both useful insects and ones that compete for plant resources? What types of native animals live on the landscape, and at what densities? Do the native animals compete with humans for plant resources? Are any of the animals dangerous? By dangerous, I mean both in the physical sense of grizzly bears, elephants, and sharks, and in other senses, such as poisonous snakes, frogs, and insects, or as vectors or reservoirs of disease.

All of these different aspects of the environment factor into how many people the land can support. But the basic physical resources and the plant and animal resources of an area are just the beginning.

Cultural Perceptions of the Available Resources

It isn't enough for resources to simply be there, in the environment. They must be defined and recognized as resources by the people who live there. Cultural perceptions of resources depend in part on knowledge. Is it edible or is it poisonous? Can it be prepared in such a way that it becomes edible? Is it defined as off-limits because of religious beliefs, or because people think it is yucky or disgusting or bad tasting?

Children around the world learn from their families, neighbors, and peers what is edible and what is not. Are some potential foods off-limits because they have totemic (religious/kinship) value? Are some potential foods off-limits because people don't know how to find them, or how to kill them, or how to prepare them? Since what we eat *becomes* us—becomes our flesh and bones—our learned cultural perceptions of, and attitudes toward, foodstuffs are deeply internalized and difficult to unlearn as an adult. People have physi-

ological reactions to just the thought of eating unfamiliar foods, or familiar foods they view as disgusting.

Two examples from my own experience illustrate this clearly. When my daughter Miranda was a toddler, we lived Mali, West Africa, where the people routinely collect termites during swarming season, fry them, and munch on them, considering them tasty, nutritious snacks. Miranda, not having any preconceived notions, ate them with gusto. As an adult, even though I knew intellectually that termites were edible, and had my own daughter telling me they were tasty, I could not bring myself to eat them.

Years later in Texas, I was waiting at the bus stop with a neighbor for our kids to arrive home from school. On the breeze we both caught the scent of meat barbecuing on the grill. My mouth began to water and I thought, "Oh man, that smells wonderful!" My neighbor, a vegetarian Hindu, commented, "Ugh. That smell of cooking meat is making me sick to my stomach. Please tell my son just to come inside when the bus arrives." Ah, the power of culture.

Knowledge and Technology

As we will see when we go through each subsistence strategy in more detail, the resources available in any environment will depend in part on what level of technology the people have available. Paleoanthropologists speculate that successful exploitation of large herbivores (antelope, mammoth, bison) for food was not possible until evolving humans had developed both the cognitive capacity for coordinated hunting, appropriate stone tool technology for spear points, and perhaps language.

Some hunters and gatherers today apply poison derived from plants or animals to the tips of their tiny arrowheads. This technology allows them to kill prey animals that are much larger than they could kill if they didn't have the poison. Some landscapes can support crops, but only if irrigation or soil enhancers are available. Others might support domestic livestock, if prevention of, or treatment for, endemic diseases is available. Likewise, it isn't possible to exploit open ocean resources unless you have ocean-going vessels and the requisite knowledge of weather, ocean currents, and the species you are hunting.

It may not be some gadget that you need, but knowledge—of the natural history of plants and animals, of when and how to grow crops, how to hunt particular animals, how to process foods to remove poisons, when and where plants will be producing fruit or nuts, when herds of animals will be migrating, and so on.

If a typical North American were dropped in the middle of the Kalahari desert, with all of Western technology available at his command, he would not see anything at all to eat and would soon perish. But a man of the !Kung San, who has lived in the Kalahari all his life, knows where to find roots, nuts, berries, birds' nests, and most importantly, water. He knows which foods are edible raw, which are edible only if cooked, which are poisonous, and so forth. Although his material technology may be simple—digging sticks, carrying containers, bows and arrows—his knowledge allows him to survive in the Kalahari.

Sometimes we might be perfectly willing to try a new food, but we don't because we don't know exactly what it is or how to prepare it. There are probably many foods in your local grocery store that you pass by, not even giving them a thought, because you don't know what they are or how to prepare them, and aren't willing (or interested enough) to find out. For some foods, it isn't obvious how they should be prepared to those who didn't grow up in a family or culture that routinely eats them: artichokes, asparagus, cactus pads, fish heads, pigs' feet, and tripe.

The same is true of foods available at restaurants. I've had students refuse to eat *couscous*, thinking it was something exotic (it's simply a form of pasta made from wheat flour). Another student reported that a meal she ordered had exotic ingredients, including the enigmatic *panko*. Panko refers to a type of bread crumbs! Others have passed on the "fried plantains," having no idea that plantains are similar to bananas. A sign on a seafood buffet, "Morton Bay Bugs," is not likely to attract many North Americans, while Australians know that "Bugs" are tasty crustaceans, related to lobsters.

Whether we are living off the land as hunters and gatherers or buying our meals already prepared for us in a restaurant, we eat only a fraction of the potential foods available in the environment. Our knowledge, technology, and learned cultural attitudes influence what we actually end up eating.

Cultural Definitions of "Successfully Support"

Remember that the carrying capacity of the environment is defined as how many individuals of a par-

ticular species can be supported successfully in a given environment. With humans, as always, there is a cultural component to this aspect. Given two groups of people who live on two identical parcels of land with the same natural resources and who have very similar attitudes, levels of knowledge, and technological capabilities, you still may find variation in how many people live on the land, even though both groups consider themselves to be supported successfully. Can you think why this might be the case?

As always in population biology, it comes down to reproductive strategies—is a species relatively **r-selected,** or relatively **k-selected?** In r-selected species, females have many offspring, each with a low probability of survival, and the parents do not provide much, if any, care. In k-selected species, females have few offspring, each with a high probability of survival, and the parents (at least the mothers) provide substantial care.

Humans, like all mammals, are relatively k-selected. We have small numbers of children, and we invest heavily in each of them through nine months of gestation, several years of breastfeeding, and many years of care and protection. Cultural beliefs and practices affect exactly how many children we have and how much care we provide.

As a general rule, *Western* attitudes toward reproduction are that it is better to have fewer children, through the use of modern contraceptives, and provide the best care that we can. As a general rule, in many *non-Western* cultures, parents are interested in having as many children as they can. We will explore this cultural difference in more detail later, in the chapter on economics. For now, suffice it to say that where children are highly valued, parents are willing to sacrifice the *quality* of each child (to a point) in order to have more children. They would much rather have six short, somewhat skinny children, than two tall, more robust ones. At some point, malnutrition from overpopulation in a region may lead to higher rates of morbidity (illness) and mortality (death), but many parents would still prefer to have four short, skinny, surviving children, out of six or eight, than only two tall, healthier children out of two. Thus, for humans, carrying capacity is not an objective characteristic of the land itself but rather a subjective characteristic based on cultural values and goals.

Cultural Definitions of "Sustainable"

Another aspect of carrying capacity is maintaining a certain population in a **sustainable** fashion, but there are many different definitions of sustainability. One way to define the term *sustainable* is to say that it means forever—into the future as far as we can predict, and beyond. If a certain environment and subsistence strategy can support, say, 100 people indefinitely, then we can conclude that their subsistence strategy is sustainable as long as the population and the environment remain stable. Stability in population size can be achieved through limiting reproduction, through death (due to malnutrition, disease, accident, or interpersonal violence), through out-migration, or through a combination of factors.

Continual improvements in technology and knowledge may allow the population to increase above 100 people and still successfully support the population in a sustainable fashion, at least for a while. This is what many people count on, assuming that human ingenuity will compensate for the steady increase in world population, while providing sufficient resources to everyone.

However, the reality is that many of the natural resources we count on to support our lifeways in the industrial and postindustrial world are either nonrenewable (such as oil, coal, natural gas, and metals), not capable of renewing themselves as quickly as they are being polluted (such as air, water, and soil), or not capable of reproducing themselves as quickly as they are being consumed (plants and animals). When species are hunted, fished, or gathered to extinction, or driven to extinction by habitat destruction, they are gone forever. When a species is overhunted, so that supplies dwindle more and more each year, like the oceans' fish, such lifeways are not sustainable. When artificial irrigation and chemical fertilizers, herbicides, and insecticides pollute the soil, intensive agriculture is not sustainable.

One of the problems with the concept of sustainability is that many people only care if a subsistence strategy is sustainable while they own the resources, or while their family is living off the land. Coal-mining companies don't expect to be in business forever—they know the coal will eventually run out or become too difficult to be mined in an economically feasible fashion. But as long as they are making a profit today, and especially if some of the costs of their activities are borne by others, they don't care.

Similarly, a commercial fishing community might well protest against limits on the number of fish they can catch, the number of days they can go out in their boats, or the number of available licenses. If you argue that the current system is not sustainable forever, they will respond that they are concerned with their family's economic survival right now. They don't care about what conditions might be like 1,000 years from now, or 100 years from now, or even 25 years from now. They need a job, they need an income, they need to support their families—*now.*

Humans and the Environment

The natural resources in the environment limit what options we have for subsistence—you simply can't be a reindeer herder or a cocoa farmer in central Texas, no matter how much that lifestyle appeals to you. You can't be a whale hunter on Lake Wobegone.

In addition, the relationship between culture and the environment is a constantly changing one. The environment is not always stable, and neither is culture. No culture is perfectly adapted to its environment, and indeed, it doesn't have to be. As long as the balance is in favor of continued survival, the subsistence adaptation will persist. In some cases, what will turn out to be a maladaptive subsistence strategy may take many years, even centuries, to be recognized as obviously maladaptive. We should not assume that because a situation exists at one point in time that it *is adaptive* by definition. Many other factors influence the course a particular culture will take.

WILD VERSUS DOMESTICATED FOODS

In order to understand different modes of subsistence, the distinction between wild and domesticated plants and animals has to be made clear. Not all of the foods that humans eat fit neatly into these two categories, but most do.

Wild Foods

Before the Neolithic Revolution, all plants and animals were *wild*. Their particular anatomical, physiological, and behavioral characteristics were shaped by a combination of all of the forces of evolution, including mutation, random genetic drift, and natural selection. Forces in the environment acted on the gene pool of each species to shape it from generation to generation, resulting in a wide array of organisms in a constant process of adapting to their ever-changing local environments.

Throughout prehistory, history, and continuing today, hunters and gatherers relied on these wild foods for their sustenance. They developed an intimate knowledge of the natural history of the flora and fauna, learning when and where different foods would be available, when trees would be fruiting or producing nuts, where different animals lived and when they migrated, and what sorts of foraging strategies returned the most food, or the most preferred food, for the energy invested.

Domesticated Foods

Around 10,000 years ago, populations living in several different areas of the world began trying to modify the wild plants and animals in their environments to make them more useful. Over time, some of these plants and animals became *domesticated*, and people began relying more and more on these domesticated sources for their food. This transition to domesticated foods is known as the Neolithic Revolution.

What exactly does it mean to say that a species is *domesticated*? The process of domestication occurs through *artificial selection*. Artificial selection works the same way natural selection works, but the selective agents are human beings rather than other forces in the environment such as the weather, diseases, or predators. Through time, people began to selectively choose those individual plants and animals that exhibited particular features that people preferred. Instead of consuming them, they were used to create future generations through deliberate breeding. By selecting which individuals reproduced, humans gradually altered the gene pool, changing the anatomy, physiology, and behavior of the species.

Domesticated Plants

For plants, changes included selection for larger edible portions (larger fruit, larger seeds, etc.), a more secure attachment of the seeds to the stalk so the seeds stayed attached to the plant until harvest, better taste (usually less bitter), higher nutritional value, resistance to disease and parasites, drought-tolerance, and so on. A plant variety is said to be domesticated when its native features have been changed to the point that it cannot reproduce, at least not in that ongoing form, without human assistance. Many modern plant crops need help with reproduction; protection from drought, disease, and pests; and the input of artificial fertilizers.

In recent decades, plants have been selected for characteristics such as the ability to continue to ripen after being picked, the ability to withstand extended storage and transportation over long distances, specific shapes of fruit that allow more product to be packed in a box, longer shelf life, and so on. Genetic engineering has been used to increase the nutritional value of some plant foods, such as golden rice, which has been modified to have a higher content of provitamin A (beta carotene).

Almost all of the plant foods available for purchase in North American grocery stores are from domesticated species. This includes all fruits, including pineapples and bananas, and nuts and berries of all kinds. It is still possible to find wild versions of these plants growing outside of farms and commercial plantations, but the wild fruits are usually smaller. The ones you find for sale in the grocery store—papayas, mangoes, blueberries, pecans, cashews, etc.—are all the domesticated varieties.

Domesticated Animals

As animals were domesticated, humans selected for a variety of characteristics, beginning with friendliness, lack of fear of humans, and the capacity to be herded and/or kept in captivity. Body size might change to become larger or smaller, depending on what was most convenient for humans. Large horns and sharp teeth might be selected against. The ability to thrive and reproduce in captivity, in more crowded conditions, and while eating different types of food than previously might be valued and selected for. If you wanted to milk your animals, you would keep cows that produced healthy calves and an abundance of milk, and kill and eat those cows that were infertile or didn't produce enough milk. If you were raising cattle for meat, you might select as the progenitor of the herd a bull that was even-tempered, healthy, fast-growing, and had lots of muscle. Other male offspring in the herd might be castrated and used as draft animals, or slaughtered for food. If you needed horses for transportation and as draft animals, you would select for strength and endurance. Horses valued for racing, on the other hand, were selectively bred for speed.

A breed of animal is said to be domesticated when its native features have been changed to the point that it cannot reproduce, at least not in that ongoing form, without human assistance. Such assistance may mean actual intervention in the reproductive process, or in the birthing process, as is necessary for many domesticated cattle and sheep, or keeping subpopulations separate so that breeds can be differentiated. For example, although dogs have been domesticated longer than any other animals, if people do not control their breeding, they quickly come to look alike—medium sized, with short hair, upright ears, and a coat that is golden or light brown in color.

In recent decades, animals have been selected for characteristics such as the ability to grow rapidly to slaughter/market weight, having highly fat-marbled meat (Kobe beef), extra lean meat (Piedmontese beef), tender and flavorful meat, larger breasts in chickens (because more people prefer white meat), and so on.

Almost all of the animal foods available for purchase in North American grocery stores are from domesticated species. For meat, these include cattle, goats, sheep, pigs, chickens, turkeys, and various products made from the meat of these animals such as hot dogs, Spam, and pet food. It is still possible to find wild versions of these animals in the world, such as wild turkeys, mountain goats, wild boar, and so on. However, most of the meats that you find for sale in the grocery store—beef, goat, lamb, pork, chicken, and turkey—are from domesticated varieties. In a European butcher shop, you might also find meat from horses, geese, rabbits, and wild game such as pheasants or deer.

Grocery stores also sell a vast array of dairy products, including milk, cream, butter, sour cream, yogurt, cottage cheese, and ice cream. Eggs from domestic chickens are ubiquitous. Honey from domesticated honey bees is widely available.

There is one major exception to the rule that most animal products found for sale in grocery stores come from domesticated animals. In the seafood department, you will find many examples of wild-caught, nondomesticated foods: lobster, crabs, shrimp, mussels, oysters, crawfish, eels, tuna, salmon, tilapia, shark, squid, octopus, and so on. Just because you buy your food in a grocery store doesn't mean that everything you eat comes from a domesticated source! Seafood can come from the oceans, or from fresh-water sources, or a combination.

Semidomesticated Plants and Animals

In addition to animals that are clearly domesticated, such as chickens, and those that are clearly wild, such as sharks, a third, in-between category deserves mention. A number of plant and animal food resources are considered *semidomesticated*. This can mean a variety of things. For example, among Lapp reindeer herders, most of the reindeer are unafraid of humans and will let humans direct their movements to a degree. Individual reindeer may be tame enough to ride or pull a sled, while others are more skittish. Many of the female reindeer will allow themselves to be milked, but some will not. In North America, ranchers raise bison in captivity, and emu ranching was briefly popular in the 1990s. Neither bison nor emu are, technically, domesticated, but when you purchase bison burgers or emu meat in the market, you can be confident that the animals were raised in captivity.

In a similar fashion, some animals are semidomesticated in the sense that they are raised in artificial ponds or lakes for commercial sale, such as catfish, crawfish, and alligators, or sheltered in fish hatcheries when they are young (trout, salmon, etc.) and then released to the wild for sports fishermen to catch.

In many regions of the world, specific wild trees (or groves of trees), berry patches, date palms, and so forth, may be claimed by individuals or kinship-based groups. Although the plants are considered wild, they are managed in some way, and only the caretakers are supposed to harvest from them. Caretaking or managing can include watering during prolonged dry spells, weeding, protecting from animals, and cutting down competing trees and shrubs that don't provide food for humans.

There isn't always a clear-cut distinction between wild, semidomesticated, and domesticated species of plants or animals. The important points to realize, in the anthropological context, are (1) that the foraging of wild foods was the mode of subsistence used while humans were *becoming humans,* and for almost all of our existence *as humans,* and (2) that some people today still live primarily as hunters and gatherers, while others rely mostly on domesticated foods but still eat some foraged or purchased wild foods.

Direct Labor versus Trade or Market Exchange

Direct Labor

When we say that foods are obtained through **direct labor,** we mean that the individual, for herself or on behalf of a small group of others (usually related),

comes by the food through her own efforts. A hunter-gatherer goes out into the surrounding countryside and shoots an antelope or gathers eggs from birds' nests. A pastoralist raises his cows and sheep, milks them, and processes the milk into a variety of foodstuffs. A farmer plants the seeds, weeds the garden patch or field, waters if necessary, and the food is harvested directly to the kitchen, the table, or the storeroom.

In a variety of contexts, people may supplement purchased groceries with additional foods that they acquire through direct labor. For example, a Malian security guard may set traps for mice in the kitchen of a restaurant; then he roasts and eats the mice he catches for a mid-evening snack. A college professor may go hiking in a state park and pick wild blackberries to make into jam. A homeless woman may make the rounds of dumpsters behind bakeries, delis, and fruit stands, collecting food that has been thrown out,

Many people around the world work producing goods or providing services for a salary. Those who work for salaries then exchange the money they earn for food provided by others. Top: a U.S. fire fighter, a barber in Malaysia, a chef in a fish restaurant. Bottom: workers at a cement factory, a potter, a medical doctor.

while another sifts through the trash cans after a baseball game, looking for scraps of hot dogs, hamburgers, and French fries.

Freegans is the name given to a small but growing subculture of anticonsumerists in the developed world (Freegans 2010):

> Freegans are scavengers of the developed world, living off consumer waste in an effort to minimize their support of corporations and their impact on the planet, and to distance themselves from what they see as out-of-control consumerism. They forage through supermarket trash and eat the slightly bruised produce or just-expired canned goods that are routinely thrown out, and negotiate gifts of surplus food from sympathetic stores and restaurants. . . . There are Freegans all over the world, in countries as far afield as Sweden, Brazil, South Korea, Estonia and England (where much has been made of what *The Sun* recently called the "wacky new food craze" of trash-bin eating), and across the United States as well. (Kurutz 2007)

In each of these examples, the food is obtained directly through the labor or work of the individual or group involved. No money is exchanged, nothing is bought or sold. In the case of full-time hunter-gatherers, all of their food comes from wild sources. In the case of full-time subsistence pastoralists or farmers, all of their food comes from domesticated sources. For the security guard and college professor, they are getting wild foods directly through their own labor. Homeless individuals and Freegans obtain food directly through their own labor—the labor of searching for and collecting the food. Like true foragers everywhere, successful homeless people and Freegans must know where and when food might be available. The only reason we don't consider them to be hunters and gatherers is because the foods they eat are mostly from domesticated sources and often are highly processed or even cooked before they are thrown away by a wasteful society.

Trade or Market Exchange

Instead of obtaining food through direct labor, many people *trade for or buy* most or all of their food, whether from wild or domestic sources. Examples range widely: Fulani pastoralists obtain milk via their cows through direct labor, and then trade some of this milk for millet from neighboring farmers, who produced the millet through their own labor. Other people work at jobs that have nothing to do with producing food—they are mail carriers, soldiers, plumbers, teachers, or car salesmen. They exchange their labor for a salary, and then later exchange part of their salary for food they purchase in a grocery store or restaurant. Most college students obtain their food in an even more indirect way. Their parents work at jobs to earn money and then send some of that money to the university for tuition and room and board. *Board* refers to the food served to college students in the dining halls. Imagine, if you will, all the many people from across the globe who actually raise, process, ship, prepare, and serve the foods you eat every day.

A man dives for food in an urban dumpster behind a restaurant.

SUBSISTENCE AND PATTERNS OF MOVEMENT

We have considered whether people are eating wild or domesticated foods, and whether they obtain these foods directly through their own labor or indirectly through trade or purchase. Next we consider how a group's subsistence patterns affect another important aspect of their lifestyle—*how they move across the landscape.* Although there are many variations and combinations, it is helpful to classify the patterns of movement into nomadic, transhumant, and sedentary. Again, think of this classification system as a *heuristic device,* not as a direct reflection of how people behave all the time.

The Nomadic Lifestyle

When anthropologists use the terms **nomad** and **nomadic,** they are referring to a way of life that requires moving across the landscape to wherever resources are available, in a context where the resources are not always to be found in the same places from season to season or year to year. The limiting resource may be water or food, but the key feature of a nomadic lifestyle is that the resource base is ever-changing and somewhat unpredictable. People "follow the rains" or go where the pastures are greenest. If a group is truly nomadic, they usually have extensive knowledge of a large region; they either predict where resources might be from clues in the environment or travel in broad arcs across the landscape searching for food and water. They may use divination to determine where to go next or rely on a network of scouts, traders, and travelers to gather information about where resources might be found. The accumulated knowledge of elders is very helpful for nomadic groups, as the elders control vast amounts of information about patterns of past resource availability. In recent drought years, the Fulani cattle herders of Mali have collaborated with NASA scientists to use satellite imagery and cell phones to help locate green pastures for their herds.

Some hunting and gathering groups and some pastoralists are true nomads. There are probably fewer nomads today than there were in the past, due to the restrictions of national borders and competition from other modes of subsistence. Farming requires settling down in one place to take care of your crops while they grow, so there aren't any nomadic horticulturalists or agriculturalists. Some people living in industrial and postindustrial societies are nomadic, traveling from place to place, wherever they can get work, not staying long in any one location.

How long nomads stay in one place before moving depends on the environment and on exactly how they make their living. Hunters and gatherers may stay in one place until game becomes scarce or plant foods are depleted, or they may move on when the campsite has become fouled with waste and garbage. Some foragers move every day or two, others once a week or once a month. Still others may stay in one place for several months before moving on to wherever the next opportunity takes them. Adjunct college professors are modern-day nomads, staying at one school for one or two semesters and then moving on to the next job, possibly in another city or another state.

The distance the group has to move before setting up camp again also depends on the environment and on exactly how they make their living. Pastoralists may need to move just to the adjacent pasture, once the herd has cropped down the current pasture. Or if the rainfall has been patchy, the people and their herds may need to move many miles in search of another good pasture. Itinerant craftspeople and tinkers may move on to the next town, or they may need to put more distance between themselves and local authorities who are bent on chasing them away.

The Transhumant Lifestyle

Also referring to movements across the landscape, but in contrast to true nomads, **transhumant** (*transhumance,* when used as a noun) indicates that there are regular patterns to the movements people make. The length of the transhumant cycle may vary, from weekly or monthly to an annual cycle based on the seasons of the year. It may involve only two different settlement sites, or three or four or more, but the key feature is that it is possible to predict where the group will be, depending on the stage of the cycle.

For foraging groups, if one location has resources that are predictable and reliable, but periodic, then they may plan their movements around this resource. The prehistoric site of Terra Amata on the south coast of France reveals that people stayed there in the spring and summer some 380,000 years ago, building "prepared living structures" (huts) on the beach and exploiting both land and coastal resources. They returned again and again to the same stretch of beach, at the same time of year.

The Shoshone of Nevada, studied by Julian Steward (1938[1970]), followed a seasonal round that included some nomadic wanderings by small family groups during the spring and summer, when a variety of foods were available across the landscape. In the fall, people would meet up with extended kin and others for communal rabbit drives and the harvesting of pinyon nuts when they ripened. The nuts were collected and stored, either at a nearby winter village site or in caches near the pine groves. Most groves produced an abundant crop only every two or three years, but good crops provided more than enough for the local inhabitants, so people came from neighboring areas to harvest wherever the crops were most plentiful.

Many pastoral groups follow a standard seasonal round based on the availability of water and pasture for their animals. The Nuer, who combine cattle herding with horticulture and fishing, move between wet season villages and dry season camps. Evans-Pritchard (1940) describes their mode of life:

> Nuer cannot, except in a few favored spots, live in one place throughout the year. The floods [from heavy rainfall during the rainy season] drive them and their herds to seek the protection of higher ground. Absence of water and pasture on this higher ground compels them to move during the drought [dry season]. Hence their life is of necessity migratory, or, more strictly, transhumant. . . . In their seasonal movements Nuer seek pasturage as well as drinking-water and they take the cattle to where they know both can be obtained. . . . Different villages and sections tend to move about the same time and to visit the same pools [of water] each year, though time and place and, to some extent, degree of concentration, vary according to climatic conditions. Usually, however, the main dry season camps are formed yearly at the same spots [around permanent water sources]. . . . Nuer are forced into villages for protection against floods and mosquitoes and to engage in horticulture, and are forced out of villages into camps by drought and barrenness of vegetation and to engage in fishing. (57–63)

Two more brief examples will illustrate the ubiquity of transhumant patterns of movement among contemporary populations. David and Dorothy Counts have studied that subset of Canadians, mostly retirees, who spend every winter in their recreational vehicles in the warmer regions of the United States. Known as Snow Birds, they practice a form of transhumant migration depending on the weather. They may travel from one RV camping site to another, or spend the entire winter in one location, such as Quartzite, Arizona, or The Slabs in California, returning year after year to camp with the same groups of people (Counts and Counts 2001; Slab City 2010).

Migrant farm workers are another contemporary example of the transhumant lifestyle. Many people come from Mexico and Central America to the United States and Canada to harvest farm and orchard crops. They may begin each season in California with the strawberry or artichoke harvest, move north to harvest cherries and apples in Oregon and Washington, then go back south to Arizona for the late-fall broccoli harvest. When there is no farm work to be had, they may return to their rural home villages or seek other work wherever it is available.

As with a nomadic lifestyle, transhumant populations vary in terms of how often they have to move, and how far. Since their movements are more predictable, it is much more likely for transhumant groups than for nomads to move in stages, with some members of the group heading on to the next site early and others following at a later time.

Many anthropology professors are transhumant, living in houses near where they teach during the school term and spending the summers at their research sites, which may be far away. Likewise, many college students are transhumant, living in their dorms during the school year and spending the summers and mid-year breaks at home with their parents.

The Sedentary Lifestyle

If people live in one location and don't have to move in order to make a living, or indeed, must stay in one place for subsistence purposes, then we say they are **sedentary.** All of the different modes of subsistence are compatible with a sedentary way of life. Complex sedentary hunters and gatherers can be found wherever the natural resources are sufficiently rich and varied enough to permit year-round settlement. The native communities of the U.S. Northwest Coast and Canada, such as the Kwakiutl and the

Haida, are examples of complex, sedentary foragers. They established large, permanent villages along the coasts and on the banks of the major rivers of the region. Salmon migrating up the rivers to spawn every year formed the basis of the food supply. Likewise, in the Central Valley of California, abundant supplies of acorns and deer furnished a comfortable living for the Maidu and other aboriginal populations.

Some pastoral economies are located in regions with adequate, reliable rainfall and therefore have pastures that can support herds of grazing animals year-round. For example, in some areas of eastern and southern Africa, pastoralists live in sedentary villages; the animals are taken out to pastures every morning.

Most horticulturalists and agriculturalists must be sedentary. They need to remain near their crops in order to tend them and harvest them when the crops are ripe. Most people living in industrial and postindustrial economies are more-or-less sedentary. They may move from city to city, or even between countries, pursuing job opportunities, but they establish permanent living places each time they move.

Dettwyler's "Stuff Theory" of Material Culture and House Form

Introductory anthropology students often misinterpret the paucity of material culture exhibited by many people around the world. "These people are so poor!" they wail. "Why don't they have any furniture, any clothes, any *stuff?*" and "Why don't they build proper houses?" are common classroom queries. A big part of the explanation for why some people have so little, and others have so much, is relatively simple. It has little to do with poverty or meagerness of the imagination, or even cultural values such as greed and materialism. Simply put, the amount of material culture of a people depends mostly on three issues related to subsistence:

• How often must they move?

• How far must they move?

• How can they transport their goods?

Frequency of Movement

Nomadic people have to move relatively often. How often depends on the local environmental conditions, and may vary across the seasons or from year to year. Transhumant people likewise have to move—perhaps not as often as nomadic people, but still several times a year, or between winter pastures and summer pastures. Sedentary populations don't have to move, they can stay put.

Distance to Be Traveled

How far people have to move each time they do move varies all across the board, from just a few miles to many hundreds of miles, including across high-altitude mountain passes or across raging rivers swollen with snow melt.

Means of Transporting Goods

In Your Arms or on Your Back

If you are a hunter and gatherer, without any domestic animals, then you must carry all of your possessions yourself each time you move—either in your arms, or on your back. You may have contraptions to help you carry more, such as backpacks, net bags, baskets, or even sledges that can be pulled. Nevertheless, you have to carry everything you want from your current location to your next location.

Help from Domestic Animals

If you at least have domestic dogs, as the indigenous peoples of eastern Siberia, Alaska, Canada, and Greenland did (until the dogs were replaced by snowmobiles), you can have the dogs carry some of the goods—using side packs, travois-like sledges, or sleds on runners. If you have larger domestic animals, such as horses, donkeys, cattle, and camels to help you move, it is much easier to transport significant quantities of material goods, including housing materials, furniture, pots and pans, young children, the sick and elderly, and so on. People sometimes press sheep and goats into service as well, heaping goods on their backs in specially-designed side packs. If you have wheeled carts and wagons, you can use your domesticated animals to pull them, allowing you to carry more, and even to have mobile homes that don't have to be packed and unpacked with each move.

How much stuff you can have and move from place to place depends on whether you must carry it all by yourself, or have the help of a wheeled conveyance or domesticated animals. Top: backpackers, a homeless man with a shopping cart, and a man moving carpets with the help of a bicycle. Bottom: a reindeer sled in Finland, a cow cart in India, and a camel in Egypt.

Mechanized Transport

If you have mechanized transport, such as cars or recreational vehicles, or access to rented vehicles such as U-Hauls or moving vans, you can move vast quantities of material goods much farther than you can feasibly move with only your own power or even with domesticated animals.

The "Stuff Theory" of Material Culture

How do these variables—frequency, distance, and means of transport—relate to material culture, as well as to house form? *The more often people have to move, the less stuff they tend to have.* Although material goods are nice and might make life easier, if you have to move very often, you soon discover that you can live without a lot of things, especially heavy things. Likewise, *the farther people have to move, the less stuff they tend to have.* It may be relatively easy to transfer the contents of your dorm room across campus if you need to— perhaps with the help of some friends, or by making

several trips, or using a hand cart. But if you are switching to a university in another state, you have to find another way to transport your stuff, or you may decide to leave much of it behind. Finally, *people who have only their own arms and back for transport will have the least stuff.* If people have domestic pack animals such as dogs, horses, donkeys or camels, then they will have more stuff than people who must carry everything themselves. Further, if people have carts or wagons pulled by domestic animals, or cars, U-Hauls, moving vans, or recreational vehicles, then they will have more stuff than people who must rely only on domestic pack animals.

People who are sedentary—who don't have to move their stuff—can afford to accumulate stuff, even heavy stuff, whether or not it is of any particular value, whether or not it is used very often. They buy or build permanent homes with lots of storage space— closets, basements, attics, and sheds. They may even rent storage facilities to store their belonging at a location other than their primary residence. They can have

Living on the water, and/or adding an internal combustion engine, can greatly increase the amount of material goods a person or family can have. An elaborate houseboat in Kerala, India (top), a houseboat in Seattle, Washington (middle), an overloaded trailer in Mpumalanga, South Africa (bottom).

large objects, and heavy objects, and vast quantities of stuff—size, weight, and number are irrelevant if things don't have to be moved.

To make this lesson more concrete, imagine that you are moving from living with your parents at their permanent home to living in your college dorm room (not a big stretch of the imagination for most of you). First, you have much less room than you did at home, so you can't bring all of your belongings with you. A bed is provided, so you don't bring your bed from home. Likewise, a desk and chair are provided. You may bring a small refrigerator, a microwave, a computer, some (but probably not all) of your clothes, and various other personal items you can't live without such as your cell phone, iPod, guitar, photographs of family and friends, and so on. Some students rent a U-Haul to move to college, while others pack everything into one or two cars, and still others come with practically nothing. At the end of the year, you pack up most of your belongings and move them back home again for the summer, only to repeat the process the next year.

Now imagine that you don't have a car or a van. Imagine that you have a small donkey on which you have to pack everything you want to bring with you, and that you have to change dorms once a month. Which things are absolutely essential, and which end up being left behind? Maybe the refrigerator and the microwave aren't so important. Let's rethink the aquarium—it's too difficult to pack on a donkey. When I was in college in the mid-1970s, we had to move stereos and speakers and ridiculously heavy albums, so we were very selective in deciding what music to take to college. Today, you can put all your music on your MP3 player and tuck it in your pocket. If you had only a donkey, you might choose a lightweight laptop computer, rather than a desktop computer with a separate monitor, keyboard, and heavy CPU. In the old days, we didn't have computers to take to campus (we were excited about our Texas Instruments SR-70 calculators!).

Imagine you must pare things down even further. You don't have a donkey, you only have a backpack. And now you must move from one dorm to another every three days, and there is no electricity in the dorms, and no beds, desks, or chairs. What else suddenly becomes less essential? You'll definitely give up the refrigerator and microwave. A pillow is nice, but then you'll have to leave your extra shoes behind. One warm coat may be necessary, but there's only room for one. Chairs are great, but would you really carry one with you from place to place? Perhaps the guitar can be traded for a harmonica? Once you stop and think about it, it is much easier to understand why people whose subsistence base requires a nomadic or transhumant lifestyle have so few material possessions, and why those without domestic animals have the least of all. It isn't just that they are too poor or they are not materialistic—they are precluded from having a lot of heavy material goods by the necessity for frequent moves.

Tales of wagon trains heading westward along the California and Oregon trails during the nineteenth century are replete with stories of people having to abandon precious heirlooms and heavy furniture as the wagons broke down, the oxen died, and the river crossings and trails over the mountains became too difficult. There goes Grandma's piano, and the rocking chair. And the china cabinet and chests full of dishes, and all but one of Patty Reed's dolls (Laurgaard 1981). Nothing like a little adversity on the trail to sharpen one's priorities about which material goods are essential and which can be left along the way.

Many homeless people in North America have few material possessions for the same reason. What little they do own, they may keep in a purloined shopping cart or a rolling suitcase. This allows them to have more than they can carry in their arms and still take everything they own with them wherever they go. Shopping carts require neither food nor gasoline and can be easily replaced if they break.

This "Stuff Theory" of material culture helps us understand why mobile foraging bands have simple musical instruments. They may use their hunting bows to make music, or just their voices. It helps explain why they don't have a tradition of carving large heavy masks for use in religious rituals and/or performances for entertainment. It is no coincidence that huge totem poles are found among the sedentary hunters and gatherers of the Pacific Northwest Coast, such as the Kwakiutl and the Haida, but not among the nomadic Hadza of Tanzania or the Aché of Eastern Paraguay. Where the climate is accommodating—warm or hot—and you have to carry everything in your arms, you probably aren't going to bother with a lot of clothing. Many Australian Aboriginal populations, at contact with Europeans, didn't wear any clothing at all, or they wore only small skirts that covered their pubic regions.

The "Stuff Theory" of House Form: Gimme Shelter

All humans need some type of shelter against the elements, at least during some seasons of the year or during storms. The types of shelters people build and live in vary tremendously, depending on the local environmental conditions, local resources available for building, as well as the patterns of movement required by their subsistence mode. People must adapt to variations in temperature, including freezing cold, stifling dry or humid heat, and intense solar radiation. Some must cope with torrential rainfall, periodic flooding, and fierce storms bringing snow, hail, rain, or desert sand. Others must design their homes to avoid mosquitoes that carry disease or to try to catch the occasional breeze. Houses and settlements may be designed to keep predators at bay, including other humans. There are also, of course, stylistic and creative differences in architectural designs that differentiate houses around the world. In this section, we will briefly explore the main types of shelter that people rely on to protect themselves and their possessions from the ravages of nature.

Nomadic Foragers

Nomadic foragers who live in warm climates and do not have domestic animals often live in small, temporary houses that may be labeled **huts.** These huts are usually quick and easy to build, are made from local materials that are available everywhere the group travels, and are left behind to fall apart when the group moves on. These huts are usually round or oval in shape, 6 to 12 feet across, 4 to 5 feet high, and able to accommodate several people for sleeping. Examples include the twig and brush shelters built by Australian Aborigines; similar shelters known as *skerms* built by the Kalahari Bushmen; and twig and leaf shelters built by the Aka, Mbuti, and other so-called Pygmy populations of Central Africa. These shelters will often be arranged with their entrances facing a central public space where a campfire is built for cooking and other purposes.

Circumpolar populations build igloos, or ice houses, made of blocks of packed snow and ice. Igloos

Simply built houses of people who move often. Mud and timber house of the Himba people, in Namibia, Africa (left), and First Nations teepees set up across the river from the Parliament buildings in Ottawa, Canada (right).

can be built in a matter of hours from materials available wherever the group decides to stop. They are wind and water tight, and temperatures inside may be much higher than outside due to oil lamps and cooking fires. Since the fires are inside the dwellings, and the dog teams need to be kept apart, igloos are usually built farther from one another than are the twig or leaf huts in desert or rain forest environments. During warmer seasons, when ice and snow are not available, Inuit peoples erect hide huts, similar to truncated teepees. Animal hides can be transported from place to place on the dog sleds. Traditionally, the Makah whale hunters of Washington built large rectangular houses with walls and roofs of cedar planks. The planks were tethered together and could be disassembled and moved as needed (Home of the Makah People 2010).

Nomadic / Transhumant Pastoralists

Nomadic and transhumant **pastoralists** have more options, as they can pack sturdier, longer-lasting building materials on their domestic animals and put up and take down more substantial shelters each time they move. The structure of the shelter may be made of heavier timbers or long poles, interwoven with smaller wooden components to form a basic framework. The framework may be round, oval, square, or rectangular, of varying sizes, and with slanting walls (teepees), curved walls (huts), straight walls (yurts), or

tents with open sides. The framework can be finished with wattle and daub (sticks and mud) construction or can be covered with a variety of materials including animal hides or mats woven from plant fibers. Fabric woven from cotton or wool can be used for tent ceilings, walls, and floors. Densely woven wool rugs may be used as floor coverings as well. Felted wool is used to make the outer covering for most yurts. Modern materials such as tarps, nylon ropes, plastic sheeting, and corrugated plastic or metal siding may be pressed into service.

Examples of such portable, more substantial dwellings include the tents of Bedouin Arabs found throughout North Africa, Saudi Arabia, and the Near and Middle East; the *ari* houses made by the Afar people of the Horn of Africa, which are covered with woven palm mats; similar structures covered with woven grass mats among the Tuareg and Fulani peoples of West Africa; the triangular teepees of Siberia and the Plains Indians of North America; and the *kotas* of the Sami (Lapps) of northern Scandinavia.

Yurts are found among many nomadic and transhumant pastoral peoples of the Central Asian Plateau, including the countries of Mongolia, Nepal, Bhutan, and Tibet. Yurts are large circular houses with vertical felt walls, built over an internal structure made of wood. Their constituent parts are lightweight and can be moved from place to place on large wheeled carts.

Some houses are more substantial, and intended to last for longer periods, but are still relatively easy to move or to rebuild if they are destroyed. A yurt in Mongolia, with solar powered satellite dish and television (right), a house built on stilts in the ocean off the coast of Borneo (bottom left), and a close-up of reed houses built on floating islands in Lake Titicaca in Peru (bottom right).

Many town and city dwellers throughout Mongolia live in permanently-sited yurts.

Sedentary Peoples

Sedentary people, whether foragers, pastoralists, horticulturalists, agriculturalists, or industrialists and postindustrialists, can have many different types of houses with many different architectural styles. Since these houses are relatively permanent, it makes sense to build them of longer-lasting materials whenever such materials are available locally or can be imported. Since they don't have to be moved, they can be very heavy and have multiple stories, glass windows, brick chimneys, tile roofs, and stone exteriors. They can be small and modest or large and pretentious. If the region has ferocious storms or seismic activity, the houses may be built of materials that can flex in response to high winds, fierce rain, and earthquakes. If

high temperatures are an issue, they can be built with thick adobe walls and thatched roofs that absorb heat and keep the interiors relatively cool during the day, then reflect heat back during the cooler nights.

Among the complex, sedentary hunters and gatherers of the Northwest Pacific Coast, substantial houses were built of lumber from the nearby forests. In many different regions of the world, people build long houses of wood or bamboo that provide shelter for a number of extended families and are topped with water-tight thatched roofs that shed heavy rainfall. The Bambara and Dogon of Mali, like the Puebloan peoples of the American Southwest, build mud-brick houses from local earth, and then cover them with mud stucco. Traditionally, Bambara houses were round, with thatched roofs. Today, they are more likely to be square or rectangular to accommodate corrugated iron roofs, although round houses and thatched roofs are still seen in rural areas. Dogon houses are built into cliffs and usually have two stories, with flat, open rooftops enclosed by low walls for sleeping outside during the hot season. Pueblos of the American Southwest may be many-storied, with adjoining walls and open rooftops similar to the houses of the Dogon.

Finally, urban regions often have multistoried communal housing, such as apartments, townhouses, or condominiums, in addition to single-family housing. Population densities can be much higher where people live stacked on top of one another, with little open space between buildings.

Sedentary people build much more substantial houses of adobe, wood, brick, or cement. They are expected to last for decades or centuries. Left: a typical adobe house in Djenne, Mali, and houses on a hillside in Guanajuato, Mexico. Below: row houses in Cambridge, England, and a castle in Europe.

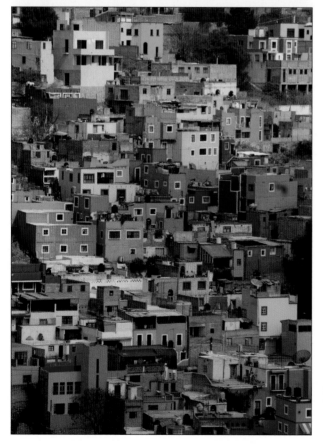

Other interesting features to note with regard to the use of space in different cultures is that in permanent settlements, people may live in nuclear family groups, with each family having its own house, or in large extended families, with clusters of houses, adjoining houses, or long-house arrangements. In North America, most everyone is familiar with suburban landscapes, where single-family homes are set in the middle of the property. Outdoor living spaces, often carpeted with grass, may be found in front of and/or behind and to the sides of the home. Most daily activities, including sleeping, cooking, working, and leisure activities take place inside the house.

In contrast, in some regions of the world where people are sedentary, each family's property is enclosed around the perimeter by a fence or wall, and the rooms are built facing a more private, inner courtyard where most work and leisure activities take place. For example, the Bambara of Mali live in extended family *compounds* with a relatively large part of the property devoted to outdoor living space. This inner courtyard is enclosed by the walls of the sleeping and storage rooms, connecting walls, and the doorway to the street outside. Cooking is done outside unless it is raining. People often sleep outside when it is too hot to sleep indoors.

Patterns of movement, environmental constraints, economic constraints, building materials, kinship and social organization, notions of privacy versus communal living, and stylistic preferences all affect the types of shelters people construct and live in.

GETTING FOOD: MODES OF SUBSISTENCE, PART II

Hunters and Gatherers in More Detail

Modern Foragers and the EEA

Why are anthropologists so interested in hunters and gatherers? First and foremost, because *this mode of subsistence was the only one practiced by humans for most of human existence.* Anthropologists assume that the conditions necessitated by a hunting and gathering lifestyle were critically important in shaping the early evolution of humans, both biologically and culturally.

Anthropologists refer to this long stretch of time—from several million years ago until about 10,000 years ago—as the **Environment of Evolutionary Adaptedness,** or EEA. A great deal of anthropological inquiry focuses on trying to understand what life was like for early human foragers, including what sorts of behaviors and cognitive capacities would have been developed through natural selection and other evolutionary processes. Cultural evolution occurs much more rapidly than biological evolution, and for some contemporary peoples, the mismatch between their evolved biological characteristics and the cultural contexts they find themselves living in can be huge and can lead to health problems as well as other concerns.

To try to understand the EEA, we can study archeological materials, social mammals, especially the nonhuman higher primates (monkeys and apes), and modern-day hunters and gatherers. We can use **ethnographic analogy** with contemporary foragers to gain insights into the evolution of our species, while being careful not to rely too much on such analogies, since today's hunters and gatherers live within modern nation-states and have various types of interactions with people who practice other subsistence modes.

The Myth of Progress

Another reason anthropologists focus on hunters and gatherers is because we hope to impress on students that hunting and gathering is a perfectly reasonable lifestyle. Not everyone abandoned foraging at the time of the Neolithic Revolution, when plants and animals began to be domesticated. Hunting and gathering is not a primitive or backward way of obtaining food, and foragers didn't simply "miss the memo" or *forget* to switch to raising their own plants and animals. Today, some people living on every continent (except Antarctica) continue to live as hunters and gatherers. Hunting and gathering is an effective and sustainable lifestyle, with much to recommend it.

Many people raised in the postindustrial world of North America have learned to view so-called *traditional* peoples with suspicion or disdain. They may assume that foragers live on the verge of starvation, desperately searching for food every day, and living lives famously characterized by Thomas Hobbes as "solitary, poor, nasty, brutish, and short" (1651[2009]). Hunters and gatherers live under a variety of conditions, and have not always been fairly treated by others, but it is clear that their lives under precontact conditions were not ones of "continual fear and danger of violent death" as Hobbes supposed (1651[2009]).

Variation among Foragers

In the following sections, I lay out a number of important findings about the foraging lifestyle that have been confirmed from many years of ethnographic research by a number of different anthropologists. Remember, though, that there is much variation in the lives of contemporary hunters and gatherers, making it difficult to generalize about them. What is typical of hunter-gatherers may vary considerably by geographic region, and even from one valley to the next (cf. Steward 1938[1970], for detailed descriptions of variation in hunter-gatherer lifestyles in the Great Basin of North America). Foragers live under different environmental conditions, from the rain forests of the Amazon, Central Africa, and Southeast Asia to the desert regions of Australia and Botswana; from the rich coastal regions of the Pacific Northwest to the arid scrubland of Tanzania and the islands of the South Pacific. In each environment, local adaptations and the specific history of a region shape the exact nature of daily life, which is neither stable nor static, but constantly changing over time.

Many foraging peoples today have a very restricted range compared to earlier times. Their lands have been invaded by pastoralists, farmers, miners, multinational corporations, government troops (and rebel resistors), tourists, and others. Many have been pushed onto marginal lands, with fewer natural resources than their ancestors had to work with. Some hunting and gathering peoples were extirpated (became extinct in the local area) by the arrival of European explorers, missionaries, and colonists, through deliberate warfare, murder, and the introduction of disease. Many other groups disappeared through assimilation to the culture of the invaders and generations of interbreeding with them. Still others were forced to abandon their traditional lifestyles and were confined to reservations, forbidden to speak their native languages or practice their religions. There are only a few surviving hunting and gathering groups who have not been seriously affected by contact with others.

Back to the Future: The Martu and the Makah

Some indigenous peoples have attempted to return to the hunting and gathering lifestyles of their ancestors. In 2003, the *Outstation Movement* of the Martu Aborigines of the Western Desert in Australia culminated with the return of 136,000 square kilometers of their ancestral lands (which had been seized by British colonists centuries before). After more than 50 years of living at sheep stations and missions, the Martu returned to a foraging lifestyle. By 2006, about 85 percent of their diet was based on traditional hunting and gathering of wild foods (Borghi 2006).

The Makah Nation of the state of Washington, likewise, has attempted to assert their treaty rights to hunt whales. The last traditional Makah whale hunt occurred in the 1920s. In 1999, after receiving permission from authorities, they resumed whale hunting. They killed one gray whale using canoes and harpoons and celebrated on the beach as the whale was butchered and the meat, fat, and oil were distributed (Home of the Makah People 2010). However, in 2002, a U.S. federal appeals court ruled that the Makah tribe's hunting of whales violated the Marine Mammal Protection Act, and all whale-hunting activities were suspended, pending further negotiations. For all indigenous groups returning to the land or sea, the goal is to find a more satisfying life than that afforded by supposedly more modern ways of living forced on them by outsiders.

Who Forages What?

In foraging societies, other than human breast milk, most of the food supply comes from wild plant and animal sources that are obtained through the direct labor of adults and older children. Although it is tempting to think that plants are gathered and animals are hunted, the reality is messier. There are many animal foods that can be gathered, such as birds' eggs taken from the nest; turtle eggs dug up from the beach; burrowing snakes pulled out of holes; insects collected from underneath tree bark or from termite mounds; and clams, crabs, and mussels collected along rocky seashores. Women are usually in charge of most of the gathering, of both plant and animal foods, taking their youngest child or children with them, while men are usually the ones who *hunt* larger and more dangerous prey such as antelopes, wild boars, and monkeys. Men may also gather plant and animal foods if they have not killed anything and/or if it is convenient for them to do so. People gather a wide variety of plant foods, including both different species and different parts of

Hunters and gatherers (foragers) obtain wild foods from the environment through a variety of means. Top: a man climbing a tree to collect sugar dates in Iraq (left), collecting crabs in Cambodia (middle), commercial crab boats in Alaska (industrial foraging) (right). Bottom: a San/Bushman hunter of the Kalahari, Namibia (left), a wild-turkey hunter in California (middle), a woman gathering wild cranberries (right).

the plant: fruits, vegetables, grasses, leaves, seeds, nuts, roots, tubers, bark, pith, flowers, and stalks.

Who provides most of the food in foraging societies? Early anthropological studies implied that men, through their hunting activities, provided the majority of the food for women and children, who were dependent on the men. Further ethnographic research revealed, however, that among many groups, most of the food comes from the gathering activities of the women, with estimates ranging from 66 percent to 75 percent or more on a daily basis. Meat may be highly

prized for its flavor and high protein value, but hunting is unpredictable and unreliable compared to the gathering of plant and animal foods.

Cultural anthropologists often stress the division of labor by sex among hunters and gatherers. Typically, men engage in the more dangerous activities, where they are more likely to be injured or killed, and may have to spend one or more nights away from camp. Women are the ones who get pregnant, give birth, and breastfeed each child for several years, and most of their tasks are ones that expose them to less danger and, perhaps more importantly, can be combined with child care. The distinction between men's and women's activities is not always clear-cut, however, and there are foraging groups where women hunt alongside the men, or where all members of the group participate, such as those who practice net hunting. Where men and women do have strict rules about who can do what, it is usually the case that both men's and women's contributions are equally valued. They are seen as complementary and **egalitarian** (equal in status), rather than the men's work or contributions being more highly valued.

In addition to generally egalitarian relationships between males and females, egalitarianism among males, and among females, is the general rule in hunting and gathering societies. Most adults know how to do most required tasks, and while a man might be admired for his hunting skills, or a woman for the fine baskets she weaves, there are no elected or enforced leaders or rulers. Group decisions are usually made by consensus, and if disputes arise they are settled through discussion or by one side moving to another group. True warfare is unknown among simple, nomadic hunters and gatherers (Fry 2007).

Other Aspects of the Foraging Lifestyle

A common ethos of **generalized reciprocity** (sharing, especially of food) is typical of hunters and gatherers. We will discuss this in more detail in the chapter on economics. Suffice it to say that most food is shared among all members of the hunting and gathering group who are spending the night at the same camp. If one man is successful at the hunt and brings home an animal, everyone shares in the meat. If the mongongo nuts are plentiful, everyone has some to eat, whether or not they, or someone in their immediate family, collected them personally.

Foragers spend most of their lives in relatively small groups of 25 to 50 people, most or all of whom are well-known to them, and related to them in multiple ways, either biologically or through marriage. People have ample time to socialize, make

crafts, and engage in creative activities such as singing and dancing. Foragers typically have a varied diet, eating many different kinds of plant and animal foods. They rarely go hungry. Many contemporary foragers trade with their farming or pastoral neighbors for foods from domesticated plants and animals, as well as commercial foods available through local stores or markets.

If they have to move often, then they have little in the way of material culture—perhaps just bows and arrows, carrying baskets and containers, and a few personal items. Each time they move, they construct new shelters out of local materials, using technology that even young children can master.

To find out more about the threats to survival of indigenous peoples, including contemporary hunting and gathering groups, visit the website of Cultural Survival (http://www.culturalsurvival.org/).

A Special Word about Fishing Peoples

Fishing and marine mammal hunting tend to get lost among the typical subsistence categories anthropologists use. If the animals are wild, as most of them are, then fishing and marine mammal hunting qualify as foraging. However, fisher-folk often lead very different lives than typical hunters and gatherers. They may live in larger, more sedentary settlements and are likely to combine fishing with other subsistence modes.

Fishing boats in Malta.

When people think of hunters and gatherers, they tend to envision the !Kung San of the Kalahari or prehistoric Native Americans. They overlook the north Atlantic fishing villages that line the coasts of Newfoundland, Greenland, Iceland, Ireland, England, Scotland, and the Scandinavian countries, as well as circum-Mediterranean fishing villages, the commercial shrimpers who sail out of ports along the Gulf of Mexico, or the swordfish and cod boats that call Maine coastal villages home. Whale hunters in the South Pacific may live on nearby islands, or in centuries past, they may have sailed out of Martha's Vineyard, Massachusetts.

People who live along the shores of lakes or rivers almost always exploit some of these freshwater resources to supplement other foods they gather, raise, or purchase. Thus, the category of hunting and gathering is an extremely broad one, encompassing many different and constantly changing ways of life.

Combining Foraging with Other Modes of Subsistence

Many foraging peoples are in regular contact with neighboring groups who grow crops, herd animals, or import food from other regions. Both trade and market exchange take place. Thus, even people who expend most of their direct labor efforts foraging for wild foods also may consume a wide array of domesticated plant and animal foodstuffs, and even commercially processed foods.

Likewise, in North America, wild plants and animals still supplement the diet of many people. During specific hunting seasons, people may hunt turkeys, pheasants, ducks, geese, doves, deer, wild boar, muskrats, and squirrels. Others fish in lakes, ponds, streams, rivers, and along the seashore, or go out in small boats near the coast. They may go clamming, crabbing, or oystering. Some people pick wild plant foods as well, including wild strawberries, raspberries, blackberries, dandelion greens, wild mushrooms, poke salad, wild grapes, and wild pecans. Living off the land contributes significantly to the diet of many North Americans, even if most of their food comes from the grocery store.

Pastoralism in More Detail

Pastoralism is a form of subsistence based on the herding of domesticated or semidomesticated animals. We can examine pastoralism from a number of different perspectives.

Typically, when anthropologists speak of pastoral peoples, they are not referring to households that may have a milk cow, a small flock of chickens, a pig or two, or some guinea pigs (yes, guinea pigs were originally domesticated in South America as a source of food and are still raised for food in some regions). When anthropologists use the term *pastoralists*, they mean societies where taking care of a herd of animals is the main way that people occupy themselves, and in return, the herd provides most of the food supply. Herd animals require water, food, protection from predators, and shelter during inclement weather. They also need preventive and curative veterinary care.

Types of Animals

Pastoral people around the world rely on many different types of animals. Some focus on a single species, while others have two, three, or more different types of domestic animals. Which animals are herded depends, in part, on the natural environment—how hot or cold it is, how much water is available, local diseases and parasites, and so on. Camels, either Bactrian or dromedary, are the hardiest domesticated animals in arid environments. If more water and pasture are available, goats, sheep, donkeys, horses, water buffalo, yaks, and various breeds of cattle can form the basis of the subsistence herds. If there is too much rainfall, combined with high temperatures, various diseases that affect domestic herbivores, such as sleeping sickness transmitted by tsetse flies, may preclude pastoralism.

Patterns of Movement

Just as hunting and gathering peoples can be nomadic, transhumant, or sedentary, the same is true of pastoralists. Pastoralists must always keep in mind their animals' needs for water and food. There are only a few remaining pastoral groups that can be classified as truly nomadic, wandering across an unpredictable environment, with scattered resources. Such nomadic pastoralists follow the rains wherever they fall, looking for pasture for their animals. It is much more common for pastoralists to be transhumant, moving between camps in different regions of their territories according to the seasons. For example, the Bakhtyari of Iran trek across high mountain passes and ford freezing cold rivers to move between winter and summer pastures for their herds. The arduous migration of the Bakhtyari

Pastoralism involves the raising of domesticated animals, whether in large herds or flocks, or just a few animals on a family farm, and whether for local subsistence needs or for sale in the marketplace. Top: goat herding in the Dominican Republic (left), guinea pigs (raised for meat in South America). Bottom: a young boy feeding goats and chickens on the farm (left), and alpacas in Chile.

was immortalized in the classic silent ethnographic film *Grass* (Cooper and Schoedsack 1925). Other pastoralists may move between winter settlements in valley bottoms and summer pastures in the high mountain valleys, such as the Kalasha of northwest Pakistan, or the goat and cattle herders of Switzerland.

Sedentary pastoralists include those who live in rich enough environments that most or all of the population can live in a permanent settlement. The herd animals may spend nights in a barn, and be turned out to fenced pastures every morning. Or they may spend nights in a corral near the village and be taken out to open pasture by adult men or young herd boys every morning and brought home every evening. In still other cases, the herd travels from place to place in the vicinity of the village, accompanied full-time by young herdsmen, who spend their nights out with the herd and return to the village only once every few days, weeks, or months.

How Pastoralists Live off Their Herds

When herd animals were first domesticated, we assume that they were viewed primarily as a captive meat source—animals that you didn't have to track, kill, and haul back to camp. When you needed or wanted meat, you simply killed a member of the herd. Some pastoralists do keep large livestock for this purpose, killing one animal at a time, as needed for food. In addition, some people raise smaller domestic animals, such as rabbits, guinea pigs, fowl, dogs, and cats, killing one or more as needed for food. However, people soon figured out that there are many ways to live off a herd of animals without necessarily killing them. You can only eat the meat of an animal once, after all.

The most important type of food that can be obtained from domesticated mammals (without killing them) is milk. All mammals, including humans, produce milk in mammary glands following pregnancy and birth. Around the world, wherever people herd camels, cattle, horses, sheep, yaks, and goats, they often milk these animals. In order to keep up a good supply of milk, the females in the herd must have adequate water and food and must occasionally be mated and give birth. Through many generations of artificial selection, humans have modified herd animals so that the females produce much more milk than their own offspring need to survive. Thus, the herd can continue to increase while providing additional milk for their human owners.

Milk can be consumed raw, or it can be transformed into a variety of other forms, such as butter, yogurt, kefir, cheese, and other fermented milk products. Across Central Asia, yak milk is churned into butter and added to hot, salty tea, which is consumed in vast quantities on a daily basis. Bovine milks may be mixed with blood and/or grain by some pastoralists before consumption.

Although milk is touted by the U.S. dairy industry as being necessary for strong bones and teeth, and as an essential part of the diet for everyone, in fact, most people in the world do not drink any milk as adults. Most humans only ever drink the milk that their own mother provides to them during childhood. Research on the natural age of weaning (duration of breastfeeding) in modern human populations suggests that human children would be breastfed for between 2.5 years and 7.0 years if our cultural beliefs didn't interfere with the natural process (Dettwyler 1995a). Indeed, around the world, including North America, many children are breastfed for three to five years, or longer (Dettwy-

ler 2004a). Following weaning in mid-childhood, most people never again consume milk products.

Since, realistically, you can't milk a wild animal, anthropologists assume that drinking the milk of other species is a relatively recent phenomenon in human experience, developing only since the Neolithic Revolution, and only in regions of the world with a long history of pastoralism as a subsistence strategy. These would include Europe (and those of European ancestry living elsewhere), Anatolia, the Middle East, South Africa, East Africa, and parts of India and Asia. In these areas, where dairying has been practiced for approximately 8,000 years, you find many people who are able, as adults, to digest lactose, the sugar in milk, due to past selection for a genetic mutation. The mutation prolongs the childhood ability to make lactase, the enzyme required to digest lactose. Today, most people in the world can digest lactose only in childhood, when they are of an age to be breastfed by their mothers. As adults, most people cannot drink animal milks or consume milk products (such as cheese or ice cream) without suffering various intestinal problems. In a few regions, animal milks are processed in such a way that the lactose is broken down by bacterial fermentation before consumption by humans, thus making some milk products, such as specific types of cheese, available for adults to consume.

Another way to live off your herd animals without killing them is to extract blood from them. Just like people who donate blood for medical purposes, this does not harm the donor, and the blood is replaced by the body within a few days to a week. Evans-Pritchard (1940) describes the practice:

> Like other pastoral peoples in East Africa the Nuer extract blood from the necks of their cattle, and this is a supplementary article of diet in dry season camps, where one may generally see at least one cow bled each evening. . . . The operation, called *bar*, consists of tying a cord tightly round a cow's neck so that the veins stand out and one of them can be stabbed, on the head side of the cord, with a small knife bound with cord or grass to prevent it entering too deeply. The blood spurts out, and when a large gourd has been filled they loosen the cord and it ceases to flow. . . . The blood is boiled by women till it is fairly consistent and can be used as a meat flavoring with porridge; or the men let it stand till it coagulates into a solid block, and, after roasting it in the embers of a fire, cut it up and eat it. (27–28)

Beef blood is a good source of high-quality protein and also contains iron and other nutrients. In a number of European countries, people make blood sausage from pig or cow blood, and black pudding—a staple of English, Irish, and Scottish breakfasts—is made from animal blood.

Although many North American students find the consumption of blood unappetizing when described this way, anyone who routinely eats most types of meat has consumed animal blood. Many people prefer their steaks rare, with blood still clearly visible in the meat. The exceptions are Kosher or Halal meats. Both Jewish and Muslim religious beliefs require specific techniques for slaughtering animals, Kosher and Halal, respectively, with the aim of removing all of the blood from the animal before its meat is consumed.

People who raise domestic birds of any type—chickens, ducks, turkeys, geese, guinea fowl, and other varieties—have eggs as an easy source of food. Or, they can allow the eggs to hatch and grow into adult birds and then eat them for their meat.

In addition to meat, milk, and eggs, some domestic animals provide renewable resources that can be harvested and used by the family or sold in the market. For example, camel, musk oxen, sheep, goats, rabbits, alpacas, vicunas, and llamas are raised for their wool or hair. Shearing the animal does not hurt it, and a new coat will grow back.

Domesticated animals can be helpful in other ways besides providing food. The owners of draft (work) animals can use them to help prepare the ground for growing and harvesting crops. Animals that can be ridden, such as horses, reindeer, donkeys, and even some types of cattle, can be used to herd other animals. Some domestic animals are pressed into service transporting a variety of things across long distances, including household items, trade goods, or people, either directly on their backs or with the use of a travois or wheeled conveyance such as a cart or wagon. Draft animals can also be rented to others for use during busy agricultural seasons, and extra animals can be sold in the marketplace.

Dogs were the first animals to be domesticated, with good evidence dating back to 12,000 years ago, and some tantalizing clues suggesting a much earlier domestication during the Upper Paleolithic some 30,000 years ago. Dogs can help with hunting and herding, and they can also pull fully loaded sledges, sleds, or travois. They can serve as sentinels, alerting humans to the approach of predators or strangers, and they are great for cleaning up debris around the house and campsite. Dogs are eaten in some parts of the world. Likewise, domestic cats are eaten in some places, but their primary usefulness is as predators to keep rodent populations under control in regions where grain is stored before being consumed.

Combining Pastoralism with Other Modes of Subsistence

Pastoralism is often combined with other modes of subsistence. For example, the Kalasha of northwest Pakistan keep herds of goats and raise field crops of wheat and corn, and tree crops such as apricots, walnuts, apples, and mulberries. In the winter, the goats are kept in barns near the village. In the spring, the men leave with the goat herds for the high summer pastures, while the women stay in the village and tend the crops.

Many pastoralists routinely trade or sell some of their meat, milk, or wool to other people who raise crops or who hunt or fish. The Fulani herders of Mali exchange milk from their cow herds for millet and sorghum, grown by their horticultural Bambara neighbors, and trade milk to the Bozo people in exchange for fish from the Niger River.

In areas of North America where the zoning allows, people may keep a cow or a goat to provide milk, and there has been a recent resurgence of interest in raising backyard chickens to supplement the diet of urban and suburban dwellers (Backyard Chickens 2010).

Horticulture and Agriculture in More Detail

The domestication of plants began during the Neolithic Revolution and has been an ongoing process ever since. The ability to grow one's own food, rather than rely on wild food sources, has been a mixed blessing. It has allowed human population size to increase dramatically, to the point where the planet now holds almost seven billion people (World POP Clock Projection, 2010). It has allowed most people to live sedentary lives, build more permanent homes, and accumulate more stuff. It has allowed some members of some populations to forego contributing to the food supply altogether and focus their time and talents on other activities. However, horticulture and agriculture have disadvantages as well, when compared to the foraging lifestyle that all humans once followed.

Horticulture and agriculture often require large inputs of labor—you have to prepare the ground; plant the seeds, seedlings, or shoots; control weeds; provide water if necessary; keep away birds, insects, and other pests; deal with crop diseases; and harvest the crops during what is usually a brief window of opportunity. Many crops then require further labor inputs for drying, storing, processing, grinding (if needed), and cooking.

Horticulture

Remember that in anthropological contexts, *horticulture* refers specifically to the growing of domesticated plants using humans as the only source of power and using a digging stick or a hoe rather than a plow. Horticulturalists may rely on a specific type of farming referred to as shifting cultivation or **slash and burn** farming. In areas where the soils are poor and where native trees and shrubs cover the landscape, the farmers must first clear the land by cutting down (slashing) the vegetation so that sunlight can reach the ground. This material is then burned to reduce it to ash, which provides additional nutrients to the soil. Thus, the phrase: slash and burn.

Crops are planted and tended for as long as the soil will support a good return. This may be only one season, several years, or many years. In tropical regions of the world, the soil is often relatively poor, and without external inputs of fertilizer, the fields quickly give out and new fields must be cleared. Old fields may need to rest, or *lie fallow*, for a brief time, or it may take many years for them to recover enough to be useful for growing crops again.

Horticulturalists can be found on all continents except Antarctica. Most are subsistence farmers, growing crops for their own needs. They usually grow a variety of crops in their fields and gardens, relying on one or two staples; several supplemental crops to provide variety, spice, and essential nutrients; and perhaps one crop that can be stored for an extended time—either in the ground or after harvest. Nonfood crops like opium poppies, tobacco, cotton, and sisal can also be grown and then traded or sold in order to obtain other goods.

Staple crops of horticulturalists include a wide variety of grains (wheat, barley, rye, corn, sorghum, mil-

let, teff, rice, etc.), root crops (taro, manioc, yams, sweet potatoes, white potatoes, peanuts, etc.) and tree crops (domestic nuts and fruits of all kinds). The plant-based diets of horticulturalists are often supplemented with wild foods gathered from the surrounding areas, including game and fish, as well as a few domestic animals who are raised around the homestead, such as pigs or chickens, a few goats or a milk cow.

Agriculture

In anthropological contexts, the term *agriculture* is used to refer to growing domesticated plants with the addition of domesticated animals as a power source and the addition of the plow as a tool. A plow completely overturns the surface of the ground prior to

Horticulture refers to growing crops of domesticated plants, using only human power and a digging stick or hoe. Many people feed their families partially or entirely through horticultural labor.

The term agriculture is used by anthropologists to refer to people who grow domesticated crops with the addition of animal power and a plow to turn over the soil. Agriculture often involves higher human labor inputs than horticulture, as people build and maintain terraces, irrigate, fertilize, transplant seedlings, and so on. Top left: plowing with a water buffalo in Thailand; top right: terraced rice fields in Bali; left: an Amish tobacco field and drying barn in Pennsylvania.

planting. Some agriculturalists are subsistence farmers, while others produce crops for sale or trade in addition to, or instead of, their own family's use.

Many crops can be grown with either horticultural or agricultural technologies, while some environments and/or crops require the additional inputs implied by the term agriculture. By adding domesticated animals to the power supply and using a plow to turn over the soil, more land can be put under cultivation and more food can be grown per acre, supporting more people. Domestic work animals must be fed and taken care of, which adds to the responsibilities of an agriculturalist. The most common domestic animals used to pull plows or other farm implements, such as levelers and harvesters, are draft horses, donkeys, mules, oxen, and water buffalo.

The Amish and Hutterites are examples of contemporary North American agriculturalists who rely heavily on their domestic farm animals to assist in cul-

tivating large tracts of land (Bennett 2007; Kraybill 1989). In Lancaster County, Pennsylvania, for example, corn and tobacco are the primary field crops of the Amish. A huge variety of vegetables, fruits, and flowers are raised for household consumption and for sale to others. Cows, goats, pigs, guinea pigs, chicken, turkeys, and rabbits also contribute to the food supply. In recent years, the Amish have turned more and more to craft production for the tourist market as a supplemental source of income, with some men making furniture, for example, and some women making extra quilts and other craft items to sell.

Intensive and Industrial Agriculture in More Detail

Recently, while preparing to teach a class titled *Anthropology and Human Nature,* I reviewed a book by social psychologist Roy Baumeister (2005). I was struck by his perspective on Western patterns of food consumption. Baumeister contrasts solitary animals, who must get food on their own, with social animals such as lions and wolves, who hunt in packs and presumably get more and better food than those operating alone. He goes on to say of humans, who he describes as *cultured animals*:

> Last, we lucky few who live in culture need considerably more inner structures, but by making use of culture we can get more and better food than even the merely social species. . . . And we do eat better than they do. Even amid the bitter chill of a midwestern winter, when all is covered in snow and ice, people can eat fresh fruit, fish, and fancy meats. Modern humans in developed countries can say, *with pride*, that they don't kill their own food nor grow their own food—they buy their food in restaurants and supermarkets. In a pinch, they call room service. (Baumeister 2005:9, emphasis added)

Wow, I thought. What ignorance; what arrogance!! Why should *we* (Baumeister means Americans) be *proud* that we don't kill our own food or grow our own food? Should all the foragers, horticulturalists, pastoralists, and agriculturalists of the world be *ashamed* of their lifeways? If someone didn't hunt, gather, or produce the food originally, there wouldn't be any food for anyone! And why is it considered better to be able to eat fresh fruit in the dead of winter, or consume fish in a region far from the source? In reality, we—as individuals and societies, and the planet as a whole—pay a huge price for the modern conveniences of consuming food bought from restaurants, supermarkets, and room service. But I digress . . .

By adding additional sources of power and additional tools and technology to the process, agriculture can be intensified and even industrialized. Farm machines such as tractors, harvesters, and balers can allow even larger tracts of land to be put under cultivation, and even more food to be harvested from a given amount of land. Terraced hillsides and sophisticated systems for capturing and channeling rain water allow intensive wet rice farming in many regions of Southeast Asia. In more arid regions of the world, mechanized irrigation systems pump water many miles from the source to irrigate crops in places that otherwise could not support agriculture of any kind.

Agriculture can also be intensified through the addition of organic and chemical fertilizers, pesticides to control insect damage, and herbicides to kill competing plant life. Although such inputs allow more food to be grown, they have disadvantages as well. In addition to the extra cost and additional labor, they contribute to pollution of the soil and water and require immense inputs of energy to produce (see below).

Industrial agriculture or factory farming refers to the intensive modification of the environment through such inputs, on enormous tracts of land owned by corporations rather than families, for the purpose of producing products to be sold to processors or wholesale distributors (who, in turn, sell to retailers, who then sell to consumers). Crops are often genetically engineered and new seed must be purchased each year from the companies who own the patents. Thousands and thousands of adjacent acres may be devoted to the raising of a single crop or a specific strain of that crop, which increases the risk of catastrophic crop failure.

Starting in the second half of the twentieth century, and continuing today, more and more of the world's food is produced using such technology. Most of the labor inputs are provided by gigantic, complex machines that require nonrenewable resources to operate (kerosene, diesel, gasoline, oil). Decisions about what and how much to grow are determined by corporate board members based on worldwide supply and demand, governmental subsidies, and import/export tariffs. Much of the food that is produced is packaged and shipped to distant markets, which requires further use of nonrenewable resources for storage, refrigeration, and transport, and results in substantially more waste.

Food Production

As you move from one subsistence mode to another, the energy efficiency of food production changes dramatically. For most foragers, pastoralists, and horticulturalists, and many agriculturalists, the main source of energy input for food production is the sun. People must clear land, plant, weed, and harvest crops, and they must care for and milk their herd animals, but most of the energy that goes into food production is solar energy, which is free, renewable, and nonpolluting. For every calorie of human labor input, more than one calorie of food is produced.

Once agricultural and pastoral intensification develop, the energy inputs soar, and the efficiency of food production declines steeply. Very quickly, many calories of energy inputs are required to produce one calorie of food, and the energy inputs tend to be costly, nonrenewable, and polluting. According to one recent study by Johns Hopkins Bloomberg School of Public Health, "The average U.S. farm uses 3 kcal of fossil energy in producing 1 kcal of food energy. Meat production uses even more energy. In the typical feedlot system—where a little more than one-half of the cattle's feed is grain—the fossil energy input is about 35 kcal/kcal of beef protein produced" (Horrigan, Lawrence, and Walker 2002). Most of the excess energy used in intensive agriculture goes toward the production of fertilizers and pesticides, which then must be transported to farms and applied to fields. These estimates don't include energy used for processing or transportation.

Food Processing

Many of the foods produced by industrial agricultural enterprises are not sold to consumers in their original form. Rather, they are sent to industrial processing plants to be processed in various ways (washed, peeled, sorted, cut up, ground up, etc.), combined with other foods, cooked, shaped, and packaged. They are eventually transformed into a huge array of different foods with extended shelf lives. Much of the

In addition to using industrial equipment to help grow, harvest, store, ship, and process food crops, such as carrots (left), many commercial nonfood crops are grown using intensive agricultural techniques, such as grapes for wine in a vineyard in Switzerland (top right), and tea on a plantation in Japan (bottom right).

food purchased and eaten on a daily basis by North Americans is highly processed and modified from its natural state. Artificial colors and flavors are added to enhance palatability, and preservatives help maintain freshness or, at least, edibility for months or even years.

Industrial processing of food requires even greater energy inputs. Citing the report of the Cornucopia Project, the Johns Hopkins report estimated that "processing accounts for about one-third of the energy use in the U.S. food system, and *each calorie of processed food consumes about 1,000 calories of energy*" (Horrigan et al. 2002, emphasis added). Many of these processed foods are then transported many miles to market and on to the consumer. Additionally, many of them require further energy inputs to refrigerate or freeze and to cook, even if they come precooked and are only reheated in the microwave. The rise of the *heat and eat* food industry is a remarkable cultural phenomenon, spurred on by the invention and widespread adoption of the microwave oven, the movement of women into the paid workforce, and the decline of cooking skills.

Think of all the people whose jobs are not to produce food directly, but to aid in the processing, transportation, and selling of foods that come from all regions of the world: the manager of the steel manufacturing plant that produces freighters; the drivers of the trucks that haul food; the folks who work in the food processing plants; the restaurant and grocery store managers; the cashiers, the cafeteria ladies; the cooks; the dishwashers; the USDA inspectors; the people who make shipping containers, cardboard boxes, glass bottles, paper labels (and the ink they are printed with), foil containers, and plastic and paper bags; even the local guy who stocks the vending machines outside your classroom. Not to mention all the people involved in getting rid of food waste: the trash collectors, the recyclers, the garbage disposal manufacturers, and construction contractors. Truly, it boggles the mind!

Excerpt from "The Blessings of Dirty Work" . . .

My generation has absorbed an implicit hierarchy of values in which working the soil is poor people's toil. The real labors of keeping a family fed are presumed tedious and irrelevant. A woman confided to me at a New York dinner party: "Honestly, who has time to cook anymore? My daughter will probably grow up wondering what a kitchen is used for."

This is modern thinking. Sorry, but we have *work* to do, the stuff that happens in an office or agency or retail outlet—waiting tables, for instance. Clicking a cash register. Driving a truck on a long-distance haul. We have risen above the muddy business of an agrarian society. People in China and India do that for us now.

On the other side of the world from that New York dinner party, another influential woman gave me an opposite perspective: It's impossible to leave behind the labor and culture of food. We only transform the tasks, she claims—and not necessarily for the better.

Vandana Shiva, director of the Research Foundation for Science, Technology and Natural Resource Policy, was trained as a physicist but is best known for her work for farmers' rights. The soil of her country, India, is home to one-quarter of the world's farmers.

Increasingly, they grow commodities for export rather than traditional, locally adapted foods for their own communities. This strategy was laid out in the 1970s, promising that one farmer with the right tools and chemicals could feed hundreds, freeing the rest of us for cleaner work.

It sounds good unless you're that one guy on a tractor in Nebraska and the price of soybeans won't quite refuel your tank and pay for your fertilizer. Elsewhere, it's worse. In India, Dr. Shiva says, 150,000 farmers have committed suicide after being bankrupted by costly chemicals in a cycle of debt created by ties to corporate agriculture. Centralized food production requires constant inputs—fertilizers, pesticides, and irrigation—that in some settings are impossible to sustain, and chemical-based farming virtually always damages the soil over time.

Industrial farming—however destructive to our land and our nutrition—has held out as its main selling point the allure of freedom: Two percent of the population would be able to feed everyone. The rest could do as we pleased. Dr. Shiva sees through that promise.

"Most of those who have moved off of farms are still working in the industry of creating food and bringing it to consumers: as cashiers, truck drivers, even the oil-rig workers who generate the fuels to run the trucks," she says.

"Industrial agriculture did not 'save' anyone from that work, it only shifted people into other forms of food service."

Surprise: There is no free lunch. No animal can really escape the work of feeding itself. We're just the only one with fancy clothes and big enough brains to make up a story like that. (Kingsolver 2007a, B1)

Excerpt from "The Blessings of Dirty Work," *Washington Post*, reprinted with permission of Barbara Kingsolver.

Food Distribution

For most of human existence, foragers hunted and gathered in a relatively small region surrounding their base camp. Women went out in the morning and returned later the same day, limiting them to a radius of only a few miles from camp. Hunters might sometimes stay out overnight, or even for two or three days, but essentially, local foods provided for all the requirements of the group. Diets varied seasonally, as different plants and animals became available. Most food was eaten fresh, and in (close to) its original form, with minimal processing.

After the Neolithic Revolution and the rise of market towns and trade routes, people's diets became more restricted. They ate less variety of wild foods, and the staples of the diet might consist of only one or two grains (wheat, or millet, or corn, or rice) and only a few types of domestic animal meats (beef, mutton, goat, pork, or chicken). Later improvements in transportation, such as camel caravans, and especially seagoing vessels, led to long-distance explorations and the discovery of exotic foods from faraway lands. Much of the colonial enterprise of claiming distant lands for European countries during the fifteenth through twentieth centuries was done in the service of making new foods available to Europeans. Spices, sugar, tea, chocolate, and coffee led the way.

Many foods grow only in certain climates, but people in distant regions may develop a taste for them and are willing to pay premium prices for them. Some foods may grow locally, but only during one season of the year. In order to eat them year-round, they must be imported from the other hemisphere. Because imported foods are often more expensive than locally grown ones, a certain status may accrue to those who can afford to buy and consume them.

According to the USDA Economic Research Service, an increasing proportion of what Americans eat is produced in other countries, up to 15 percent in 2005, when measured by volume. Figures for specific categories of food are more revealing. Based on volume, between 2000 and 2005, the United States imported an estimated 79 percent of the fish and shellfish, 32 percent of the fruits and nuts, 16 percent of the wine and beer, 13 percent of the vegetables, 12 percent of the grains and grain products, 11 percent of the sweeteners and candy, and 10 percent of the red meats the population consumed (Jerardo 2008). According to Pirog and Benjamin (2003:1), "The typical American prepared meal contains, on average, ingredients from at least five countries outside the United States."

The average distance food travels from where it is grown to where it is purchased or consumed—a concept known as **food miles**—is steadily increasing. Even when food is produced domestically, rather than imported, it often is transported over great distances. For the United States, estimates of the average distance food travels have surpassed 1,500 miles (Pirog and Benjamin 2003). All of this moving of food resources from one side of the globe to another, or from farm to factory to store, requires huge inputs of energy in the form of nonrenewable resources such as oil—for the freighters that carry raw materials and processed foods across the world's oceans; for the planes that bring fresh seafood and produce to inland cities; and for the trains and trucks that move food from ports to processing plants, distribution centers, and local grocery stores.

The environmental impact of food production, processing, transport, and distribution also depends on other factors. It may be more energy efficient, despite transportation costs, to grow tomatoes in Spain and export them to the United Kingdom, than to grow the same tomatoes locally in a heated greenhouse during the winter (Smith et al. 2005). Likewise, it may be more energy efficient to import lamb from New Zealand, where the pastures are lush and the sheep can graze outside year-round, than to raise sheep in areas with poor pastures and cold winters (McWilliams 2007).

In addition to transportation issues, much of the food in industrial and postindustrial contexts is produced long before it is consumed. It may then be stored for months or years before processing, and stored again after processing, before transport to distribution centers and retail grocery outlets many miles or continents away. A variety of nutrients are removed from some foods to make them last longer, while others have chemical stabilizers, artificial colors and flavors, and preservatives added so the food won't become moldy or taste stale. The finished product often bears little resemblance to the original resources.

All of these characteristics of the *modern* food system—that many foods come from far away, are not remotely fresh, and are highly processed—make our diet less nutritious, more costly for consumers, and devastating for the environment.

Contamination of the Food Supply

Another consideration when evaluating the modern system of food production is the possibility of accidental and deliberate contamination of the food supply. In recent years, a number of different food products have been inadvertently contaminated by bacteria, including *Salmonella* and *E. coli*. The number-one source of *E. coli* poisoning in the United States is ground beef sold directly to consumers as well as to fast-food outlets. The second most common source of *E. coli* infection is green leafy vegetables, such as spinach, lettuce, and green onions. In 2009, a peanut processing plant was identified as the source of an outbreak of *Salmonella* poisonings in the United States, and the plant was shut down when it was revealed that corporate managers had known of the contamination for some time before it was reported in the news media but did not issue a recall for the affected products or even shut down the production line. In January 2010, a number of *Salmonella* cases were traced to contaminated black pepper imported from Vietnam by a manufacturer of salami and other cured meats. Hepatitis A, a viral infection, has also been spread from contaminated factory and restaurant workers to the general public, including a 1988 outbreak in China that affected some 300,000 people who had consumed tainted clams.

Accidental food contaminations of this kind are common, and our current system of food processing and distribution means that one contaminated provider—of ground beef, green onions, peanuts, etc.—can affect different types of foods in many locations, including restaurant and institutional food services as well as home kitchens. The U.S. Centers for Disease Control maintains a centralized reporting system for outbreaks of food- and water-borne diseases (NORS 2010).

Deliberate contaminations of the food supply are rarer, but more alarming. China has been the source of many food products later found to have been deliberately adulterated with the industrial chemical *melamine*, which can cause kidney problems and lead to death. The China-melamine connection first came to light in March 2007, when many brands of dog and cat food were recalled in North America, Europe, and South Africa after reports of kidney failure in pets. The kidney problems were traced to melamine contamination of pet foods and pet food ingredients that originated in China. Melamine is inexpensive, and in China, and perhaps other countries, is commonly added to both pet and human food to inflate the apparent protein content. A few months after the pet food recall, melamine was discovered in Chinese sources of vegetable protein used to make chicken feed in the United States.

The most amusing example of melamine contamination of the human food supply came in the fall of 2008. Levels of melamine more than 100 times the legal limit were discovered in several chocolate-flavored erotic spreads imported to Britain from the Chinese manufacturer, *Le Bang*, including "Chocolate Flavored Willy Spread" (*Daily Mail* 2008). On a more serious note, the most disturbing example came that same fall, when 22 Chinese manufacturers had to recall tainted infant formula, which had sickened close to 300,000 babies in China. At least six infants died of kidney failure, and 860 were hospitalized.

The Chinese infant formula scandal highlights the fact that artificial infant formula is especially vulnerable to accidental contamination, manufacturing mistakes, and deliberate consumer fraud through dilution (or cutting of the powdered form) with cheaper ingredients. Just in the past decade, infant formula in North America has been recalled for the following reasons: too much magnesium; too little iron, protein, or Vitamin C; and contamination with *Enterobacter sakazakii*, polyvinyl chloride, or metal particles (Walker 2007).

FINAL THOUGHTS

No matter how much we may appreciate the relatively cheap food supply we enjoy in many Western countries, as well as the convenience, wide range of food choices, and interesting flavors provided by industrial foods, we also need to recognize that this system of food production carries significant costs at all levels—to the individual, the group, and the environment.

The 2002 book, *The Fatal Harvest Reader: The Tragedy of Industrial Agriculture,* edited by Andrew Kimbrell, dispels each of the major *myths* that many North Americans hold about industrial agriculture: industrial agriculture will feed the world; industrial food is safe, healthy, and nutritious; industrial food is cheap; industrial agriculture is efficient; industrial food offers more choices; industrial agriculture benefits the environment and wildlife; and biotechnology will solve the problems of industrial agriculture. All myths.

The reality is that food production using industrial agriculture and pastoralism is incredibly inefficient in terms of energy use. We will never be able to feed the world adequately, as the human population continues to increase faster than our ability to increase food production. Industrial food isn't all that safe. Many deaths and diseases are caused by contaminated foods, whether that contamination was deliberate or accidental. Raw materials contaminated in one place get distributed throughout the country, indeed, throughout the world. Industrial food isn't always healthy and nutritious—many important nutrients are removed from foods to give them longer shelf lives, and many disease-causing agents are introduced during processing. Industrial food isn't really cheap. It only seems cheap because of government subsidies and the fact that no one, so far, has had to pay for cleaning up the environmental damage caused by its production. Although some industrial foods benefit from economies of scale (it is cheaper per chicken to raise 1,000,000 chickens on one farm than 10 chickens each on 100,000 farms), this only holds as long as the environmental costs are not factored in. Industrial agriculture and pastoralism waste nonrenewable resources and pollute the land and water supplies. By relying on only a few main crops and domestic animals, we risk catastrophic failure of the food supply should a new disease or unusual weather conditions wipe out a significant portion of the food resources we depend on. Finally, biotechnology is the devil we don't know—it has the potential to bring great benefits, but also great harms that may not be apparent until years down the road.

There is much to commend the traditional modes of subsistence that Baumeister so cavalierly dismisses. More and more people in the industrial West are starting to realize the high price we pay for industrial foods, and a variety of grass-roots movements have begun to take hold to address these issues, including: being a vegetarian or vegan; eating locally and seasonally, to reduce food miles; eating fresh foods to reduce processing and increase nutritional value; growing your own meat (cf. Backyard Chickens); and growing your own vegetables in a home garden.

The future of subsistence for the entire world may indeed be that each person, or family, returns to producing much of his own food supply through direct labor or purchasing food from local farmers, herders, and fisherfolk.

Key Concepts Review

Anthropologists typically classify subsistence modes into hunting and gathering (foraging), pastoralism, horticulture and agriculture, and intensive and industrial agriculture.

This classification is merely a heuristic device, as most people today consume food from a variety of sources.

Anthropologist Julian Steward emphasized that a group's mode of subsistence affects many other aspects of their culture, including settlement patterns, material culture, religion, arts, and more.

Foods are said to be domesticated when their genetic profiles—and consequently their anatomy and physiology—have been substantially modified through artificial selection by humans.

Foodstuffs can be obtained through direct labor or indirectly, through trade or the marketplace.

Subsistence affects how people move across the landscape, including nomadic, transhumant, and sedentary lifestyles.

Dettwyler's "Stuff Theory" of Material Culture and House Form relates how much stuff people have, and the kinds of houses they live in, to three variables: (1) frequency of movement, (2) distance to be traveled, and (3) means of transporting goods.

Hunting and gathering was the only human mode of subsistence during the Environment of Evolutionary Adaptedness (EEA) and some people today still live as hunters and gatherers; wild foods continue to contribute to diets all over the world.

Pastoralists can live off their herds without necessarily killing their animals for meat.

Domesticated crops provide most of the food for the world's current population, but intensive and industrial agriculture are neither sustainable nor efficient.

The true costs of industrial food would include the costs of intensive production, processing, and distribution, as well as the health risks from accidental or deliberate contamination.

Even in industrial and postindustrial economies, where most people don't forage for wild foods or grow their own food, many people are engaged in the processing and distribution of food and ancillary industries.

Sign for public toilets in Thailand.

3

LOVE IS ALL WE NEED

Sex, Gender, & Sexual Orientation

If I was in charge of the world, it would be a world where one's talents, skills, interests, genetic capabilities, occupation, social status, and personal value were not thought to be limited by one's sex chromosomes, hormone levels, internal or external anatomy, sexual preferences, or sexual behavior.

Once a group's basic needs for food and shelter have been satisfied, the next major goal to accomplish is the reproduction of the group. This involves many different aspects of life, including controlling sexual behavior, dealing with pregnancy and childbirth, and keeping your kids alive and healthy. It also requires that adults provide children with everything they need to know to be proper, functioning members of the group—all of the knowledge, beliefs, attitudes, practices, and behaviors that constitute culture. All cultures make some distinctions in how they treat children and what they teach them, or allow them to learn, based on the (perceived) sex of the child. Further, all cultures construct elaborate sets of beliefs and behaviors that shape and modify how the child's sex is expressed in terms of the gender roles available in the culture.

In this chapter, we will begin with a thorough explanation of the difference between **sex** and **gender,** which is much more complex than you might imagine. We then move on to a discussion of **sexual orientation** (sex object preference). These are particularly important topics to understand, as many people use the terms sex and gender interchangeably, even though they refer to very different aspects of identity. Additionally, typical *Western* cultural beliefs about sexual orientation cause untold confusion and grief in many societies. Misperceptions about these topics make it difficult for many North Americans to understand how sex, gender, sexual orientation, and related issues play out in unfamiliar cultures.

THE STANDARD NORTH AMERICAN CULTURAL VIEW

Most contemporary North Americans are raised to believe in a very specific cultural view about how the world works with respect to sex, gender, and sexual orientation. This standard *cultural view* can be summarized in three statements:

1. *Biological sex is a dichotomous variable.* There are only two sexes—male (XY) and female (XX). A person's sex is determined by his or her sex chromosomes, which determine hormone levels, which determine internal and external anatomy, capabilities, interests, and personality traits. A person's sex is not subject to environmental influences or cultural interpretation.

2. *Gender is a dichotomous variable.* There are only two (legitimate) genders—masculine and feminine—and they correspond exactly to biological sex. Males are automatically masculine and females are automatically feminine. All aspects of gender vary together. Male/masculinity is considered the superior category.

3. *Sexual orientation is a dichotomous variable.* There are only two sexual orientations, and only one of them is considered normal. People of one sex/gender are supposed to want to have sexual relationships only with people of the opposite sex/gender (referred to as *sexual orientation* or *sex object preference*). If you are normal, you are labeled a *heterosexual*. If you prefer

having sex with people of the same sex/gender as yourself, you are labeled a *homosexual*. Heterosexuality is considered the superior category.

The same information is presented in table 3.1.

The reality of how the world actually works is much messier, much more complex, and much more affected by environmental factors and cultural beliefs than most people realize. It is also *much more interesting* than the simplistic view presented above. In the following sections, we will unpack and examine each of these three cultural beliefs.

BIOLOGICAL SEX

What Determines Whether You Are Male or Female?

Sex is not a clear-cut dichotomous variable. Different cultures define biological sex differently; there is no standard definition, even in Western biomedical contexts, about the basis by which a person should be considered either male or female. There is also disagreement about how to classify people who don't fit neatly—in terms of their anatomy, physiology, or behavior—into the two main categories. A simple male/female dichotomy is not sufficient to understand issues of sex, gender, and sexual orientation in cross-cultural perspective (Fausto-Sterling 2002).

Typically, people's sex chromosomes determine the level of reproductive hormones that circulate in their body at various times during their life. Hormone levels, in turn, affect the development of internal and external anatomy, physiology, and many aspects of behavior. Most humans have 23 pairs of chromosomes, with the twenty-third pair designated as the sex chromosomes. This pair comes in two varieties, X and Y. Typically, each male has an X from his mother and a Y

from his father. Each female has two X chromosomes, one from her mother and another from her father.

Under ordinary circumstances, genes on the Y chromosome cause male fetal testicular tissue to start producing the hormone testosterone at about 12 weeks after conception. It is the presence of testosterone in the system during fetal development that makes the person anatomically, physiologically, and behaviorally male. Females have only X chromosomes, and no testicular tissue to make testosterone during gestation. In the absence of testosterone during gestation, development proceeds in the default mode, which is female, and the fetus develops into a person who is anatomically, physiologically, and behaviorally female. At puberty, a female's ovaries and adrenal glands will begin to produce tiny amounts of testosterone that affect her libido, bone density, and general mood.

Biological influences via hormones may also come from the environment through exposure to chemicals that either are exactly the same as human sex hormones or function in a manner similar to these hormones.

There are specific sensitive periods during which the body and brain are particularly susceptible to the effects of hormones, whatever the source. The **first sensitive period** is during gestation, **in utero.** All fetuses have external genitalia that appear female to begin with. Regardless of your chromosomes, if you are exposed to testosterone during gestation, you will develop to look more like a male on the outside—you will develop a penis, rather than a clitoris, and the folds of skin on either side of the developing genitals will fuse across the midline to form the scrotum. If you are *not* exposed to testosterone, or your tissues don't recognize testosterone properly, you will develop to look more like a female on the outside—you will develop a clitoris, rather than a penis, and the folds of skin will not fuse across the midline, but rather will develop into the labia on either side of the vaginal opening. The time of onset, duration, and levels of testosterone exposure during fetal development will affect exactly how your external and internal genitalia form.

The **second sensitive period** happens only in typical XY males, and is a postnatal surge of testosterone from the testicles that occurs when the baby boy is *three to six months* of age.

Table 3.1	Standard North American cultural view		
Chromosomes	**Sex**	**Gender**	**Normal Sexual Orientation**
XY	Male	Masculine	Female—Hetereosexual
XX	Female	Feminine	Male—Heterosexual

The **third sensitive period** happens in *both sexes at puberty*, when the testicles of typical XY males begin producing testosterone at much higher levels, and the ovaries of typical females begin producing estrogen at high levels. All males and females produce both male hormones (such as testosterone) and female hormones (such as estrogen), but in different amounts. Estrogen is produced mainly by the ovaries but also by fat tissue, and there are plant (phyto-) estrogens, especially from soy products, that mimic estrogen in the body. Testosterone is produced mainly by the testicles in males but also by the adrenal glands in both sexes. Other hormones are involved as well, but estrogen and testosterone are by far the most important.

In the vast majority of cases, development proceeds as it should, and individuals with XY chromosomes develop into anatomically, physiologically, and behaviorally typical males; individuals with XX chromosomes develop into anatomically, physiologically, and behaviorally typical females. But not in every case.

Atypical Chromosomes

There are several atypical sex chromosome possibilities, in addition to the standard XY/male and XX/female. People can have an extra piece of a sex chromosome, or an entire extra sex chromosome. They can also be missing a piece of a sex chromosome, or an entire sex chromosome. There are many variations, but only two will be mentioned here.

Some people have an extra sex chromosome. They may be XXY, or XYY. The presence of the Y chromosome means that testosterone is produced during fetal development, which makes these individuals male. In some cases, there may be minor biological and behavioral side effects from the extra chromosome, but many XXY and XYY individuals are never diagnosed as such.

Some people are missing a sex chromosome. They are born with one X, and no matching chromosome. This condition, designated XO, is known as Turner's Syndrome. The lack of a Y chromosome results in their being anatomically female, although their internal reproductive organs may not develop properly. Women with Turner's Syndrome are often noticeably short, usually won't go through puberty without additional estrogen treatments, and usually are not fecund (capable of getting pregnant). The comparable situation of having only a Y chromosome but no X is fatal early in embryonic development. Thus, there aren't any people walking around with just a Y chromosome.

Normal XY Chromosomes, Atypical Testosterone Production or Hormone Receptors

Some individuals have typical XY chromosomes—their Y chromosome makes them chromosomally male. However, because of other genetic variations, they either (1) do not produce testosterone at all, or not in sufficient quantities, or (2) produce testosterone normally, but the relevant target cells in the body have nonfunctioning testosterone receptors, so the testosterone has no impact, or (3) do not produce testosterone in utero or at three to six months of age, but do begin producing testosterone at puberty.

In all three situations, these individuals appear to be female at birth. If there has been no testosterone present at all during fetal development, they will have normal female external genitalia. If low levels of testosterone were present, they may have somewhat ambiguous genitalia but are usually thought to be female.

In the first two cases—no testosterone produced, or faulty receptors on the target cells—the children are raised as little girls and are not diagnosed with anything until they fail to go through puberty (i.e., they don't develop breasts or menstruate). If they seek medical help, they may be diagnosed as chromosomally male. At this point, most choose to take exogenous female hormones to develop female secondary sexual characteristics such as breasts and broader hips relative to shoulders. They will not menstruate or be fecund, however, because they don't have a uterus or ovaries. They think of themselves as females and are recognized as females by society.

Externally, individuals of type 3 are anatomically female at birth and are raised as girls. However, at puberty, their testicles (located in their labial folds) begin to produce testosterone, and they start to develop male secondary sexual characteristics such as facial hair and a deep voice, and their clitoris grows somewhat larger (though not to typical penis size). At this point, most choose to switch their sexual identity to males. They think of themselves as females during childhood, but their circulating testosterone levels cause them to identify as males at puberty, and they are recognized as males by society once puberty progresses.

Normal XX Chromosomes, Extra Androgen

There are two situations in which fetuses who are XX—chromosomally typical females—are exposed to extra androgens (male hormones) during prenatal development, which may lead to variations in anatomy, physiology, and behavior.

The first situation is when an XX female fetus is exposed to *external* androgens, leading to the development of ambiguous genitalia or external male genitalia at birth. Usually, these babies are identified as males at birth and spend their childhood as little boys. They are not diagnosed with anything until they fail to go through puberty (i.e., they don't have a growth spurt, they don't develop facial hair or deeper voices, their penis does not begin to grow larger). If they seek medical help, they may be diagnosed as chromosomally female.

At this point, some may decide to switch their sexual identity to female. They can take female hormones to develop a more feminine physique. Their uterus and ovaries may not have formed properly, so they may not be able to reproduce. They may consider themselves females, even though raised as boys, and live their lives as women after diagnosis. Some, however, take a different path after diagnosis. These individuals consider themselves to be male, due in part to the effects of prenatal testosterone on the brain. They choose to keep their male identity and may take male hormones to develop male secondary sexual characteristics.

There are many variants of this condition, depending on the timing of exposure to exogenous androgens, the length of the exposure, and the strength of the exposure. Most exogenous androgens come from chemical contamination of the mother's environment or from prescription drugs she is taking while unaware that she is pregnant.

The second situation is Congenital Adrenal Hyperplasia (CAH), when an XX female fetus is exposed to excess levels of *internal* androgens (male hormones), produced by their own adrenal glands during prenatal development. Depending on the amount and timing of these extra androgens, the individual may or may not be diagnosed. If the circulating levels of male hormones affect the appearance of the external genitalia, making them appear slightly masculinized, then tests may be done for clarification of the child's sex. However, in many cases, the exposure is at such a low level that the internal and external anatomy form as a typical female, but the brain is nevertheless affected by the circulating androgens during fetal development.

The research on behaviors and personality traits of individuals diagnosed with CAH shows them to be somewhat masculine in behavior and feelings, but they still consider themselves to be normal females. There probably are a number of females in every population who have mild, undiagnosed cases of CAH. They are undiagnosed because their internal and external anatomy appear fully female and function normally, and they are fecund. A girl or woman might suspect she has a mild case of CAH if she enjoys activities culturally defined as typically male (in North American culture, she is considered a *tomboy* as a child) or if she disdains some activities culturally defined as typically female (in North American culture, she doesn't like to play with dolls, never daydreams about her perfect wedding, and doesn't care about shoes). On the other hand, many women *without* CAH rebel against the activities their culture tells them they should enjoy. Not all tomboys have CAH.

Now that you have some idea of how complicated sex can be, let's move on to an even more complicated topic—gender.

GENDER

Sex and gender are two different concepts, both of which are complicated and both of which are influenced by biological variables and cultural shaping. The standard Western belief system usually conflates these two categories, acting as though they are interchangeable—as though there are only two gender categories, *masculine* and *feminine*—and as though every male is automatically masculine, and every female is automatically feminine. In such a schema, if your biological sex doesn't match your gender, then there must be something wrong with you, rather than the classification scheme. In reality, sex and gender are *not* the same, and gender is a much more complicated concept than sex.

Defining Gender

In this textbook, *gender* is defined as follows: a set of socially and culturally constructed categories, many aspects of which flow from typical biological (chromosomal/hormonal) differences between the two sexes, and many aspects of which are completely random, arbitrary, culturally defined, and change over time. By this, I mean that every culture has one or more sets of beliefs concerning what males and females are supposed to be like—a set (or sets) of rules of appropriate behaviors, feelings, predilections, talents, capabilities, and so on. These rules may include what kind of clothes you wear, how you fix your hair, how you move and speak, what occupations you pursue, what hobbies and interests you prefer, what talents you have, and so forth. Nevertheless, as shown in the evidence from the research on CAH females (discussed above), *gender* is not 100 percent social/cultural.

Across cultures, gender categories always include the stereotypically masculine and feminine personas associated with typical males (XY) and typical females (XX). Many or most people will, indeed, fit comfortably into the gender categories that their apparent sex indicates and will wonder what all the fuss is about. However, there are also a number of cultures and subcultures around the world where the gender classification system includes more than two gender categories. Some have three, some four, and some even more.

Typically, if there is a third formal gender category, it will be for people who are apparently male but prefer to behave in feminine ways, at least in some respects. If there is a fourth category, it will be for people who are apparently female but prefer to behave in masculine ways, at least in some respects. If there is a fifth category, it may be one such as the *Two-Spirit* of some Native American tribes. People assigned to this classification are considered to be equally masculine and feminine at the same time—to have the gender attributes of both sexes.

The typical Western view supposes that *masculine* and *feminine* categories are clear-cut, distinct, and mostly nonoverlapping. In reality, gender is more properly viewed as a continuum, ranging from hypermasculine ("real men") at one end of the spectrum to hyper-feminine ("real women") at the other, with everything in between. In many cultures, there will be a broad range of overlap and many characteristics will be considered equally appropriate and acceptable for both masculine and feminine individuals.

The Western perspective also supposes that gender identity is a single suite of characteristics that always vary together. That is, if you express any aspect of one gender, then you should express all aspects of that gender. In reality, gender is more properly viewed as having many different aspects, which don't necessarily vary together. An individual may rank as masculine on some gender aspects, as defined by the local cultural belief system, and as feminine on other aspects. Some cultures may stress one aspect more than another in terms of defining a person's gender identity.

Finally, the Western view supposes that gender identity and sexual orientation vary together—that if a male is feminine, then he is also homosexual; if a female is masculine, then she is also homosexual. In reality, just as sex and gender don't necessarily go together, *a person's gender can vary completely independently of his or her sexual orientation*, and sexual orientation itself is defined very differently in different cultures.

Although many cultures assume that most people will automatically fit into the gender category that their apparent sex indicates and will be sexually attracted to members of the opposite sex/gender category, it is universally recognized that these *natural* rules need to be *culturally* reinforced. The rules are both implicitly and explicitly taught to children and reinforced over and over again, to make sure that everyone behaves as they should, with punishments for transgressions. When children express feelings or act in ways that are not considered appropriate to their sex or gender, cultures vary in how they deal with the situation. If more than two gender categories are available, the child may be slotted into one of the alternatives.

Aspects of Gender

The specific parameters of gender categories vary greatly from culture to culture and within cultures, and of course they change over time. There are all sorts of rules you are expected to learn and follow, as well as attitudes and predilections you are supposed to have naturally because of your sex. Some aspects of behavior are allowed a lot of variation, while others are more narrowly defined, depending on the culture. The following discussion, modeled after Nanda (2000), is not exhaustive.

How are you defined as belonging to a gender category? People are assigned to categories, whether the standard two, or an alternative classification, according to many different criteria. If you express the appropriate sentiments and behave in the standard ways for someone of your sex, then you are assumed to belong to the standard gender that goes with your sex. If you only fit some of the parameters, or act in atypical ways only in certain circumstances, or at certain times, then the situation becomes more complicated. Others may tolerate such variation without requiring you to change genders. Other than your apparent sexual identity based on external anatomy, cultures vary in terms of which criteria are the most important in defining a person's gender.

Cultures also vary in terms of how a person gets defined officially as a *gender variant*—either a male who acts feminine, a female who acts masculine, or something else. An alternate gender identity may become apparent in childhood, or only at puberty, or only after you reach adulthood. Sometimes, there may be a supernatural sign that indicates a person belongs to an alternate category.

Likewise, cultures vary with respect to whether they believe one's gender identification is voluntary or innate. In other words, do males choose to be masculine and females choose to be feminine, or is it part of their biology? Do gender variants choose to be different, or is it the result of unusual biological forces such as extra or missing sex chromosomes or receptors, or hormonal effects during fetal development? In some cases, where gender identification is believed to be voluntary, parents will deliberately assign their children to an alternate category (for various practical reasons) and then expect them to behave according to the rules of the category they have been placed in. Or, if a child expresses sentiments and behaviors that don't match their sex, they may be punished, or people will try to talk them out of it.

Likewise, cultures vary with respect to whether they think a person's gender classification is permanent or transitory. Some cultures allow people to change their gender classification if they want, or even assume that it will automatically change as a person gets older.

Finally, cultures vary greatly in terms of how gender variants are thought of and treated by members of the two dominant sex/gender categories. In some places, members of the alternate gender categories are regarded as powerful—they may be expected or encouraged to become ritual or religious specialists. In some cultures, gender variants are valued as entertainers, and in still others, they are shunned and looked down upon. In other circumstances, they may be accepted as long as they "stay in their place." For example, in the United States, males who behave as flamboyantly cross-gender may be accepted more readily as interior decorators or dancers than they would be as soldiers or judges.

Gender and Biological Sex Differences

Males and females are different. There are clearly biologically based differences in the anatomy, physiology, and behavior of typical males and females, as well as enormous overlapping ranges of variation in all of these factors. It is impossible to pin down all of these biological differences because of the complications that culture introduces, and many of them are tendencies, rather than absolute differences, but they are real, nonetheless.

Gender categories may be culturally defined in such a way as to *be generally congruent* with the typical biological tendencies of each of the two primary sexes (male/XY and female/XX). They may build on, support, and be in harmony with, any underlying biological differences.

On the other hand, gender categories may be culturally defined in such a way as to *not be congruent* with the typical biological tendencies of each of the two primary sexes. They may be *more restrictive* than the normal range of variation in biological tendencies. They may *exaggerate the differences* between the biological sexes, as in the "cults of masculinity" described in Gilmore's *Manhood in the Making* (1991). Or, gender categories may be culturally defined in such a way as to be in *direct opposition* to the biological tendencies of each sex, thereby *downplaying the differences* between the sexes, as Margaret Mead (1935[2001]) described for the Arapesh of highland New Guinea (see also Mead 1949[2001]).

The take-home message is that culture can be very powerful in shaping your thoughts, your feelings, and your behaviors. You can learn to suppress your natural tendencies, if they are not valued or acceptable for people of your sex/gender. You can also learn to fit in.

You may participate and even enjoy activities solely on the basis of enculturation as a child, whether or not they fit naturally with your sex/gender.

Relationships between Gender Categories

Whether you have two categories, or more, the gender categories may be very distinct, with a vast "no person's land" in between, or they may overlap a little, a lot, or 99 percent. Additionally, they may be **egalitarian,** or **hierarchical.** For simplicity, we will explore these issues using only the two standard categories of masculine and feminine and recognizing that most people in the masculine category are male and most people in the feminine category are female.

When the two categories are egalitarian—equally valued—as they usually are among hunters and gatherers, they tend to be quite distinct. Hunting and gathering societies have essentially *separate but equal* gender categories. Men and women will have different responsibilities, engage in different subsistence and household tasks, and be expected to exhibit different personality types, appropriate to their sex. However, men's and women's contributions to the survival of the group are considered complementary—both are considered important.

In a hierarchical system, the personality traits, occupations, and value of one category are considered to be superior to those of the other category—their contributions to subsistence are considered more important, their personality traits and activities more valuable. Where the two categories are hierarchical, the male/masculine category *always* has the higher status. There are no societies that have hierarchical gender categories with female/feminine having the higher status, with the possible exception of the Mosuo of China.

In the United States and Canada today, the gender categories overlap substantially in some respects—women are now allowed much more freedom to pursue occupations that were regarded traditionally as only for males, such as being a firefighter or a veterinarian. They have many more opportunities to engage in organized competitive sports and can choose whether to wear a dress or a pair of pants. However, most male/masculine occupations and activities are still accorded higher value than female/feminine activities, and most stereotypically female/feminine occupations and activities are still devalued in general.

Since male/masculinity is the more highly valued category, people think it only reasonable that girls and women should aspire to achieve the higher statuses accorded to males and male occupations. But many people view with suspicion males who aspire to belong to the inferior category. Since female/femininity is the discriminated-against category—the *contaminating* category—any hint of feminine feelings or behavior in a boy or man may serve as evidence, to the individual himself and/or to others, that he has a "gender identity disorder" (and may likely be "homosexual" as well). This is ridiculous, of course, but is a logical consequence of the belief system most North Americans buy into, including many medical professionals (Swidey 2005). We will explore this in more detail below.

Goodness of Fit

The influence of culturally defined aspects of gender begins before birth (in your parents' perceptions of you, if they know your sex) and is overwhelming from birth on. In most cultures, boys and girls are dressed differently, given different toys to play with, given different household chores and responsibilities, and given different opportunities for development. Girls and boys are usually held to different standards of behavior and are aware that their parents have different expectations for what they will accomplish in life. Even one's given name may matter—a girl with a very feminine name, such as Tiffany or Ann Marie, may feel more pressure to act feminine than girls named Charlotte or Alexandra who go by Charlie and Alex. A boy named Leslie or Francis may feel the need to act conspicuously masculine to overcome the stigma of his ambiguous name, while Dirk or Craig have no such problems.

Children learn the appropriate behaviors for their sex/gender category the same way they learn other aspects of their culture—through observation of others; through overt, deliberate teaching by their parents, extended family members, friends, neighbors, and teachers; through various forms of media such as radio, TV, music, and the Internet; and by being teased, ridiculed, or seriously punished when they break the rules or transgress the boundaries. We take for granted many of the gender differences we see around us and assume that they are biologically based and similar across all cultures.

In every population, many people will be comfortable fitting into the gender category that their culture assigns to their sex. They will be perfectly happy following the rules and will not experience any difficulties or problems. They will assume that gender categories are *natural* and that all people feel the same way.

At the same time, many people will be *comfortable with most aspects* of the gender category that their culture assigns to their sex but will chafe at the restrictions placed on them for other aspects of their gender category. When I was growing up, girls were ostracized for being tomboys, and some, including me, chafed at rules that said we couldn't play competitive sports, and shouldn't even want to. Even today in North America, boys may be teased for being overly interested in cooking and fashion, while still fitting in otherwise with their "more masculine" peers.

In every population, some people will be *uncomfortable with most aspects* of the gender category that their culture assigns to their sex. If there are only two gender categories, masculine and feminine, they may feel as though they don't belong to the gender category usually assigned to their sex. Does that mean they belong completely to the opposite gender category? Not at all. They may wish there was a third gender category to which they could belong. If there are no other options, and there are extreme penalties for not behaving as expected, individuals may conform (at some cost to their own well-being), or they may live as they wish and accept the penalties, or they may become depressed and eventually commit suicide. This is especially problematic where it is generally accepted that there are only two clear-cut sexes and only two legitimate gender categories, and everyone is expected to automatically fit in. In such cases, there may be little tolerance for variance from the rigid cultural rules.

In contexts where there are more than the two standard categories, some people may fit more or less easily into one of the available categories and mold their behaviors to correspond to the rules for that category. There will probably always be a few individuals who find that they don't fit into any of the options that are defined as acceptable.

Sexual Identity and Gender Identity

In addition to all these variations in sex and gender, there is a further complication: how a person feels about him- or herself. Some people, for no apparent biological reason, feel that they have been born into the wrong body—that they really are of the opposite sex, in mind and spirit, regardless of their chromosomes, hormones, and internal and external genitalia. We can ask, "What is an individual's perception of his or her own sex in terms of male versus female, and his or her gender in terms of masculinity or femininity?"

There are some people who are typical females in terms of chromosomes, hormones, and anatomy but feel, nonetheless, as though they are males. Likewise, there are some people who are typical males in terms of chromosomes, hormones, and anatomy but feel as though they are females. Sometimes, where this is an option, these people change their anatomy and hormones to match their internal vision of who they are. The term **transsexual** may be used to refer to these cases, whether or not people take steps to have their bodies match their internal feelings about themselves.

The terms *transgender* and *transsexual* should refer to different things, but in the contemporary United States the terms themselves seem to be hopelessly confused and conflated, not to mention defined differently by every person one asks. The important thing to realize is that you can be disgruntled with your particular society's limitations on the gender category that people of your sex are usually assigned to, without concluding that you actually belong to the opposite sex. *Sex and gender are different things.*

Is Gender 100 Percent Culturally and Socially Defined?

Some people would like to define *gender* as a 100 percent cultural/social construct, and deny that there are any biological differences in abilities, behaviors, or feelings between males and females. Research has shown conclusively that this is *not* true. Males and females are different.

Cross-cultural evidence supports this, as traits assigned to *masculine* or *feminine* gender categories do not vary randomly across the world. There are places where males are taught culturally to curb their aggressive tendencies, just as there are cultures where males are taught to exaggerate and publicly express their aggressive tendencies. But you don't find that in half of all cultures, men are considered more aggressive by nature and act that way accordingly, and in the other half, women are considered more aggressive, and act that way. In most cultures, it is recognized that males are, on average, more aggressive than females.

There are cultures where men weave and women do not—such as the Hopi and the Bambara—but in the overwhelming majority of cultures, only women weave. There are cultures where men participate more in child care than in others (Hewlett 1992, 1993), but there aren't any cultures where the men routinely do even 30 percent of the childcare, let alone more.

The story of David Reimer serves as a dramatic example of the fact that gender cannot be imposed on children through the force of cultural beliefs alone. In the latter part of the twentieth century, some experts claimed that in contrast to biological sex, gender was completely malleable and could be *culturally assigned* up to about 18 months of age. The most famous example of this is the case of David Reimer, one of a set of identical twin boys born in Canada in 1966 (Colapinto 2001). When he was eight months old, his penis was seriously maimed in a circumcision accident. The following year, acting on the advice of Dr. John Money, a well-known U.S. psychologist and gender specialist, his parents agreed to have his testicles removed and raise him as a girl.

However, David's brain had already been masculinized by the presence of testosterone *in utero*, as well as the postnatal surge that happens at three to six months of age. Despite being treated as a girl, and taught the appropriate gender role for females in Canada in the 1960s and 1970s, David *felt* that he was a boy, and struggled throughout childhood to make sense of his life. His parents gave him estrogen therapy so he would develop breasts and a more feminine body and face. At the age of 14 years, he learned the truth, and subsequently lived his life as a man. He had his breasts surgically removed and changed his hormone treatments from estrogen to testosterone. He eventually married a woman and adopted her children, and seemed to be coping. Then, in 2002, his twin brother committed suicide. Following the breakup of his marriage in 2004, David also killed himself (Usborne 2004).

The case of David Reimer, the research on females with Congenital Adrenal Hyperplasia, and the cross-cultural distribution of gender attributes clearly show that there are biological underpinnings to many aspects of the differences between gender categories. Many aspects of gender are based in part on true underlying bi-

ologically based differences between males and females. The influence of testosterone on the developing brain is profound and irreversible. Gender is *not* a 100 percent socially and culturally defined construct.

Is Gender 100 Percent Biologically Determined?

Some people believe that just like biological sex, gender is completely determined by biology and is not influenced by culture. Research has shown conclusively that this is *not* true. Many aspects of gender are based on seemingly random and arbitrary cultural distinctions that change over time and vary across cultures. The rise of the feminist movement in Western cultures will be used as an illustration.

Within most Western cultures, the prefeminist cultural construction of the biological differences between the sexes (still alive and well in some places) and, therefore, the proper roles for men and women in society, had two basic premises. First: "Women can't do the things men do because all women are (a) too weak (physical limitations, especially strength); (b) too stupid (cognitive limitations, especially for science/math); and (c) morally deficient (too emotional, not capable of rational reasoning)." Second: "Only the things that men do—productive activities in the public sphere—are important." A corollary of the second premise is that the things that men specifically *can't do* because of their biology—menstruate, conceive, gestate, give birth, and lactate—are *unimportant*. These reproductive activities are part of the private, domestic sphere; they were (and are) "taken for granted" as being what women do since women aren't capable of achievement in the men's world of true/real accomplishments.

Many Western feminists have devoted much of their time arguing against the first proposition (and rightly so), claiming, and going on to demonstrate, that at least some women are capable of, and interested in, traditionally male productive activities and deserve to have the opportunities to pursue them if they want.

When I was growing up in the United States in the 1950s and 1960s, girls *naturally* didn't whistle, didn't serve in the armed forces except as nurses or Donut Dollies, weren't allowed to take high school calculus classes, and didn't participate in organized or competitive athletics. After much lobbying, I was allowed to practice running hurdles with the boys' track team in high school—I was faster than any of the boys. I was even allowed to ride the bus and attend the meets, but I wasn't allowed to compete, simply because I was a girl.

Thanks to the feminist movement, the United States now has female politicians, female fighter pilots (since 1993!), female mathematicians and physicists, and females who participate in organized and competitive sports from an early age. *Times change.*

When I taught at Texas A&M University in the late 1980s and the 1990s, women in the Corps of Cadets (members of any of the military ROTC programs) were routinely treated with disrespect by their male peers, who felt that the Corps should have remained all-male. Female students were urged by male advisors not to apply to medical school or veterinary school, because they would be taking a seat away from a man who would, after all, need a job to support his family!

These images of women in occupations once reserved exclusively for men illustrate how female gender roles have dramatically changed during the past 50 years in many countries. Top: chef, firefighter, miner; middle: mathematician, future submariner, veterinarian; bottom: research scientists, future fighter pilot.

All around the world, traditional cultural beliefs about appropriate gender roles have limited the opportunities available to women. The United States Agency for International Development supports a variety of programs to expand options for girls and women to receive education and training for salaried employment. Above: Cambodia's male population suffered severely under the Khmer Rouge regime. Today, more than half of the population is female, and many women are widows. To help women assume new roles in business and in the family, Women for Prosperity, with USAID's support, is training women to participate in local governing councils and lobby for more representation of women in National Party lists. Left: the ADAPT alliance in Vietnam aims to prevent trafficking by giving girls and women educational and professional support and opportunities, and it encourages community and parental involvement to limit obstacles that prevent girls from attending school. In one region, participants received bicycles to help them make the daily trek to schools, which are up to five miles away.

Thanks to the feminist movement, the United States now has approximately equal numbers of men and women entering professional schools to become lawyers, doctors, and veterinarians. *Times change.*

At the same time, some of the same feminists who worked so hard, over so many years, to provide wider opportunities to women, have accepted—lock, stock, and barrel—the second premise outlined above. They have agreed with the general male view that only the things men do are important, and that the things *only* women can do, because of biological differences between the sexes, are unimportant. In their view, anything that detracts a woman from pursuing success, as defined in a male/masculine way, is viewed as oppressive, because women's contributions as the reproducers of the population, both biologically (through pregnancy, birth, and breastfeeding) and culturally (through

child rearing) have been devalued in traditional Western cultural belief systems.

Fortunately, a number of other, perhaps more radical, feminists have rejected *both* premises. They have worked just as hard, over the same time period, to change Western cultural devaluations of female reproductive labor, insisting that women's contributions to the production of children and society are vitally important. Thanks to the work of these feminists, women have made great strides in achieving better standards for maternity leave and support for mothers of young children, although more progress has been made in many European countries and Canada than in the United States. Support for breastfeeding—including better education and laws that protect women's rights to breastfeed in public—has resulted in much higher rates and longer durations of breastfeeding in all Western countries. Instead of automatically dismissing the things women can do and men cannot, women are being more valued for the effort they put into producing and raising the next generation. *Times change.*

Multiple examples of cross-cultural variation in gender categories can be found in the work of Nanda (2000) and Gilmore (1991). Many aspects of *gender* are based on completely random, arbitrary, culturally defined beliefs. They change over time, even as the biology remains essentially the same. Gender is *not* a 100 percent biologically defined construct.

SEXUAL ORIENTATION/ SEX OBJECT PREFERENCE

Sexual orientation (sex object preference) is yet another arena in which the standard Western cultural perspective is very simplistic and misleading and can make it difficult to understand sexual behavior in one's own culture, let alone in other populations.

The standard Western belief system views sexual orientation as a dichotomous variable—as though there are only two options, a person is either a *heterosexual* or a *homosexual*—and as though all *normal* people are automatically heterosexual. In such a schema, if you prefer to have sex with people of the same sex as yourself, then there must be something wrong with you. In reality, sexual orientation is much more complicated than this and is culturally defined in different ways around the world.

A number of critical points will be explored in the following sections: distinctions among sexual lust, romantic love, and affectionate love; distinctions between preferences and behavior; the fact that sexual orientation is not a dichotomous variable, but rather a continuum; the fact that sexual orientation is an independent variable that doesn't necessarily go along with either one's biological sex or one's gender identity; and finally, the fact that different cultures define *homosexuality* according to varying criteria.

Lust, Romantic Love, or Affection?

To begin, people have various types of relationships with others. First, there is sexual lust—what type of people, or specific individuals, arouse you sexually and cause you to desire to have sexual intercourse with them? Most people are sexually attracted only to very specific other types of people and tend to ignore, or not even consider, the sexual relationship potential of the vast majority of people they interact with.

Second, there is romantic love, which may or may not be associated with sexual lust. Romantic love as the basis for a sexual relationship or marriage has very specific cultural, geographic, and temporal limitations. Many marriages around the world are not based on romantic love. Additionally, you can be *in love* with someone and yet not desire them sexually, just as you can desire someone sexually without having any feelings of romantic love for them.

Third, there is affectionate love, which is neither sexual nor romantic. You can love your parents, your children, your siblings, your close friends, and even your pets in this fashion. It never occurs to you to lust after them, and you clearly recognize that these feelings are very distinct from romantic love. In many cultures around the world, affectionate love is accompanied by physical contact including holding hands, walking with your arms around each other, sitting right next to each other, shoulder and foot massages, even kissing. But none of these activities necessarily have anything to do with sex.

In North America, many people think that any close physical contact between two people *must* have sexual connotations. If they see two men walking along holding hands, as in the ethnographic film, *The Nuer*, they may assume that the men are homosexual. They are not; it is considered quite acceptable for Nuer men to express affectionate regard for one another through physical contact, including holding hands or walking with their arms around each other's shoulders. One of the first things young adult male Nuer refugees learn upon arrival in the United States is not to touch other men in public, because people will interpret their behavior as homosexual (Mylan and Shenk 2004).

Similar beliefs underlie the objection some people in North America have to parents cosleeping with their children. They think that any two people who sleep in the same bed must be sexually involved, when of course this is not true at all. Around the world, most children sleep with their parents and siblings.

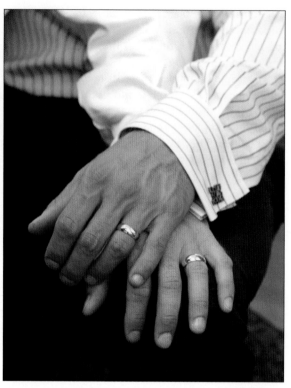

Images of "homosexual" men, as defined by Western cultural standards. The photographs reveal affection and romantic love, including legal marriage. When two males make a couple, it isn't always apparent if they are heterogender or homogender.

Preference Is Not the Same Thing as Behavior

People can have a clear-cut preference for people of the same biological sex as themselves (in terms of lust or romantic love) but not necessarily act on such feelings. Depending on the local cultural context, such feelings may not even be acknowledged as existing, let alone be considered acceptable. Or people may live for many years in denial of their feelings, because they've been taught that such feelings aren't appropriate. Other times, the punishment for acting on their feelings may be severe. In such instances, people are so afraid to risk their reputation, or even their life, that they suppress their feelings and do not act on them. Many a person who would *prefer* to have long-lasting sexual and romantic relationships with people of the same biological sex as

themselves nevertheless get married and raise a family with someone of the opposite sex—because that is what is expected and allowed in their culture, at the time.

In general, men have a greater sex drive than women and may seek sexual release with whoever is handy, in the absence of their preferred sexual partners. There are a number of contexts in which men who would otherwise *prefer* to have sex with women will have sex with other men or boys instead, either because no women are available (such as in all-male prisons) or because their cultural beliefs demand it.

The Sambia of highland New Guinea, studied by Gil Herdt (2005), are sometimes cited as an example of a culture where males "change their sexual orientation" across their life-spans (cf. Miller 2009:155). Among the Sambia, during traditional male rites of passage, teenage boys were required to perform fellatio (oral sex) on older men. This behavior was based on a deeply—and sincerely—held belief that it was necessary for boys to ingest semen in order for them to grow up and be able to reproduce. Once Sambia boys became adults, they married women and had children. Their sexual orientations did not change over time, merely their behavior. Likewise, some U.S. Navy personnel who served on diesel submarines in the 1970s engaged in anal sex as part of a standard hazing ritual for every new member of the all-male crew (Anon., pers. comm. 1975). They did not consider themselves *homosexual* in any sense of the term, and indeed most viewed themselves as hyper-masculine in terms of gender identity and entirely heterosexual in terms of sexual orientation.

The failure to distinguish between preference and behavior leads to much confusion in the literature. Further misinterpretations come from the failure of many people, including some anthropologists and other scholars, to realize that sexual orientation is not a dichotomous variable.

Sexual Orientation Is a Continuum

The standard Western cultural view assumes that people are either 100 percent heterosexual (preferring and having sex with members of the opposite sex only) or 100 percent homosexual (preferring and having sex with members of the same sex only). Since homosexuality is the discriminated-against category—the *contaminating* category—any hint of homosexual feelings or behavior may serve as evidence, to the individual himself (or herself) and/or to others, that a person *is homosexual*.

In fact, this isn't the way sexual orientation works. As the famous zoologist/sex researcher Alfred C. Kin-sey and his colleagues pointed out more than 60 years ago, sexual orientation is a continuum (Kinsey, Pomeroy, and Martin 1998a; Kinsey, Pomeroy, Martin, and Gebhard 1998b). Kinsey et al.'s *Sexual Behavior in the Human Male*, first published in 1948, included this now famous quote:

> Males do not represent two discrete populations, heterosexual and homosexual. The world is not to be divided into sheep and goats. Not all things are black nor all things white. It is a fundamental of taxonomy that nature rarely deals with discrete categories. Only the human mind invents categories and tries to force facts into separated pigeon-holes. The living world is a continuum in each and every one of its aspects. The sooner we learn this concerning human sexual behavior the sooner we shall reach a sound understanding of the realities of sex. (1998a:639)

The table below shows how Kinsey divided the continuum into a seven-point scale, ranging from exclusively heterosexual (0 on his scale) to exclusively homosexual (6 on his scale).

In addition to Kinsey's seven categories, there should probably also be a category for those who are generally uninterested in sex with anyone.

Sexual Orientation Is an Independent Variable

The standard Western cultural perspective on sex, gender, and sexual orientation assumes that all three variables are supposed to vary together. If you are male, then you should be masculine, and be attracted to females. If you are female, then you should be feminine, and be attracted to males. Thus, if you are a feminine male, it is assumed that you are attracted to

Table 3.2	Kinsey et al.'s Scale of Sexual Orientation (1948)
Scale Point	**Definition**
0	Exclusively heterosexual
1	Predominantly heterosexual, only incidentally homosexual
2	Predominantly heterosexual, but more than incidentally homosexual
3	Equally heterosexual and homosexual
4	Predominantly homosexual, but more than incidentally heterosexual
5	Predominantly homosexual, only incidentally heterosexual
6	Exclusively homosexual

Many individuals do not fit into stereotypical gender categories of male/masculine and female/feminine. Top: androgynous people (a man and a woman). Middle: a feminine woman with short hair and a biological male dressed as a female. Bottom: two U.S. "drag queens"—men who deliberately dress up as parodies of sexy women. Nothing about their appearance or clothing tells an observer how any of these individuals feel about their sexual and gender identities, what their sexual orientations might be, or how they behave in situations of affection, love, and lust.

males, as most feminine females are. If you are a masculine female, it is assumed that you are attracted to females, as most masculine males are. In fact, sexual orientation is *not necessarily* linked to other aspects of gender—it can vary independently.

There are males who are somewhat (or very) feminine, and are heterosexual, homosexual, bisexual, or somewhere else along Kinsey's continuum of sexual orientation. There are females who are somewhat (or very) masculine and are heterosexual, homosexual, bisexual, or somewhere else along Kinsey's continuum of sexual orientation.

Likewise, there are some males whose gender identity is hypermasculine, but whose sex object preference is other males, and some females whose gender identity is hyperfeminine, but whose sex object preference is other females. In some cultures and/or contexts, taking on a gender usually associated with a member of the opposite biological sex *does involve* what Westerners would describe as homosexual behavior. In other cases, you can belong completely to the other gender, but still have a person of the opposite sex as your sex object preference. For example, you can be a man who likes to dress in women's clothing, and perhaps prefers women's work, but who is heterosexual by preference, is happily married to a woman, has sex with her, and has children by her.

Different Cultures Define Homosexuality According to Varying Criteria

In the standard Western perspective, if two people are of the same biological sex and engage in sexual intercourse, then they are both labeled "homosexual." In other cultures, other criteria than the biological sex of the two people involved carry more weight.

In some belief systems, the role one takes in sexual intercourse is a more important determinant of both one's gender and sexual orientation than one's biological sex. "Male/masculine" usually implies that you take the role of penetrator/inserter, while "female/feminine" usually implies that you take the role of penetratee/insertee. In cultures where your behavior during sexual intercourse is the prime determinant of your sexual orientation label, if you take the role in sex that typically goes with your biological sex, you are viewed as *heterosexual*—regardless of the biological sex of your partner. For example, in some cultures a man who is masculine—and has sex with others only as the penetrator—is not considered a gender variant or homosexual, whether he has sex with males or females. In the same culture, a man who takes the role of penetratee/insertee (through oral or anal sex) is considered both a homosexual and a gender variant, because he is "not masculine" (Nanda 2000).

In some cultures, as long as the two individuals are of different *genders*, one masculine and one feminine, it doesn't matter what their biological sex is. As long as they are **heterogender,** they are considered normal and not unusual. Conversely, if the two individuals are the same gender, even if they are of different biological sexes, this would be viewed as a **homogender** relationship, and the pair would be considered quite odd.

Conclusions about Sex, Gender, and Sexual Orientation

How humans define what it means to be male versus female, masculine versus feminine, heterosexual versus homosexual, and everything in between, constitutes one of the most complex and fascinating topics within cultural anthropology. It stands alongside religion as a major source of confusion, conflict, and misunderstanding in the world. It is important to real-ize that one's own cultural interpretation of how sex, gender, and sexual orientation work is just that, *a cultural interpretation*.

It is also important to realize that the standard Western cultural perspective on these issues is very restrictive and causes a lot of grief to individuals, their families, and society. If I were in charge of the world, it would be a world where one's talents, skills, interests, genetic capabilities, occupation, social status, and personal value were not thought to be limited by one's sex chromosomes, hormone levels, internal or external anatomy, sexual preferences, or sexual behavior.

REPRODUCTIVE STRATEGIES OF MALES VERSUS FEMALES
THE GREAT INEQUALITY

We turn our attention now to several important features of basic human biology that help explain many aspects of cultural variation including matrilineality, veiling, honor killings, and female circumcision. Without an exploration of the evolutionary forces that have shaped human physiology and behavior, these cultural

Images of "homosexual" women, as defined by Western cultural standards. The middle photo was taken at a wedding in Belgium, where marriages between two men or two women are legal. Note that in each pair of women, one is more masculine, while the other is more feminine, making them heterogender couples.

attributes seem to be merely random strange ideas and practices that people persist in following even though they make no sense. In reality, they all constitute cultural solutions to basic inequalities between males and females when it comes to reproductive strategies.

The Great Inequality and Paternity Uncertainty

A man can theoretically have many more children than a woman but struggles with **paternity uncertainty** (knowing that his children are genetically related to him); a woman is biologically limited to having many fewer children than a man, but every woman has **maternity certainty** (she always knows who her children are).

For all sexually reproducing species, the measure of reproductive success over evolutionary time is the number of offspring raised to adulthood. In each generation, those individuals who reproduce most successfully, for whatever reason, will have the most copies of *all* of their genes in the next generation. Therefore, any gene variants (known as alleles) that code for behaviors that *increase* reproductive success will be more frequent in the following generations. Gene variants that code for behaviors that *decrease* reproductive success will be less frequent in the following generations (unless they are linked to other genes that are selected for). Therefore, each individual carries genes that promote behaviors that maximize reproductive success. However, the pathways to reproductive success are very different for males and females.

Female Limits

Women are limited in the number of offspring they can possibly bear by three *biological factors*. First, women are capable of reproducing only after **menarche** (the onset of ovulation/menstruation) and before **menopause** (the end of ovulation/menstruation). The average age of menarche worldwide is 15 years, and the average age of menopause is 45 years, allowing about 30 years for reproduction overall. Second, gestation in humans takes about nine months, on average, the longest for any primate species. Third, human babies need to be breastfed for several years in order to develop normal immune systems and cognitive capabilities that will ensure a good chance of survival. The natural age of weaning for modern humans, based on

phylogenetic and physiological evidence, is between 2.5 years and 7.0 years. This suggests a birth interval of four to seven years.

Prior to the development of antibiotics, immunizations, clean water, modern sanitation technology, and artificial feeding technologies (bottles and infant formula), *not* breastfeeding was usually fatal to the infant. In areas of the world where these amenities are still not available, artificial feeding is often fatal. Even today in the United States, many children die because they are not breastfed at all, not breastfed long enough, or not breastfed exclusively for the first six months. A recent study by Bartick and Reinhold (2010:e1048) concluded: "If 90% of US families could comply with medical recommendations to breastfeed exclusively for 6 months, the United States would save $13 billion per year and prevent an excess 911 deaths, nearly all of which would be in infants ($10.5 billion and 741 deaths at 80% compliance)."

Breastfeeding helps suppress ovulation in the mother, sometimes for years, so she usually does not get pregnant again while she has a young child who is nursing frequently, especially at night. This absence of ovulation and menstrual cycles during intensive breastfeeding is known as **lactational amenorrhea.** There is great variation in how long lactational amenorrhea lasts. Frequent nursing, especially at night, without any long stretches of time where there is no breastfeeding, leads to longer lactational amenorrhea. Negative energy balance in the mother (taking in less energy than she expends) will also prolong lactational amenorrhea (Ellison 2001).

If an average woman is fecund (capable of becoming pregnant) for about 30 years, and each child takes a minimum of three years to gestate and nourish by breastfeeding, then a typical woman could have a maximum of about 10 children surviving to adulthood. Twins and triplets might increase the number, but under pre-industrial circumstances, multiples have a lower survival rate. Women can also cut down the length of time that they breastfeed, and many women have, which increases the number of children born but also tends to increase the number of children who die. When the birth interval falls below two to three years, the mortality rate increases. It increases sharply when birth intervals are less than two years. Hunters and gatherers usually have children spaced about four years apart.

Among the Hutterites, a North American religious community, the women and children have plenty of food and good medical care. Without contraception, and using artificial feeding, they have managed to increase their fertility, such that many women have between 10 and 15 children who survive to adulthood. This probably represents the maximum for human females. More common are figures of four to eight surviving children in pre-industrial, nonmodern-contracepting populations around the world.

In the industrialized West, because of cultural beliefs and practices, including later marriage, later childbearing, temporary and permanent birth control, and the acceptance of childlessness for adults, many countries now have a total fertility rate below replacement levels (fewer than two children per couple). This has become a social and political issue in some European countries, including France and Italy, where some people are worried that their native populations are dwindling, even as immigrants from other countries are reproducing at much higher rates.

All of which is just to say that *there are biological and physiological limits to the maximum number of children a woman can have.* The range of variation for female reproductive success is narrow—from a low of zero surviving children to an upper limit of 10–15 in certain circumstances.

Female Strategies

In evolutionary terms, human females have no way to control what genes they inherited from their parents, or which ones they pass on to their children. Therefore, a woman's best strategy for maximizing the number of surviving offspring she has is to try to maximize the potential genetic fitness of her offspring by being very picky about whom she has sexual intercourse with when she is fecund. She needs someone intelligent, strong, and healthy. She will also benefit if she picks someone who gives indications that he will stick around and help her raise the children. She needs to behave in such a way that her husband/sexual partner will be convinced he is related to the children, whether he is or not. It is to her advantage to act in ways that do not arouse her husband's suspicions about who the father of the children might be.

Finally, for the woman—in terms of successfully raising her children—her husband's extramarital activities (or his co-wives in polygynous societies) will not have any direct bearing on her reproductive success, unless he starts devoting his time and energies to another woman's offspring, rather than to hers, or if he brings home a sexually transmitted disease that affects her fecundity and health. As long as the father of the children continues to care for her and her offspring, and stays uninfected by STDs, his indiscretions and other offspring will not threaten her reproductive success. She continues to concentrate her time, energy, and resources on the children of her own body, who she knows are hers. She knows because she gave birth to them—she was there when they came out of her body.

At the same time, it doesn't increase her reproductive success to have sex with lots of men, although she might try to get better sperm than that available from her husband if the opportunity comes along. In many cultures, women have little choice about who they marry, but they may be able to exercise some choice extramaritally in terms of who they get pregnant by—though usually at great risk to the woman if she is caught. If the woman doesn't have much choice in who she marries, she may try to improve the genetic quality of her children by having sex with a man she perceives as genetically better than her husband, if and when the opportunity arises. Estimates from studies in a number of societies suggest that as high as 25 percent of all children are not fathered by the woman's legal husband, whether he knows it or not.

Male Limits

For males (both human and nonhuman), the situation is different, and thus we expect that men's reproductive strategies will have been shaped very differently through evolutionary processes. What limits the number of children a man can have? He has age limits, just as females do, but males begin to produce sperm at an earlier age than the age at which females begin ovulating. These early sperm may be few and/or not very functional, but it only takes one to make a woman pregnant. Men continue to produce sperm for many years. The number and vitality of sperm begins to decline when men are in their thirties, but many men continue to make viable sperm into their eighties and nineties. Additionally, a man produces sperm all the time—he doesn't stop making sperm just because he has gotten someone pregnant, nor is his fecundity affected by caring for an infant once it is born. Rather

A man with multiple wives can have many more children than a man with only one wife. Joseph F. Smith is shown with his wives and children, circa 1900. Joseph F. Smith was the nephew of Joseph Smith, Jr., the founder of the Church of Jesus Christ of Latter-day Saints, which encouraged polygyny in its earlier years.

than the three years per child that women must invest in order to produce a healthy child, for men it potentially takes only a few minutes.

What limits the number of children a man can have? The only limitation is the number of women he can convince or force to have sex with him. For a small investment in the "chase and capture," a few minutes of his time, and a little bit of protein, he can potentially produce another child. His supply of sperm is, for all intents and purposes, limitless. His investment can be minimal, but the return can be very large. Consider a man who has 10 wives, and each wife has 10 children. He then has 100 legitimate children, for very little reproductive effort. If he also has 20 long-lasting but unofficial relationships, he might have another 20 to 30 children, or more. Add to those some one-night stands with 30 or 40 women, and he may have additional kids—perhaps children he doesn't even know about. Not all of the women he has sex

with will get pregnant, and not all of the children that result will survive to adulthood, but the man loses very little, and it doesn't usually affect his future reproductive success, if he takes advantage of every opportunity that comes his way to impregnate a female.

For a man, it makes sense to contribute to the care of children who are related to him by protecting them, providing them with food, shelter, education, or whatever they need to survive to adulthood. A man's own biological children are related to him by sharing 50 percent of his genes. His sibling's children are also related to him; they share 25 percent of his genes. However, even if a man doesn't contribute to the care of his biological children, some of the children he begets will survive to adulthood—because their mother takes sole care of them and/or because unrelated men take care of them, thinking that they are related; or because men related in other ways help raise them (such as the mother's brothers).

Male Strategies

What, therefore, is the best reproductive strategy for a man? First, he should behave in ways that maximize the number of women who will have sexual intercourse with him over the span of his lifetime. Second, he should not be particularly selective about most of these women in terms of their intelligence, strength, or health—the key characteristic is someone who will have sex with him, without taking up too much of his time and energy. Third, he shouldn't waste too much time and effort on females who are either too young to get pregnant (before menarche/breast development) or too old to get pregnant (after menopause). Fourth, and most importantly, if a man is going to "settle down" with one or several women in a marriage, and contribute to the care of these women and their children, so that the children will have a better chance of survival, he wants to be *absolutely sure* that he is contributing to the care of children who are related to him.

Paternity Uncertainty

This brings us to the second part of the great inequality between men and women caused by our different biologies. To wit: a woman always knows, beyond any shadow of a doubt, that her children belong to her, that they are related to her by sharing 50 percent of her genes, because they are born from her body. Men, on the other hand, can find it difficult to be sure of paternity. This is known as the problem of *paternity uncertainty*. Among our closest relatives, the Great Apes (chimpanzees, bonobos, gorillas, and orangutans), males do not know who their offspring are, and the females take on all of the responsibility for child rearing.

However, humans have culture. And there are ways to set up systems of cultural beliefs and practices that increase a man's chances of being biologically related to the children to whose welfare he is contributing (or at least increase his confidence in the belief that the children are related to him).

Solutions to the Great Inequality and Paternity Uncertainty

Cultural solutions to the conundrum of paternity uncertainty fall into two broad categories. On the one hand, a society can use matrilineal kinship and descent as a way to solve the problem. On the other hand, societies can combine nonmatrilineal kinship and descent systems with some type of control over female sexual behavior. Each of these solutions tends to be nonoverlapping—once you have developed a way to deal with paternity uncertainty, you don't need to implement the other solutions.

Solution #1: Matrilineality

One solution to the issue of paternity uncertainty is for a man to take care of his sisters' children, rather than his wife's children. In matrilineal descent systems, a child takes its identity from its mother—the child belongs to the mother's lineage. Thus, a man knows absolutely that his sister's children are related to him because he knows that his sister is related to him. They have the same mother; they were both born from *their* mother's body. They may also have the same father. Likewise, a man knows absolutely that his sister's children are hers because they came from her body. Thus, he knows that he shares 25–50 percent of his genes with his sisters, and half that (12.5–25 percent of his genes) with his sisters' children. This isn't as high as the percentage of genes he shares with his biological children, which is 50 percent, but he can't be sure which children *are* his biologically. Through matrilineality, a man can be 100 percent sure that he is contributing to the welfare of children who are related to him through his sisters.

Implications of Solution #1: Matrilineality

Under the matrilineal solution to paternity uncertainty, men and women still grow up and marry and have relationships with their biological children. However, a man's investment of significant resources of time, effort, and money will be directed to his sisters' children. Likewise, a man's biological children will receive care from their maternal uncles, their mother's brothers. In cases where the mother has no brothers, all the adult men of the child's mother's lineage will see that the child is provided for.

With matrilineality, there is little concern for controlling female sexual behavior, because a woman's brothers care for her children, regardless of who the father might be. That doesn't mean that a man wouldn't be upset if his wife had sex with someone else, but just that it isn't as great a concern in general. Women have more sexual freedom in such contexts and are not likely to be punished or killed for infidelity or for getting pregnant or having a child before they are married.

Likewise, a woman has greater power with respect to ending an unhappy marriage because her children belong to her lineage and cannot be taken away from her if the marriage ends. Therefore, she doesn't have to put up with a husband who is abusive or lazy, or who deserts her. She likely can divorce him without any social or economic sanctions, since her brothers will continue to take care of her and her children, as they always have. After a divorce, or the death of her husband, she usually has the choice to marry again or to remain single.

Solution #2: Control Female Sexual Behavior

If a man lives in a society that uses a nonmatrilineal kinship and descent system, then he must follow a very different strategy. The **cultural logic** behind all the variations of controlling female sexual behavior is as follows: it is assumed that women are highly sexual beings with sex drives equal to, if not greater than, men. It is assumed that most women are not capable of controlling their sexual urges and will therefore be tempted to have sex before marriage, or to have sex with men other than their husband after marriage. These supposedly natural attributes of women's behavior cast doubt on the paternity of children they give birth to. The solution, then, is twofold.

First, a man needs to be somewhat selective about the woman/women he marries, the women whose children he is going to invest in. He will likely look for intelligence, strength, health, virginity, and good morals as evidenced by coming from a good family. Second, after marriage, he needs to keep that woman's (or women's) sexuality under extremely strict control, so that he knows that the children she bears are his biological children. If a man has chosen the strategy of concentrating a lot of his personal resources of time, effort, and money in assuring the survival and success of his wife's children, rather than his sisters' children, it is imperative that he is raising his own children and not someone else's. He will share 50 percent of his genes with any child he fathers, and 0 percent of his genes with any child fathered by someone else. Any sexual activity by his wife with another man directly threatens him, by raising the possibility that he is wasting his resources raising children who are not related to him.

There are *four basic ways* that a society can be structured to keep a woman's sexual behavior under control. Remember that any one society will tend to use *only one* of these solutions, and that these categories represent simplified descriptions of a much more complex reality.

Solution #2a: Keeping Women under Physical Control

If a society develops this solution, then a woman (literally, her body) will always be under the physical control of one or more related adult men. Before she is married, this task falls to her father, uncles, and brothers. After marriage, this task falls to her spouse and his relatives. When girls are young and prepubertal, they often are allowed much physical freedom—they can run and play outside, go to the market, run errands for their elders, and go to school. Once a girl nears puberty, however, the rules change. She is mostly confined to the house. If she does go out, she must be chaperoned by her father, uncles, brothers, or several adult women from the family. She typically is not allowed to attend school any longer, or work at a job, or drive a car, as these might allow her to be in contact with unrelated males without supervision.

When out in public, she must cover herself to varying degrees—sometimes just her hair, other times her whole body, using a variety of veils and concealing clothing known in different languages by different terms (burka, chador, veil, modest clothing, etc.). Such modest clothing is meant to show that she is respectable and also avoids arousing male sexual ardor or giving even the impression that she might act improperly with an adult man who is not her husband. Physical control by members of her family guarantees that the woman is a virgin when she is married. In some societies, the bride is expected to publicly display the bloody sheet on the morning following the wedding night, so that everyone can see that intercourse with her husband ruptured her hymen, resulting in bleeding, and thus proving her virginity. This also shows everyone that her family fulfilled its duty to keep her safe and chaste before marriage.

After she is married, it is up to her husband, his brothers, and perhaps his parents to make sure she has no opportunities to have sex with anyone other than her husband. Again, she is mostly confined to the house and must be chaperoned and veiled when she goes out in public. If these precautions are followed,

Images of women from around the world wearing modest dress. Top: Central Asian woman (wearing garb known as a *paranja*), two Muslim women in Kolkata, India, and two Catholic nuns in Italy. Bottom: Rajasthan, India, Hindu woman, and Afghan women in burkas buying jewelry.

then when she gets pregnant and gives birth, her husband can be certain that the children are his biological children, and he willingly contributes to their care.

Implications of Solution #2a: Physical Control

Under such a system, women have little or no sexual freedom and may be punished or killed if they are caught (or even suspected of) having sex with anyone other than their husband. This is true even if they are the victims of sexual assault or rape. An unmarried girl's male relatives are responsible for controlling her behavior and for protecting her and her virginity. She is at risk if she deliberately misbehaves by leaving the house without a chaperone for any reason, especially at night. It is considered partly her responsibility if she misbehaves and is harmed, but it is also viewed as a failure by her male relatives to keep her under control and protect her. Thus, both she and her male relatives are blamed if she is caught engaging in voluntary sexual activity. Likewise, both she and her male relatives are blamed if she is sexually assaulted. After marriage, if she is caught engaging in voluntary sexual activity with a man who is not her husband, or if she is sexually assaulted, again it is partly her fault and partly a failure on the part of her husband to properly control and protect her.

Such events bring great shame and dishonor to the woman and her extended family. Not only was she (apparently) not properly brought up, but her male relatives failed in their duties. The family likely will be ostracized and lose important friendships and economic and political relationships in the community. In some cultures, the only way to overcome this shame and dishonor is for the woman's family to kill her. By taking on the responsibility for killing her, they somehow restore the family's honor. Tahira Khan's *Beyond Honour* (2006) explores honor killings from an historical materialist perspective.

Such **honor killings** have been reported from a number of countries including Bangladesh, Great Britain, Brazil, Ecuador, Egypt, India, Israel, Italy, Jordan, Pakistan, Morocco, Sweden, Turkey, Uganda, Afghanistan under Taliban rule, Iraq, and Iran (Mayell 2002).

Although people in cultures that do not practice honor killings often view such behaviors as barbaric, these killings do make sense within the local cultural context. It should not be assumed that a girl's (or woman's) male relatives are happy or eager to kill her. Indeed, they are often devastated that the events have transpired, and horrified that they are required to kill her. The job of killing the girl may fall to the youngest capable male in the family, because in many cultures an honor killing is still considered murder. A young killer, such as the girl's younger brother, will often get a shorter prison term than the girl's father or paternal uncles would if they carried out the task.

The following excerpt from the novel *Birds Without Wings* (2004) by Louis de Bernières provides some idea of what a tragedy such situations can be for all concerned. Bezmialem is the daughter of Yusuf the Tall and his wife Kaya, who are Muslim and who live in a small town in Turkey. Bezmialem has become pregnant before marriage by her boyfriend, who is a Christian. Her father Yusuf knows that the only way to restore the family's honor is for someone in the family to kill her.

Excerpt from *Birds Without Wings* . . .

Overtaken, finally, by weariness, Kaya had given up pleading with him, partly because she herself could see no other way to deal with what had occurred. If it had been a Muslim, perhaps they could have married her to him. . . . Perhaps they could have kept her concealed in the house, unmarried forever, and perhaps the child could have been given away. Perhaps they could have left it at the gates of a monastery. Perhaps they could have sent her away in disgrace, to fend for herself and suffer whatever indignities fate and divine malice should rain upon her head. It had not been a Muslim, however, it had been an infidel. . . .

When his sons were before him, Yusuf took his pistol from his sash, weighed it in his hand, took it by the barrel, and handed it to his second son, Sadettin. Sadettin took it by the butt and looked at it in disbelief. At first his voice seemed to fail him. "Baba, not me," he said.

"I have tried," said Yusuf, "and I can't. I am ashamed, but I can't."

"Not me, Baba. Why me?"

"You have courage. Great courage. And you are obedient. This is my command."

"Baba!"

Yusuf beheld the spiritual and moral agony of his second son, and the surprise, but he would not relent. . . .

Father and second son looked at each other for a long moment. "I command it," repeated Yusuf the Tall.

"I would rather kill myself," said Sadettin at last.

"I have other sons." Yusuf placed his hand on Sadettin's shoulder. "I am your father."

"I will never forgive you," replied his second son.

"I know. Nonetheless, it is my decision. Sometimes . . ." and here he hesitated, trying to name whatever it is that takes our choices away, ". . . sometimes we are defeated." . . .

Sadettin entered the haremlık. It was dark because the shutters were closed, and it smelled comfortingly of things feminine and mysterious. In the corner, glowing and glittering with terror in the half-light, he saw the eyes of his sweet sister, Bezmialem, of all his sisters the most gentle, and the one he loved the best. . . .

Sadettin raised himself up and realized that after all he would have to defile his right hand. He transferred the pistol, threw his left arm around his sister's neck and embraced her. They stood together, trembling. Softly she put her arms around him, as if he were a lover. He felt the soft pulse of her breath on his neck. He placed the muzzle of his pistol against her heart, clenched his eyes shut, muttered "In the name of God . . ." and fired. He held Bezmialem to him as she choked and the spasms and convulsions overcame her. He thought that they would never end, and the dread came over him that he might have to go out, reload the pistol and shoot her again. For a desperate few seconds he wondered if it might not be possible to take her to a surgeon and save her. At last her head fell on his shoulder, and finally he let her down gently to the floor. He knelt and kissed her, the arc of his motion so familiar because so akin to the rituals of the mosque, and then he rested his forehead on hers.

When Sadettin emerged into the selamlık, his shirt was glistening with the dark blood that his sister had coughed up, and it was as if he had become another man. He threw the gun down at his father's feet in a brutal gesture of contempt, held his father's gaze, and wiped his hands so roughly together that they made a sound like clapping. "I have defiled my right hand because of you. I am finished with you all," he said. (De Bernières 2004:138–141)

From *Birds without Wings* by Louis de Bernières, copyright © 2004 by Louis de Bernières. Used by permission of Alfred A. Knopf, a division of Random House, Inc.

This quote is intended to impress upon you the idea that honor killings are not necessarily the actions of brutal, uncaring men.

Another major implication of solution #2a, physical control, is that it effectively removes women from any significant participation in public life. They do not have the freedom to contribute to their societies through economic, political, religious, or creative activities, except indirectly through their male relatives.

On the other hand, there are some advantages to this type of system. Women in such societies have, for the most part, freedom from worrying about being sexually assaulted or raped—they are seldom or never out alone at night where they might be at risk. They have freedom from sexual harassment in the classroom, the workplace, and while walking down the street. There are very few pregnancies before marriage, and thus few, if any, abortions, abandoned babies, or single mothers. There will be few divorces due to infidelity on the wife's part, and very few children grow up without a father.

Solution #2b: Female Circumcision

In some societies, the solution that has developed to solve the problem of paternity uncertainty involves circumcising every female in order to reduce her sexual desire and the physical pleasure she gets from sexual intercourse. Female circumcision is known by a number of different terms, including **genital cutting** and the more value-laden **female genital mutilation.** Most of the time, the procedure involved is a so-called **simple clitoridectomy**—cutting off the woman's clitoris.

Clitoridectomies are done in a number of cultures across the world, including many regions of Africa, and some parts of the Middle East, as well as wherever natives of these regions have migrated to. There are many cross-cultural variations in terms of the age at which the procedure is done, ranging from infancy to puberty or just before marriage. There are differences in terms of whether it is carried out as a mundane private event or as part of a significant, celebratory, public ceremony. There is variation in exactly how much of the clitoris and surrounding tissue is removed, who does it, what instruments are employed, if anesthesia is used, if it is part of a rite of passage, if other physical or status-marker changes accompany it, and so forth.

The *cultural logic* behind female circumcision of this type is as follows. It is assumed that all women are highly sexual beings with sex drives equal to, if not greater than, men. It is assumed that most women are not capable of controlling their sexual urges and will therefore be tempted to have sex before marriage, or to have sex with men other than their husband after marriage. This casts doubt on the paternity of any children they give birth to. The solution, then, is to perform a clitoridectomy. It is assumed that women who have been circumcised have had their sex drives dampened and will be capable of controlling their desires and behaviors and acting appropriately both before and after marriage. Through circumcision, they become clean, trustworthy, respectable, and marriageable. Without circumcision, they are assumed to be dirty, out-of-control, wanton harlots, willing to have sex with just

about any man they encounter—not the kind of person a woman wants her daughter to grow up to be, not the kind of person a man wants to marry, and not the kind of person most women want to be thought of as!

Most people in these contexts think that women can be trusted to behave if they have been properly circumcised and enculturated to follow the rules of their society. Thus, they don't have to be kept inside the house, or veiled when they leave the house. Everyone knows who is circumcised and who is not, who is respectable and who is not. Husbands trust their wives to behave in their absence.

A Word about Islam

Many people believe that genital cutting and Islam are somehow directly connected, but this is not true. Nothing in the official doctrines of Islam requires, or even recommends, female circumcision. Indeed, many of the most deeply religious communities of Muslims, including Saudi Arabia, Iraq, and Afghanistan, do not practice genital cutting.

The confusion stems from two sources. One is the tendency of people to explain their traditions to outsiders by citing religion. They claim: "We do it because it is part of our religion," rather than saying "It is part of our culture," or "It is part of our tradition," or "We do it because we do it. Doesn't everybody do it?" The second source of confusion comes from people who truly believe that their religion requires them to do these things, whether it officially does or not. Religious leaders may justify and reinforce such behaviors by appealing to their religious significance, and many people have no idea that their religion does not really require these things.

Thus, some Muslims may say, "We circumcise our daughters because we are Muslim," just as some Christians may say, "We handle rattlesnakes and drink strychnine because we are Christian." In both cases, people sincerely believe that their religion requires these actions, but many or most other members of the religion disagree, and there is no official doctrine within the religion that supports the view that these things are required. Female circumcision is found in parts of Africa, including Egypt, and the Middle East, including Yemen and Oman. It is relatively unknown in most other parts of the Muslim world, including South and Southeast Asia, southern Africa, and Saudi Arabia. Most Muslims do not practice female circumcision, and where it is common, the people are not necessarily Muslim. In Mali, most ethnic groups practice female circumcision, whether they are Muslim or Christian or follow local traditional religious beliefs.

Implications of Solution #2b: Circumcision

There are a number of implications, both positive and negative, for people living in societies that use solution #2b. A wide variety of health problems may result from circumcision, depending on the cleanliness of the instruments used, the skill of the operator, and the quality of postsurgical care. In addition to the physical and emotional pain of circumcision, the girl may lose a lot of blood. If the incision becomes infected and is not treated, she may die. Scar tissue may form that will later interfere with intercourse or childbirth.

Many Westerners are concerned that women who have been circumcised miss out on the sexual pleasures of intercourse and orgasm. While this is certainly an important issue to some people, it may not be very important to everyone. In much of the world women don't experience orgasms on a regular basis (with or without a clitoris) and attach very little significance to sexual pleasure, as it simply isn't a big part of their experience. It is also possible to get sexual pleasure through most any part of the body. A clitoris is not a prerequisite for sexual pleasure, nor indeed for an orgasm.

Positive aspects of circumcision, relative to other solutions for controlling female sexual behavior, are mainly that it allows girls and women freedom to move about the society, in public. Circumcised women are allowed to go to school, to work at jobs outside the home, to travel alone, and to generally move about as they wish. They can contribute economically, politically, religiously, and creatively to public life. They are not confined to their homes, nor do they have to wear modest clothing such as veils or chadors. Since they are, for the most part, trusted to behave themselves, they may be able to take lovers if they are discreet. If they get pregnant by someone other than their husband, chances are that no one will ever know.

Two examples from my research among the Bambara of Mali in the 1980s illustrate how women manipulate this system to their advantage. First, Bambara women claimed that a pregnancy could last anywhere from four months to more than three years.

Men acquiesced to women in all matters of knowledge pertaining to pregnancy, childbirth, and breastfeeding. If a man was gone on a trip for a year, and his wife had a baby six months after his return, no one would be suspicious—it was simply a short pregnancy. Likewise, if he was gone for three years and returned to find his wife with a one-year-old child, that was also explicable.

Second, I worked with one family where an elderly man had three wives and many children. While perusing the birth certificates of the children, I noticed that the first wife, who claimed several of the children as her own, was not listed on their birth certificates. She explained that she had been unable to get pregnant and so had encouraged her husband to marry a second, and eventually a third, wife. Each of these women had "given" her a couple of their children to raise as her own within the extended family compound. Later, she confided that it was actually the husband in the family who was sterile. When the second wife also did not become pregnant, the first wife figured it out. Rather than embarrass their husband, or face childlessness or divorce, the first wife encouraged the second wife to go out and find some sperm, which she did. Eventually, the third wife joined the family and did not become pregnant either—at which point she was told what was going on, and she also went out and found some sperm in order to have children. The first wife decided it would be too suspicious if she suddenly became pregnant, so she never had any children of her own. The husband never knew.

In Mali, all circumcised women are treated with respect, and since it is assumed that all women are circumcised, this means all women are treated with respect. Sexual assault and rape were unheard of when I did my field work in Mali in the 1980s. Women and young girls felt free to travel alone or in groups, anywhere, at any time of the day or night.

Solution #2c: Infibulation

In a few regions of the world, the solution that has developed to solve the problem of paternity uncertainty involves a more severe form of female circumcision that not only reduces a woman's sexual desire and the pleasure she gets from sexual intercourse, but physically prevents her from getting pregnant. Known as **infibulation,** this procedure involves cutting off the girl's clitoris, cutting off some or all of her labia minora and labia majora, and then fastening the open edges of the labia majora together across the midline. The labia then heal together, creating a layer of tissue that prevents penetration of the vagina. A small hole is left open to allow for the passage of urine and menstrual blood.

The *cultural logic* behind infibulation is that you want to prevent a girl from getting pregnant before marriage or after marriage, if her husband is absent for any length of time. Infibulation does not prevent her from engaging in other types of sexual behavior such as manual, oral, or anal sex. It works very well, however, to prevent pregnancy, as the penis cannot enter the vagina, and the other forms of sex do not lead to pregnancy.

As with clitoridectomy, there are many variations in when, how, and under what circumstances infibulation takes place. Usually the procedure is done in late childhood, as the girl nears puberty (and becomes capable of pregnancy). Once she is married, the layer of scar tissue must be cut open enough to allow her husband access, so he can have sex with her and make her pregnant. During labor, the opening will be enlarged enough for the birth of the child. Often she is sewn up again after giving birth, to make a tight vaginal opening that will provide maximum sexual pleasure for her husband. Thus, she will have to be cut open and resewn with each birth experience. In societies where infibulation is practiced, a woman may be completely sewn up if her husband plans to be gone for a long time, such as going away for college or post-graduate work, or for employment in a distant city or another country. Again, this prevents her from having children by other men while he is away, but does not prevent her from having other sorts of sexual relationships.

Such practices are not limited to distant and exotic groups. Until the 1990s, it was quite common in the United States for women to have their natural vaginal opening enlarged during labor and delivery through a surgical incision called an episiotomy. Theoretically, this allowed more room for the baby's head as it emerged from the birth canal. After delivery, in many cases, the mother's vaginal opening would be sewn up so that it was tighter than it was before giving birth. This was done for her husband's sexual pleasure and not always with the woman's knowledge.

Episiotomies have fallen out of favor in the United States in recent decades, but **vaginoplasty** not related

to childbirth is becoming more and more common. Women are encouraged to have their labia trimmed (to improve their appearance), to have the hood of their clitoris removed (supposedly to increase their own pleasure and shorten the time to orgasm), and to have their vaginal openings tightened up (to increase their partner's pleasure). As an example, see the website of Dr. Royal Benson III of Bryan, Texas. Dr. Benson specializes in: "Clitoral Hoodectomy or Clitoral Circumcision, Labiaplasty or Labia Minora Reduction, Vaginoplasty or Tightening of the Vagina, and In Office Tumescent Liposuction" (Benson 2010).

Implications of Solution #2c: Infibulation

The implications of infibulation are almost all negative. Although women do have freedom of movement, in contrast to being physically confined, chaperoned, and/or veiled, they pay a much higher price in pain and health than with simple circumcision. Infibulation carries a much higher morbidity and mortality rate. Many girls and women die from loss of blood and infection. Scarring can be extensive and create major problems for passing urine and menstrual fluid, for having sex, and for giving birth. Poorly done infibulations can lead to urinary and fecal incontinence, which can result in ostracism by other members of the society. Repeated cutting and reinfibulation after the birth of each child creates an ongoing risk of blood loss and infection. And of course, the physical and emotional pain of infibulation is unimaginable for those who have not experienced it.

Infibulation implies that women are not trusted to behave and therefore must be physically prevented from becoming pregnant by anyone other than their husband. This leads to much suspicion and mistrust of daughters by parents and of wives by husbands.

Solution #2d: Double Standards

The last option, which doesn't work nearly as well as any of the others to solve the problem of paternity uncertainty, is for the society to have double standards—different rules for men and women to follow with respect to sexual behavior. This is the main solution found in industrial and postindustrial societies such as the United States, Canada, and much of Europe. Females are taught to be modest, and to view their virginity and reputations as something they should guard. Girls and women are allowed to go to school, to work outside the home, and to be friends with unrelated boys and men, even going on unchaperoned dates. However, teenaged girls usually have stricter rules than teenaged boys such as: when they can begin dating, how late they can stay out, whether or not they can have friends of the opposite sex in their bedrooms with the doors closed, and so forth.

A teenage or young adult male may be praised for his sexual prowess and boast of how many sexual conquests he has made. A teenage or young adult female will be stigmatized if she has many sexual partners and be viewed as immoral and nasty—not the kind of girl one takes home to meet the parents, and not the kind of girl one marries. If an unintended pregnancy results from sexual activity before marriage, it is often only the female who faces the shame and bears the responsibility for the child. Males are required to pay child support only if it can be proven that they are the biological father. If a newborn is found abandoned or discarded, whether alive or dead, it is often only the mother who faces prosecution.

Until the advent of no-fault divorce in the United States, in many states a man could divorce his wife for infidelity, but she could not divorce him for the same behavior. It was considered reprehensible if she cheated on him, as he might end up supporting a child who wasn't his (this was pre-DNA testing, when paternity couldn't be proven). But if a man cheated on his wife, it was viewed as insignificant, as long as he continued to be a good provider to her and her children. Many wives simply ignored their husband's philanderings because they needed his financial support for themselves and their children.

Implications of Solution #2d: Double Standards

A system of double standards has many advantages over any type of female genital cutting, and over the stricter physical control of women's bodies found in Solution #2a societies. Women keep their clitorises, and are able to experience normal sexual pleasure and orgasm. Women do not face the health problems inherent in circumcision or infibulation. Women are free to move about society and contribute to the public arena through economic, political, religious, and creative activities. Women can choose with whom they have sex, and who they marry, within some limits. However, societies that choose double standards as their solution pay a very heavy price as well.

Sexual assault and rape are much more common in societies where women are, in general, not respected and where there are many opportunities for a predatory male to find a woman alone and vulnerable to attack. Women in the United States may have the *freedom to* work late and walk alone to their cars in the parking garage without everyone assuming they are whores, but they do not have the *freedom from* worrying about attacks from strangers in the parking garage. They may have the *freedom to* date whoever they want, to be alone with men they are not married to, and even to have sex with them if they wish. But they do not have the *freedom from* worrying about date rape, or from actually experiencing it. Where there is no automatic respect conferred by circumcision or infibulation, a man may judge a woman's character by the clothes she wears, the way she walks, or whether her behavior is viewed as inappropriately flirtatious or provocative. Many a rapist has been acquitted based on the notion that the woman somehow asked to be assaulted. Even if a woman is never sexually assaulted, she invests an enormous amount of emotional energy worrying about the possibility and altering her movements and behaviors to try to prevent an assault.

Societies that give women relative freedom to move about and be alone with unrelated men have much higher rates of unintended pregnancies, which leads to higher rates of abortion and abandonment of unwanted newborns. It also leads to many women raising children without the help of a partner, and children growing up without the guidance of a father. On the other hand, in cultural contexts where women are allowed to do so, such as the Scandinavian countries, those women who are willing and able to raise children without the help of men enjoy freedom from many of the limitations described above. Under these circumstances, paternity becomes mostly irrelevant.

Final Thoughts

All societies have come up with some sort of solution to the problem of paternity uncertainty—some set of cultural beliefs and practices that reassure men that they are indeed related to the children they are supporting. Generally, societies choose *only one* of these solutions, although #2d, double standards for male and female behavior, may be found to some degree in addition to each of the others, as well as by itself. Matrilineality as the solution is relatively rare. Most societies fall into the categories of #2a, #2b, or #2c. It is important to reiterate that, usually, solution #1 and #2a–c are *nonoverlapping*. If you know that a group is matrilineal, you can be confident that the women are not physically confined or veiled and are not subject to genital cutting. Likewise, you don't usually find physical confinement where there is circumcision or infibulation, or circumcision or infibulation where there is physical confinement and the wearing of modest clothing.

Solutions #2a–c (physical control, circumcision, and infibulation) involve erecting a whole array of cultural and social rules and practices whose end result is to ensure that women come to the marriage bed either as virgins, or at least as never having been pregnant, and that after marriage they only have sex (that can lead to pregnancy) with their husband.

There are numerous lines of evidence that support the idea that the amelioration of paternity uncertainty and the establishment of the legitimacy of all children are the primary underlying reasons for all of these cultural beliefs and practices, whether this is explicitly recognized by the members of the population or not. For example, in cultures that allow, permit, or encourage sexual activity between a female and a male she is not married to, such behavior is usually limited to the times of her life when she cannot become pregnant—either before puberty (menarche) or after menopause, or both. For males, there are usually no comparable limits.

Years ago, among traditional Maasai communities in Kenya, young prepubescent girls would be allowed to visit the unmarried male warriors, known as *morans,* in their cattle camps. Sex was allowed between willing girls and these teenaged and young adult males, as long as the girls showed no evidence of approaching puberty. Once their breasts started to develop, however, the girls were no longer allowed to leave the village to visit their boyfriends among the morans. Instead, each girl prepared for her rite of passage to the status of a marriageable woman who had been circumcised. Then she would be married to a much older man (not to one of the morans she had previously consorted with). For the Maasai, virginity at marriage was not important. Not being pregnant before marriage was critical. During marriage, a Maasai woman was expected to remain faithful to her husband until she went through menopause. Older wives

and widows were allowed to take young men from among the morans or older married men in the community as lovers.

Like the Maasai, many cultures that physically control women through in-house confinement, chaperoning, and veils greatly relax these rules once the woman has gone through menopause and is considered too old to become pregnant. As reported in the classic ethnographic film *Kypseli: Men and Women Apart*, made in Greece, if a woman's husband dies, she is thought to stop menstruating (Aratow, Cowan, and Hoffman 1973). She never remarries, and she automatically *becomes* a postmenopausal woman in the eyes of her neighbors, with all of the expanded freedoms this status includes. Presumably, she must be very careful not to become pregnant, which would spoil the ruse!

Among the Kalasha of Pakistan, a girl is betrothed at a very young age to a much older man as her first husband. A girl's first marriage is arranged by her parents. The girl will eventually go through puberty and begin having sex with her husband (and perhaps other men). Any children born to her are considered to be automatically the legitimate children of her first husband. As she grows up, she may often pick someone else as her *heart-struck* husband, one she chooses of her own accord under notions of romantic love. She will then divorce her first husband, marry her true love and have more children by him. The result of marrying all girls before puberty is that it prevents unwed mothers and illegitimate children. For the Kalasha, virginity is not important or expected for heart-struck marriages, while having all children be legitimate is very important.

In his book *The Last Lion, Winston Spencer Churchill, Visions of Glory 1874–1932,* historian and biographer William Manchester explains most eloquently why members of the British aristocracy of the 1800s were less concerned with *children of the mist* (the illegitimate children of either the husband or the wife) than were the members of the newly developing middle class. The system of inheritance in wealthy families involved primogeniture and entail—all of the family's resources were passed down only to the first legitimate son. Extra children inherited nothing and therefore were tolerated. Middle-class children all inherited a share of the family's wealth, so it was more important that they all be related to the father. Thus:

[The servants] understood why there was one standard for their masters and mistresses and another for the rest of England. Victorian morality arose from the needs of the new middle class. As the lord chancellor explained when divorce courts were established in 1857, *a [middle class] woman lost nothing by her husband's infidelity and could absolve him "without any loss of caste," while "no one would venture to suggest" that he could pardon her adultery, which "might be the means of palming spurious children upon him." This was important; such children shared a middle-class legacy.* In titled families it was meaningless. Only the legitimacy of the first patrician child counted. Professor McGregor writes: "The sexual waywardness of aristocrats . . . did not endanger the integrity or succession of family properties regulated by primogeniture and entail. Countless children of the mist played happily in Whig and Tory nurseries where they were no threat to the security of family property or to the interests of the heirs." (1983:88, emphasis added)

A final example comes from the practice of using eunuchs (castrated males) to guard the harems of wealthy men in some regions of the Middle East and India. Although castration (removal of the testicles) does reduce testosterone levels, and therefore dampens male sexual desire to a degree, eunuchs could and certainly did on occasion have sex with the women in the harem. The important point was that they could not make the women pregnant, but could protect the reproductive assets of the women in the harem, keeping the women inside and keeping out anyone who could make the women pregnant, other than their husband.

Thus, understanding the great inequality between men and women in terms of number of children and certainty of parenthood helps explain a wide array of cultural patterns, from matrilineality to female genital cutting, from honor killings to the wide sexual license given to many postmenopausal women and some prepubescent girls. Only matrilineality is free of disadvantages for the women. It is probably not the solution of choice in most cultures because the genetic relationship between a man and his sisters' children is not as strong as that between him and his own biological children. Where men are willing to enact and enforce the cultural rules for controlling women's sexual behavior, they stand to get many more copies of their genes into future generations.

OTHER ASPECTS OF HUMAN SEXUAL BEHAVIOR
DISPELLING MYTHS

In this final section, I briefly touch on several other interesting aspects of human sexual/reproductive behavior that have emerged out of biocultural and cross-cultural research, dispelling some common myths about human sexuality.

How Important Is Sex?

Not everyone is as concerned (one might say obsessed) with sexuality and sexual behavior as people in Western cultures, particularly the United States, seem to be. Karl Heider's work among the Dani of highland West New Guinea is an excellent example of an entire population that simply doesn't spend much time thinking about, agonizing over, or participating in sexual intercourse. Heider writes:

> The Grand Valley Dani of Irian Jaya, Indonesia (West New Guinea) have an extremely low level of sexual interest and activity. Especially striking is their five year postpartum sexual abstinence, which is uniformly observed and is not a subject of great concern or stress. This low level of sexuality appears to be a purely cultural phenomenon, not caused by any biological factors. . . . The norm of a long postpartum sexual abstinence is neither supported by powerful explanations nor enforced by strong sanctions. Most people have no alternative sexual outlets. No one shows signs of unhappiness or stress during their abstinence. (Heider 1976:188)

Looking back on his research among the Dani some 25 years later, Heider concludes:

> [But] the long Dani postpartum sexual abstinence remains a significant instance of the bio-cultural model, the cultural shaping of a biological feature basic to *Homo sapiens*. Sexual intercourse between male and female is common to all human groups, but there is a wide latitude in how different cultures perform it and construe it. (Heider 2002:94)

Sexual Dimorphism and Mating Systems

Among the nonhuman primates, there is a clear relationship between the degree of sexual dimorphism and typical mating patterns in terms of how many females are associated with each male.

In general, monogamous primates have little or no sexual dimorphism (di = two, morph = forms). Males and females are about the same size, shape, and coloring, and it is difficult to tell them apart without looking closely at their genitals. In these species, the typical mating pattern is one female per male, or *monogamy*. One male and one female form a lasting bond and mate only with each other, for the most part, and raise their offspring together. Several species of New World Monkeys as well as gibbons and siamangs (Lesser Apes of Asia), fit this pattern.

Most primates are polygynous (poly = many, gyn = female), with one male having access to several or many females, and most primates exhibit some degree of sexual dimorphism. Sexual dimorphism most commonly takes the form of the male being larger than the

female in overall body size, but there may be other anatomical differences as well, such as larger canines in the male, different patterns of hair/fur color and distribution, or different colors of skin on the face.

Polygynous primates vary in two parameters. First, in some species, one male is considered the *alpha* male in the dominance hierarchy and does most of the matings with females in **estrus**—a short time period around ovulation when she is both fecund and willing to have sexual intercourse, and during which time the males are sexually interested in her. Sexual dimorphism is quite marked in such species, such as among gorillas and orangutans, as well as many monkeys. Gorilla males are about twice as large as females, with much larger canines and more heavily muscled physiques, and the dominant male develops a silver saddle of fur on his back. Orangutan males are much larger than females and develop extraordinary flaring cheek

The greater the degree of sexual dimorphism in a species (differences in size and shape between males and females), more females are usually associated with a single male. The photo above shows pygmy marmosets that have monogamous (one male–one female) social organization. In monogamous species, there is little or no sexual dimorphism—it is impossible to tell the male from the female. The photo on the left, macaques, shows the significant degree of sexual dimorphism typically found in species with one male–multiple female social organization; in this case the female is much smaller than the male. Human sexual dimorphism falls between these two extremes, suggesting a basic pattern of limited polygyny, with one male and several females.

pads on their faces. In other species, a female in estrus may mate with numerous males, a pattern found among chimpanzees and bonobos. Sexual dimorphism is typically less in these species, but still sufficient to make it fairly obvious what sex an individual is.

Second, polygynous primates vary in how many females are associated with one male, from those where each male controls many females to those where each male is associated with more than one, but perhaps only two or three females. Typically, *the more females a male controls, the greater the dimorphism between the sexes in that species.*

Sexual dimorphism in humans is moderate— more than would be found in a monogamous species, but not as marked as that seen in intensively polygynous species where one male dominates many females. Among humans, males are about 15–20 percent larger than females. On average, they are somewhat taller and heavier, with broader shoulders and larger hands and feet. Males typically have more body hair, more facial hair, more sweat glands, and deeper voices. They tend to have bigger muscles for the same amount of strength (an artifact of higher testosterone levels). Be aware that average differences in strength between males and females are determined almost entirely by culture. Where women do most of the hard physical labor, especially starting at a young age, the women will be stronger than the men. Where men and women do equal amounts of labor, they will be equally strong.

Nonhuman primates with the degree of sexual dimorphism found in modern humans are either moderately polygynous (one male, several females) or live in multimale/multifemale groups. It seems clear that, without cultural influence, *the natural system of mating in modern humans would be moderate polygyny.* Indeed, around the world, most cultures allow men to have more than one wife if they can support her and her children economically. The important point to remember is that humans are *not* naturally monogamous— monogamy among humans is a cultural phenomenon of limited geographic and temporal distribution.

Human Uniqueness

Estrus

Although humans are unique in many ways, their distinctiveness is often overstated. For example, among primates, only the female prosimians (small, so-called primitive primates such as lemurs and lorises) have estrus. None of the anthropoid primates (larger primates including New and Old World Monkeys, Lesser Apes, Great Apes, and humans) exhibit estrus. All of the anthropoid primates are willing and able to have sex throughout their reproductive cycle, although sex is often more frequent around the time of ovulation, including in humans (Dixson 1999).

Visual Signaling of Ovulation

Among Old World Monkeys and apes, only a few visually advertise ovulation with conspicuous sexual swellings around their vaginal openings. You see pink or bright red sexual swellings in a few Old World Monkey species and in chimpanzees, bonobos, and gibbons. Most monkeys, and gorillas, orangutans, and humans do not exhibit such obvious visual markers of ovulation. Like these other primates, humans use more subtle behavioral and pheromonal (chemical) cues to indicate ovulation and willingness to have sex (Dixson 1999).

Positions for Sex

In terms of positions for sexual intercourse, humans are often cited as being unique among mammals for having sex face-to-face (ventral-to-ventral, in anatomical parlance), rather than front-to-back (ventral-to-dorsal, or doggy style, in anatomical and common parlance). In fact, face-to-face sex is neither the most common nor the most preferred position for sexual intercourse in humans around the world. The most common position is, like all other mammals, front-to-back, with the male behind the female. In humans, this is most often accomplished while both are lying down on their sides, rather than the female on her hands and knees with the male behind her on his knees. The use of the term *missionary position* to refer to face-to-face sex derives from the primarily European practice of having sex face-to-face with the man on top. This unusual position for sex apparently startled and/or amused any number of native peoples who were visited by European missionaries.

Face-to-face sex recently has been documented among gorillas, orangutans, and bonobos, thus even further blurring the lines between what might be considered natural and what is clearly cultural.

The human couple is merely cuddling in bed, but this image illustrates the most common position for sexual intercourse among humans—with the male behind the female, the same as with all other mammals (such as elephants).

Privacy

When it comes to privacy, some scholars have claimed that humans are the only species that requires privacy for sexual intercourse. Cross-cultural research shows that in most human communities, most of the time, children and other related adults are in close proximity when two people are having sex. Most sexual activity does take place at night, in the dark, but there seems to be no overwhelming requirement for absolute privacy. In many cultures, children sleep in the same room with their parents and siblings and are used to the sounds and sights of their parents having sex. Most of the time, sexual intercourse is relatively brief, and relatively quiet, and no one seems to care or mind. Only when illicit sexual encounters are taking place do people try to seek privacy from prying eyes and ears.

Similar secretive behavior is found among nonhuman primates when females are mating with males other than their usual partners (in monogamous species such as gibbons) or other than the top-ranking males (in chimpanzees and orangutans, for example).

Beauty and the Breast

Finally, I can't leave this subject without saying a few words about breasts. The belief that women's breasts are naturally erotic is limited mainly to the United States and a small number of other (mostly Western) cultures. The mammary glands play no role in sexual behavior in any species other than humans, and most cultures do not define women's breasts as sex objects. Extensive cross-cultural research in the 1940s and 1950s, published by Ford and Beach (1951), found that, of 190 cultures surveyed, only 13 viewed women's breasts as sexually attractive. Likewise, 13 cultures out of 190 involved women's breasts in sexual activity. Of these lat-

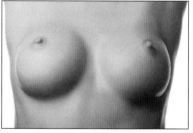

Only a few cultures around the world teach children to consider women's breasts to be erotic sex objects and a measure of a woman's femininity and beauty.

The image on the left shows a mother breastfeeding her child—the biological purpose of human breasts. The image on the right is of a woman who has had breast augmentation surgery (mutilation of her mammary glands). Note the unnatural shape and size of her breasts, the abrupt way they protrude from her chest wall, and the misplacement of the nipples and areolas several inches too high.

ter 13, only three are also listed among the 13 where breasts are considered sexually attractive.

In most regions of the world, breasts are viewed solely as functional body parts for feeding children, just as a typical North American male views women's elbows as devices to bend arms. Thus, in most cultures, it doesn't matter whether breasts are covered or not, or how big they are; husbands do not feel jealous of their nursing children, and women don't have to be discreet when breastfeeding their children or worry that someone will accuse them of nursing too long.

Unfortunately, Western cultural beliefs about the sexual nature and allure of breasts are being spread to many other regions of the world. This is problematic for several reasons. Even as breastfeeding becomes more common in Western cultures, people in other parts of the world are turning to infant formula, viewing breastfeeding as old-fashioned and too loaded with sexual meaning. Following the lead of North American women, women in other areas are clamor-

ing for surgery to increase the size, or improve the appearance, of their breasts in order to be more sexy and attractive to men. Both trends increase the number of health problems that women and children face (Dettwyler 1995b).

Of course, males in a variety of cultures have isolated different female body parts, often in less-than-natural configurations, and turned them into sexual fetishes. Foot-binding in China, stacks of neck-rings among the Karen of Myanmar (Burma), exposing the nape of the neck in Japan, large posteriors across much of West Africa (and among many men of West African descent in North America), and long hair in many cultures, all serve as examples of how powerful cultural beliefs can be.

Research in human behavioral ecology has identified only two aspects of female appearance that are considered attractive across most cultures and may therefore be presumed to have some genetic basis, due to natural selection over many generations. The first

People in some cultures define women's breasts as sexual fetish objects. In other cultures and times, people have focused on elongated necks, such as those of the Karen (Kayan) women of Myanmar, or tiny, deliberately deformed feet known as Golden Lotuses. Chinese foot-binding was common in some regions of China until it was outlawed at the beginning of the twentieth century. Today, there are only a few surviving elderly Chinese women who had their feet bound as children.

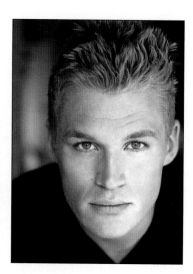

Three people with very symmetrical faces. Studies show that both men and women, in cultures around the world, equate facial and body symmetry with health and attractiveness in others.

is to have bilaterally symmetrical facial features, which may reflect underlying genetic fitness and health. The second is to have a specific waist-to-hip ratio of approximately 70 percent (hips broader than waist). A ratio of 70 percent has been associated with optimal levels of estrogen and lower risks of diabetes, cardiovascular disorders, and ovarian cancer, com-pared to higher ratios (thicker waists). Waist-to-hip ratio predicts mortality in older women—those with-out much of a waist indentation are more likely to die sooner. The most direct connection to reproductive success is that wider hips relative to waist may reflect adequate room for successful childbearing in young adult females.

Key Concepts Review

Sex and gender are two different aspects of human identity.

Sex is chromosomally, anatomically, and hormonally complex; it is not a simple dichotomous variable, with only male and female categories.

Gender categories are culturally defined and complex; gender is not a simple dichotomous variable, with only masculine and feminine categories.

Some cultures recognize three, four, or more gender categories.

Gender categories are based partly on observations of biologically based differences between males and fe-males; gender categories are based partly on random and arbitrary cultural beliefs about what behaviors are appropriate for males and females.

Sex and gender don't automatically match.

Sexual orientation is complex; it is not a simple dichotomous variable, with only heterosexual and homosexual categories, but rather it varies along a continuum.

Sexual orientation does not follow automatically from either one's sex or one's gender identity; all combinations are possible.

Gender categories may be separate or overlapping to various degrees; they may be egalitarian or hierarchical; when hierarchical, masculine always trumps feminine.

A man can theoretically have many more children than a woman but struggles with *paternity uncertainty* (knowing that his children are genetically related to him); a woman is biologically limited to having many fewer children than a man, but every woman has *maternity certainty* (she always knows who her children are).

Realistically, most women are limited by their biology (menarche/menopause, gestation, breastfeeding) to a maximum of about 10 children.

A woman's optimum strategy is to get the very best sperm she can to reproduce with, and to take care of her children to the best of her ability.

Men are limited only by the number of women they can impregnate; thus, a man's optimum strategy is to have sex with as many women as he can, focusing on those who are capable of becoming pregnant (not too young, not too old, not already pregnant).

Cultural solutions to paternity uncertainty include matrilineality and various means of controlling women's sexual behavior, including physical control, honor killings, female circumcision, infibulation, and double standards, all of which make sense within their respective cultural contexts.

Each of these cultural solutions has advantages and disadvantages.

Based on the degree of sexual dimorphism seen in humans, the natural mating system for humans is polygyny, not monogamy.

Humans are similar to some nonhuman primates in *not* having estrus, *not* having visible signs of ovulation, and having sexual intercourse mostly in the *ventral-to-dorsal* (front-to-back) position.

Breasts are not naturally erotic; viewing breasts as erotic and involving them in sexual activity is a cultural phenomenon limited to only a few (mostly Western) cultures; other cultures may fetishize other female body parts.

The only universal examples of features of females that men find attractive are symmetrical faces and a waist-to-hip ratio of around 70 percent.

A Touareg man pours tea into traditional glasses.

4

GOOD HEALTH, GOOD FOOD, GOOD SEX

Medical, Nutritional, & Reproductive Anthropology

The subfields of medical, nutritional, and reproductive anthropology are among the most rapidly growing and the most fascinating areas of research in contemporary anthropology. They combine cultural and biological perspectives to help us understand many aspects of human experience around the world.

Medical, nutritional, and reproductive anthropology are among the most rapidly growing topical areas within anthropology. Medical anthropology encompasses both biological and cultural perspectives and is concerned with many different aspects of human health and wellness. Some anthropologists study worldwide patterns of disease and the health consequences of how humans interact with their physical and biological environments. Others focus more on cultural factors that directly or indirectly cause injury or lead to poor health, including the political economy of health at the global level. Some medical anthropologists are interested in how people define illness, what sorts of healing therapies and medical experts exist in different places, how people make decisions in their "quest for therapy," and how effectively different medical systems work. Nutritional anthropologists focus more narrowly on health issues related to food and nutrition, with substantial overlap into the "anthropology of food," which is more concerned with cuisines and the cultural meanings of food. Reproductive anthropologists examine family planning, contraception, pregnancy, and birth in their cultural contexts.

Because the health and well-being of people at both the individual and group levels affect all other aspects of life, the anthropological perspective on these subjects is both important and enlightening.

MEDICAL ANTHROPOLOGY

Most discussions of medical anthropology begin with a distinction between illness, disease, and sickness, where **illness** is viewed as individuals' subjective experience of how they feel, **disease** refers to the Western scientific (theoretically more objective) diagnosis of what is causing the illness, and **sickness** refers to how patients are supposed to act—the role they are expected to take in interactions with others, including healing experts. Likewise, it is useful to distinguish between physical **injuries** such as a broken bone or a cut, **systemic diseases** such as polio or influenza, and **conditions** such as color-blindness or albinism. Additionally, we can define diseases or conditions differently depending on whether they are viewed as affecting the body (somatic or physical illness) or the brain/mind (mental illness), though such distinctions are defined culturally, and therefore a single definition will not apply in all cultural contexts. People everywhere have to deal with a variety of health issues, but the specific problems they face will depend on the local environment as well as the cultural shaping of health and wellness.

In addition to temporary illnesses, injuries, or conditions, many people are either born with or acquire some permanent impairment in their ability to function. How such individuals are treated in different cultural contexts provides a valuable window into the local cultural meanings of health and wellness as well as what it means to be a human.

Conceptually, it is useful to make distinctions between impairment, disability, and handicap. Following the World Health Organization classifications (1980), an **impairment** can be defined as "any loss or abnormality of psychological, physiological or anatomical structure or function." A **disability** is defined as "any restriction or lack (resulting from an impairment) of ability to perform an activity in the manner or within the range considered normal for a human being." Finally, a **handicap** is defined as a disadvantage for a given individual, resulting from an impairment or a disability, that prevents the fulfillment of a role that is considered normal (depending on age, sex and social and cultural factors) for that individual."

Both disability and handicap are heavily shaped by a number of cultural variables. Cultural coping mechanisms may partially or completely offset the disability that results from impairment. For example, people who cannot walk may be able to get around fine with the help of a wheelchair or crutches in an environment that has universal access. People who cannot hear may be able to communicate through sign language. If everyone around them understands and speaks the same sign language, then their impairment—ears that don't hear—does not constitute a disability. Likewise, cultural attitudes toward difference will determine whether the "inability to perform an activity" constitutes a handicap for that individual. Where people with mental illness or mental retardation are stigmatized, ridiculed, and/or separated from others, there is a significant handicap. Where they are welcomed and incorporated into the fabric of society at all levels, and treated with respect and affection, there may be no handicap associated with their impairment, however disabling it might be.

Many people will experience some degree of disability during their lifetime, whether due to injury, illness, or a health condition, and whether short- or long-term. Thus, disability is a near-universal human experience, not something that happens only to a few members of a population. Cultural beliefs and accommodations can go a long way toward alleviating the constraints of a disability and determine whether the disability constitutes a handicap.

The Equation of Human Health and Medical Care

The health status of an individual or a population is a result of many complex interactions between the physical environment, the biological environment, genetic factors, developmental factors, and cultural factors. There are four more-or-less distinct components to the equation of human health and medical care:

1. Ultimate causes: Explanations of *why* (the *reason* someone was injured or became sick or died, or was born with, or developed, a particular condition)

2. Proximate causes: Explanations of *how* (the *mechanisms* by which someone was injured or became sick or died, or was born with, or developed, a particular condition)

3. The natural coping mechanisms of the body (genetic and physiological)

4. The cultural coping mechanisms (systems of medical beliefs and practices) available to the individual and/or the group

Ultimate causes might include: accident, fate, God's will, evil intentions of supernatural beings or other humans, the unintended consequences of some other act, and so forth. Immediate proximate causes might include: a car accident, a dog bite, an infection with a virus or bacteria, and so on. In addition, there may be several intermediate levels of causation between ultimate explanations of why and proximate explanations of how. It is the interaction of the causes, the natural coping mechanisms of the body, and the cultural coping mechanisms of medical care that determine a person's state of health.

As a gross simplification and overgeneralization, we can say that Western Biomedicine (WBM), as a group of cultural coping mechanisms, focuses on counteracting or combating the proximate causes of poor health, while so-called Traditional or Alternative Medicine, as a group of cultural coping mechanisms, focuses on ultimate causes, with therapies aimed at strengthening the natural coping mechanisms of the body while also combating the ultimate causes of poor health. Both approaches include a variety of beliefs and practices with varying degrees of effectiveness. In other words, both approaches work, to some degree, for some people, some of the time. For some conditions, a WBM approach of attacking the proximate cause holds the best hope for restoring good health. For other conditions, a traditional/alternative approach of strengthening the body's ability to cope holds the best hope for restoring good health. Since the two systems tend to work in very different fashions, a combination of approaches may work better than one or the other.

Ultimate Causes

Seldom do people attribute misfortune to bad luck or to the idea that "stuff happens" for no reason. More typically, in many societies around the world, the prevailing cultural belief is that nothing happens without a reason, including injury, sickness, and death. People believe that there are no such things as accidents or coincidences, or simple bad luck. Stuff doesn't just happen—it has a cause. If a person is injured or becomes sick, or is born with an impairment, it must be due to some well-defined cause, the most common of which are briefly described below.

Violations of Taboos

First, it may be because the person violated some taboo or rule of proper behavior, and the health-related consequences follow automatically from this behavioral breach of etiquette. Presumably, people sometimes find it difficult to follow all the rules of their society, and failure to follow the rules may result in injury or illness. People may unintentionally violate the rules, or they may do so intentionally but with the thought or hope that they can get away with it.

Supernatural Intervention

A second ultimate source of deliberately caused injury/poor health is supernatural intervention. Supernatural entities may harm humans through injury or illness, or even death, for a number of different reasons. The supernatural entity may be a god or goddess, an ancestor spirit, a ghost, a demon, or a nature spirit. According to Murdock, the most widespread concept of this type is spirit aggression, which he defines as "the attribution of illness to the direct hostile, arbitrary, or punitive action of some malevolent or affronted supernatural being" (Murdock 1981:20).

Human Intervention

A third ultimate source of deliberately caused injury/poor health is human intervention. Again, for a number of different reasons—anger, envy, frustration, revenge, mental illness, or pure maliciousness—some people may harm others, causing injury, illness, or death. The harm may be accomplished through covert magical means, such as witchcraft and sorcery, or through more straightforward overt means such as physically injuring the victim or deliberately exposing the person to disease organisms or toxins. Sometimes, the victims themselves are held to be at fault; they are held to be responsible for their own problems—they did something even though they knew it was dangerous and carried some risk of harm.

"Stuff Happens"

Finally, in a few cases, on either an individual basis or as part of a shared belief system, people may ultimately attribute injury or poor health to "the luck of the draw." This may be expressed as a belief in predestination, fate, bad luck, or considered just an accident or coincidence—"stuff happens." In these cases, nothing could have been done to prevent it, and no one can be held responsible for the consequences—neither the victim, nor any human or supernatural agent had anything to do with the injury, disease, or condition. It isn't anyone's fault. Bad things sometimes happen for no reason at all.

Proximate Causes

In almost every society around the world, people recognize that there are many sources of injury or ill-health at different levels of causation. It is important to distinguish between ultimate *why* explanations, described above, and proximate *how* explanations, described below. These are two different aspects of health, and failure to understand the difference leads to much confusion about what people in different cultures believe about the causes of ill-health and how patients should be treated. The following sections list the major categories of **proximate causes** that can adversely affect health. Remember that such a listing of variables by category glosses over the fact that the health status of an individual or a population is a result of many complex interactions between the physical environment; the biological environment; and genetic, developmental, and cultural factors.

Physical Environment

The physical environment consists of all the nonliving components of the environment. Precipitation, or the lack thereof, can have profound impacts on health. The amount and form of precipitation (snow, sleet, rain, hail, mist, dense fog), the humidity or aridity of the air, and the yearly, seasonal, and daily variations in precipitation all play a role in human health. Many diseases can be spread through contaminated water, and parasites often enter through the skin when people work, wade, or play in stagnant ponds or slow-moving streams.

Temperature also affects health, in terms of both the extremes of high and low temperatures and the duration of extreme temperatures (100 days over 100 degrees, or three months below freezing, etc.). In different regions of the world there are yearly, seasonal, and daily variations that affect health directly as well as modify the impact of other variables. Heat stroke, hypothermia, and frostbite are all direct consequences of exposure to extreme temperatures.

Sunlight, or the lack thereof, affects both physical and mental health. Levels of ultraviolet radiation vary with latitude and altitude. Near the Equator, people are exposed year-round to high levels of UV radiation. UV levels decline gradually as you travel toward the poles. UV radiation is more intense at high altitudes and is affected by plant cover. Desert and savannah-dwelling populations have more exposure to sunlight than people who live in dense tropical rain forests. Too much UV radiation is harmful, as it decreases the levels of folic acid circulating in the bloodstream. Adequate amounts of folic acid are necessary for successful reproduction. Deficiencies of folic acid in women during pregnancy can lead to miscarriages or improper development of the brain and spinal cord (spina bifida) of the fetus. Folic acid deficiencies in males disrupt sperm production.

At the same time, too little UV radiation is also harmful, as the body needs sunlight to produce adequate Vitamin D, which is needed for the proper absorption of calcium from the diet. Calcium, in turn, is needed for the growth and development of strong bones during fetal development and throughout childhood. Human skin color varies across the globe as a result of natural selection attempting to strike a balance between sufficient folic acid and sufficient Vitamin D. In temperate regions where the amount of sunlight varies with the seasons, people develop tans with exposure to UV radiation, and the color of their exposed skin adjusts with the seasons to protect against the amount of UV radiation present.

The amount of sunlight available, the seasonal and daily variations in hours of sunlight, and the angle of the sun's rays also influence what sorts of plants and animals can survive in a particular region. These variations affect whether mosquitoes can flourish and act as vectors of disease, and whether sunburn and skin cancer are significant health problems. Lack of adequate sunlight has been linked to depression and seasonal affective disorder, as well as rickets (bowed bones, deformed legs, and constricted pelvises) due to insufficient calcium absorption during childhood.

Wind patterns also influence health, including the direction from which the wind usually blows and at what speeds. Winds can carry particulate matter, such as the fine grains of sand carried by the Harmattan winds that blow south off the Sahara Desert, and affect people's eyes and lungs. Winds contribute to the spread of many contagious diseases. In Mali, people say that measles "comes on the wind"—and indeed it does, as winds spread the virus from one infected village to another. Winds also distribute everyday industrial pollution, sometimes from thousands of miles away, affecting lung function and contributing to a number of health problems.

In 1986, the Chernobyl nuclear power plant in the Ukrainian Soviet Socialist Republic experienced a catastrophic failure. A plume of highly radioactive material was released into the atmosphere; this material contained more than 400 times the amount of radiation released by the 1945 atomic bombing of Hiroshima, Japan. Most of the radioactive material fell in Belarus, but the plume drifted over much of Europe and even reached eastern North America. Thousands of people were permanently evacuated from the region around the power plant, and accurate estimates of the number who died, or whose health was adversely affected, including birth defects in subsequent generations, have never been determined (Petryna 2002).

Also in 1986, Lake Nyos in northwest Cameroon emitted a large cloud of deadly carbon dioxide gas. The lake sits on top of volcanic magma, which leaks carbon dioxide into the lake. The lake burped, as it were, perhaps as the result of an underwater landslide, and deadly carbon dioxide gas bubbled to the surface and spread throughout the surrounding valleys. The cloud of carbon dioxide, which is heavier than normal air, hugged the ground and flowed down hillsides into nearby villages. More than 1,500 people died of suffocation, as did 3,500 livestock.

The soils of a region can contribute to health issues both directly and indirectly. If the soils in a region are generally poor, crop yields may be low and the nutritional status of the local populations may be affected. If the soil is deficient in one particular element, then crops grown on the soil will also have low levels of that element. For example, dietary iodine deficiency due to poor soils leads to the development of thyroid hormone deficiency. The body responds by increasing the size of the thyroid gland, and a goiter develops on the front of the neck, more frequently in women. Severe iodine deficiency during pregnancy can lead to mental retardation in children, a condition known as endemic cretinism. In previous centuries, cretinism was common in Alpine villages of southern Europe, and it continues to be a problem for any populations living far from the sea in areas where the soil is deficient in iodine.

Soils that are contaminated with toxic chemicals can also cause health problems. Between 1961 and 1971, the United States sprayed more than 21 million gallons of Agent Orange, a powerful herbicide and defoliant, across the forests of Vietnam as part of the Herbicidal Warfare Program. During the manufacturing of Agent Orange, 2,3,7,8-tetrachlorodibenzo-p-dioxin (TCDD), was formed as a by-product. TCDD is a known carcinogen and is suspected as a contributing factor in a number of serious health conditions. At the time, the poisoning affected not only the people of Vietnam but also U.S. soldiers who served in areas sprayed with Agent Orange, and the children and grandchildren of both populations. Dioxin from Agent Orange still lingers in the soil and is incorporated into the crops grown and consumed in these regions of Vietnam. People continue to be sickened from direct exposure to the dioxin as they work the land and eat the crops grown on the land, and it leads to birth defects and illnesses.

The Ministry of Foreign Affairs in Vietnam estimates that close to five million Vietnamese people have been affected by Agent Orange, including some 400,000 deaths and disabilities, and 500,000 children born with a variety of birth defects including cleft palate, mental retardation, hernias, missing or deformed limbs, and congenital deafness and blindness. The U.S. Department of Veterans Affairs lists the following diseases as being related to exposure to Agent Orange: prostate cancer, respiratory cancers, multiple myeloma, type II diabetes, Hodgkin's disease, non-Hodgkin's lymphoma, soft tissue sarcoma, chloracne, porphyria cutanea tarda, peripheral neuropathy, chronic lymphocytic leukemia, and spina bifida (in children of veterans).

Altitude is yet another environmental variable that affects health. Populations living at very high altitudes above sea level must cope with reduced levels of oxygen in the air (hypoxia), cold temperatures, and high levels of ultraviolet radiation. Crops often grow poorly at high altitude, so nutritional stress becomes an additional burden. Reproduction can be affected by the low levels of oxygen available to the fetus.

Finally, natural disasters of various types contribute both directly and indirectly to morbidity (poor health) and mortality (death) in most regions of the world. Earthquakes and volcanic eruptions, and subsequent tsunamis (tidal waves), kill and injure people directly and contribute to the destruction of food and water supplies, which may lead to more deaths. Storms such as tornadoes, hurricanes, cyclones, and typhoons also wreak havoc on the health and well-being of human populations in multiple ways.

Biological Environment

The biological environment also poses many dangers for humans. Macrofauna (animals), both wild and domestic, including mammals, reptiles, amphibians, bird, insects, and arachnids, can contribute to human injury and disease. They may be the source of diseases such as anthrax, avian flu, tuberculosis, and rabies. Insects may serve as the vectors of disease, including mosquitoes that transmit malarial parasites, tsetse flies that transmit trypanosomiasis (sleeping sickness), and black flies that spread onchocerciasis (river blindness). River blindness is caused by the body's inflammatory response to the release of bacteria from parasitic nematodes (*Onchocerca volvulus*). An estimated 18 million people worldwide are infected with this nematode, and 300,000 of them have suffered permanent blindness.

The mode of transmission of health problems between animals and human can be through bites, through close contact with the animal or its feces, or through contaminated water. Some individuals may experience severe, even fatal, allergic reactions to contact with animals, and some amphibians, reptiles, fish, arachnids, and insects have evolved poisonous secretions or venom that affect humans. Animals can also be the sources of injury through attacks with claws, hooves, horns, and teeth.

Microfauna include bacteria, viruses, prions (infectious agents composed primarily of protein), and numerous parasites, which adversely affect human health. The most common viral diseases are diphtheria, pertussis (whooping cough), tetanus, polio, measles, mumps, rubella, chicken pox, influenza, and the common cold. Smallpox took an enormous toll on human populations before it was eradicated through a World Health Organization campaign that ended in the late 1970s.

The main bacteria that infect humans include *Streptococcus* and *Staphylococcus, Pseudomonas, Salmonella*, tuberculosis, and cholera. Cholera is caused by enterotoxin-producing strains of the bacterium *Vibrio cholerae*. Transmission of cholera is most often through contaminated food and water supplies, or from patients to health-care workers, and many water sources can serve as reservoirs of the bacteria. Cholera is highly contagious; spreads rapidly through refugee camps, slums, and crowded cities; and is one of the most rapidly fatal illnesses known. From the onset of symptoms, death from dehydration can occur within hours. Only rapid treatment with antibiotics and intravenous fluids can forestall death. Although some parts of the world have access to antibiotics to combat bacterial infections such as cholera, they are still not available in many regions or are not available in sufficient quantities to deal with epidemics, or they are exorbitantly priced.

Microfauna enter the body via skin-to-skin contact, by inhaling particulate matter in the air, or by eating poorly cooked meat (trichinosis in pork, many intestinal parasites such as tapeworm) or other foods (*Salmonella* from eggs, chicken, or peanut butter, *E. coli* in undercooked hamburger, etc.).

Parasites such as malaria, hookworm, tapeworm, and schistosomiasis can infect the human bloodstream, the lungs, or the gastrointestinal, urinary, or reproductive tracts. Malaria is transmitted by the bite of an infected mosquito. Hookworm can be acquired through walking across contaminated soil. Schistosomiasis is acquired by wading, playing, or working in slow-moving streams and irrigation canals. The prions that lead to bovine spongiform encephalitis (Mad Cow Disease/Creutzfeld-Jacob Disease) may be ingested in food or may enter the body through the skin during food preparation or even surgery.

In this photograph, the president of East Timor, left, receives a soccer ball with an antimalaria message from the U.S. ambassador to celebrate the launch of a program to distribute mosquito nets to families with young children in East Timor. Malaria is transmitted by mosquitoes and is one of the leading causes of child mortality in tropical regions of the world. Unfortunately, the only way to develop immunity to malaria is to survive multiple bouts as a child. By protecting young children from malaria, such prevention programs save lives in the short term but also result in populations that are more susceptible to malaria throughout their lives.

Flora (plants) can also affect human health. Wild plants can cause allergic reactions, and many, such as acorns, contain toxins that must be carefully removed by processing and/or cooking before they are safe for consumption. Relying on one or two staple crops may lead to nutritional deficiencies if the crops are naturally missing some essential amino acids. Even domesticated plant crops may contain toxins, such as the cyanide in some varieties of manioc/cassava. Likewise, manioc has almost no protein—it is a good source of calories, but only if another source of protein is available in the diet. Some people have allergies to certain components of some plant foods, such as peanuts, tree nuts, and mangoes. Some plants contain hormones that can have an impact on human physiology, such as the high levels of phytoestrogens (estrogen-like compounds) in soy products.

The demographic structure of the human population likewise affects health. The larger the population, and the closer people are in contact with one another (through crowding, public transportation, etc.), the more likely the transmission of disease from one person to another. If the group is small and nomadic, sanitation is less likely to become an issue. If the group is large and sedentary, then oral–fecal transmission of disease is more problematic. If a population has lived in one region for many generations, genetic and developmental adaptations to local diseases have time to develop. But new modes of transportation and patterns of migration can bring new diseases to people, or expose people to new diseases in new environments.

Genetic Factors

There are a number of genetic factors that contribute to human health, both directly and indirectly. Direct effects include diseases/conditions caused by specific alleles of a gene, such as cystic fibrosis, achondroplastic dwarfism, or sickle-cell disease. Other diseases/conditions are caused by extra or missing (but otherwise normal) genetic material, such as Down syndrome (an extra copy of chromosome 21), Huntington's Disease (extra copies of stretches of DNA on chromosome 4), or Turner's syndrome (a missing sex chromosome). Diseases/conditions caused by having two copies of a recessive allele will be more common in populations that are small and endogamous (marry within the group).

Genes can also contribute indirectly to health through the inheritance of predispositions to develop certain diseases or conditions, especially given other genes or specific environmental circumstances. Examples for physical health include Tourette's/autism, breast cancer, diabetes, colon cancer, asthma, and substance abuse. Examples for mental health include schizophrenia, depression, bipolar disorder, obsessive-compulsive disorder, and others.

Cultural Factors

In addition to all of the physical and biological environmental dangers lurking around to harm humans, a number of cultural factors can lead either directly or indirectly to injuries or disease. Direct examples for physical health include child abuse and neglect, sports injuries, car accidents, sharing needles among IV drug users, circumcision and infibulation, and tobacco and alcohol use and abuse. Examples for mental health include child abuse and neglect (again), tyranny, imprisonment, torture, high levels of crime, and warfare or the threat of warfare.

Indirect cultural factors are those aspects of cultural beliefs and practices that may contribute to injuries or poor health, especially given other genetic or environmental circumstances that also contribute to the same problems. Examples for physical health include over- or underavailability of food, sedentary jobs and leisure activities, factories that produce pollutants, lack of access to modern housing (exposure to lead in old paint), and crowded transportation. Various aspects of sanitation, ranging from hand-washing practices; availability of soap and hot water; and food preparation, storage, and disposal options; to the adequacy of the sewer system, all impact on physical health. Examples of indirect cultural influences on mental health include the many types and sources of emotional stress; unrealistic expectations; overemphasis on certain qualities such as beauty and thinness, intelligence, or athletic ability; tolerance of bullying; lack of cultural acceptance of atypical personality types; and so forth.

Natural Coping Mechanisms of the Body

The third component of the equation of human health involves the body's natural ability to cope with the consequences of whatever health challenges it faces. It isn't simply a matter of being exposed to disease-causing organisms or physical or emotional trauma. In fact, we face multiple health challenges every day, but most of the time our bodies and minds are able to cope. Only when conditions overwhelm the body's natural coping mechanisms do symptoms begin to appear.

There are many different factors that affect an individual's ability to cope with disease, injury, trauma, and physical and emotional stressors. Some people will be very resilient, able to withstand extraordinary conditions that would sicken, disable, or even kill others. Other individuals are less able to cope and may succumb to the first health challenge they encounter, however minor. Why is there so much variation?

Natural Selection / Genetic Factors

Throughout millions of years of evolution, natural selection has favored individuals who were able to survive and reproduce successfully in the face of a variety of diseases, conditions, and injuries. In premodern populations, many infants and children died before reaching reproductive maturity, thus leaving only the fittest, sturdiest individuals to reproduce. Even today in parts of the world without access to immunizations, antibiotics, antimalarial drugs, and proper nutrition, up to 50 percent of children die before they reach the age of five years. That we have managed to survive and flourish as a species is a testament to our natural coping mechanisms—our fundamental ability to recover and heal from injury and disease—and to our continued biological evolution in the never-ending race against the evolution of disease organisms, even without the addition of any cultural coping mechanisms.

Just as there are genetic factors that contribute directly and indirectly to poor health, so there are genetic factors that affect a person's response to health challenges. For example, while having two copies of the sickle-cell anemia allele causes the disease itself, having only one copy of the sickle-cell allele and one unaffected copy provides some degree of natural immunity to malarial infections. The allele for sickle-cell is most common in populations that have had long experience with malaria as a selective force, such as those living in the tropical regions of Africa (and today in places where people of African ancestry live). Likewise, a mutation of the CCR5 gene, known as the Δ-32 allele, provides resistance to both plague bacteria and the Human Immunodeficiency Virus (HIV) that can lead to AIDS. One copy of the Δ-32 allele provides some resistance, and two copies provide even more. The Δ-32 allele of CCR5 is most common in populations that experienced plague epidemics as a selective force in previous centuries, particularly in Europe (and today in places where people of European ancestry live).

Sometimes, genetic variation leads to a poorly functioning immune system, as is the case for individuals with Trisomy 21 (Down syndrome), so they are more susceptible to *any* disease-causing organism that comes along. They are more likely to become sick, to have more severe symptoms, and to take longer to recover.

Developmental Factors

Researchers use the concept of resilience (**positive deviance**) to describe people who seem better able to cope with health challenges in general. Some of this ability to avoid illness or to respond quickly and effectively to setbacks is thought to be due to genetic variations as yet undiscovered. In addition, developmental factors during childhood also affect how well the body can respond. Among the most important developmental factors are whether the person was breastfed or not, and for how long. A normal, well-functioning immune system requires several years of breastfeeding, along with other aspects of good nutrition such as adequate calories, protein, vitamins, and minerals from other foods. People who were not breastfed, or only for short durations, are at greater risk of many diseases throughout life, not just in childhood. Breast milk functions in a dose-response fashion—the longer a person is breastfed, the better their life-long health. At the population level, this can make a tremendous difference in quality of life.

Current Health Status and Stress

Ongoing factors also influence how well an individual can respond to health challenges, including recent and current nutritional status, physical fitness (heart and lung function, stamina/endurance), the co-occurrence of other health problems, and other sources of physical or emotional stress such as temperature extremes, severe thirst or hunger, overexertion, or prolonged anxiety or fear. Social support is also important. The greater the social support available, in the form of family, friends, and societal or government levels of support, the more likely people are to remain healthy and to recover from disease. Some research suggests that the *perception of social support, or its lack,* may be just as critical as actual support. Likewise, the perception of the cause of the illness or condition may affect how well a person copes.

Stress plays an important role in whether we succumb to infections. Often, our bodies harbor colonies of bacteria, viruses, and fungi that are either beneficial or at least cause us no problems, as they are kept under control by other beneficial microorganisms or by the body's defenses such as white blood cells. When we become run-down due to malnutrition, another disease, or stress, we overload our body's ability to cope, and we *catch* the disease, which we actually have had all along.

For example, cold sores (also known as fever blisters) are caused by a flare-up of a normally quiescent infection with the Herpes Simplex I Virus. Almost everyone becomes infected with herpes in childhood, through contact with family members and friends. It typically lies dormant in the mucous membranes of our oral cavities. Usually our own defenses keep the virus in check. Under stressful conditions, however, the virus may overrun the body's ability to cope. Thus, you may develop a cold sore just before your senior prom, during finals week at school, or on the day of an important job interview.

Another Herpes Simplex I Virus is responsible for chicken pox, which is usually acquired in early childhood. Some populations have access to a recently developed vaccine, which provides partial protection. Most chicken pox infections are relatively mild, and the victim recovers in a few days. Afterward, however, the virus is not necessarily eliminated from the body. It may lie dormant in the roots of spinal nerves as they exit the spinal column. When you are elderly or, for example, undergoing chemotherapy for cancer (very stressful on both physiological and emotional levels), the chicken pox virus may reemerge as *shingles*—a very painful and debilitating skin condition.

Bacterial infections can also be asymptomatic. Many people have *Streptococcus* bacteria residing in their upper respiratory tracts; usually the body's defenses keep it in check. Under stressful conditions, the bacteria may be able to multiply rapidly, erupting into a full-blown infection known as strep throat. Vaginal yeast infections in women serve as a fungal example of the same phenomenon. All women have yeast in their vagina; usually the yeast beasts are kept in check by good bacterial flora in the digestive and reproductive tracts. However, if you take antibiotics for an infection, the good bacteria are killed off along with the bad. This allows the yeast to flourish and overwhelm the body's defenses, and symptoms of a yeast infection develop.

Cultural Coping Mechanisms

The final part of the equation of human health and medical care concerns the cultural coping mechanisms, by which I mean the systems of medical beliefs and practices available to the individual and/or the group. A variety of perspectives can be used to examine cultural coping mechanisms.

Distinction between Western Biomedicine and Traditional Medicine

It is common to divide the world's systems of cultural coping mechanisms into the dichotomy of **Western Biomedicine (WBM)** and so-called **Traditional Medicine** (also known as complementary or alternative healing systems). This can be a useful *heuristic device* to begin with, as long as one keeps several important points in mind. First, such a distinction is an oversimplification, and most people have access to, and may utilize, multiple overlapping systems of therapy. Second, remember that Western Biomedicine, contrary to popular belief, is only loosely based on scientific research and evidence. Third, Traditional Medicine is not based entirely on superstition and hocus-pocus—popular portrayals of witch doctors in the Western media are not accurate. Fourth, research shows that practitioners of Traditional Medicine are often very knowledgeable about how to effect healing through manipulation of the social environment as well as the psychological resources of the patient. And finally, I emphasize that practitioners of both approaches to healing may understand neither the mechanisms by which a particular disease causes problems nor why a particular treatment works. *Effective treatments do not necessarily hinge on knowing the exact physical or physiological mechanisms of either disease or cure.*

At the beginning of this discussion, I pointed out that, as an oversimplification and overgeneralization, Western Biomedicine focuses mainly on combating the proximate causes of poor health, while Traditional Medicine focuses mainly on strengthening the natural coping mechanisms of the body (sometimes through supernatural means). Both approaches include a variety of beliefs and practices of varying degrees of effectiveness. In other words, they both work, to some degree, for some people, some of the time.

Birth Defects / Congenital Abnormalities

Around the world, every day, children are born with a variety of atypical physical and physiological features. If the abnormalities are obvious, parents may take steps to kill the infant. Although this may seem callous to some, it is often the most practical choice where there is little chance that the child will survive. In some cultures, it is considered too difficult to care for twins, and one or both members of a set of twins may be killed at birth. Children who are missing limbs, are anencephalic (born without a brain), have severe spina bifida, or other major physical abnormalities may likewise be killed.

In North America, due to the development of prenatal diagnostic testing, many pregnancies are screened for such abnormalities and, if an abnormality is found, the pregnancy is usually terminated. For conditions that are not diagnosed until the time of birth, North American parents do not have the option to kill their child outright, but in most circumstances they may leave the child in the hospital's neonatal intensive care unit while withholding food, water, and medical support until the child dies.

In other cases, a child seems normal and healthy at birth but fails to develop in the normal fashion. Among the Bambara of Mali, people would refer with sadness and regret to children who "weren't really children"—children who never learned to sit up or talk. In some regions, such children were believed to be snakes or other wild animals and were taken into the bush outside the village and abandoned. The children were never seen again, and it was assumed that they had turned back into snakes and slithered away, reinforcing the belief that they had not been human to begin with.

Dealing with Impairments, Disabilities, and Handicaps

Every culture and time period has different beliefs about the value of individuals with impairments or disabilities and different ways of treating them and accommodating their needs (or not). One of the best ethnographies of impairment is Nora Groce's book, *Everyone Here Spoke Sign Language: Hereditary Deafness on Martha's Vineyard* (1985). Populations living on Martha's Vineyard in the nineteenth century and the early decades of the twentieth century were the descendants of a small group of settlers from the region of Kent in England. As time passed, and people married distant relatives, some of them inherited two copies of a recessive allele for hereditary deafness that was present in the original Kentish population. Eventually, as more and more individuals on the island were born deaf, a full-fledged sign language developed, and both hearing and deaf islanders were able to communicate with everyone else. Because *everyone spoke sign language*, being deaf was neither a disability nor a handicap.

The sign language of Martha's Vineyard fell into disuse in the 1920s and 1930s as children who were deaf began to attend a school for the deaf on the mainland and brought back the newly developed American Sign Language system, to which they had contributed some Martha's Vineyard Sign Language features. Some of the deaf islanders married people from off-island who were hearing, or who were deaf for different genetic reasons, thus more hearing children were born on the island. Martha's Vineyard Sign Language no longer exists. However, the same phenomenon has been documented for a remote village of Bedouin Arabs in Israel, where linguists are currently studying the development of an indigenous, spontaneous sign language among hearing and deaf members of the community (Fox 2008, discussed further in chapter 11).

The cross-cultural study of impairments, disabilities, and handicaps is still in its infancy, but holds great potential for providing insight into how people in different cultures conceive of the so-called *normal* body and how far they are willing to go to make accommodations for people who are different.

First Aid and the Popular Sector in Healing

In every culture, some people have a basic knowledge of first aid—how to treat simple injuries, such as minor cuts, splinters, scrapes, bruises, and sprains. There may be specialists who treat more severe injuries, including stitching up major wounds, performing surgery, manipulating parts of the body, and setting broken bones. These specialists are often different individuals than the experts who treat organic disease or psychological/behavioral problems. Bioarcheological evidence dating as far back as the time of Neanderthals reveals that some people have been able to survive severe injuries, including crushing blows to the skull, multiple fractures, scalping, animal attacks, amputations of limbs, and being hit by projectile points (from spears or arrows) that healed over and remain embedded in their bones.

Likewise, many people will have basic knowledge of how to treat minor symptoms of illness such as fever, headache, and stomachache, as well as head colds, heat rashes, or malaria. They may massage a friend's or relative's shoulders to relieve tension and muscle knots. This level of common knowledge and ready access to basic medicines and treatments is sometimes referred to as the **popular sector** in healing.

Medical care takes many forms. Knowledge of first aid for minor injuries and treatments for common, mild illnesses is often widespread among the general population, while treatment for serious conditions may require someone with more specialized training. Likewise, some medicines are available "over the counter" for anyone to buy, while others require a prescription from a medical expert. Top: a mother in Japan puts a bandage on her young son's scraped knee, an osteopathic physician manipulates the patient's body physically to relieve pain, and a team of doctors prepares for surgery. Bottom: a healers' market in Peru sells herbal remedies for many problems—physical, psychological, and spiritual; a Chinese herbal pharmacy requires a doctor's prescription, as does a U.S. pharmacy with its stock of mass-produced medicines.

Musculoskeletal and Energy Therapies

Until recently, medical anthropologists paid little attention to healers who specialized in musculoskeletal therapies (often called *bone-setters*). The first edited volume on this type of healing was published in 2004 (Oths and Hinojosa 2004). The editors write: "The time has come for anthropologists to balance their extensive documentation of exotic, supernatural healing practices with studies of healing based on the pragmatisms of ordinary human anatomy, physiology, and pathology" (Oths and Hinojosa 2004:xiv).

Musculoskeletal therapies include chiropractic manipulation, therapeutic massage of all types, joint manipulation, physical and occupational therapy, and energy healing. Manual traditions emphasize the importance of the "laying on of hands" for diagnosing medical conditions as well as treating them through manipulations of the bones, muscles, and connective tissues. Most insur-

ance companies in North America now cover chiropractic care, orthopedic treatments, and occupational and physical therapy. Some even cover therapeutic massage. In some European countries, massage is often the first therapy a doctor prescribes for muscle aches and pain.

Energy healing therapies or bioenergetics (reiki, acupuncture, polarity therapy, etc.) are based on the idea that illness can be caused by blockages or imbalances in the body's energy fields or meridians. Although many WBM practitioners are skeptical of the underlying beliefs about how energy healing works, they acknowledge that patients often improve after such therapies, and most insurance companies in North America now cover acupuncture treatments for some conditions.

Herbalists and Pharmacology

All healing systems have experts in pharmacology—the use of natural chemical compounds derived from animals, plants, or minerals, or manufactured synthetically, which can be used to treat disease or relieve symptoms. As with first aid, basic knowledge of such chemical compounds may be widespread, but often this is a specialized area of knowledge limited to experts. Around the world, many populations have figured out that plants containing the chemical acetylsalicylic acid (Aspirin) can reduce fevers and relieve pain when ingested or administered transdermally (across the skin, through washing, soaking, or poultices). Thousands of such medicines have been developed, tested, and used in different cultural contexts. Some work better than others, some may not work at all, and still others may work, but not in the way people think they do.

Some medicines are used to treat highly specific conditions, such as newer chemotherapy drugs that target only cells that are cancerous, or they may work on a broader basis, as older chemotherapy drugs do, killing all cells that are rapidly dividing. Such a broad approach kills cancer cells but also kills other useful cells of the body that divide rapidly such as hair follicles in the scalp or the lining of the gastrointestinal and urinary tracts. Other treatments are meant to strengthen the body's immune system, to treat a wide variety of infections (broad-spectrum antibiotics), or to "calm the nerves."

Many medicines have side effects that can range from merely unpleasant to lethal. People often must make complex decisions, weighing the risks and benefits of treatment against the risks and benefits of doing nothing, or of alternative treatments. For example, in Mali, mothers whose children had malaria were often reluctant to take them to the doctor for an injection of chloroquine, because sometimes the doctor accidentally hit the sciatic nerve in the back of the child's leg with the needle. The chloroquine would probably cure the malaria, but damage to the sciatic nerve might leave the child unable to walk. Tamoxifen, a heavily marketed drug used in North America in the 1990s and early 2000s to lower the risk of breast cancer, had a side effect of increasing the risk of uterine cancer and is no longer prescribed.

Within the system of Western Biomedicine, we have much more detailed knowledge of the chemical structures of pharmacologically active compounds and the mechanisms by which they work. At the same time, researchers still don't know how many of the drugs used to treat mental illnesses work within the brain. By no means have we perfected the treatment of illness using natural or synthetic compounds. Many researchers are studying local plant-based medicines from a wide range of cultures around the world, looking at their efficacy. Where effective and where economically feasible, new medicines are being developed from these plants or are being synthesized directly from their chemical constituents.

Shamanic and Community Healing

In addition to bone-setters and herbalists, many traditional/alternative systems of medicines use a variety of beliefs and practices to strengthen the body's physical and emotional defenses and help people heal on their own. Often, though not inevitably, these approaches involve calling on supernatural forces to aid the expert in diagnosing and treating the illness, or to aid patients directly in their recovery. Individuals who are experts in these procedures are often referred to as **shamanic healers.** Their ability to communicate with the world of the supernatural is most often used to provide medical care and healing to members of the community.

Shamans may enter into a trance with the aid of drumming, music, dance, or perception-altering drugs. They then may travel to the spirit world and gain access to information to help explain what type of disease the person has, what the ultimate cause might be, and what the patient needs to do to recover. Sometimes the patient also enters into a trance as part of the healing ceremony. These rituals are often public, with friends, family, and other community members turning out to participate and show their care and support for the individual seeking treatment. Participation may include community praying, singing, dancing, and offering sacrifices to the spirits. Follow-up care may require the patient to make amends for prior transgressions committed against the spirits or ancestors, or against fellow community members. In this way, shamanic healers may act as community psychologists, bringing conflicts out into the open where they can be resolved.

There are a number of issues to consider when evaluating approaches such as shamanic and community healing rituals. Western popular imagination often ridicules shamanic healers, referring to them as *witch doctors* and assuming that what they do is just mumbo-jumbo, hocus-pocus, based in superstition and

Traditional healers, sometimes referred to as shamans or even witch doctors, are usually religious leaders as well, who have special abilities to communicate with the spirit world for help in diagnosing and treating health problems. They may use trance, dance, music, touch, smoke, talk therapy, and herbal preparations in their work. Top: a shaman of the Urarina people of the Peruvian Amazon, and a woman selling herbal remedies and other ritual offerings for healing in La Paz, Bolivia. Bottom: a healer of the Shona people close to Great Zimbabwe, Zimbabwe, and an Amazon forest shaman.

without any real efficacy. Nothing could be further from the truth. *Shamanic healing is an ancient form of the healing arts and has much success in curing disease and illness,* even though Western Biomedicine may not yet understand all of the mechanisms by which it works. Shamanic healing often involves the healer touching and manipulating the patient's body, and thus it incorporates aspects of musculoskeletal and energy healing modalities. Many patients who go to Western medical practitioners also pray for divine intervention and ask their friends and family to pray for them, or to envision them surrounded by healing white light.

It is also possible that when people *believe* that supernatural forces and shamanic healing rituals can help them, such beliefs affect the body's natural coping mechanisms in a positive way. In some regions of the world, such as northern Peru, shamanic healing rituals have become syncretized (melded) with Catholic religious beliefs imported from Europe during colonial times (Glass-Coffin 1998). It is possible, of course, that supernatural spirits of various types actually do help people heal if appealed to properly.

Many community healing rituals, such as the dance ceremonies of the Kalahari *Ju|'hoansi* (!Kung or San) serve to focus attention on the patient and reinforce the importance of the individual to the community (Katz, Biesele, and St. Denis 1997). It doesn't really matter whether these rituals work through a real transfer of healing energy via the laying on of hands, as many people believe, or through some mechanism of compassionate touch that is not yet understood by Western Biomedicine, or if they work (merely) psychologically through a placebo effect, as some skeptics insist. The goal is always for people to feel better and recover from their illness, and these treatments often work.

Practical Access to Medical Care

In addition to issues of belief, there are many practical concerns that affect health, such as access to medical care. Not all types of treatment are available in all communities. Distance and transportation may mean that it isn't feasible to travel for preventive or curative medical care. While immunizations have eradicated many serious childhood diseases in Western countries—diphtheria, pertussis, tetanus, measles, mumps, rubella, chicken pox, and polio—they are not available equally in all parts of the world. After manu-

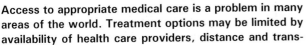
Access to appropriate medical care is a problem in many areas of the world. Treatment options may be limited by availability of health care providers, distance and transportation issues, or economic constraints. Left: Count Bleed-Ya-Dry, a giant Dracula-like puppet, appears at a health care reform rally in Seattle, Washington, in 2009. The hovering bats are labeled "insurance company," "drug industry," and "HMO." Count Bleed-Ya-Dry is a project of the Backbone Campaign (http://www.backbonecampaign.org). Many people in countries without socialized medicine cannot afford health insurance or health care. Right: a community-based reproductive health agent in Ethiopia connected a young woman with the services she needed to heal her obstetric fistula. Obstetric fistulas are caused by difficult labors and deliveries, leaving many women around the world with urinary or fecal incontinence, which causes them to be ostracized.

facture, most vaccines must be kept refrigerated, making it very difficult to transport them to the many regions of the world that do not have electricity. Deciding to have your child immunized is much easier if you can hop in your car and drive a few miles to the pediatrician's office. It is another matter altogether if you have to walk, carrying your child, more than 10 miles in intense heat or cold, to reach a regional clinic, which may or may not have a supply of the vaccine.

In some areas of the United States, you can even get flu shots at a drive-through facility ("Would you like fries with that?"), or nurses will travel to work sites and child care facilities to give immunizations.

Economic Access to Medical Care

Economic constraints also play an important role in health. Whether payment consists of a chicken or a bag of rice brought as a gift to the local traditional healer, $20 for the co-pay for a prescription drug covered by an insurance policy, or $200,000 for a heart transplant that isn't covered by insurance, many people cannot afford medical care. In some Western countries, such as Sweden, people pay a high percentage of their income as taxes that are used to provide a basic level of medical care to everyone. In the United States, the cost of medical care varies widely based on the region of the country, the type of insurance coverage you have, and many other constraints. Where people have little access to money, either because they live in a subsistence economy, or due to poverty, they sometimes face choices between medical care for one sick family member and food for the other family members. As medical anthropologist Nancy Scheper-Hughes has shown through her research in Northeast Brazil, mothers sometimes decide not to invest any more resources, whether money, time, or effort, in a child who is not expected to survive (Scheper-Hughes 1993). It is difficult for many people to even imagine having to make such a choice.

Decision Making and Individual Agency

It can be misleading to assume that in all situations the patient (or the patient's parents, if the patient is a minor) is the one who makes the decisions about when to consult an expert for an injury or disease, which expert(s) to consult, and whether or not to follow their advice. Not everyone is a free agent when it comes to these decisions, or many others. The social structure of the extended family may mean that someone else, such as an elder male, is the gatekeeper for knowledge and decisions about medical matters for all family members. A mother-in-law may control access to medical care for her daughters-in-law and their children, or a husband may control access for his wife. Adult children may take over medical decision making for an elderly parent.

Under Western biomedical systems of care, it is often the insurance companies who act as the gatekeepers, determining which doctors, clinics, and hospitals a person may use; which drugs will be paid for; which services are approved; and which are denied because they are supposedly experimental or ineffective. In addition, hospital ethics committees, guardians, and courts at various levels sometimes intervene in decisions about the care of individuals deemed not able to decide for themselves, such as infants and people with mental retardation, autism, or mental illness. In North America, medical controversies have erupted over the rights of parents to withhold surgical care, food, and water from children born with birth defects and over the rights of parents to impose their religious beliefs—such as refusal of blood transfusions or chemotherapy—on their minor children. Children of various ages have fought for their rights to have some input into decisions about their medical care.

In order to fully understand how people access and use the treatment options available to them, in addition to matters of convenience, transportation, and cost, we need to know the broader cultural context in which medical decisions are made. Western Biomedicine and legal structures often assume that only the patient is involved in such decision making and is a free agent, but this is often not the case, even in the West.

Typical Life-Span versus Life Expectancy at Birth

A common misunderstanding plagues many discussions of mortality across different cultures, populations, and time periods. The confusion stems from a failure to appreciate the distinction between the **typical life-span** of members of a species and **life expectancy at birth,** a statistic generated from data on ages at death of members of a particular population.

The concept of *typical life-span* refers to the oldest typical age to which an individual will live if he survives infancy and childhood (the usual periods of greatest risk of death). Those who survive childhood will continue to die of injuries and diseases through-out their adult years, but at a much lower rate. As the limits of typical life-span approach, the mortality rate increases again, subject to amelioration by the cultural coping mechanisms available. For humans as a spe-cies, the typical life-span is approximately 60–65 years for populations without access to high-tech, advanced medical care. In populations with access to modern medical care—antibiotics, surgery, blood transfusions, organ transplants, joint replacements, intravenous feeding, mechanical ventilators (breathing assis-tance), and chemotherapy of all types—some individ-uals will live to be 80 or 90 years old, or even longer. It is rare to find individuals this old in communities without access to modern medical care.

When we consider that human females are gener-ally capable of reproduction between the ages of 15 and 45 years, and that each human child needs the care of its mother for approximately 15 years, we see the influence of natural selection. In the past, women who survived until their last child was capable of sur-viving on its own had relatively more offspring, pass-ing along their genes for surviving until 60–65 years of age. Some researchers have also suggested that women can enhance their reproductive success by contribut-ing to the care of their grandchildren once they are past menopause (and are no longer having children of their own). This *Grandmother Hypothesis* has garnered much attention in the research literature, but the data are not clear in terms of how significant grandmater-nal care has been, or continues to be, for the survival of human children. A typical life-span of 60–65 years is consistent with only direct maternal care being of significance for reproductive success in humans—a woman needs to survive until her last child, born when she is around 45 years of age, has reached the age of 15 years or so [45 + 15 = 60].

The concept of *life expectancy at birth*, or average life expectancy, on the other hand, is a completely dif-ferent animal. Life expectancy at birth is a statistic that reflects the *average* length of life for all members of a specific population. It is calculated by adding up the ages at which people died, and then dividing by the number of people who died to get the average length of life for members of the population, including everyone, even those who died in infancy and early childhood.

Average life expectancy can be very misleading. In each of the following examples, the average life expectancy is

40 years of age, yet the underlying data reflect vastly dif-ferent experiences for members of each population.

- *Example A*
  Ages at death: 6 months, 18 months, 78 years, and 80 years
  Sum of ages at death/# of dead = 160/4 = 40 years

- *Example B*
  Ages at death: 38, 39, 41, and 42 years
  Sum of ages at death/# of dead = 160/4 = 40 years

- *Example C*
  Ages at death: 10, 30, 50, and 70 years
  Sum of ages at death/# of dead = 160/4 = 40 years

Thus, to know that each of these populations has a life expectancy at birth of 40 years tells us very little about the structure of death in the population. Gener-ally, *populations with very low life expectancies at birth ex-perience very high infant and child mortality*. Every child who dies at three days of age, or one week, or one month, pulls the average age of death down dramati-cally. For example, Afghanistan has an average life ex-pectancy at birth of 42 years, but that doesn't mean that no one lives past that age, or that most people die in their early 40s. It means that many children die in infancy and childhood.

The Infant Mortality Rate (IMR) is a statistic that indicates how many children die between birth and one year of age, per 1,000 children born. The most re-cently available data for Afghanistan, from 2006, show an infant mortality rate of 165. Another 92 chil-dren out of every 1,000 died between one and five years of age. In other words, many children die in in-fancy and childhood. However, for those children who survive to age 15 years, more than half will live to age 60 years or beyond. Once they reach 60 years of age, mortality rates begin to increase as the immune sys-tem ceases to function as well and as various organs succumb to organic deterioration and the diseases of old age (heart failure, cancer, etc.). Afghanistan has only two doctors and four hospital beds per 10,000 people. By comparison, the United States has 26 doc-tors and 32 hospital beds per 10,000 people.

At the other end of the spectrum, populations with very high life expectancies at birth are those in which two conditions are present, both attributable mainly to modern medical care. First, infant and childhood mortality rates are very low due to immuni-zations, antibiotics, adequate nutrition, and relatively sophisticated systems for providing clean water and for handling sewage. Second, mortality rates among adults are reduced due to the availability of modern medical care (antibiotics, surgery, blood transfusions, organ transplants, joint replacements, intravenous feeding, mechanical ventilators, and chemotherapy).

As can be seen from table 4.1, Japan has the highest average life expectancy at birth, at 83 years. Japan also has among the lowest infant mortality rates, with only three children per 1,000 dying during the first year of life, and only one more succumbing in the next four years of life. For those children who survive to age 15 years, fully 93 percent will live to age 60 years or beyond. Japan has 21 physicians and 141 hospital beds per 10,000 people. Although the density of physicians is not particularly high, compared to other urban-industrial countries, the number of hospital beds available per 10,000 people is more than four times as high as either the United States or Canada.

Table 4.1 provides comparative data for several countries for a number of variables relating to life expectancy and health care access. To summarize, a low average life expectancy at birth means a lot of infants and children die by the age of five years. In such populations, for those who live to age 15 years, fewer than half will die before the age of 60 years, and more than half will survive beyond that age. A high average life expectancy at birth means very few infants and children die by the age of five years. For those who live to age 15 years, few will die before the age of 60 years of age, and 88–94 percent will survive beyond age 60 years. The *typical life-span* for humans as a species remains approximately 60–65 years for populations without access to high-tech, advanced medical care.

Final Thoughts

All of these topics, and many more, are the subject of research by medical anthropologists. Learning how people define and interpret health and wellness, and how they cope with accidents, diseases, birth defects, and natural disasters, provides a fascinating window into many aspects of cultural beliefs and social organization.

Many of the diseases affecting modern human populations are the result of recent developments. Some are due to the evolution of new disease-causing organisms such as the human immunodeficiency virus and the Ebola and Marburg viruses, or the evolution of multiple-drug-resistant strains of old diseases such as tuberculosis and *Staphylococcus*. Some are due to the negative consequences of technological progress, including diseases related to coal, asbestos, and uranium mining; to air and water pollution; and to contamination of the soil with toxins ranging from DDT to

Table 4.1 Comparative data showing the relationship between life expectancy at birth and mortality rates during the first year of life, the next four years of life, and between 15 and 60 years of age, as well as two indicators of access to modern medical care*

Country	Life Expectancy at birth (years)	Infant Mortality Rate (0–1 year) per 1,000	1–5 Mortality Rate (1–5 years) per 1,000	Adult Mortality Rate (15–60 years) per 1,000	Percent of 15-year-olds who live more than 60 years	# of doctors per 10,000 pop.	# of hospital beds per 10,000 pop.
Afghanistan	42	165	92	473	53%	2	4
Mali	46	119	98	427	57%	<1.0	3
India	63	57	19	241	76%	6	N/A
China	73	20	4	116	88%	14	22
United States	78	7	1	109	89%	26	32
Canada	81	5	1	72	93%	19	34
Sweden	81	3	1	64	94%	33	N/A
Japan	83	3	1	67	93%	21	141

*From WHOSIS, www.who.int/whosis/data/ Latest available data as of February 2010 (most of the data reflect conditions between 2000–2006)

heavy metals. Diseases of old age become more prevalent and noticeable as more people survive longer and as more diseases are recognized through advanced diagnostic techniques.

No doubt there is still much to learn about the multiple factors that contribute to patterns of modern health and disease. It is important to understand the complexity of the interactions between genetic factors, environmental factors, cultural/social factors, and stress—throughout development and during adulthood and old age—that contribute to human health and wellness. It is also critical that we be open to new understandings of how the mind and body work in concert to deal with stress and to recover from accidents and disease, and how Western Biomedicine and Traditional/Alternative medical approaches can contribute to better health for everyone.

NUTRITIONAL ANTHROPOLOGY

Nutritional anthropologists are interested in a variety of issues having to do with food, cuisines, food security, nutritional adequacy, and malnutrition (both over- and undernutrition). Nutritional status is one of the major contributing variables affecting health and disease, thus nutritional anthropology and medical anthropology overlap significantly. Nutritional anthropology is an eclectic and rapidly growing field, with many different perspectives, most of which combine elements of social-cultural anthropology with methodologies and data from biological anthropology. This brief overview will introduce a number of the major issues to which nutritional anthropologists devote their time and attention.

Primate and Early Hominid Diets

Primates

Most members of the order Primates (*pry-MATE-eez*), including humans, have generalized teeth and a generalized diet—we are omnivores. We eat a wide variety of foods from across the spectrum of other life forms, including all manner of plants, animals, and fungi. Among our closest primate relatives, gorillas subsist mainly on vast quantities of green leafy vegeta-

tion from the forest floor, while chimpanzees and bonobos are known to eat more than 200 different species of plants, including fruits and nuts as well as leaves and blossoms.

Chimpanzees also eat insects, small game such as deer and wild pig, and other primates, including prosimians, monkeys, and even, on occasion, other chimpanzees. Chimpanzees craft fishing sticks for probing termite mounds to extract termites, an excellent source of protein and fat. They have been observed cracking open hard nuts using stone anvils and hammers and fashioning simple spears for hunting galagos, which are nocturnal primates that sleep in nests inside tree trunks during the day. If a chimpanzee finds a sleeping galago, it will search for an appropriate stick, sharpen the ends to make it into a spear, and then thrust it into the nest to kill the galago, in order to eat it. Additionally, groups of male chimpanzees carry out organized hunts of monkeys in the treetops. One monkey will be chosen as the target, and the male chimpanzees cooperate, chasing their prey through the trees, surrounding it, and then killing and eating it. Female chimpanzees sometimes attack other chimpanzees' newborn infants, killing and eating them.

Early Hominids

Current thinking in biological anthropology is that the common ancestor of chimpanzees/bonobos and humans lived some six million years ago in Africa and had a diet similar to that of modern-day chimpanzees and bonobos, consisting of a wide variety of plant foods, as well as animal foods when they were available. Evidence for the first bipedal hominids places them in woodland-savannah environments in East Africa, between five and six million years ago. Bipedalism permanently frees the hands from locomotor functions while on the ground and allows for the gathering and transporting of food across long distances. As far as we can tell, these early hominids (human ancestors) continued to have a primarily plant-based diet, but with ever more sophisticated abilities to obtain animal foods as time went by. Sources of animal foods include passive scavenging (picking the bones of carnivore kills after the carnivores, hyenas, vultures, and other scavengers have had their fill), active scavenging (chasing competitors away from carnivore kills while there is still a lot of meat on the bones), and opportunistic hunting including young, sick, or injured animals. Additionally, slow-moving animals such as baby birds, tortoises, grubs, and other insects can be gathered.

Cooperative Hunting

As these early hominids evolved, evidence for sophisticated, coordinated hunting of larger animals becomes more and more common. Much speculation has been put forth suggesting that larger amounts of meat in the diet contributed to the dramatic increase in brain size that occurred beginning about 2.0 million years ago. Others have hypothesized that adding roots and tubers to the diet, acquired with the help of sharpened digging sticks, may have provided the extra nutrients necessary for an expansion of the brain, as well as a larger population of hominids. *Only stone tools and fossilized animal remains survive from these time periods, so it is impossible to know exactly how and when techniques for cooperative hunting were developed, or how much meat was in the diet of early hominids and prehistoric humans even through the Upper Paleolithic.* Evidence of net hunting and the use of sharpened wooden spears or digging sticks is seldom preserved in the archeological record.

Fire

At some point, humans developed the ability to control and use fire. Evidence of hearths in archeological sites dates back almost one million years, but at first these may have been used mainly as sources of light and heat, or to keep other animals away, rather than for cooking. Eventually, however, someone discovered that foods could be modified by applying heat either directly, such as roasting meat or fish over an open fire or burying tubers in hot ashes, or indirectly, through cooking in liquids using fire-proof containers. Cooking can transform food resources, making some of them easier to chew and digest, and increasing the ability of the human gut to absorb some nutrients.

Domesticated Foods

It wasn't until the Neolithic Revolution, beginning about 10,000 years ago in several areas of the world, that some populations began to have access to domesticated plant and animal food resources, radically changing the human diet. Throughout most of our existence as a species, humans have relied on hunted and gathered foods only, eating across a broad spectrum of wild plant and animal species, eating what was locally and seasonally available, and experiencing some periods of abundance interspersed with periods of hunger or even starvation.

Following the Neolithic Revolution, as more and more of the human diet came from domesticated food sources, the variety of foods consumed dropped sharply. In some areas, meat-eating became more significant, while in others, a few carbohydrate staples came to play a central role in the diet. As populations grew and social life became more complex, obtaining or producing food became the province of only some members of the population, putting the rest at the mercy of the food producers.

In the following section, I begin at the beginning and examine the original source of food for all human infants—breast milk.

Breastfeeding and Breast Milk

The first food for all mammals is their mother's milk, produced by the mammary glands (called *breasts* in humans) through the process known as lactation. Breastfeeding is a way to provide protective immunities and health- and growth-promoting factors to children. The *nutritional* function of breast milk appeared relatively late in the evolution of mammary glands and lactation. Primates in general have slow-growing, large-brained offspring, who, like other mammals, depend on breast milk as a significant part of their diet throughout infancy. Note that **infancy** is defined by zoologists and anthropologists as the time from birth to the eruption of the first permanent teeth. Among primates, humans have the slowest-growing, largest-brained offspring, whose first permanent teeth are the first permanent molars, which erupt behind the deciduous (baby) teeth, at about the same time the baby front teeth are falling out—around the age of six years.

Research on the composition of primate milks and on the nursing patterns of various nonhuman primates, as well as cross-cultural comparisons of human populations, provides some insight into what the underlying physiological pattern of breastfeeding and weaning would be in humans if we didn't alter it through culturally biased beliefs and practices.

Frequency of Nursing

During gestation, the fetus is fed continuously from the mother's bloodstream, 24/7, through the placenta via the umbilical cord. After birth, all of the child's food, as well as most of its protection from pathogens, must come from its mother's breasts. In cultures where infants are carried all the time by their mothers and allowed to nurse whenever they wish, the typical pattern is for the baby to nurse several times an hour throughout the day and multiple times at night. As the child gets older, she will eventually sleep for longer time periods, especially at night, and may shift to patterns of nursing less frequently but for longer stretches each time in response to the mother's urging. However, in populations where mothers continue to allow children to nurse as often as they want, the pattern of nursing several times an hour throughout the day and multiple times at night may continue for several years. As solid foods are added to the diet, children gradually nurse less and less, although in times of sickness, stress, injury, or fright, they will return to a more frequent pattern of nursing.

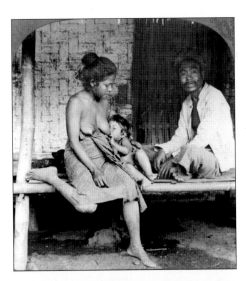

A normal, well-functioning immune system requires several years of breastfeeding, along with other aspects of good nutrition such as adequate calories, protein, vitamins, and minerals from other foods. People who were not breastfed, or breastfed only for a short duration, are at greater risk of many diseases throughout life, not just in childhood, and in all regions of the world, not just developing countries.

Supply and Demand

During the first four months of life, milk supply is determined by how often the baby nurses—the more often the baby nurses, the more milk is produced, through an endocrine (hormone-based) feedback mechanism. Additionally, the more often the baby nurses, the higher the fat content of the milk, which helps the infant's brain develop normally. Around the four-month mark, control of milk production switches to autocrine control, and the amount of milk produced is thereafter regulated by how much milk the child removes from the breast through suckling, rather than the frequency of suckling.

Where cultural rules dictate relatively infrequent nursing bouts, especially in the first few months of life, the mother may not develop an adequate milk supply. She may then find that her supply drops at around the four-month mark, when control switches from endocrine to autocrine. She may have to supplement the child with other foods earlier than is ideal, or else the child's growth and health may falter. Widely spaced feedings and solitary sleeping based on maladaptive cultural beliefs result in low milk supply in many mothers, poor growth in many children, and generally unhappy children. Unfortunately, this may reinforce the belief that some Westerners hold that many modern women are *not capable* of producing enough milk for their children, rather than a recognition that scheduled feedings and solitary sleeping interfere with the establishment of an adequate milk supply.

Colostrum

The first milk produced by the breasts after the baby is born is referred to as *colostrum*. It is thicker and darker than the mature milk, which will begin to appear a few days after birth. Colostrum is very nutrient dense and rich in fat and has very high levels of immune factors that help prepare the infant's digestive system for life outside the womb. In some cultures, people regard the colostrum as unhealthy and express the breasts by hand to remove the colostrum and then discard it. Although this is generally regarded by Western Biomedicine as an unfortunate misunderstanding of the value of colostrum, it should be noted that colostrum only gradually transitions to mature breast milk over the first few weeks of life. Removing the colostrum for the first day or two may not have a significant impact on the child's health, and indeed a few researchers have speculated that this practice may serve to rid the mother's body of environmental and dietary toxins that have accumulated up to that point. More research is needed to clarify the health impacts of discarding the initial colostrum.

Flavour Programming during Breastfeeding

The experience of breastfeeding can have profound effects:

> [Breastfeeding is] one of the first ways that mothers pass on to daughters and sons their gastronomic culture. This body of research reveals that, like other mammals, the foods eaten by women during pregnancy and lactation flavour amniotic fluid and mothers' milk respectively. Such experiences bias acceptance of particular flavours and may program later food preferences. (Mennella 2009:113)

Thus, the culturally specific solid foods that a child eats will contain flavors that are already intimately familiar, if the child was breastfed. The lack of flavour programming in bottle-fed children may explain why so many North American children (even college students) are reluctant to try new foods, spicy foods, or "ethnic" cuisines, preferring to subsist on relatively bland and taste-free foods such as chicken fingers and French fries.

Addition of Solid Foods

For nutritional purposes, solid foods typically are introduced during the second half of the first year of life, around six months of age, although there is substantial cultural variation in this process. The American Academy of Family Physicians (2010), the American Academy of Pediatrics (2005), and the World Health Organization (2003), all recommend adding safe and appropriate solids at around six months of age, following the baby's lead in terms of interest.

Most populations have various cultural beliefs about what the first foods should be, when and how they should be prepared and administered, and who should control what and how much the baby eats. Often, the dietary staple is ritually offered as a first food. Other first foods will be those considered easy to chew and digest, not likely to cause choking, and particularly suited to children in various ways. In most cultures, children gradually transition from only breast milk to only nonbreast-milk foods over a period of several years.

There are many different belief systems about which foods are safe for children and which are dangerous, which are preferred, which are extravagances, and which are forbidden for various reasons. Much of the nutritional anthropological literature is devoted to the topic of infant and young child feeding and addresses both the underlying cultural beliefs and practices that determine what and how much children eat, and what the consequences are for their subsequent growth and development, health, and survival. When children don't want to eat (anorexia), often due to gastrointestinal illnesses, their mothers may encourage or even force them to eat, or they may allow them to go for days or weeks without eating very much.

A Time to Wean

My own research on nonhuman primates, looking at a variety of life-history variables that correlate with age at weaning, predicts that a natural age of weaning for humans would range from 2.5 years to 7.0 years (Dettwyler 1995a). Some children may wean earlier on their own, while some will nurse longer if allowed. The World Health Organization (2003) and the American Academy of Family Physicians (2010) recommend *a minimum of two years of breastfeeding for all children*, with no upper limit. Likewise, the Koran enjoins Muslim mothers to breastfeed for *a minimum of two years*. The American Academy of Pediatrics (2005) recommends a minimum of one year, with no upper limit, and no adverse consequences regardless of how long children nurse. In cultures around the world, where children are allowed to nurse as long as they wish, most wean on their own between three years and five years of age.

Breastfeeding is influenced by a variety of cultural beliefs, some directly related to breastfeeding itself and others pertaining to a woman's role in society, to the proper relationship between mother and child and between mother and father, and even to beliefs about breasts themselves. For example, in a few Western cultures, many people believe that breastfeeding serves only a nutritional function, should only be done in private, and is only appropriate for young infants. Additionally, the unusual and relatively rare cultural belief that breasts are sexually charged casts a different light on the breastfeeding of children through toddlerhood and beyond. Together, these beliefs may make it difficult for women to carry out breastfeeding and weaning practices that are biologically normal for our species (Dettwyler 1995b).

Even in such discouraging Western cultural contexts, however, there are many women who breastfeed their children for three years or longer. Research carried out in the 1990s in the United States showed that, for women who nursed longer than three years, the average age of weaning was 4.2 years (Dettwyler 2004a). Similar results have been reported for mothers and children in Australia (Gribble 2008). Although today relatively few children worldwide are breastfed to seven years (the estimated upper limit for modern humans) *there is no evidence to suggest that there has been any genetic or evolutionary change in human physiology.* Weaning before the age of six or seven years is the result of direct and indirect cultural influences, including beliefs about how long is appropriate and the availability of more foods that young children can digest as a result of the discovery of fire/cooking and the domestication of plants and animals.

Consequences of Early Weaning or No Breastfeeding At All

Most often, when children are not breastfed, or are weaned early, artificial infant formula (based on cows' milk, soy, or corn) is used as a substitute for breast milk. Even when water supplies are clean and there is sufficient money to purchase formula, there are a number of adverse consequences that follow from early weaning, or from not breastfeeding at all. For the children, these adverse consequences include higher rates of death and disease, both in childhood and throughout life (including coronary heart disease and multiple sclerosis, which don't manifest until middle-age or later), and lower IQ scores due to less than optimal cognitive development. Breast milk provides important immunities and nutrients, especially for growing brains, as long as the child is breastfed. It is a source of physical and emotional comfort to a child, and for the mother, it is the wellspring of the important mothering hormones, prolactin and oxytocin.

Ordinarily, childbirth is followed immediately by breastfeeding, with its flood of prolactin, the mothering hormone, and oxytocin, the hormone of love and affiliation. Both hormones elicit caretaking, affectionate, and protective behaviors by the mother toward her child. Mothers who do not breastfeed have low levels of these hormones, as would be the case if the baby had died, because the death of the newborn infant is the only natural situation in which pregnancy and childbirth would not be followed by lactation/breastfeeding. Mothers who do not breastfeed have a higher risk of postpartum depression and greater difficulty dealing with the tasks involved in caring for a young infant and later a toddler. The formula-fed child will experience more illnesses and be fussier than a breast-fed baby, and the mother must cope with her cranky baby without the calming and nurturing influence of prolactin and oxytocin in her own bloodstream.

In addition to the effects on her mothering experience and her relationship with her child, the mother who doesn't breastfeed at all, or only for short periods, faces a higher risk of all reproductive cancers (breast, uterine, cervical, ovarian), as well as higher rates of osteoporosis later in life.

The Infant Feeding Transition

One way of thinking about cultural influences on breastfeeding initiation and duration is based on the model of the Demographic Transition, in which societies move from a pretransition stage of high birth and death rates, through a transitional stage of high birth but falling death rates (resulting in rapid population growth), and eventually into a posttransition stage of low birth and death rates.

Margaret Mead was the first to recognize an analogous Infant Feeding Transition (Raphael 1979). Every culture begins in a pretransition stage of almost everyone breastfeeding for several years and then moves through a transitional stage of bottle-feeding with artificial infant formula. Three main forces conspire to move women away from breastfeeding: (1) the separation of their productive labor and their reproductive labor, as societies shift from subsistence-based economies to wage labor-based economies, and/or women are taken away from both productive and reproductive work to be their husband's social partner; (2) increasing confidence in the power of science to provide "better living through chemistry," coupled with decreasing confidence in the ability of women's bodies to function normally; and (3) the rise of commercial interests intent on making a profit by convincing women that breastfeeding is less healthy, difficult, primitive, and/or shameful. This transition is initiated by women with more education and higher incomes, who turn to shorter and shorter durations of breastfeeding and eventually only wet-nursing (in previous centuries) or bottle-feeding with artificial infant formula from birth (in the twentieth and twenty-first centuries).

As time goes by, women with less education and lower income levels emulate their social superiors and adopt bottle-feeding as well. By the time the last of the lower classes have adopted bottle-feeding as being modern and scientific, the well-educated, upper-class women are returning to breastfeeding, first for short periods, and then for increasing durations. They have moved on to the posttransition phase. The return to breastfeeding by well-educated, upper-class women is fueled by several factors, including: (1) research documenting the negative consequences of formula use for maternal and child health and child cognitive development; (2) feminists' insistence that women's reproductive powers are of great value; and (3) a general backlash against the infant formula companies, particularly Nestlé, for promoting their products in unethical ways. In the United States, women have fought for legislation at state and federal levels to protect the rights of

women to breastfeed in public and for better maternity care and on-site child-care facilities.

There are still many pretransition cultures in the world, in which all women breastfeed each child for several years, but Western influence—particularly in the form of aggressive infant formula marketing strategies and the diffusion of Western cultural beliefs about breasts as sex objects—is affecting many regions of the world. Korea, for example, is in the early stages of the transition from universal long-term breastfeeding to the adoption of bottles. Survey data reveal a decline in breastfeeding incidence and duration from the 1960s to the 1990s, led by upper-class, well-educated urban Korean women (Ro and Dettwyler 1995). China, likewise, has begun the transition to bottle-feeding, experiencing a rapid decline in the prevalence of breastfeeding in urban and periurban areas. Not surprisingly, China has been specifically targeted by the infant formula companies as the next great market for their products.

Australia, Canada, and the United States represent societies farthest along in the Infant Feeding Transition, with women of higher incomes and more education initiating breastfeeding in great numbers, as high as 75–80 percent reporting breastfeeding at hospital discharge, and with increasing durations as well. In the United States and Australia, breastfeeding to the age of three years or beyond is becoming more common, as is breastfeeding siblings of different ages, known as **tandem nursing** (Dettwyler 2004b). In the last decades, the biggest leaps in initiating breastfeeding in the United States have been among clients of WIC (the federally funded Special Supplemental Nutrition Program for Women, Infants, and Children). These women tend to be poor and less well-educated. This trend reflects both a trickle-down effect of breastfeeding from the upper classes, as well as the success of WIC Peer Counselor training programs.

Exactly how a particular region responds to influences from Western industrialized nations and from multinational infant formula companies depends on many different social, political, and economic factors. This makes it difficult to predict how the infant feeding transition will look in a specific region, or how long the bottle-feeding stage will last (Simopoulos, Dutra de Oliveira, and Desai 1995).

As cultural beliefs and practices in densely populated areas of the world, such as India and China, move farther and farther away from the underlying physiological pattern of frequent nursing for a number of years, a rising proportion of health problems worldwide will be attributable to the use of artificial infant formula. Only a return to more natural breastfeeding patterns will halt this decline in health.

Other Cultural Beliefs about Breastfeeding

Among the Bambara of Mali (in the early 1980s), people believe that breast milk is made from a woman's blood. Just as a father is related to his children through the transfer of a white fluid, semen, so is a mother related to her children through the transfer of a white fluid, breast milk. Breastfeeding is the primary means by which a mother establishes a connection with her child—merely being pregnant and giving birth are not considered sufficient!

In Mali, the process of breastfeeding creates a special relationship between a child and the woman who breastfeeds that child, whether or not the woman is the child's biological mother. Likewise, breastfeeding creates a bond among all the children who nurse from the same woman, whether or not they are biological siblings. Having *milk-siblings* expands one's kinship network, providing more people one can call on for help in times of need. However, these kinship ties also prohibit marriage between the related children. In order to reduce the impact on potential marriage partners, women generally breastfeed other women's children only if they would already be excluded as marriage partners. Thus, a woman might wet-nurse the children of her co-wives, the children of her husband's brothers, or her grandchildren, while avoiding breastfeeding the child of her best friend, who she hopes will grow up to marry one of her own children. Similar beliefs about the *milk tie*, as it is known, are found among people in Haiti, Papua New Guinea, the Balkans, Burma (Myanmar), and the Badawin of Kuwait and Saudi Arabia.

In a wide variety of cultures, males are breastfed longer than females, sometimes much longer. These practices are supported by a variety of cultural beliefs, including the ideas that earlier weaning for girls ensures a much-desired earlier menopause (Taiwan), that boys must be nursed longer so they will be willing to take care of their aged parents (Ireland), and that breast milk is the conduit for *machismo*, something boys need, but girls do not (Ecuador). Additionally, a number of societies have noted that males are physiologically weaker than females, prone to more illnesses and earlier deaths, so mothers nurse their sons longer to help ensure their survival (Dettwyler 2004b).

Modern-Day Cuisines

One of the most fascinating subfields within nutritional anthropology is the anthropology of food, which focuses more on what and how people eat and the cultural meanings people ascribe to food, than on the nutritional and health consequences of different eating patterns.

North American Eating Patterns

In North America, a typical evening meal for many people consists of a relatively large portion of meat (usually beef, chicken, pork, or fish), accompanied by smaller portions of carbohydrates (potatoes, rice, pasta, or corn) and vegetables (green beans, peas, carrots, or green salad). Most people don't produce any of the food they eat, and many foods have been imported from other regions of the country or the world.

Meat from domestic animals is relatively cheap because it comes from intensively managed factory farms, known as concentrated or confined animal feeding operations (CAFOs). Likewise, industrial farming methods are used to produce most of the fruits, vegetables, and grains that make up the side dishes. With the decline of home gardening and cooking from scratch, much of the food we eat at home comes already processed—washed, chopped, cooked, and combined with other foods and spices. The invention of the microwave oven further revolutionized eating habits in North America, and now many people buy their meals already prepared and cooked. They just have to be reheated in the microwave and they are ready for consumption.

Carbohydrate-Based Cuisines

In contrast to this typical North American meal pattern featuring meat, in many regions of the world one or two carbohydrate staples provide the major source of calories at each meal. Whether people grow this staple themselves, or purchase it in the market, the carbohydrate staple is the center of the meal. Across Europe, wheat, barley, oats and potatoes are the major crops. In savannah regions of Africa, sorghum, millet, corn, rice, wheat, and teff are the major grain crops. In more tropical regions, root crops such as potatoes, manioc, yams, and cocoyams (taro) form the staple. In some regions of Africa, plantains are a major food source.

Rice is the most important carbohydrate staple in the world. Rice feeds more people around the world than any other single crop—more than half of the world's population (Sharma 2005). Three of the world's four most populous nations—China, India, and Indonesia, more than 2.5 billion people—rely on rice as their main food, and many people consider that they have "eaten" only if they have had a meal that included rice. Rice comes in different varieties and was domesticated independently at least twice, once in Southeast Asia, and once in West Africa. In South America, potatoes of many different kinds form the basis of the diet in the Andes, along with grain-like crops such as quinoa and amaranth. Guinea pigs and chickens supplement the Andean diet, and populations along the coast also have access to fish and other marine resources. In Central America, various combinations of rice, corn, beans, squash, and plantains form the basis of many cuisines. In the South Pacific, the processed pith of the sago palm tree, which grows wild, provides the carbohydrate staple wherever sago palms grow. Yams form the basis of the subsistence economy in other regions of the South Pacific, including New Guinea.

In northern Mali, the staple is millet, first pounded into flour in a large mortar with a wooden pestle and then cooked with water in a pot over an open fire to form a thick paste. The foods most comparable in taste and texture that might be familiar to North America readers would be thick Cream of Wheat or grits. Large portions of cooked millet, known as *toh*, are served with a sauce or gravy made from various vegetables, such as onions, tomatoes, okra, and squash; green leaves from domesticated or wild plants; spices; and occasionally fish paste (from smoked, dried fish) or small amounts of meat. In remote villages during the lean season, every meal of the day may consist of millet toh with a thin sauce made from the leaves of wild baobab trees. Across Mali, wherever peanuts are grown, they are ground to a fine paste and made into a tasty sauce.

In central Mali, the staples are likely to be millet or sorghum or rice. The farther south one travels, the more likely one is to find corn as the basis for toh, cooked in the same way—pounded into flour and cooked with liquid to form a thick paste, served with a sauce of vegetables and spices. In Guinea and Cameroon, in contrast, root crops such as yams or manioc are used as the carbohydrate basis for meals, and beans provide the protein missing in these staple crops.

Flavorings and Spices

Different cuisines have developed over time depending on the availability of local foods, including various flavorings and spices. Many plants used as flavorings are indigenous to tropical regions of the world, including cinnamon, nutmeg, cloves, and peppercorns. The "flavour principle," first developed by Elizabeth Rozin (1992), refers to the characteristic use of specific flavorings and spices, or combinations of flavorings and spices, in cuisines from around the world. For example, various Asian cuisines make frequent use of combinations of ginger root, garlic, soy sauce, rice wine, fermented fish sauce, brown sugar, sesame seeds, chili, and basil. Italian cuisines make frequent use of oregano, bay leaves, basil, rosemary, and thyme. Greek cuisine is distinguished by the use of olive oil, lemon, and oregano. Indian cuisines often feature the "C" spices: cumin, coriander, cardamom, cloves, cinnamon, and chili. Hundreds of varieties of chili peppers are grown all over the world and incorporated into many different cuisines. Onions and garlic are also staples of many cuisines. Every year since 1979, Gilroy, California, has been the site of the Gilroy Garlic Festival, where garlic, known as the scented pearl or the stinking rose, is celebrated for its contributions to the cuisines of the world (Blank 1980).

Opposite page: **People cook and eat a variety of foods around the world. Top: a family cooks steak and corn in the backyard for a summer barbecue, a woman in the American Southwest bakes bread in an outdoor oven called a** *horno,* **and a man with Down syndrome prepares goulash in a large kettle over an open fire in Hungary. Middle: a typical U.S. meal, heavy on the meat and potatoes; an Indian curry meal based on rice,** *naan* **(Indian bread), and vegetables in a sauce; and a plate of Japanese sushi. Bottom: an assortment of chili peppers; Turkish spices; and Indian spices, illustrating the** *flavour principle.*

Meal Frequency

Variation in how often people eat—how many times a day—serves as a perfect example of how *cultural beliefs can modify human behavior, but only within the limits set by our underlying physiology.* In North America, people typically eat three meals a day: breakfast, lunch, and dinner, although many skimp on breakfast, having only coffee, or skip breakfast altogether. Snacking between meals, often on different foods than those served at formal meals, is also common in many communities. In England and Ireland, the traditional pattern is to eat a full, cooked breakfast, including meat, followed by lunch, tea in the late afternoon, and dinner in mid-evening. The actual cup of tea is usually accompanied by some sort of biscuit, scone, or cake, or even small sandwiches. Throughout much of Europe, a leisurely and filling lunch may be the most substantial meal of the day, with a lighter meal in the evening.

In Mali, people typically eat breakfast, lunch, and a late dinner. Young children are also offered a fourth meal, in the late afternoon, and may be asleep by the time the evening meal is served. In many cultures, there are two meals a day, one in the morning before starting work, and one at the end of the day. In some regions of highland New Guinea, people eat only one substantial meal a day, in the late afternoon, after the day's work is completed. Nowhere do we find cultures where people routinely eat only every other day, or once a week—such patterns are not compatible with normal human activities and physiology.

Other Cultural Beliefs about Food

In addition to rules about what and how often to eat, there are many other cultural beliefs surrounding food. For example, in many regions, people use their left hand to wash themselves with water after going to the bathroom (they consider the use of dry toilet paper to be gross and disgusting). The left hand may also be used to blow one's nose. The right hand, therefore, is reserved for conveying food to the mouth, shaking hands, and giving and receiving items. Left-handed people must learn to eat with their right hands in these contexts!

Food may be conveyed to the mouth with the fingers or hands, or with utensils such as forks, knives, spoons, or chopsticks. One of the more distressing images found in any ethnographic film is that of an Inuit toddler placing a large chunk of meat in his

Army Specialist Stacy R. Mull, a 20-year-old Okemah, Oklahoma, native, and Creek Indian, kneads ingredients to make a Native American-style fried bread during a pow wow at Camp Taqaddum, Iraq, in 2004. The U.S. Army's 120th Engineer Combat Battalion, an Okmulgee, Oklahoma-based reserve unit then deployed in Iraq, held the event to promote cultural understanding of Native American heritage with other service members and to bring a piece of home to many of the Native Americans serving in Iraq. Nearly 20 percent of the 120th's soldiers are of Native American descent. Highlights of the festivities included storytelling, dancing, music, a class on pow wow etiquette, and the chance to sample traditional food.

mouth and then cutting off a bite right next to his lips, using a large, razor-sharp knife (Abrams and Bishop 1994). It is hard not to cringe when viewing this scene if you come from a cultural background where toddlers are presumed to be incapable of safely handling sharp knives.

There may be very specific techniques for eating with one's hands, depending on the culture and the nature of the food being consumed. In the United States, many foods are eaten with the hands or fingers, including sandwiches, hot dogs, chicken wings, and pizza, but using one's hands for spaghetti or ice cream would be considered inappropriate.

Meals may be eaten individually, with each person having his or her own plate and food, or they may be eaten communally, with people sitting around a large container of food and sharing with others. Even where sharing is the norm, there are rules about who eats what, how far one may reach into the bowl, and who gets the best morsels of scarce food items such as meat. In some cultures, males eat with other males, and females with other females; spouses do not eat together. Children may eat separately from their parents. In some circumstances, the males eat first, and the females eat whatever is left over.

Food taboos, often based on religious or health beliefs, affect what foods are not allowed to be eaten, either by certain individuals or groups, or by entire societies. Jewish dietary laws forbid the eating of any animals that are cloven-hoofed but do not chew their cud (thus no pork or camel meat), as well as animals that come from the ocean but do not have scales (thus no shrimp or lobster). Hindus are urged to abstain from eating any kind of meat. Members of the Church of Jesus Christ of Latter-day Saints (Mormons) aren't supposed to consume alcoholic or caffeinated beverages. Muslims usually don't eat pork or consume alcohol.

Some meat eaters abstain from eating red meat, allowing chicken, pork, and fish, but not beef or lamb, while others restrict themselves to fish. *Vegetarians* come in many varieties, including those who will eat animal-based foods that don't involve killing the animal, such as dairy products and eggs. Strict *vegans* don't eat any animal-based foods, not even Jell-O or candy corn, which contain gelatin made from cows' hooves, or Worcestershire Sauce, which contains anchovies (tiny fish).

Some food taboos may be related to kinship, such that people will not consume the flesh of their totemic animal. Others have their roots in other aspects of culture. Most people in the United States consider it inappropriate to eat any animal that is kept as a pet, whether in reference to entire species such as dogs, cats or horses, or to specific individual animals, such as a pet pig or goat. Many North Americans have no idea that guinea pigs were domesticated in South America for use as a conveniently sized package of animal protein for dinner.

A new movement gaining popularity around the world, and growing partly out of the Slow Food Movement of the 1980s and 1990s, is referred to as being a **locavore** (Kingsolver 2007b; Pollan 2008). Locavores try to eat only those foods grown within a certain distance from their house, and they shun imported foods that carry a high energy cost for transport. More and more people are growing their own vegetables in their backyards or in urban community gardens (Sustainable Urban Gardens 2007–2008). Some people also keep backyard chickens for eggs and meat, while others participate in Community Supported Agriculture (CSA), where individual subscribers pay in advance for a share of the produce grown on a local farm. Organic foods have become more important in industrial and postindustrial diets, as people become concerned about the health and environmental consequences of the use of herbicides, pesticides, and synthetic fertilizers.

Cooking Techniques and Fuel

Local cuisines are influenced by available cooking technologies and sources of fuel, and much of the world still relies on wood to fuel their cooking fires. In such places, grains are often pounded into flour first to reduce the amount of time, and therefore fuel, needed for cooking. Cutting meat and vegetables into small pieces before cooking likewise reduces fuel consumption. Wood fires must be constantly attended to maintain the proper temperature, so they require both lots of fuel and lots of time and attention.

Herders often live in environments where wood is scarce, but they make use of the dried dung of their animals to fuel their cooking and heating fires. Dung fires usually burn at lower temperatures than wood fires, so the food requires longer cooking. Charcoal is another source of cooking fuel. Charcoal is especially efficient for cooking small amounts of food or heating water for tea. Where fuel is plentiful and women have

In many cultures, most cooking is done outside, over an open fire, as shown in this 1916 photo of an Inupiat (Eskimo) kitchen in Nome, Alaska. The type and availability of fuel for cooking will determine, in part, what sorts of cooking techniques are feasible and whether foods are cooked whole, cut in small pieces, or ground into paste or flour before cooking.

many other tasks to attend to, slow cooking in a stew pot may work better, as the stove can be set on low and then ignored for hours, like a Crock-Pot or slow cooker in a North American kitchen.

Oven technology is not universal. Where ovens are found, leavened bread is often a staple of the diet. Ovens may be found in every home kitchen, or there may be a communal village oven where all the women take their dough to bake every morning. Where ovens are not available, grains may be pounded into flour, mixed with liquid to form dough or batter, and then cooked briefly on a flat surface or grill over an open fire or on an electric or gas-powered stove. Such un-leavened flatbreads include corn and wheat tortillas, *pita* (Circum-Mediterranean), *lavash* (Armenian), *piadina* (Italian), *piki* (Hopi), and *chapatti* (India), among many others.

Drinks

Anthropologists tend to pay much less attention to what people around the world drink than to what they eat, but water is also essential for life. Finding a drinking water supply that is both safe and adequate is not always easy. Where people live near streams, rivers, lakes, and springs, these may serve as sources of drinking water. In other areas, people dig wells to reach the water table, and then pull the water up using ropes and buckets, or pumps of various kinds. In areas where rainfall is plentiful, people may collect rainwater from their roofs and store it in rain barrels or cisterns.

Water must be imported from distant sources for large communities, not only for drinking, but also for washing, irrigating crops, manufacturing, sewage disposal, and other purposes. Some villages will have one central water pump, fountain, or stand pipe where everyone comes to get water. Having clean, running water in one's house—especially heated water—is a luxury for many people; those who are used to having it tend to take it for granted.

Contamination of drinking water is a serious health issue around the world, as people often bathe, wash dishes and clothes, and water their domestic animals in the same places they obtain their drinking water. Many diseases are easily transmitted from one person to another through contamination by animal and human waste. Even in cities with sophisticated water treatment and delivery systems, the water supply may contain lead, iron, *E. coli*, or other contaminants.

Although many people drink only plain water, a variety of other beverages have been developed as part of different cuisines and lifestyles. For example, coffee beans were first discovered and eaten in Ethiopia more than 1,000 years ago. Soon, traders from Arabia took the beans back home, further domesticated the plants, and figured out that roasting, grinding, and soaking them in boiling water produced a flavorful brew that gave people energy. Soon coffee spread to Turkey and thence around the Mediterranean and across the world. Public coffee houses sprang up as a place for people (mostly men) to gather and exchange news; play cards, dominoes, or chess; and discuss politics. Eventually, coffee plantations and export systems were developed, and coffee became an essential part of daily life for many people. Coffee's popularity in the United States is attributed, in part, to early protests against the British, who were, and indeed still are, known for their tea-drinking habits.

Teas of various sorts are also important beverages in many regions of the world. Tea is consumed, both at meals and at snack time (elevenses, High Tea) throughout the United Kingdom and the former British empire. The practice of drinking multiple cups of very strong, sweet tea is found in regions surrounding the Sahara desert and is attributed to Muslim influence. Like coffee drinking in Mediterranean coffee

Many cultures consume hot drinks based on tea leaves or ground coffee beans. The methods of preparation and cultural contexts vary greatly from one place to another. In Rajasthan, India, a woman prepares tea in her outdoor kitchen.

shops, tea drinking in some cultures is a social activity that is limited primarily to males. Visitors are always offered tea and friends gather early in the morning and late in the afternoon to share three cups of tea. In Mongolia, tea is mixed with butter and salt and consumed as a staple part of the diet for all people.

Carbonated, sweetened soft drinks (sodas or pop), such as the ubiquitous Coca-Cola, rose to prominence in the second half of the nineteenth century in the United States. Originally touted as a health drink, flavored water infused with carbon dioxide quickly gained a loyal following. During the twentieth century, consumption of soft drinks grew steadily, and many companies began exporting their products overseas. Today, Coke and other soft drinks can be found around the world, alongside regional variations such as nonalcoholic ginger beer, which is popular in East Africa and the Caribbean. The term **coca-colonization** is often used pejoratively to imply that American cultural values are taking over the world, to the detriment of the local culture and local products, through a process of economic colonization.

In addition to water, coffee, tea, and sweetened carbonated soft drinks, beverages containing alcohol are found in many cultures around the world. In 1986, Katz and Voight suggested that the first domestication of cereal grains in the Middle East some 10,000 years ago might have involved the growing of barley for the purpose of brewing beer. Local brewing traditions rely on a variety of carbohydrates as the base—whether potatoes, wheat, barley, or other grains. In some regions, palm wine is produced by tapping palm trees, much as maple syrup is obtained from maple trees.

Drinking alcoholic beverages is a part of many different cultural rituals and celebrations, as well as part of daily meals in some regions. As with coffee and tea, men may gather together and drink, apart from women, as a standard part of male socializing. In many instances of cultural conflict and forced assimilation, the people whose lands have been invaded and whose lifeways have been forcibly changed often resort to drinking alcohol as a means of coping. Additionally, people with chronic physical or emotional pain, or a variety of mental illnesses, may self-medicate with alcohol to reduce their symptoms. Chronic alcoholics may eventually succumb to liver disease or malnutrition.

The culture of binge drinking on American college campuses is especially troubling. Alcohol is an addictive and toxic depressant; used to excess, it can lead to death from acute alcohol poisoning merely by drinking too much, too fast, for the liver to process. As blood alcohol levels rise above .03, drinkers experience impaired alertness, judgment, coordination, and concentration. As levels climb toward .08 and beyond, the impairments worsen, inhibitions are lowered, and aggressive tendencies are increased.

Most deaths from alcohol in North America come from acute alcohol poisoning, from vomiting and then aspirating the vomit into the lungs, or from vehicle accidents. The Gordie Foundation (GORDIE 2010) tracks alcohol-related deaths of middle school, high school, and college students across the United States. They report more than 1,700 deaths each year of college students, many due to hazing rituals at college fraternities and sororities. Most often, friends of the victims think they have simply passed out and can be left alone safely to sleep it off. In reality, their blood alcohol content may have risen so high that it depresses breathing and the people die in their sleep.

The culture of binge drinking on college campuses has become a major health crisis in the United States. Many students believe that it isn't possible to have fun without becoming drunk and will drink before going to a party, or other activity, and then drink more once they get there. Students gain social status by recounting narratives of how drunk they were the night before, what ridiculous behaviors they engaged in, and how close they came to being arrested. Fraternity hazing rituals are particularly dangerous because they involve pressuring pledges to drink enormous amounts of alcohol in a very brief time in order to gain admittance to the fraternity. I'm sure that some readers of this text will recognize themselves or their friends in this description of campus alcohol abuse.

Problems of Malnutrition: Undernutrition

Despite the efforts of many people over many years to alleviate hunger through crop improvements, nutrition education programs, the amelioration of poverty, and emergency food aid, many people in the world still suffer from undernutrition. Undernutrition may be temporary, the result of a periodic drought, crop failure, or the disruption of food supplies during political turmoil. Or it may be seasonal, as among the Lese farmers of the Congo, who experience significant weight loss every year during the preharvest hunger season (Ellison 2001). In other cases, undernutrition is chronic, and people may never have quite enough to eat for optimal growth and development.

Protein-Energy Malnutrition (PEM)

Protein-energy malnutrition (PEM) is due to an overall lack of food, and is most common among children under the age of five years. With protein-energy malnutrition, the diet is lacking in both calories and protein. PEM can have both environmental and cultural causes, which often interact in complicated ways. Environmental causes may include poor soils for raising crops, chronic drought conditions that make it difficult to keep enough livestock alive to provide milk and meat, and many diseases and/or parasites that drain the body's resources. The main cultural cause is poverty, which itself has multiple complex political and economic bases.

Sometimes, the main issue for small children is that the dietary staple consists of a bulky carbohydrate that is filling but is neither calorie- nor nutrient-dense. Adults may be able to eat enough food to satisfy their needs, but young children, with smaller stomachs, physically may not be able to eat enough to meet their relatively greater needs for calories and protein to use for physical activity, disease fighting, and growth.

When I was conducting research among the Bambara of southern Mali in 1989, I was repeatedly told that young children didn't need much food, and they especially didn't need or deserve the better foods that were only occasionally available, such as meat or fresh fruit. Parents felt that as long as their children could eat their fill of the carbohydrate staple, it was appropriate to reserve the best-tasting foods for adults, especially the elderly. Both within and between a small group of rural villages in southern Mali, I found a negative correlation between the nutritional status of the mothers and the nutritional status of the children. In villages where the women were the plumpest, more of the children were undernourished, and families with the best-nourished adults had more severely undernourished children. People did not understand the distinction between quantity and quality of food. They had no idea that their children's poor health and slow growth was due to their cultural beliefs about food distribution—they knew only that their children were eating a lot of food and not going to bed hungry.

Chronic protein-energy malnutrition leads to growth faltering and stunting (being short for your age). PEM may manifest itself as early as six months of age, when children who have been exclusively breastfeeding or bottle-feeding are not supplemented with appropriate solid foods. Children with PEM appear skinny, with easily visible ribs, and knee and elbow joints larger than the limbs above and below them. They are often listless and quiet. Children who are undernourished may not have the energy for ordinary play activities, cannot contribute as much to the household economy, have greater difficulty dealing with disease, and don't do as well in school. The most severely undernourished will die before they reach the age of five years, but some individuals will survive for many years even though undernourished. Those who survive may exhibit delayed puberty. As adults, they will be unable to sustain heavy labor activities compared to their better-nourished peers and therefore may not be able to produce as much food or earn as much money.

Kwashiorkor

A very specific condition of malnutrition, known as **kwashiorkor,** develops when a child's diet has adequate, or more than adequate, calories but is severely deficient in protein. Kwashiorkor is seldom seen in children who are still breastfeeding, as the protein in breast milk is sufficient to prevent the condition. However, once a child has been weaned, if the dietary staple is very low in protein, symptoms of kwashiorkor may appear. The main symptom of kwashiorkor is edema (fluid retention) in the face, abdomen, hands, and feet. Children with kwashiorkor are very apathetic and often stop playing and talking. They may exhibit reddish hair and a flaky skin rash.

When the dietary staple is low in protein, or has no protein at all, the body begins to metabolize its own muscles in order to obtain the protein necessary for daily metabolic needs. The by-products of muscle protein metabolism then spill into the bloodstream and wreak havoc, leading to edema and other symptoms of kwashiorkor. Unlike PEM, a child cannot live for very long with kwashiorkor and usually succumbs quickly once the symptoms have become manifest.

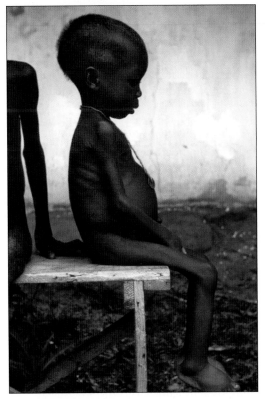

Undernutrition in children is usually due to a combination of different factors, including drought, poverty, illness, and political turmoil. Other factors include the nature of the food available for young children and cultural beliefs about who should decide what, when, and how much children eat. Top left: several young children share a common bowl of thin, carbohydrate-based gruel, without supervision by an adult—a recipe for undernutrition. Top right: a mother directly feeding her infant by placing food in his mouth. Bottom left: a severely malnourished child from the Nigerian-Biafran War of the 1960s. Bottom right: yet, there are many well-nourished healthy young children in Africa, contrary to Western stereotypes.

Since the child may be eating a lot of food, including high-calorie foods such as avocados and bananas, the parents seldom suspect a dietary cause for the child's illness. Kwashiorkor is found mostly in areas where the carbohydrate staples are entirely lacking in protein, such as parts of West Africa where manioc or white yams form the bulk of a young child's diet, or regions of the South Pacific where cocoyams (taro) hold the same position. Although not high in protein, diets based on corn, rice, millet, or sorghum usually are sufficient to prevent kwashiorkor. Even small amounts of additional protein from peanuts, fish, or insects can satisfy a young child's need for protein.

Specific Nutrient Deficiencies

In some situations, the diet is generally adequate, both in terms of calories and protein, but one or more specific nutrients may be missing. The most common nutrient deficiencies are iron deficiency, which can lead to anemia (especially in women); zinc deficiency, which can lead to delayed growth and puberty (especially in boys); iodine deficiency, which can lead to the development of goiters and endemic cretinism; Vitamin A deficiency, which can lead to an impaired immune system and impaired eyesight; Vitamin D deficiency, which can lead to rickets; and deficiency of folic acid (Vitamin B9), which can lead to birth defects in children and lower sperm counts in adult men. Hunter-gatherers usually eat a varied diet that is nutritionally balanced. Thus, specific nutrient deficiency diseases are more often found in horticultural populations relying on one staple crop.

Nutrition Intervention Programs

Numerous nutrition education and intervention programs have been developed to try to counteract local deficiencies in one or more nutrients and to improve the overall diet in populations whose calories, protein, or both, are insufficient. For example, programs to increase Vitamin A levels in the diet in Mali have ranged from distributing Vitamin A capsules to encouraging people to eat more liver and carrots, to finding mango trees that naturally produce fruit with higher-than-average levels of Vitamin A, and then distributing cuttings from these trees to villagers for planting.

Rural outreach programs are funded by many different governmental and nongovernmental organizations and may involve nutrition education, microloans to allow people to earn money to buy foods to supplement their diets, the introduction of new crops, or the modification of techniques for processing traditional crops to increase their nutrient value, such as the malting of grain. Many people trained in cultural and biological anthropology work as researchers and consultants for such programs through the World Health Organization, CARE, and other organizations.

Problems of Malnutrition: Overnutrition

Even as we make progress against undernutrition in many regions of the world, overnutrition is rapidly becoming a worldwide health problem. Overnutrition refers to eating more calories than one needs, or too much of specific nutrients such as saturated fats or sugar. Like undernutrition, overnutrition has multiple causes. In some cases, it is partly due to the overabundance of nutrient-dense foods and the relative inexpensiveness of food.

Thrifty Genotype Hypothesis

In the Environment of Evolutionary Adaptedness, or EEA, we assume that our hunter-gatherer ancestors were eating a wide variety of foods. Most of these foods would have been relatively low in fat, sugar, and salt, and food availability would have varied from abundance to scarcity. People who were inclined by their genetic predispositions to eat lots of fat, sugar, and salt, when available, or to be more efficient at processing and metabolizing their dietary intake, could store extra calories as fat. During lean times, they would have a survival advantage over their more slender counterparts who either did not take advantage of foods when they were abundant or were not efficient at storing extra calories as fat.

The **Thrifty Genotype Hypothesis,** originally proposed by James Neel in 1962, suggests that individuals in a population who were able to survive the lean times, through whatever means, were more likely to pass their thrifty genes on to future generations. As long as the food supply remained varied, low in fat, sugar, and salt, and hovered around the adequate level, they would thrive, and soon entire populations would exhibit this thrifty genotype as an adaptation.

Health problems arose only when these populations experienced a major cultural and dietary transition, usually after contact with Europeans. Access to an abundant diet based on less variety, but with higher levels of fat, sugar, and salt led first to obesity and then to obesity-related health problems such as diabetes and heart disease. Native populations of the South Pacific and the Pima Indians of Arizona represent two examples of this phenomenon. Among the Pima of Arizona, who eat a modern diet and have much lower levels of physical activities than their ancestors, diabetes rates reach 50 percent among adults, and 95 percent of adults with diabetes are overweight. In contrast, in a study of 35 adults from the genetically similar Pima Indians of Mexico, who eat a traditional diet and maintain high levels of physical activity, only three had diabetes, and the population was not overweight (National Diabetes Information Clearinghouse 2009).

Too Much Food, Not Enough Activity

Even in populations not exhibiting the Thrifty Genotype, obesity is becoming a major health threat. The overabundance of relatively inexpensive, nutrient-dense foods, the sheer variety of different foods available in some cultural contexts, and the decrease in physical activity that has accompanied life in postindustrial societies contribute to this epidemic of obesity. The increasing popularity of fast food, larger portion sizes in restaurant meals and at home, the decline in cooking from scratch, the high consumption levels of carbonated soft-drinks, and the higher cost of healthier foods likewise contribute to this crisis of overnutrition.

Reductions in activity levels have been especially rapid and severe in North America, where children seldom play outside, physical education programs in schools have been cut or eliminated, communities are structured so that cars are necessary to get from one place to another, and more and more people turn to electronic media for entertainment and recreation.

REPRODUCTIVE ANTHROPOLOGY

Reproductive anthropology encompasses a variety of issues including menstruation, pregnancy, childbirth, population structure (demography), and family planning (contraception). This is an active and grow-

ing focus of interest within both biological and cultural anthropology, and the following discussion touches only briefly on the main areas of research interest. Like medical and nutritional anthropology, reproductive anthropology is particularly concerned with the interaction between biological variables, which have been (and continue to be) shaped by evolutionary forces, and cultural beliefs and practices that modify the biological variables. I begin with a brief discussion of the evolutionary context of human reproduction, including both **fecundity** (ability to become pregnant) and **fertility** (number of children actually born).

Evolutionary Context

Although evolution proceeds through a variety of different forces, our main concern here is with natural selection. Under natural selection, any genetic factors that contribute to reproductive success, whether their influence is on anatomy, physiology, behavior, or some combination, will lead to there being more copies of these genetic factors in future generations. Given that humans are large-bodied, large-brained, slow-growing and slow-maturing primates, the underlying reproductive pattern seems to be: birth after a nine-month gestation; breastfeeding for five to six years; rapid brain and body growth for the first several years, with brain growth being mostly complete by the age of six years; slow, gradual growth during mid- and late childhood; and an adolescent growth spurt accompanied by sexual maturation around 15 years for females and a few years later for males, followed by the cessation of growth in the late teens.

For most females, the achievement of reproductive maturity is quickly followed by the first pregnancy; then several years of breastfeeding and lactational amenorrhea (suppression of ovulation and fecundity due to breastfeeding), with perhaps an interval of several months with menstrual cycles; then the onset of the next cycle of pregnancy, breastfeeding, and lactational amenorrhea. This pattern continues until the onset of menopause at around 45 years of age. Birth spacing is probably intended to be six to seven years in humans.

However, those women who manage to raise the most children to adulthood (defined as 15 years of age, in this context), will have the most copies of their genes in future generations. For most women, the only way to have more children is to reduce the birth-spacing through shortening the duration of breastfeeding and lactational amenorrhea. Two major cultural developments—first the discovery of how to control fire to cook food, and much later the domestication of plants and animals—contributed to the possibility of shortening birth intervals without increasing the mortality rates of the children who had already been born. Much later, cultural innovations such as sanitation systems for clean water and sewage disposal, immunizations, antibiotics, and the development of artificial infant formula have allowed some populations to drastically shorten breastfeeding or to dispense with it altogether (though not without cost in terms of mortality and morbidity). Under such conditions, birth spacing may be as short as 11 to 13 months.

Menstruation

The worldwide average age of menarche is around 15 years of age. Rates of growth in childhood and timing of sexual maturity depend on diet and health. Populations with excellent nutrition and good health will have earlier menarche and earlier attainment of adult height. In the United States, the average age of menarche is 12.6 years, a figure that has not changed since the 1960s. This probably represents the lowest average age for sexual maturity possible for humans as a species. Populations with substandard nutrition and poor health can have an average age of menarche as high as 18 or 19 years.

Different cultures celebrate, ignore, or denigrate menstruation and hold diverse beliefs about what it means, what effects it has on society and the individual, and how you should talk about and feel about it. In some cultural contexts, menarche is viewed as a significant milestone in a girl's life, as it marks the end of her childhood and the beginning of her life as a potential mother. There may be public feasts and rituals to celebrate the occasion, as Farrer describes for the Mescalero Apache (Farrer 2011). Where marriage takes place close to menarche, the first pregnancy usually follows quickly.

In other cultural contexts, menarche is not particularly noted or celebrated. It may be considered a taboo subject for discussion, and girls may start bleeding from their vaginas at puberty without understanding what is happening. Where sexual activity and marriage are postponed for many years after menarche, or where contraceptives are common, young women may experience many menstrual cycles before their first pregnancy—month after month after month after month after month, year after year after year after year after year!

In some places, menstruating women are considered powerful (typically in a negative way), and are viewed as a source of ritual and/or actual contamination. When ethnographers describe the women of a culture being confined to the menstrual hut during their menstrual periods, forbidden to work in the fields or to cook for their families, many Western readers think "how oppressive" or "how disruptive to everyday life." In reality, women in many societies rarely have a menstrual period. Between menarche and menopause, they are usually either pregnant or experiencing lactational amenorrhea and seldom have the opportunity to take a few days' rest from their chores and responsibilities, to relax and hang out with other women in the menstrual hut (Buckley and Gottlieb 1988; Strassman 1997). Attitudes among women about the rules and restrictions surrounding menstruation will vary both within and between cultures.

Pregnancy

As with all human endeavors, pregnancy is surrounded by multiple layers of cultural meanings and an amazing variety of rules and regulations that are intended to ensure a positive outcome. These range from special diets and modified activities for pregnant women to rituals meant to safeguard the mother and child. There are guidelines for how to decide if you are pregnant, how to tell if the baby is a boy or a girl, when you should announce the pregnancy to others, and whether, or for how long, you can continue with your daily activities. There are different beliefs about how one becomes pregnant—is it through sexual intercourse, or is the spirit world involved? If you have a nursing child when you become pregnant again, should that child be weaned? If so, what harm might befall the child if it nurses from a pregnant mother? What are the rules about sex during pregnancy? Is it forbidden or encouraged? What are the consequences for breaking any of these rules? If the child is born and has some type of atypicality such as albinism, cleft lip, or hydrocephaly, is this attributed to something the mother did or didn't do during the pregnancy?

Much depends on whether the pregnancy is considered legitimate—is the mother old enough? Is she married? Is her husband clearly also the father? Is it too soon after the marriage, or after the birth of the previous child? If the pregnancy has been long-awaited and is greeted with joy, there may be celebrations and extra precautions taken to ensure a healthy baby. If the pregnancy is unexpected and/or unwanted, there may be recriminations and punishments for both mother and father.

During the pregnancy, the mother may be under the care of a specialist, such as an obstetrician, a family-practice physician, a health care professional in a neighborhood clinic, a traditional midwife, or her own mother and other women who have given birth previously. Depending on the specific cultural context, it is possible that the mother may not feel the need for any special attention.

In Western biomedical contexts, the mother may not only have access to, but may also be encouraged or compelled to use, a wide array of diagnostic technology to confirm the pregnancy, predict the due date, test for sexually transmitted diseases, such as HIV, and assess the "health" of the fetus. If a problem with the fetus is detected, the mother may be urged to terminate the pregnancy (Rapp 2000).

Many women in North America follow a pattern of going to college and then working through their 20s and 30s, and then find they have difficulty getting pregnant. A variety of assisted reproductive technologies have been developed to help infecund couples have children, either with their own sperm and eggs or from donors. In addition, surrogate motherhood is also available as an option, where one woman provides the egg and another provides the womb. A number of reproductive anthropologists have explored the ever-changing cultural landscape of prenatal diagnosis and new reproductive technologies (Rapp 2000; Rothman 1986).

Childbirth

Evolution of Childbirth

Several anthropologists have focused their research efforts on understanding how the experience of childbirth in humans has been shaped by evolutionary and cultural forces. Wenda Trevathan and Karen Rosenberg have focused on evolutionary forces: because humans are bipedal (walk on two legs) instead of quadrupedal, our pelvises are shaped very differently from those of our closest relatives the quadrupedal chimpanzees, bonobos, and gorillas. Humans also have been selected for increased brain size, which we achieve by giving birth to large-brained babies, whose brains then grow more after birth than those of any other primate. The combination of a relatively small bony pelvis and a large-brained baby means that there is a very tight fit between the baby's head and the mother's pelvis. The baby must twist and turn as it passes through the birth canal and ends up emerging with the back of its head facing up. This makes it difficult, if not dangerous, for the mother to pull on the baby to help it emerge.

Trevathan and Rosenberg conclude that social birth—actively seeking out the company of helpers during labor and delivery—is an evolutionary adaptation among humans. In almost every culture, humans give birth with the assistance of others, or at least in their presence. This stands in contrast to the nonhuman primates, which, like most mammals, give birth alone, apart from the social group (Rosenberg and Trevathan 1995, 2003; Trevathan 1987).

Childbirth in Cross-Cultural Perspective

Building on the pioneering work of Brigitte Jordan and Margarita Kay, a number of anthropologists, most notably Robbie Davis-Floyd, have examined various aspects of childbirth in cross-cultural perspective (see Jordan and Davis-Floyd 1993; Kay 1982). As predicted by Trevathan and Rosenberg, births are often attended by other females, such as the woman's own mother, aunts, co-wives, and friends. Where traditional birth attendants such as midwives exist in a culture, they may be called to the woman's house to help with the delivery, or the woman may travel to the midwife before the birth. In most cultures, men are not allowed to view childbirth and don't participate in any way.

In Minnesota, two public health nurses decided to show a group of Nuer female refugees, recent immigrants to the United States, an educational video about U.S. hospital birth:

Suddenly in the video a man appeared sitting on the bed of the woman in labor. "Who was this man?" they wondered, and when they realized that it was not a male doctor, but rather the woman's husband, the women exploded—some in uncontrollable laughter, others in horrified screams! Nuer men do not attend childbirth, and the very idea was alien and shocking to the women. [Later in the video] He leaned over his laboring wife, rubbed her head, and gave her a gentle kiss. With this, the women exploded even more uncontrollably than before, in laughter and in screams. One woman, eight months pregnant, leaped up, screaming; she ran out of the apartment, down two flights of stairs, out of the building, and began running down the street! . . . If childbirth is increasingly seen in American culture as the ultimate moment of togetherness for a couple, to the Nuer it is the quintessential context for the separation of male and female spheres. (Holtzman 2008:82–83)

Who is allowed to be present in the immediate vicinity when a woman is in labor and delivering her baby is more than just a curious example of differing cultural beliefs and practices. Like all placental mammals, humans in labor experience a slowing down of contractions and delayed labor when they are emotionally or cognitively stressed. The presence of multiple strangers in the delivery room is the norm for North American hospital births—the doctor, who may or may not be known to the woman, the labor nurses on duty, medical students, orderlies, and so on. If the woman is stressed by being surrounded by strangers, and not in control of her own body and actions, this may lead to delayed labor, which often leads to more interventions.

Criticisms of Industrial Childbirth

From the Western biomedical perspective, birth is thought to be difficult and dangerous, and it is assumed that many women are unlikely to be successful without multiple medical interventions. Especially in North America, fear of the pain of childbirth leads many women to request epidural anesthesia and/or analgesics, even though these procedures have many adverse side-effects on both mother and baby. Rates of Cesarean-section (surgically removing the baby from the mother's uterus) have risen drastically in North America in the last few decades for many reasons, few of which have anything to do with improved outcomes for mother or baby.

Much of the rich anthropological literature on childbirth is critical of the high-technology-based approach to birth that has developed in North America (cf. Davis-Floyd 1992; Davis-Floyd and Sargent 1997; Davis-Floyd et al. 2009). Many sophisticated technologies have been shown to have no effect on improving the outcome of labor and delivery in terms of healthy

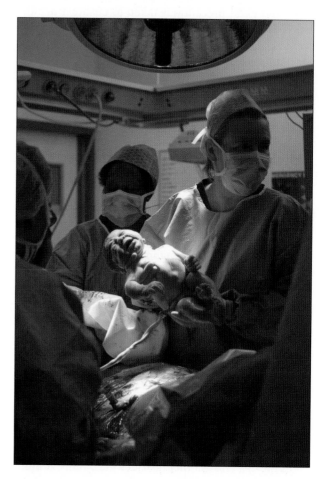

Research has repeatedly shown that the best outcomes for both mothers and babies (in terms of survival and health) result from maternity care systems where most babies are born at home or in birthing centers with assistance from a knowledgeable midwife, where mothers and babies are kept together after birth, and where only high-risk pregnancies take place in hospitals under a doctor's control. Typical industrial childbirth interventions such as epidurals, episiotomies, electronic fetal monitoring, and Caesarian sections cause more harm than good for mothers and babies.

mothers and babies. The countries with the best records in that regard are those where midwives handle all of the normal pregnancies and babies are delivered at home or in birthing centers and where physicians and hospital birth are only involved in high-risk labor and deliveries.

Postpartum Practices

The most significant aspects of the postpartum period, from a cultural perspective, are the differing beliefs and practices that guide what the mother and baby may or may not do, and for how long, following the birth. In cultures that employ the hot-cold theory of health—where some conditions are considered one temperature and the treatment involves the opposite or balancing temperature—childbirth is considered cold, thus mothers are kept warm after birth. They may stay close to the fire and drink hot tea or consume hot soup prepared by a special recipe. There may be different ideas about how long the mother should rest before resuming her usual workload, ranging all the way from the few days typical for the Bambara of Mali, to the very generous one-year maternity leaves provided in most Western European countries and by some Canadian employers.

There are different ideas about what should be done with the placenta. In many species of mammals, including strepsirhine primates and monkeys, the mother eats the placenta, a practice known as **placentophagy.** According to Wenda Trevathan:

> The pattern is more variable in the pongids [Great Apes]: only about one-half of the gorilla and chimpanzee births observed have been followed by consumption of the placenta. This may relate to a suggested function of placentophagy: avoidance of detection by predators. The smaller, more vulnerable species routinely consume the placenta and all fluids associated with birth, while the two least-preyed upon primates species are as likely not to consume the placenta as they are to do so. (1987:104–105)

Most humans live in cultures that have specific prohibitions against placentophagy, and it is not a routine part of postpartum behavior in any human society. Trevathan, citing Janszen, writes:

> An exception to this practice of not consuming the placenta can be seen among some contemporary home-birth populations in the United States. Janszen (1980) estimates that placentophagy accompanies 1–2% of home births in the eastern United States and about 5% of those along the West Coast, especially California. She concludes that the practice is part of the "back to nature" movement and is founded, to some extent, on *the belief that placenta consumption is common in other cultures* and is part of the human heritage. (Trevathan 1987:106, emphasis added)

Here we have a curious example of one group of humans basing their beliefs and behaviors on erroneous ideas about the beliefs and behaviors of other groups of humans!

In many Western contexts, the placenta is usually ignored or treated as offensive medical waste and incinerated by the hospital. But in most human cultures, the placenta and umbilical cord are treated as significant objects that should be treated with respect and disposed of in culturally appropriate ways. For example, among the Hmong of Laos, where babies were traditionally born at home, the placenta would be buried under the floor inside the house. That way, after the person died, his or her spirit could return to the house, retrieve the placenta, and wear it like a jacket for protection on its trip through the spirit world (Fadiman 1997).

Cultures have different rules about separation of the mother and infant. In some cultural contexts, mother and baby are secluded for a week, a month, or more, away from the general population, but together as a pair. This allows the mother time to rest and an opportunity to bond with the baby and establish breastfeeding, and also serves to reduce the newborn's exposure to germs from visitors.

A typical U.S. hospital birth involves some separation, as the baby is typically taken away right after birth to be washed, examined, weighed, have its footprints recorded, have blood drawn for tests, and other procedures. Research on mother–baby separation has shown that these practices have negative consequences for the baby, delay or impair maternal–child bonding, and make breastfeeding more difficult. Newer, evidence-based practices are gradually taking hold in North American hospitals. These include placing the baby on the mother's abdomen for skin-to-skin contact, allowing the baby time to find the breast and begin breastfeeding on its own, and postponing other procedures such as bathing and blood-draws until breastfeeding is well-established. The Baby-Friendly

Hospital Initiative (World Health Organization 2009) and the Mother-Friendly Childbirth Initiative (Coalition for Improving Maternity Services 1996) are two social change movements aimed at improving maternity and postpartum care.

A significant amount of international public health research has focused on improving maternity care to women in remote, rural locations around the world through training programs for traditional midwives. Emphasis is placed on retaining traditional midwifery knowledge, such as the ability to turn a poorly positioned baby in the womb (external version) and the ability to monitor the baby's heart rate using just one's ear or a simple stethoscope (instead of a fetal heart monitor). At the same time, traditional midwives are taught how to assess complicated or obstructed labors, so that women can be transported to a nearby clinic or hospital in a timely manner. Lack of transportation or nearby medical facilities continue to be serious problems in some areas.

Postpartum Sex Taboos

In many, if not all, cultures, there are specific rules about how long a woman should wait following the birth of a child before she resumes sexual intercourse. These are referred to as **postpartum sex taboos.** Typically, women in North America are told to wait for six weeks, and for the permission of their physician, before resuming sexual relations. The six-week rule is based on the notion that it takes that long for the woman's vagina to physically recover from the wear and tear of childbirth.

In other contexts, postpartum sex taboos are geared more toward spacing pregnancies apart, and the postpartum sex taboo may last until the current baby is walking or talking well, is completely weaned, or reaches some predetermined chronological age. Among the Bambara of Mali, people say that a toddler should not continue to breastfeed once its mother has become pregnant again. Preferably, this doesn't happen until the older child has been weaned, around two years of age. If the mother does become pregnant while still nursing a toddler, women say the breast milk will make the child sick. Thus, as soon as a new pregnancy has been confirmed, the toddler is weaned. In contrast, among the Dani of highland New Guinea, Heider reports that children breastfeed for about two

years on average, but the postpartum sex taboo lasts for five years (Heider 1976).

The combination of postpartum lactational amenorrhea and postpartum sex taboos—both of which may last for several years—functions to space births out among most human populations. In addition to these mechanisms, many societies employ a variety of contraceptive practices to regulate childbearing.

Patterns of Fertility and Child Spacing

How many children a woman has, and the timing of those births, depend on many biological and cultural factors. The biological factors—menarche, menopause, gestation, and lactational amenorrhea—were discussed in chapter 3. Cultural factors include both direct and indirect influences and vary depending on many other aspects of the physical and cultural environment. *Fecundity* is the term that refers to a woman's ability to become pregnant. Women are infecund before menarche and after menopause, during pregnancy, and for much of the period of lactational amenorrhea. Women can also be infecund because of nutritional status, disease, and mechanical blockages or surgical procedures. *Fertility* refers to the number of children a woman actually gives birth to, and **reproductive success** refers to the number of children who survive to adulthood.

Fertility and Child Spacing in the Environment of Evolutionary Adaptedness

The presumed original pattern of reproduction for humans during the EEA was one in which cultural means of contraception were rudimentary, and lactational amenorrhea was the primary means of spacing children. Where children were nursed intensively for five to six years, that meant a typical birth spacing of six to seven years, and a total of five children per woman. This fits well with the comparative nonhuman primate data. However, the development of fire and the domestication of plants and animals both contributed to an ability to keep children alive while shortening the birth spacing through reducing the intensity and duration of breastfeeding and introducing solids earlier and in greater quantities. As human nutritional status improved overall, women found themselves getting pregnant again sooner than they perhaps desired, and a variety of techniques were developed to enable women to postpone pregnancy, to terminate an unwanted pregnancy, or to avoid pregnancy altogether. Changing cultural attitudes toward the value of children also play an important role in shaping fertility patterns.

The Demographic Transition

Like the Infant Feeding Transition discussed earlier, the concept of a demographic transition is a *heuristic device* that helps us understand changing patterns of fertility. In the first stage, before the transition, populations are characterized as having natural fertility levels, meaning that people are not making conscious decisions to limit the number of children or manage the timing of births. Typically, birth rates are high, limited primarily by lactational amenorrhea and postpartum sex taboos. Infant and childhood mortality levels are also high, resulting in relatively stable population size, or very slow growth. During the transitional period, infant and child mortality rates fall due to cultural innovations, but people continue to have as many children as they can, resulting in very rapid population growth. Gradually, as people come to believe that more or most of their children will survive, they begin to voluntarily reduce the number of pregnancies and births through the use of various forms of contraception. In posttransition populations, both the birth rate and the infant and child mortality rates are very low, resulting once again in relatively stable population size, very slow growth, or very slow decline.

Another way to think about fertility is to compare reproductive patterns across different subsistence strategies. As long as we keep in mind that *cultural patterns vary over space and time, and that any generalizations we make are just that—generalizations, as well as simplifications*—this can be a useful exercise. Also keep in mind that from an evolutionary standpoint, those humans who have the most offspring surviving to adulthood get the most copies of their genes into subsequent generations, so there continues to be natural selection in favor of behaviors that result in having many surviving children.

Fertility and Child Spacing in Traditional Foraging Societies

Among hunters and gatherers, fertility levels and infant and child mortality rates all fall in the moderate range. Hunter-gatherer women typically have relatively late menarche and early menopause. They breastfeed their children often, both day and night, and experience several years of lactational amenorrhea with each child, resulting in typical birth intervals of four years. They may experience some stretches of infecundity or subfecundity due to negative energy balance (taking in less energy than they expend) as a result of their low-fat diets and high energy expenditures.

Studies of the Kalahari *Ju|'hoansi* of Botswana and Namibia reveal a cultural ideal of unassisted birth as a test of a woman's physical and spiritual courage (Biesele 1997). Among the *Ju|'hoansi*, women average four or five live births over their reproductive careers and usually have several children who survive to adulthood.

In foraging populations, direct means of contraception to limit the number of children or increase the birth interval include rules concerning postpartum abstinence, induced abortion, and infanticide. Rarely do people feel the need to try to increase the number of pregnancies or reduce the birth interval through cultural interventions. Children are usually viewed as valuable and important in their own right, and a source of joy and entertainment.

Fertility and Child Spacing in Pastoral, Horticultural, and Agricultural Societies

Many populations following these modes of subsistence experience relatively high fertility levels as well as relatively high levels of infant and child mortality. Children are highly valued for several reasons. As among foragers, children are appreciated and loved for themselves. In patrilineal societies, the number of children a man has, especially the number of sons, contributes to his social status, his wealth, and his importance among his peers. Children also make significant contributions to the workforce, with children as young as three or four years beginning to help with domestic chores, leading calves to pasture, watching pigs as they forage, caring for younger siblings, and so forth. Thus, children become net resource providers to the family very early on, rather than being only consumers of their parents' time, energy, and resources. In old age, parents rely on their children to help take care of them when they become incapable of providing for themselves due to age and/or infirmity.

Although children are very highly valued—a perspective known as **pronatalism**—people also lose many children to combinations of malnutrition and disease. Thus, women want to give birth to many children, in order to ensure that enough survive to provide status, help with the work, and help in old age. As diet and health improve, and infant and childhood mortality levels decline, women may be more interested in limiting the total number of children they have or in spacing their births farther apart.

All of the same factors affect fecundity in these populations as in foraging populations—timing of menarche and menopause, lactational amenorrhea, and infecundity or subfecundity due to negative energy balance. Breastfeeding patterns may change to become less frequent, and the availability of a wider range of solid foods for infants and better nutritional status for mothers may all contribute to shorter durations of lactational amenorrhea. Postpartum sex taboos may begin to break down, especially in parts of the world where Islamic and Western cultural beliefs—that a 40-day postpartum abstinence is sufficient—have replaced earlier traditions of waiting until the child could walk or talk or was completely weaned. Induced abortion and infanticide continue to affect fertility rates. Birth spacing may be quite short, on the order of two to three years, but most people realize that as birth intervals decrease, infant mortality levels increase.

Where bearing and raising children are considered the main purposes of a woman's life, being infertile is a calamity. People may resort to medical or ritual means to increase fertility, including limiting the duration of breastfeeding. Among the Bambara of Mali, if a child was healthy and thriving, he might be weaned early, before the cultural ideal of two years, in order for the mother to become pregnant again sooner. During my fieldwork, many women encouraged me to wean my daughter Miranda, once she was older than two years, in order to hurry up and have a son for my husband. On the other hand, one mother in my research study had given birth to nine children, all of whom had survived, and she was not interested in having any more. She convinced her brother to pose as her husband and go with her to the pharmacy to get birth control pills. She then convinced her husband that she had gone through menopause and encouraged him to marry a younger wife (which he did), since he still wanted more children. Although no one would talk about it openly, it was rumored that herbalists in the market sold concoctions that could be used to induce abortions for unwanted pregnancies.

Fertility and Child Spacing in Industrial and Postindustrial Societies

A number of factors contribute to posttransition patterns of relatively low fertility and low infant and child mortality. Improvements in access to clean water, modern sewage systems, immunizations against childhood diseases, and antibiotics all reduce the levels of morbidity and mortality among infants and young children. Gradually, people begin to accept that most, if not all, of their children will survive to adulthood, so it isn't necessary to have quite as many. The introduction of formal educational systems and cultural notions of *childhood*—as a time of life that is relatively stress-free and devoted to school—act to reduce the value of children as part of the family workforce. As productive labor becomes distinct from domestic and reproductive work, paid labor in an industrial economy is often structured to make it incompatible with child care. Thus, as women enter the workforce in record numbers, and their value as wage earners becomes more important, their ability to produce and raise children is correspondingly devalued.

Where childbearing and rearing is considered incompatible with productive labor, women who want more than one child may decide to have them close together in age. Overlapping the children's most intensive times of need, birth to three years, serves to limit the number of years the mother must devote to the care of young children. Some women cite the desire that their children be playmates and companions, while others cite the need to concentrate their time out of their careers into as few years as possible as their reasoning behind short birth intervals. Others are concerned that they have waited too long to begin reproducing and must hurry up and give birth before their fecundity declines or they get too old. Very close birth spacing means, however, that each child gets much less individual time and attention than they need and increases sibling rivalry. It also means that breastfeeding must be curtailed in order to shorten lactational amenorrhea.

In industrial and postindustrial economies, marriage may be postponed until several to many years after menarche, and childbearing postponed even after marriage until the woman has completed her education, accomplished specific career or life goals, or accumulated the resources thought to be necessary before beginning to reproduce. Some women wait so long to begin childbearing that when they finally begin to try, they discover that their fecundity has declined and they can't get pregnant. They may resort to various assisted reproductive technologies such as chemically induced ovulation, *in vitro* fertilization, donor sperm or eggs, or even surrogate mothers. Some people choose to adopt, either nationally or internationally, especially from countries where many female children are available in orphanages because of local cultural devaluation of girls and women.

In industrial and postindustrial economies, children become more expensive to raise, as they no longer contribute much, if anything, to the household economy, and they may come to be seen as burdens. Additionally, as the general society becomes less and less tolerant of children (**antinatalist**), it becomes more acceptable to contract out the work of motherhood to others in the form of day-care providers and nannies. It becomes even more acceptable for women to have only one or two children or to be childless by choice. Women who have, or express a desire to have, large families may be viewed as irresponsible. Ironically, at the same time as small families or being childless becomes the norm, a few families in the upper socioeconomic strata in the United States are returning to the view that children represent status, and that if you can afford them, the more the merrier.

The decline of breastfeeding in many Western populations during the first half of the twentieth century, combined with the shortening of postpartum sex taboos to 40 days, contributed to the need for alternative forms of birth control. A variety of contraceptive methods have been developed including temporary ones (birth control pills, condoms, transdermal patches, injections, intrauterine devices, diaphragms, spermicidal sponges, and so on) and permanent ones (tubal ligations and vasectomies). These have given women unprecedented control over whether they become pregnant and have made it possible, not only to postpone childbearing, but also to choose birth intervals at will and cease reproducing whenever they want to.

At the same time, there are still many unplanned and unwanted pregnancies, and abortions become an alternative, postconception form of birth control. Likewise, as prenatal diagnostic technologies develop, many women choose to carry to term only those pregnancies that pass quality control assessments. Thus, in some countries, fewer female children are born, and many children with genetic or developmental disabilities are aborted. It is now possible to screen for genetic conditions either before *in vitro* fertilization or following *in vitro* fertilization but prior to implantation of an embryo, thus reducing the need for prenatal diagnosis and abortion.

Where pronatalist religious ideologies coincide with the availability of clean water, modern sewage systems, infant formula, immunizations, and antibiotics, women may be able to forego breastfeeding and lactation amenorrhea altogether, while still keeping most or all of their children alive. This results in extremely short birth intervals of only one to two years, and very large families. The Hutterites of North America are reported to have the highest completed fertility rates, with each woman having 12–16 children, and most or all of them surviving. Mennonites, Amish, Mormons, and Catholics have similar fertility profiles wherever formula is embraced and contraception avoided. One extreme example of this approach would be the Duggar family of Arkansas. Their first child was born in 1988. In 2009, 21 years later, Mrs. Duggar gave birth to her nineteenth child (she had two sets of twins along the way). Such a fertility pattern is only possible where a mother does not breastfeed her children and rejects the more common cultural attitude that children are not of particular value.

Some European countries have become concerned about their population's declining fertility, sometimes below replacement levels (fewer than two children being born, on average, for each adult woman). Concerns arise about whether smaller future generations will be able to support an aging population of Baby Boomers (those born between 1946 and 1964), and whether local native populations will be swamped by the children of immigrants from other parts of the world. A number of European countries, including Ireland, Germany, and Austria, have established various government subsidies intended to encourage people to have more children, including excellent maternity leave, monthly payments for each child, and subsidized or completely free child care and kindergarten.

Key Concepts Review

Medical, nutritional, and reproductive anthropology combine biological and cultural anthropology; they represent three of the most rapidly growing research areas in the discipline.

The health status of an individual or a population is a result of many complex interactions between the physical environment, the biological environment, genetic factors, and cultural factors.

We can divide the "equation of human health and medical care" into ultimate causes, proximate causes, the natural coping mechanisms of the body, and the cultural coping mechanisms of the individual and/or group.

Western Biomedicine tends to focus on proximate causes, with therapies aimed at counteracting the proximate causes; *Traditional Medicine* tends to focus on ultimate causes, with therapies aimed at strengthening the natural coping mechanisms of the body.

All societies have a variety of different approaches for preventing health problems and for treating injuries, illnesses, and many assorted conditions that impact health.

Healing specialists include herbalists/pharmacists, bone-setters/orthopedists, physical therapists, and shamans; popular conceptions of *witch doctors* are inaccurate and misleading.

Typical life-span and *life expectancy* are two different concepts; the typical life-span for all humans is approximately 60–65 years without access to modern medical care; populations with short life expectancies are those in which many infants and young children die.

Primates are generally omnivores; eating a wide variety of foods helps prevent nutritional deficiencies.

Women's breasts produce breast milk for children, which keeps children healthy, as well as providing the appropriate nutrition needed for normal brain growth and immune system development.

Physiological breastfeeding includes nursing several times an hour, including at night, to establish an adequate milk supply in the first four months.

Solid foods are usually added to the diet around six months of age, and breastfeeding can continue for many years; the physiological norm for weaning in humans is between 2.5 years and 7.0 years.

Artificial infant formula is harmful to children throughout the world, including North America, resulting in higher rates of illness and death throughout life, impaired cognitive development, and impaired immune system development.

A mother who doesn't breastfeed will have a different relationship with her child than if she had breastfed, and she has a higher risk of reproductive cancers and osteoporosis later in life due to not breastfeeding.

The *anthropology of food* examines the cultural dimensions of food and mealtimes; cultures vary with respect to what foods people eat, how often they eat, and how meals are structured.

Rice and other cereal grain crops provide the staple food in most cuisines, modified by local traditional combinations of flavorings and spices.

Finding adequate supplies of safe drinking water is a critical issue facing the world today.

Problems of under- and overnutrition affect many populations.

Reproductive anthropologists study patterns of fecundity and fertility, as well as the cultural meanings assigned to menstruation, pregnancy, childbirth, and child rearing.

Many anthropologists are critical of the high levels of medical interventions used in childbirth in North American hospitals, because such interventions seldom improve mother–infant outcomes and often interfere with bonding and breastfeeding.

Physiological child spacing for humans would be six to seven years, with each child being breastfeed for sev-eral to many years and therefore not needing to share the resources of parents with other young siblings.

Populations have used a variety of cultural resources to affect reproduction, including late marriage, postpartum sex taboos, lactational amenorrhea, contraception, abortion, and infanticide.

The value of children to a society depends on its subsistence mode and other factors, but natural selection will always favor those individuals who have the most surviving children.

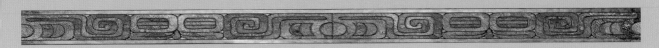

Father's brother's daughter's son.

5

ORGANIZING PEOPLE INTO GROUPS

Kinship, Descent, & Common Interest

*Kinship groupings are based on a variety of relationships—
who you are descended from, who is descended from you,
who you share common ancestors with, who you are married to,
as well as other ties of biological, legal, and fictive kinship. By choosing
which elements of such relationships to emphasize, and which
to downplay or ignore altogether, people create a limited number
of complex but adaptable systems of social organization.*

All populations need to find a relatively efficient way to organize people into different groups for a variety of purposes. Cultural rules about marriage, kinship, and descent—how individuals are related to one another biologically and legally, at one point in time, and from generation to generation—can be used to create sophisticated systems of social organization. As the population grows larger, and people interact on a daily or weekly basis with others to whom they are *not* related, other bases of organization are needed in addition to kinship. Many groups are created based on the common interests of the members or on chronological or developmental age.

This chapter begins by exploring some of the cultural variation surrounding marriage, kinship, and descent and discusses the nature of the groups created by these rules. Next, is a look at the functions of such groups—the tasks they can accomplish—while comparing kinship-based social organization to common-interest-based social organization, which can be used to accomplish the same tasks among larger populations. The last section of the chapter explores how different cultures define and use chronological or developmental age as yet another way to organize people.

MARRIAGE

Kinship and descent represent aspects of a continuous cycle of formation and the growth of families from one generation to the next. I start by describing the basic cultural rules that govern the beginning of a new family—rules about marriage.

Defining Marriage

Developing a definition of marriage that works across many different cultural contexts is more difficult than one might think. From the cross-cultural perspective, marriage is not always limited to two people, and even when it is, the two people are not necessarily of opposite sex. Yet there are many aspects of the structure and function of marriage that are similar across cultures, and with one possible exception (the Mosuo of China), some form of marriage is a cross-cultural universal. What sorts of things does marriage, as an institution, have in common across all cultures?

Marriages Are Formal Unions

First, marriages are publicly sanctioned and recognized unions between two or more people. The marriage ceremony may be civil or religious or both, but in all cases, other members of the society recognize the links between the parties as being legitimate and as having economic, political, legal, social, and even

Weddings are publicly sanctioned and recognized unions. For the official religious or civil ceremonies that change their legal status, people may wear special clothes, perform rituals, and celebrate with friends and family members, often with food, drink, music, and dance. These images show weddings in Senegal, West Africa; India; and the U.S.

medical consequences. We can describe legal marriage as being a formal institution, in contrast to informal relationships, such as unmarried cohabitation.

Marriage Affects the Status of Children

Second, marriages form a context in which children are given social legitimacy as being products of the marriage. This may be important for reasons of personal identity, class, status, inheritance, lineage membership, and so on. The desire to produce children, and to have those children clearly identified as legitimate members of a family and society, drives much of the structure of marriage across cultures.

Marriage Entails Rights and Responsibilities

Third, marriage establishes certain rights and responsibilities between the husband and wife, between the couple and their children, between their extended families, and between the couple and the state. Formal marriage gives each partner certain rights, such as the right to sex (usually exclusive) with the other party to the marriage, the right to share in the fruits of the other's labor, and the right to have children together who will be recognized as products of the marriage and legitimate members of the society. Formal marriage also establishes certain rights for the couple with respect to local, state, and federal laws and regulations.

Typically, society expects the wife to provide various types of labor for the household that is created by the marriage, including domestic labor, productive labor, and reproductive labor. Domestic labor refers to such activities as cleaning the house; hauling water; gathering and chopping firewood; processing and cooking food; washing dishes; making, repairing, and washing clothes; and keeping the household running on a daily basis. Productive labor refers to the woman's contribution to the food supply or other economic re-sources of the family, including gathering food; plant-ing, tending, and harvesting crops; tending livestock; producing goods to sell; or working at a job outside the home. Reproductive labor refers to all the work in-volved in reproduction, from being pregnant and car-rying children to term, to giving birth, breastfeeding, and providing most, if not all, of the child care.

Typically, society expects the husband to provide various types of labor for the household as well. He usually doesn't have as many domestic labor responsi-bilities but may be expected to build or provide the house and carry out necessary repairs. His main contri-bution will be in the realm of productive labor, contrib-uting to the food supply or other economic resources of the family, including hunting; gathering; breaking new ground for gardens; planting, tending, and harvesting crops; herding animals; producing goods to sell; or working at a job outside the home to provide funds for household expenses. Reproductive labor for men in-volves providing the sperm, at a minimum. Fathers' or maternal uncles' contributions to child care vary dra-matically from one culture to another, and even from one family to another, and may change over time. Adult males may be expected to entertain babies, care for toddlers, provide discipline and training for older children, and provide the financial resources necessary for housing, clothing, and education. Barry Hewlett's work on fatherhood across cultures documents the wide array of contributions that fathers and maternal uncles make to the reproductive labor involved in rais-ing the next generation (Hewlett 1992, 1993).

Marriage establishes certain rights and responsi-bilities between the couple and any children they may have (whether by birth or adoption). These may be in-formal cultural beliefs and practices, or they may be codified into law. The type of descent system deter-mines whether all of these rights and responsibilities extend to both mother and father equally or primarily apply to one parent.

Marriages often establish certain rights and obli-gations between the members of the bride's and groom's extended families. In patrilineal polygynous marriages, the addition of another wife to the family creates a series of expectations and relationships be-tween the new wife and an already established wife (or wives). Under a matrilineal system, many of the productive and child-care responsibilities usually as-signed to the husband (father) are filled by the wife's brothers (maternal uncles), but husbands in a matrilin-eal society may have other specific duties to the fam-ily. In some cases, a daughter-in-law may be expected to perform certain services for her mother-in-law, or a son-in-law may provide specific amounts of labor to his wife's family. Grandparents or godparents may play special roles in the raising of children. Marriages between families from two different groups may serve to create or strengthen political and economic ties be-tween the groups or help resolve long-standing con-flicts. Thus, for many reasons, marriage functions as more than just a union of two people and may have much broader significance than the relationship be-tween the husband and wife.

With respect to laws and regulations, nations and their subdivisions (states, provinces, counties, and so on), exhibit enormous variation in terms of the conse-quences of marriage, or its absence, for the partici-pants. Some, like Sweden, make little distinction, fo-cusing all tax and benefit regulations on the individual, which makes it irrelevant whether a person is single, married, or cohabiting (living with someone without being married). Others, like the United States, confer substantial benefits to spouses in legally married unions. These benefits may not be available to those who are single or cohabiting without being married. For example, in the United States, both partners in a cohabiting couple (whether of the same sex or different sexes) own property individually. In communal prop-erty states, all of the assets of a legally married couple are considered to belong to both of them jointly. If one partner in a cohabiting couple dies, the other has no le-gal rights, whereas a surviving spouse has many rights.

In the United States, while you are a child under 18 years of age, your parents have the right to make medical decisions for you and to have full access to your medical records. When you get married, those rights automatically transfer to your spouse (unless you make other legal arrangements). Without a mar-riage certificate, even if you have been living together for many years in a committed relationship, your part-ner may have no legal standing with respect to health issues. If one partner in a cohabiting couple is sick or injured, the other has no legal rights to visit that per-son in the hospital, to be informed about his or her status, or to make medical decisions should the person become incapacitated.

If the relationship dissolves, married couples have access to the courts to help decide who gets what property and who gets custody of the children. If the couple is merely cohabiting, there are no regulations to cover who gets what in terms of real estate and other property. If the unmarried cohabiting couple has children, in most cases, custody automatically goes to the mother. The father will have to prove paternity to claim any rights. If both partners are the same sex, only one of them can be the legal parent of any children they have, and only the legal parent can make medical decisions and gain custody.

For tax purposes, in the United States, married couples can file their income taxes jointly, which pro-vides substantial tax advantages. Cohabiting couples must file separately. In terms of various benefits such as health care insurance, retirement benefits, and Social Security, legally married spouses and their dependents are entitled to coverage. If the couple is cohabiting, the partner and his or her dependents are not necessarily entitled to coverage under the other partner's health care, retirement, or Social Security benefits.

In recent years, much discussion and debate has taken place in the United States about whether or not the distinctions between married and merely cohabit-ing couples is fair, especially in cases involving two in-dividuals of the same sex. In states where same-sex

People disagree within and between cultures about what marriage means and what it should entail. In 2008, the Church of Jesus Christ of Latter-day Saints (Mormons) took an official stance against gay marriage. This, in turn, led to protests against the LDS Church, including this New York City protestor's reference to the fact that some Mormons advocate and practice polygyny.

In some Catholic religious orders, nuns consider them-selves to be married to Christ. "A religious habit identi-fies a sister as a bride of Christ. People know that she belongs to God and His Church in a particular and spe-cial way. It allows people to know that she is not avail-able for marriage, because she is already married to Christ. . . . The scriptures tell us that a 'woman's glory is her hair' and therefore reserved for her husband's view. This is part of the reason why religious women wear a veil" (http://www.torsisters.com/faq.htm).

marriage is legal, all the benefits that accrue to a married couple are available to all citizens in formal, long-term committed relationships, regardless of their sex. A number of individual companies have extended spousal benefits to domestic partners, but there remains much opposition to this practice, as well as to legalizing same-sex marriages at the federal level. Some people think marriage, and its legal and financial benefits, should be limited to marriages that involve one male and one female only.

Do Women Need Men?

Primate Foundations and Paternal Care

As discussed in chapter 3, mating systems are related to the degree of sexual dimorphism found in a species. Nonhuman primates that exhibit similar levels of sexual dimorphism as modern humans are either polygynous, with each male having access to several females, or live in multimale/multifemale groups. In these primates, the adult males in the group provide no care for the young—the females raise the young with essentially no help from males.

Given that marriage and some contribution to child care by genetically related males are nearly universal in humans, it is safe to assume that these cultural elaborations of the underlying primate mating and child care system began early on in the development of human culture and have proven to be biologically adaptive. The development of marriage, which makes clear which males and females are supposed to be having sex with each other (however poorly it works in some instances), probably led to a significant decrease in male–male competition for females and a concomitant decrease in aggression and violence between males.

Likewise, the addition of varying forms and degrees of male contributions to child care probably led to an increase in the survival of children. In other words, on average, more offspring survive when males contribute to their care, and males are most likely to contribute to the care of children they are related to. Given that all stages of the life-span are elongated in humans relative to the other Great Apes—longer gestation, longer infancy, longer time to reproductive maturity—culturally based male contributions to child care were likely critical for the survival and expansion of the species. Humans may have been too successful in their quest for child survival, as overpopulation of the Earth by humans now threatens the planet itself.

Mothers without Partners

Women need men, primarily for the sperm they provide. It is certainly possible to imagine a world in which women, like their nonhuman primate sisters, do all of the work of provisioning themselves and their children, and some women indeed do just that in contemporary societies. Around the world, mostly in industrial and postindustrial contexts, more and more women are reproducing and raising children with little or no contributions from the children's father(s). Sometimes the woman gets married, but the marriage ends in divorce or widowhood, and she raises the children on her own. Other times, no formal marriage takes place, and the informal relationship, known as cohabitation, ends. In many cases, the woman is able to provide for herself and her children through paid

Women everywhere provide the majority of child care. Where men are unable or unwilling to contribute significant financial resources to a family, for whatever reason, women may find that it makes more sense to remain single and raise their children on their own. Men who find themselves as single fathers are much more likely to remarry, in order to have a wife and a mother figure for their children.

employment. *Where men are unable or unwilling to contribute significant financial resources to a family, for whatever reason, women may find that it makes more sense to remain single and raise their children on their own.*

The Case of Sweden

In some countries, the government subsidizes mothers of young children, sometimes completely, eliminating the need for a male partner to provide economic support. For example, in Sweden, high taxes provide revenue to fund universal health care for children and other child-friendly programs. Mothers get one year of leave from their jobs following the birth of a baby, at 80 percent of their salary, and the guarantee of an equivalent job when they return to the workforce. They can take an additional six months of leave with a further reduction in pay. Swedish parents are also provided a child allowance by the government for each child they have (payments are made directly to the mother or father) and a housing allowance to offset the costs of a home large enough to accommodate children. There are no financial incentives to marry, as all government taxes and benefits accrue to the individual, whether married or not. As of 2005, only about 60 percent of Swedish women marry, and 56 percent of all births are to unmarried women. Of all heterosexual couples living together, 28 percent are unmarried. At the same time, women who are not involved in a stable relationship—whether marriage or unmarried cohabitation—are not allowed to have in vitro fertilization, and anonymous sperm donation is illegal (Popenoe 2005). David Popenoe writes of the high level of couple breakups in Sweden:

> [The] high breakup level is testimony to the fragility of modern marriage in which most of the institutional bonds have been stripped away—economic dependence, legal definitions, religious sentiments, and family pressures—leaving marriage and other pair-bonds held together solely by the thin and unstable reed of affection. (Popenoe 2005:10)

The Case of the United States

In the United States, the only guaranteed time off for having a baby is the 12 weeks of unpaid leave mandated by the Family & Medical Leave Act. Private companies may have more generous policies, and/or individual women may be able to negotiate better leave, but few have benefits as generous as Swedish mothers. There are financial incentives to marry in the United States, including spousal health coverage and retirement benefits as well as tax breaks and other legal rights. As of 2005, more than 85 percent of women in the United States will marry; approximately 35 percent of all births are to unmarried women, most of whom are not in long-term cohabitation relationships. Of all heterosexual couples living together, only 8 percent are unmarried. In contrast to Sweden, sperm banks and in vitro fertilization are available to anyone who can pay, which makes it substantially easier for women in the United States to have children without benefit of a partner (Whitehead and Popenoe 2005).

How Are Marriages Formed?

In many cultures around the world, marriages were traditionally arranged by the extended families of the potential bride and groom, sometimes with the help of a formal or informal matchmaker. Today, notions of romantic love and choice of partner by the prospective bride and groom are growing in popularity worldwide. Such relationships are referred to as **companionate marriages.** Societies typically have a variety of rules, based on different sorts of considerations, that determine who is considered an eligible marriage partner and who is not.

Proscriptive rules, or rules of **exogamy,** are those that define specific people or categories of people you are *not allowed to marry.* Prescriptive rules, or rules of **endogamy,** are those that define specific people or categories of people you *should marry.* All societies make use of both types of rules for clarifying and influencing how marriages should be formed. The most significant proscriptive rule—the rule against incestuous matings and marriages—is a cultural universal.

Incest Avoidance

Incest (matings between parents and offspring or between biological siblings) is rare among the nonhuman primates, presumably because the increase in genetic variation from mating outside one's family is more likely to lead to better health and greater reproductive success. Incest is also rare among people who were raised together as children, whether they are biological relatives or not. But in addition to such natural prohibitions, all societies express some culturally elaborated version of the **incest taboo**—rules or laws against marrying close relatives, especially parent–child and brother–sister marriages. Only a few exceptions have been noted, usually in royal families where brothers married their sisters in order to keep resources and power within the family. How far the incest taboo extends, in terms of which relatives are forbidden as marriage partners, depends on local cultural beliefs. For example, in the United States, some states allow first cousins to marry, while such unions are illegal in other states. In contrast, some cultures prefer that a person marry a specific kind of first cousin, while other types of first cousins are not acceptable as marriage partners.

Endogamy

Endogamy refers to rules that specify that you should choose a marriage partner from *inside a certain group*, whether based on kinship or non-kinship-based criteria. In some societies, beyond the immediate relatives who are forbidden by incest taboos, marriageable partners are specified by the kinship terms you apply to them. In other words, although you cannot marry your parents or your siblings, you may be expected to marry specific other types of more distant relatives, under a system of prescriptive marriage rules. Thus, you may be expected to marry a particular type of cousin, related through your mother in some instances, or through your father in others.

Occasionally, the specific type of relative is not defined, or you may be forbidden from marrying any relative, but you are still expected to marry someone from within a particular group. For example, many people believe it is important to marry someone who shares the same religious beliefs or who defines him- or herself as belonging to the same ethnic group or who holds the same national citizenship status. For other families, political leanings may be more important, or they may hope that their child marries someone of a similar social status and/or someone who shares core values concerning education, child rearing, gender relationships, and other lifestyle choices.

Exogamy

Exogamy refers to rules that specify that you should choose a marriage partner from *outside a certain group*. Again, the group may be defined based on various aspects of group membership, such as sex (typically, you are expected to marry someone outside your own sex category), or on geographic considerations, but most are based on wider kinship variables. For example, a person in a unilineal society may be told that she can marry a person from any lineage other than the one she belongs to. Groups of related villages may follow a practice of village exogamy and regional endogamy—you should marry someone from a different village, but stay within the general area in your search for a marriage partner, so that you speak the same language and share many basic cultural beliefs and practices.

Hypergamy

In most societies, women marry men who are the same age as they are, or older (in some cases, much older). Likewise, women usually marry men who are the same height as they are, or taller. Finally, women usually marry men who have equal or greater social status or educational attainment than they have. These trends are known as **hypergamy** (marrying up), based on the woman's perspective. To put these in terms of proscriptive rules, a woman's family may caution her not to marry anyone who is younger than she, shorter than she, or of lower social status than she currently enjoys. Because children take on the social status of their father in most descent systems, marrying up is often the major strategy a woman (or her extended family) may employ to improve the social standing of her children.

In many cases, marriage rules will include both endogamous and exogamous exhortations. These may be hard-and-fast rules, or they may be merely expectations on the part of parents and other extended family members. They may even reflect unspoken attitudes and prejudices that one absorbs growing up in the family and community. And there may be a sliding scale of disapproval for certain choices. For example, in my *natal family* (the family I was born into), my parents never expressed any preferences in terms of ethnicity or religious or political leanings, but they made it clear that they expected me to marry someone who was well-educated, had a good job, and who didn't smoke.

Marriage rules of various types can be elaborated into incredibly complex systems that may specify exactly who you must marry or who you absolutely must not marry, or they may serve merely as general guidelines for you to take into consideration as you think about who you might marry or as your extended family arranges a marriage for you.

Arranged Marriages

Where marriages are arranged by members of the extended family, it is usually the parents and grandparents who have the most influence, but in some cases aunts, uncles, and/or a matchmaker may also be involved. Matchmakers are usually older women, who make it their business to keep track of which families have children approaching marriageable age and which matches would be most advantageous for specific families or individuals. The matchmaker may act as a liaison, setting up meetings and overseeing negotiations between members of the two families involved. Even if formal matchmakers are not part of a particular culture, interested parties outside the family may make explicit suggestions or arrange meetings between young adults they think would make successful marriage partners.

Much variation exists in exactly how arranged marriages come to be arranged. In some cases, neither bride nor groom has any say in the matter, and they meet each other for the first time on their wedding day. In other cases, the bride, the groom, or both may be allowed rights of refusal. In such cases, their family can present a candidate, and they can then say no if they don't want to marry the person. Or the parents may present several potential candidates and give them opportunities to get to know one another through supervised visits or chaperoned dates, and the bride- or groom-to-be can then express a preference for one candidate.

Where arranged marriages are the tradition, the social standing and character of the family are more important than the specific personality traits of the individuals who are being married. The marriage is viewed as a way to establish a household and raise children. If the bride and groom come to feel affection, or even love, for one another, and provide mutual companionship and emotional support over the years, that is considered a bonus but not a necessity for a successful partnership.

For example, in Mali, where most marriages are still arranged, a woman hopes that her husband won't be too old, or in ill-health, and that he will be a good provider and treat her well. A man hopes that his wife will be good-natured, hardworking, fecund, and faithful. Neither expects that they will fall in love, and typically they don't count on their spouse for emotional support and companionship. Rather, when a woman marries and moves into her husband's household, she has a whole range of new people to establish relationships with, including her husband's parents, his other wives, his brothers' wives, and his unmarried sisters, as well as new neighbors. Eventually, the new wife will have children and get significant emotional satisfaction from her relationships with her children, especially her sons (who will always live with her), and her grandchildren. She will also maintain close ties with her own parents, siblings, and other members of her extended natal family, unless she has moved far away. Because she does not expect her husband to be the sole source of love and affection in her life, she is less likely to be disappointed if they don't get along. She has her work, her neighbors, her friends, her children, and other relatives to create a multistranded web of kinship that provides her with ample affection and emotional support.

Likewise, for a man in Mali, his wife's most important roles are as mother to his children and partner in the economic operation of the household. She is obligated to have sexual relations with him, but for friendship and companionship he is more likely to rely on his brothers, lineage mates, and friends.

In addition to members of one's extended family deciding whom one should marry, people sometimes turn to others for advice about whom *not* to marry. The example of Tay-Sachs is quite illuminating in this context. Tay-Sachs is an autosomal recessive inherited disease that is more common among Jewish families of Ashkenazi (Eastern European) descent than other populations. Tay-Sachs is not treatable and leads to death in early childhood. In order to reduce the number of children born with this genetic condition, a number of genetic screening programs and registries have been established in the United States, which has a large population of people with Ashkenazi Jewish ancestry. *Dor Yeshorim* in New York City is one such screening program. Young adults are screened to find out if they are carriers of Tay-Sachs, but are not given their results. When a couple is considering marriage, they ask the organization if they are compatible or not. An incompatible match would be one in which both partners are carriers for Tay-Sachs. This doesn't mean they are not allowed to get married, but lets them know that they have a one in four chance, with each pregnancy, of having a baby with Tay-Sachs. They may decide not to marry, or not to have children, or they may just take their chances.

Marriages Based on Ideals of Romantic Love

In some contexts, emotional bonds of love and affection between husband and wife are considered one of the primary benefits of marriage and the basis by which marriages are formed, but this is by no means a cultural universal. Marriages based on **romantic love** or companionship have their deepest history in Western industrial and postindustrial cultural contexts.

Even without formal rules about who you may or may not marry, where arranged marriages are not found, and in contexts where young people think they have complete freedom to choose a marriage partner based on notions of romantic love, cultural beliefs and practices may limit the range of people you view as potential marriage material. All of the beliefs and attitudes and prejudices of your social environment—including your parents and other relatives, your peers, your teachers, and so on—will affect whether you view another individual as a potential marriage partner, or pass right by him without giving him a thought. If you believe that marrying someone from the same religious background is critical, you will probably notice (or find out) another person's religious preference early in your acquaintance. If someone from a different ethnicity would be anathema to your parents, even as a friend, then you aren't likely to pursue a romantic relationship with that person—it may never even cross your mind. If education is vitally important to you, you aren't likely to become interested in someone who dropped out of school in the sixth grade.

Many social institutions have as a primary or secondary purpose the goal of offering a chance for appropriate marriage partners to become acquainted with one another. The British and U.S. upper-class practice of having young ladies be presented to society at cotillions and debutante balls is one example. Many young people in North America meet their future spouses in college or on the job. If you are from a wealthy family and have good grades, you will attend a different sort of college or university, and meet a different pool of potential mates, than if your family is poor and you attend a community college and work at the local mall to pay the bills.

Probably the strongest foundation underlying the American system of marriage (and divorce) is a cluster of beliefs about romantic love. Many people believe that romantic love should be the basis for choosing a marriage partner, and that this love will last forever—"until death do us part"—as long as you have managed to find your one true love, your soul mate. People fall in love, often after not knowing one another for very long, and may be attracted to one another based on trivial and/or transient characteristics. People get married because they are "in love." Then they expect their spouse to be perfect—to be their soul mate—and to meet all of their emotional needs. This, in addition to whatever else they expect!

Of course, some of the time, things don't work out. Their spouse turns out not to be perfect and/or not able to meet all of their emotional needs. Practical difficulties may arise, such as a job loss or illness, and the couple seems to pull apart, rather than facing the situation together. One, or both, falls out of love. One, or both, decides that the problem with the marriage is the specific person they married, rather than their unrealistic expectations for the relationship. They get divorced, and set off once more in search of their perfect mate, to try again.

Understanding this cultural belief system goes a long way toward explaining why people in the United States have such a high divorce rate, and why **serial monogamy** (the practice of being married to only one person at a time, but to several different spouses over the course of one's lifetime) has become so prevalent. It also helps us understand why the concept of arranged marriages seems so foreign to most Westerners. It isn't just the notion of having someone else pick your spouse and being expected to have sex with, and reproduce with, someone not of your own choosing. Even more significantly, it is the absence of romantic love that makes an arranged marriage seem so unlikely to lead to happiness. Westerners are not used to having their emotional needs filled by a variety of other people—a group of relatives, friends, neighbors, and coworkers.

Advantages of Arranged Marriages

In addition to providing a broader network of support—an entire group of people who can be called on in times of need—systems of arranged marriages have other advantages:

- There is less chance of disillusionment with marriage when one's emotional expectations are not so high; therefore, there is less motive for divorce.
- Everyone knows they will eventually get married to someone appropriate (as judged by their parents and

other relatives). This means a huge reduction in teenage/young adult angst:

"Will I get married?"

"Will I pick the right person?"

"How will I know it's the right person?"

"Will the person I think is right for me also want to marry me?"

"What if I never meet the right person?"

"What if the person I marry turns out not to be my soul mate?"

- Females in societies with arranged marriages are more likely to focus their energies on their studies, or on productive work, and not spend so much time focusing on their physical appearance:

"Do I weigh too much? Should I go on a diet?"

"Am I pretty enough? Are my breasts large enough?"

"How do I look? My clothes, my shoes, my hair, my makeup?"

"How do I get that guy's attention?"

Modern Loves

It may be difficult for someone raised on notions of romantic love to appreciate the advantages of arranged marriages. In recent years, the concept that the partners should have some say in who they marry, and that husband and wife are entitled to emotional as well as physical intimacy, is gaining a foothold in many cultures where traditionally most marriages are/were arranged without the participation of the prospective bride and groom. Jennifer Hirsch and Holly Wardlow's *Modern Loves: The Anthropology of Romantic Courtship and Companionate Marriage* provides a series of case studies documenting this global transformation of marriage ideals. They write:

> This volume discusses how women and men from Mexico, Papua New Guinea, Brazil, Pakistan, India, Nigeria, North America, and Singapore negotiate courtship, love, and marriage. Collectively we show how people in a variety of settings are coming to emphasize emotional intimacy as the source of ties that bind. The chapters explore similarities and differences in shifting expectations for marriage, the growing perception that intimacy and pleasure are fundamental elements of modern relationships and modern personhood, the cultural forms—popular videos, advertisements, Christian tracts—that facilitate the globalization of a companionate marriage ideal, and the ways that these claims of modern love relate to

changing gender ideologies [as well as political and economic forces]. (Hirsch and Wardlow 2006:2)

Marriage Types

Marriages can be classified according to how many people are involved, and their sex.

Monogamy

Monogamy (mono = one, gam = marriage) is traditionally defined as marriage between one man and one woman, one husband and one wife. In some societies, monogamy is the only officially sanctioned form of marriage, and spouses are expected to stay married to one partner all of their lives. With *serial monogamy,* the dissolution of the first marriage—for whatever reason—is followed by a second marriage to a different spouse. This marriage may be followed later by a third marriage, and so on.

Polygamy

Polygamy (poly = many, gam = marriage) is a general term that refers to culturally sanctioned marriage forms involving more than two people in one marriage. Polygamy is divided into polygyny and polyandry, depending on which sex/spouse is represented by more than one person. Because the overarching term polygamy is so vague, it is seldom used in anthropology.

Polygyny

Polygyny (poly = many, gyn = female) is the specific term that denotes a marriage between one man and more than one woman (one husband and multiple wives). This is likely the natural mating system for humans and is the most common allowed or preferred form of marriage around the world. Approximately 80–85 percent of societies allow polygyny and see it as the most desired situation for all concerned—the husband, his wives, and all of the children. For a man, the ability to have more than one wife allows him to increase his reproductive success in terms of legitimate children born within culturally sanctioned unions. For a woman, polygyny does not significantly affect her reproductive success; she is more limited by her own biology than by how many other wives her husband has.

Most societies that allow polygyny place constraints on the number of wives a man can have or the conditions under which he can marry multiple times. For example, there have been cases throughout history, and from around the world, where members of the ruling families or the very wealthy were allowed to have more wives than the common folk. As part of the development of Islam, the prophet Mohammed decreed that Muslim men were henceforth to be limited to a maximum of four wives and that, in all cases, each wife must be considered to have equivalent legal status and must be treated fairly. A Muslim man is allowed to have more than one wife only if he can afford to support each wife and her children and keep all of them housed, fed, clothed, and educated according to local standards.

Polygyny is found most often in societies where women do significant amounts of hard physical labor, including domestic, productive, and reproductive work. In most of the world, women do the majority of the domestic labor (cleaning the house, hauling water, gathering and chopping firewood, processing and cooking food, washing dishes, making, repairing, and washing clothes, and keeping the household running on a daily basis). In addition, women do much of the productive labor—gathering food, planting, tending, and harvesting crops, milking animals, producing goods to sell, or working at a job outside the home. Finally, women do the vast majority of the reproductive labor—carrying children to term, giving birth, breast-feeding, and providing most of the child care.

Men's contributions to the various forms of labor necessary for life can range from zero or minimal for domestic and reproductive labor, to as much as or even more than the women's in terms of productive labor. Where the burden of labor falls mostly on the wife in a marriage, a woman often welcomes a co-wife to help ease the load. The more wives there are, the more hands there are to share the work, including child care. If one wife is sick, her children can be cared for by a co-wife. If there are multiple wives, they can take turns cooking for the entire family, or divide up the chores according to preference, with one doing more of the laundry and the other doing more of the firewood chopping; one may prefer pounding millet, while another is happy to sit in the market selling herbs.

Women also receive friendship, companionship, and social and emotional support from their co-wives. Co-wives may join forces to convince or coerce their husband to behave in a particular manner. When a

man has multiple wives, he is more likely to follow postpartum sex taboos, allowing each wife a break from sexual relations after the birth of a child, thus making it more likely that she will have adequate time to recover, and resulting in longer birth intervals and lower child mortality rates.

In some polygynous societies, women are confined to the house, and thus have limited opportunities to contribute to the family's economic resources. In such cases, the husband must provide all the productive labor or income for the family. Thus, a man must work very hard and/or be relatively wealthy to be able to support more than one wife and the children she bears. In such cases, wives may resent one another if they feel that resources are spread too thin, or that one wife and/or her children are being favored over another.

Enormous cultural variation exists in how polygynous families are formed. In some cases, a man will marry two or more sisters. This is known as **sororal polygyny,** and carries the advantage that the co-wives will already know one another and will be genetically related to each other's children. In other societies, sororal polygyny is considered quite peculiar, and co-wives usually come from unrelated families. In some cases, it is the first wife who petitions her husband to marry a second wife to help her with her work. This request often comes once the first wife has several young children who need care, but who don't yet contribute much to the household economy. The first wife may suggest potential candidates or simply pester her husband until he makes arrangements for a second wife to join the family. As a wife nears the end of her reproductive career, at menopause, she may encourage her husband to find a much younger bride, preferably one who is strong and healthy and will help with the work as well as provide sex and more children to the husband. Much older first wives may accumulate enormous respect and power and delegate most or all of the labor to the younger wives.

Another variation has been described for the Mpondo, a Xhosa-speaking people who were living along the southeast coast of Africa in 1737 when a ship was wrecked in a winter storm and tossed up five survivors, including an English girl about 7 years old, named Bessie. She has been described as having pale skin, long black hair, and blue eyes. She grew up among the Mpondo and eventually became the *Great Wife* of Tshomane, who was the "Great Son of the

Tshomane chief Matayi, a prince of the blood, descendant of the ancient Mpondo kings, whose line dated back to 'time immemorial'" (Crampton 2006:32). Bessie would have been of marriageable age (16–18 years) around 1746 to 1748:

> Tshomane already had several other wives, so he was probably older than she was. A chief usually married his first wife soon after his initiation into manhood . . . and as he grew in stature and wealth he acquired more and more wives—but no matter how many he had, none were as important as his Great Wife, whom he usually only married later in life. This was possibly in order to avoid disputes about succession (although it did not always work) since it was only through his Great Wife that the chief's line could continue; even if, as was often the case, he already had several children by his existing wives, he was not considered to have an official heir until such time as his Great Wife bore her first son (the Great Son). Consequently the most important marriage of a chief was to his Great Wife, and it just so happened that Tshomane had not yet taken his Great Wife when Bessie reached marriageable age. . . . Since a chief did not normally choose his own Great Wife, Bessie would first have had to win the approval of Tshomane's amaphakati or

> counselors, men of proven wisdom and influence before whom all matters of importance were discussed and decided. (Crampton 2006: 33)

Through her descendants, Bessie's line can be traced down through the generations to "many present-day Xhosa, Thembu, Bomvana and Mpondo royal families" (Crampton 2006:316).

In addition to multiple wives, men may also have unofficial wives—concubines or slave-wives—or mistresses who may or may not be known to the official wife or wives or recognized publicly. In this way, a man may harness the reproductive power of numerous women, while having formal legal responsibilities only to his official wife or wives and their children.

More on Polygyny: Bridewealth versus Dowry

Most patrilineal, polygynous cultures exhibit one of two institutional forms relating to the exchange of resources that take place at or near the time of the marriage. These two systems, known as **bridewealth** and **dowry** are usually mutually exclusive and reflect very different underlying cultural beliefs about the value of women and the nature of marriage.

Bridewealth consists of resources (often livestock) transferred from the groom's family to the bride's family. In contrast, dowry consists of resources (often practical household goods for the new couple) transferred from the bride's family to the groom's family. Left: the traditional, formal presentation of the dowry—money and jewelry, in this case—at an engagement ceremony in Thailand. Right: a photograph of Fahra Izhak Eadeh on her wedding day in Ramallah, Palestine (sometime between 1898 and 1914), wearing her traditional dowry clothing and headdress.

Bridewealth, also called bride-price, refers to *resources transferred from the groom's family to the bride's family at the time of the marriage in exchange for certain rights* (figure 5.1). Bridewealth may take the form of land, livestock, money, consumer goods (alcohol, cigarettes, cloth, appliances, and so on), or some combination. Bridewealth is amassed from the joint resources of the groom's patrilineage, who must give their permission for the transaction. The exact amount and form of the bridewealth is often negotiated between the families, and it may be paid all at once or in several installments. Once the bridewealth has been paid, the groom and his family are considered to have acquired specific rights, including, but not limited to: the person of the bride (she leaves her natal family and goes to live with her husband's family); rights for the groom to have exclusive sexual access to the bride; rights to her domestic, productive, and reproductive labor; and, most significantly, *rights to affiliate the children she gives birth to with the groom's family and lineage.* If the bridewealth has been paid, then the children belong to the husband's lineage.

Some Westerners have viewed bridewealth negatively as a system of buying women or treating them as commodities. In reality, bridewealth reflects the relatively elevated status of women in societies where a woman's ability to make other people (have children) is highly valued. The bride's family is giving up a significant and valuable resource—the reproductive potential of their daughter—and the groom's family must compensate the bride's family for this loss.

Dowry is a very different institution from bridewealth, and is more variable in form and meaning. Like bridewealth, dowry may take the form of land, livestock, money, consumer goods, or some combination. Like bridewealth, the exact amount and form of the dowry is often negotiated between the families, and it may be paid all at once or in several installments. Dowry appears, in some ways, to be the opposite of bridewealth, because resources flow from the bride's family to the groom's family (figure 5.2). However, nothing substantial is received by the bride's family in exchange for their daughter, her labor, her reproductive potential, and her dowry.

In many societies, dowry includes furniture, appliances, household linens, pots and pans, and other goods to be used by the bride and groom in their married life. In situations such as these, the dowry repre-

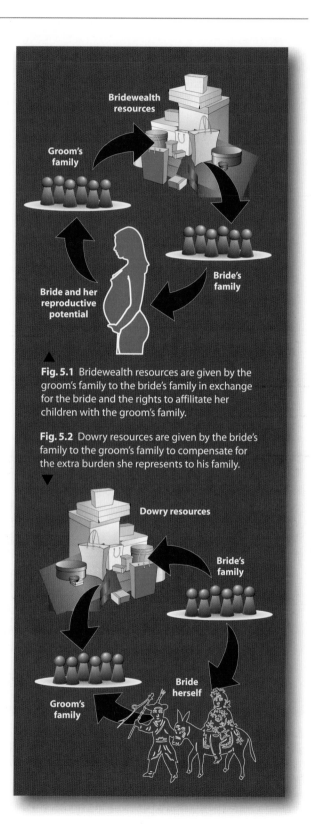

Fig. 5.1 Bridewealth resources are given by the groom's family to the bride's family in exchange for the bride and the rights to affiliate her children with the groom's family.

Fig. 5.2 Dowry resources are given by the bride's family to the groom's family to compensate for the extra burden she represents to his family.

sents a daughter's share of her family's wealth—she inherits her share when she marries, and the sons of the family inherit the rest when the parents die. If the resources actually go to the bride and groom, and are enjoyed by them and used to establish their own household and support their future children, then dowry can serve a useful purpose.

The tradition in the United States of the bride's family paying for the wedding can be viewed as a lingering vestige of a dowry system. Each guest invited to the wedding and reception is expected to bring a gift for the couple of approximately equal value to the guest's share of the cost. If there are 100 guests and the total cost is $1,500 (because the reception is held at the local fire hall, catered by the bride's aunts), then the cost per guest is $15, and each guest's gift should be worth approximately that amount. If the total cost is $20,000 (because the wedding is held at a fancy country club with steak and lobster, and an open bar), then the cost per guest is $200, and each guest's gift should be worth at least that figure. In this way, resources are, in essence, transferred from the bride's family to the newlywed couple via the guests. The couple's friends and relatives get to enjoy the celebration, and the newlyweds have household goods or money with which to begin their life together.

However, in some situations, dowry reflects a belief system that devalues female children and women in general. In some patrilineal, polygynous societies, women are held in very low esteem, in part because children are not viewed as valuable in and of themselves, so a woman's ability to produce children is less important. Daughters are viewed as burdens on the household—they are expensive to clothe, feed, and educate, and when they grow up, they require expensive dowries in order to secure a husband. Then they leave their natal family and go off to work and reproduce in their husband's household. Their family gets nothing in return. In order to secure a husband from a good family, potential brides' families compete to see who can offer the largest dowry. The bride's family, in essence, pays the groom's family to assume the burden of caring for the woman.

Under such circumstances, the birth of a daughter may be a disappointment rather than a cause for celebration. Daughters may be discriminated against within the family, receiving less food, education, and medical care than their brothers. Typically, the dowry itself (whatever its form), goes to the groom's parents and extended family, not to the bride and groom themselves. Sometimes, after the dowry has been negotiated and the marriage has taken place, the groom's family comes back and demands further dowry from the bride's family in order to ensure her safety in her new home. If the bride's family cannot or will not meet their demands, the bride may suffer. Deliberate murders of young brides, known as dowry deaths, are usually passed off as tragic household accidents. In northern India, where dowry deaths are a particular problem, a common explanation is that the bride accidentally set herself on fire while cooking. Although such deaths are viewed with suspicion, few are prosecuted and even fewer result in punishment for the groom or members of his family. The dowry resources are not returned, since the bride died accidentally. The groom is then free to search for another wife, who will bring her own dowry with her.

Polyandry and Other Cultural Solutions to Limited Resources

Polyandry (poly = many, andr = male) refers to a form of marriage in which one woman is married to more than one man (one wife and multiple husbands). Polyandry is exceedingly rare among humans and is found only under very specific environmental and economic circumstances. Polyandry is found where population growth must be kept at a minimum and where a family's resources would not be sufficient to support all the sons if they each had separate wives and separate sets of children. In such cases, several brothers may marry one woman, a system known as **fraternal polyandry.** In this way, the next generation is limited to the number of children one woman can produce. The men share their wife in terms of sex and domestic and productive labor. From each husband's perspective, any children his wife bears are either his own children or his brother's children, to whom he is also related. Thus, the children born to the family are related to all of the husbands.

From an evolutionary perspective, it is less adaptive for a man to share his wife's limited reproductive potential with other men, even if they are related to him. There are likewise no advantages to the woman of having to provide sex, as well as domestic and productive labor, to more than one man. Not all populations facing limited resources solve this problem through polyandry, as there are other cultural solutions that don't require men to limit their reproductive potential, which is another reason why polyandry is so rare among humans. One such alternative is exemplified by large Catholic families in Western Europe in cases where the family's land holdings and other resources were sufficient to provide for only one married couple and their children in each generation. These families used the practice of **primogeniture,** in which the eldest legitimate son was designated as the heir and inherited most or all of the family land and resources. Traditionally, the second son was promised to the church, meaning that he became a priest or a monk, and he would go to live wherever he was assigned and be supported by the church. As a celibate priest or monk, he neither married nor was obliged to support children.

The second daughter was often promised to the church as well, and became a nun, supported by the community. Nuns likewise didn't marry or have children. Other daughters would plan to marry and leave the family estate to live with their husbands, or would "go into service" as servants for wealthier families. Younger sons would be expected to leave home when they reached adulthood and make their own way in the world. They might become merchants or explorers, or join the military, or go to sea. During the sixteenth to twentieth centuries, many emigrated to European colonies such as the fledgling United States, Canada, Australia, and New Zealand, and to colonial outposts in Latin America, Africa, Asia, and the islands of the South Pacific.

Contemporary Industrial and Postindustrial Monogamy

Many people living in Western societies find it difficult to understand why a woman would be content to share her husband with a co-wife. Where marriages are arranged by the future bride and groom themselves, and based primarily on notions of romantic love and sexual attraction, jealousy is often perceived as the major obstacle to sharing a husband. Even the potential advantage of sharing the burdens of domestic and reproductive labor with a co-wife are not enough to overcome objections to polygyny.

In contemporary industrial and postindustrial monogamous families, both husband and wife may work outside the home at salaried employment, and many of the traditional domestic duties of men and women have been contracted out to others. Those who can afford to will often pay other people to do the housework, including cleaning, laundry, dishes, and so forth. They may pay someone to shop for, prepare, and serve food, or they may pay a premium for already prepared food from the grocery store or restaurants (either dining at restaurants often, or eating takeout at home). Some people pay a service to run errands, such as going to the post office, bank, dry cleaners, and so forth. Duties once taken care of by the husband such as yard work, plumbing, carpentry, electric repairs, keeping the car running—even cleaning up the dog poop in the yard—may also be contracted out to others.

The same is true for reproductive labor. If the family has children, much of the care of the children may be contracted out to nannies, babysitters, mother's helpers, or child-care facilities, beginning as early as six weeks postpartum. Wet-nursing—paying another mother to breastfeed one's children—is experiencing a bit of a renaissance in the contemporary West. Some wealthy women even hire surrogates to undertake the work of pregnancy and childbirth for them, either because they are too old themselves or don't want to take the time off from work and other activities. Older children may have a dedicated driver who takes them to and from school and to various activities (soccer practice, piano lessons, karate, etc.), supervises homework, and fixes dinner.

Contemporary Industrial and Postindustrial Polygyny

Polygyny is illegal is most Western societies, but that doesn't mean that all marriages are monogamous. In the United States, polygynous marriages are found in several different contexts. Members of the breakaway Fundamentalist Church of Jesus Christ of Latter-day Saints follow original church teachings encouraging polygyny, in defiance of current church doctrine and U.S. law. Polygyny has also emerged among some evangelical Christians in the United States, facilitated by websites where already established families advertise for additional wives. Muslim families in the United States are *unlikely* to be polygynous because Islam requires that each wife have the same legal status, and that isn't possible under American law.

How Marriages End

Widows and Widowers

There is great cultural variation in how marriages end, and what happens after they do. For example, if one spouse dies, the other may remarry immediately or after some period of mourning has passed. In some circumstances, a woman might be taken in by one of her husband's brothers, either as a full-fledged wife (especially if she is young and can still bear children) or as a charity case (if she is beyond reproductive age). Nuer *ghost marriage,* discussed below, is one example of how a widow can remain part of her husband's family even after his death. Across much of southern and eastern Europe during the twentieth century, women who had lost their husbands in World War I or II were not expected, and in some cases not allowed, to remarry. For the rest of their lives they wore the traditional black clothing of mourning/widowhood. Much of the time, if it is the wife who dies, the husband remarries, especially when there are young children who require care.

Divorce

Marriages may also end because the couple finds that they cannot get along, or because one spouse is unfaithful. Every local group will have formal laws as well as informal rules about what constitutes grounds for dissolving a marriage. Where one of the main functions of the marriage is to produce children, an infecund woman may be returned to her natal family, either in exchange for a refund of the bridewealth or for another female as a replacement. In the United States, before no-fault divorce, most states had laws allowing a man to divorce his wife if she was unfaithful, but not the reverse. If he was the unfaithful spouse, the reasoning went, it didn't really affect her. But if she was unfaithful, there was a chance that a child born to the marriage might not belong to her husband, and this was considered sufficient reason for her husband to divorce her. This provides further support for the notion that marriage is mostly about controlling women's sexual behavior in order to ensure paternity certainty for the male acting in the role of father or social provider.

In some societies, divorce is not an option, usually backed by religious sanctions that forbid it. When spouses do not get along, they can still continue to live together and even have and raise children together. In patrilineal societies, a woman may be unwilling to leave her husband and return to her natal family because it means leaving her children behind, since they belong to their father's lineage.

In matrilineal societies, women usually have more power when it comes to divorce. Their children belong to their own lineage and therefore cannot be taken away. If a woman's husband is neglectful, abusive, lazy, alcoholic, or displeases her in any other way, she is more free to divorce him. Her brothers and other male members of her lineage will take care of her children, regardless of whether she is married or divorced. Thus, women in matrilineal societies tend to be less tolerant of inappropriate behavior on the part of their husband.

Contemporary Industrial and Postindustrial Divorce

Divorce became more common in many industrial and postindustrial societies in the second half of the twentieth century. A number of factors contributed to this trend, including the advent of no-fault divorce, which allowed women the same rights as men to end a marriage on the basis of infidelity, and added "incompatibility" as an acceptable reason for divorce. Another factor was the increasing educational and economic opportunities that began to open up for women during and after World War II.

In the first half of the twentieth century in the United States, with few exceptions, women were not allowed or encouraged to pursue higher education and were not allowed to work outside the home. They (and their children) were economically dependent on their husband's income, and knew they would be destitute if they divorced. Being divorced also carried an enormous social stigma, especially for women. Gradually, as cultural attitudes changed, more and more women finished high school and attended college; some pursed postgraduate degrees. More women entered the workforce and began to earn their own income, so that they were no longer completely financially dependent on a spouse. General disparities in income between men and women still exist in most countries, and many women stand to lose economically after divorce, but women no longer face such strong economic incentives to stay with an unsatisfactory spouse. As divorce has become more and more common, the social stigma has all but disappeared.

As discussed above, another consequence of women's increasing ability to support themselves without the aid of a husband has led many women to form temporary or long-term unions with men, but to forego marriage, even when children come along. And in contexts where the nation-state provides a minimum level of support for all citizens, such as Sweden, women increasingly find few reasons to get married. *Where men are unable or unwilling to contribute significant financial resources to a family, for whatever reason, women may find that it makes more sense to remain single and raise their children on their own.*

The Importance of Reproductive Success and the Legitimacy of Children

Two examples from the Nuer of the southern Sudan illustrate the importance of reproductive success, and especially establishing the legitimacy of children, in determining marriage forms.

Ghost Marriage

The first example is known as **ghost marriage** (Evans-Pritchard 1940). Suppose that a Nuer woman has married a man from another lineage, and his family has paid her family the requisite bridewealth (in livestock, money, or other resources) in exchange for the rights to affiliate her children with her husband's lineage. The marriage is a happy and productive one, and after several years, she has given birth to two children. Then her husband dies unexpectedly, leaving her a widow with two young children, long before she has completed her reproductive years.

Theoretically, she could return to her natal family. However, that would involve leaving her children with her husband's family (to whose lineage they belong), and her family would have to return part of the bridewealth. Another option would be for her to remain at her husband's household and live out the rest of her life as a celibate widow. She would be able to continue raising her children, but the rest of her reproductive potential would go untapped, and her husband's family would only get two children in exchange for the bridewealth they paid. Under *ghost marriage*, the young widow is still considered to be married to her husband, even though he is dead (thus the name); she is able to remain with her children, as part of her husband's family; and she continues to have children who are considered his legitimate heirs, and who belong to his lineage. The biological father of these children may

be one of her husband's brothers, or someone else of her own choosing. In this way, she is able to remain with her children, her family isn't obliged to repay the bridewealth, and her husband's family gets full advantage of her reproductive potential in the form of children for their lineage.

Female–Female Marriage

The second example is usually referred to as **female–female marriage** and is found among the Nuer as well as several neighboring East African populations, with minor variations (Evans-Pritchard 1940). How does female–female marriage work? Typically, children are born in approximately 50/50 ratios by sex—half sons and half daughters. Under the Nuer system of patrilineality, as daughters reach marriageable age, they are married to men from other lineages in exchange for bridewealth and leave the family to live with their husband's family and have children for their husband's lineage. The bridewealth resources brought in by the daughters of the family are then used to help secure wives for the sons of the family. Thus, cattle and other forms of bridewealth circulate one way through the system, while women and their reproductive potential circulate the other way.

Suppose that a middle-aged Nuer man has a wife and many children, but most of his children are daughters. Perhaps he has only one son, who will marry and whose wife will produce children for the lineage (grandchildren for the Nuer man). One by one, as his daughters marry and move away, the Nuer man accumulates lots of resources as bridewealth. What he really wants, however, are many descendants who are members of his lineage, but his grandchildren through his daughters all belong to their fathers' lineages. One solution is to choose one of his younger daughters and designate her as a son. Everyone knows she is his daughter, and is female, but she agrees to play the role of husband in a marriage to a female from another lineage, and to be the social father of any children born to the marriage. The Nuer man pays bridewealth to the bride's family, and the bride comes to live with her female husband, who continues to live in her natal household.

This marriage between two females does not involve homosexual feelings or behavior. Both women have sex with men and produce children. All of the children belong to, and are considered legitimate members of, their *father's* lineage (even though for some of them, their father is, biologically, their mother).

The biological fathers of the children may be a succession of different men, or one or both of the women may form long-lasting relationships with men who have no wives of their own because they cannot afford to pay bridewealth. The female husband, in these cases, is usually happy that she gets to stay with her natal family and has some choice about who she has sex with and produces children by. Her children will belong to the same lineage that she does, so no one can separate them from her. Her wife, likewise, is most often fine with the arrangement, as her family still gets bridewealth in exchange for her children belonging to her (female) husband's lineage, but she also enjoys more choice about who she has sex with and produces children by. Through this system of female–female marriage, the Nuer man who had mainly daughters is still able to have numerous grandchildren who belong to his lineage.

One way for people to be biologically related to one another (consanguineal kin) is for one person to be descended from another. Here, four generations of a Buryat (Mongolian) family are represented: three young children seated in front of their parents, with their grandmother (far left), and their great-grandmother.

KINSHIP: DIFFERENT WAYS TO BE RELATED

Biological (Consanguineal) Kinship

From the Western scientific perspective, there are two basic ways for people to be biologically (genetically) related to one another, and both ways are acknowledged by societies around the world, whether or not they are aware of the genetic basis of these relationships, or conceive of them in other ways. These kin generally are referred to as **consanguineal kin** (con = with, sanguin = blood).

Descent of A from B

The first way for people to be biologically related to one another is when one person is related to another because they are *descended from* that person. This is how parents are related to children, and vice versa. You are related to your biological mother and father because you are *descended from* them. Likewise, you are related to both sets of biological grandparents because you are *descended from* them through your parents. The same is true of your four sets of great-grandparents, eight sets of great-great-grandparents, and so on, back into the mists of time. At the same time, you are (or will be) related to your children because they are *descended from* you. Through your children, your grandchildren will be descended from you, and your great-grandchildren and great-great-grandchildren and so on, forward into the future. Thus, each person, or *Ego* in anthropological kinship terminology, serves as a node linking past and future relatives who are biologically related to one other by being descended one from the other.

Descent of A and B from a Common Ancestor

The second way for people to be biologically related to one another is when one person is related to another because they are *both descended from a common ancestor*. This is how you are related to your full siblings, with whom you share both a mother and a father. If you go back a generation and look at all the people who are descended from a common set of grandparents, but through different parents, you include the people referred to as *first cousins* in Eskimo kinship terminology (the form of kinship terminology used most often among English-speaking peoples). People who share a common set of great-grandparents, but different grandparents and parents, are called *second cousins.*

You are also biologically related to people who are descended from the same ancestor(s) but at different generational levels. If you go forward a generation to the children of your siblings, they are referred to as your nieces and nephews. Your parents are their grandparents (common ancestors, but at different generational levels). The children of your first cousins are your first cousins once-removed. And so on. Heading up the generations, your parents' siblings are referred to as your aunts and uncles—your grandparents were their parents. This can seem a bit confusing at first, as most North Americans do not live near or interact frequently with distant relatives. We tend to lose track of the exact relationships with relatives as they move farther away in genealogical as well as geographic distance.

Such is the power of breastfeeding and breast milk that, in many societies, nursing from one woman is thought to create special biological ties between children. This **milk tie,** known from cultures around the world, unites all the children who nursed from one woman in a special relationship similar to siblings, whether or not they are biologically related. In Mali, a man will distinguish among his brothers according to whether or not they share the same mother. Those who have the same mother are referred to as *shin ji* (breast milk brothers), in contrast to ordinary brothers, who merely share the same father. Likewise, if an unrelated child is routinely nursed by a woman, that child becomes shin ji to that woman's children as well.

Legal (Affinal) Kinship

In addition to biological relatedness to your consanguineal kin, people are, of course, related through ties of marriage. These kin are referred to as your **affinal kin.**

In-Laws

When you get married, you acquire a spouse (husband or wife). In addition, you become related, through the marriage, to all of your spouse's consanguineal kin, and vice versa. You may acquire a mother-in-law and father-in-law, brothers- and sisters-in-law, and so forth. Eskimo kinship terminology does not distinguish between more distant relatives who are consanguineal versus affinal kin. Thus, the terms *aunt* and *uncle,* as well as *niece* and *nephew,* may refer to people related to you either through ties of blood or marriage.

Stepparents and Half-siblings

In addition to inlaws, other types of affinal kinship relationships

Another way for people to be biologically related to one another is to be descended from one or more common ancestors. The four Dettwyler brothers (above)—Rick, Jack, Bob, and Steven—share the same parents, Jeanne and Bill. Steven (far right) is the author's husband.

exist. For example, if a parent remarries, you may acquire a step-mother or step-father, step-brothers and step-sisters, as well as more distant step-relatives. If your parent then has children with her new spouse, you will have siblings with whom you share only one parent in common. In Eskimo kinship terminology, these would be called your half-sisters and half-brothers. The personalities of the specific individuals involved, and how they get along, will determine what sort of relationship you have with them. A step-father-in-law may be more significant in your life than your own father. You may be closer to your younger half-sister than to your much older full sister.

Adoption and Fostering

Relatives can also be acquired through formal and informal adoption and fostering. In most cases, adopted children are accorded the same or similar status as biological children, and in the Eskimo kinship terminology system they are not distinguished by separate terms.

Fictive Kin

Many people around the world accord kinship status to beloved individuals who are related neither through biological links nor marriage. These **fictive kin** may be called by the kinship term assigned to the relative who holds the most similar position in the family. Thus, my husband's best friend Andrew is referred to as "Uncle Andrew" by our children. Women without children may play the role of favorite aunt to their friends' children, who call her by that kinship term. Fraternities and sororities are explicitly modeled after fictive sibling relationships—fraternal means brotherly, and sororal means sisterly.

The Web of Kinship: Multiple Strands

Finally, in societies where people intermarry with distant relatives, or have few options for marriage partners, two individuals may be related in multiple ways. Two of my father's brothers, William and Earl, married sisters, Nellie and Marie, who then became sisters-in-law as well, and double sisters-in-law to their brothers-in-law. Years later, after Marie had died, Earl married Esther, the widow of another brother (Abraham); thus, Esther became Earl's wife in addition to being his former sister-in-law. Incredibly complex webs of kinship can be created through such pro-

cesses, and people may be able to pick and choose which kinship relationship they use when approaching a relative to ask a favor or negotiate a deal.

An 1861 photo of famous adoptee Naduah ("Someone Found"). Born Cynthia Ann Parker, she was an Anglo-Texan girl of Scots-Irish descent who was kidnapped at the age of nine by Comanches during a raid on her family's residence at Fort Parker in East Texas. She grew up among the Comanches, married an influential chief, Nocona, and had three children, forgetting her earlier life. She and her two-year-old daughter Topsanna were among a Native American party captured in 1860 by the Texas Rangers, who refused to let them return to their Comanche family. Her son Quanah became an important Comanche chief and a leader in the Native American Church. He had five wives and 25 children.

KINSHIP: MAKING DISTINCTIONS AND TRACING DESCENT

Axes of Distinction

People in every society around the world divide all their many relatives—consanguineal and affinal, close and more distant—into different categories for various purposes. We will talk about the functions kin groups can fulfill shortly. First, we need to talk about the *three main axes of distinction* that people use to create kinship categories and descent groups. Not all societies use all three axes, or place the same degree of importance on them. **Kinship terminology,** the names by which people refer to their different relatives or groups of relatives, provides a window into how these categories are established, which variables are considered most important, and how people in the different categories are view and treated.

Ego and AlterEgo

Anthropologists usually talk about kinship systems from the perspective of one individual, who is labeled **Ego.** Traditionally, Ego was male, but in recent years, Ego is sometimes female. In either case, the other person to whom one is tracing a relationship out from the starting point of Ego is referred to as **AlterEgo.** When tracing genetic/biological relationships, the people through whom one passes when tracing the path from Ego to AlterEgo are referred to as the *links.*

Sex of AlterEgo

The *first main axis of distinction* that all kinship systems use is *whether AlterEgo is a male or a female.* Thus, in Eskimo kinship terminology in English, we recognize distinctions between mother (female) and father (male), between brother (male) and sister (female), between daughter (female) and son (male), between grandmother and grandfather, aunt and uncle, niece and nephew, grandson and granddaughter, and so on. There *do exist* English terms such as parent, sibling, and child, which don't refer to the relative's sex, but they are seldom used in common speech. You aren't likely to say "My sibling is coming to the football game this weekend," or "That was one of my parents on the phone"—you specify whether it is your brother or your sister, your mother or your father.

Genealogical Distance

The *second main axis of distinction* that all kinship systems use is *whether AlterEgo is a close relative or a more distant relative.* This is reflected by the different terms used in Eskimo kinship terminology for brothers and sisters versus cousins. We use a different term for siblings (who share the same parents), than for cousins (who merely share the same grandparents). Notice also that in the Eskimo system, we don't have separate terms for male versus female cousins.

Different terms of address will distinguish whether relatives belong to the same generation or are separated by several or many generations. For example, we have parents, grandparents, great-grandparents, and so on; children, grandchildren, great-grandchildren, etc. Likewise, in the Eskimo kinship system, we have first cousins, second cousins, third cousins, as far as you want to take it. If the two relatives are different numbers of generations away from the common ancestor, they may be described as "eighth cousins, four times removed" and so on. Such terminology allows us to tell immediately whether a relative is close genealogically or quite distant. Kinship systems other than Eskimo will have different ways of indicating genealogical distance through the terms used to refer to specific relatives.

Sex of the Links When AlterEgo Is a Cousin: Are They Both the Same Sex, or One of Each?

Studying how people refer to their cousins enables anthropologists to learn a lot about a group's kinship system. We will examine the rules for distinguishing among cousins as a means of exploring the *third main axis of distinction* used by some kinship systems. The third axis is based on the *sex of the links between Ego and AlterEgo.* From Ego's perspective, there are two links between Ego and his AlterEgo cousin. The first link is one of Ego's parents (either his mother or his father), and the second link is one of Ego's parents' siblings (his father's brother or sister, or his mother's brother or sister). Cousins, then, are the children of Ego's parents' siblings. This third axis of distinction focuses not on whether the two links themselves are male versus female, but rather on whether both links are the *same sex* (female-female or male-male) or include one relative of each sex (female-male or male-female).

Because this axis of distinction is not used in the Eskimo kinship system, many students in North

American and European universities find this the most difficult aspect of kinship to understand. It is really quite simple if you understand the rules. In anthropological terminology, those cousins who are related to Ego through two links of the same sex, both male or both female, are referred to as **parallel cousins** (such as father's brothers' children). Those cousins who are related to Ego through two links of opposite sex, one male and one female, are referred to as **cross cousins** (such as mother's brothers' children). The *cultural logic* behind this system is as follows:

For each of Ego's parents, their siblings of the *same sex* are considered equivalent to the parent; thus, father and father's brothers are all called *father* and are treated pretty much the same. For example, if you owe respect to your father, you also owe it to his brothers. Thus, father's brothers' children, your parallel cousins, are like your own siblings and are treated as being the same type of close relatives as siblings. Parallel cousins may even be referred to as brother and sister. Considering your mother, her sisters are all called *mother* and expect to be treated the way you treat your mother. Thus, mother's sisters' children are also parallel cousins and are treated like brothers and sisters too. The main difference this makes in daily life is that since one does not marry one's brothers and sisters, in any culture, *parallel cousins are not considered potential marriage partners.*

For each of Ego's parents, their siblings of the *opposite sex* are considered to be quite different—father's sisters and mother's brothers are not considered to be equivalent to mother and father, respectively. Thus, your father's sisters' children and your mother's brothers' children are lumped together as more distant relatives, your *cross cousins.* They are referred to by different terms than those used to refer to siblings or parallel cousins. As more distant relatives, they may be considered potential marriage partners and are sometimes preferred over unrelated marriage partners.

In a culture where this is the prevailing system, a male Ego may be expected to choose a bride from among his female cross cousins. This group would include all the unmarried daughters of his father's sisters and his mother's brothers. Where people have large families, there may be quite a variety of young girls to choose from. In some cases, it may be further specified that Ego must marry only a paternal cross cousin—one of his father's sisters' children.

Cousins and Kinship Terminology

In an introductory text, we only have time to scratch the surface of the complexities of kinship terminology systems. Kinship terminology systems were named by anthropologists after the Native American groups among whom they were first identified, although each is found across the world. It was originally assumed that kinship systems would be endlessly creative and variable, but as it turns out, most people in the world use one of a handful of systems. The Eskimo kinship system makes use of the distinction between male and female AlterEgos, and between close and more distant relatives, but ignores the sex of the links between Ego and his cousins. Thus, the terms brother and sister are limited to those individuals who share one or both parents, and those people who share grandparents are all called cousin, regardless of whether they are parallel cousins (two links of the same sex) or cross cousins (one link of each sex).

In the Hawaiian kinship system, all members of Ego's generation who share the same grandparents—one's siblings and all one's cousins—are considered equivalently close relatives, are all known as brothers and sisters, and are therefore taboo as marriage partners.

In the Iroquois system, parallel cousins are referred to by the terms used for brother and sister, while cross cousins are referred to by different terms, indicating that they may be available, or even preferred, as marriage partners.

In addition to Eskimo, Hawaiian, and Iroquois kinship terminology systems, there are also Omaha, Crow, Dravidian, and Sudanese. Sudanese, also known as descriptive kinship, identifies each relative specifically by naming all of the links between Ego and AlterEgo.

Tracing Descent through Male or Female Links

As we have seen, kinship systems may distinguish different sorts of cousins from one another, or they may classify some cousins as siblings. Descent systems—how the generations relate to one another—also make use of the distinction between male and female links in tracing familial ties through time. The three most common systems include: tracing links equally through both males and females, tracing links only through males, and tracing links only through females.

Bilateral Descent

Bilateral (literally *two-sided*) **descent** systems trace relationships outward from Ego to other relatives through both male and female links. This is the most common type of system in North America and Western Europe and is often associated with Eskimo kinship terminology. Under a bilateral system, Ego's *mother's* mother is his grandmother, just as his *father's* mother is his grandmother. His *brother's* children are his nieces and nephews, just as his *sister's* children are his nieces and nephews. *The sex of the links between Ego and AlterEgo are irrelevant.*

Unilineal Descent in General

Unilineal (literally *one-line*) **descent** systems trace relationships outward from Ego to other relatives only through links of one sex or the other, but not both. **Patrilineal** *descent systems trace relationships through male links only.* **Matrilineal** *descent systems trace relationships through female links only.*

Unilineal descent is much more common throughout the world than bilateral descent, and most unilineal descent systems are of the patrilineal type. Membership in a unilineal descent system is automatic, by virtue of your birth to your parents. In a patrilineal system, Ego automatically belongs to the lineage of his or her father; in a matrilineal system, Ego automatically belongs to the lineage of his or her mother. Lineage membership is not voluntary, nor is it changeable. It is a lifelong part of a person's identity and denotes the group of people to which one belongs—the people one can count on for certain rights and support and the people to whom one owes allegiance and has responsibilities. Most societies that use unilineal descent use only patrilineality or matrilineality, but there are a few societies with more complicated systems.

Unilineal descent divides all of one's relatives into those who are members of the same lineage, and those who are not. These groups are clearly defined—they are unambiguous, and they are not open to negotiation. The existence of these specific groups allows the society to base solutions to many different problems on the lineage system. It is often the lineage, rather than the individual members of the lineage, that owns real property and other significant resources. One inherits from the lineage, not necessarily from one's father or mother. The functions of unilineal descent systems will be discussed in more detail below.

Unilineal Descent through Males Only: Patrilineal Descent

In patrilineal descent systems, only *male* relatives can serve as links between Ego and all of the AlterEgos who are considered to be part of Ego's lineage. The patrilineage itself will include both male and female members, all of whom are linked through male relatives. When tracing kinship connections outward from Ego, any time you come to a male relative, you include him and continue on through him to both ascending and descending generations. Any time you come to a female relative, you include her in the lineage, but then you stop, as *females cannot serve as links in a patrilineal system.*

Marriages in patrilineal descent systems are almost always between members of different lineages. Women in a patrilineal system belong to the lineage of their father, sisters, and brothers, and their brothers' children, and do not change lineage membership upon marriage. Thus, a woman's children will belong to their father's lineage, a different lineage than their mother belongs to.

Starting from a male Ego in a patrilineal system, the following relatives would be members of his patrilineage:

- Ego's brothers and sisters, who are related to Ego through the father they share
- Ego's children, both sons and daughters
- Ego's sons' children (grandchildren through sons), but not his daughters' children
- Continuing down through the descending generations indefinitely as long as there is a male link
- Ego's father, but not his mother
- Ego's father's siblings (aunts and uncles), and his cousins through paternal uncles (his father's brothers' children, but not his father's sisters' children)
- Continuing up through the ascending generations indefinitely as long as there is a male link

Once again, to recap, a patrilineal system divides all of Ego's possible relatives up into two groups. One group consists of his patrilineage, which includes both males and females, his lineage mates, all of whom are related to him through male links. The other group consists of his other relatives, who are recognized as being related to him, but are members of other lineages and don't have the same obligations to him (nor does he have the same obligations to them as he does to his lineage mates). In a patrilineal system, Ego's lineage mates are also known as his **agnates.** Females in a patrilineal system belong to the same lineage as their father, brothers, and sisters, but a different lineage than their husband and children.

Unilineal Descent through Females Only: Matrilineal Descent

Matrilineal descent works the same way as patrilineal descent, but in matrilineal descent only *female* relatives can serve as links between Ego and all of the AlterEgos who are considered to be part of Ego's lineage. The matrilineage itself will include both male and female members, all of whom are linked through female relatives. When tracing kinship connections outward from Ego, any time you come to a female relative, you include her and continue on through her to both ascending and descending generations. Any time you come to a male relative, you include him in the lineage, but then you stop, as *males cannot serve as links in a matrilineal system.*

Marriages in matrilineal descent systems are almost always between members of different lineages. Women in a matrilineal system belong to the lineage of their mother, sisters and brothers, and their sisters' children, and do not change lineage membership upon marriage. Thus, a woman's children will belong to her lineage, a different lineage than their father belongs to.

Starting again from a male Ego in a matrilineal system, the following relatives would be members of his matrilineage:

- Ego's brothers and sisters, who are related to Ego through the mother they share

- *Not* Ego's children, who belong to their mother's matrilineage

- Ego's sisters' children (nieces and nephews through his sisters), but not his brothers' children

- Continuing down through the descending generations indefinitely as long as there is a female link (his nieces' children, and so on)

- Ego's mother, but not his father

- Ego's mother's siblings (aunts and uncles) and his cousins through maternal aunts (his mother's sisters' children, but not his mother's brothers' children)

- Continuing up through the ascending generations indefinitely as long as there is a female link

Once again, to recap, a matrilineal system divides all of Ego's possible relatives up into two groups. One group consists of his matrilineage, which includes both males and females, his lineage mates, all of whom are related to him through female links. The other group consists of his other relatives, who are recognized as being related to him, but are members of other lineages and don't have the same obligations to him (nor does he have the same obligations to them as he does to his lineage mates). Females in a matrilineal system belong to the same lineage as their mother, brothers, sisters, and children, but to a different lineage than their husband.

In matrilineal systems, all the members of a matrilineage take care of the children of the matrilineage. This means that a man, along with his brothers and his other male lineage mates, has responsibility for his sisters' children and the children of his other female lineage mates. His own children are cared for by the adult male members of their matrilineage, who are his wife's brothers (their maternal uncles) and her other male lineage members. There will always be adult males in every matrilineage, so even if a specific woman has no brothers, there will be other male members of her matrilineage who will help her raise her children.

As wives and mothers, women in matrilineal societies have several advantages over women in patrilineal societies. In a matrilineal society, a woman does not have to stay with an abusive or neglectful husband, as her brothers will provide for her children if she divorces or leaves her husband. Likewise, if she decides to end the marriage, the children automatically stay with her, so she is never at risk of losing her children or having to leave them behind with their father's family. In some matrilineal societies, valuable resources such as land or a house are passed down from mothers to daughters.

Matrilineality does not *necessarily* give women any more real power than patrilineality. In most communities, it is typically a group of men who hold the economic, political, and religious power. The only difference is in how the men are related to one another—through male links in a patrilineal system, and through female links in a matrilineal system.

Lineages, Clans, Phratries, and Moieties

As the generations pass, lineages will grow in size, and eventually will need to be divided up into smaller segments, based on more recent ancestors. Related lineages may still be clustered together into larger units known as clans, which in turn may be linked with related clans in the same phratry or moiety. The term moiety is used only when an entire group of people is divided into two clusters of phratries or clans—where everyone belongs either to one moiety or the other.

This system forms a nested hierarchy of levels of relatedness, also known as a **segmentary lineage system,** which can be adapted for many different uses in the realms of politics, economics, and marriage. U.S. Major League Baseball serves as an excellent analogy for understanding how nested hierarchies work.

Major League Baseball (MLB) includes all of the professional baseball teams that play at the highest level of competition in the United States and Canada. MLB is divided into two leagues, the American League and the National League. In the idiom of kinship, these would be referred to as **moieties**—all teams belong either to the American League or to the National League. There are no other leagues, and each team belongs to only one league.

Each league, in turn, is divided into three divisions based on geography: East, Central, and West, for a total of six divisions. Divisions can be thought of as **clans.** Each division is composed of four to six teams, or franchises. The teams can be thought of as **lineages.** Each team is composed of all the members. Individual ball players are the smallest unit, just as individual people are the smallest unit in the lineage-clan-phratry-moiety system. Table 5.1 provides a graphic representation of this information.

For political and social control purposes, members of one lineage stand together against another lineage—just as each baseball team plays other teams in its division. All the lineages belonging to one clan will put their differences aside and stand together in a dispute against another clan—just as the best team in each division competes against the best team from the other divisions to see which division is the best in each league. All the clans that belong to one moiety will stand together in a dispute against the other moiety—just as the American League championship team

Kinship and Descent in the United States

Most people living in the United States follow the pattern of a woman changing her last name to match that of her husband upon marriage and giving her children their father's last name, so last names are usually assigned patrilineally. I was originally Katherine Small but changed my surname to Dettwyler when I married my husband, Steven Dettwyler. Our three children have the surname Dettwyler, as do all of Steven's brothers and their children. My grandson is Henry Hannam, because his father, my daughter's husband, is Mark Hannam. Even in cases where the parents are not married, the children are often given their father's surname, so if siblings have different fathers, they will have different last names from their mother and from each other. These examples reflect patrilineal beliefs.

In the United States, legal custody of children in cases of divorce is usually awarded to the mother. In addition, adult daughters in the United States often maintain stronger ties with their natal families than adult sons, reflected in the saying "Your son is your son 'til he takes him a wife, but your daughter's your daughter for all of her life." Both of these examples reflect variations on matrilineal beliefs.

For most other purposes, people in the United States follow *bilateral descent*, considering the sex of the relative or the sex of the link(s) between two relatives to be irrelevant.

Table 5.1   Major League Baseball as an example of a nested hierarchy

League/Moiety	Division/Clan	Team/Lineage	Team Name/Totem
American	East	Baltimore Orioles Boston Red Sox New York Yankees Tampa Bay Rays Toronto Blue Jays	Orioles Red Sox Yankees Rays Blue Jays
	Central	Chicago White Sox Cleveland Indians Detroit Tigers Kansas City Royals Minnesota Twins	White Sox Indians Tigers Royals Twins
	West	Los Angeles Angels Oakland Athletics Seattle Mariners Texas Rangers	Angels Athletics Mariners Rangers
National	East	Atlanta Braves Florida Marlins New York Mets Philadelphia Phillies Washington Nationals	Braves Marlins Mets Phillies Nationals
	Central	Chicago Cubs Cincinnati Reds Houston Astros Milwaukee Brewers Pittsburgh Pirates St. Louis Cardinals	Cubs Reds Astros Brewers Pirates Cardinals
	West	Arizona Diamondbacks Colorado Rockies Los Angeles Dodgers San Diego Padres San Francisco Giants	Diamondbacks Rockies Dodgers Padres Giants

plays the National League championship team in the World Series.

One's identity shifts depending on the context—you may root for the Philadelphia Phillies during the regular season, but if they don't win the divisional title, you may still root for another National League Eastern Division team to win. If the Arizona Diamondbacks win the divisional title, you may root for them, as the National League team, during the World Series.

This is the baseball-based equivalent of shifting one's geographic identity based on the context. At college, if a classmate asks where you are from, you tell him the city, or the nearest big town if you live in a rural area. If you travel to the other side of the country, and someone asks you the same question, you may reply with your state or province. If you travel to another country, you probably respond with your country. In Paris, France, you might say you are from Canada or India or Kenya—you wouldn't say "I'm from Orangevale" (because no one knows where the heck Orangevale is). If you are visiting another planet, you would tell a local that you were an *Earthling*, and if speaking to someone from another galaxy, you would say you were from a planet in the Milky Way.

A famous Arabic proverb expresses the kinship-based nested hierarchy of loyalties as follows: "Me against my brother, me and my brother against my cousin, me and my brother and my cousin against the world."

"Why So Much Bother?"— The Functions of Group Organization

Descent groups based on ties of kinship can be mobilized to accomplish many different goals and can serve multiple purposes. They are convenient devices for solving a number of specific challenges that commonly confront human societies. *Cultural anthropologists have devoted much time and attention to understanding patterns of marriage, kinship, and descent precisely because so many societies base much or all of their social organization on these structures.* We have examined the structures in some detail. In larger populations, groups may also be formed on the basis of **common interest**—people band together with others who share certain beliefs, practices, or interests, but membership is non-kinship-based. Such groups can serve the very same functions as kinship-based social organization, as described below.

Groups as Corporate Owners of Resources

One of the most important functions that a lineage (or sublineage or clan) may serve is to act as a **corporation** (an entity that exists above and beyond its current members) *that holds resources in trust for the use of members.* In this way, valuable property is held in common by the group, and no individual member may use, sell, or destroy the property for her own profit. Members may use the property only with the permission of the group as a whole, and it is the entire group, or its designated leaders, who make decisions about the use and disposal of the property. For example, among the agro-pastoral Nuer, it is the lineage that owns the herds of cattle, goats, and sheep. Animals may be assigned to specific people for some purposes, such as individual care and milking, but the herd itself belongs to the lineage. When a man wants to marry, he or his father approaches the lineage elders and ask for cows from the herd to use as bridewealth. If an important elder has died, and a sacrifice is needed for the funeral, all of the elder's descendants will join together and choose one or more oxen from the herd to serve this purpose.

An analogous example not based on kinship would be the manner in which businesses are incorporated. For example, a fraternity on campus may own land, on which sits the fraternity house and all its furnishings. These resources are owned by the fraternity as a corporate body. Every year, freshmen join the fraternity, and seniors graduate and move on. Individuals come and go, but the fraternity as a corporate entity persists over time. Bedrooms in the fraternity house are assigned to specific members for their use while they are in school, but the occupants of the rooms change from year to year. If you are assigned a bedroom, you may live there (you have what are known as *usufruct* rights), but you may not sublet your bedroom to a local family or sell the furniture to fund a Spring Break trip or run an illegal business out of it. Likewise, a Nuer man cannot kill one of the lineage cows just because he is hungry for a steak.

Federal or state ownership of land, or groups such as the Nature Conservancy, illustrate how corporate ownership can be used to protect resources for the use of all members in perpetuity. In Delaware, the state owns a large tract of land known as White Clay Creek State Park. The first blocks of land were donated to the state by branches of the Dupont family, with the provision that the land serve as public parkland and preserve the watershed of White Clay Creek, which has been designated as a federally protected National Wild and Scenic River. Over the years, the state has continued to add to the park holdings by buying adjacent or nearby properties as they come up for sale.

In 2005, the state had the opportunity to purchase a country club and golf course located between two areas of the park. In order to add to the parklands and protect the open spaces and forests, the state purchased the property and incorporated it into the park. In this manner, they were able to protect the area from residential or commercial development, creating a large contiguous stretch of Appalachian Piedmont forest for the enjoyment of the native wildlife and humans alike. Local residents can use the parklands for hiking, biking, fishing, and bird-watching, and now have a public golf course and country club to enjoy as well. They cannot build houses on the property or cut down the forests, and hunting of deer is limited to certain seasons.

Different groups can own resources in common. Left: national parks, such as Grand Canyon National Park, are owned by all citizens of the United States. Middle: this building at Dartmouth College is owned by the Theta Delta Chi fraternity. Right: the Trump Tower in New York City is owned by one of Donald Trump's many corporations.

Groups as Sources of Labor and Money

A second important function that a lineage (or sublineage or clan) may serve is to provide a large number of people who can be called on in times of need, either to perform work that needs to be done quickly in order to be effective or to contribute money for a purchase that would otherwise be too expensive. For example, if a barn accidentally burns to the ground, it needs to be rebuilt quickly to shelter the livestock. Assume the barn will require 1,000 man-hours of labor to rebuild. One man, working by himself, would have to work for 10 hours a day, 7 days a week, for more than 3 months to rebuild his barn, during which time he couldn't get any other work done and his livestock would be without shelter. Clearly, doing it all by himself is not an effective solution. If he can call on 19 lineage mates to come and help him,

they can finish in five days. If he can expand his pool of workers and call on 39 relatives, they can finish it in two-and-a-half days. Throw in some food and drink at the end of the day, and perhaps some music, and you've got yourself a barn-building party.

Other kinship-based examples might include:

- The members of a lineage are called to help harvest a crop before a hail storm.

- All the members of an extended family are asked to contribute to a fund to send one particularly promising young family member to college in the capital city.

- One member of the clan loses his shrimp boat in a hurricane, and has no insurance; all the members of his extended clan chip in to buy him another boat.

An analogous example based on common interest rather than kinship might be our unfortunate farmer

Well-defined groups, whether based on kinship or some other common feature, can be called upon to provide a large number of people in times of need. Left: a group of people come together near Toronto, Canada, to build a barn in one day, a practice known as barn-raising. Right: members of the county sheriff's department and local search-and-rescue volunteers launch a boat to check on residents along the flooded Red River in Minnesota in March 2009.

whose barn burned to the ground. If he doesn't have an extended kinship network to call on, but needs the barn rebuilt quickly, he can hire a crew of local carpenters. He must pay them to do the work, but their relationship is then over—he isn't obligated to work with them in the future or help build anyone else's barn.

Other non-kinship-based examples do involve ongoing ties of commitment based on relationships other than kinship. These might include:

- Members of a local church congregation who take turns providing meals for other church families who have a new baby or are dealing with an accident or illness.

- Members of the Firefighters' Auxiliary, who hold bake sales and car washes to raise funds to buy a new fire truck.

- A shrimp-boat owner who has insurance; when his boat is destroyed in a hurricane, his insurance company replaces his boat, using a small portion of the revenues collected from all of their subscribers.

- The town's Lions' Club sponsors a college scholarship for a promising student from the local high school.

Groups as the Basis of Identity: Longing to Belong

A third function of discrete groups, whether based on kinship or not, is to provide an identity to the members. This identity allows them to call on other members of the group for support, even when they are far from home. For example, in patrilineal societies, women most often marry and move away, but they remain members of their father's lineage. Suppose that, years later, a young man is traveling through a potentially hostile region and is challenged to identify himself. Even though he is a stranger to everyone personally, if he can claim lineage ties to one of the women who married into the village years ago, then he can be classified as a "relative" and welcomed into the village.

Many people take advantage of kinship ties to help them establish a place to live and a job when they move to a big city, following others from their family, lineage, or clan. Nuer refugees in Minneapolis/St. Paul, Minnesota, and other major cities in the United States have found that clan-based mutual assistance organizations function very well to assist with many practical issues. At the same time, similar organizations based on larger groupings, such as "all Nuer" or "all Sudanese" (including Nuer, Dinka, Anuak, Shilluk, and other tribal groups) have not been nearly as successful as clan-based organizations (Holtzman 2008).

Likewise, non-kinship-based groups can serve the same function of providing automatic entry into another branch of an organization to which a person be-

Through extended family kinship ties, people can often find relatives in distant places. For example, in 1975, H. B. Le left Vietnam with his family and did not return until 2009, as the commanding officer of a U.S. Navy guided-missile destroyer, the *USS Lassen* (DDG-82). In this photo, Cmdr. Le poses with members of his extended family who stayed behind in Vietnam, as well as with members born since 1975.

People can also belong to groups not based on kinship, but that have branches in numerous locations. This photograph shows the local members of the Independent Order of Odd Fellows (IOOF), located at Silliman University in the Philippines. IOOF, also known as the Three Link Fraternity, is a worldwide altruistic and benevolent fraternity located in approximately 29 countries.

longs. If you are a member of the Bahá'í faith, anywhere you travel in the world, other Bahá'í will provide you with hospitality, a place to stay, food, and whatever type of help you need. If you join a fraternity at one university, and then transfer to another, your fraternity membership is transferable—you are automatically allowed to be a member of the group at your new school. If you belong to La Leche League (an international breastfeeding organization with local support groups around the world) and move to a new city, or even a new country, you can meet other mothers of young children through League meetings, and you can count on a warm reception. If you are a member of the Goth clique at the local high school, and your family moves to a new city, you may be quickly accepted by the Goth community at your new school, as they assume, correctly, that you share cultural beliefs and practices in common.

Non-kinship-based ties may be based on employment. For example, if you work as an elephant keeper at the Portland Zoo, you can visit other zoos around the world and get special behind-the-scenes tours of their elephant facilities. At the end of spring semester in 2009, I was visiting the university my son would attend the next fall. I was granted permission to use the anthropology department's computers to submit grades for my classes at the University of Delaware, where I teach. By virtue of being a member of the same tribe—the tribe of anthropology professors—I was welcomed into the department and offered use of an office and computer, as well as hospitality. Membership in a group with local chapters in many different locations allows an individual to travel far from home yet be classified as, or transformed into, "a member of the group," rather than being viewed as a stranger.

Nested Hierarchies as a Way to Contain and Settle Disputes

Another function of kinship-based social organization is the settlement of disputes, which will be discussed in more detail in chapter 6. In a nutshell, if a dispute is between two members of one family, then only members of that family get involved. If a dispute is between two members of one lineage, then only members of that lineage get involved. If a dispute is between members of two different lineages, then all members of both lineages get involved. This is an excellent system for containing and settling disputes in the absence of state-controlled, autonomous criminal justice systems such as police, courts, and jails.

Non-kinship-based organizations may also use a similar model of dispute settlement, rather than bringing in an outside agency or mediator. For example, if two Army privates get into a fight on base, the local military police handle it. But if a group of U.S. Army privates are out at a bar in a foreign country and get into a dispute with a group of U.S. Marines, military police from both organizations, or even the local municipal authorities, may be called. If the brawling Army men and Marines are challenged by a group of men from the local region, the Americans immediately meld back into "American soldiers" and join forces to fight the enemy, in which case authorities from several countries eventually may be involved. The segmentary or nested hierarchical structure of such organizations allows them to be very adaptable, splitting or fusing together, as the situation demands.

Non-kinship-based organizations serve many of the same functions as kinship-based groups, yet they differ in a number of important ways. These differences are highlighted in table 5.2.

AGE AS THE BASIS FOR GROUP FORMATION

Chronological age and/or developmental age are often used as another basis for dividing people up into subsets of the larger population. In many cases, age-based classifications cut across those based on kinship and common interest. Because age-based systems are so widespread, and play a significant role in both Western and non-Western cultural contexts, we will explore them in some detail.

Chronological versus Developmental Age

Chronological Age

Chronological age refers to a system of keeping track of how old individuals are, based on Western notions of linear time. Age may be reckoned from the date of conception, the date of birth, or some other beginning time point. The following discussion refers to the typical calculation of age in North American cultures, where chronological age is considered an important value, and where one's life is usually considered to begin on the day of one's birth.

Table 5.2   Comparing aspects of kinship-based social organization and common interest groups

Criteria	Kinship/Descent Groups	Common Interest Groups
Becoming a member	Happens automatically at birth, by virtue of who your parents are, and the kinship and descent rules operating in your society	Not automatic—you must join, which may require certain credentials or achievements, or approval of current members
Type of membership	Usually mandatory, you cannot opt out	Usually voluntary, you may join or quit as you please (with limits)
Cost of membership	Free, except that you have duties or obligations to all other members of the group, just as they have to you	May involve ongoing payment of dues or contributions of work, time, or money
How identified as a member	Your surname or lineage name, or the ability to trace common ancestry; perhaps facial scarification or tattoos or particular types of clothing that identify you	Identification card, perhaps with a photo, or knowledge of the secret handshake; perhaps wearing of particular tie or types and colors of clothing or jewelry
Boundaries	Very clear-cut, unambiguous, not subject to negotiation or change	Less clear-cut, may be different levels/degrees of membership and activity, may be negotiated, or may change over time

In the first year of life, age may be calculated in terms of weeks, or months. Sometime during toddlerhood, years become the primary signifier of age, and many people mark their annual birthday with celebrations that may include a party, special food, and gifts. Chronological age is used as the time marker for when certain rights and responsibilities are assigned to individuals. Examples from the United States include:

- Your parents can claim you as a tax deduction for the entire year, beginning with the year you were born, even if you were born at 11:59 PM on December 31.

- You must be five years old by the cut-off date in order to qualify for publicly funded kindergarten.

- Immunization schedules for childhood diseases are based on chronological age.

- You must be a specific chronological age to get a driver's license, to vote, to legally consent to sex, to get married, to join the military, to enter into certain legal contracts, and to drink alcohol legally.

- Once you reach a certain age, if you are male, you are required to sign up for the Selective Service.

- Once you reach the age of 18, your parents are no longer legally responsible for you—they don't have to contribute anything to your care.

- Supplemental Security Income (SSI) eligibility begins on your 18th birthday if you are disabled and unable to support yourself.

- Once you reach the official chronological age for Social Security retirement benefits, which varies based on your year of birth, you are entitled to benefits if you have paid into the system.

In some cultural contexts, specific birthdays have greater personal and social significance than others, whether or not they are accompanied by changes in legal status. For example, in Jewish culture, the Bar or Bat Mitzvah at age 13, and in Latin American cultures, *La Quinceañera* celebrations for 15-year-old girls, mark the transition from childhood to adulthood. Turning 30 or 50 or 100 years of age is also considered a milestone in the passage through life for most Americans.

In Mali, social and political power depends, in part, on relative chronological age. The older people become, the more power and respect they are accorded, relative to others who are younger. Thus, not only do children show respect to adults, but young adults show respect to older adults, and older adults express great deference to the truly elderly. Within a family, a son who is 68 automatically has higher status than a son who is 64, and the eldest son always defers to his father, even if the son is 52 and the father is 78. People often do not know exactly how old they are in years, or when their birthday is, but they know precisely who is older than they are and is due respect, and who is younger and should show them respect.

Developmental Age

In many non-Western cultures, chronological age holds no particular significance. People may not have birth certificates and may not know when they were born, or may know only the year or the season. Birthdays may not be noted or celebrated in any way. At the same time, virtually all societies do pay attention to the physical growth of children, the achievement of developmental milestones, reproductive maturity, and various other achievements over the course of a lifetime. Transitions from one culturally defined category to another may be marked by biological transformations, such as the development of secondary sexual characteristics, giving birth, or going through menopause. Other transitions are marked by cultural transformations such as circumcision, tattooing, scarification, a new name, and so on. Among traditional Nuer of the southern Sudan, a boy's transition from childhood to manhood usually took place in his early teens, whenever he felt he was ready, and was marked by the cutting of a series of deep parallel grooves across his forehead. During the twentieth century, among traditional villages of Gikuyu in Kenya, many of a woman's achievements as a mother were marked by rituals and celebrations, including marriage, the birth of her first child, the weaning of her first child, the circumcision of her first child, the circumcision of her last child, the birth of her first grandchild, and so on (Davidson 1996).

There are many different categories of developmental age that may be marked in various contexts, including *before naming*, which may be postponed until some days or weeks following birth. Other categories might include: before the child can walk (or walk well); before the child can talk (or talk well); before the child has developed common sense and can be expected to understand right from wrong; the child is still breastfeeding versus has been weaned; the child is the youngest child versus the next-to-youngest child; and so on. **Uncircumcised** and **circumcised** are important distinctions in some cultures. The age at which circumcision occurs may vary from culture to culture, as well as within a single culture, if circumcision ceremonies take place only once every few years. **Not-yet-menstruating** and **menstruating** are important in some contexts, as the first menstrual cycle (menarche) is used to mark the boundary between childhood and adulthood for girls in some societies, regardless of how old they are when they begin to menstruate.

In contrast to defining adulthood based on chronological age or physiological maturity, some cultures withhold full adult status until an individual has married, or until he has become a parent. In such situations, if you never marry, or marry but don't have children, you will be considered immature in some sense, a legal minor, no matter how old you get.

Even after death, you may continue to advance through developmental stages, moving from "recently deceased" to "long-deceased but still survived by people who knew you personally," and eventually to "one of the ancients."

When Does Life Begin?

Humans express a wide variety of cultural beliefs about when life begins. Typically in Western societies, the differences in worldview are characterized as being clear-cut—either life begins at conception or it begins at birth. A closer examination of the cross-cultural evidence reveals that individuals in many cultures, including Western ones, maintain a rather more complicated set of beliefs about the gradual development of humanness.

Conception or Before?

Some people maintain that human life begins at conception, at the moment that the woman's egg allows the man's sperm to enter, creating a single cell with 46 chromosomes and the potential to develop into a human being. In many societies, however, the prevailing view is that children exist in spirit form long before they exist as a fertilized egg (DeLoache and Gottlieb 2000). They may be thought to live in a spiritual realm, along with ancestors, and may themselves be spirits who have lived previous lives as humans and who can be reincarnated multiple times. The moment

of conception holds no special significance when the child has had former lives and spent time living in the spiritual world.

Quickening

Across Western Europe, a widespread traditional Christian belief was that although pregnancies began several months earlier, God didn't place a soul in the developing fetus until around the fourth month of pregnancy. This event was known as **quickening** and coincided with the first time that the mother could feel the fetus' movement. The kicking of the baby was considered a sign that the pregnancy was now viable and the baby had a soul. People seldom talk about quickening any more, and women in the United States are more likely to define the pregnancy as "real" either when they first see the image of the fetus on the ultrasound screen around 12 weeks into the pregnancy or when they get the results of an amniocentesis test and make a conscious decision to continue the pregnancy (Rapp 2000; Rothman 1986).

At the same time, more Americans support a woman's right to have an abortion during the first two trimesters (the first six months of a nine-month pregnancy), than during the last trimester. After this point in the pregnancy, there is a much better chance that the baby could survive on its own outside the womb. Thus, a person might support an elective abortion early in the pregnancy but object to a government-ordered abortion against the mother's wishes at 8.5 months of pregnancy, as has occurred in China under the "One Child Rule."

The Gradual Nature of Becoming Human

When considering how pregnancy losses and later childhood and adult deaths are treated, it is clear that many Americans adhere to a belief that the longer you are alive, *up to a point*, the more human you become, and the more significant and tragic is your death. For example, many people expect that a woman's grief over a miscarriage will be proportional to the duration of the pregnancy. In other words, if you miscarry at six weeks into the pregnancy, within days of discovering that you are pregnant, most people think you will be sad, but they also think that you shouldn't dwell on your loss. You are not expected to name the child, bury the remains, or mourn for years. Most people would consider a late miscarriage to be much more distressing than an early miscarriage. A stillbirth or death immediately following delivery is considered even more upsetting than a late miscarriage.

Likewise, the death of a two-month old is considered (by those not directly involved) to be less of a life-altering event than the death of a three-year-old or a 12-year-old or a 16-year-old. Judging from reactions following the death of a young person, it appears that the prevailing cultural belief in the United States is that the death of a teen or young adult is the most tragic, both for the individual and for his or her parents, family, and friends. Of course people mourn loved ones who die at any age, but the death of someone in their 30s, 40s, or 50s is usually considered sadder than the death of someone in their 80s or 90s, but not as upsetting as the death of a teenager. When my husband's grandmother, Hannah Hughes, died in 2002 at the age of 104, members of her family were all sad. She was a lovely person and was active and alert until right before she died. At the same time, her death was not a surprise, and although we miss her, we also feel that she enjoyed a good long life.

In cultures where infant and child mortality rates are very high, parents expect that some of their children will die and therefore do not mourn them to the same extent that parents do in contexts where hardly any children die. In some places, children are not considered to be fully human until they have survived to a particular age or developmental stage, or until they have survived whatever diseases routinely kill children in that society.

Organizing Groups Based on Age

In addition to kinship- and common-interest-based social organization, many societies around the world use chronological age, developmental age, or stage of the life-span as the basis for organizing people into groups. There are two broad types of age classifications, *age grades* and *age sets*. Although they have similar names, they are quite distinct concepts.

Age Grades

The term **age grade** refers to a classification based on age or stage of the life-span that a person enters and then, after some period of time, exits. *Age grades are not permanent.* The most obvious example in North American societies would be grades in public school. Most school districts have strict rules about the minimum age for entry into kindergarten (five years) or first grade (six years). Thus, most kindergarteners are five to six years old. As you move through the grades, there may occasionally be a student who skips a grade, or a few students who fail and repeat a grade, but most of the children will be within a year of each other in age. Except for those who are held back, you are a first-grader for only one year, then you become a second-grader, and then a third-grader, and so on. In high school, your first year you are a freshman, then a sophomore, then a junior, then a senior. You spend one year in each grade, then you move on. As a college student, you will never be a high school senior again.

Age grades can be based on developmental age, rather than chronological age. For example, most children go through a stage of being able to sit, but not yet crawl. Then most move on to a stage of crawling, but not yet walking. Walking comes next, followed by running and jumping. Children may vary in the chronological age at which they reach these stages of motor development, but most go through the same stages, in the same order. Likewise, you might characterize children into developmental stages based on dental eruption patterns: no teeth, some deciduous teeth, all deciduous teeth, some permanent teeth, all deciduous teeth gone, and all permanent teeth, including the third molars or wisdom teeth (the last to erupt).

Age grades can be based on achievement as well. Many voluntary associations have progressively higher ranks that an individual may move through based partly on age and partly on achievements. Most military organizations have ranks of this sort, as do the Boy Scouts, Little League, and many secret societies such as the Masons. As you move further and further up the ladder, chronological ages at each rank become greater, and the range of ages within each rank also increases, since some people remain at one rank for many years or even for the rest of their lives.

Finally, age grades can also be based on stage of life. People who have just gotten married for the first time are referred to as *newlyweds*. There may be little consensus on how long the newlywed period lasts, but after 30 years, my husband and I are clearly no longer newlyweds! Women who are first-time mothers, whether they are 18 or 28 or 38, have much in common, and may join together in various types of local groups for information and support. You can be a first-time mother only once in your life. Many American parents go through a "PTA, car-pooling, soccer-coaching" phase.

Retiree communities may have a minimum age, usually 55 years, and all the residents have their retirement in common—they are no longer working at a job or career. Couples in the United States typically go through a series of stages, from dating to engaged, married/newlywed, still married but without children, parents of their first child, who goes from being a baby to a toddler, to a child to a teenager, to an adult (with perhaps more children along the way). Eventually, their last child will leave home and, in the United States, they are then referred to as *empty nesters*. They will share many things in common with other parents who are at the same stage of life, even though the chronological ages of the parents will vary widely.

Essentially, any age or stage that you go through and then exit out of can be the basis for age-grade or-ganization. Common interest based on chronological or developmental age, or stage of the life-span, can be the basis for banding together with others for many different purposes.

Age Sets

In contrast to age grades, **age sets** are based partly on chronological or developmental age, but *are permanent entities to which one always belongs*. You enter into a named age set based on specific criteria, but you never leave that age set—you will always be a member, and membership in the group will always be a part of your identity. The simplest example for college students would be your high school graduating class. I was a senior in high school in 1972. I was a high school senior for only one year—that was an age grade. But I will forever and always be a member of the Class of 1972 from Casa Roble High School in Orangevale, California, an age set to which I belong.

In many places, children of the same or similar ages are grouped together for school and sports activities. As they get older, they move on to the next age grade. For example, U.S. preschools typically enroll children who are three or four years old. When they are five, they begin kindergarten. Top: Captain Bette Bolivar, commanding officer of Naval Weapons Station Yorktown, reads a book to preschool children at the station's Child Development Center. Bottom: Little League players and U.S. Sailors participate in a ceremony to dedicate the ball field in Mount Washington, Kentucky, as "Navy Field." As the children grow up, they will move on to different divisions of Little League.

Age sets are groups to which a person always belongs. In 2009, World War II veterans of the battle of Peleliu held their 56th reunion in San Diego aboard the battle's namesake ship, the *USS Peleliu*. More than 400 friends, family members, Sailors, and Marines were in attendance. Their joint participation in the battle has bound these veterans together for life in an age set.

A second clear example of an age set would be the different named generations identified during the past century. Those who were adults during World War II, who fought in the war, have been dubbed *The Greatest Generation* by journalist Tom Brokaw, and men and women who fought during the war will always be World War II veterans regardless of what else they do or how old they get. After the end of World War II, birth rates soared, creating a much larger cohort of young children than existed prior to or following this time. The term for this large group of people, *Baby Boomers*, includes anyone born between 1946 and 1964.

Some scholars have described the Baby Boom Generation as being analogous to a rat moving through the digestive system of a snake! I was born right in the middle of the boom. When I was growing up, there were more young children than any other segment of the U.S. population. When I was a teenager and young adult, we continued to represent the largest segment of the U.S. population, with significant influence on politics, entertainment, fashion, and music. Baby Boomers often delayed marriage and child rearing, so their offspring are spread out over a much greater range than the 18-year spread of the original Baby Boomers. However, there was a notice-

able spike in childbearing among Baby Boomers in the 1970s and 1980s—a Boomlet. Children born during these decades to Baby Boomer parents are called Echo Boomers.

At the end of the first decade of the twenty-first century, the Baby Boomers are beginning to retire in huge numbers, and as we age, we will put an enormous strain on the Social Security and health care systems.

Age sets are found in a number of societies around the world, including many of the East African cattle-herding societies. For example, among the Maasai, young boys are initiated into named age sets every six to ten years, beginning with a ritual of initiation that includes circumcision. All of the boys who are circumcised at the same time will belong to their named age set for the rest of their lives. Going through circumcision together is the first of many experiences that will bond them tightly together as a group of similarly aged men, or age-mates. The group composed of one's age-mates cross-cuts groups based on ties of kinship.

Among the Maasai, members of one age set will pass through the different grades as a group. First they will be newly circumcised, newly initiated youths. After a period of instruction in the skills of cattle raiding and warfare, accompanied by a number of food taboos and the wearing of special clothing, they advance to the rank of junior warriors, or *morans*. During this time, they traditionally live away from the villages, but they keep watch, protecting the villages and herds, killing lions who attack the livestock and raiding other groups to acquire more cattle. After a number of years as morans, the group as a whole advances to the status of senior warrior, to be replaced by the next set of junior warriors. Senior warriors return to the villages, get married, and begin raising families. Eventually, as a group, the age set advances to the final status, that of respected elders, those who make important decisions for the entire population.

FINAL THOUGHTS

The main take-home message of this chapter has been that human populations have been able to solve a number of problems by organizing people into groups for various purposes.

The simplest type of group is the new unit that is created through marriage, which may eventually include more than two partners to the marriage. Marriages then become the basis for producing legitimate children and are thus the foundation of all larger kinship-based groups. All societies, with the possible exception of the Mosuo of China, have institutions of formal marriage.

Larger kinship groupings are based on a variety of relationships—who you are descended from, who is descended from you, who you share common ancestors with, who you are married to, as well as other ties of biological, legal, and fictive kinship. By choosing which elements of such relationships to emphasize, and which to downplay or ignore altogether, people create a limited number of complex but adaptable systems of social organization. The groups formed by such kinship and descent-based systems can then own property, can be mobilized to accomplish a number of tasks, can serve to give individuals and groups a well-defined identity within the system, and can be used as the basis for social order and control.

Social organization can also be based on other shared characteristics besides kinship. Common interest is the primary basis by which non-kinship-based organizations are formed, including businesses, clubs, associations, and so forth. Distinctions based on age or stage of the life-span can also serve as the basis for group membership and social organization. Groups based on common interest or age can serve the same functions as kinship-based groups and may be found instead of, or in addition to, kinship-based social organization. Generally, the more individuals who interact on a daily or weekly basis, the smaller the role kinship plays in social organization.

Anthropologists pay so much attention to kinship-based organization because it is often the main way small-scale societies are organized, and it continues to be important even in industrial and postindustrial societies.

Key Concepts Review

Marriages are publicly recognized, formal unions that affect the status of children and establish the rights and responsibilities of the parties to the marriage.

Marriages are culturally defined institutions that may involve more than one individual of each sex, or may involve two individuals of the same sex.

Marriage is nearly universal in human cultures and probably developed early in human cultural development as a way to reduce male–male aggression and encourage males to contribute to child care.

Where men are unable or unwilling to contribute significant financial resources to a family, for whatever reason, women may find that it makes more sense to remain single and raise their children on their own.

In many cultures, marriages are arranged by the families of the prospective bride and groom and are based on economic, political, and religious considerations, as well as shared values, and the bride and groom are not expected to be romantically in love with each other.

The notion of companionate marriage, based on romantic love, is spreading from many Western cultures to other regions of the world.

Every culture has both prescriptive and proscriptive rules about who makes an appropriate or inappropriate marriage partner, including incest avoidance, endogamy, and exogamy.

Many women marry men who have a higher status than they do, a practice known as hypergamy.

There are advantages of arranged marriages over the system of companionate marriage most common in North America, especially for women.

Marriages can be classified according to how many people are involved, and their sex, including monogamy, polygyny, and polyandry; polygyny is the most common allowed marriage form around the world, while polyandry is the rarest.

There are advantages to polygyny for the co-wives in contexts where women do most of the physical labor.

Bridewealth is the transfer of resources from the groom's family to the bride's family and is found in cultures that value the ability of women to make other people.

Dowry is the transfer of resources from the bride's family to the groom's family and is found in cultures that generally devalue women's reproductive abilities.

In many Western cultures, much of the labor of running the household is contracted to outsiders, not performed by the husband and/or the wife.

Among the Nuer, ghost marriage and female–female marriage show the importance of children to the concept of marriage.

Biological (consanguineal) kinship comes either from one person being descended from another or from both being descended from a common ancestor.

Affinal kinship is established through cultural rules of marriage and adoption.

For tracing kinship outward from Ego, people use up to three basic axes of distinction: the sex of AlterEgo, the genealogical distance, and the sex of the links between Ego and AlterEgo.

Systems of kinship terminology are named after Native American tribes and can be distinguished based on what siblings and cousins are called, which often determines which individuals are potential marriage partners.

For tracing descent outward from Ego, people can use links of both sexes (male and female) to create bilateral kinship systems, or they can use links of only one sex to create patrilineal systems (male links only) or matrilineal systems (female links only).

Patrilineal descent is the most common system found around the world; most Western societies use bilateral kinship; under matrilineal systems, men take care of their sisters' children.

There are advantages to matrilineal kinship systems, especially for the women.

Patrilineages and matrilineages contain both male and female members, and men usually have the majority of the economic, political, and religious power—the main difference is how the men in the lineage are related to one another.

Lineages in either system can be grouped together into larger organizational levels known as clans, phratries, and moieties.

Whether people are organized into groups based on kinship or common interest, such groups can be used to fulfill many important functions, including: corporate ownership of resources, providing labor and money, providing a sense of identify and belonging, and containing and settling disputes.

continued

Kinship-based organization is automatic, is unambiguous, and provides a safety net of support for all members of the group.

Chronological age and/or developmental age can be used to organize people into groups that cut across kinship and common interest.

"When does life begin?" is a question whose answer is shaped by cultural beliefs and is more complex than merely a choice between conception and birth.

Age grades are groupings that you move into and then out of, like grades in school, and can be based on chronological age, developmental age, achievements, or stage of life; examples include being a senior in high school, a newlywed, or a new parent.

Age sets are groupings to which you permanently belong; like age grades, they can be based on different factors; examples include being a member of your high school graduating class, a military veteran, or an Eagle Scout.

Anthropologists pay so much attention to kinship-based organization because it is often the main way small-scale societies are organized, and it continues to be important even in industrial and postindustrial societies.

6

GETTING PEOPLE TO BEHAVE

Enculturation, Rules, & Politics

The most powerful tool that any group has at its disposal for getting people within the group to behave is the enculturation of children. From the moment of their birth, children are exposed to the social norms— the values, the ethics, the standard ways of thinking and behaving— that comprise their cultural heritage.

Every culture has rules of behavior—guidelines about what is acceptable, what is frowned upon, what is absolutely forbidden, and so on. Without some sort of guidelines for how to behave, it would be very difficult to organize large groups of people into more-or-less functioning societies. Where the rules are clear-cut, and everyone follows the rules, even large, complex societies can function very smoothly. Where the rules are less clear-cut, are ambiguous, and/or where some or many people don't follow the rules, the society may function somewhat inefficiently, or it may not function very well at all. The main disadvantage in a conformist society, where everyone knows and follows the rules, is that personal freedoms are stifled and there is little tolerance for variation in beliefs and behavior. The main disadvantage in a society where personal freedoms and choice are more highly valued, and where there is more tolerance for variation, is that conflicts are more likely to arise, and in general, the society functions less efficiently. What happens when two groups with different sets of rules come into contact?

All cultures have to develop organized means of creating and revising the rules and deciding who has the legislative power and/or authority to do so. Likewise, cultures need some means of deciding who is responsible and who gets punished when a rule is broken, and who carries out the legal sanctions. Groups may operate by a code of individual or corporate responsibility, with very different results.

Who is allowed to administer justice? In some cases, the person who was harmed can take individual revenge against the perpetrator of the crime **(self-redress).** In other cases, any member of the victim's kin group may take revenge against the perpetrator and/or other members of his kin-group **(feuding).** Eventually, these **privilege rights** of prosecution and the imposition of legal sanctions are shifted over to clearly defined public officials representing the society as such, through some type of criminal justice system (after Hoebel 1967, quoted in Fry 2007). **Warfare** as a means of resolving disputes has only been part of human behavior for the past 10,000 years, and many cultures today remain peaceful and do not participate in warfare.

My understanding of these issues draws heavily from anthropologist Douglas P. Fry's brilliant and exhaustive analysis of sociopolitical organization and conflict resolution, *Beyond War: The Human Potential for Peace* (2007). All of the different levels and aspects of getting people to behave via the political and legal systems are interrelated and feed back on one another. It is hard to know where best to start our explorations—we begin with different types of cultural rules.

TYPES OF RULES

Formal Rules

Not all societies have written languages or the bureaucratic machinery for devising and modifying rules

200

that might be recognized as explicit *laws*. In hunter-gatherer societies, there are seldom written laws, but there are still formal rules, backed by historical tradition and/or religious mythology that outline what the formal rules are. In all societies, there will be mechanisms for making sure that children learn the rules as they grow up. In more complex societies, the formal rules may be codified into laws, which may be written down.

Formal rules are often based on geographic distinctions, so that there may be different rules and regulations at the community, city, county, state, national, and international levels. Formal rules may also be based on common interests, so, for example, there are laws governing financial institutions, the military, trade and commerce, and so on. There will be rules for making the rules, and rules for changing the rules, and rules for punishing those who break the rules. There may be general rules, or there may be very specific and explicit rules concerning minute details of behavior.

In societies where the laws are written down, most people do not have access to them, and haven't read them, but there is a general consensus about the notion of a **rule of law** and agreement that people are supposed to obey the laws or suffer the consequences. If people disagree with the laws, there are usually legal mechanisms in place to change them.

Formal rules may be explicitly taught to children, or to newcomers to the group of any age. There may be training sessions or handbooks or policy manuals or even websites that lay out the formal rules. These documents may explain the justification behind the rules, as well as lay out the punishments for breaking the rules. Many organizations require that people agree—orally, in writing, or by the click of a mouse—with the stated rules before they may participate in the group.

Informal Rules

In addition to the formal rules that a group establishes, there will also be a number of less stringent, more ambiguous, informal rules that govern behavior in different circumstances. These are often just as important, or even more important, than the formal rules. However, it can be more difficult to find out what these informal rules are, who established them, how they might be changed, and what will happen if these informal rules are broken. Informal rules are often implicit,

and a person only becomes aware of the rules by the reactions of others when the rule is broken.

For example, university campuses seldom have dress codes, but if someone showed up for class in a bikini, a clown costume, or a tuxedo, people would probably make fun of him or her. And if you are interviewing for a job in the business world, there are informal rules about what to wear and what not to wear (no flip-flops, no glam-rock makeup). You won't get arrested if you show up in flip-flops, but you are unlikely to get the job.

In many parts of the world, the left hand is used to clean oneself after urinating and defecating. Even though people wash their hands afterward, the left hand is still not used for shaking hands, transferring objects to another person, or eating. If you come from a culture where this is not the custom, and especially if you are left-handed, it may take some practice to learn to follow this important informal rule. People will usually let you know, through the way they look at you, through body language, or with words, that what you are doing is inappropriate.

For many people, it is the informal rules that are the most problematic when entering a new culture, whether that involves traveling overseas or merely switching jobs from one company to another. The informal rules are seldom articulated and usually are not written down. People who are familiar with them take them for granted and so won't even think to mention them. "Of course you can't have photographs of your family in your cubicle—that would be unprofessional!" Or, "Yes, it's true that you officially get an hour for lunch, but if you want to be promoted, you'll eat a quick sandwich at your desk and continue working."

Rules for Breaking the Rules

In addition to formal and informal rules, there also will be unspoken rules about which rules absolutely must be obeyed and which are more flexible. In other words, in many contexts, there are additional rules about breaking the rules. Which rules can one break with impunity? In what ways? Some written rules and regulations are seldom honored, yet they stay "on the books."

My favorite practical examples of this phenomenon come from traffic laws. Every country and state, and even some smaller municipalities, will have a variety of traffic laws. People are supposed to obey the

All societies have formal rules, informal rules, and even rules for breaking the rules. Left: an intersection in southern California displays 12 different signs telling drivers and others what they can and can't do, including no left turn, no U-turn, no skateboarding or rollerblading, and "Watch out for illegal aliens from Mexico crossing the border" (sign at top right of family running). Below: a car in Vancouver, British Columbia, Canada, blithely ignores two prominent "no entry" signs. Very likely, people who live on this street routinely break the rule.

rules, more or less, in order to ensure safety and the smooth flow of traffic. In Western countries, traffic lights have different colors with different meanings. Red means stop, green means go, yellow is supposed to mean *slow down*. But many people behave as though yellow means *go faster*. If you come from a region where everyone speeds up for yellow lights, and you are driving in a region where everyone slows down, you may find yourself running into the person in front of you. When the light turned yellow, you expected the car in front of you to speed up and get through the intersection, but instead it slowed down. Crash! When I lived in Texas, it was common practice for people to speed up at yellow lights and for cars to continue through the intersection if the car ahead of them had gone through, even if the light had turned red. As long as cars were whizzing through the red light one after another, the people in the cross-street would sit waiting patiently, even though their light was green. Everyone knew the rule for breaking the rule about slowing down and stopping when the light turned yellow, and then red.

In Delaware, people are more likely to slow down at a yellow light and stop. On the other hand, if a car has stopped in its lane waiting to turn left across oncoming traffic, people in Delaware often drive around the car using the right-hand shoulder—which is illegal! Likewise, drivers in Delaware often behave as though the bicycle lanes were right-hand turn lanes (they are not), and students on campus routinely ride their bikes on the sidewalk or the wrong way in a one-way bike lane (both illegal). If you want to avoid an accident when you move to a new place, you need to quickly figure out which laws are routinely followed, and which ones ignored.

Customs

Even more amorphous than informal rules are the generic customs or traditions of a group—standards of behavior that don't even rise to the significance of rules or regulations and carry no clear negative sanctions if they are not followed. They are just "the way things are" or "how we do things in this place." Visitors become aware of these customs and often follow along without really questioning them. They unconsciously adopt the local customs and styles, and don't even realize it.

For example, French fries are served with catsup in the United States, and with mayonnaise in Belgium; people in some communities engage in social chit-chat before getting to the point of a conversation, but in Finland, people get right to the point; apartments in Germany are usually rented with an empty kitchen—each new renter brings his own cabinets, countertops, appliances, and light fixtures. Clothing styles, hairstyles, slang terms, popular songs, styles of interacting with others, variations of handshakes—all vary from one group to another and are constantly changing.

WHO MAKES THE RULES?

There are too many variations on this subject to go into detail here. Suffice it to say that in small-scale, band societies, the rules are more likely to be made via discussion and consensus, with all adults having approximately equal power in the decision-making process. As sociopolitical organization becomes more complex, a smaller subset of people may take on the authority for rule making and rule changing. There may still be discussion and input from everyone, but some people's views and opinions are accorded more value. There may be elected representatives chosen by a group of people to represent their interests in the legislative process. Or all of the power may be concentrated in one individual (dictator) or a small group of influential individuals, who maintain their positions through economic strength, hereditary kinship connections (such as royalty), military might, religious mythology, or some combination of sources of power.

In many tribal societies and small chiefdoms, a group of elders, usually all men, will make decisions for the entire group, or they will advise the leader, who may or may not follow their advice. This type of political organization is known as **gerontocracy** (led by the elders), and may function at the family level as well as the village or regional level. State-level societies have official legislative bodies and laws that set out how other laws can be made, or how old laws can be changed.

In voluntary organizations, such as clubs and associations, there may be elected officials such as a president, vice president, secretary, and treasurer, or a team captain and squad leaders. Often, whoever founds the group initially gets to determine the initial rules and regulations and sets up the mechanism by which power is transferred from one generation to the next. On the playground, whoever owns the ball gets to say what the rules are!

People participating in any group may not agree with all the rules. However, they may have a limited number of options for handling their objections, including leaving the area (if the group is geographically based), leaving the organization altogether, attempting to change the rules through the current system (rebellion), attempting to change the rules by overthrowing the current system (revolution), or simply ignoring the rules and hoping no one notices. In some cases, those who are disaffected may opt to leave and begin their own group, with rules and regulations more to their own liking.

In hierarchical contexts, it may be that the people at the bottom aren't dissatisfied with the rules themselves, they are merely unhappy with their position in the hierarchy. If they can move up to positions of power, they are happy to maintain the system itself. For example, some of the recent political woes of Liberia in West Africa can be traced to its founding by freed slaves from the United States in the mid-1800s. They had experienced the plantation/slave system in the United States, with themselves as the slaves. After they attained their freedom, they returned to Africa, to the newly formed U.S. colony of Liberia, where they promptly set up a similar system, but with themselves as the plantation owners and local native Africans as the slaves (Huffman 2005). Descendants of the two groups have been in conflict ever since.

TEACHING AND LEARNING THE RULES

The most powerful tool that any group has at its disposal for getting people within the group to behave is the enculturation of children. From the moment of their birth, children are exposed to the social norms—the values, the ethics, the standard ways of thinking and behaving—that comprise their cultural heritage. If the society does a good job of instilling its worldview about what is appropriate and what is not, then such internal controls function extremely well for encouraging conformity in thought and deed. However, external controls also play a role, both in creating and reinforcing internal controls and in motivating people to behave even when they would rather not. We begin with a discussion of internal controls.

Internal Social Controls

Enculturation: Internalizing Beliefs and Behavior

Through enculturation by family, friends, school teachers, peers, and the media, children are taught what is appropriate and what is not appropriate in their cultural group. Sometimes children are taught explicit rules to follow, such as "Always say please and thank you," or "Never look an adult in the eyes," or "Always exchange items with others using your right hand." Other times they learn through trial and error, through the reactions of others to things they say and do. A child may be rewarded when he does something that is approved of and valued but be corrected or punished when he does something that is inappropriate or forbidden. The majority of enculturation takes place simply through living in a society. You learn through watching others and imitating what they say and do. You come to realize: "This is the way things are done."

Enculturation begins from the moment of birth, if not before. Children soak up their surroundings, learning through observation and imitation, direct instruction from older children and adults, and reactions from others to things that they do, whether those reactions are favorable, such as cheers, or unfavorable, such as a spanking. Children exposed to only one way of doing things take their cultural rules for granted and just assume that everyone shares the same beliefs and follows the same rules. Left: Amish children at a Farmer's Market; middle: U.S. upper-class children playing a computer game; right: a little girl in India, part of a family of beggars, eating watermelon.

Eventually, you *internalize* these beliefs and they guide your behavior, in terms of both encouraging you to act according to the norms and discouraging you from violating the norms. Most of these internalized beliefs are not easily articulated; they form **tacit knowledge** (things we don't know that we know). We don't necessarily even realize that these are beliefs that we hold, which guide our behavior. Notions of personal space provide an example—we learn how far apart one should stand or sit when interacting with strangers, versus friends or relatives. We think it is just natural to maintain whatever distances we have learned. We follow the rules without being aware of them. We assume that others understand the world in the same way and therefore will behave similarly.

Internalized beliefs provoke automatic responses. They don't require that we think about our options and make conscious choices—we just act. Alternative courses of action simply don't occur to us; they are unheard of, unknown, literally unthinkable. If explicitly presented with different notions, we may find them difficult to comprehend—"Why would anyone do that? Why would it even occur to anyone to think of doing that?"

In some countries, people dodge to the right as they approach others, either walking on a pathway or driving a car. In other countries, the custom is to pass on the left. If everyone shares the same customs, pedestrian and automobile traffic can flow more freely. In an international airport like Heathrow in London, British and non-British passengers all hurry about in cramped quarters with many near collisions and traffic jams, as *going right* versus *going left* customs intersect.

Internal Sanctions: Positive and Negative

When enculturation is incomplete, or you have come to question what you learned as a young child, you may find that you disagree with the rules and expected behavior patterns of your cultural environment. It may occur to you to think or act in a manner contrary to the prevailing norms, but still you may curb your inclinations to question authority and to misbehave. These more conscious controls on thought and behavior, or internal sanctions, may take several forms. First, consider what you feel inside when you do something you know is wrong, whether or not anyone else knows about it. You may experience *negative* feelings of shame, guilt, or fear: shame because you

have been taught that you aren't supposed to think that way, or act that way; guilt because you know you have broken the rules; and fear that someone will find out. Even if no one is likely to know what you have done, or what radical ideas you have entertained in the privacy of your own mind, you may be constrained by these internal feelings of shame, guilt, and/or fear, which you find most unpleasant. By teaching children that some things are not allowed, we attempt to invoke such feelings in them internally so that their conscience will guide their behavior and help them make the appropriate choices—even when they consciously disagree, and even when no one is around to remind them of how to behave or to chastise them if they misbehave.

Second, consider what you feel inside when you do something you know is right, whether or not anyone else knows about it. You may experience *positive* feelings of pride or satisfaction, knowing that you have upheld the beliefs and values of your family or community. For example, you may take pride in a job well-done, based on the work ethic instilled in you at an early age; you see the neighbor's dog wandering the streets, so you return him to his backyard—because it's the right thing to do, and it makes you feel better about yourself to have done it; you find a wallet on the street and return it to its owner, because the satisfaction of behaving correctly far exceeds the value of the money inside.

Religious Sanctions: Positive and Negative

People may be influenced by internal expectations of punishment or reward through supernatural forces, either in this life or after death, through enculturation into the religious beliefs of their culture. Young Christian children in North America may behave especially well during the weeks leading up to Christmas, because Santa Claus is coming to town, and they know he is watching to see if they've been good or bad, and making up his list accordingly. Religious belief systems may contain general guidelines for behavior or many very specific rules. You may not truly believe in supernatural beings but figure that if such entities exist, it doesn't hurt to accumulate "brownie points" in your favor by doing good deeds.

You may have been taught that if you do something good, you will be rewarded, and if you do something wrong, you will be punished through God's wrath or divine retribution—if not in this life, then in the next. Such beliefs encourage people to follow the rules of their culture or religion, lest they suffer the consequences. Systems of morality don't have to be based on supernatural rewards and punishments, but in many cases, they are.

External Social Controls

External social controls are those imposed on a person from outside his or her own conscience. They are sanctions imposed by other members of society and are either positive sanctions (rewards) for doing right or negative sanctions (punishments) for doing wrong. Expected responses from others can be powerful motivators that shape our behavior, either reinforcing approved actions or extinguishing inappropriate ones.

Positive Sanctions from Others

Positive sanctions for behaving appropriately can range from simple and fleeting to complex and long lasting. Examples include:

- A smile from a friend when you say hello
- "Nice job, A+" on the top of a term paper when it is handed back
- Compliments on one's appearance or accomplishments
- A promotion to a higher-paying position as a result of hard work and initiative
- A commendation for saving a swimmer's life at the beach
- A Medal of Valor, a Nobel Prize, a Lifetime Achievement Award, a Genius Grant

Although people may not be consciously working toward or expecting such rewards, most people are pleased when they receive positive feedback from others, and it can serve as a powerful motivator to work hard and excel, according to the standards of one's culture.

Negative Sanctions from Others

Negative sanctions for behaving inappropriately or transgressing the norms can likewise range from simple and fleeting to complex and long lasting. Examples include:

- A glare from your mother when she overhears you cursing
- A D+ on the exam you didn't study for
- Teasing from friends if you come to class dressed in a suit and tie
- Getting arrested for public drunkenness and spending the night in jail
- Losing your job because you are often late and goof around too much
- Going to prison for 10 years for robbing a bank

People are not always aware of the negative sanctions that might be imposed on them (they are ignorant of the law). Or they may be well aware of the negative sanctions they will face if caught but are convinced they won't be caught. However, most people are mortified when they receive negative feedback from others, and the possibility of being caught and facing negative sanctions can serve as a powerful motivator to conform to the norms of one's culture and a powerful deterrent (a preventive sanction) against breaking the rules.

Witchcraft beliefs can serve as a powerful preventive sanction. In cultures where people believe in witchcraft, anyone who behaves in any way out of the ordinary runs the risk of being accused of being a witch and then facing negative sanctions, including ostracism or death. Describing witchcraft beliefs among the Xhosa of Southern Africa, Hazel Crampton points out that such beliefs help explain why a family or community might suffer one misfortune after another, but they may also serve a political purpose:

> [But] witchcraft was also a useful tool in the maintenance of the status quo—as one observer put it, a "state engine for the removal of the obnoxious." To accuse someone of witchcraft was a sure-fire means by which a chief and his counsellors could rid themselves of powerful rivals and seize their cattle wealth. It was also a means of isolating, or removing from the community, individuals who were perceived as being divisive. (Crampton 2006:209–210)

Both positive and negative sanctions can range along a continuum based on the power of the behavior and the emotions attached to it. Sanctions may be verbal or physical; they may be primarily emotion-based; they may have monetary consequences; or they may result in fame or infamy. Likewise, sanctions may be formalized into rules, regulations, and laws at different levels and enforced by an authorized political body. In other cases, sanctions may be informal and enforced by whoever cares to enforce them.

"It Takes a Village"

The famous African proverb that "It takes a village to raise a child," refers to a common belief in many cultures that *all adults are responsible for all children.* In cultures where all adults are empowered to watch over, protect, and care for all children, the adults also have the right, indeed the responsibility, to chastise the kids if they are doing something wrong. This approach stands in stark contrast to the typical view in North America that only a child's parents have the right to correct her behavior in public. Since children are often unsupervised by their parents, this allows for much mischief and wrongdoing, with few or no consequences for the children. This creates tension within the culture between the desire to give parents as much freedom as possible in raising their children as they see fit—to accommodate lots of variation in child-rearing philosophies—while at the same time ensuring that all children are relatively safe and properly cared for, don't annoy others, don't damage property, and follow the rules.

POLITICAL ORGANIZATION AND CONFLICT

Levels of Political Organization

Traditionally, discussions by anthropologists of political organization use a four-level classification: bands, tribes, chiefdoms, and states. This system can be used to describe contemporary cultures, but it also implies the evolution of cultural complexity, with bands being the simplest and earliest form of political organization, and states the most complex and recent. Over time, as populations become larger, more sedentary, more hierarchical, and more complex, they face different sorts of problems in getting people to behave, and new forms of political organization develop to solve these problems. Thus, we turn now to a comparison of the features of societies at these four distinct levels of political organization.

Bands

The term **band** refers to the type of sociopolitical organization found among *contemporary hunters and gatherers* and among *all humans for most of our existence.* Bands are usually small in size, ranging from 25–50 people, and the people are nomadic or seminomadic foragers. Most of the individuals are well-known to each other and are related to one another through bilateral kinship ties. Band composition is flexible and changes often, as people come together or disperse, or as some individuals move to another group. Bands are politically egalitarian—males and females have similar status, and no adult man has a higher status than any other man. There are no hereditary or elected leaders, and most decisions are made through discussion and consensus. Individual autonomy is emphasized and group leadership is minimal. When conflicts arise, they are usually settled without aggression or violence. Sharing, cooperation, and egalitarianism are explicit cultural values that are taught to children. Nonviolent values and behaviors are promoted, and competitiveness and aggression in children are typically punished, not encouraged. Notions of masculinity do not include militaristic or warrior values, and avoiding conflict is often seen as the sensible thing to do, not as cowardly behavior (Fry 2007).

Tribes

Tribes represent the next level of political organization, where there are more people who must be organized into larger groups while still getting along with one another most of the time. Tribal organization is relatively recent—it dates back only to the beginning of the Neolithic Revolution, some 10,000 years ago. Tribal organization is typically found among sedentary horticulturalists and herders (such as the Nuer). Groups of 50–100 or more can be organized relatively effectively in a tribal system. Leadership may be vested in a headman or **big man**—someone who may be articulate and charismatic and who can gather a group of loyal followers. In some tribal societies, leadership may be assigned automatically to the oldest male in the group, or to a group of elders who make decisions for the rest of the tribe. For many purposes, social organization is still largely egalitarian, and tribal leaders generally lead through persuasion and example, rather than by coercing people. Tribal organization may be based on the segmentary lineage and clan system that develops from unilineal rules of kinship and descent (either patrilineal or matrilineal). Because they often are sedentary, tribal societies are more likely to have strong ties to the land and to defend their borders against intruders.

Chiefdoms

Chiefdoms are much larger political systems that arose in some regions of the world after tribal organization was well established. Chiefdoms can range from relatively small to very large, organizing hundreds or thousands of people into cohesive societies. Chiefdoms are hierarchical, ranked societies that divide the population into at least two levels—chiefs and commoners; some chiefdoms include a slave class as well.

Chiefdoms are typically based on farming or fishing as the subsistence mode and are sedentary. Complex, sedentary hunter-gatherers such as the natives of the Northwest Coast of North America qualify as having chiefdom-level sociopolitical organization. It is rare for foragers to be sedentary, but in resource-rich marine environments, complex social organization can develop.

The chief himself (chiefs are seldom female) may have limited power over his subjects, or he may wield lots of influence over major decisions as well as matters of everyday life. Chiefs and their families often get special privileges such as the rights to wear special clothing, hunt in areas that are off-limits to commoners, assign land to commoners for farming, have more wives and children, have a better diet, and so on. Commoners may be required to pay tribute to the chief in the form of money, part of their crop or fish harvest, or labor. A wise chief redistributes at least some of this wealth back to his or her subjects, either in the form of a major feast and redistribution of material goods or by using it to carry out projects that benefit everyone. Chiefdoms themselves may be organized into multilevel hierarchies that include neighborhood chiefs, village chiefs, and regional chiefs, with sometimes a paramount chief at the top of the hierarchy, ruling over a vast region with the help of the lower-level chiefs.

Chiefs may be elected or selected by some or all of the local population, or the position may be hereditary, with assorted mechanisms for the transfer of power from one generation to the next. The chief may rule as a virtual dictator, or he may lead or rely on a council of advisors, who themselves may have been elected or may hold their positions through inheritance. Authority in chiefdoms may be backed up through economic or military power, force of personality, traditions, religious mythology, and/or the threat of force.

States

State-level societies (sometimes referred to as *civilized societies* or simply *civilizations*) are quite recent. Archeological evidence points to the rise of the state in several different regions of the world only 5,000–6,000 years ago. **States** are characterized by higher population densities, larger settlements, permanent buildings, ceremonial areas, differences in status revealed by differences in nutritional status and health, and different burial practices for the elite. In early state-level societies, the subsistence and economic system is based on intensive agriculture. Later on, commercial agribusiness, manufacturing, industry, and trade come to characterize state-level societies. Some scholars have suggested that states originally developed out of the need to control and manage water for irrigated, intensive agriculture. Building and maintaining complex irrigation systems, they argue, led to the rise of state-level political organization.

In states, political power is concentrated among a small group of individuals at the top of a multitiered social hierarchy. Many people live in rural hinterlands, but more and more people flock to centralized towns and cities or ceremonial centers. There are numerous social classes or ranks, with slaves, indentured servants, and captives of war on the bottom. The middle ranks may be composed of commoners, artisans, petty bureaucrats, and tradespeople. Rulers have more power than chiefs, and their power is supported by a military organization with permanent armies led by specially trained commanders. Political and religious power may be connected, with the political rulers also serving as religious leaders, or a special class of religious experts may advise and legitimize the power of the ruling class.

States may have other specific features that arise only when the population grows sufficiently large and the social organization reaches a certain level of complexity. Such characteristics might include a written system of communication; the use of mathematics; a state-controlled criminal justice system (police, courts, and prisons); public works (roadways, plazas, and parks); large buildings for meetings or sports competitions; and monuments to the gods, the ancestors, or the rulers themselves. The trend toward urbanization and the development of multiple layers of civil bureaucracy continues in contemporary nation-states.

Fry's extensive analysis of the archeological and ethnographic record clearly shows that increasing sociopolitical complexity is accompanied by the development of different strategies and tactics for resolving conflicts (Fry 2007).

Aspects of Disputes

One of the main points Fry makes in *Beyond War* is that discussions of human nature and warfare are confounded by the failure to clearly and consistently distinguish among different aspects of disputes. Thus, we begin with some definitions:

- **Conflict:** The term conflict is defined as "a perceived divergence of interests, where interests are broadly conceptualized to include values, needs, goals, and wishes, between two or more parties, often accompanied by feelings of anger or hostility" (Fry 2007:24).

- **Aggression:** The term aggression is defined as "the infliction of harm, pain, or injury on other individuals. Sometimes aggression is subdivided into verbal and physical aggression. A central point is that conflict need not involve any aggression whatsoever. Aggression and conflict are not synonymous" (Fry 2007:24).

- **Violence:** The term violence is limited to "severe forms of physical aggression, including war and feud. Violence entails forceful attacks, usually with weapons, which can result in serious injury or death" (Fry 2007:24).

- **Warfare:** The term warfare is defined very specifically as: "A group activity, carried on by members of one community against members of another community, in which it is the primary purpose to inflict serious injury or death on multiple nonspecified members of that other community, or in which the primary purpose makes it highly likely that serious injury or death will be inflicted on multiple nonspecified members of that community in the accomplishment of that primary purpose" (Prosterman 1972, cited in Fry 2007:16).

All groups of people who live and work together experience conflicts from time to time. It is unrealistic to expect that the members of any group will always be in agreement about every subject. We are justified in concluding that *it is part of human nature to disagree with our fellow humans.* However, not all conflicts are resolved using aggression, violence, and warfare. It is clear that the techniques used for managing conflicts vary systematically depending on the society's level of political organization. Warfare, as defined above, only appears in the archeological record beginning about 10,000 years ago, coinciding with the beginning of the Neolithic Revolution. Archeological and historical evidence for warfare becomes more obvious, more frequent, and more devastating with the rise of *civilization* and complex state-level political organization, a mere 5,000 to 6,000 years ago. *Violence and warfare are cultural phenomena, not part of an intrinsically dark human nature.*

Before we proceed to the different ways in which disputes might be resolved, we need to clarify the distinction between two different cultural belief systems regarding who is held to be responsible for breaking the rules during conflicts.

Defining Responsibility

There are two fundamentally distinct concepts for assigning blame for transgressions of the social rules and for meting out punishment: **individual responsibility** and **corporate (group) responsibility.** Without a clear understanding of which belief underlies the justice system in a particular situation, people's behavior may make little sense.

Individual Responsibility

Under a code of justice based on the notion of individual responsibility, only the person who actually committed a crime, or transgressed a rule, is responsible for that act. It is assumed that people have free will, can act independently of others, and control their own actions. Thus, a person who chooses to break the law is the only one responsible for that act, the only one who should be held responsible by others, and the only one who should be punished. Many modern nation-states have criminal justice systems based on this concept, and it is also used in many everyday situations.

Once a crime has been reported, enormous effort goes into identifying the person(s) who are thought to have committed the crime, capturing them, and then proving in court that they are indeed the specific individual(s) responsible. The fields of crime scene investigation and forensics are dedicated to establishing links between the crime and the individual or individuals who committed it. Investigators gather eyewitness accounts, use lineups of suspects, and collect fingerprints and trace evidence (hair, saliva, blood, semen, clothing fibers, tire tracks, dirt, pollen, and so on) from the scene and from potential suspects as evidence. If the physical evidence and/or witnesses can place the accused at the scene of the crime as an active participant, then there is a good chance that a court trial will result in a conviction or that the suspect will plead guilty or strike a plea bargain with the prosecutors and be punished. Enormous amounts of time, effort, and money go into identifying the individual(s) responsible and tying them to the crime.

Examples of situations in which individual responsibility is the guiding principle include:

- Students work in groups to write up a joint lab report—when one student is caught making up data, only she gets a failing grade.

- When one member of a gang kills a member of a rival gang, the police try to track down the killer.

- Timothy McVeigh was convicted of blowing up the Alfred P. Murrah Federal Building in Oklahoma City in 1995, thus killing 168 people; McVeigh was tried and sentenced, and died by lethal injection in 2001.

There are cases where people other than the individual(s) who carried out the crime are held to be partly or equally responsible. For example, anyone who aids and abets a criminal by serving as a lookout or a get-away driver, or who provides funding or material help (guns, keys, wire taps, etc.), or who provides a false alibi, or who can be shown to be the mastermind behind the crime, may be held responsible as well. Some nation-states have racketeering laws that specifically target large organized groups of criminals, and anyone who contributed directly or indirectly to the criminal activity may be held responsible.

Corporate Responsibility

Standing in stark contrast to the notion of individual responsibility is the concept of corporate responsibility. Under a system of corporate responsibility, *all members of the group to which the person who committed the crime belongs are held to be equally responsible for the crime.* Like the previous system, under corporate responsibility, it is assumed that people have free will and can act

independently of others. However, it is also assumed that all members of a group are jointly responsible for the actions of each and every member of the group. Thus, a person who might be inclined to break the law should be prevented from doing so by the other members of his own group. If people fail in their responsibility to control an individual's actions, they have only themselves to blame and must accept equal responsibility for the crime. They are jointly held to be liable for whatever damages need to be paid or for whatever punishment is meted out.

With corporate responsibility, each member of the group is considered *fungible*, or interchangeable, with every other member. If one member of the group commits a crime, *any* member of the group may be retaliated against. Alternatively, several or many members of the group may be punished, even if the actual perpetrator of the crime is not included in the group receiving the punishment. In some cases, all members of the group are punished. Many local systems of justice are based on this concept and it is also used in many everyday situations.

Under a system based on corporate responsibility, it isn't necessary to identify the specific individual who committed a crime. All you have to know is the group to which he or she belongs. One of the difficulties with corporate responsibility, of course, is that individuals belong to many different groups. In contexts where the system of kinship and descent are used for political organization and social control, the appropriate corporate group to be held liable will depend on the relationship between the perpetrator and the victim. If a member of lineage A harms a member of lineage B, then the members of lineage B may retaliate against any member of lineage A. If a member of Tribe C harms a member of Tribe D, then the members of Tribe D may retaliate against any member of Tribe C. And so on.

At the same time, one of the advantages of a corporate system of responsibility is that no one has to spend time, effort, and money identifying the specific individual who committed the crime. It is usually either obvious to which group the perpetrator belongs, or people assume that they know—no need to have an eyewitness who can identify the individual, no need to have physical evidence that ties the individual to the crime. But who decides which group is the appropriate target for corporate responsibility? Is it based on nationality, sex or gender, sexual orientation, ethnic identity, age, religion, or some other group to which one belongs?

Examples of situations in which corporate responsibility is the guiding principle include:

- When one student athlete is late to football practice, the coach makes all members of the team run wind sprints.
- When one member of a gang kills a member of a rival gang, the victim's gang tries to kill any member of the other gang.
- When the Murrah Federal Building in Oklahoma City was bombed, an all-points bulletin was sent out to local, state, and federal law enforcement officials; a number of vaguely Middle-Eastern-looking men were detained and questioned before Timothy McVeigh—a "quintessential white guy"—was identified as the perpetrator.

When Individual and Corporate Responsibility Collide: The Achille Lauro

One particular case is presented in detail to illustrate how individual and corporate responsibility differ and to underline the important role that such cultural differences can play in international politics. When a cultural group that believes primarily in individual responsibility comes into conflict with a cultural group that operates by the code of corporate responsibility, the level of misunderstanding and violence can quickly escalate—as though two teams are trying to play a game, but one is playing baseball and the other is playing cricket.

In 1985, the Italian cruise ship Achille Lauro was hijacked in the Mediterranean Sea by four members of the Palestine Liberation Front (PLF), a faction of the Palestine Liberation Organization (PLO). The hijackers were led by a man named Mohammed Abbas. In return for the release of the ship and its passengers, the PLF members wanted Israel to release some Palestinian prisoners. During the course of negotiations, one of the ship's passengers, Leon Klinghoffer, an elderly man confined to a wheelchair, was shot to death by the hijackers and his body was thrown overboard.

The PLF and PLO have long been in conflict with Israel, and with the United States for their support of Israel. Leon Klinghoffer himself never hurt anyone and didn't know any of the hijackers. He probably didn't know any Palestinians at all, but that wasn't relevant. He wasn't killed because he personally had done anything to harm the hijackers. He was killed as a representative of all Americans and as a representative of all Jewish people. The PLF members were operating by the code of corporate responsibility. According to their beliefs, Israeli people (and by extension all Jewish people) have harmed Palestine and Palestinians; the U.S. government (and by extension all Americans) has supported Israel in this conflict. Therefore, it is just to retaliate against anyone who is Jewish and/or an American. Klinghoffer was both.

The hijackers eventually gave up control of the ship and tried to fly to their headquarters in Tunisia. Ronald Reagan, the U.S. president at the time, sent U.S. warplanes to intercept them and forced the hijackers to land at a base in Sicily that was under joint United States and Italian control. Thus, Mohammed Abbas and the other three hijackers were in custody at one point, but the Italians refused to extradite them to the United States, and Abbas was allowed to leave the country. He was eventually tried in absentia and sentenced by the Italian courts to multiple life terms in prison; however, no one knew where he was. In 1995, Abbas was granted immunity for the hijacking as part of an Israeli–Palestinian peace agreement.

Over the years, the United States continued to try to track down Abbas—the one individual who had masterminded and carried out the hijacking of the Achille Lauro, and who had shot and killed Leon Klinghoffer—in order to arrest him and hold him responsible for his crimes. They were finally successful, and Abbas was captured by the U.S. military in Iraq almost 18 years after the crime, in April 2003. According to published reports, Abbas died of a heart attack in March 2004 while in U.S. custody.

Members of the U.S. government were operating by the code of individual responsibility. According to prevailing U.S. beliefs, Mohammed Abbas was the primary person responsible for Leon Klinghoffer's death, and justice would not be served until he had been punished. Abbas died before he could be brought to trial.

Types of Dispute Settlement

Nonviolent Conflict Resolution

A number of methods of resolving conflicts do not involve physical aggression or violence, and these techniques are used throughout the world, even in societies that do occasionally resort to violence and warfare. In industrial and postindustrial countries, the widespread reporting of *news* via personal gossip, radio, television, print newspapers and magazines, and the Internet tends to overemphasize and distort our view of how common violence is. Peace is not news, just as the lack of natural disasters, car accidents, and homicides are not news. Fry writes:

> In actuality, the vast majority of people on the planet awake on a typical morning and live through a violence-free day—and this experience generally continues day after day. The overwhelming majority of humanity spends an average day without inflicting any physical aggression on anyone, without being the victim of physical aggression, and, in all likelihood, without even witnessing any physical aggression with their own eyes among the hundreds or thousands of people they encounter. (Fry 2007:22)

Fry discusses many different techniques for dealing with conflicts without resorting to physical aggression or violence, including:

- *Avoidance:* people cease to interact with problematic others; they avoid them temporarily or permanently.
- *Toleration:* people agree to disagree and don't discuss the issue that divides them.
- *Resolve conflict:* people talk over the issue, they debate and discuss, perhaps they even argue verbally, but eventually they reach compromises and negotiate solutions, perhaps involving the payment of compensation or damage, or a verbal apology.
- *Forgive and forget:* people reconcile and forgive one another.
- *Third-party approach:* people agree that a third party can act as a mediator or adjudicator to help people resolve their differences (Fry 2007).

These techniques are often successful at diffusing anger and hostility, and peace returns to the group. When such techniques do not work, the conflict may escalate. The ethnographic evidence suggests that much of the violence that does occur is not random. Rather, it happens when people are defending their rights against others who would infringe on them, or have infringed on them in the past. In other words, much violence happens when people are attempting to correct real or perceived injustices (Fry 2007).

There is a clear relationship between the type of conflict resolution and the level of political organization: as societies become more complex, the level of violence escalates.

Sudan residents of Kapoeta, Eastern Equatoria, do a traditional peace dance at a rally where the Comprehensive Peace Agreement text was distributed. Eighteen months after the agreement that ended Sudan's two-decade civil war had been signed, few Sudanese knew its details. That began to change in April and May 2006, when USAID launched an initiative to help more than 150,000 people in five Southern Sudanese states access details of the agreement and participate more fully in implementing the peace. Documents in Arabic and English were distributed to all government officials in the south, and an official summary was developed and published in English and Arabic. The Sudan Radio Service created audio versions of the summary in seven languages—Moro, Arabic, simple Arabic, Toposa, Shilluk, Dinka, and Nuer—and the *Sudan Mirror* published 22,000 summaries to be included as supplements in its Easter edition.

Self-Redress or Individual Assaults/Homicides

When members of a band society feel compelled to resort to violence to achieve justice, it almost always takes the form of self-redress or revenge. By self-redress, we mean that a person with a grievance takes action against the person who has harmed him. The person who was originally harmed is considered the only one who should seek revenge, and he is expected to seek revenge against, or redress of the grievance from, the individual who was responsible, under the code of individual responsibility. Redress may take the form of an apology, payment of compensation in some form, or punishment of the aggressor by the victim. The conflict may escalate if the parties disagree about who started it, who was harmed, whether the redress was appropriate and/or sufficient, and so on. If one person kills another, the victim's close relatives are considered the appropriate people to seek redress from the killer. Self-redress is most common among band-level societies and decreases in use as political organization shifts toward tribes, chiefdoms, and states. Within many modern nation-states, self-redress—taking the law into your own hands—is expressly forbidden by the legal system.

Feuding

With the development of farming and herding as subsistence modes, and the tribal level of political organization, feuding becomes more common as a way to settle conflicts. Feuding refers to situations where one kin-based organization is pitted against another—family against family, lineage against lineage, clan against clan, tribe against tribe. Feuding uses the concept of social substitutability (corporate responsibility or fungibility), whereby each and every member of the group is responsible for the actions of each and every other member of the group. Once a conflict begins, one or several members of the victim's kin-based group may seek redress from, or revenge against, any member or multiple members of the aggressor's kin-based group, not just the aggressor himself (or herself, though most violent aggression is carried out by males).

The major drawback of feuding as a means of settling conflicts is that people seldom stop the violence after the initial cycle of harm and redress. Feuding is supposed to resolve the conflict, but often it simply begins a new round of violence. Back and forth, one side attacks, then the other side attacks, then in retaliation the first side attacks again. Blood feuds of this sort between lineages, tribes, neighboring villages, or countries can go on for hundreds of years, and the conflict can be passed down the generations. Even when peace has been restored and former enemies have been living side-by-side in harmony for many years, resentments may simmer just below the surface of neighborly amity. A single new act of aggression can stir up old resentments and trigger the resumption of a blood feud.

Kinship-based conflicts can be classified as feuds. The famous feud between the Hatfields and the McCoys lasted from 1878 to 1891. Pictured above is the Hatfield clan in 1897.

Failure to distinguish between feuding and true warfare has led to much confusion among historians and prehistorians. These images from 2006 show men of the Dani tribe of highland New Guinea. The man on the right is climbing one of the towers from which men watch for the enemy. The famous ethnographic film *Dead Birds* was filmed among the Dani in 1965 and documented their intervillage conflicts, which qualify as feuding, but not warfare. In the film, the skirmishes appear more like a soccer match: rules govern the activities; some players are on the field, while others watch from the sidelines; there are coaches calling plays, time-outs, and even cancellations because of rain or darkness.

Warfare

As defined by Fry, warfare, as a distinct set of behaviors, entails *relatively impersonal lethal aggression between communities.* This definition clearly excludes individual homicides and blood feuding or revenge killings, where known individuals are targeted.

Evidence for true warfare is not found in the archeological record until about 10,000 years ago and seems to accompany the development of chiefdoms and especially state-level political organization. Different sorts of archeological remains can be interpreted as clear evidence of warfare, including:

- Specialized weapons such as clubs and daggers not used for hunting
- Depictions of martial (military) scenes in artwork
- A substantial number of burials with projectile points either embedded in the bones or lying within the framework of the skeletal remains
- Evidence of massive fires followed by a change in artifact types and styles (reflecting occupation by the victors)
- A reduced number of male burials in cemeteries—perhaps reflecting deaths elsewhere in battle
- Repetitions of the same patterns in several archeological sites in the same region at the same time

Such archeological evidence is rare before the rise of chiefdoms and states within the last 5,000 years or so. At the same time, warfare is not a necessary part of all chiefdoms or state-level societies. In an appendix to his book, Fry lists more than 70 geographically defined cultures worldwide that can be classified as *nonwarring,* based on the specific definition of warfare he employs. These groups may have homicides, including revenge homicides, and protracted blood feuds, but they don't have warfare involving *relatively impersonal lethal aggression between communities* (Fry 2007).

Fry points out that until the arrival of Europeans, warfare was virtually unknown across the entire continent of Australia, where all of the indigenous peoples were nomadic hunters and gatherers. In addition, a number of modern nation-states have not engaged in war for many years. Fry cites Sweden, which has not been to war in 170 years, Switzerland (over 200 years), Iceland (over 700 years), and Costa Rica (since the end of World War II) (Fry 2007:18).

Fry points out that "among nation-states, social substitutability can facilitate war, as one act of violence (for instance, a terrorist attack) provokes retaliation not solely against the actual perpetrators, but against anyone labeled as belonging to the same national or religious group as the attackers." (Fry

2007:95). Although retaliators may try to confine their revenge to military targets, a high level of collateral damage—the acknowledged killing of innocent civilians, including women, children, and the elderly, and the destruction of nonmilitary buildings and other infrastructures—has come to be accepted as a normal part of modern warfare.

When Individual and Corporate Responsibility Collide: The 9/11 Attacks

Consider the September 11, 2001, attacks on New York City's World Trade Center Towers and the Pentagon. Osama bin Laden, a citizen of Saudi Arabia, has claimed responsibility for planning these attacks. According to bin Laden, the 9/11 attacks on the

True warfare—relatively *impersonal* lethal aggression between communities—is found only among state-level societies. Top left: an aerial view of the site of the September 11, 2001, terrorist attacks on the World Trade Center in New York City, taken on September 17, 2001. Top right: a U.S. Soldier on patrol in the Middle East. Bottom left: in 2009, Special Warfare Combatant-craft Crewmen (SWCC) assigned to Special Boat Team 20 teach members of Boy Scout Troop 300 of Williamsburg, Virginia, about modern weapon systems to give them a look at Naval Special Warfare life. Bottom right: an unmanned predator drone armed with Hellfire missiles flies over Afghanistan. Such drones represent the ultimate in *impersonal* lethal aggression by one community against another community.

United States were specifically in retaliation for U.S. support of Israel's invasion of Lebanon in 1982. This is a prime example of corporate responsibility: all people living in the United States, as well as Americans abroad, are considered culpable for the invasion of Lebanon almost 20 years earlier, which led to the deaths of many Palestinians and the destruction of many buildings in Beirut.

Bin Laden's *corporate responsibility* perspective is considered highly unjust by people who believe in individual responsibility. Most likely, not a single one of the individuals killed at the World Trade Towers or the Pentagon were directly responsible for the deaths of any individual Palestinians in Lebanon. Some of them hadn't even been born in 1982.

The divergence in views also reflects the tendency of many Westerners to focus on the present and the future and either be ignorant of, or dismiss, the past. To this day, many Americans have no idea what happened in Lebanon in 1982, or what relevance it has to the 9/11 attacks. This is in sharp contrast to the tendency of people in many non-Western cultures to focus on the past. They remember and continue to resent insults against their ancestors, dating back not just a few decades but hundreds of years, or longer. The Korean concept of *han* captures this latter perspective elegantly.

In his study of the cultural meanings of autism around the world, cultural anthropologist Richard Roy Grinker interviewed Seung-Mee, the mother of a child with autism. Seung-Mee explained:

> I inherited the resentment of my ancestors, my people's *han*. "*Han*" is a word that can't be translated easily from Korean. It refers to one's consciousness of ongoing trauma, the agony of injustices unresolved. *Han* can grow and be passed on to successive generations, who look to a utopian future when, in whatever manner—through revenge, revolution, reconciliation, or generosity—they can overcome it. (Grinker 2007:286)

A focus on *individual responsibility* contributed to the frustration many people felt following the 9/11 attacks, which were carried out by suicide bombers. U.S. authorities were quickly able to identify the men who hijacked and crashed the airplanes, but they had no way to punish them—because the hijackers perished during the attacks. The U.S. government then turned its attention to those who helped plan the attacks, focusing specifically on Osama bin Laden. Alleged links between Saddam Hussein and the 9/11 attacks were used as one of the justifications for the invasion of Iraq in 2003. Likewise, purported links among bin Laden, al-Queda, and the Taliban continue to be the basis for the wars in Afghanistan and Iraq.

Because bin Laden is a Muslim, some Americans have extended their animosity to all Muslims, and/or to anyone from the Middle East, Afghanistan, Pakistan, or even India. In turn, many Muslims characterize U.S. military actions as a war on Islam. Notions of corporate responsibility abound. On the other hand, although bin Laden is originally from Saudi Arabia, his nationality has not been used as a justification to attack Saudi Arabia, which continues to be an ally of the United States. Although bin Laden is very tall, tall people have not come under suspicion since 9/11. We pick and choose which groups, and how far, to extend the code of corporate responsibility.

Who Administers Justice?

When modern nation-states resort to warfare to settle disputes between communities and countries, they are essentially *feuding* on the basis of much larger political entities, way beyond local kinship divisions. The people engaged in the fighting may not necessarily have been personally harmed by the enemy, and they don't personally know the people they have been told to kill.

As international warfare continues around the globe, people continue to face harm from others within their local population, including people they know, as well as complete strangers. Typically, however, in chiefdoms and state-level societies, individuals and/or their kin groups are no longer allowed to seek justice on their own either from the perpetrator or from members of the perpetrator's kin group. Rather, as Fry puts it:

> The tendency is to shift the privilege rights of prosecution and imposition of legal sanctions from the individual [as in self-redress] and his kin-group [as in feuding] over to clearly defined public officials representing the society as such [as in courts of law] . . . [such that] well-developed chiefdoms and states usurp from individuals and kin groups the right to administer justice. . . . States claim the right and duty to administer justice. (Fry 2007:92–93)

Fry is referring here to criminal justice systems in all their manifestations. Once you reach a certain level of social complexity, chaos would ensue if everyone were allowed to take justice into their own hands and seek redress of grievances. The bloodshed would escalate out of control. Thus, over time, some crimes come to be defined as *crimes against society*, not just against the individual who was harmed or his kin group. Institutions develop that are designed specifically to administer justice. Thus, in contemporary nation-states, officers of the law are charged with keeping the peace at various levels: campus, local, city, county, state, federal, and international. Just as with a kinship-based social control system, the various branches of the justice system have specific jurisdictions. When a crime is committed, the victim or a witness, or whoever discovers the crime, is supposed to call the appropriate authorities, and only these authorities have the rights to proceed in investigating the crime.

For example, in the United States, if you commit a crime in one state, you are considered to have harmed all the people of the state. The state criminal justice system is the level at which you are prosecuted and punished if found guilty. However, if you commit a crime that involves crossing state lines, then you are considered to have harmed all the people of the country (the federal level), and you are prosecuted and punished through the federal court system. Crimes that involve more than one nation may involve cooperation between the federal systems in the countries involved, or they may involve Interpol or the International Court of Justice.

Part of the criminal justice system is designed to identify, find, and capture the suspected perpetrator(s). Another branch gathers evidence for and against the suspect. Still others (lawyers or barristers or their equivalent) argue in court before a judge, a panel of officials, or a jury of peers, and then a decision is rendered. There may be different evidentiary standards required for different courts. Once a person has been judged guilty by the authorities, then another branch of the criminal justice system takes over to impose the legal sanctions (administer the punishment), which may include a fine, forfeiture of property, community service, public humiliation, loss of privileges and rights, jail, prison, maiming, or execution.

Giving up one's individual or kin-based rights to respond to harm caused by others, and acknowledging the rights of public authorities to prosecute and punish wrongdoers, is part of a belief in the *rule of law*. A number of people believe that we need a worldwide authority for adjudicating disputes between countries, an alternative to modern warfare, where, currently, individual countries assert their rights to take revenge against the group to which their enemy belongs. Others protest that such international courts would have too much power and would usurp the rights of sovereign nation-states to seek justice on their own.

Carabanchel Prison was built in Madrid after the Spanish Civil War to house political prisoners. After Franco's death (1975), the inmate population included "common criminals and terrorists." It was one of the biggest prisons in Europe, and was infamous for the cruelty of both guards and prisoners. After it was closed in 1998, the building was heavily looted, and the prison walls were covered with graffiti. The photo was taken in 2008, shortly before the building was torn down.

LOCAL POLITICS

Even among hunters and gatherers living in small bands, there will be conflicts and disputes, and some people will have more influence than others, either through force of personality or through natural leadership abilities that others recognize and to which they defer. As groups get larger, more complex political organization is needed to keep things running smoothly. In this section, we will explore only a couple of aspects of local politics. Then we will move on to a more detailed examination of disputes between larger political entities in the form of one population invading another.

Power versus Authority

When talking about politics at any level, it is important to distinguish between the two related concepts of power and authority.

Power

Generally, anthropologists use the term **power** to mean the actual ability of one person (or group) to make another person (or group) do something. Power can have many sources and can be deployed using a variety of strategies. For example, wealth can be a source of power, as can hereditary position, family connections, or who you know. Education and experience can be sources of power, either in the form of knowledge, wisdom, and skill, or from the status that is automatically conferred on specific educational credentials or years on the job. Some people gain power through the force of their charismatic personalities, especially their ability to speak eloquently, to clearly articulate what others are thinking and feeling, to persuade people to carry out their wishes, and to motivate others to action. Other people gain power through their ability to fool and manipulate others through lies, cons, scams, and schemes that mislead people and convince them to behave in certain ways.

Power and authority do not always go hand-in-hand. The G8 summit is an annual meeting of the leaders of the eight most economically powerful countries in the world (Canada, France, Germany, Italy, Japan, Russia, the United Kingdom, and the United States). The G20 summit is also held yearly, and is made up of the finance ministers and central bank governors of 19 countries (the G8 plus Argentina, Australia, Brazil, China, India, Indonesia, Mexico, Saudi Arabia, South Africa, South Korea, and Turkey) and the European Union. The G8 summit is designed to be a forum for the world's top leaders to meet face-to-face and discuss current world problems and how to fix them. The G20 summit focuses specifically on economic issues. Both groups have significant authority, but little real power, as leaders are often unpopular at home and it is overwhelmingly difficult to get people to agree to meaningful reforms. On the other hand, the summit meetings serve as a forum for individuals and groups to get public support for their causes, thus increasing their power. The photo on the left shows some of the G8 leaders at the 2010 summit. The photo on the right shows a peaceful protestor serenading the police at a G20 protest in 2010.

And of course, there is the power that comes from brute force—from being bigger and stronger, from having more, bigger, or better weapons in a fight. Consider the famous scene in the film *Indiana Jones: Raiders of the Lost Ark* set in the Cairo, Egypt, marketplace. Indiana Jones, armed with his bull whip, is confronted by an angry scimitar-wielding opponent. After considering his options, Indy pulls out his gun and shoots the other man dead. That's the power of brute force.

Authority

In contrast to power, the term **authority** refers to the publicly recognized and sanctioned permission given to one person (or a group) to make another person (or groups) do something. It is sometimes called *legitimate* power. Often, positions of authority are very powerful—not only does the person have the publicly acknowledged right to wield power, she actually has power to wield. The president of a country, the head of a company, the principal of a school, the hereditary chief of the village, the captain of the football team—these are all positions of authority that may indeed include a lot of real power to bend others to one's own will and to make or influence important decisions for the group.

However, power and authority do not necessarily coincide. There may be people in positions of authority who have little or no real power to get things done, and there may be people without any authority who nonetheless have significant power that they wield behind the scenes. A few concrete examples should clarify these distinctions.

Examples of Positions of Authority without Any Significant Power

- The king of Sweden (currently Carl XVI Gustaf) has only ceremonial and representative duties; by law he has no political power, although he is popular and well loved by most Swedes.
- The governor of Texas has very little power; the lieutenant governor wields the real power, even though his position of authority is technically lower.
- A corporation's chief executive officer's every move must be approved by the board of directors—they wield all the power.

Examples of People or Groups Who Wield Power without Any Position of Authority

- The wife of the president of the United States can significantly influence events through her husband, even though she is not elected to any office. "Only the First Lady and the president determine the extent of her power, though frequently she has operated without his knowledge or permission" (Anthony 1990:8).
- Industries, such as artificial infant formula manufacturers, wield enormous influence over governments, including the United States, via their control of vast sums of money (Walker 2007).
- Often, the lowest-paid employees in any organization, such as the secretaries and the cleaning staff, wield enormous power through their detailed knowledge, their institutional memory, and their role as gatekeepers controlling access to people and resources (it is always a good strategy to cultivate their friendship).

Power Struggles within a Group or Community

Political conflict within a group or community usually takes the form of some sort of power struggle. When people without power are unhappy with how things are being handled by those in power, they may try either to overthrow the current leaders and assume the same positions of power themselves (rebellion) or to completely do away with the current power structure and replace it with something else (revolution). There are numerous strategies and tactics for manipulating political organization, ranging from legal to illegal, moral to immoral, nonviolent to violent, and persuasion to physical coercion.

In a democracy, some power struggles are settled through elections, although many factors influence elections other than the simple notion of "one person, one vote." In a dictatorship, dissenters may be silenced through censorship of all types of media, including the blocking of Internet and phone traffic, as well as through violent government suppression of protests and the threat of arrest, exile, death, or disappearance. In some organizations, there are structured means for making and changing rules, while in others, the rules are established by fiat and cannot be easily changed. Some groups use a process of consensus building, by which each decision must be discussed and debated until a compromise is reached that everyone supports.

If the organization is a voluntary one, such as a club or team, rival factions may split off and establish a separate group if they are unable to get what they want within the structure of the original organization.

For example, the Fundamentalist Church of Jesus Christ of Latter-day Saints split from the founding LDS church in the early twentieth century over disagreements about polygyny.

One major source of conflict within nation-states has to do with who has **jurisdiction** over a particular

Democratic forms of government are based on both the rule of law and the use of elections where, at least theoretically, each person can vote (once) for the candidate or option of his/her choice. Left: in this image from 2005, an Iraqi national drops his voting ballot for the election for the new Iraqi constitution into a ballot box at a polling station in Barwana, Iraq. Bottom left: in January of 2009, Salh Mohammad, from Farah City in Afghanistan, registers to vote at the Voter's Registration Center for men. Bottom right: April Sikorski from Brooklyn took this photo as she waited in line to vote for Barack Obama for president of the United States in the November 2008 elections.

region or topic—who has the authority to exert control over specific activities, people, or places. It helps if the lines of authority are clearly drawn, so that there is no room for ambiguity. For example, in the U.S. criminal justice system, with only a few exceptions, if a crime is committed entirely within one state, that state has the authority to address the crime. If a crime is committed that crosses state boundaries, such as a kidnapping or illegal interstate commerce, then the federal government has authority, through the FBI. Most college campuses have their own police forces, who have jurisdiction over crimes committed on campus, although they cooperate with local town or county-level authorities. If the criminal activity involves immigration, then the Immigration and Naturalization Service is in charge of the investigation. If it involves drugs, then the Drug Enforcement Administration takes over. Of course, many criminal cases involve multiple issues, and therefore multiple agencies.

Likewise, there may be disputes over which entity has to pay for some service that is provided by the government. For example, if a person is mentally ill, then one agency is in charge, whereas if the individual has a substance-abuse problem, then another agency is supposed to pay for treatment and rehabilitation. Often, people who are mentally ill self-medicate with legal or illegal substances, and rather than compete to see who gets to provide services, both agencies try to avoid having to treat people classified with dual diagnoses. "His main problem is that he has schizophrenia—that's *your* responsibility" versus "No, his main problem is that he is an alcoholic—that's *your* responsibility." Rather than fighting to see who has control, the agencies fight to *avoid* taking responsibility.

Detailed analyses of political conflict within groups and communities will be left to the political scientists. In the following sections, we examine larger-scale political disputes that involve one country or population invading another country or population.

THE STRUCTURE OF
POLITICAL DISPUTES

For most of human evolutionary history, people lived in small flexible bands of 25 to 50 people. They foraged for wild foods and moved across the landscape as their subsistence needs dictated. Most disputes were handled nonviolently, through discussion, avoidance, or by one or more individuals moving away to join another band either temporarily or permanently. If violence did erupt, it was usually in response to some real or perceived injustice—often two men arguing over a woman—and took the form of self-redress, where the victim sought to restore justice by directly confronting whoever had harmed him or her.

With the development of state-level societies some 5,000–6,000 years ago, followed by the rise of the modern nation-state, the scope of violence between groups increased manyfold, and modern warfare as we know it became more common. Around the world today, multiple conflicts are taking place simultaneously, whether in the form of civil war (within one nation-state) or between two or more nation-states (international conflicts). Contemporary political disputes, as well as those of the past few hundred years, differ widely in terms of the weapons used, the parties involved, the scale of the devastation, and the specific causes and justifications offered for the carnage. Despite all of this variation, the basic *underlying structure of political disputes* is essentially the same, wherever and whenever they occur.

Almost all historical and current political disputes can be characterized as conflicts between two opposing populations—the **invaders** and the **invadees.** In this discussion, the *invadees* are assumed to be the original inhabitants of the land and can be referred to by a variety of terms, including indigenous peoples, native peoples, First Nations, or autochthonous peoples. We begin our discussion with the *invaders*.

Invaders/Conquerors

Reasons for Invasion

Almost all political disputes are based on the premise that the invaders want someone else's land (and/or the resources on or below the land). Their reasons for invading and laying claim to the land typically fall into one of four types: (1) the invaders want to travel across the land safely to get somewhere else (e.g., American settlers wanted to travel across the Great Plains and western deserts to get to colonies in California and Oregon); (2) the invaders want to use the land for the same purposes that the indigenous people are using it for (e.g., they want to hunt on the land where the natives have always hunted, or they want to raise cattle where the natives have been raising cattle); (3) they want to use the land for different purposes than the indigenous people are using it for (e.g., they want to raise sheep where the natives have been hunting and gathering, or they want to grow crops where the natives have been herding animals); or (4) the invaders don't really care about what happens on the surface of the land, but they want access to the resources underneath the land, such as water, oil, gold, diamonds, copper, coal, platinum, and so forth. In addition, the invaders may exploit the indigenous people as a source of cheap labor. These reasons for invasion may overlap, or they may change over time. For example, settlers initially may come to raise livestock, but then gold is discovered in the region.

Justifications for Invasion

Invaders usually justify their behavior, and rally others to join them, by invoking one or more of the following sets of cultural beliefs:

1. *Terra nullis:* "The land is unoccupied, no one lives here, therefore it is fine for us to claim it." For example, hunting and gathering typically requires more land than other subsistence modes. Thus, large sections of land used by foragers can appear empty to outsiders, who are unfamiliar with how foraging works.

2. *Manifest destiny:* "Our god wants us to have this land." It is supernaturally ordained that the original inhabitants be removed in some fashion so that God's Will can be achieved.

3. *The indigenous people aren't really people:* "These creatures aren't human, or aren't fully human, or aren't civilized, and therefore have no rights to the land." Since they aren't human, they can be killed with impunity.

4. *"Finders keepers" doesn't count:* "Just because they were here first, it doesn't give them rights to the land and resources." This is a variation of the notion that might makes right—military power trumps possession.

5. *Retaliation for attacks on peaceful settlers:* Peaceful settlers from the invading group have a right to take some of the land and should not be attacked by the local inhabitants; the *savages* kill *innocent homesteaders*, especially women and children. In order to make the region safe for settlers, the murderous locals must be exterminated.

6. *"It's for their own good":* The invaders (often sincerely) think, "The indigenous people will be better off following the introduction of our obviously superior cultural beliefs and practices. They should be grateful."

Techniques for Invasion

There are many different techniques used by the invaders either alone, sequentially, or simultaneously, to effect a change in control over the land and its resources. Common techniques include:

- *Disease:* Perhaps the most powerful technique for getting rid of local populations is to kill them off by introducing new diseases to which they have no biological immunity, and with which they have no cultural experience for preventing or treating. Diseases may enter a new territory unintentionally, carried by explorers, missionaries, traders, or military scouts (see Diamond 2005; Farmer 2004; McNeill 1976); sometimes the introduction of disease is intentional.

- *Superior numbers:* The local population can be overwhelmed by the arrival of many invaders and settlers; being overwhelmed can impair their ability to resist (and thus back up the invaders' claims to legitimacy, especially where the indigenous people are foragers living at low population densities).

- *Superior military technology:* Guns are more powerful than bows and arrows, machine guns more powerful than rifles, cannons more powerful than grenades, and so forth, with nuclear missiles and chemical and biological weapons as the most deadly—superior firepower usually prevails.

- *Outright murder:* The deliberate killing of individuals in cold blood (not in battle) is employed for the express purpose of ridding the land of its original inhabitants, including surprise raids on undefended villages, bounties paid for each person killed, or rounding people up and executing them *en masse*. Hundreds of thousands of people have *disappeared* in many regions of the world during political disputes.

- *Direct and indirect attacks on locals as part of a counterinsurgency policy:* Such tactics include raids by small groups of soldiers, sniper attacks on insurgents (those locals who fight to defend their rights), and economic sanctions, such as blockading food and medicine, resulting in deaths from malnutrition and disease.

- *Moving people off their land, or restricting them to a small part of it:* A special *reservation* or homeland may be created where the indigenous people are confined, either for their own protection (according to the invaders) or for more efficient administration and control, freeing up land for the invaders. The reservations may encompass a small part of the original homeland or be located far away, in a different part of the country, even in a different environmental zone. The reservations may combine groups who have little in common other than their common fate as invadees. Over time, the reservations may be reduced in size or moved to a different region.

- *Forced change in lifeways:* Many aspects of the invadees' culture may be subject to new rules imposed by the invaders, such as:
  — A forced change in subsistence practices (nomadic pastoralists forced to settle in permanent villages; foragers expected to become farmers)
  — Forbidding people from speaking their native language
  — Outlawing traditional religious beliefs and practices, which are dismissed as merely superstition, devil-worshipping, or worse
  — Making people change their clothing and hairstyles
  — Curtailing the rights of women in egalitarian societies
  — Taking away rights, such as the right to own land or to choose their own leaders

- *Removing the children for education elsewhere:* The invaders try to break the cycle of transmission of culture from one generation to the next by sending the children to boarding schools far from their parents, often in the guise of providing education to those who "haven't had any opportunity to go to school."

- *Treaties that promise compensation to the invadees for cooperation:* Treaties—formal agreements that establish what rights and resources each party is entitled to—are rarely honored by the invaders, especially when valuable resources are discovered on or below the land initially assigned to the indigenous people.

- *Assigning all rights to land and resources to the government set up by the invaders and allowing others to purchase or lease those rights:* When a nation-state has been established by the invaders, and that nation-state encompasses a number of different indigenous groups in remote regions, the initial invaders may have little contact with some of the indigenous peoples. Decades may go by in relatively peaceful co-existence before the government decides to "open the region" to exploration for natural resources. They may do it themselves, or have outsiders do the exploring. The very process of exploring for resources can damage the environment and disrupt the lifeways of the indigenous peoples. If valuable resources are discovered, the government may allow outside companies to purchase or lease the rights to exploit the resources. Contemporary examples include drilling for oil in Ecuador and in the Arctic National Wildlife Refuge; the extraction of gold, silver, and copper in the New Guinea highlands; the logging of forests in Indonesia; and the establishment of wildlife reserves for ecotourism in East Africa (for example, Homewood, Kristianson, and Trench 2009).

- *Alcohol:* The introduction of alcohol, or making alcohol more readily available, has had a devastating effect on invadee populations in some instances. Crampton, describing the introduction of Cape Brandy to the Xhosa of Southern Africa in the early 1800s, writes:

> [Cape Brandy's] impact on the country's history cannot be underestimated: "If dagga [marijuana] and tobacco were the first tiny storm clouds to appear in the sky, brandy was undoubtedly the raging thunderstorm itself." So many chiefs succumbed to alcoholism that [alcohol] must rank as one of the most effective weapons in the colonial arsenal; not only in South Africa but in Australia, the Americas, and throughout the world, indigenous people let their land slip through their fingers as they opened their hands to grasp the bottle. (Crampton 2006:190)

Invadees/The Conquered

Invaders will encounter a variety of reactions and responses from the indigenous peoples, depending on the history of the region and the specific groups and individuals involved. However, the underlying structure of responses is similar across a wide variety of conflicts. Where the indigenous population is relatively homogeneous, egalitarian, and united in cul-

The fate of invadee populations and their descendants varies widely from one political dispute to another. Invadees are sometimes wiped out entirely. Left: this image shows the last four surviving Palawa people (Tasmanian Aborigines), including Truganini (far right), who was the final survivor of the British campaign to wipe out the natives of Tasmania and surrounding islands. She died in 1876. The middle image shows nine members of the Chiricahua Apache nation, who fought valiantly against the invasion of their homelands by European Americans from the 1700s until 1886. At that time, Geronimo and Naiche and their small band of followers surrendered to 5,000 U.S. Army troops and were taken as political prisoners. Although many Apache people were killed by Mexicans, U.S. Army Soldiers, and "settlers," or died while imprisoned in Florida and Alabama, enough survived that the Chiricahua Apache still form small cultural communities in Oklahoma, Texas, Arizona, and New Mexico. Right: Stephen Kearney, a contemporary New Zealand rugby player of Maori ancestry. The Maori peoples of New Zealand arrived on the previously unoccupied islands in the 1300s. Although the population declined due to diseases and conflict brought by Europeans in the seventeenth and eighteenth centuries, a significant proportion of the population survived. A revival of traditional Maori culture and language has been underway since the 1960s.

tural worldview, people tend to sort themselves into one of three categories: **resistors**, **cooperators**, and the **silent majority** (people just trying to stay out of the way) *based on individual circumstances and predilections.* Where the indigenous population is made up of distinct subgroups, with different social statuses, ethnicities, languages, religions, and so on, relationships between subgroups are often hierarchical. Some groups have more power than others before the invasion, and the subgroups may have very different worldviews and different responses to the experience of invasion. They will also vary in terms of the proportion of the population they represent. In the following discussion of heterogeneous populations, I will use a fictitious example with only two subgroups, those who are "In Charge" and those who are "Oppressed." Following an invasion, the same three types of responses are found: resistance, cooperation, and just trying to stay out of the

way. Members of the subgroup "In Charge" will tend to gravitate to the resistor category, while those who had little power, the "Oppressed," are more likely to choose cooperation with the invaders.

Homogeneous Population of Invadees—Resistors

Among the people being invaded, there will be some who view the invasion as being manifestly unjust and who are willing to resist. They may be labeled by the invaders as resistance fighters, insurgents, rebels, guerillas, or even terrorists. To those who support them, they may be viewed as freedom fighters. These are the individuals who fight to save their land, their people, and their lifeways from invasion by outsiders. They "would rather die on their feet than live on their knees" in subservience to the invaders.

Among the resistors, there may be disagreements about how best to resist, with three different strategies:

violent resistance, nonviolent resistance, and moderate approaches. Violent resistors believe that any and all means for fighting the invaders are justified. They may assemble armies or militias of their own or form small groups to carry out ambushes and raids on invaders, especially on isolated farmsteads, trading posts, or forts. In the decades of conflict between the Chiricahua Apache and the Mexican and U.S. armies, the group of resistors led by Geronimo and Naiche attacked settlers and army troops throughout their territory in retaliation for the invasion of their land. Geronimo was specifically motivated by the unprovoked murder of his wife, mother, and children by the Mexican Army in a raid on an undefended Apache village.

Contemporary violent resistance may take the form of suicide bombings, sniping, road-side explosives, kidnappings, tampering with infrastructure (destroying bridges and roads), use of biological weapons such as poison, and so on, depending on the sophistication and resources of the group.

Other resistors may agree that resistance is justified but believe that nonviolent means are either more appropriate morally or have a better chance of success than violent resistance. Nonviolent resistors may engage in peaceful protests, marches and sit-ins, chaining themselves to fences or trees, facing down tanks and soldiers with flowers, widespread work stoppages, fasting, appealing to outside groups for assistance, and so on. Nonviolent resistors often cite their religious beliefs as the basis for their nonviolent approach, refusing to meet the violence of the invaders with more violence.

The third category of resistors includes those we call moderates, whose tactics fall between the extremes of violent and nonviolent resistance. These individuals typically believe that they can work through the system to restore justice and counteract the force of the invaders. They may appeal to local, national, or international courts for support, or count on world opinion to affect the actions of the invaders. They make great efforts to report what is happening to them; in recent years, they have turned to new media such as websites, YouTube, and even Twitter to garner support for their stance.

Among the resistors, then, there may be disagreements about how best to proceed. Those who advocate violence may view the nonviolent resistors as cowardly or foolish. The nonviolent resistors and moderates may be morally opposed to violence, for any reason, and/or may resent the violent resistors for making peace more difficult. And, of course, not everyone wants to be a resistor.

Homogeneous Population of Invadees—Cooperators

In most cases, the invadee population includes some individuals who are willing to cooperate with the invaders. They may be labeled as traitors by the resistors, and be viewed as allies by the invaders. Usually they are willing to cooperate because they think resistance is futile. They "would rather live on their knees than die on their feet." They may see the invading force as being too overwhelming, too powerful, too superior in number and/or firepower for resistance to have any chance of success. Although they may be unhappy that their lands have been invaded and their resources confiscated, they believe that the best long-term strategy is to cooperate with the invaders. They may provide clandestine services to the invaders such as spying (providing intelligence), sniping against resistors, even infiltrating insurgent groups to find out their plans. They may provide material support to the invaders in the form of food, water, shelter, manpower, supplies of various kinds, medical care, and so on.

Cooperators are often very resentful of resistors, viewing the actions of resistors as completely pointless and likely to lead to more bloodshed, perhaps even the annihilation of the entire population. During the 1880s, a number of Chiricahua Apache men volunteered as scouts to help the U.S. Army track down and capture Geronimo and Naiche, and their followers. Still other Apaches didn't actively help the invaders, but neither did they view Geronimo as a hero. On the contrary, they were angry with him for his persistence in fighting against the Mexican and U.S. invaders and felt that he was doing all Apache tribes a disservice. When the resistors were finally captured, the cooperative Apache scouts who had helped find them and convince them to surrender were summarily declared prisoners of war as well. They were sent to prisons in Florida along with Geronimo and Naiche and the other resistors.

Homogeneous Population of Invadees—
The Silent Majority

In some cases, a large segment of the invadee population is marginally involved in the conflict. Many political disputes take place primarily in the major cities and towns. In the hinterlands, far from the seat of power, hunters and gatherers may move through the forests unaffected by who runs the government. Farmers and herders in remote regions of the country may not even know that their nation-state has been invaded, or that resources in a distant part of the country are being exploited by outsiders. They prefer just to be left alone, to raise their corn, beans, and squash, or to herd their sheep, or to fish their rivers, in peace.

Often this is possible, but sometimes these innocent bystanders get caught in the crossfire between the invaders and those who are cooperating with the invaders on the one hand, and the insurgents/resistance fighters on the other hand. Many rural villagers have found themselves placed in a position of threat from both sides. If they don't provide aid and support to the insurgents, they may be shot by the insurgents. If they do provide aid and support to the insurgents, they may be shot by the invaders, by company officials, or by government forces who are backing the invaders or corporate exploiters. What happens when the invadees are comprised of many different subgroups with varying interests?

Heterogeneous Population of Invadees—Resistors

Although members of both groups, those who are "In Charge" and those who are "Oppressed," may be unhappy that their land has been invaded, those most likely to participate in an organized resistance will be *those who have the most to lose* if the invaders are successful at imposing their own culture on the invadees. Who stands to lose the most, both in terms of political power and economic wealth? Those who were "In Charge" before the invasion. Thus, we expect to find that when a heterogeneous population is invaded by outsiders, the resistance will come mainly from those "Formerly in Charge."

In all other ways, the resistors are likely to behave similarly to those in a homogeneous population, being divided among those who advocate violent resistance by any means possible, those who prefer nonviolent forms of protest, and those who are moderate and try to work within the system.

Heterogeneous Population of Invadees—Cooperators

Although a few members of the "Formerly in Charge" group may, for various reasons, decide to cooperate with the invaders, the vast majority of cooperators will be drawn from the "Formerly Oppressed" subdivision of the population. They have less to lose, since they started with less to begin with. And they potentially have much to gain if they can ally themselves with the invaders. By cooperating with the invaders, they may be able to switch positions with those "Formerly in Charge" and gain both political and economic power relative to their previous status. Cooperators, therefore, may hail the invaders as heroes who have come to save them from oppression. Some will hope to establish a more just and fair sharing of resources among all the people, but others will be interested only in taking over the positions of their former oppressors—with the support of the invaders—thus gaining power, including the opportunity to punish those "Formerly in Charge" for their past behavior.

Heterogeneous Population of Invadees— The Silent Majority

And again, there will be large segments of a heterogeneous population who are just trying to stay out of the way and get on with their daily lives. Perhaps, as members of small ethnic minorities or obscure religious factions, they weren't really players in the political and economic arenas before invasion. It makes little difference to their lives who is in charge, and they just wish to stay out of the conflict altogether. Those living in remote regions may be able to do just that, while those living in the midst of the fighting may find themselves caught between three different groups— the resistors, the cooperators, and the invaders.

Real-World Examples: Former European Colonies

In a number of actual cases, European governments invaded other regions of the world and set up new nation-states, protectorates, or colonies, with colonial administrations. The artificially created political units that resulted often split cohesive cultural or ethnic groups among several different nation-states, or lumped together a number of distinct, hierarchically related, and antagonistic cultural groups in one new political entity, or both. The cultural/ethnic group with the most members—the majority of the region's population—may have been in charge formerly by virtue of their superior numbers. They may have justified their position, and their oppression of other groups, by claiming that they were of higher status, or were taller and more regal looking, or had the better religion.

They resisted the colonial takeover most strongly, because they had the most to lose, but were ousted from power and replaced by colonial administrative officials.

Other cultural groups who had been in inferior positions were more likely to cooperate with the European colonial administrators. In some cases, they were singled out for positions of power and influence, and many young men were sent overseas to receive an advanced education under the system of the colonial rulers. They learned the culture, the language, the style of dress, the habits of eating, and so forth, of their colonial masters and took on much of the colonial worldview while maintaining their resentment of their former native oppressors. At the end of the colonial era, in the middle of the twentieth century, many of these colonized countries gained their independence from their European masters. Once control of the colonial administration was turned over to the local elites, who were still a minority in terms of population size, long-simmering resentments boiled over and disputes among the different local groups turned violent. Many of the ongoing conflicts in former European colonies in Africa, the Middle East, and Asia have their roots in practices of the invaders pitting resistors against cooperators and exploiting the differences among subgroups within the invadee population.

Real-World Example: The Case of Iraq

Iraq was created as a modern political entity at the Cairo Conference of 1921, following the defeat of the Ottoman Empire during World War I. A group of 40 politicians and military leaders, including Winston Churchill, T. E. Lawrence (Lawrence of Arabia), and Gertrude Bell, met in secret and discussed how best to reconfigure the former Ottoman Empire. Their primary goal was to ensure Western European, primarily British, political and economic interests by securing sources of oil and installing leaders who would follow British advice. Three separate divisions of the Mesopotamian part of the former Ottoman Empire—Kurds in the north, Sunni Muslims in the middle, and Shia Muslims in the south—were consolidated into the single country of Iraq, whose borders were drawn by Gertrude Bell. The British installed Lawrence's friend and collaborator, Faisal, as the first king of modern Iraq.

Today, most Muslims belong to one of two main sects, Sunni and Shiite (Shia). Traditionally, the United States has supported Sunni Muslims across the Middle East. In Iraq, the United States helped Saddam Hussein, a Sunni, attain and maintain power. Hussein's forces oppressed many of their fellow Iraqis, including the Shia, who constitute the majority of the population. The Shia shared Arab ethnicity with those in power but remained separated by their religious differences. At the same time, government policies targeted the minority ethnic Kurdish population in the north of the country, even though they were Sunni Muslims. If the traditional Kurdish homeland in the north had been bereft of resources, the Kurds probably would have been left alone. However, the most lucrative oil fields in Iraq are to be found in the north. Hussein moved many of the Kurds south and brought in Sunni Arabs to occupy and settle the northern region of the country and control the oil.

Since the United States invaded Iraq in 2003, it has been, and continues to be, mostly the "Formerly In Charge" Sunnis who lead the insurgency, and the "Formerly Oppressed" Shia who cooperate most with U.S. forces, as one way to seek justice from their former oppressors. The Kurds, meanwhile, have retaken control of their region of the country and are pressing for autonomous political authority within Iraq, while dealing with Kurdish extremist factions who advocate violence against their Turkish neighbors. The Turks also have a long history of oppressing the Kurds who live within their borders. The world is a mess.

FINAL THOUGHTS

In many cases, specific political disputes will be enormously more complicated than the presentation above. There may be multiple competing groups among the invadees who jostle and compete for power when presented with the opportunity by virtue of an outside invading force. Among the resistors, internal disagreements about how best to resist may lead to assassinations of moderate leaders by more radical ones, and vice versa. Likewise, among invaders, in addition to the actual forces involved in the invasion, there will be many back at home who are not actively participating. Some of them may be gung-ho supporters of the invasion, while others may be strenuously protesting their government's actions. Some, perhaps most, remain part of a vast clueless majority. They don't really know what the reasons for the invasion were or which of the justifications, if any, are valid, and they may not particularly care, as long as it doesn't directly impact their lives. For Fry, the fundamental question remains:

> How can we improve the quality of life for all humanity, reduce the social and economic inequalities that

foment hostility, hatred, and terrorism, and create new procedures and institutions for providing justice and resolving differences without war? In short, at the global level, how can we replace the law of force with the force of law? (Fry 2007:xv)

Key Concepts Review

Every culture has rules of behavior—guidelines about what is acceptable and what is not.

Rules are established and changed through a variety of methods.

The most powerful tool that any group has at its disposal for getting people within the group to behave is the enculturation of children.

Sanctions can be either positive or negative, internal or external, natural or supernatural.

Conflicts and disputes are found in all human groups, but the vast majority are resolved using nonviolent means such as compromise, avoidance, or discussion.

Anthropologists typically classify political organization, based on complexity, into bands, tribes, chiefdoms, and states.

Disputes or conflicts can be resolved nonviolently, or they can be resolved through aggression, violence, and/or warfare.

A code of individual responsibility holds only the individual actor liable for anything he or she does, while corporate responsibility means that all members of a group are held liable for the actions of any member of the group.

Humans are not innately aggressive and violent.

Justice seeking moves from mostly self-redress in band societies to mostly blood feuds in tribal societies; warfare is recent—it arose with the origin of chiefdoms (10,000 years ago) and became more common with the rise of state-level societies (5,000–6,000 years ago).

The concepts of power and authority are distinguished by the fact that authority is publicly recognized and sanctioned; people behind the scenes, who have no authority, often wield much of the power.

As societies become more complex, the state usurps the rights of individuals and kin groups to redress grievances and administer justice—a criminal justice system is developed that is administered and enforced by clearly defined public officials.

All political disputes have a similar underlying structure, with the invaders or conquerors exhibiting a limited number of reasons for invasion, justifications for invasion, and techniques for invasion.

Likewise, invadees tend to fall into one of three response categories—resistors, collaborators, or "the silent majority"; when hierarchical societies are invaded, those who were formerly in charge usually resist the most, and those who were formerly oppressed are the most likely to cooperate with the invaders.

7

ACHIEVING ECONOMIC GOALS

Markets, Trade, & Exchange

People have many different motivations other than profit, and the majority of economic transactions provide returns in multiple ways. Individuals usually act rationally with respect to economic transactions, given the cultural constraints within which they must work, and their specific goals and values.

conomic anthropologists combine the perspectives of anthropology with the theories and methods of economics to analyze human culture and behavior. Since economics is embedded within larger social systems and grounded in the local and regional environment, it is often difficult to draw clear boundaries about what constitutes economic behavior and what falls outside this realm. Thus, a wide variety of cultural beliefs systems and behaviors come under the scrutiny of economic anthropologists, ranging from studies of risk and decision making using game theory to the importance of gifts and long-term social relationships, from global economic trends and Internet merchandising to local marketplaces where people meet and gossip, from value placed on monetary profit to calculating wealth by the number of children one has, and much more.

THREE BASIC ECONOMIC PRINCIPLES

Traditionally, cultural anthropologists describe economic principles as belonging to one of three types: market exchange, redistribution, and reciprocity (which itself has three varieties). This is a useful *heuristic device* for starting to think about the underlying structure of economic transactions in cultures around the world. However, there are many situations where two or more principles are operating at the same time, and many cases where the superficial differences between systems or contexts may disguise the underlying similarities. Learning to look beneath the surface to the deeper levels, and recognize the economic principle or principles at work, will go a long way toward helping you understand why people behave the way they do in economic transactions. In a later section of this chapter, we will explore the various goals that motivate people to act the way they do and the different sorts of returns one might get for spending one's time, money, and effort. Our exploration begins with an explanation of the three types of economic principles.

Market Exchange

Market exchange is often the easiest principle for members of industrial and postindustrial societies to understand, because we partake of it multiple times every day. **Market exchange** *refers to the exchange of resources between two parties where the two parties agree that the exchange involves resources or currency of equal value.* Resources can takes a variety of forms: people (slavery), livestock, food, water, alcohol, cigarettes, all types of natural and manufactured products, services of all types, labor, knowledge, the rights to do things in the future, and many others.

Most market exchanges are voluntary. I don't have to buy your goods, and you don't have to sell them. But if you have something I want or need, and I have something you want or need, we may agree to trade or swap our resources. In many cases, one side of the exchange involves **currency**—some form of money that we both agree can temporarily *hold the value* of what I get from you until you find something else you wish to exchange the money for, often with a different trading partner. However, it is important to realize that currency is not necessary for an exchange to be classified as market exchange. If two strangers meet in an abandoned building and exchange sex for illegal drugs, this qualifies as market exchange, even though no money was involved. Likewise, if people connect through U-Exchange and trade items—an aquarium for a bike—that is also market exchange. We will explore the idea of money in more detail below.

Most market exchanges involve agreement between the partners on the approximate worth of the resources under consideration. In most Western markets, the prices are set by someone other than the two individuals involved in the transaction, and the seller has no flexibility to adjust the price. If the buyer thinks the price is too high, she can look elsewhere, or go without. The Western system of fixed prices is based on the underlying belief that goods and services have some intrinsic value based on their quality, the associ-

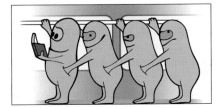

The three basic economic principles: Top: market exchange in Morocco; along the Ginza shopping street in Tokyo, Japan; and at an upscale mall in the U.S. Middle: redistribution at a Native American potlatch; the Girl Scouts "Operation Thin Mint" delivering cookies to U.S. Navy personnel in Japan; and the dessert end of a potluck serving line, somewhere in the U.S. Bottom: generalized reciprocity, such as a stranger helping change someone's flat tire; balanced reciprocity, such as two friends helping a third pack and move his belongings; negative reciprocity, such as pickpockets on a subway.

Not all market exchanges involve commodities (material goods). In many regions of the world, men and women, boys and girls, make money by having sex with strangers. Around the world, the part of a city where prostitutes can be found is referred to as the "red-light district." The image above shows a street in St. Pauli, the red-light district of Hamburg, Germany.

and forth go the offers and counteroffers until either a compromise is reached or the negotiations break off. Marketplace bargaining is a fine art, one with many and varied informal rules that may be difficult to learn as an outsider. Frustration can occur on both sides when one side is expecting a fixed price and the other is expecting one or more rounds of bargaining to precede the exchange.

Where prices are fixed, market exchange can be relatively impersonal—it takes place between people who do not necessarily have any personal relationship with each other and may never interact again. This type of system can be very efficient, especially in terms of time: you go into the market, make your choice, pay for it, and leave. No time is spent on social interaction, and the price is set, so there is no need for bargaining. At the same time, these conditions increase the potential for fraud and deception, as both partners in the exchange may be trying to get more value than they give, and expect never to see the other person again.

Market exchange can become incredibly complex in industrial and postindustrial societies. However, even in these complex societies, economics includes much more than market exchange, as we explore below.

Redistribution

Redistribution is a particular form of economic exchange that involves, first, the gathering together of resources from many and varied sources in a central location. Second, some publicly recognized authority is charged with collecting, storing, organizing, processing, and repackaging these resources. Third, the resources are sent out again—*redistributed*—to a number of recipients. Redistribution underlies many different economic activities in a variety of societies, from the smallest scale to entire nation-states, and even operates at the international level. We will explain each step in turn and then look at some concrete examples of redistribution at work.

The accumulation of resources can take many different forms. It may be voluntary, as when people contribute money or goods to charities. It may be required, in the form of taxes that people are obligated to pay—taxes on their income, their expenditures (sales tax), their property, or their agricultural production. In some cases, rather than money or a portion of

ated prestige value, and/or other considerations. Prices are set partly on the basis of how many there are of an item (supply) and how many people want the item and what they are willing to pay for it (demand). If a product doesn't sell, then the price is lowered, and if it still doesn't sell, then it will no longer be produced. People *vote with their wallets* in terms of what is popular, at what price, and what is considered not worth buying no matter how low the cost.

In many non-Western markets, people operate with a different set of beliefs, including the idea that an item is worth whatever a person is willing to pay for it, and therefore, prices are flexible. Often, the sellers are the ones who grew or produced the product, or are offering the services themselves, and they have the power to negotiate a different price for each buyer, even for identical items. Bargaining for goods in the marketplace is viewed as a sport, or as performance art, in some contexts, with both sides starting at extreme values—the seller asking a ridiculously high price, the buyer offering a ridiculously low price. Back the crops, people are obligated to donate their time, labor, or knowledge.

The publicly recognized authority that collects the resources may be one or more levels of government or it may be a local or regional leader or organization. Redistribution systems vary in terms of how the resources are collected; whether they must be moved from one location to another; whether they must be stored, processed, or repackaged; and how they get to their final destinations. Despite this variety, the underlying structure of redistribution systems will be similar across a wide variety of circumstances.

Redistribution, likewise, can take many forms. Sometimes the resources are collected and then redistributed in similar or modified form to the same people who contributed them. Other times, the resources are sent out to those who couldn't afford to contribute to the system, in which case the redistribution serves as a way to spread out the wealth of the society and reduce disparities in income and standard of living. Economic anthropologists refer to this as a **leveling mechanism**—a way of reducing economic differences between people. In some instances, everyone contributes to the common pool of resources, but only those who need them, as a result of some crisis, benefit from them. Sometimes the resources are used to build or maintain facilities that anyone can use who wants to, or that only a small portion of the society will directly use, but that everyone benefits from in the long run. The following concrete examples will clarify what sorts of economic transactions fall into the realm of *redistribution:*

- All levels of government taxation in the United States, including:
  - *U.S. federal taxes,* collected by the Internal Revenue Service and redistributed in the form of federal government services, including the Department of Commerce, the Department of Defense (all branches of the military), the Department of Health & Social Services, the CIA, the FBI, the interstate highway system, Medicaid, Medicare, Social Security, NASA, National Oceanic and Atmospheric Administration, federal courts and prisons, federal parks, the Veterans Administration, etc.; plus federal contributions to funding for a number of regional and local infrastructure projects (roads, dams, electrical power plants) and social programs for the homeless, the mentally ill, the intellectually disabled, the poor, and so on. Every federal employee's paycheck, every desk chair, every ream of paper, every stapler, every computer, the electricity to run the buildings, the gas to power the cars, every airplane and gun and missile, every cell phone, every coffee pot— all of these are expenses incurred by the federal government and are paid for through federal taxes contributed by the vast majority of citizens.
  - *State taxes,* collected in the form of income tax or sales tax, or both, fund state-level programs including the Departments of Motor Vehicles, Transportation, Education, Natural Resources, etc.; the state-level criminal justice system (police, judges, jails, DA's office, etc.), state highway systems, state hospitals, and state contributions to infrastructure projects and social programs.
  - *County and local taxes* may pay for local road maintenance, local fire and police departments, local parks, and so on.
  - *Local property taxes* are often used to fund the local school systems, which is why wealthier areas of the country have better schools, with new facilities, better equipment, and more extracurricular programs, and why wealthier areas can attract the best teachers through higher salaries.

- Charities that collect money in a variety of ways (donations, fund-raising dinners, walk-a-thons, bike rides, bake sales, silent auctions, and so on); some of the money pays for overhead expenses (to raise the money), but most of it is redistributed to the designated recipients:
  - Medical charities may distribute the money in the form of research grants to scientists working on prevention, detection, or a cure; they may fund educational outreach programs for a specific illness, or subsidize screening programs, or provide financial and counseling support to affected families; they may pay for a lobbyist who can influence legislation that affects research priorities or the lives of people living with the condition.
  - Girl Scouts of America collects boxes of Girl Scout cookies each year to ship to U.S. troops serving overseas.
  - The Seamen's Center of Wilmington, Delaware, is supported by donations from the community and provides a variety of services to the crew

members of the ships from around the world who dock at the Port of Wilmington.

- Insurance companies are paid premiums by the subscribers, and companies pay out benefits only as needed. Most people who own cars and homes have insurance, and they pay their insurance premiums every year, hoping that they never get any of that money back, because that would mean they had sustained damage. Insurance may be mandated by law, but most people are willing to pay for the peace of mind that comes from knowing they are covered in the case of an accident or crisis; they don't mind their premiums being used to fund repairs for other people who need it.

- University campuses charge tuition and fees (and parking fines), augmented by government funding, research grants, and alumni donations; the administration redistributes the resources to pay for faculty and staff salaries, building and grounds maintenance, electricity bills, computing resources, food for the dining halls, books and subscriptions for the library, equipment for the sports teams and marching band, research facilities and travel funding for faculty, and so on.

- Everyone who is invited to a pot-luck dinner brings a dish of food to share, and then all the guests fill their plates with small portions of the food provided by each guest. In a true pot-luck, you never know what people will bring, which is part of the fun and surprise.

There are many different varieties and forms of redistribution around the world; the above examples are merely meant to help you understand the concept. Kwakiutl potlatches and South Pacific yam feasts, discussed in a later section, are also examples of the economic principle of redistribution in action.

Reciprocity

The third economic principle at work in all human enterprises is that of reciprocity. Reciprocity comes in three different forms—generalized, balanced, and negative—and each will be discussed in turn, with examples.

Generalized reciprocity simply means doing things for others—giving them resources, time, labor, knowledge, and so forth—with no expectation of payment or any other form of return directly from the recipi-

ent(s). It may help to think of it as a one-way system, with the resources constantly being passed onward to others. If you do something for me (or give me something), I am in your debt. However, instead of paying *you* back, now or in the future, I *pay it forward*. I do something for someone else, who in turns does something for yet another person. This concept is embodied in such axioms as "What goes around comes around," "Pay it forward," and "Practice random acts of kindness."

The *cultural logic* behind generalized reciprocity involves two steps. First, people who have resources that others can benefit from, whatever form those resources may take, help out those in need whenever they can. They do so not because they are being paid, or because they expect something in return from the person they have helped, but simply because they can and are expected to—they have been enculturated to do so. Second, if enough people participate in the system, and put good deeds out into the world, then the world will be a better place, and eventually each person who contributes will end up receiving something in return. It may be from different people, it may take a different form, and the giver may not reap the benefits for many years, but the belief is that eventually each person will get back at least as much as he put into the system. Examples abound.

Among most foraging peoples, who live off of wild plants and animals, generalized reciprocity is standard practice. At the end of the day, when those who have gone out hunting or gathering meet up with those who have stayed in camp, everyone shares whatever food has been collected. If a hunter has been successful, he doesn't keep all the meat for himself, or share it only with his family, or save it for later; nor does he try to sell it to other members of the group. He freely shares whatever meat he has with everyone. There may be rules about who gets which part, with choice cuts going to the hunter's family or to the person who made the arrow or to the sick or elderly, but everyone shares—no one goes hungry. In the long run, each hunter will be successful only some of the time, but everyone gets to partake of whatever meat any of the hunters have returned with.

Generalized reciprocity takes many forms, from putting quarters in other people's parking meters to stopping to help someone whose car has run out of gas; from contributing to charitable causes to parents caring for children, who will then grow up and care for their own children, down through the generations. Many people participate in informal networks of generalized reciprocity without ever giving a thought to the economic principle involved.

The key point for distinguishing generalized reciprocity from other forms is that *the giver does not expect to be paid back by the recipient*, either right away or at a later date, either directly or indirectly. Rather, the giver expects the recipient to play the role of giver to someone else, in the future, whenever and however he is able.

Balanced reciprocity involves two people who know one another and have a positive social relationship—they are relatives or friends or acquaintances or trading partners. Both provide resources to the other when needed, again in the form of money, goods, services, support, or other forms of help. The recipient is not expected to pay for this help, or to reciprocate in kind, or within a specific time frame. However, it is expected that, over time, both parties to the relationship will benefit and help each other out.

If the friends have equal access to resources, then it is generally expected that the value of the goods and services they exchange will work out to be approximately equal, although no one is keeping close tabs. Examples of balanced reciprocity include: exchanging birthday presents with friends, neighbors taking care of each other's dogs when each are on vacation, and mothers who exchange babysitting as needed. The pastoral Fulani of Mali establish trading relationships with Bambara millet farmers and Bozo fishermen and exchange milk for millet or fish, but with a time lag, as the various foodstuffs aren't necessarily available at the same time. *Balanced reciprocity differs from market exchange because the two partners have on ongoing social relationship, resources flow back and forth at different times, and no one keeps an exact accounting of the balance on either side.*

Balanced reciprocity doesn't necessarily involve equal value in terms of the monetary value of the resources exchanged. Between people of equal social status and income, it is expected that over time the value of the exchanges will be about the same. However, balanced reciprocity can also occur between two parties of different social status or income levels, and each acknowledges that while the monetary value of the exchanges may be uneven, the thought and feeling that go into the exchange are what is important. For example, parents in Western cultures often give their children gifts that cost more than the gifts the children give in exchange (ceramic figurines and macaroni art), but no one minds. Or two friends may take turns paying for lunch, and the one with the better-paying job selects a more expensive restaurant.

Negative reciprocity is the term used to denote those cases where one partner to the exchange tries to cheat the other partner by offering something of lesser value, by failing to repay the favor in a timely manner, or by contributing less than 50 percent to the relationship. We've all known people like this, who seem to be friends, people we may enjoy, but they ask for favors all the time yet can never quite return them somehow. Like the person who never seems to have any money when it comes time to pay the bill at a restaurant, but promises to pick up the check next time, and next time never comes. Or the person who always needs a ride somewhere and promises to contribute gas money, but never does. Or the person who routinely asks for favors, but is never able to reciprocate—"Gee, I'd love to help you move, but I have to get my cat spayed this weekend." When one person consistently doesn't hold up her end of the implicit agreement, the other partner may break off the relationship either openly, telling the person that she is inconsiderate, or by reducing the number of favors given and eventually refusing to grant favors or cutting off contact.

Market exchange, redistribution, and reciprocity are overlapping systems and operate independently as well as in combination in all cultures. Even a single transaction can combine elements of all three different principles. Other economic principles are also at work in many contexts, including bribery, corruption, blackmail, and black market exchange.

THE FLOW OF WEALTH

When we talk about wealth, we are referring to economic resources of all kinds, including money, goods, knowledge, and services. There are two distinct patterns to the flow of wealth between and across generations in different societies around the world. Although it is a gross simplification to say that "all Western cultures" tend to exhibit one pattern and "all non-Western cultures" tend to exhibit the other, it is still useful to explore these two approaches. Understanding the difference between them helps to explain an often misunderstood aspect of culture—how people decide how many children to have.

The *Western* Pattern

Remembering that this is only a generalization: typically, in Western (industrial and postindustrial) contexts, wealth tends to flow down the generations. By this, I mean that resources of all kinds tend to be passed from parents to children and grandchildren. In a typical nuclear family, one or both parents may contribute to the economic base of the family, but the children do not. Parents earn the money (or produce the food) and children consume it. Parents pay for their children's housing, utilities, clothes, transportation, entertainment, travel, medical care, education (parents often pay for college), and so forth. Parents do the majority of the domestic labor to keep the household running, such as the cooking, cleaning, laundry, yard work, paying the bills, and child care. Some children do contribute domestic labor, helping with chores, running errands, babysitting their siblings, and so forth, but many do not, or not until they are teenagers. Older children may have jobs that bring in money, but that money often goes toward their own wants (clothes, gas, movies, iTunes), rather than augmenting the household income to pay for basic needs such as housing and food.

Essentially, each nuclear family household has one or two adult wage earners, who also provide most of the services. The children act mostly as consumers, as drains on their parents' time, energy, and money. Even when they are old enough to help with domestic chores, they are often not expected to. These patterns of behavior stem from a number of widespread cultural beliefs: (1) that *childhood* is a special time—a time for playing and enjoying oneself; (2) that a child's main job is to go to school, do homework, study hard, and participate in extracurricular activities, which leaves no time for helping around the house; (3) that it is the parents' responsibility to provide everything that the household and the children need; (4) that children will remain financially dependent on their parents at least until they finish their formal education, and sometimes beyond; and (5) that children do not have to pay their parents back for all of this investment of

resources, but rather will *pay it forward* to their own children someday.

Under such a belief system, where the entire family must be supported by one or two adults, *the more children the family has, the further the resources must stretch.* There is a limit to how much money the parents can earn, and a finite amount of time and energy to expend on domestic labor and other services. Therefore, it is obvious that the more children there are, the fewer resources each child will get. Under this type of system, if poor parents continue to have more children, those of higher birth order (the fifth or sixth child, for example) may not be as well-nourished and may have to make do with hand-me-down toys and clothes, or go without.

As an example, I like the metaphor of buying pizza. Suppose there are two students in the dorm who contribute money for pizza, $5 each, and they order in one large pizza and split it between them; each gets three slices. Both are happy and satisfied. Now, suppose that before they can begin eating, a nonpaying neighbor catches the aroma, drops in, and says, "Hey! Can I have some?" If three people share the pizza, then each gets only two slices. If three additional neighbors come by and want pizza, each person gets only one slice, and the hosts are probably getting annoyed. There is a finite amount of pizza, and if it is to be shared equally, then as more people join the party, each person gets a smaller and smaller portion. The more party guests, the less pizza each one can have. It makes sense to lock your door and keep your pizza to yourself (or to go out for pizza).

In a cultural system where wealth flows down the generations, from parents to children, the same relationship obtains between the number of children in a family and the resources each child has. Under these circumstances, *it makes economic sense to limit the size of one's family to the number of children the adults can support at the standard of living they find acceptable.* It makes no sense to have more children than you can afford.

The *Non-Western* Pattern

Remembering that this is only a generalization: typically, in many non-Western contexts, particularly in pastoral and horticultural societies, although some resources do flow down the generations, *significant resources flow up and across the generations.* By this, I mean that resources of all kinds flow not only from older to younger generations but also from children to parents and grandparents, as well as from individuals of all ages to their siblings and cousins. In a typical extended family (the most common family form in pastoral and horticultural societies), not only do one or both parents contribute to the economic base of the family but the children do as well, from a very early age. Starting as young as three or four years of age, children are taught to contribute both domestic and productive labor to the best of their abilities. Very young boys may be assigned pigs to watch over as they forage or calves to take to pasture or cattle dung to carry out of the village every morning. Girls as young as four or five years of age may be enlisted as babysitters for the next youngest child, freeing the mother for other responsibilities for much of the day.

The specific details of which tasks are assigned to which sex, at what ages, varies greatly from culture to culture, but the general pattern is that children are expected to spend a significant part of their day helping support the family in some way. Children may contribute labor directly to any of the domestic and productive needs of the household, or they may take over some of the relatively easier or safer tasks, thus freeing their parents and older siblings for more productive labor.

For example, in rural Mali, young girls help gather and chop firewood, haul water, pound millet, sweep the compound, cook and serve food, wash

In many Western cultures, children are viewed as (and are raised to be) consumers of their parents' time, money, and effort; thus, the more children there are in a family, the less each child can have. In many non-Western cultures, children are expected to help from an early age, and are net income producers for the family; thus, the more children there are in a family, the more each child can have. Top: teenage girls in the U.S. spend their parents' money buying clothes. Middle: sisters in India bring water home from the river for their family to use. Bottom: in 1912, the Mortaria family of New York City makes flower wreaths at home. The three-year-old on the left was actually helping, putting the center of the flower into the petal, and the family said she often worked until 8:00 PM. The other children, 9, 11, and 14 years old, worked much later, until 10:00 PM. The oldest girl said her father was a soap-maker, making $3.00 a day for three years.

dishes and clothes, and help watch over the younger children. By the age of nine or ten years, most of them know how to do all the tasks that will be required of them as adult women in Bambara society, and they have developed incredible upper body strength, which allows them to be a real help to the family. While the mother prepares food to sell in the market, her six-year-old daughter may be walking around with the tray of food for sale, collecting money and making change, with a baby or toddler strapped to her back. Children as young as three or four years of age may be sent off to the market, and are expected to navigate the streets of the community, bargain for a fair price, and come home with the correct change.

In Mali (and many other cultural contexts), children also wait on their elders, fetching water, food, cigarettes, newspapers, and so on, or delivering messages from one household to another. Young boys in Mali lead relatively more carefree lives than their sisters, but they still provide significant domestic and productive labor, including herding goats. In southern Mali, young boys provided a significant percentage of their own protein needs by roaming the countryside with their slingshots, killing, cooking, and eating small animals such as birds and lizards while away from the village. In addition, they are roped into helping with horticultural labor as needed.

Essentially, each extended family household has multiple adult wage earners, as well as a number of children who *contribute more resources than they consume* from an early age. Children require intensive care for the first few years but then begin to help out, rather than acting only as drains on their parents' time, energy, and money. As with the patterns described above for Western cultures, these very different patterns of behavior stem from a number of widespread cultural beliefs: (1) that *childhood* doesn't exist as a separate and distinct phase of life; (2) that the main job of children is to help their parents and other members of the extended family and do whatever they are asked—children go to formal schooling only if it is available and affordable, and if they can be spared; (3) that it is everyone's responsibility to contribute to the needs of the household; (4) that as they get older, children will gradually become more and more useful to the family and become income producers for the family at a relatively early age; and (5) that children will be repaid for their labor when they are adults and have children and grandchildren of their own to wait on them and take over much of the burden of daily chores.

Under such a belief system, where the extended family is supported by multiple adults and numerous children, *the more children the family has, the greater the resources they have to share.* The more children there are, the more income, the more hands to help with the work, the more services that can be provided to whoever needs them, thus, the more resources each child will get. This is reflected in the nutritional status of children in Mali: children of higher birth orders—the eighth, ninth, or tenth child in a family—will have better growth and be less likely to be malnourished than children of lower birth orders (first, second, or third). By the time a family has their tenth child, there are many older children and adults contributing to the family's resource base.

The pizza metaphor looks quite different in cultures where the resources flow up and across as well as down the generations. Suppose there are 10 people in the dorm who contribute $5 each for pizza, and the organizer orders in a number of pizzas and everyone eats their fill, with some left over. Since it only costs $4.50 to buy as much pizza as one person can eat, the organizer pockets the left-over money, $.50 per person. If the word spreads that a bunch of folks are having a pizza party, then more people contribute $5 each. If you get 100 people participating, the organizer ends up with $50 extra. The more people who participate, the more resources there are, because each person contributes more than they consume.

In a cultural system where wealth flows up and across the generations, from parents to children but also from children to parents, and from older children to younger children, the same relationship obtains between the number of children in a family and the resources each child has. Under these circumstances, *it makes economic sense to maximize the size of one's family, as the more children there are, the better the standard of living that everyone can enjoy.* It makes no sense to limit the number of children you have.

The important point to take away from this detailed discussion is that *having more children makes economic sense in many cultural contexts*—wherever children contribute to the household economy, having more children makes one richer, not poorer.

MONEY

Money is an interesting aspect of economics to study cross-culturally because it takes so many different forms. The notion of **money** was created to facilitate economic transactions whenever two parties to an exchange didn't have resources of equal value, and/or mutual exchanges couldn't take place simultaneously. Something was needed to serve as a common measure of value, equivalent across many different resources and as an instrument of exchange. Money acts as a **repository of value,** a way to measure value, to store value over time, and to easily transport value over space. The power of money resides in the shared ideas in people's heads—the partners to the transactions must agree that the units of money have a specific value. People must be willing to accept money in exchange for the real goods, services, or information they are giving up. And they must trust that they can keep it for some time, take it somewhere else, and find others who also agree on its value, so it can be exchanged for other resources of equivalent value. To be most efficient, money, in whatever form it takes, should be easy to transport, easy to measure, easy to divide into smaller units, and in consistent demand. The three most common forms of money are currency (coins and bank notes), commodities, and electronic data residing inside computer networks.

Money in the Form of Currency

In many regions of the world, and for thousands of years in some places, money has meant *currency*—originally coins made of metal, and then bank notes (paper bills) issued by the government or another authorized agency. Many countries mint their own coins and print their own bank notes. This form of currency is called national money or fiat money. In addition, there are regional currencies such as CFA and Euros. CFAs (Communauté financière d'Afrique, or West African Francs) are the official currency of the eight countries that belong to the West African Economic and Monetary Union. Likewise, the Euro is the official currency of many of the countries that belong to the European Union, and Euros are accepted in some other EU countries that still have their own national currency. U.S. dollars and Euros are accepted in many places around the world, but certainly not everywhere.

In addition to national or fiat money, numerous local municipalities, businesses, and organizations produce their own currency that can only be spent in restricted areas and/or for special purposes. These forms of currency may be referred to as local, community, alternative, or complementary currencies. For example, since 1987, Disneyland has printed Disney Dollars, which can be purchased for their equivalent in U.S. dollars but can only be spent at Disneyland and Disneyworld. A variant on community money, known as Time Dollars, can be found in many small towns in a number of countries. One Time Dollar represents one hour's worth of a person's time—his labor, skills, or knowledge. Time Dollars can't be used to purchase goods or commodities, but they serve quite well to facilitate the exchange of services such as hair styling, lawn mowing, math tutoring, babysitting, and so on, among people in a local region.

Money in the Form of Commodities

The shared cultural value of money doesn't have to reside in currency in the form of coins and paper bills. The term **commodity money** refers to any objects or goods whose value people generally agree on, and which can be pressed into service for use as money. Examples of commodity monies used around the world include:

- *Cowrie shells:* These small white sea shells are used across much of Africa and some parts of Asia as currency and are thought by some to have intrinsic, even mystical, value.

- *Venetian trade beads:* Beautifully colored and intricately designed, these art-glass beads were made by the Venetians beginning in the 1400s for use as currency by European traders traveling to Africa and Asia; they are still used as money in some regions of the world, and valued by collectors for their beauty and historical significance.

- *Cigarettes:* During World War II (and later in Korea and Vietnam), members of the U.S. armed forces were issued a ration of cigarettes in addition to their paychecks; because they were in high demand, but not everyone smoked or needed all of their ration, cigarettes became a widespread commodity money both within the military and in occupied territories such as Japan following WWII; cigarettes are still used as units of exchange in many prisons.

Other examples of commodities used as currency include alcohol, legal and illegal drugs, gold, ivory, cloth, and livestock. Among many pastoral peoples, there is common agreement about the value of various kinds of livestock. For example, a goat may be valued the same as a sheep, while a certain number of either are equivalent to one cow or camel. Economic anthropologist Harold K. Schneider writes:

> Goats and sheep are important secondary livestock throughout East Africa, but that they are considered distinctly inferior to cattle and camels cannot be overstated. When calculating ratios for exchange of sheep and goats (which look alike because the sheep are hairy, like the goats) the animals usually are aggregated as "goats" and equated to cows (i.e., female adult cattle) at a rate of five or ten "goats" to a cow. Thus a goat is perceived as, at best, worth only one-fifth of a cow or even as little as one-tenth. (Schneider 1979:44)

In some contexts, livestock have an agreed upon, intrinsic value, regardless of their size, their age, or the state of their health (within limits). When a well-meaning Western-trained agricultural agent tries to get an East African herder to exchange his herd of 20 stunted, skinny cows for five big healthy cows, the East African likely refuses, because a cow is a cow is a cow. For monetary purposes, it doesn't matter if the cow is skinny or fat. Likewise, an American college student is unlikely to exchange her torn, dirty, crumpled $20 bill for two clean, crisp, brand-new $5 bills

that her anthropology professor is offering. The perceived value of the bills, like the value of the individual animals in the herd, lies in people's minds and is not affected by their physical condition.

Money in the Form of Electronic Data

Since money is a shared cultural concept, it can exist without physical form once systems of information technology and computer hardware and software have been developed. In other words, as long as people agree to allow electronic data to serve as a repository of value, one can do away with currencies and commodity monies altogether. In their place, we need various mechanisms that can accomplish the transfer of value in the form of electronic data, moving the value from one account to another over computer information networks. These mechanisms for electronic money transfer include direct deposit of paychecks, where employees are paid for their labor not with currency or a paper paycheck to take to the bank but with an electronic transfer of funds from the employer to the employee's bank account. The employee then can turn around and pay bills such as the mortgage, car loan, utilities, food, clothing, education, and so on via his computer. Nothing physical changes hands, only the idea of value formerly captured in currency and commodity money is transferred from one owner to another. An account owner can even set up an auto-

Where livestock have intrinsic value, regardless of their size, age, and condition, one cow is worth the same as every other: The fat cow (above left) is worth $50, and the two skinny cows (above right) are worth $100. It wouldn't make economic sense for a person to trade his two skinny cows for one fat cow, any more than it would to trade an old, crumpled $100 bill for a crisp new $50 bill. The new bill is in better condition, but condition is irrelevant.

matic system whereby money is transferred from one account to numerous others on specific dates, for specific amounts.

In addition to direct deposit and online bill payment, other mechanisms for shuttling value around include credit cards, debit cards, and electronic benefit transfer cards. In a system analogous to community money, many college towns participate in the Off-Campus Meal Plan system, whereby students can purchase meal credits through their university, which can be spent at participating restaurants and stores near campus. Value is added to the card electronically and then subtracted by the merchants in exchange for food and service using an electronic card reader.

The development of electronic money has made many economic transactions faster and more efficient, especially over great distances, but it also has its disadvantages. Many people find it much easier to spend electronic money than value embodied in currency or commodities. When people can use the credit card system to spend money they don't really have, money that doesn't really exist because it hasn't been earned yet, they can quickly get into serious debt—it somehow isn't as real to pay for an item with your credit card as to exchange cash for it. Another disadvantage, one that electronic money shares with local currencies, is that some forms of electronic funds transfer are not accepted in some places. Just as one can't buy groceries at a corner market in Cairo, Egypt, using Lithuanian *litas*, and a German soft-drink machine won't accept U.S. quarters, not everyone accepts American Express or the Off-Campus Meal Plan card.

The sheer variety of electronic money has made it less efficient than currency in some ways and creates a lot of frustration when people find themselves in a situation where the forms of money they have are not accepted. For example, at the University of Delaware parking garages, you can pay with cash or check, but not with credit or debit cards. Likewise, many merchants in the United States today no longer accept legal currency in the form of large-denomination bank notes, such as $50, $100, or $500, because of the problems of counterfeiting.

Still, it is pretty amazing when you can travel to Romania and the automatic teller machines will accept a small plastic debit card from a U.S. bank and spew out Romanian paper currency in exchange! How clever, how efficient, how convenient!

CONCEPTS OF OWNERSHIP

What Can Be Owned?

Varying notions of ownership can be found around the world, not only in terms of what can be owned, but also who can own it, who can use it, and what ownership itself means in different cultural contexts. These belief systems influence many aspects of economic behavior and have been a major source of conflict in human history, sometimes with disastrous consequences.

Land and Water

In *Ishmael*, his novel of anthropological philosophy, author Daniel Quinn makes a distinction between **Takers** and **Leavers.** According to the main character, Ishmael (a telepathic gorilla), Leavers include all hunting and gathering peoples, from the origins of human culture some two million years ago to contemporary foragers. The fundamental principle of the Leaver philosophy is, "Man belongs to the world," just as all other living things do. In this worldview, people cannot *own* resources in the sense of being able to claim them, isolate them, and prevent others from using them. Although certain groups may traditionally hunt in one area, or get water from particular water sources, they would never deny access to these resources to other individuals or groups of people who need them.

In contrast, Takers develop a very different philosophy, beginning with the Neolithic Revolution some 10,000 years ago, when they start to domesticate plants and animals. The fundamental principle of the Taker philosophy is, "The world was made for man." Of this premise, Ishmael says: "It's a very simple notion and the most powerful in all of human history" (Quinn 1992:60).

The Taker worldview leads to a logical, but devastating, conclusion: "If the world was made for us, then it *belongs* to us and we can do what we damn well please with it" (Quinn 1992:61). For Takers, everything in the world can be owned—land, water, goods, knowledge, even other people. Owners stake a claim to their resources, isolate them, prevent others from using them (or charge for their use), and defend them against attempts by others to take them away.

Quinn's dichotomy is overly simplistic, but it serves as a useful *heuristic device* for beginning to think about different concepts of ownership. For some indigenous peoples, land is not something that can be owned. Like water and air, land is thought of as existing prior to, and separate from, human experience. When asked by invaders, "Who owns this land?" they responded, "No one." But they meant, "No one—because no one *can* own the land." The invaders interpreted their response to mean, "No one owns this land, so feel free to claim it for yourself, or your king and queen." The idea that the newcomers would eventually block access to the land, and kill anyone who trespassed on it, was unimaginable to the original occupants.

Within the general idea that land can be owned, distinctions may be made. Some land is owned by nation-states, by the government. In the United States these are referred to as federal lands and include all of the national parks, as well as national monuments and cemeteries. Other land is owned by smaller governmental units such as states, counties, townships, cities, and towns. Some land is owned corporately by businesses, educational institutions, and charitable organizations. And some land is owned by private individuals, such as the land on which a person's house is built (assuming the mortgage has been paid off—before then it belongs, at least partly, to the mortgage lender).

Land ownership raises a number of interesting questions. For example, is it just the surface of the land that is owned? Or can an individual or corporate entity own the rights to resources underneath the land—water, oil, coal, natural gas, precious metals, or cultural objects such as grave goods and human skeletons—either in addition to, or instead of, the surface itself? A major problem with some underground resources is that they don't necessarily have the same boundaries as the land above them. If one person drills for oil or gas or water, he is tapping into underground reserves that may stretch for miles in many directions, reaching into areas that are underneath other people's land. This is especially problematic with aquifers, which are underground sources of water. Removing water by pumping it to the surface in one location may deplete the water in all the surrounding neighbors' wells, lowering the water level and causing some wells to run dry. How to regulate who owns or has access to underground resources is thus a difficult problem to overcome. A related problem crops up when activities on one piece of land pollute the ground water, which then leads to contamination of other people's water.

Another issue related to land ownership is whether or not owning the land gives a person the right to do whatever she wants with it, especially if it has the potential to adversely affect neighboring properties. Restrictions, in the form of zoning laws, may be placed on what sorts of activities can take place. In some areas, you can't have a business on your property if it is zoned for residential use only. In others, you can't have domestic food animals; dogs or cats are fine, but not chickens and pigs. In some, there are restrictions on the type of house you can build, how tall it can be, how much noise you can make, and so on. Similarly, there are restrictions on how far you can go to protect and defend your property from wild animals, the neighbor's dog, and trespassers. There are a number of different cultural beliefs about what sorts of rights go along with land ownership, and what would be reasonable limits on those rights.

Above-ground water flows from one region to another, passing over lands that may belong to many different private individuals, as well as corporations or government entities. Disputes over rights to the water continue to plague many populations around the world. How much water can be diverted by folks living upstream and how much must be left in the creek or river for the use of people downstream? What happens if one group pollutes the water, which then carries toxins downstream, into the sea?

Bodies of water may serve as boundaries between two political entities, but the dividing line isn't necessarily the middle of the lake or river. For example, the Twelve-Mile Circle is a geographic entity created in 1682, when the Duke of York ceded all the land within a 12-mile radius of the courthouse of New Castle, Delaware, to William Penn. The northwest portion of this arc forms the boundary between Delaware and Pennsylvania. Within the Twelve-Mile Circle, Delaware owns all of the Delaware River and the land beneath it, up to the low-tide mark on the shore of the New Jersey side of the river. In recent years, Delaware has prevented New Jersey from building a large natural-gas off-loading and storage facility that would extend out into the river, since the river itself belongs entirely to Delaware at the planned location.

There are legal limits to how far out into the ocean a nation-state's jurisdiction extends. *Territorial Waters* extend from the mean low-water mark on land out as far as 12 nautical miles, and these waters are considered part of the sovereign territory of the state, including the airspace over the water and the seabed below. From the outer edge of the territorial waters, up to 24 nautical miles from the coast, we find the *Contiguous Zone,* over which the state exerts more limited control. From the coast extending out for 200 miles, the waters are called the *Exclusive Economic Zone.* Within this broader zone, the state controls all the potential economic resources, including fishing, oil drilling, and mining, as well as threats to economic resources, such as pollution or trespassing by foreign fishing fleets.

Controversies have emerged in recent years over previously unclaimed land and ocean resources. The UN Commission on the Limits of the Continental Shelf is currently pondering the claims of several countries to all or parts of the land surrounding the North Pole in the Arctic, which is estimated to contain about 25 percent of the world's oil reserves. In 2007, a Russian submarine traveled to the region and left a capsule containing a Russian flag on the seabed, thereby claiming the land for Russia. In the future, we may see disputes over who owns real estate in space, such as the moon and other planets. This may seem farfetched, but the United States bombed the moon in the summer of 2009, an action that outraged many people.

Russia has claimed territorial sovereignty over the land surrounding the North Pole, which is estimated to contain 10 billion tons of oil and natural gas deposits. Their claim is disputed by a number of other nations. In this photograph, the submarine *USS Honolulu* surfaces about 280 miles from the North Pole and is investigated by curious polar bears. Because the United States has not ratified the UN Maritime Convention (pending since 1982), it does not have a seat on the International Seabed Authority, which is the body that oversees the UN Maritime Convention and controls areas outside national jurisdictional limits, including the area in question around the North Pole.

People

Slavery exists today despite the fact that it is banned in most of the countries where it is practiced. It is also prohibited by the 1948 *Universal Declaration of Human Rights* and the 1956 *UN Supplementary Convention on the Abolition of Slavery, the Slave Trade and Institutions and Practices Similar to Slavery.* Women from eastern Europe are bonded into prostitution, children are trafficked between West African countries and men are forced to work as slaves on Brazilian agricultural estates. Contemporary slavery takes various forms and affects people of all ages, sex and race. ("What is modern slavery?" 2010)

Around the world, many people believe that one person cannot legitimately own another person, that it is morally reprehensible and philosophically untenable, and that each person is, by definition, an autonomous individual with rights of his or her own. When someone refers to **slavery,** many people think of the trans-Atlantic African slave trade, which flourished from the fifteenth century well into the nineteenth century, and brought an estimated 10–12 million people from regions of West and Central Africa to the New World to live and work as slaves, mostly on agricultural plantations. Importing slaves to the United States was outlawed in 1808, and the Thirteenth Amendment to the U.S. Constitution in 1865 freed all slaves and made it illegal for one person to own another in the United States. However, slavery existed in many forms long before the fifteenth century, in Africa and elsewhere, and continues around the world today.

Accurate data concerning the numbers of individuals involved, the specific form of slavery, and the geographic distribution of slaves are difficult to find, but an estimated 27 million people live as slaves in the world today. The majority of slaves are found in Africa and India, but more than 14,500 slaves are trafficked into the United States each year. Some are **chattel slaves,** meaning they earn no money at all and are held against their will, often forced to perform labor through violence or threats of violence to themselves or their families. Others, sometimes referred to as **bonded labor** or **indentured servants,** borrow huge sums of money to pay to be smuggled into another country and then work for years at low-paying, menial jobs in order to pay off their debts. Around the world, most slaves work as mining, agricultural, food service, or garment industry workers; or as sex slaves; or as domestic (household) slaves. In several regions of the world, women and young girls and boys are held as sexual slaves, earning money for their owners through the services they provide to paying clients, including sex tourists from Western countries.

In a radically different example, the relationship between parents and children involves some aspects of one person owning another. For example, in the United States, until children are 18 years of age, their parents have extensive rights to determine what medical care they receive (or do not receive), even against the child's express wishes. And if a man and a woman create embryos using in vitro fertilization, the parents usually have exclusive rights to decide what happens to those embryos. They can be used to produce children for the couple, or they may be donated or sold to other couples or to research facilities, or they may be destroyed. Under some circumstances, individuals who are mentally retarded, mentally ill, or have age-related cognitive problems may be declared incompetent by the courts and lose their rights to make decisions about where and how they live. In Japan, young children often are considered an extension of their mother, and if she kills them and then commits suicide, it is deemed *oyako shinju* (double suicide) rather than murder-suicide (Goodman 2000, cited in Montgomery 2008). In Japanese culture, the general belief is that the mother owes it to the children to kill them, rather than leave them motherless.

Underlying these belief systems about personhood is a common premise—that some individuals are not human, or not fully human, and therefore don't have the same rights as those who are. In many cultural contexts, women and children do not have the same rights as adult men, and many ethnic or religious minorities are denied rights that are enjoyed by whichever group constitutes the majority and/or sets the rules.

This is a very complicated subject, and I have only touched on it briefly here, but it is important to remember that there are still people in the world who view other people as commodities—as resources to be bought and sold, used and used up, exploited and harmed.

Nonhuman Animals

The people Ishmael would describe as Takers, who form the vast majority of people in the world today, usually view nonhuman animals as commodities that can be owned and exploited. People own livestock, such as cattle, goats, and sheep. They own horses, which may be raced, used in rodeos, worked on ranches, used for competitive or recreational riding, or eaten. They own cats, dogs, hamsters, fish, birds, ferrets, guinea pigs, and on and on. Only a few groups of people, those Ishmael would describe as Leavers, would claim that nonhuman animals cannot be owned any more than people can be owned. When my son Alex was little, a Native American man at a pow wow patiently explained to him that the tame wolf who was with him did not *belong* to him, because wolves can't be owned by people.

Other Stuff

In addition to the ownership of land and water, and human and nonhuman animals, plants can be owned, all sorts of nonliving objects can be owned, and ideas can be owned. **Intellectual property** is the term used to refer to specific ideas, inventions, and knowledge, and creative output such as writing and music. There are a number of different perspectives on the extent to which such intangible resources can be *owned* in any meaningful sense.

In recent years, the view that such resources should be free and available for anyone to use has been gaining momentum in the United States and elsewhere, facilitated by the ease with which music, photographs, writings, and other intellectual property can be transmitted around the world instantly via the Internet. At the same time, some countries have allowed the patenting of life forms, either in their entirety, or in the form of individual genes, such as Monsanto's patent on certain genes found in soy beans. Others find the idea of owning genes to be ridiculous. This remains a source of debate and controversy around the world.

How Are People and Things Owned?

Private or Individual Ownership

There are several different ways that ownership—whether of land, people, objects, or ideas—can be assigned. The concept of **private property** refers to the notion that a single individual has full control over whatever is owned; she has the right to claim the property—she inherited it, purchased it, found it, or made it—as well as the right to use it for her own purposes, including selling it or destroying it. The property belongs to a single person, and no one else has any legal claim to it. Concepts of private property are widespread around the world, but there are some cultures in which very few resources are held as private property, and most property is held by a group larger than the individual.

Corporate Ownership

Any group—whether it is based on ties of kinship or is a business corporation or an informal cooperative—may own resources in common. Under **corporate ownership,** the group or corporation is understood to have an existence above and beyond the specific individuals who belong to and participate in the group at any one time. Over time, individuals will both join the group and leave the group. Resources belong to the group itself, not to the individuals that comprise it at a specific point in time. As members of the group, individuals have some rights to use and enjoy the resources, but they don't have the right to sell or destroy the resources. Rights of use, also known as **usufruct rights,** often carry restrictions or limits.

For example, a village may own agricultural land in common, with the chief of the village having the right to assign land to individuals for cultivation. The same family may farm that land for generations, but it still belongs to the village as a whole—the family cannot sell the land to developers. If they no longer need it for growing crops, it returns to the general pool of village resources. Likewise, in pastoral societies, the lineage may function as the corporate entity that owns livestock. If a lineage member needs cattle for bride-

wealth, or for a sacrifice, the lineage elders must agree and grant permission. A fishing cooperative may consist of several men, each of whom owns his own fishing boat, while together they own the fish-processing facility at the dock, which processes the fish that all of the co-op members catch.

Universities may act as corporations, owning the land the campus sits on, the buildings that house classrooms and offices, the books in the library, the football stadium, and the dormitories with all their fixtures and furnishings. When college students live in dormitories, they pay for the right to live in their room; use the restrooms, lounges, hallways, and other common areas; and enjoy whatever other resources the university supplies, including heating and air conditioning, water, electricity, phone and Internet access, and so on. Students who live in a dorm room are not allowed to sublet it, to operate a business out of it (though some do), or to destroy it. As a group, the students who live in a dorm one year cannot sell the building to a developer—the students have limited usufruct rights, but not the rights of ownership. The resources are thus preserved, to be used in subsequent years by a steady influx of new students each fall.

Government Ownership

Government ownership of resources is a special case of corporate ownership. Different levels of the government bureaucracy may serve as property owners, as mentioned previously. For example, the government of a nation-state may own land outright and/or economic rights over resources found on or under the land. The government may own buildings, furnishings, vehicles, and so forth. The limits of governmental rights depend on the form of government. Under a system of democracy, government leaders may have the right to sell or lease land and resources to other entities—such as the leasing of logging rights or oil exploration rights on federal lands in the United States to business corporations.

GOALS AND VALUES IN ECONOMIC BEHAVIOR

One of the most interesting aspects of studying economic exchanges from an anthropological perspective is realizing that people have different goals in mind as they engage in economic activities. Sometimes one goal is paramount. Sometimes the strategy is to achieve several goals at once, goals that may be overlapping or, in some cases, contradictory. People born and raised in a capitalist society, where much economic activity occurs in a relatively impersonal marketplace, may take it for granted that everyone acts in pursuit of monetary profit. Certainly the profit motive is an important one in many societies, but there is much more to economic exchanges than making money.

Maximizing Profit

We'll talk about profit first, to get it out of the way. When people act so as to maximize their profit, they are trying to increase the total value of their material resources, including various monetary instruments such as bills and coins, but also property, other real estate, livestock, goods, and so on. The goal is to exchange A for B, where A and B are both material objects, and where B has more value than A. **Profit** is the increase in value of B over A. With this profit, people may reinvest in their economic enterprises, accumulate more goods and services for themselves and others, gain power and/or prestige, or save for any of these uses in the future. The profit motive is a powerful force driving much economic activity, especially in industrial and postindustrial societies. However, strategies that have the potential to return a high profit usually carry a high risk as well. Alternate goals are also pursued in most societies, and in some cases the profit motive takes second or third place to other goals.

Minimizing Risk

For many people, high risks are unacceptable because if things go wrong, the person or the family is left destitute and starving. Many factors go into people's perceptions of risk, and how much risk they are willing to take or feel comfortable with. If you have extra money to invest, you may be willing to invest in a scheme that has high risks but high potential profit. If it doesn't work out, you will still be fine. However, if you are trying to decide how best to invest your efforts in order to procure food for your family, you can't afford to participate in risky enterprises. If you gamble

and lose, then you and/or your family starves, or loses their home, or loses their ability to make a living.

It may be more important to have a steady, if modest, income than to take a risk of perhaps becoming wealthy, but also perhaps becoming a pauper. Let's look at a couple of concrete examples. Suppose you are an East African cattle herder with 100 cows that need to be assigned to five different herders (young adult male members of your lineage) to be taken to distant pastures. There may be two excellent pastures, two mediocre pastures, and one really poor pasture. It might seem obvious that you should split the herd into two groups of 50 cows each, and divide them among the two excellent pastures. That way, you can be assured that there will be plenty of food and the cows will grow fat and happy, reproduce successfully, and provide lots of milk.

However, there are other considerations. There is always a chance that members of neighboring pastoral tribes may raid your herd and steal some or all of your cattle, and that carries some risk of injury or death for the young herders. In some areas, predators are more common, and you risk losing some of the newborn calves to lions, leopards, or hyenas. Every location carries some risk of disease, such as rinderpest or sleeping sickness. There may be a trade-off between the availability of good water for the herd and the availability of fodder. The better pastures may be farther away from potential buyers, and the cattle may start out weighing more but will lose too much weight on the trail to market.

Your top priority may be to minimize your risk—to send some cattle to each of the five different pastures and hope that enough will survive and thrive that your family will have enough for food and religious sacrifices. Even if one group gets stolen by thieves, or suffers many losses from disease or tainted water, chances are the other groups will survive. By spreading your investments in your cattle out among a variety of potential pastures, you are minimizing the risk that you will lose all of them. Whenever there are multiple ways to lose one's investment, and no way of accurately predicting or influencing what might happen, the wisest strategy is to distribute the risk as broadly as possible, assuring some minimal return.

As an example from a postindustrial context, let's examine the finances of a married couple, Steven and Kathy. Steven is confident in the stock market and invests most of his retirement money in high-risk/high-return stocks, bonds, and mutual funds (which operate similarly to the cattle example above). Kathy is more risk-averse, and she puts all of her retirement money in a fixed-interest savings account, where it earns much less than Steven's money when the stock market is doing well, but where it continues to earn the same amount even when Steven is losing money due to the stock market tanking.

Steven is trying to maximize his profit, but at a high risk. Kathy is trying to minimize her risk and therefore earns smaller returns. Since neither knows what the overall economy and market will do in the time they have left until retirement, they can't predict which strategy will turn out to have been the best until they retire. They hope their combined mixed strategy works.

The take-home message? *Don't assume that everyone is always going to act in such a way as to maximize profit.* Many times, people pursue strategies that minimize risk instead.

The Favor Bank

Maximizing Debts That Others Owe You (Future Assets)

Another strategy that some people pursue, in addition to either maximizing profits or minimizing risk, is to act in such a way as to maximize debts that others owe you. This is a way of accumulating value in what some writers refer to as the *Favor Bank*. If you have plenty of resources (land, time, money, goods, or whatever), and you give or lend these resources to others, then they owe you something in return. It may be as significant as loaning someone the money to start her own business in exchange for some percentage of the future profits, or as modest as giving a friend a ride home for the weekend, knowing that sometime in the future, if you have occasion to ask this friend to do something for you, the person will feel obligated. It may involve putting in a good word for a friend's child who is job hunting, or introducing two business associates to one another. Many a savvy businessman or woman has followed this strategy, going out of their way to do favors for others—friends, family, colleagues, even acquaintances. You do things for others when you can and don't ask for anything in return. People think you are generous and helpful. Later, if you call on them for support, they aren't necessarily obligated to return the favor, but they will feel obliged.

This may sound a lot like balanced reciprocity, but the distinction is this: In a relationship of balanced reciprocity, both sides mutually participate on an ongoing basis, to the benefit of both. By maximizing debts that others owe you, you are stocking up *assets for the future*. If you don't need to, you don't ever ask for a favor in return. But at the same time, you know that a vast network of recipients of your past largesse exists out there in the world, and they serve as a way to bank favors for the future. You do things for others when it costs you the least, and then they (hopefully) will feel obligated to return the favor if and when you ask. They may return the favor quickly, or not for years; they may return the favor by doing something similar or something completely different. A series of small favors may be repaid by one big favor. If you are always successful, you may never need to cash in these deposits to the Favor Bank, but they form a safety net, providing security.

Minimizing Debts That You Owe Others (Future Debts)

The flip side of maximizing debts that others owe you is to minimize debts that you owe to others. You try to remain as independent as possible and ask for help only when absolutely necessary. This relieves you of worrying about when you might be called on to return the favors that have been granted to you in the past. If it is necessary to accept help from others at some point, you can repay them as soon as possible, so that you maintain control over your assets.

Economic Transactions as Social Relationships

Maximizing Social Relationships

In some cultures, the profit motive takes a distant backseat to the goal of maximizing social relationships among people. The long-term result of such a strategy may be to increase profit, but often the social relationships themselves are the main reward. In small-scale communities, where many people know one another, economic activity is not anonymous, and people place a higher value on their friendships than they do on saving money or making a profit.

Vending machines can be economically efficient, allowing the sale of goods without a human vendor present. They also appeal to people who prefer to minimize social relationships and thus try to acquire the things they need without interacting with others. The photos show vending machines for worms in Spain (presumably for fishermen) and memorial candles at a cemetery in Germany.

For example, the word *customer* literally means "one who is in the custom of coming to a particular vendor to purchase goods or services." You want as many people as possible to get in the custom of coming back to you whenever they want or need whatever it is you provide. At the beginning of these relationships, you may offer people a cheaper price, even to the point where you lose money on the transaction. At the same time, you are building social relationships with people—you learn their names, who they are, what their tastes and preferences are, what concerns they have going on in their lives. You may see them only in the vendor–customer context (you don't have to become best friends), but the social relationship becomes an important part of the transaction. More is going on than just exchanging money for something else.

For example, in Malian fresh food markets, all the tomato sellers can be found along the same row. Each woman has essentially the same product for sale, at the same price, and they all clamor for your attention, your *custom*. By establishing a social relationship with one specific vendor, you get more than tomatoes for your coins—you get a social exchange, you swap news, you joke and laugh. Once a relationship has been established, the other vendors leave you alone. Your tomato lady may give you a discount if you buy

a large quantity, or she may put aside especially lovely tomatoes and save them until you arrive at the market, or toss in some extra red peppers for free. Even if she charges you slightly more for the nice tomatoes, you appreciate it and are willing to pay more. You both look forward to the exchange.

On occasion, these relationships turn out to be valuable—people cut you some slack or treat you better because you know each other. This sort of approach to economic exchanges—maximizing the social relationship aspect—is important in many cultures. People don't necessarily view economic exchange as impersonal interactions; they expect to have ongoing relationships with others. This can be unsettling or confusing to people who are used to viewing economic transactions as purely utilitarian—I pay you for a six-pack of Coke, and neither of us says a word because we have no social relationship and never expect to see each other again.

Minimizing Social Relationships

Of course, some people are not interested in making small-talk with tomato vendors. They want the best value for their money, the cheapest price, the quickest transaction, and that's it. Some people actually abhor the sort of small-talk and chit-chat that these social relationships entail, and they go out of their way to avoid them.

If your highest priority is getting the lowest price for gas, you go wherever the lowest price can be found. If you're in a hurry, you go where the lines are shortest. If you'd rather not talk to anyone, you go to the station that accepts credit cards at the pump, even though the price is higher. You duck down a different row at the library than the one you need, in order to avoid someone else in the row. You'd rather come back later than listen to someone blathering on and on about their research or their current relationship drama.

The important thing to remember is that although people almost always act rationally according to their own goals, maximizing profit is only one of many possible goals. Rather than dismiss economic behavior that seems unreasonable to you, stop and think about whether people are pursing different priorities than you, and why.

What Sort of Return Are People Getting for What They Give/Exchange?

Economic behaviors can be analyzed from additional perspectives as well. There are all sorts of returns that people might get for whatever they give or exchange with others. These returns may be primary motivators, or may nudge a person in one direction versus another. People will value these returns differently, depending both on their enculturation into the norms and values of the group they grew up amidst and on their individual personalities, which develop over the course of a lifetime. Additionally, some people are better at getting what they want—they have more sophisticated skill sets and can figure out how best to manipulate others and/or the market, to their benefit. Understanding these other motives goes a long way toward making sense out of people's behavior that appears mystifying when judged by one's own priorities.

Social Prestige (Others Think More Highly of You)

A powerful motivator for many people is social prestige—what others think of you. If other people will think more highly of you if you follow one course of action rather than another, that may make a difference in your choices and behaviors. Often, people do things that seem economically irrational, in the sense that they end up with less value in terms of goods or

money (they give things away, or sell them for less than their cost), or they expend enormous effort for seemingly little or no personal return. But if they can acquire and accumulate social prestige, and turn that into higher rank, or power over others, then they may be following a very astute strategy indeed.

A classic example from the ethnographic literature is the **potlatch** of Northwest Coast Indians such as the Kwakiutl, where wealthy leaders would accumulate vast stores of goods and distribute them publicly to other members of the group during a huge celebration and feast. The practical effect was for a chief to redistribute goods from those who had excess to those in need, and in the process, the chief acquired immeasurable amounts of social prestige. Likewise, Big Men of the South Pacific islands would distribute yams, birds of paradise, and other items, and host big celebrations as one way of increasing their political power and adding to their legions of followers. In postindustrial consumer societies, wealthy families may compete via their children to see who can throw the most lavish Sweet 16 birthday party, or the most expensive wedding. When two high-society families are united in marriage, the cost for the wedding and reception may run as high as a million dollars and will be written up in the society pages of the *New York Times*.

When philanthropists give vast sums of money to charitable causes, or when wealthy supporters go to a black-tie fund-raiser that costs thousands of dollars per person to attend, they appear to be generous and selfless, donating their money to a good cause. In reality, they are paying for what they receive in return—higher public acclaim and the maintenance of their position at the top of the hierarchy. Their photographs and descriptions appear in the media, they are able to hobnob and make connections with other wealthy and influential families, furthering their economic interests and/or setting the stage for advantageous marriages among their offspring. They may get their names on the new wing of the hospital or the new arts center at the university.

In order to attend a charity banquet or ball, people may spend hundreds or thousands of dollars on travel to distant locations, and on tuxedos and designer gowns, in addition to the required donation to attend. In return, they get to eat a rubber chicken dinner worth $7.50 and publicly flaunt their wealth and position in the company of others who also qualify as rich and famous. If their goal was truly selfless, they would have stayed home in their bathrobes eating mac and cheese and donated the money, including what they would have spent on travel and clothes, directly and anonymously to the charity.

In these, and many other ways, members of the upper class increase and maintain their positions of power. On the surface, a potlatch and a charity ball may seem to be two entirely different cultural phenomena, but the underlying structure and purpose are the same—to *redistribute wealth in exchange for social prestige.*

Self-Esteem (You Think More Highly of Yourself)

Many people behave in what would otherwise appear to be economically irrational ways because it makes them feel better about themselves. They do things for others quietly, anonymously, without telling anyone or bringing attention to their own good deeds. People donate money or time to charitable causes without any public recognition; they perform community service, volunteer in the public schools, take their pets to visit the elderly in nursing homes, deliver hot meals to the homebound, and many other activities because it brings them a feeling of accomplishment—they are proud of themselves for their efforts, even though they may toil without pay, recognition, or public acclaim.

Sometimes, their activities even bring them scorn or disdain from others. When I go to my neighborhood park to pick up trash, neighbors driving by will tease me—"What have you done this time, to be sentenced to community service as a punishment?" When I tell them that I find it a useful and satisfying way to spend my time, and view it as a way to give back to my community, they are perplexed. Why not spend my time doing something fun or something that will earn me money? Some people can't imagine getting personal satisfaction out of doing things for others at some cost to oneself of time, effort, and money. Luckily for the world, there are many people who do.

Brownie Points (in a Cosmic Reward, Religious Belief, Afterlife Sense)

Some people are motivated by their religious belief system to do things for others, including engaging in economic transactions that reduce their profit margin. For example, some people donate a percentage of their income to the religious organization they belong to. Although they might not cite supernatural reward

in this life or the next as a justification, it probably plays some role. Likewise, people who are not adherents of any specific religion may, nonetheless, be spiritual and have some vague notion that *if* there is a supernatural force keeping track of our behavior, it can't hurt to do good once in a while, even if it costs time, effort, or money.

Examples might include: stopping to rescue a turtle crossing the road by moving it over to the edge of the roadway; turning in a lost set of keys to the nearest lost and found; stopping to move a branch out of a bicycle path for those following behind, and so forth.

Tax Breaks

Some economic transactions are carried out because they provide a tax break to the donor, which means that they don't cost as much as they appear to. If you inherit a parcel of land that you never plan to use, and you donate it to the local nature conservation organization, you can claim the value of the land as a charitable donation and reduce your tax bill. In some cases, that ends up costing you less than paying inheritance and income taxes on the land itself, in addition to ongoing property taxes and upkeep in the future.

Enjoyment

Some people engage in certain activities simply because they get personal enjoyment out of them, even though these activities may not make much sense economically. For example, they donate their time to various organizations or jobs because they get personal pleasure and satisfaction out of volunteering, whether or not it affects the way they feel about themselves in terms of self-esteem (as in the park cleanup example above). That's one reason why more people will volunteer for some enjoyable activity—reading to kids, caring for injured birds, being involved in an Earth Watch research project in Costa Rica—than for an activity that most people find unpleasant, such as scrubbing restrooms, cleaning out the grease trap behind a restaurant, or processing fish.

And of course, some people get personal enjoyment out of spending money in general. Shopping is a hobby for some people in industrial societies, perhaps particularly in the United States, at least before the economic downturn of the late 2000s. A middle-aged man may buy a red convertible sports car for the pleasure it gives him in driving with the top down—not because it is a practical way to get back and forth to work. A woman may spend thousands of dollars on jewelry or furs because she loves the way she feels when she wears them. Collectors of all sorts will pay a premium price for rare items that increase the size and meaning of their collection, even if they collect something that has no practical value, such as Hummel figurines or signed first editions of books by famous authors. They might claim that their acquisitions are an investment—that it does make economic sense to pay thousands of dollars for an old book, because it will increase in value. In many cases, however, they have no intentions of ever selling the item(s), so the investment-value claim is mostly a justification. There isn't any way to put a price tag on the pleasure of owning something that is meaningful to you.

Final Thoughts

People have many different motivations other than the profit motive for engaging in economic transactions. Additionally, many, perhaps even the majority of economic transactions, provide returns in multiple ways.

For example, the McDonald's corporation donates money to support the Ronald McDonald Houses near children's hospitals, where families of sick children can stay at a reduced cost. The corporation gets huge tax breaks for its charitable donations, and no doubt it makes the people involved feel better that McDonald's is doing something good with a small percentage of its profits. McDonald's minimizes risk by supporting a noncontroversial endeavor that no one could possibly object to. Some in the corporation may view this as good corporate citizenship, while others may see it strictly as a business strategy to increase sales by improving the corporate image. People are convinced that they are helping the world by purchasing Happy Meals.

Bill and Melinda Gates, through their eponymous foundation, donate millions of dollars toward various global health initiatives, including paying to train graduate students in international public health fields. They do much good in the world, and certainly not because it brings them more monetary profit or because they need more social prestige. They are truly being altruistic, in part because it brings them enjoyment, and perhaps for religious motivations as well.

WEALTH AND STATUS

In complex, hierarchical societies, people may compete for power and seek the admiration and esteem of others. They may work diligently using a number of different strategies to acquire whatever attributes are valued in their local social environment. Before we leave the subject of economics, we will spend a little time exploring what sorts of attributes are valued in different cultural contexts.

Ascribed versus Achieved Status

There are two basic ways to achieve high status in any complex society. One is to be born into high status by virtue of who one's parents are. This is known as inherited or **ascribed** status. Studies of nonhuman primates who live in complex hierarchical social groups repeatedly have shown that much of an individual's status is determined by the status of his or her mother. High-ranking females give birth to automatically high-ranking offspring, and low-ranking females give birth to low-ranking offspring. Many human societies also exhibit this type of ascribed status, where aspects of a person that are inherited—whether genetically or culturally—contribute greatly to his status as an adult. For example, in many cultures, children of higher-status parents likely enjoy better nutrition, better medical care, and better educational opportunities than the children of lower-status parents. If status is dependent on one's skin color, facial features, ethnicity, religion, or social connections, parents will pass on these attributes to their children.

Often, individuals who have high ascribed status take it for granted that they somehow earned these advantages, rather than having acquired them merely by virtue of their birth into the specific culture, times, and family they live in. An excellent analysis of the automatic benefits of being born into the high-status group can be found in McIntosh's *White Privilege: Unpacking the Invisible Knapsack* (1988[1990]).

Status can also be **achieved** in many cultural contexts, by which we mean that a person's status can change over the course of their lifetime if value is awarded by others for the individual's own accomplishments. Where high status can be achieved, it may be easiest for children born with relatively high status to move even further up the hierarchy, but even those at the bottom levels of society have opportunities for improving their status. There may be many routes to improving one's status, such as performing acts of strength and bravery, getting an education, developing one's leadership skills, or working hard and practicing to become an expert in some skill, such as sports, music, art, or any other arena of talent. Wealth and status, whether ascribed, achieved, or some combination, may be expressed in a variety of ways in different cultures.

Wealth and Status in the Form of Money

In some contexts, the main route to wealth and status is to accumulate lots of money, whether by inheritance, strategic investing, hard work, criminal activity, or a lucky break such as winning the lottery. There are many ways that people advertise how much money they have, including lists publicized through the media of the wealthiest people in the world. Occasionally, one hears of quiet, unassuming people who have scrimped and saved all their lives, made good investments, and accumulated millions of dollars. After they die, it is revealed that they bequeathed their fortune to charities or to an educational institution, to the surprise of all who knew them. Thus, having lots of money doesn't automatically translate into high status—you have to let people know that you have lots of money. Most people who have lots of money flaunt it in many ways, including the conspicuous consumption of material and consumable goods.

Wealth and Status in the Form of Material Goods and Lavish Lifestyles

Wealth and high status are often reflected in the material goods one owns. In *some* cultural contexts, the more money people have, the more land they own, the larger and fancier their house (or they have multiple houses), the more expensive their car, yacht, clothing, jewelry, furniture, and other items. They may collect expensive art and travel often and widely while staying in the fanciest hotels and eating expensive meals at gourmet restaurants. They may have servants such as a butler, housekeeper, groundskeeper, chauffeur, pool person, cook, and nanny. People who live "lifestyles of the rich and famous" may be respected, admired, and envied (Conniff 2002).

Where high status is measured partly by the *stuff* one has, people may go out of their way to acquire expensive items and to make sure that others know they have them. They go to expensive events in their expensive cars, wearing their expensive clothes, and flashing their gold and diamond jewelry. It isn't only the people at the very top of the social status rankings who try to maintain or manipulate their status through the acquisition and consumption of expensive material goods.

Extravagant wealth may be displayed through conspicuous consumption of material goods. Top: the Bugatti Veyron doesn't have a set price—the cars are hand-built to order and customized options mean the price can differ from car to car—but *Car & Driver* quotes around $1.9 million as a base price for a Veyron. Bottom: for older men, being accompanied by a beautiful young woman, while one stays in luxury hotels, is one way to display wealth and status. Possibly the most expensive hotel room in the world is the Bridge Suite at the Atlantis Hotel in the Bahamas, at $25,000 per night.

In cultures where material goods are the main measure of success, some people at every level try to acquire the best they can afford, even going into debt to buy a bigger house than they need or to buy a new car even though their old one runs fine. Some people may try to convince others that they have a higher status than they actually do—they buy designer knock-off handbags, wear faux-furs, rent an expensive car for the evening, or steal a pair of the hottest shoes.

In the United States, many people spend more than they earn on a regular basis and find themselves deeper and deeper in debt—but their status comes from their material possessions, which are obvious to others. Their debt is private, at least until they must declare bankruptcy. Even people who earn the highest salaries may be living paycheck to paycheck, as they spend enormous sums every month on their mortgages, car payments, vacations, expensive private schools for their children, and so on.

However, it is important to realize that judging the value of a person by how much money she has, or the quantity and quality of her possessions, is a cultural phenomenon. In some cultures, having lots of money or material items is not the goal, not a significant measure of success, and not what people are respected and admired for.

Wealth and Status in the Form of Children and Other Dependents

As I have pointed out in prior contexts, what counts in terms of evolution and natural selection is getting the most copies of your genes into future generations. In many societies, the cultural belief system likewise focuses on how many children (and other dependents) one has as a measure of status. This emphasis on procreation—on parenthood and children as status markers—is reflected in a number of ways. In some cultures, full-adult status may not be conferred on individuals until they have reproduced, regardless of their age and other accomplishments. Unmarried and childless men may have little or no political or economic power.

If inheritance can go only through the male line, from father to son, then even having daughters doesn't count. King Henry VIII of England divorced two wives, had two more executed, and even broke away from the Roman Catholic church to found his own

separate branch of Christianity (the Church of England) in his attempts to father a son who could inherit his throne. In many patrilineal pastoral societies, a man's status and influence over others depends heavily on the number of children and grandchildren he has.

Likewise, in many cultures, the bearing and raising of children helps cement a woman's position in her husband's family and increases her value and status. In both patrilineal and matrilineal cultures, women can exert significant influence over their children, even after they reached adulthood. Where increasing age also confers higher status, older women with many adult children and grandchildren wield immense power. Writing about women in northern Thailand, Marjorie Muecke states:

> Motherhood has long been essential for Thai women. In fact, it has superseded royal rank as a status marker for women. Young reported that among turn-of-the-century nobility in Bangkok, "great respect [was] shown to the condition of motherhood, a wife of low rank with children being of far more importance in the family than even the chief wife, should she be childless." (Muecke 1984:462)

The general overall trend around the world in the past century has been toward smaller families, and many societies are shifting some of the traditional status value of children to material goods ranging from radios and bicycles to electricity and refrigerators. Muecke's analysis of northern Thai women, cited above, examines the shift from making babies to making money as a measure of status.

At the same time, a recent trend in the United States among wealthy families is to have more than two children as a way of flaunting one's financial success. Ronald Bailey says of families in New York City who have more than two children:

> These added kids provide many opportunities for status signaling. Wealthy parents can talk endlessly at the country club about the costs of Maine summer camps, high-school semesters abroad, little Andrew's sailing trophies, and what hunt Sarah rides with regularly. And of course, there are schools and universities. Did they prep at St. Albans or Choate? How well are they doing at Harvard, Yale, or Middlebury? Being able to provide lavishly for a large number of children shows that you've really got it made. This is not to say that rich people don't love their kids. Rather, kids today are not only little bundles of joy but also are perhaps

the ultimate symbols of worldly success and status. Perhaps we are now seeing a new social phenomenon—trophy kids. (Bailey 1997)

FINAL THOUGHTS

In this chapter, we have only scratched the surface of all the topics that economic anthropologists study and analyze. There are many studies going on that examine how local economies interact with global economic forces, and the short- and long-term impacts of development aid, including the World Bank and the International Monetary Fund. Other research focuses on micro-credit programs such as the Grameen Bank, founded by Muhammad Yunus. Yunus and the bank itself shared the Nobel Peace Prize in 2006 for their work providing small-scale loans to poor people, especially women.

Economic anthropology also has a rich and contested theoretical history, with formalism, substantivism, and culturalism being the three main branches of economic theory. The approach taken in this chapter is really a combination of all three theoretical schools and can be summed up as follows:

- Individuals usually act rationally with respect to economic transactions, given the cultural constraints within which they must work and their specific goals and values.

- Economic goals and values are shaped by many different aspects of culture, but people also have individual preferences that affect the choices they make.

- People seldom, if ever, have complete and accurate information about the short- and long-term consequences of the economic choices they make and the strategies they pursue, so there will always be some measure of risk and uncertainty.

- If it seems as though people are behaving in an economically irrational manner, go back and explore what they truly value, as individuals and as members of a family and various cultural groups, and also determine what methods they have to reach their goals and what local cultural constraints they must work through.

Key Concepts Review

The three basic economic principles are:

Market Exchange—the exchange of resources between two parties where the two parties agree that the exchange involves resources or currency of equal value

Redistribution—a particular form of economic exchange that involves the gathering together of resources from many and varied sources in a central location, where some publicly recognized authority is charged with collecting, storing, organizing, processing, and repackaging these resources, and redistributing them

Reciprocity—comes in three forms, generalized ("Pay it forward."), balanced ("You scratch my back and I'll scratch yours."), and negative ("Trying to get something for nothing.")

Wealth usually flows down the generations in *Western* societies (more kids = fewer resources per kid), and up and across the generations in *non-Western* societies (more kids = more resources for everyone).

Money acts as a *repository of value*, a way to measure value, to store value over time, and to easily transport value over space. The power of money resides in the shared ideas in people's heads and can take the form of currency, commodities, or electronic data.

People have disparate cultural beliefs about what, exactly, can be owned and who does the owning, including private ownership, corporate ownership, and government ownership.

In Daniel Quinn's book *Ishmael*, the world is divided into Leavers ("Man belongs to the world.") and Takers ("The world belongs to man.").

People pursue different goals and values with respect to economic behavior:
  Maximizing profit or minimizing risk
  Future assets and debts—the Favor Bank
  Maximizing or minimizing social relationships
  Social prestige (others think more highly of you)

Self-esteem (you think more highly of yourself)
Brownie points (in a cosmic reward, religious belief, afterlife sense)
Tax breaks
Enjoyment

Wealth and status may be ascribed (you were born into it) or achieved (you earned it); many people with high ascribed status (the luck of their birth to a particular family) mistake their position for achieved status (something they worked for and deserve).

Wealth and status can be measured in many ways, including how much money you have, how much "stuff" you have, and how many children you have.

In Mexican folk culture, the Catrina, a high-society woman, is one of the most popular figures of the Day of the Dead celebrations.

8

MAKING SENSE OF THE WORLD

Religion, Spirituality, Philosophy, & Worldview

Around the world, people believe in supernatural beings, they believe in magic, they believe in the spirit world. Such beliefs help them explain what they experience as they go through life, provide comfort under trying circumstances, and help them cope with grief, loss, and disaster. Such beliefs encourage us to be better people.

This chapter explores the anthropological perspective on the topic of religion. Religious beliefs and practices can be a touchy subject for many introductory anthropology students, both because religion is primarily an emotional experience and because many systems of belief include the basic proposition that all other systems of belief are invalid. It is often easier for students to be open-minded and tolerant of other peoples' kinship systems, or styles of music, than it is to accept that other religious beliefs are as valid as one's own. Nevertheless, this chapter will dive headfirst into an exploration of all the many different facets of religious belief and expression around the world. As always, you don't have to accept all of the propositions presented herein—but you are expected to make a concerted effort to understand the anthropological perspective on this topic, as on all the other topics covered in this text.

AN ANTHROPOLOGICAL PERSPECTIVE ON RELIGION

Our first task is to try to define our subject matter. We can say that **religion** refers to those beliefs and practices that help humans make sense of the often nonsensical world they inhabit. Whether we call it religion, spirituality, philosophy, worldview, systems of thought, or use some other term, we can think of religions as systems of nonscientific beliefs and practices that help people explain and deal with the otherwise inexplicable.

When we say that religious beliefs are nonscientific, we mean that they are not testable, and therefore not disprovable. Testability is the defining characteristic of a scientific hypothesis. Using the **scientific method,** we can make observations, perform experiments, and gather information from the natural world, and then use these data to test our hypotheses. Scientific hypotheses can be supported or refuted (not supported). They can never be proven, they can only be disproved. Religious beliefs, on the other hand, are explicitly *not* scientific, because they cannot be tested or disproved.

Another way of thinking about religion is to say that it involves belief in supernatural entities, such as gods, goddesses, nature spirits, ancestor spirits, and the like. As we shall see, however, not all worldviews or systems of thought require beliefs in supernatural beings.

If you were born and raised in the United States or Canada, you may be used to thinking of religion as a relatively discrete, separate part of your identity. Although a majority of North Americans define themselves as *Christian* (more about labels later), the United States was founded, in part, on the principle of religious freedom. Today, there are hundreds of different religions practiced in North America, as well as many people who consider themselves humanist, agnostic, or atheist. Much of the time, our religious identification is of little relevance to other aspects of our lives—we may go to school with, work alongside, and socialize with many different people and have no idea what their religious beliefs are, or how such beliefs are translated into practice. Most large nation-states today include a variety of different ethnic groups and religious belief systems within their borders, so that knowing that someone is from India, for example, does not tell you what that person's religion is. Likewise, knowing that someone is Jewish or Catholic does not tell you specifically what his religious beliefs might be, how important they are to him, or how they are manifested in practice on a daily, monthly, or yearly basis.

However, in many cases, *religion* cannot be defined as a separate domain of culture. In such contexts, religious beliefs and practices may be inextricably intertwined with subsistence, with ethnic identity, and/or with economic, political, and kinship relationships. Thus, it isn't always easy to tease out religious beliefs and practices from other aspects of daily life. In some circumstances, ethnic identity and religious identity are virtually isomorphic (most Kurds identify themselves as Sunni Muslims, most Italians identify themselves as Roman Catholics, most Dogon people of Mali still identify themselves as followers of the Dogon religion). In other cases, people of one ethnicity living in the same country may express a wide variety of religious orientations. For example, some African Americans are Jewish, some are Christian, including both Catholic and Protestant, some are Muslim, some are Unitarian Universalist, some are atheist, and so on. As with all things having to do with human beings and culture, religion is a complex issue. An important point to remember is that *you shouldn't make assumptions about a person's religious beliefs and practices based on her nationality or ethnicity, surname, or skin color.*

What we *can* say is that all societies have religion. Not every member of each group subscribes to all of the tenets of their religion, and some may not believe at all, but every known culture has a complex, sophisticated set of religious beliefs and practices. *There are no societies that do not have religion.* The earliest evidence of religious beliefs and practices can be traced back at least 40,000 years, to the first appearance of anatomically modern *Homo sapiens sapiens* in the fossil record, and perhaps much further.

Glimmers of what contemporary humans typically think of as religious sentiments have been noted among chimpanzees. In addition to the chimpanzee waterfall dances described in more detail later in the chapter, chimpanzees are unusually fascinated by pythons. Jane Goodall reports:

Suddenly, Fanni gave a soft "huu"—a sound signifying wonder, puzzlement, just a little fear. Fifi moved closer and started down, following the direction of Fanni's gaze. Then she too gave a "huu" followed, almost at once, by the spine-chilling "wraaa," the chimpanzee alarm call. This acted as a signal to the other chimps and I found myself in the centre of a fearsome chorus. The males, hair bristling, suddenly began spectacular arboreal displays, leaping from branch to branch, shaking and swaying the vegetation.

As yet, I had seen nothing, but all at once, as Satan leapt, with a fierce call, almost to the ground, I saw it too, or part of it: an extremely large python, as big around as a man's thigh. So perfect its camouflage that I never would have seen it had not Satan's display set it moving slowly, through a patch of sunlight.

For the next twenty minutes the chimps and baboons hung around. No longer scared, they were curious, fascinated. First one, then another, would move down, closer and closer, only to leap back, with startled exclamations, if the python moved. But gradually, as the snake glided into dense undergrowth and disappeared from sight, the spectators lost interest. (Goodall 2000:134)

The archeological site with the earliest evidence for human rituals also features pythons. Anthropologist Sheila Coulson studied a 70,000-year-old site located inside a cave in the Kalahari Desert in Botswana, in an area with the world's largest concentration of rock paintings:

The hills are still sacred to the San, who call them the "Mountains of the Gods" and the "Rock that Whispers." San mythology holds that mankind descended from the python. . . . [The cave contains] a rock resembling a huge python's head . . . the six-meter-long by two-meter-tall (20 feet by 6.6 feet) stone bore more than 300 dents that she [Coulson] argues are man-made. "You could see the mouth and eyes of the snake. It looked like a real python. The play of sunlight over the indentations gave them the appearance of snake skin. At night, the firelight gave one the feeling that the snake was actually moving." . . . An apparent secret chamber lay behind the python stone, she added, and parts of its entrance were worn smooth, suggesting many people had passed through it over the years. (Research Council of Norway and *World Science* staff 2006)

Religion seems to be something humans need in order to survive and be successful, just as they must come up with a way to get food (subsistence), a way to preserve social order (kinship and politics), and a way to express themselves creatively (music, arts, sports, and so on).

Four Basic Principles

The anthropological perspective on religion can be expressed in four basic principles.

1. ***All Religions Are "true":*** Each and every religion is *true* to the people who believe in it. There are thousands of different religions in existence/practice around the world, and for people who believe in them, their explanations of the world *are true for them.* Religion is important to most people, to their sense of self, and to their lifeways.

2. ***No Religion Is "True":*** No religion is *True* (with a capital T) in the sense of having any scientific evidence of its literal truth. Religious beliefs are, by definition, nonscientific, and therefore, all religious beliefs are equally not testable. In some sense, that's the whole point of faith—you believe because you believe, because you were taught to believe, and because it helps you to believe, not because there is any scientific evidence that your religious beliefs are True (and all other peoples' religious beliefs are False). Unfortunately, many systems of belief include the tenet that they alone *are* the Truth (with a capital T) and that all other systems of beliefs are False, which has led to much violence, hatred, and bloodshed. From the anthropological perspective, all religions are equally *true* to the people who believe in them, and all are equally *false* with reference to scientific validity.

3. ***Religious Beliefs Are a Consequence of Time and Place:*** If you had been born to a different family and/or into a different culture and/or at a different time in history, your religious beliefs probably would be very different from whatever they are now. Religious beliefs are not genetic, they are not biologically encoded. Your religious beliefs are primarily the product of your enculturation during childhood (through your family, your community, and your peers). For many people, their religious beliefs and practices may be modified or completely transformed as they grow up and conduct their own search for spiritual knowledge and comfort.

4. ***Morality ≠ Supernatural Beliefs:*** Systems of morality and ethics do not have to be based on religious beliefs (though many are). You can be an exemplary, moral person, without deriving your system of morality from any beliefs in religion or the supernatural, or in divine punishment or reward, either in this life or an afterlife. At the same time, being a member of any particular religion does not automatically make you more honest, more moral, more loving, more ethical, and so forth, than members of other religions, or people who are humanists, agnostics, or atheists. For examples of systems of morality and moral behavior that are not based on beliefs in supernatural beings, visit the websites of the Unitarian Universalist Association of Congregations (www.uua.org) or the Ethical Culture movement (www.aeu.org).

FUNCTIONS OF RELIGION

As with all other aspects of culture and social organization, religious beliefs and practices can be examined from a structural-functionalist perspective. Religion fulfills a number of specific functions for the individual and society and can be viewed as having both advantages and disadvantages. Although it is not possible to compare or judge religions according to their *truthiness,* it is possible and useful to examine how well different sets of beliefs and practices fulfill the functions usually assigned to religion.

Answering Unanswerable Questions

At the beginning of this chapter, we said that religion refers to those beliefs and practices that help humans make sense of the often nonsensical world they inhabit and that we can think of religions as systems of beliefs and practices that help people explain and deal with the otherwise inexplicable. One primary function of religion, then, is to provide answers to unanswerable questions. As large-brained, highly intelligent and complex primates, humans seem to be innately curious about the world and our place in it. We seem to thirst for knowledge to explain what we experience and to guide us in our lives. As far as we know,

From the anthropological perspective, all religions are equally true to the people who believe in them, and all are equally false with reference to scientific validity; thus, each of the religions depicted above is equivalent to any of the others. Top: a Zoroastrian fire temple (depicted on an Azerbaijan postage stamp); the Church of Scientology building in Boston, Massachusetts; and a Falun Gong float in the Fourth of July parade in Washington, D.C. (2008). Middle: a statue of Confucius; Christianity, as represented by the painting *Madonna and Child* attributed to Leonardo da Vinci; and the Dogon religion of northern Mali, as represented here by a masked dancer. Bottom: the Islamic mosque in Djenne, Mali; Buddhist monks in Laos; and a Jewish woman lighting the Sabbath candles.

we are the only sentient creatures on the planet who are conscious of our own mortality and can ponder such existential questions—questions that cannot be answered with any certainty through scientific ways of understanding.

Where Does All This Stuff Come From?

Perhaps the most fundamental unanswerable question is: "Where did the universe, the Earth, and living things come from?" We can certainly use scientific reasoning and evidence to understand history and prehistory and track the evolution of life on Earth back to its beginnings some 3.6 billion years ago (give or take a few years). We can study the fossil record to understand the origins of bipedalism among apes some 6 million years ago and the subsequent development of

All religious belief systems include a story about how the world was created and where humans came from. Among the Batak ethnic groups found in the highlands of North Sumatra, Indonesia, people believe that the earth was created by Naga Padoha, a female snake. The snake's movements through the "ancient waters" brought dry land to the surface and thereby created the world. This photograph shows one of the oldest Batak books (ca. 1850), made of tree bark, with a carving of Naga Padoha on the top.

these early hominids into modern humans. Physicists trace the origins of the universe back to the *Big Bang* some 13.6–13.8 billion years ago. Nonetheless, no matter how far back we go, and how much we understand about the mechanics of the processes of physics, geology, and evolution, we eventually come to a point where we can only wonder "What came before that?" What was there before the Big Bang? Is it possible to know? Even more profoundly, we ponder the question of "Why?" *Why is there anything instead of nothing?* Why did the universe form the way it did? Why did life on Earth develop as it did, and not some other way?

Every religion that has ever been studied and described provides some sort of answer to these questions. Whether it is the Abrahamic story of God creating the heavens and Earth in six days, and creating all living creatures, including Adam and Eve, or the Puebloan creation story of Spider Grandmother spinning the world into creation, or the Toraja people's belief that they came from the constellation Pleiades—all religions have some story or myth that explains how the world was created and how humans originated. In many creation myths, the original humans consist of one male and one female. Sometimes they are twins, brother and sister; often they are some version of Mother Earth and Father Sky. Creation myths tell the stories that relate humans to the world, to other living things, and to the supernatural being(s) who supposedly created it all.

One objection many scientists have to teaching so-called Intelligent Design in science classrooms is that it is simply one version, the Abrahamic version, of the creation myth. Since all creation myths should be accorded the same footing, it would take all the time the teacher had, and more, to explore the creation stories of all the religions of the world. This is a fascinating subject, but it is not part of a scientific explanation of the world. And the theory of Intelligent Design has the same flaw as the Big Bang theory—if all that we know of the universe today implies that it was designed by an intelligent creator, then where the heck did that entity come from? Surely the Intelligent Designer must have had a mother!

What's the Point? What Are We Here For?

Is there a purpose to human existence? Why do we exist, anyway? Are we here for some higher purpose, or simply to live and die as all living creatures do, in Mufasa's Great Circle of Life? If there is a purpose to human existence, what is it? Is it unchanging, or constantly in flux? Some religions provide very specific answers to these questions, while others offer only generalities such as "We are here to do good in the world," or "The purpose of human existence is to learn important lessons so we can move on to the next (or at least another) plane of existence."

What Happens after Death?

All humans recognize the distinction between life and death, between a living person and her corpse after death. Whether they define this difference as the presence, in a living being, of a soul, life force, spirit, anima, or something else, all humans look to religion to understand what happens to this animating life force once the physical body is no longer functioning. Since no one has ever come back from death to tell us what happens, if anything does, there is no way we can know—in the scientific sense of knowing through evidence and hypothesis testing—what happens after we die.

The idea that there may be nothing after death is very unsettling to many people, and religious belief systems often provide reassurance. Many religions include extremely complex and elaborate ideas about what happens after death. Some tell of an afterlife based on either punishment or reward for behavior in this life (such as Christian notions of Heaven and Hell). Others propose that the spirit is reincarnated, sometimes as a human being again, sometimes as a different type of life form. Sometimes the spirit transfers immediately from a deceased person into the body of a fetus or newborn. Other times the spirit spends varying amounts of time in the spirit world before deciding whether or not to return, and in what form. In some religions, the spirit leaves the body at death and joins the all-encompassing life force of the universe.

Whatever the specific beliefs found in any religion, their function is to provide comfort and reduce fear and anxiety about impending death in the one who is dying, to provide comfort to the grieving survivors, and to reinforce cultural norms about how to behave so as to be certain of the best possible outcome following departure from this life.

A photo of the Hale-Bopp comet, taken in Croatia in the spring of 1997. For most people, the comet was a remarkable natural phenomenon, a curiosity in the evening sky. For the members of a small religious group in southern California, it was a sign that their transport to the next "evolutionary level" had arrived. The religion was founded by Marshall Applewhite and Bonnie Nettles in the early 1970s and came to be known as "Heaven's Gate." The belief system included components of Christianity but also incorporated concepts of evolutionary advancement and travel to other worlds and dimensions. Applewhite convinced 39 followers to commit suicide with him, so that their souls could be free to leave the Earth, rise up, and board the spaceship that was traveling in the shadow of the Hale-Bopp comet. Many religious belief systems include such concepts as eternal souls, some type of existence following the death of one's physical body on Earth, alien beings, and multiple lives, either on Earth (reincarnation) or in different dimensions.

Why Are the Gods So Distant?

If supernatural beings exist, why can't humans see them, talk to them, and interact with them? Why are they so mysterious? Many religions have a myth explaining why the gods are not available for personal interaction with humans. Oftentimes, the story points out that originally, humans were able to interact with a personal god and that this supernatural being set up some specific rule for humans to follow. Humans being humans, they disobeyed, angering the deity and precipitating consequences. These consequences included a separation between humans and the god. Sometimes the consequences also included a change in status for humans from immortal to mortal. However, it isn't always humans who anger the gods.

For example, Evans-Pritchard relates a story from the Nuer of the Sudan, who conceive of their deity, Kwoth, as being a spirit who is *in the sky* or *of the sky,* which is viewed as heaven:

> God's separation and remoteness from man are accounted for in a myth recorded by Father Crazzolara which relates that there was not always a complete separation of heaven and earth and that there might never have been but for an almost fortuitous event. . . . The myth relates that there was once a rope from heaven to earth and how anyone who became old climbed up by it to God in heaven and after being rejuvenated there returned to earth. One day a hyena—an appropriate figure in a myth relating to the origin of death—and what is known in the Sudan as a durra-bird, most likely a weaver-bird, entered heaven by this means. God gave instructions that the two guests were to be well watched and not allowed to return to earth where they would certainly cause trouble. One night they escaped and climbed down the rope, and when they were near the earth the hyena cut the rope and the part above the cut was drawn upwards towards heaven. So the connexion between heaven and earth was cut and those who grow old must now die, for what had happened could not be made not to have happened. (Evans-Pritchard 1956:10)

Why Is There Pain and Suffering in the World?

People in all cultures find it difficult to understand why life isn't fair, and especially why bad things happen to good people (we tend not to worry or care so much about why bad things happen to bad people!). Whether in reference to a car accident, a death during war, a failure of the crops due to drought, or massive death and destruction caused by an earthquake or other natural disaster, people want to know why, and especially, "Why me or my loved ones?" This quest for meaning and comfort in the face of life's struggles is one of the most important functions that religion serves. If your religious belief system provides an explanation, an understanding, for why bad things happen, you may be better able to cope than someone who feels at the mercy of an arbitrarily cruel and capricious world.

What Is Human Nature?

Are people mostly good, or mostly bad, or are we blank slates at birth, waiting for culture to write the scripts of our lives? Are newborn babies born into sin, as Puritan parents of New England believed in the seventeenth century?

> Your child is born in sin, depraved, and prone to sin. Only through constant teaching of the Scripture within the home, from morning to night, may you help your child gain salvation and enter the kingdom of heaven. . . . Conceived in sin, your baby should be baptized as soon as possible after birth. . . . Now [around the first birthday] is when you shall see the behaviors that indicate that your infant was, indeed, born in sin, that all infants are born evil, and thus are the root of rebellion against God and man. . . . It is your duty to break and beat down the natural pride and stubbornness that may develop. (Reese 2000:47–52)

Or, on the contrary, are newborn babies divine? Contemporary Balinese mothers, who are almost all Hindu (with some Buddhist influences), have very different religious beliefs than Puritans about the nature of babies:

> It is wonderful that you are becoming a parent, for your children will be a source of great joy to you, your husband, and your families. . . . At birth, your child will be divine, closer to the world of the gods than to the human world. Having just arrived from heaven, your infant should be treated as a celestial being. . . . You should hold your newborn high, for gods and members of higher rank should always be elevated relative to their inferiors. For the first 210 days (or 105 days, depending on region and status), never put your baby down on the ground or floor, which is too profane for a god. Until then, your baby should be carried at all times. (Diener 2000:98–105)

Are people fundamentally good, merely led astray by fear, anger, or greed? Or are people fundamentally bad, behaving properly only because of their enculturation into beliefs in natural and supernatural retribution if they commit sins or crimes? What are the *natural* relationships between males and females? Between parents and children? Between *us* and *them*—however those groups are defined? Most religions provide some justification of the status quo, some purportedly *natural* explanation for why the world works the way it does, an explanation of who gets to be in charge, and why. The myths that explain the status quo often make it very difficult, if not impossible, to challenge or change it. Thus, those in control have a vested interest in keeping things the way they are and in convincing those not in control that nothing can or should be done to change the system.

Providing Help and Comfort in Times of Crisis

If answering unanswerable questions, explaining the inexplicable, is one of the main functions of religion, what other functions does it serve? Certainly, people turn to supernatural entities for help in times of crisis, in times when they themselves can do nothing—or think they can do nothing—to address the problem. If you are sitting in your living room watching TV and realize you are hungry, you don't pray to God to provide you with food somehow. Rather, you get up and go into the kitchen to find something to eat, or you call out for pizza. But if you have fled your homeland due to civil war and are living in a refugee camp with thousands of others who are also starving, and you have no way to get food for yourself or your children, then you will very likely turn to whatever supernatural beings you believe in, asking and praying for divine intervention.

Another example: if you have a headache, you go take some Advil. But if your child is dying of bacterial meningitis, and everything medically possible has been done, then you appeal to the gods for deliverance, for an exception to the usual rule that meningitis is fatal. This strategy—of taking care of things yourself when you can and appealing to the gods only when you can't—is the underlying logic of the famous phrase, "There are no atheists in foxholes" (foxholes being the defensive ditches and holes that soldiers hide in on the battlefield during wartime).

People living in different circumstances will have different perceptions of how much they can control, as well as varying resources and abilities to take care of business on their own. If you live at the mercy of natural forces such as earthquakes, volcanoes, tsunamis, floods, droughts, and plagues of locusts—things that you cannot control in any way—then you turn more often to the supernatural world for protection, coping, and recovery. If you live at the mercy of other people's actions (drunk drivers, asymptomatic carriers of the flu, an oppressive political system) or of calamities you cannot understand (a miscarriage, cancer, or a fall that results in a broken bone), then you likewise may ask for protection and support from supernatural forces. Anthropologist George Peter Murdock expressed it this way, citing Sumner:

> William Graham Sumner (1906:6–7) has called attention to "the *aleatory* [random] element in life, the element of risk and loss, good or bad fortune. This element is never absent from the affairs of men. It has greatly influenced their life philosophy and policy. On one side, good luck may mean something for nothing, the extreme case of prosperity and felicity. On the other side, ill luck may mean failure, loss, calamity, and disappointment, in spite of the most earnest and well-planned endeavor. . . . The aleatory element has always been the connecting link between the struggle for existence and religion. It is only by religious rites that the aleatory element in the struggle for existence could be controlled." (Murdock 1980:83–84)

Murdock himself claims:

> It is perhaps unnecessary to insist that, unlike the physical and social environments, the ideational environment is totally illusory and has no actual existence outside of peoples' minds. There are, for example, no such things as souls, spirits, or demons, and such mental constructs as Jehovah are as fictitious as are those of Superman or Santa Claus. Neither ghosts nor gods exert the slightest influence on men or their behavior. But men can and do influence the behavior of one another, and the ideas they hold can have a serious bearing on how they behave. (Murdock 1980:54)

Both Murdock and Sumner approach life's difficulties from the perspective that sometimes *stuff happens,* and there is no meaning to such occurrences, no reason behind them, no lessons to be learned, no one to blame, no way to prevent them, and no supernatural help for coping with them. For many people, in

cultures all around the world, such an approach is untenable. People require more meaning, a better answer than "stuff happens" and "you can't do anything to prevent it or deal with it." Whether through one's own actions or through appeal to the supernatural powers they believe in, most people need to feel that they have some control over their lives. "If I do things correctly—sacrifice to the gods, say my prayers, honor my ancestors, observe all the taboos, and get my yearly mammogram—then I am less likely to suffer hardship." And, "If I do find myself in a situation where I can't do anything to fix it, then I'll ask the gods for help." Sometimes our prayers are (seemingly) answered, and sometimes they are not, but people go on believing and getting comfort from such beliefs.

Similar sentiments have been reflected in songs such as "Plastic Jesus" (Rush and Cromarty 1962) and "Jesus Take the Wheel" (James, Lindsey, and Sampson 2005). The driver in the latter song asks Jesus to help her—to take the wheel—only when her car is spinning out of control on black ice, not when she's cruising down the turnpike on a sunny day.

Many cultural anthropologists would take exception to Murdock's dismissal of beliefs in *any* supernatural beings, pointing out that scientific reasoning cannot explain all of the different experiences people have. Some people see things, and hear things, and feel things that others cannot detect. People experience trance, mystical/religious ecstasy, and feelings of reverence (whether in nature, in a synagogue or church, or at the Vietnam Memorial Wall in Washington, D.C.). Several neuroscientists have explored the genetic and biochemical factors that affect perception and brain functioning and may therefore account for why some people are more likely to have spiritual feelings and experiences than others (Newberg and Waldman 2006).

In his classic ethnography *In Sorcery's Shadow*, anthropologist Paul Stoller documents his research among the Songhay of Niger and his absolute conviction that sorcery is real (Stoller and Olkes 1989). Likewise, Edith Turner has written in detail about her experiences while participating in an intense community healing ceremony, the Ihamba tooth ritual, among the Ndembu of Zambia. She writes:

> Quite an interval of struggle elapsed while I clapped like one possessed . . . while Singleton pressed Meru's back, guiding and leading out the tooth—Meru's face in a grin of tranced passion, her back quivering rapidly. Suddenly Meru raised her arm, stretched it in liberation, and I *saw* with my own eyes a giant thing emerging out of the flesh of her back. This thing was a large gray blob about six inches across, a deep gray opaque thing emerging as a sphere. I was amazed—delighted. I still laugh with glee at the realization of having seen it, the *ihamba*, and so big! (Turner 1992:149)

Many anthropologists, as well as ordinary folks, have had similar experiences, events that they cannot explain through what is commonly referred to as rational, scientific reasoning. To point out that, from a functionalist perspective, beliefs in supernatural beings help people understand what they have experienced and provide comfort in times of crisis is not to state with authority that such beliefs are purely creative fictions that spring from the minds of human beings. It would be the height of folly to claim that everything that exists, and everything that people experience, can be studied, analyzed, and understood from the perspective of Western science.

Opposite page: **People turn to their religious beliefs and to supernatural beings such as saints, gods, goddesses, and the ancestors for help and comfort in times of grief and distress. Appeals for help may take the form of ritual actions, prayers, or sacrifice. Top: lighting a candle is one way to ask for help (Christianity and other religions); burning sacred herbs (some Native American traditional religions), and dancing (Jains in India) are other paths. Middle: prayer is found in most, if not all, religious traditions, including Judaism (a man praying at the Western Wall in Old Jerusalem), Islam (Muslims praying at a mosque in Istanbul), and Christianity (a Catholic woman with her rosary beads). Bottom: sacrifice is another way of convincing the gods to help you, and can take many forms, including the sacrifice of one's own comfort (during the Thaipusam festival in Singapore, devotees of the Hindu deity Subramaniam pray for divine help and make vows; they show their sincerity by piercing their body in multiple places and pulling or carrying heavy loads on a pilgrimage to some sacred caves); the sacrifice of animals, as in Eid Al-Adha, also known as Tabaski, in which Muslims commemorate the willingness of Abraham to sacrifice his son, and was then given a reprieve by God, who let him sacrifice a ram instead; and in offerings of eternal fires to Buddha in a temple in Nepal.**

Providing a Blueprint for *Right Living*

Another function that many religions serve is to act as the basis for the individual's and group's system of morality and ethical behavior. As explained previously, an individual or a group doesn't necessarily *have* to base their moral and ethical system on beliefs in supernatural beings, but many people around the world do. Their religious beliefs and myths serve as guides to acceptable behavior, and fear of supernatural punishment, either in this life or the next, may help convince people to behave according to the rules of their religion. Cross-culturally, many religions share a common theme that can be summed up as some version of the Golden Rule: "Treat others as you would want to be treated by them." Or, expressed negatively, "Don't do anything to another person that you wouldn't want to have done to yourself or those you love."

Some religions have a limited number of general injunctions about how to behave **(prescriptions)** or not to behave **(proscriptions),** such as the Ten Commandments shared by the Abrahamic religions. Some religions have lots and lots of very specific rules about how to behave, including how to dress, how to wear your hair, what to eat or not eat, under what circumstances sex is allowed, how to pray and worship the gods, and so on. If you have committed yourself to such a belief system, with lots and lots of rules about daily life, then you no longer have to make such decisions for yourself.

Researchers who study religious **cults** (however defined) have cited the detailed instructions about how to live a good life as one of the attractions for followers of charismatic cult leaders. Life can be simple, safe, and reassuring when all decisions are taken out of your hands and made for you by others. If the founder or leader is believed to be speaking on behalf of a supernatural deity, and considered a prophet, then his proclamations carry even more weight.

Social Solidarity versus Discord and Conflict

Finally, shared religious beliefs can play a role in establishing and strengthening social solidarity. Members of the same religion (or subgroup within a religion) may share many beliefs and practices and come together to form communities that provide safety and support. In societies where extended kinship networks are not available, one's religious community may serve many of the same functions, such as providing meals or hospital visits to sick members, helping cope with the death of loved ones, or sharing in the celebration of good news.

Unfortunately, religion can also play an important role in creating discord and conflict within and between groups, leading in some cases to mistrust, misunderstanding, hatred, war, and even genocide. Often, the basis of this downside to religious belief is simple ignorance and misunderstanding. Followers of every religion are not necessarily well versed in all the tenets of their own belief system, the one they claim to follow. For example, I have had Catholic students who did not know they were supposed to believe in the literal Transubstantiation of the Host (the Communion wafer and wine literally transforming into the flesh and blood of Christ, thus rendering the taking of communion an act of cannibalism). Likewise, I have had Muslim students who cannot explain the differences between Shia and Sunni sects of Islam, except to say that whichever one they belong to is the right one.

People may know even less about the component beliefs and practices of other religions, but accept whatever they have heard, no matter how reliable the source or how outrageous the claim. Even when accurate and from credible sources, general descriptions of any religion will mask the diversity to be found within. For example, **fundamentalists** in any religion may believe and act in ways that are quite dissimilar to most of the people belonging to the same religion. When Fundamentalist Church of Jesus Christ of Latter-day Saints members (Fundamentalist Mormons) are criticized for practicing polygyny, many non-Mormons assume that all Mormons approve of polygyny; most Mormons do not.

Students in many introductory anthropology courses watch the classic ethnographic film *The Holy Ghost People*, about a fundamentalist Christian church in rural Appalachia. In the film, worshippers are seen in trance, speaking in tongues, handling snakes, and drinking strychnine (poison) without adverse consequences (at least until one man is bitten by a snake). All of these practices are based on New Testament Bible verses, are interpreted by church members as evidence of their bodies being inhabited by the Holy Ghost, and are viewed as evidence of their sincere beliefs. Although these people are clearly devout Christians, most Christian religious services do not include these activities.

We will return to the topic of religious diversity later in the chapter. For now, we will shift gears somewhat and discuss the structure of religious beliefs.

THE STRUCTURE OF RELIGIOUS BELIEFS

Definitions

To begin our discussion, we need to clarify the meaning of a number of terms and concepts that are used when discussing the supernatural realm. First, we need to distinguish among atheism, theism, animism, and animatism.

Atheism

Atheism can be defined as the absence of a belief in deities (gods and goddesses) and other supernatural phenomena. Among self-described atheists, there is no one ideology or set of behaviors that they all share in common.

Theism

Theism refers to a belief in one or more deities. People may refer to these deities as gods (male) or goddesses (female). Deities are presumed to be supernatural beings that exist in a form different from that of any living creature on Earth. They may be thought to have human form or to be formless, to have different personality characteristics (loving, vengeful, angry, helpful, indifferent to daily problems, nosy busybodies, etc.), and to have different powers. There may be only one deity, or there may be an entire hierarchy of deities including a supreme being as well as lesser gods and goddesses, angels, and so forth.

Most of the so-called *major religions* of the world are theist religions, including all of the Abrahamic religions (Judaism, Christianity, Islam, and the Bahá'í Faith). Greek and Roman pantheons can be described as theist religions. Some religions, such as Buddhism and Jainism, do not require belief in a supernatural deity but are structured along traditional theist lines in many other ways.

Animism

Animism is a term often used in introductory anthropology textbooks to describe *traditional* religions of the world. However, this use of the term is confusing and inaccurate. Animism is not a specific religion, any more than theism is. Rather, theism refers to the belief in all-powerful, somewhat amorphous, supernatural beings, as described above. Theist religions encompass a huge variety of beliefs and practices. Likewise, *animist religions encompass a huge variety of beliefs and practices*. In contrast to theism, however, *animism refers to the belief in specific spirits associated with nature and natural phenomena*. In animist religions, living things (plants and animals, including humans) are thought to have both a physical body and an animating spirit or soul (anima), which conveys life to the body. Sacred places or locations may also be thought to have an animating spirit, and even inanimate objects may be animated by spirits.

Animist beliefs vary widely. In some animist worldviews, while all living creatures have a spirit or soul, some have more significant spirits. Thus, in Mali, enormous (and therefore ancient) baobab trees are thought by some people to have spirits and to exist as sentient beings. When I was doing research there, I found that to be a perfectly reasonable belief. When a North American Plains Indian killed a buffalo and then thanked the buffalo spirit for the meat and other resources it was providing to his family, he was displaying an animist belief. Whenever an albino (all-white) buffalo was born, local American Indians interpreted it as a living avatar of the Great Buffalo Spirit. The famous Golden Spruce of British Columbia's Queen Charlotte Islands is an example of a specific tree that was revered by the local Haida Indians and considered by them, as well as many non-Haida, to be sacred and sentient. When it was chopped down in 1997 in an act of eco-vandalism, it was deeply mourned, as though a person had died (Vaillant 2005).

In addition to living creatures, people may believe that specific places have spirits as well. Sometimes the general term **sacred** is applied to the location, rather than a conception of a specific spirit entity. Thus, there may be a spirit who lives in the volcano, in the lake, at the bottom of the river, or in a grove of trees. Places

Animism refers to the belief in specific spirits associated with nature, natural phenomena, and inanimate objects. The photos above all represent different versions of animistic beliefs. Top: sacred places animated by spirits, including the Sacred Cenote at Chichén Itzá in Mexico, used by the ancient Mayans for making sacrifices to the rain god Chaac; the Vietnam War Memorial in Washington, D.C.; and Mato Tipi (Devil's Tower) in Wyoming. Middle: a white buffalo, sacred to some Native American Plains Indian groups; the sacred crocodiles of Bazoulé, Burkina Faso (West Africa); and an ancient baobab tree in Africa. Bottom: the *Liberty Belle*, a fully restored U.S. Boeing B-17 Flying Fortress airplane from World War II; an adult woman sleeping with her special "lovey"; and a relic—in this case a skeleton encased in golden armor, but not the saint himself—from the Holy Catacombs of San Pancrazio in Rome, Italy.

where significant events occurred, or where specific events are commemorated, may be thought of as having their own powerful spirit, or as being sacred.

For example, the Sanctuary of our Lady of Lourdes in France is considered sacred by Catholics because of claims that the Virgin Mary appeared multiple times to a local girl in 1858. Spring water from the grotto is believed by many to have healing properties, and each year more than five million pilgrims visit the site (Lourdes-France 2010). The Vietnam Memorial Wall in Washington, D.C., a monument to all the soldiers killed in the Vietnam War, is another example of the spirit of place. Many visitors to the Wall, even those who did not personally know anyone who died in Vietnam, are overwhelmed with grief and sadness and describe it as a special place, with its own spirit (National Park Service 2010; Vietnam Veterans Memorial 2010).

Mato Tipi in Wyoming (also known as Bear Lodge or Devil's Tower) is considered sacred to some Native American tribes. In response to protests by Native Americans that recreational rock-climbing desecrates their sacred land, the National Park Service asks people not to climb the Tower during the month of June, when many ceremonies traditionally occur (Glass 2005; National Park Service, Devils Tower 2010). Similarly, Uluru-Kata Tjuta National Park, in central Australia, is home to Uluru (also known as Ayer's Rock), which is sacred to local Aboriginal tribes (Australian Government 2010). Each of these cases is an example of a belief in the anima, soul, or sacred quality, of a place.

In addition to living beings and geographic locales, inanimate objects may be animated by spirits who inhabit them either temporarily or permanently. In many West African religious belief systems, carved wooden masks are worn by human dancers in religious performances. A specific spirit may be said to live in the mask, and when the wearer dons the mask for the dance, the spirit who lives in the mask takes over the dancer's body and is alive and present for the ceremony. Over time, the mask ages and become cracked or eroded from use. Eventually a new mask will be carved to replace the old one, and a specific ritual ceremony will accomplish the transference of the spirit from the old mask to the new mask. Afterward, the original mask reverts to being "just a piece of old wood," with little significance to the local people. These masks may then be sold to collectors on the world art market for many thousands of dollars—their high value as *authentic* African masks being due to the collectors' beliefs in contagious magic (more about contagious magic later).

Another interesting example concerns the Sacred Pole of the Omaha tribe. Since 1888, he had resided at Harvard's Peabody Museum in Massachusetts. After more than 100 years, he was repatriated to the Omaha tribe. The pole was returned to the tribe in part through the efforts of anthropologist Robin Ridington:

> [My story] tells about my relationship with a person of the Omaha tribe. That person is Umon'hon'ti, "The Venerable Man" or "The Real Omaha," known in English as the Sacred Pole of the Omaha tribe. He is a physical object, a cottonwood pole, but he is also a person. He is alive as the Omahas are alive. My story touches on his long and venerable life among his own people, on his more recent century of living in the care and custody of anthropology, and on my own witness to his return to the tribe in 1989. I first met Umon'hon'ti in 1962, when I began graduate studies at Harvard's Peabody Museum. The Sacred Pole was on display in a glass case there. I had no idea then that he might be something other than a physical object, although I did understand that the Pole had been sacred to the people who once cared for him. . . . I have come to know Umon'hon'ti as a real person, a "real Omaha." (Ridington 1995:133 and 145)

In addition to the sacred, religious nature of many animistic beliefs, some beliefs about inanimate objects are not usually acknowledged as having any religious significance, yet still serve as examples of *animism*. Every year I ask my students how many of them had a special blanket or stuffed animal that held great importance to them as children. Many North American children develop a close physical and emotional relationship with an inanimate object, in part because they are often raised without close physical and emotional relationships with other people (many are bottle-fed with formula as infants and sleep alone in a separate bed and room, from birth). Psychologists who study child development primarily in Western cultures refer to these relationships as **inanimate object attachments,** and some even view them as normal and necessary aspects of childhood, although they are rare or absent in most cultures around the world.

Not only do many North American college students report that they had a special blanket or stuffed animal as a child, a large percentage admit that they brought these special objects with them to college. The belief that the objects are more than just their physical selves is a belief in animism. Likewise, in wartime, pilots often name their planes, endow them with personalities, and talk to them while on missions, which is yet another example of animism.

Animatism

The last concept to be introduced is that of **animatism.** Because it looks and sounds so much like *animism*, many students get the two confused, even though the concepts are fundamentally different. Animism is the belief in specific, personal spirits that inhabit living beings, places, or inanimate objects. *Animatism*, in contrast, is a belief in one general, impersonal spirit or power source that exists out there in the universe, rather than in any specific creature, place, or object. This concept was originally described by anthropologists using the Oceanic language term *mana*, based on concepts found in Polynesia, Melanesia, and Micronesia. A number of other religious traditions embody similar notions using a variety of terms.

Unlike animistic spirits, which may be good or evil, playful or serious, weak or strong, the power of animatism is morally neutral. It is simply power. Under specific circumstances, individual humans may be able to tap into this power source and shape and guide it for either beneficial or nefarious (evil) purposes. In order to harness this power, typically you must either know the specific techniques (words and rituals), or you must have sufficient faith in the power, or both. Sometimes people inherit mana from powerful ancestors, while others acquire it during warfare. Objects may also possess a piece of mana and are respected and valued for the power they embody and for their ability to accomplish things.

Contemporary anthropology students may be familiar with the concept of mana/animatism through The Force from George Lucas' series of *Star Wars* films. In the original film, a young Luke Skywalker is trained by Yoda, an elderly Jedi Master, to become aware of the power of The Force and to use it for honorable purposes. In the climactic battle of the original film, Luke must *trust in The Force* and relax, simply allowing the power of The Force to flow through him as he guides his X-wing toward the Death Star. Luke's father, the dastardly Darth Vader, was once a noble Jedi Knight, but he was "seduced by the dark side of The Force," and uses its power for evil.

Supernatural Beings

Different religions incorporate beliefs in, and worship of, many different types of supernatural beings. We will take a brief look at the variety to be found in different religions, including several not covered in our previous discussions.

Gods and goddesses form one significant category of supernatural beings. A religion may have only one god or goddess (**monotheism**) or it may have many gods and/or goddesses (**polytheism**). Where there are multiple gods/goddesses, the deities may have equal standing (an egalitarian system), or they may be hierarchical, with one supreme deity and other lesser deities.

In some religions, it is possible for every person to have direct communication with the deity or deities. They can talk to *God* (however they conceive of him, her, or them) and/or *God* can talk to them. In other religions, the deity or deities are thought to be imposing, distant entities, who must be approached through intermediaries. These intermediaries may be specially trained human religious specialists such as priests, ministers, or shamans. In other cases, the intermediaries may be other supernatural beings or spirits who were once alive as humans and now exist in the spirit world as ancestors or saints.

For example, in Roman Catholicism, a person can pray for the intercession of saints who are thought to be especially effective at petitioning God for intervention with specific types of problems. Thus, Saint Jude is considered the patron saint of lost causes, and Saint Gerard Majella is the patron saint of motherhood. If your house has been on the market for months without selling, you might buy a small statue of Saint Joseph and bury it upside down in your front yard. This practice often reverses the trend, and your house sells. Additionally, many churches provide candles that can be purchased for placing in front of a statue of a specific saint. This practice implores the saint to acknowledge and act on the candle purchaser's prayers.

In Islam, an unbridgeable gulf is held to separate humans from Allah, and there are no intermediaries between the creator and his creations. Any attempt to intercede between humanity and Allah is considered inappropriate, as well as ineffective.

Supernatural deities such as gods and goddesses may be thought of as abstract entities, or they may have representational form. Some are conceived as having human form—Zeus, Apollo, Hera, and Jesus Christ. Others are viewed as real or imaginary animals—eagles, jaguars, spiders, or rainbow or feathered serpents. Others take on natural forms (see below under nature spirits). In Islam, Allah (God), is thought to not have any specific form, and indeed, it is considered offensive to portray Allah, Muhammad, or indeed representational art of any kind in drawings, paintings, textiles, or architectural forms.

The deities in any religion may be thought of as having particular personality traits and attitudes toward human beings and life on Earth. They may be generally good and helpful, or generally bad. They may be loving, jealous, caring, vengeful, or all of these at the same time. In some religions, such as Hinduism, some deities will be said to embody some of these attributes, while other deities have different ones.

Ancestor Spirits

A second category of supernatural beings includes ancestor spirits—the animae or souls of individuals who were once alive, walking and talking as part of the concrete world, who have since died and gone on to, or back to, the spirit world. There is great variation in the specific content of beliefs in ancestor spirits. The important ancestors may be those traced through female links (matrilineal), male links (patrilineal) or both (bilateral). In some cases, only famous ancestors are viewed as being significant. For example, The Mayflower Society is open only to descendants of the Pilgrims on the Mayflower, and its members preferentially honor these specific ancestors. There will be variation in how many generations back ancestors are traced for veneration or worship.

In some Central African groups, people are thought to have distinct stages of life. First, you are alive and living in the regular world. Then you die, but you continue to live on in the memories of everyone who knew you when you were alive. At this stage, you may remain vitally interested in the everyday activities of your descendants and provide help to them in times of crisis, while expecting honor and respect through prayers, sacrifices, and rituals. Eventually, all of the people who knew you as a living person will die as well, and you move on to a more distant, less involved status as one of the distant ancestors—people may know who you were, and may remember you occasionally, based on stories they have been told, but you are now thought to no longer have much interest in, or direct impact on, your distant descendants' lives.

We need to distinguish between *belief in* ancestor spirits and *worship of* ancestor spirits. Believing that a person's soul or anima lives on after the death of their corporeal body does not necessarily mean that you worship that person the way you might worship a deity. Even determining what exactly it means to say "I believe in ancestor spirits" can be difficult.

For example, my father died several years ago, basically of old age. At some level, I do not believe that he exists any more, or that he is experiencing another form of existence, or that he watches over me and knows what I am up to. At the same time, ever since he died, I have been finding pennies on the ground, almost every day, and I pick them up. Somewhere along the way I decided to believe that these pennies were little messages of love and affection from my father—that he placed them where I would find them, so I would know that he was thinking of me. On the one hand, it is probably a matter of simple coincidence that I find so many pennies. Or I could attribute it to my practice of scanning the ground everywhere I walk (a habit left over from an undergraduate archeological survey course). No doubt it also has something to do with the fact that most people won't pick up pennies if they drop them, or if they see them on the ground, or at least won't pick up pennies that have fallen tails up because they think it is bad luck. All of which means that there are lots of pennies lying around in public places for me to find.

Sometimes I find nickels, dimes, or quarters, and occasionally even paper money (usually just one-dollar bills). In 2008, I found a $100-bill on the ground in a parking lot! Do I *really* think my father sends me this money? No, at some level, I don't believe that at all. Nonetheless, whenever I find a penny, I put it in my pocket, smile, and think of my father, keeping his memory alive.

Nature Spirits

Spirits of Place or Inanimate Objects

We have already discussed nature spirits in some regard. Nature spirits may consist of supernatural beings associated with specific natural places or objects—volcanoes, mountaintops, groves of trees, waterfalls, rivers, oceans, lakes, lagoons, grottoes, caves, and so on. Celestial objects—the sun, the moon, stars, constellations (Orion, the Pleiades), and planets, such as Venus as the morning or evening star—may be viewed as supernatural beings.

Likewise, sporadic celestial objects and events such as comets, meteor showers, supernovas, or specific unusual arrangements of celestial objects with relation to one another may be viewed as meaningful. Tracking and predicting eclipses of the sun and the moon are thought to have been the purpose of monumental architectural constructions such as Stonehenge in England and El Caracol, the round observatory built by the ancient Mayans at Chichén Itzá. Written texts from China and Japan report a *guest star* visible in the sky in July and August of AD 1054. These sightings document the implosion of a massive star, which gave birth to the Crab Nebula. The AD 1054 supernova also was noted by a Near Eastern traveler, the Christian doctor Ibn Butlan, who blamed the "spectacular star" in Gemini for the outbreak of the plague in Turkey and Egypt that year (Williamson 1984:184).

An unusual alignment of the crescent moon with the planets Jupiter and Venus was visible in North America in the fall of 2008, and some people attributed mystical significance to the celestial vision. Many people living in temperate regions of the world rely on the more regular movements of celestial objects to mark the equinoxes and solstices and to plan their agricultural activities or patterns of migration across the landscape. While not always given religious significance, celestial phenomena are often incorporated into religious belief systems, including creation myths, and may serve as omens of divine retribution.

Tectonic- and Weather-Related Spirits

Natural geological and meteorological phenomena may also be associated with supernatural beings. Volcanic eruptions, earthquakes, and tsunamis may be thought of as expressions of supernatural displeasure. Destructive weather such as tornadoes, typhoons, and hurricanes may be attributed to divine retribution (punishment for something humans did to displease the gods). Clouds and rain, thunder and lightning, the appearance of beams of sunlight coming to the ground, monsoons, floods, and droughts may all be thought of as the result of the actions of supernatural beings. Likewise, the appearance of a rainbow may be viewed as a positive sign from a supernatural being, as it was interpreted by Noah after the flood in the story from Genesis in the Christian Bible.

Totems

As mentioned previously, nature spirits may take the form of living animals or plants. An individual or a group of people, sometimes related by kinship (as a lineage or clan), may adopt a particular plant or animal as their **totem.** A totem is thought to be special or sacred to the individual or group. Members of the group may have a special relationship with the animal, such as rules against killing or eating it, rules that members of other groups do not have to observe. They may view their totem as providing assistance and protection or as exhibiting traits that they admire and hope to cultivate in themselves.

We have very early evidence for people doing interesting things with animal parts, extending 300,000 years back in the archeological record to Neanderthal sites in Europe and Western Asia. We can't know for sure how prehistoric peoples thought or felt about these animal bones, teeth, and horns. We have no way of knowing whether or not they were viewed similarly to totems among contemporary peoples. Jean Auel's fictional series about Neanderthals and Cro-Magnons opens with Ayla, a young Cro-Magnon girl (who has been injured and marked by a cave lion), being discovered by the Clan of the Cave Bear, who are Neanderthals. The clan, an extended kinship group, views the majestic and frightening cave bear as their totem, whereas Ayla, the protagonist of the story, has the cave lion as her personal guardian and protector (Auel 1984).

The closest things we have to totems in contemporary North American society are the mascots of sports teams, such as the Halifax Mooseheads (hockey), the Pittsburgh Steelers and their mascot, Steely McBeam (football), the Toronto Argonauts (football), the University of Delaware's Fighting Blue Hens, or the Banana Slugs of the University of California at Santa Cruz. Typically, totemic mascots chosen for sports teams are meant to be fierce and intimidating; thus, there are many teams known as the Jaguars, Grizzlies, Sharks, etc. In the case of the UCSC Banana Slugs, "The students' adoption of such a lowly creature for a team mascot was their reaction to the fierce athletic competition fostered at most American universities" (UCSC 2008). Fraternal and service organizations in North America sometimes have animal totems/mascots as well, such as the Benevolent and Protective Order of Elks, Moose: The Family Fraternity, or the Flintstones' fictional Loyal Order of Water Buffaloes.

Religion, Environment, and Subsistence

The lessons of anthropologist Julian Steward—that the environment matters, and that subsistence strategies influence all aspects of culture—is perhaps nowhere as obvious as in the realm of religion. You might expect to find an infinite variety of beliefs and phantasmagorical supernatural beings, deities who exist with no clear link to anything in the natural environment. Instead, it is clear that *people usually craft their supernatural beings both to reflect the local environment and subsistence strategies and to fit their need for some measure of control over the most aleatory elements of their lives.*

Some of these relationships seem obvious once they are pointed out. The sun is the most fundamental environmental phenomenon. It is universal across the planet, ultimately providing the basis for all life on Earth, regardless of subsistence strategy. It has been, and continues to be, the focus of many religious beliefs. On the other hand, volcano gods are only found in areas with volcanoes; spirits of the ocean are found only among sea-faring peoples; the Hopi of Arizona honor and worship Mother Corn, while the rice growers of Bali make sacrifices to The Rice Maiden. Others are more subtle. The Puebloan creation story of Spider Grandmother spinning the world into existence is based on people's knowledge of actual spiders and their ability to spin webs. Although many creation myths around the world feature snakes, the Maori (native New Zealander) creation myth does not, perhaps because the island of New Zealand has no snakes.

Among the Hopi, where subsistence strategies are based on rain-fed horticulture, cloud and rain spirits figure prominently in the pantheon as *kachina* spirits. Plagues of locusts, which can devour an entire season's grain harvest within hours, are used as divine retribution only by the gods of horticulturalists and agriculturalists. It would make little sense for an angry god to send a plague of locusts to the whale hunters of Lamalera in East Indonesia. It is probably no coincidence that the story of Cain and Abel in the Old Testament pits farmers against shepherds, or that Jesus exhorts his followers along the Sea of Galilee to become fishers of men. One finds mountain gods only in regions with mountains, spirits of the river or lake only in areas with these features, and so on.

Sacred places and things are often unique and unusual, including Uluru in Australia, Mato Tipi in the United States, and the Golden Spruce in Canada, which was special due to the extraordinary golden color of its needles.

Extraterrestrial (non-Earth) civilizations and beings play a role in some religions. Scientology founder L. Ron Hubbard claimed that humans were immortal spiritual beings, known as Thetans, trapped in Earthbound bodies during this lifetime. During previous lifetimes, Thetans lived in a variety of extraterrestrial civilizations. The Toraja tribe of the island of Sulawesi, Indonesia, say that their ancestors came from the constellation known to astronomers as the Pleiades. Their unusually shaped houses are said to resemble the spaceships they used to travel from the Pleiades to the Earth. Most anthropologists assume that these beliefs are the result of creative human minds. Then again, no one knows for sure.

THE STRUCTURE OF RELIGIOUS PRACTICES

Anthropologists also study religions in terms of the types of human behaviors and ritual activities that express the underlying religious belief system. Religious activities may be carried out by individuals or by groups of varying size, including the whole community if the occasion calls for it. They may be private, semiprivate, or public. For example, the Hopi of northern Arizona allow spectators at some of their religious rituals, but not all, and cameras and recording devices may not be used by onlookers. Religious practices may be carried out often, such as the five daily prayers of devout Muslims, or the daily mass attended by some Catholics. Or they may be held weekly, monthly, yearly, or at even longer intervals.

Among the Dogon of northern Mali, the Sigui ceremony to celebrate the renewal of the world is held only once every 60 to 65 years and can take several years to complete. Masked dancers travel from village to village throughout the region of the Bandiagara Escarpment, where the Dogon live. The last Sigui ceremony was held from 1967 to 1973. Because a number of the Dogon people have converted to Islam, and a few to Christianity, it is not at all clear that the next Sigui ceremony, scheduled to begin in 2032, will take place.

Types of Religious Behavior

Ritual

When anthropologists use the term **ritual,** we are referring to a series of actions that are carried out in essentially the same order and format every single time. First you do *this*, then you do *that*, followed by the next step or stage, with little or no variation. There has been much research on the comforting and reassuring qualities of participating in ritual activities, especially when carried out simultaneously with others who share your beliefs. Knowing what to expect, having the experience be the same every time, contributes to the power of rituals to help humans cope with their often confusing and disordered worlds. In many societies, rites of passage and rites of intensification are designed to accomplish specific goals, such as changing a person's status or evoking group pride.

Rites of Passage

Rites of passage are used to accomplish, or at least mark, changes in status for individuals, couples, or groups. Anthropologist Arnold van Gennep was the first to clearly outline the common structure shared by rites of passage around the world. Van Gennep divided rites of passage into three stages. The first stage marks the separation of the individual from his or her prior status, as well as from ordinary daily life and activities. The middle stage is referred to as the **liminal stage,** or liminality. During this in-between time, the person is in transition, no longer having her previous sta-

tus, but not yet settled in the new status. The third stage involves the reincorporation of the individual back into society under her new status (van Gennep 1960).

Rites of passage in some societies are complex, elaborate mixtures of private and public ceremonies, carried out with much pomp and circumstance. As an-

Many societies conduct rites of passage and rites of intensification, often with a religious basis, though not always. An adolescent boy of a Sepik River tribe in New Guinea is held by an older man while undergoing ritual scarification as part of his rite of passage to adulthood in 1975. Note the woman's hand in the lower right quadrant; it illustrates the former custom of amputating the finger joints of young girls when a relative had died, a combination rite of passage for the deceased and rite of intensification for the surviving relatives.

More examples of rites of passage and intensification. Left: a Hindu rite of passage ceremony for young boys, the Bratabandha Pooja, in Nepal in 2008. The first group Bratabandha ceremony to be held in the United States took place in July 2010 in Maryland. Right: a Jewish rite of passage ceremony for 13-year-old boys, a bar mitzvah, held at the Western Wall in Old Jerusalem in 2005.

tidotes to the ordinariness of everyday life, they are often eagerly anticipated by participants and onlookers alike. They have been of particular interest to anthropologists because they reveal so much about what is important to people.

Rites of passage include ceremonies that accomplish significant transitions or mark important stages of the life cycle, including birth, puberty/adulthood, marriage, becoming a parent, and death. In some societies, puberty rituals for males may last for several years and involve circumcision, tests of strength and courage, vision quests, and the learning of essential adult knowledge and/or esoteric religious knowledge. Some societies mark female menarche with elaborate ceremonies as well, recognizing that the onset of menstruation is a clear sign of a woman's value through her ability to produce children. Weddings, graduation ceremonies, and funerals are other examples of rites of passage.

Traditional Tibetan Buddhist "Sky Burial" involves ritually cutting a human corpse and placing it on a mountaintop, where it can be feasted on by scavenger birds and it can decompose through exposure to the elements. Buddhism teaches that the soul is reborn. Once a person has died, the body can be disposed of in a manner that is practical for a land where the ground is too hard and rocky to dig a grave, and there isn't enough wood for a cremation fire.

Rites of Intensification

In contrast to rites of passage, where one or more people change status, rites of intensification serve to uphold and reinforce the status quo of the group. Rites of intensification serve to strengthen group bonds, generate enthusiasm, and/or celebrate important events in the history of a people. A huge variety of activities fall under the category of rites of intensification. In the United States, they range from the Burning Man Project to political rallies, from gay pride parades to Midnight Yell Practices before Texas A&M football games, from Cinco de Mayo and Juneteenth celebrations to family picnics on the Fourth of July, complete with fireworks. In Canada, May 24 is celebrated as Victoria Day, to mark the birthday of the current Canadian monarch. July 1 is Canada Day, and celebrates the 1867 Confederation and establishment of dominion status.

Some rituals are both rites of passage and rites of intensification simultaneously. The funeral of an important and well-loved public figure can be both. Likewise, national political conventions, where the party's nominees are selected, fulfill both functions. The inauguration of a new president every four years in the United States is yet another example. Part of the ceremony transforms a president-elect into the new president, while all the other activities are meant to strengthen patriotic feelings and pride in one's country.

Prayer

Religious activities often include prayer—silent, spoken, or written; individual or group; spontaneous (free-form) or learned. Prayers may reflect honor, respect, or worship for the deities or other supernatural beings addressed, or they may be petitions asking for help, protection, healing, success in various endeavors, forgiveness for wrongdoings, or any number of other requests for good things to happen and bad things not to happen.

Music, Song, and Dance

Many religious activities are accompanied by music, singing, dance, or some combination. Again, there are seemingly limitless variations on how these aspects of human creativity are used to express and reflect religious sentiments, ranging from Gregorian chants to the whirling dervishes of Sufi Islam (who whirl in reverence of Allah), or the temple prayer wheels of Buddhism.

Jane Goodall has reported that among the chimpanzees of Gombe, several have been observed performing rain dances and waterfall displays during thunderstorms:

> As we drew near, the roar of falling water sounded ever louder in the soft green air. Evered and Freud [chimpanzees], hair bristling, moved faster. Suddenly the waterfall came into sight through the trees, cascading down from the stream bed fifty feet or more above. . . . All at once Evered charged forward, leapt up to seize one of the hanging vines, and swung out over the stream in the spray-drenched wind. A moment later Freud joined him. The two leapt from one liana to the next, swinging into space. . . . Frodo charged along the edge of the stream, hurling rock after rock now ahead, now to the side, his coat glistening with spray. For ten minutes the three performed their wild displays while Fifi and her younger offspring watched from one of the tall fig trees by the stream. Were the chimpanzees expressing feelings of awe such as those which, in early man, surely gave rise to primitive religions, worship of the elements? Worship of the mystery of water, which seems alive; always rushing on, yet never going; always the same, yet ever different. (Goodall 2000:241–242)

Parades, Progressions, and Pilgrimages

Some religions include public parades, festivals, elaborate progressions through the streets, or pilgrimages to sacred places, such as the Hajj to Mecca for Muslims, or a Roman Catholic's trip to Lourdes to petition the Virgin Mary for help with an illness. Carnival/Mardi Gras celebrations around the world may be raucous, explicitly licentious, and sexual, but they have their roots in deeply held religious beliefs.

Sacrifice

Sacrifice is a common aspect of many religions. Sacrifices may include libations, which are liquids poured onto the ground, over a religious figure, or over an altar. The liquids may include special water (holy water), alcoholic beverages, or blood from an animal that has been killed especially for this purpose. In some cases, people sacrifice parts of their bodies (male foreskins, finger joints, hair), or kill animals and offer the head or entire body as a sacrifice to the supernatural beings. Food and drink may be left for the gods at altars and temples. People may give up something, either temporarily or permanently, in hopes of pleasing the supernatural beings and increasing the chances of a petition being favorably answered, or simply to show respect and piety.

Rules for Living

As discussed previously, many religions involve specific lifestyle practices that members are expected to follow. Examples include injunctions against alcohol, caffeine, and various foods. Or they may be prescriptive, in the form of rules about how to dress, how to wear your hair, the presence or absence of facial hair in men, when and how to worship, fasting during certain times, giving alms to the poor, and so forth. Such daily lifestyle customs may be obvious to others, such as hair and dress, marking a person as a member of a specific religion, or they may be private, hidden from public view.

Fire

Another intriguing aspect of human religious behavior is the near universal involvement of controlled fire. This may take the form of a bonfire, around which people gather to sing, dance, pray, and worship, or in the more controlled form of torches to light nighttime processions or candles that may be held by individuals or lit on an altar. Persian Zoroastrianism is usually credited as being the first religion to establish an eternal flame that was tended by a dedicated priest, some time around the sixth century BCE (before the common era). The Abrahamic religions are thought to have adopted this concept from the Zoroastrians.

Over the years, field research on the nonhuman primates has shown that many behaviors once thought to distinguish humans from all other animals are actually not unique to humans. For example, chimpanzees, orangutans, gorillas, and Japanese macaques pass local traditions down through the generations by learning—in other words, they have culture. Chimpanzees have been observed making and using tools, hunting other primates with wooden spears, communicating through charades, dancing at waterfalls, and living in caves. Japanese macaques are known for their innovations, including the discovery and subsequent transmission of sweet potato washing, wheat washing, fishing, hanging out in hot springs, and noisily playing with stones. However, *no animals other than humans make and control fire.* All nondomesticated animals and most domesticated animals seem terrified of fire. Thus, the near-universal use of fire in rituals express-

ing religious beliefs may be one of the few things that clearly distinguishes humans from other animals.

Contemporary examples of the use of fire in spiritual contexts include the many eternal flames that burn at sites around the world to honor specific individuals, soldiers who died in wars, victims of genocide, and prisoners of conscience. The secular tradition of holding up a lit match or a cigarette lighter during a music concert is another example. As North American cultural patterns changed, with fewer people smoking and more having cell phones, concert-goers today hold up their lighted cell phone screens instead of a match or lighter. The iPod Touch even has a special screen showing a lighter with a flame. This screen can be held up at concerts to convey the same sentiments of solidarity and common group membership once expressed by actual flames.

Material Culture

In addition to special words, songs, dances, prayers, and the use of fire, we can also examine cross-cultural patterns in the material culture associated with religious beliefs. Material culture in this context includes the architecture of sacred spaces and places of religious worship or pilgrimage, special altars that hold religious objects, special clothing or other textiles used during religious rituals, and a huge variety of statues, paintings, crosses of all types (not just Christian), prayer beads, masks, hats, jewelry, staffs, and more. It is not always obvious to the outside observer when objects have religious significance, or what meanings they hold for believers.

Trance

Meditation, trance, and/or religious ecstasy are aspects of many religious traditions around the world. Trance is often misunderstood by people who have neither seen nor experienced it, especially in a religious context, so it is worth further description and discussion.

What Is Trance?

A trance is defined as an altered state of consciousness, during which the individual has experiences different from those encountered during normal awake states or while dreaming. There are different levels of trance, ranging from very light to very deep, and people in deep states of trance may become unconscious and no longer capable of controlling their movements. During a trance, the individual's brain wave patterns are altered in specific ways. Trance is not fake, it is not acting, it is not pretend. It is simply another state of consciousness that many people around the world use as part of their religious and/or healing activities.

Most people are familiar with a number of altered states of consciousness, such as deep sleep (when delta brain waves predominate), lighter REM sleep (when theta brain waves predominate, and when dreams and nightmares occur), the transitional stage that happens after your alarm goes off and you hit the snooze button for the tenth time (moving up from delta through theta into alpha brain waves), and active wakefulness (when beta brainwaves predominate). In addition, a person will be hyper-aware and alert due to an adrenaline rush during times of danger or excitement. Or you can drift off into a theta state while driving, and daydream even as part of your brain continues to pay attention to traffic, allowing you to drive safely.

Entering Trance

There are many different ways to go into trance. People often begin with some sort of external trigger that helps them achieve the trance state. Such triggers commonly include meditation (focused breathing and patterns of thought) and music and dance, especially repetitive percussion (drumming) at specific rhythms and intervals. Sensory deprivation can prepare the mind for the trance state, and deprivation of food, water, sleep, or some combination, may be used. Group effects have been noted, where entire groups of people enter trance at the same time, through drumming and dancing (sensory overload) or sensory deprivation.

In some cases, mind-altering drugs are ingested as a means of jump-starting the trance experience. These may include tobacco, psychoactive cacti infusions (peyote, San Pedro, Peruvian Torch), other plant extracts, and/or alcohol. They may be eaten, imbibed, snorted up the nose, absorbed through the skin, or inhaled through the lungs. In cultures where such substances are used to induce trance, they are seldom if ever used for recreational purposes, but rather are recognized as potentially dangerous; they are used only during supervised religious rituals. Individuals who are not in trance often help control the movements of those in trance, to prevent them from hurting themselves by falling into the fire, running off into the night, turning knives on themselves, falling to the ground, or other such behaviors.

Eventually, many practitioners develop the ability to go into trance and to negotiate different levels of trance at will, whenever they want, without the use of any external substances or triggers.

The Experience of Trance

To the outside observer, people in trance appear to move and behave in similar ways, no matter where they live or what the context of the trance experience. They may move in slow-motion or dance with jerky movements. They may appear to be having a seizure and writhe about on the ground. They may speak in a language that no one understands.

People seem to have a limited range of experiences while in trance, but how those experiences are interpreted depends almost entirely on the cultural belief system in which the behavior is embedded. Many people returning from the trance state report auditory, visual, and other sensory hallucinations. They may encounter a variety of spirit beings, ancestors, demons, and animal totems. They may experience feelings of flying, stretching, traveling through a long tunnel, seeing bright lights, hearing voices, and so on. They may interpret such trips as travel to the underworld, the spirit realm, a parallel universe, or the future. They may say that they feel as though their body has been taken over by another entity. Whether that entity is recognized and interpreted as a demon, an ancestor, the Holy Ghost of Christianity, the individual's totemic animal, or some other explanation depends on the cultural belief system.

Religious healers may enter trance to travel to the spirit world to diagnose illness, determining both the cause and the appropriate treatment that will help someone heal. They may gain insight into interpersonal conflicts that are causing stress. Some people report being able to accomplish feats of strength, or do other things that are not ordinarily possible during regular consciousness, such as lowering their heart and respiratory rates to such low levels that they appear dead, or sleeping outside under conditions of severe cold without suffering any ill effects. These accomplishments seem to be limited to those who have devoted many years to training and practice, such as Tibetan monks. The take-home message is that *trance states are real, people do have experiences that must be explained outside the realm of ordinary, everyday life, and religious beliefs systems often provide such explanations.*

WITCHCRAFT, SORCERY, AND OTHER FORMS OF MAGICAL THINKING

Like trance, beliefs in witchcraft, sorcery, and various types of magical thinking are often misunderstood by outsiders to cultures where such beliefs are found. In some cases, people don't even recognize that they themselves hold such beliefs until they are explicitly pointed out to them. In this section, we will briefly discuss the concepts that underlie the anthropological meaning of the terms *witchcraft* and *sorcery*, and then move on to an exploration of sympathetic and contagious magic.

Witchcraft

Defining Witchcraft

The terms *witchcraft* and *sorcery* are used in many different ways in different situations, but they have specific meanings within anthropology. Not every anthropologist agrees on the details, but most use the framework presented here. **Witchcraft** is thought to be the result of an innate, inborn quality that some people possess. If a person is a witch, it is not by choice, it is an inherent quality of the person—he has both a special power and a propensity for evil. Witches are thought to be particularly envious of others and often cause misfortune through use of the **Evil Eye** (looking at someone with envy or malice). The misfortunes attributable to witchcraft are not the result of deliberate misbehavior on the witch's part; the witch is not able to control whether or not bad things happen to themselves, to others, or to the group, as a result of their being a witch. Note that this is a very different use of the term *witch* than how the term is used by followers of Wicca and other pagan (nature-based) religions.

The Cultural Logic of Witchcraft Beliefs

Where people believe in witchcraft (in the anthropological sense), adverse occurrences such as the death of a child, a series of weather catastrophes, failure of the crops, or other misfortunes may be attributed to the presence of a witch in the group. The *cultural logic* is that if the witch can be identified and removed, conditions will improve. In a world where many aspects of life are not controllable by direct human action, the ability to place the blame on an individual, and then take steps to get rid of that individual, provides some measure of control and comfort.

Identifying the Witch

The first problem is how to identify the witch. The witch doesn't know that he is the problem, so the person can't confess, willingly or unwillingly. In some cases, a trial of some sort is proposed to identify the witch. My favorite has always been one used during medieval times in Europe, where the suspected witch was bound and thrown into a cistern of water. If the person floated, that indicated guilt, and the individual was pulled out of the water and burned at the stake. If the person sank instead, and drowned, that proved his innocence, but of course the person was still dead. Either way, it got rid of someone that others suspected of being a witch. And if the first accused person was innocent and drowned, it was usually easy to point the finger at another suspected witch.

In societies with witchcraft beliefs, a person is at risk of being singled out as a suspected witch if she acts in any way out of the ordinary. Thus, a woman who speaks her mind and practices healing, in a culture where such activities are not allowed for women, might draw suspicion to herself. Anyone who is unsocial, a loner, uncommunicative, a chronic troublemaker, or who disappears for stretches of time without explanation might be accused of being a witch when bad things start happening.

Functions of Witchcraft Beliefs

One of the functions of witchcraft beliefs, then, is to encourage people to behave according to the local norms and standards. Despite how you might wish to act, knowing that you might be accused of being a witch is a powerful motivator to act as you are supposed to. Likewise, if the group contains a troublesome individual, an accusation of witchcraft is one mechanism to get rid of that person.

Witchcraft beliefs are common in a number of places around the world. Witchcraft/evil eye beliefs are found all around the Mediterranean, including North Africa and the Near East, and in their respective colonies, such as the colonies of Spain and Portugal in both the Old World and the New World. Sub-Saharan Africa also includes many societies that believe in witchcraft (though not necessarily evil eye) as a significant cause of misfortune. Where witches are thought to exist, people may say prayers, adorn their children with amulets, or engage in other protective behaviors to ward off the ill effects of potential witches in their midst.

Sorcery

Defining Sorcery

In contrast to witchcraft, **sorcery,** as anthropologists use the term, refers to deliberate, conscious activities that individuals engage in to try to affect themselves or others. The techniques of sorcery may be learned by anyone, but typically some people are more powerful and effective than others. In some societies, sorcerers are highly trained, powerful specialists, who may charge others for their services. Sorcery is often thought of in negative terms, like witchcraft, as causing only harm to others, but sorcery can also be used to prevent harm, to undo or cancel harmful spells cast by other sorcerers, to make someone fall in love with you, or to protect someone on a journey.

Sorcery involves the sorcerer doing something active to cause the desired change. Typical techniques include verbal spells, prayers, or curses; placement of foreign objects into the victim to cause pain, illness, or death; use of *exuvia* of the victim (hair, fingernail clippings, feces, or an item of clothing) to cause harm; administration of magical poisons or protective substances; sending an alien spirit to posses the victim's body; or capturing the victim's soul. Beliefs in sorcery are found throughout the world and may overlap with beliefs in witchcraft. It can be difficult to get rid of sorcerers, as they are thought to be too powerful, able to kill anyone who tries to harm them. Instead, people try to stay on the good side of their neighbors, especially anyone they think might be a sorcerer, so that the sorcerer will have no reason to harm them.

The Cultural Logic of Sorcery Beliefs

Where people believe in sorcery (in the anthropological sense), adverse events that happen to individuals, such as difficulties conceiving, a lingering illness, or a series of accidents, may be attributed to the actions of a sorcerer in the group. Sorcerers usually single out specific individuals to harm, rather than the whole group. Sorcerers may act on their own or on behalf of someone who has asked or paid them to influence the victim. The *cultural logic* is such that if sorcery is suspected, the victim or the victim's family may be able to identify who has harmed him, and take steps to fight back, either directly or through counter-sorcery. In a world where many aspects of life are not controllable by direct human action, the ability to place the blame on sorcery, and then take steps to counteract it, provides some measure of control and comfort.

Functions of Sorcery

Bonnie Glass-Coffin's book *The Gift of Life* (1998), is about the mix of Roman Catholicism and indigenous sorcery beliefs in northern Peru. Glass-Coffin points out that beliefs in sorcery, like beliefs in witchcraft, can be very useful. A straying husband, discovered by his jealous wife, may blame his behavior on the other woman. He can claim that she put a love spell on him, causing him to act as he did. If his wife believes him, this may absolve him of direct responsibility, and paves the way for forgiveness and reconciliation. Even if she doesn't really believe him, it allows her to accept him back without appearing weak. Sorcery allows people to explain misfortune and offers options for actions dealing with the problem.

Magical Thinking

Magical thinking is a part of most, if not all, societies. There are many types of magical thinking, but we will focus on the two most common types found cross-culturally. Keep in mind that humans are complex and contradictory and that not all beliefs and behaviors can be easily classified.

Sympathetic Magic

Sympathetic (or imitative) magic operates through the magical connection between a person or thing and something that looks similar, is similar in some way, or has some sort of sympathetic connection with the actual person or thing. One example is burning someone in effigy. In former times, if a criminal had escaped his captors, the sentence, such as hanging or burning, might be carried out on a dummy. In more recent times, effigies may be made to resemble detested political figures and hanged in a public place to express the sentiments of the protestors. Voodoo dolls work in a similar fashion—you purchase or craft a small image of a specific individual, and then you harm the doll in some fashion, with the intent/belief/hope that the person will experience the same fate.

Objects can gain power through sympathetic magic if they resemble something else that has power. In 1994, a woman in Florida was making a grilled cheese sandwich when she noticed an unusual pattern in the grill marks on the toast. To her, it looked like an image of the Virgin Mary. She saved the sandwich for 10 years and eventually sold it on eBay for $28,000. The value of the sandwich comes from the image, which resembles the Virgin Mary to some viewers. Personally, I think it looks like Shirley Temple Black as a child, but readers are encouraged to view it online and judge for themselves (BBC News 2004).

Another form of sympathetic magic is found in behaviors that are associated with good fortune; the idea being that if you repeat the behaviors, you increase your chances of repeating the good fortune. Examples might include wearing your lucky underwear to every final exam (since you had them on when you aced your calculus final), my habit of carrying a small silver pelican charm with me whenever I fly on an airplane (haven't crashed yet), or nighttime routines of checking under the bed and inside the closet and making sure everything on the bed is arranged just so, in order to keep the scary monsters at bay. Many women in North America believe that if they breastfeed their children, eat a low-fat diet, and get their yearly mammogram, then they won't get breast cancer. While the first two behaviors can lower one's risk of breast cancer, there unfortunately isn't any magic that connects mammograms to prevention—they only allow early detection of cancer. In his classic study of baseball magic, George Gmelch explores the daily rituals and body movements during games that baseball players, especially pitchers, employ to increase their chances of success (Gmelch 1992).

Contagious Magic

Objects that have contagious magic get their power from a prior physical connection with something or someone of power. The key to contagious

magic is that the object was actually in contact with the original source of power at some time and retains some of that power even once the two things are no longer physically connected. The sorcerer's technique of using exuvia (hair, fingernail clippings, feces, or an item of clothing) relies on the magical connection between a person and parts of her body, or items the person once owned, in order to work.

Although many people associate contagious magic with traditional cultures or exotic others, in fact, beliefs in contagious magic are alive and well in even the most supposedly rational, technologically advanced, postindustrial societies. Any souvenir that a person keeps because it came from a special travel destination, or was touched by a famous person, has value only because of that connection. For example, my friend owns a napkin that, she claims, was used by Paul McCartney to wipe his mouth during a concert. He discarded it, and she collected it after the show was over and still has it, some 30+ years later. For her, the napkin is special and significant because Paul McCartney's lips once touched it.

Autographed first editions of books are valued by collectors over mere reading copies for the same reason—because the author not only wrote the book but actually touched that specific first edition copy and signed his name in it. Any type of signed sports memorabilia, first day cancelled stamps, movie props, or other collectibles likewise gain their value through their previous contact with someone or something valued by the collector.

Many Roman Catholic churches in Europe own and display relics (reliquaries) of the saints (usually bones from the hands or feet, or fingers and toes with flesh still on them), or pieces of the True Cross, or important statues sculpted by famous artists such as the *Pieta* by Michelangelo in St. Peter's in Vatican City. Each of these objects gains most or all of its power by association with the original living being, be it a saint, Jesus, or the artist.

An example of the power of contagious magic comes from the recent discovery that a painting owned by Australia's National Gallery of Victoria was a "fake." The painting, *Head of a Man,* had been attributed to Vincent Van Gogh for more than 70 years. It was purchased by the museum in 1940, as a Van Gogh, for $3,500. The gallery claimed it was worth about $5 million today as a Van Gogh, but others said that on the art museum market, it could have sold for more than $20 million, if authentic. Today, it is estimated to be worth less than $500,000 (BBC News 2007).

The misattribution was discovered in 2006, when the painting was on tour in Scotland. Following intensive research and analysis, Van Gogh experts concluded that the painting most likely was *not* a Van Gogh. The painting itself remained exactly the same— not a single atom of the painting changed. It was just as beautiful, just as aesthetically pleasing, just as well-executed as it had been the day before. Yet one day it was a highly valued part of the museum collection, and the next day it was comparatively worthless. Its primary value came via contagious magic—the fact that people thought it had been painted by a famous person.

When people speak of the sentimental value of any object—their grandmother's plain golden wedding band, passed down through the family; a souvenir program from the circus you saw as a child; a note from a friend you've carried in your wallet for years— all of these are examples of the power endowed by contagious magic onto ordinary objects.

Around the world, people believe in supernatural beings, they believe in magic, they believe in the spirit world. Such beliefs help them explain what they experience as they go through life, provide comfort under trying circumstances, and help them cope with grief, loss, and disaster. Such beliefs encourage us to be better people. Religious beliefs are important, but what is also important is understanding that, from the anthropological perspective, every system of religious beliefs has equal standing with every other system of religious beliefs. There is no way to prove the rightness or wrongness of anyone's religious beliefs, and there is no point in trying to do so.

HAVE SCIENTIFIC EXPLANATIONS REPLACED MAGICAL THINKING?

Many students assume that people living in Western industrialized societies view the world rationally, using scientific reasoning to explain how and why things happen. This would be in contrast to so-called traditional peoples whose lives are filled with supersti-

tion and fear, who must resort to magical thinking because they don't have the knowledge or the logical capability to understand how the world really works.

As we have just seen, however, sympathetic and contagious magic beliefs are alive and well in Western societies. If beliefs in witchcraft and sorcery are not as prevalent in Western contexts, it may be because they have been replaced by either faith in God's will or cosmic destiny or by a rather more cynical approach to life's travails expressed as "Life is tough, then you die," or "Stuff happens. Deal with it."

In a classic example from the ethnographic literature, British social anthropologist E. E. Evans-Pritchard analyzed the collapse of a granary in Azande land, in the southern Sudan. People had a habit of sitting in the shade of a granary in the heat of the day, talking, playing games, or working on some craft. If the granary collapsed and injured the people sitting underneath, the Azande would say that, over many years, termites had eaten away the support poles. However, they would also say that witchcraft is the proximate cause for why the granary collapsed at that specific moment. "If there had been no witchcraft people would have been sitting under the granary and it would not have fallen on them, or it would have collapsed but the people would not have been sheltering under it at the time. Witchcraft explains the coincidence of these two happenings" (Evans-Pritchard 1976:23).

In 2008, one of my freshmen students died of alcohol poisoning while attending an off-campus fraternity party. Every Thursday, Friday, and Saturday night, a startlingly high proportion of college students engage in binge drinking and other risky behaviors. According to the Gordie Foundation, approximately 1,700 students die each year in the United States from alcohol-related causes (GORDIE 2010). Nevertheless, most binge drinkers, the vast majority, do not die as a result of their behavior. So why did this student die? Did he drink too much, too fast? Did his peers, part of the *culture of excessive campus drinking*, urge him on? Did he have some underlying genetic condition (such as variants of the alcohol dehydrogenase or aldehyde dehydrogenase genes) that impaired his body's ability to metabolize alcohol? If he had eaten more first, would that have saved him? If someone had taken him to the emergency room when he first collapsed, would that have made a difference?

No one knows the answers to these questions, but I never heard anyone postulate that witchcraft or sorcery were involved in his death. Some of his friends blamed him for making poor choices. Others blamed the fraternity brothers who were watching over him after he passed out. Others viewed it as one of those mysteries of life that can never truly be understood. Some took great comfort from their sincere belief that he was in heaven (his family was Roman Catholic). Still others viewed it as a pointless tragedy, the result of stupid mistakes, with no deeper meaning than that of a random accident.

Terrible things happen to people, in every culture, in every corner of the world. Few of us will go through life without having one or more awful things happen to us or to those we care about. Even with the most detailed understanding of the scientific explanation of the sequence of events—"The bullet ricocheted off the lamppost and then came through the wall of the apartment, striking the sleeping child in the head," or "The American tourist forgot that traffic in England comes from the right, and she only looked left before stepping off the curb, right into the path of the speeding taxi," or "A mosquito carrying malarial parasites hitched a ride on an airplane from West Africa and bit a man sitting in his backyard on Long Island; his doctors never suspected a tropical disease as the cause of his high fever and headache"—we are still at a loss to understand *why,* in the ultimate sense, any of these people died.

For some people, saying that stuff happens is sufficient explanation, even though it provides little solace. Most people, however, search for a deeper understanding of life's travails. Religious beliefs help us make sense of our experiences, and they provide some degree of needed comfort as we deal with grief and loss.

DIFFICULTIES OF CLASSIFYING BELIEVERS

One problem anthropologists face when talking about religion in cross-cultural perspective is how to set up different categories of religious belief, and how to assign people to these categories.

There are no objective or universally accepted criteria for making categories or assigning people to them. If a person says that she is Hindu, what does that mean, exactly? Do you automatically believe the person, or do you ask for some sort of proof? What kind of proof? Do all Hindus agree on who is Hindu and who is not, and how to tell the difference? And if it isn't based on self-reporting, then how do you determine what religion a person belongs to?

People may, for various reasons, want to disguise their true religious beliefs under certain circumstances to avoid argument or oppression, or perhaps even for personal gain. It may be easier to let people assume you are a Christian, if the majority of people around you are Christian, than to declare that you are an atheist or a Pastafarian (a follower of the tongue-in-cheek Flying Spaghetti Monster religion). During times of religious conflict, it may mean the difference between life and death to be able to pass as a member of a religion other than one's own. Young adults may let their parents think they still follow the religion they were raised in, even as they question it or fall away from it entirely.

During my field research in Mali, people would often say they were Muslim, if directly asked what their religious affiliation was, as that is what they felt they were supposed to be. In private, many still followed traditional religious beliefs and practices, especially with respect to traditional medicine. Rural villagers might build and attend a lovely mud-brick mosque with graceful staircases to the roof, but also participate in spirit possession cults (*jine-don*) and initiation societies (*ntomo* and *korè*). Sacred and powerful ritual objects are usually kept hidden, out of the sight of visitors as well as the uninitiated. When asked by an outsider, women might respond that the small beehive-shaped structures seen around some villages are simply chicken houses, rather than admit that they are shrines containing statues of *gwan* fertility figures or other religious materials.

In cases where people are free to proclaim their true religious affiliation without suffering any consequences, many people may identify themselves as belonging to a particular religion. At the same time, other people who also claim to belong to this same religion may disagree, saying that the others aren't "true" or real members of the religion, based on their own personal criteria.

In some regions of the United States, anthropology professors encounter students who deny that Roman Catholics are Christians (one student at Texas A&M famously complained that she had specifically asked for a Christian dorm mate but was instead assigned a Catholic). Pope Benedict XVI approved a declaration in 2007 asserting that the Roman Catholic Church is "the one true church of Christ" and that Orthodox and Protestant groups are merely "ecclesial communities," not proper churches. Discrimination against Jehovah's Witnesses and Mormons (members of the Church of Jesus Christ of Latter-day Saints) can be found in some regions of the country, where other self-identified Christians deny that these groups qualify as Christians. The take-home message is that *there is no one standard, universally accepted test for being a member of any religion.*

Another important issue is that people who identify themselves as belonging to the same faith may in fact hold wildly varying beliefs and may also express their beliefs in different patterns of behavior. Within Judaism, there are several branches with differing beliefs and practices, including Orthodox, Conservative, Reform, Humanistic, and others. Many Jewish people who eat pork and never go to synagogue still consider themselves to be Jewish. Christians who go to church only on Easter and Christmas, and follow few if any of the teachings of Jesus Christ, may still identify themselves as Christians. Members of the Dogon people of Mali who have converted to Islam or Christianity may still believe in many of the tenets of their traditional religion.

Likewise, lumping all traditional animist religions together, as some textbooks do (African Traditional Religions, Native American Traditional Religions, and so on) conceals the fact that these religions may be quite distinct from one another, even if they are geographically contiguous. Even more importantly, it downplays the reality of the situation. Each and every traditional animist religion is a complex, coherent, sophisticated system of thought and practice. People who still use stone tools, and/or practice hunting and gathering for their subsistence mode, can have religious belief systems of overwhelming complexity.

In some religions, the higher levels of esoteric knowledge are limited to those who have moved up the hierarchy and been initiated, and to the anthropologists who have studied the religion under the tutelage of elders. I met a young Dogon man in Texas who admitted that I probably knew more about Dogon religion than he did, because I had read several of the published ethnographies about their complex and elaborate belief system, while he had only been initiated into the lowest levels, due to his age (and he wouldn't dream of reading the ethnographies). Nevertheless, he is a believer, while I remain only a curious outsider.

Perhaps most problematic is the tendency for one group of people to deny that another person's or group's belief system qualifies as a religion. This was (and continues to be) the mind-set behind many missionary efforts to bring religion to the "natives," who are assumed not to have a *real* religion. The ethnographic film *The Drums of Winter (Uksuum Cauyai)*, about the Yup'ik people of Alaska, focuses on the resilience of Yup'ik religious beliefs, drum music, and dancing in the face of Western pressure to convert. The film includes quotes from letters written years ago by Jesuit missionaries to their superiors, decrying the devil-worshipping activities of the native people. The priests even disapproved of the native practice of sharing resources with one another during the difficult winter months via potlatch ceremonies, suggesting instead that starvation might be good for the Yup'ik (Elder and Kamerling 1988).

A contemporary example comes from the struggle of Wiccans to get the United States government to recognize Wicca as a legitimate religion and to add the Wiccan pentacle (a five-pointed star inside a circle) to the list of approved *emblems of belief* for government-furnished headstones or markers for deceased veterans. Although the military has allowed Wiccans to hold services on military bases in recent years, it wasn't until 2007 that the Department of Veterans Affairs, facing lawsuits and widespread criticism, stopped its campaign against the Wiccans. The Wiccan pentacle now joins 38 other symbols allowed on military grave markers, including many versions of the Christian cross, the Jewish Star of David, the Muslim crescent moon, the Buddhist Wheel of Righteousness, the Unitarian Universalist chalice, the Native American Church of North America symbol (a teepee with feathers), the humanist emblem of spirit, and even an atomic symbol for atheism. Neo-Druid vets are still working on getting the Awen symbol added to the list, but there is, as yet, no campaign for the Flying Spaghetti Monster.

There is a tendency for one group of people to deny that another person's or group's belief system qualifies as a religion. The photograph on top shows children responding to a gospel presentation at a summer 2007 Bible Camp sponsored by the Christian Assembly of God denomination. Quite likely, members of such congregations would deny the status of "religion" to the Flying Spaghetti Monster religion. The photograph on the bottom shows adherents, who refer to themselves as Pastafarians or Pirates, preparing to participate in a Summer Solstice Parade in Seattle, Washington, in 2009. At the same time, many people who consider themselves Christian would be critical of the ecstatic, trance-like behavior of the Assembly of God girls, claiming that they must not be "real" Christians.

ABRAHAMIC RELIGIONS

This exploration of religion will end with a very brief history lesson on the **Abrahamic religions,** as many North Americans (perhaps especially those raised as Christian) have no idea that Judaism, Christianity, Islam, the Bahá'í Faith, and Mormonism are historically related and all worship the same deity. Given the role that religious intolerance plays in today's economic and political world, it is important to clearly understand the relationship among these major world religions.

All of the Abrahamic religions are classified as monotheistic, believing in a single, all-powerful supernatural entity known variously as Jehovah, Yahweh, God (in English), or Allah. All of these names are applied to the *same* supernatural entity, the same creator-being. These religions are referred to as Abrahamic because they all trace their human ancestry back to Abraham, who was born in Mesopotamia approximately 2,000 years before Christ. According to Genesis, Abraham was the father of both Ishmael (progenitor of all Arabs) and Isaac (progenitor of all Jews). Of Islam, Carol Delaney points out: "Jews and Christians are generally unaware that Muhammad's role was not to create a new religion but to call the people back to the one true, monotheistic faith of Abraham" (Delaney 2000:119). Note that other major religious traditions that comprise a similar level of classification as the Abrahamic category would be the *Dharmic* religions of India and the *Taoic* religions of East Asia.

In the Jewish tradition, Moses is the most important prophet, and the Torah is the sacred book. The *Torah* refers to the first five books of the Hebrew Bible; these same writings make up the first part of the Christian Old Testament. Jewish tradition holds that a Messiah, or Savior, will eventually arrive, reunite all the Jews in Israel, and bring peace to the world.

As a distinct religious tradition, Christianity developed during and after the lifetime of Jesus Christ (AD 1–33). In the Western world, we count our calendar years as starting at the year of the birth of Christ, counting backward in time from this point (years BC, for Before Christ) and counting forward in time from this point (years AD, for Anno Domini). Under the new tradition, Jesus, who was Jewish, came to be viewed as both human and supernatural, both a real living person and the son of God, who was sent to Earth to save mankind from its sins. He was accepted by many Jewish people, as well as members of other religions, as the Messiah who had been predicted to arrive.

In Christianity, although many human figures are important (Mary and Joseph, the apostles), Jesus Christ himself is the main figure who brings information from God to people. The books of the Christian Bible included in the New Testament are thought to reflect the teachings of Jesus. Note that there is no universal agreement among Christians on which books belong in the Old and New Testaments or on the translation of the writings from the original Hebrew, Greek, and Aramaic into other languages.

Islam, as a religious tradition distinct from Judaism and Christianity, can be traced to the life of its great prophet, Muhammad, who lived during the sixth and seventh centuries (AD 570–632). Muslims view Muhammad as the recipient of revelations direct from God (*Allah* in Arabic). These revelations were collected into the text known as the Qur'an (Koran). Rather than establishing a new religion, Muhammad and his followers view his work as the restoration of the original monotheistic faith of Adam, Abraham, Moses, and Jesus. The Hadith is an additional book of the sayings of Muhammad. According to standard Muslim teachings, Jesus was born to the Virgin Mary (Maryam) and was an important prophet, but not the son of God. He was taken up into Heaven by Allah before he could be crucified.

The Bahá'í Faith is a monotheistic religion that developed out of Shia Islam. It was founded in Persia in the nineteenth century by the prophet Bahá'u'lláh. According to the Bahá'í Faith, all of the major world religions have a similar underlying message, and over the centuries, God has sent a variety of divine messengers to Earth, including Abraham, Jesus, Muhammad, Krishna, Buddha, and others. The prophet Bahá'u'lláh (AD 1817–1892) is considered the last of these divine messengers. There are a number of sacred Bahá'í texts. The social principles of the Bahá'í Faith include a belief in the unity of all humankind, equality between the sexes, the elimination of all forms of prejudice, the harmony of religion and science, and world peace (Internet Sacred Text Archive 2010).

The Church of Jesus Christ of Latter-day Saints (Mormonism) developed out of Christian traditions, with the addition of further information conveyed by God to humans via the prophet Joseph Smith, Jr. (AD 1805–1844), both directly during Smith's first vision in 1820 and later via the angel Moroni, beginning in 1823. The Book of Mormon is the main sacred text for members of the faith and is regarded not only as scripture but also as an historical account of God's interactions with prehistoric Native Americans.

The purpose of this whirlwind tour of the history of the Abrahamic religions is to counter the common misperception that these religions are not connected. In fact, they constitute varying stages or forms of a single, developing, monotheistic religion, which began in the Middle East some 4,000 years ago. All members of the Abrahamic religions *worship the same god*, no matter what name they know him by.

Religion remains one of the more elusive and enigmatic aspects of human experience, difficult to pin down, difficult to define, difficult to understand.

Key Concepts Review

Religions are systems of nonscientific (not testable/not disprovable) beliefs and practices that help people deal with things that are inexplicable, usually through belief in supernatural beings; every known society has religious beliefs.

You shouldn't make assumptions about a person's religious beliefs and practices based on his or her nationality, ethnicity, surname, or skin color.

The anthropological perspective on religion can be expressed in four basic principles:

1. All religions are *true.*
2. No religion is *True.*
3. Religious beliefs are a consequence of time and place.
4. Morality ≠ supernatural beliefs; morality and spirituality can exist without reference to supernatural beings.

Religious beliefs and practices can be examined in terms of the specific functions they fulfill for the individual and society, as well as their advantages and disadvantages.

The functions of religious beliefs and practices include:
   Answering otherwise unanswerable questions
   Providing help and comfort in times of crisis
   Providing a blueprint for right living
   Establishing and strengthening social solidarity

It is important to understand religious terms including atheism, theism, animism, and animatism; many people use the term *animism* incorrectly.

Each so-called *traditional or animist religion* is a complex, sophisticated system of thought in its own right.

Most religions include beliefs in supernatural beings, ancestor spirits, and nature spirits (spirits of living beings, place, or inanimate objects, tectonic- and weather-related spirits, and totems).

People usually craft their supernatural beings both to reflect the local environment and subsistence strategies and to fit their need for some measure of control over the most aleatory (random) elements of their lives.

Religious behavior includes rituals of all sorts—including both rites of passage (through which an individual or group changes status) and rites of intensification (through which group identity is reinforced)—prayers, sacrifices, parades, processions, pilgrimages, rules for living, and fire, as well as material culture with religious significance.

A trance is an altered state of consciousness during which the individual has experiences different from those encountered during normal awake states or while dreaming; trance is not fake, it is not acting, it is not pretend; it is simply another state of consciousness that many people use as part of their religious and/or healing activities.

Beliefs in witchcraft and sorcery are found in many cultures and help people explain their experiences as well as gain some measure of control over adverse circumstances.

All peoples everywhere believe in things that are obviously *not true;* they engage in magical thinking, have superstitious beliefs, and express beliefs in *sympathetic magic* (similar appearance has meaning) and *contagious magic* (prior contact has meaning).

Scientific explanations of phenomena may explain *how* bad things happen, but they can't address the ultimate question of *why* or provide much emotional comfort.

It is not easy to classify people as belonging to specific religions, as there are no universal, objective criteria for what constitutes a *real* religion, or a *true believer* of any religion.

The Abrahamic religions, including (minimally) Judaism, Christianity, Islam, the Bahá'í Faith, and Mormonism, are historically related, share some of their sacred texts, and worship the same deity.

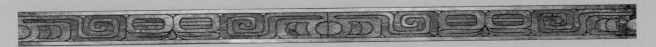

The *morin khuur* is a traditional Mongolian bowed stringed instrument, and is considered a symbol of the Mongolian nation.

9

THE THINGS WE DO FOR FUN

Music, Sports, & Games

Humans have a truly breathtaking capacity to learn information, solve problems, and develop elaborately structured social worlds; we also seem positively compelled to express ourselves creatively. Around the world, people devote considerable time and energy to various types of creative activities that provide pleasure— it's not all just living and reproducing.

Humans have the largest brain-to-body-size ratio of any animal, which affords us a truly breathtaking capacity to learn information, solve problems, and create elaborately structured social worlds. In addition to developing innovative solutions to practical problems of daily survival, humans seem positively compelled to create. Whether this is an artifact of our large and complex brains, or a fundamental part of being human, creativity reaches its fullest expression through human activities such as architecture, music, the visual and performing arts, storytelling, play, games, and sports.

All mammal babies play when they are young— they chase, they wrestle, they tickle, they sneak up and pounce on others, they amuse themselves with bits of flotsam and jetsam from the environment such as a leaf or a feather. They may be fascinated with a dripping faucet or the play of light and shadows on a windy day. Japanese macaque youngsters use vines to swing out over a stream, then let go and drop into the water with a splash; young chimpanzees swing back and forth on slender branches until they are dizzy.

As they mature, most mammals outgrow this playful stage and settle into more serious adult pastimes such as surviving and reproducing. To a greater extent than any other mammal, humans seem to hang onto this playfulness throughout their lives, finding endless ways to amuse themselves and have fun. They still must survive and reproduce, but along the way, significant time and effort are dedicated to the pursuit of happiness. The next two chapters will examine how

cultural anthropologists have approached the study of human creative expression and the things we do for fun from evolutionary and cross-cultural perspectives. I begin with some general observations that apply to all aspects of human creativity and then move on to discuss music, sports, and games in more detail. The following chapter will take a closer look at the visual and performing arts.

THE ORIGINS OF HUMAN CREATIVITY

Most anthropologists target the beginning of the Upper Paleolithic (40,000 years ago) as providing the first unequivocal evidence of human creativity. Prior to the Upper Paleolithic, archeologists find only a few glimmers of creative expression in the archeological record. Most behavior of humans and proto-humans prior to this time was dedicated to surviving and reproducing, with presumably little time for frivolous activities. But right around the time of the appearance of the first anatomically modern humans, some 40,000 years ago, the archeological record shows a virtual **creative explosion** (Mithen 1998; Pfeiffer 1982). This flowering of creativity includes local styles of tool-making, evidence of beads made of shell or bone, and small objects formed out of clay or carved from stone, bone, or ivory. One of the most famous Upper Paleolithic figurines, the Woman of Willendorf, dated at 24,000–26,000 years old, appears to be wearing a knitted cap on her head (Barber 1994). The earliest musical instruments appear. Around the same time, cave and rockshelter paintings begin to appear around the world, from South Africa to the Sahara, all across Asia, and most famously in the extraordinary paintings of animals found in caves such as Lascaux in Western Europe. And it turns out that the most elaborate cave paintings are situated at the places in the cave galleries with the best acoustics (Lawson and Scarre 2006).

As time passed, human creative expressions took on many different forms and evolved over time as new ideas were brought forth and new techniques and styles were invented and shared. We have little hard evidence for the *origins* of music, storytelling, games, and sports as aspects of human behavior, but we can see from the study of contemporary cultures that these expressions of creativity and the other things we do for fun play a very important role in modern human life and reflect underlying cultural beliefs as much as subsistence, economics, politics, and religion do.

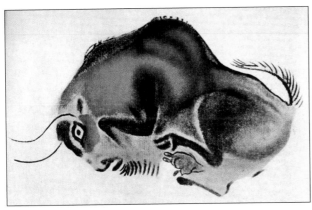

Early undisputed artworks have been found at many locations around the world. Top left: a single example from hundreds of cave paintings from Altamira Cave, in Spain. This exquisite bull is painted on the ceiling, and dates to about 15,000 years ago. The cave is designated as a UNESCO World Heritage Site. Top right: a panel of petroglyphs including a giraffe and a lion from the Damara (Twyfelfontein) site in Namibia, also a UNESCO World Heritage Site. This site contains at least 2,500 rock carvings, as well as rock paintings, and was created over a number of years ranging from 10,000 years ago to as recently as AD 1000. Bottom left: the famous Woman of Willendorf, a four-inch-tall statue of a plump woman found in Austria and dating from more than 20,000 years ago. She is carved out of a type of limestone not local to the area and tinted with red ochre. Bottom right: a bas-relief carving of a similarly shaped woman known as the Venus (Woman) of Laussel, from France, approximately 25,000 years ago. She was also tinted with red ochre. In her right hand she holds a horn that is notched with 13 marks.

Different Aspects of Human Creativity

When considering creative expression and fun, there are a number of different questions one can ask about the activity in any particular cultural setting. These are presented as dichotomies, but they are better viewed as varying along a continuum. Although this chapter is primarily about music and sports, these preliminary ideas apply equally well to the visual and performing arts.

Solitary versus Group

Is the activity something done by a single individual, a group, or either? If a group of people are doing something together, how large can the group be, and/or are multiple groups involved? Examples of solitary activities include playing the piano, reading a book, surfing the Internet, knitting socks, or playing solitaire. Group activities include barbershop quartet singing, a musician's jam session, square dancing, bowling in a league, playing soccer, quilting at a quilting bee, or playing bridge. Larger groups may participate in an orchestra or marching band performance, the Boston Marathon, or the Super Bowl, either as participants or spectators.

Public versus Private

Is the activity usually carried out in a private setting, or is it better described as a public performance? A person may play the piano by himself, for his own enjoyment, or the person may play at a small party of close friends, or before a large audience. A couple may play Scrabble after dinner, or they may participate in a competitive, televised Scrabble competition. The production of art may be a solitary undertaking, as when a painter or sculptor works in his or her studio, or a novelist sits alone at the computer. The end product, if a painting or sculpture, may end up in a private home, in a museum setting, or hanging on the wall of a corporate office; if a book, it may end up in the personal collections of only a few people, or it may become a best seller, be made into a movie, and be read and discussed by local book clubs or citywide reading programs such as *Seattle Reads*.

Large sculptures, such as Anish Kapoor's *Cloud Gate* in Chicago (known to locals as *The Bean*), are

meant to be outside, where the public can view and interact with them in an urban setting (Millennium Park, Chicago 2010). Storm King Art Center in New York exhibits large-scale sculptures and landscape artworks on their 500 acres of rural land. Visitors are encouraged to view the natural landscape as an integral part of the viewing experience of the artworks. American architect Frank Lloyd Wright built *Falling Water* as a private residence for the Kauffman family in the 1930s. In 1963, it was donated to the Western Penn-

"Falling Water" (top) in Western Pennsylvania, was designed by architect Frank Lloyd Wright as a private residence but is now open to the public. Alexander Calder's huge metal sculptures were designed to be viewed by the public, in outdoor settings. "Black Flag" (bottom) can be seen at Storm King Art Center in New York.

sylvania Conservancy and opened to the public. However, its remote location means that many fewer people have ever seen it in person than have seen New York City's Guggenheim Museum, also designed by Wright. The Taj Mahal in Agra, India, was built in the seventeenth century by Mughal Emperor Shah Jahan as a mausoleum for his favorite wife, Mumtaz Mahal. A mixture of Persian, Indian, and Islamic architectural elements, it has been designated by UNESCO as a World Heritage Site, and is one of the most popular tourist sites in the world.

Participant versus Observer and Amateur versus Expert

Most musical or artistic endeavors and sports activities can be enjoyed as a participant, as an observer, or both under different circumstances. For many creative pursuits, any person with the basic skills and resources can participate at the amateur or recreational level—anyone can play soccer or chess; anyone can make a pot out of clay or paint a picture; anyone can sing, dance, play the piano, or go swimming. In other cases, only a few individuals actually participate or perform, and the other people are involved as observers—they form the audience.

The participants may be highly trained and possess sophisticated artistic or athletic skills. For example, during an international ice skating competition, or a professional ice hockey game, the skaters will have trained and practiced for years, while the spectators may never have been on ice skates. The same is true for a military air show or a concert by a famous rock band or a professional orchestra. One can enjoy playing football with friends at home and also enjoy watching high school, college, or professional teams compete, on TV or in the stadium. Many people enjoy the vicarious thrill of watching others perform dangerous activities such as bull riding, bungee jumping, tightrope walking, or car racing. Some people enjoy the anticipation and fulfillment of getting to see spectacular crashes, or participants injured or even killed—the bloodier the better.

Cross-cultural comparisons show that in some contexts, there are only a few expert participants but many observers, while in others, almost everyone in the society participates in one way or another—there are no designated professionals and no separate audience.

Competitive or Cooperative

Another aspect to be investigated is whether specific artistic and athletic activities are carried out in a spirit of cooperation and fun for all, or are highly competitive and exclusionary. Many sports in Western cultures are highly competitive, with strict rules about age and skill levels, and only those who have talent are able to participate, even though any sport could be played competitively or cooperatively.

For example, during the past few decades in the United States, youth sports have greatly expanded in scope. Soccer in particular has experienced huge growth, with leagues that begin with children as young as three or four years of age. Typically, even leagues for young children are highly competitive, and only the best players get a lot of time on the field or make the all-star team. The focus is on winning, and coaches and parents alike urge the kids on with shouts of encouragement or dismay from the sidelines. Most kids who participate think this is as it should be, and though they may be disappointed if they aren't good enough to play very much, or don't get promoted to the next level, they seldom question the overall belief system. They agree that the better players should play more, in order to win, and that winning the game (or the divisional, state, or regional title) is the goal. They celebrate with wild enthusiasm when they win and are devastated and go home moping when they lose. They express animosity toward the members of competing teams and are harsh critics of themselves or their teammates if a mistake is made.

To counter what they viewed as an overemphasis on competition and winning, and the exclusionary nature of youth soccer, a group of parents in Katy, Texas, began an alternative program in 1986, called Fair, Fun, Positive Soccer (FFPS 2010). The program accepts children at any skill level, including children with special needs (physical or intellectual disabilities). The focus is on learning the rules of the game, getting exercise, making friends, and having fun. Each player gets the same amount of time on the field and rotates through every position, and there are no all-star teams. Parents and coaches are allowed to make only positive comments, and everyone goes out to celebrate together at the end of the game.

Music and other artistic endeavors can also be either competitive or cooperative. For example, in 2009, the Smithsonian Institution announced the winner of an architectural competition to design the National Museum of African American History and Culture, slated to open in 2015 on the Mall in Washington, D.C. Each of the competing architectural firms submitted its own design. Only one was chosen by the panel of judges, even though each of the other proposals had some excellent design elements. Cooperation among the interested architectural firms was not an option. In contrast, a number of public art projects have involved multiple individuals and groups from the community in the creation of large-scale murals. The editor of a recent book on cooperative street art in San Francisco's Mission District writes:

> Muralismo is a chaotic art movement, an American twenty-first-century mix of style, content, and multi-culturalism. The individual and collective efforts challenge boundaries of ownership, space, and social agency. Painting styles range from WPA formalism to Zap Comix to punk urban oddities to day-glow expressionism. Descendants of Bruegel and Bosch create complex social satires with wry observations of human foibles. (Jacoby 2009:30)

The Tour de France bicycle race is a combination of competition and cooperation. Riders on each team cooperate among themselves but compete against other teams. Only one team will be declared the overall winner, but riders can earn individual honors for best overall time (yellow jersey), King of the Mountains (polka-dot jersey), most points for sprinting (green jersey), and best rider under 25 years of age (white jersey). American Lance Armstrong won the Tour de France seven times, both because he was an outstanding athlete and because his teammates cooperated to help him win.

In some cultural contexts, most of the sports and artistic endeavors are carried out cooperatively, with little or no emphasis on score keeping and deciding winners versus losers, or first, second, and third place. In others, almost every activity is turned into a competition, and winning becomes the primary motivation for participating. Whether the focus is on cooperation or competition, or some of each, artistic activities and games give an outside observer insight into the cultural beliefs and values of the group.

Is It Just for Fun, or Does It Have Other Purposes?

Some artistic and athletic endeavors are carried out just for the fun of participating or watching. But these activities may have other purposes as well, which may be just as important, or more important, than simple enjoyment. The goals of games and sports may include increasing physical fitness, strength, and coordination. There may be religious meanings to music, architecture, and art. Many people emphasize the educational value of participating in art, music, and sports, pointing out that such participation involves learning about history, politics, economics, leadership, and decision-making skills. For others, such pursuits are seen as a route to economic success and high social status, whether through selling the crafts or fine arts they produce, making a living as an actor or musician, or becoming a professional sports star. In some contexts, people play golf with current and potential business partners in order to secure contracts or make sales.

Economic Aspects of Participation

Artistic and athletic pursuits may be limited by the cost of participating; as such, they reflect economic and class distinctions within a society. Sports such as swimming, ice skating, skiing, gymnastics, golf, yacht racing, English equestrian jumping, and polo require specialized equipment and facilities, and huge investments of time and money. Wrestling, foot races, martial arts, and many forms of ball play are found all around the world and typically require little equipment and relatively inexpensive facilities. Soccer is the most popular sport worldwide at least in part because it requires only a ball and a relatively flat, open space.

To be a professional singer, you need inherent talent, a good voice, absolute (perfect) pitch or the ability to learn relative pitch, voice lessons, a good work ethic, and a few lucky breaks. Only the lessons require money. To be a classical violinist, in addition to all the resources listed above, you need many years of expensive training or schooling and a high quality (expensive) violin, as well as money to travel for lessons, auditions, competitions, and performances.

People with talent and opportunity may be able to make a living performing music, creating art, or playing professional sports. In some instances, however, this requires stifling creativity. Someone who makes a living from selling her artwork may have to cater to the changing whims of the market (what buyers want to purchase), or the artist may be commissioned to create specific works based on a wealthy patron's desires. In Mali, some producers of *bògòlanfini* (mud cloth) stick to traditional patterns and designs, while others retain the traditional techniques but create unique designs that become their signature style. Still others allow buyers to choose from a selection of patterns and then create a piece of cloth to order (to create virtual bògòlanfini yourself, see http://www.mnh.si.edu/africanvoices/mudcloth/html/index_text?showhtml#bogolanfini). A few professional musicians may write and perform their own compositions, and some styles of music incorporate improvisation. However, most professional musicians who play for orchestras must play the notes exactly as written, with direction from the conductor as to timing and emphasis. Similarly, professional football players must take direction from coaches and captains. There is limited room for improvisation and creativity for professionals in the orchestra pit or on the football field.

Technological Innovation and Culture Change

When ideas and technology spread from one place to another, they may be altered to better fit local cultural conditions and values. One famous example is Trobriand Cricket. The British game of cricket was introduced to the Trobriand Islands (now known as the Kiriwina Islands) in the South Pacific in 1903 by Western missionaries, who were hoping to reduce ritual warfare between tribes, which the missionaries viewed as too violent. The Trobrianders were happy to adopt cricket as a replacement for their previous skirmishes, but they modified it to suit their needs. They added erotic dancing and chanting to their opening and closing processions and during the game itself, and changed some of the rules. In Trobriand Cricket, the home team always wins, and after the game, they host a giant feast for everyone involved.

In 1998, an article on an obscure British pastime known as *letterboxing* was published in *Smithsonian* magazine (Granstrom 1998). Letterboxing can trace its roots back to 1854 and was popular only among a small group of eccentrics in the British countryside

who spread the idea and the rules by word of mouth. In the *Smithsonian* article, letterboxing was presented as a quaint and unusual British pastime involving tramping over the moors searching for hidden boxes with unique, hand-carved rubber stamps inside. In response to the article's publication, two Americans began a U.S. version of letterboxing on a modest scale. From humble beginnings, the sport has morphed into a variety of different forms, including the high-tech version known as *Geocaching,* which uses GPS systems, websites, and e-mail alerts; the urban-literary version known as *bookcrossing;* and the minimalist *Where's George?* a website for tracking dollar bills. Within a decade, letterboxing, Geocaching, and other variants have exploded in popularity across the United States and, indeed, around the world (Kettlewell 2002).

The type of media available for transmitting ideas, including sound (beginning with telephones and radios), writing (beginning with hieroglyphics and other early forms of writing, and moving on to handwriting, printing presses and the Internet), and pictures (from cave paintings and petroglyphs, all the way up to photography, television, and film), also influences the rate of transmission and the geographic spread of creative output of all kinds. The advent of the Internet and sophisticated search tools such as Google enable people all over the world to participate as spectators in all manner of athletic competitions and artistic performances; to read books, newspapers, and other printed materials; and to see sights once available only to local readers or travelers. One can even play games via the Internet with people who live both near and far away. Various forms of media have become, in themselves, a source of knowledge and entertainment across much of the world.

Technological innovations such as the digital camera, cell phones that can take pictures and record video, and websites such as YouTube have dramatically transformed contemporary society. Some have called the phenomenon of information and opinion sharing via the Internet the **democratization of the world,** as anyone with the technical skill and equipment can upload their creative output to the Internet for viewing by potentially billions of people around the world. This has allowed many more people access to audiences for their creative work. Unfortunately, misinformation, half-truths, and rumors can be spread as rapidly as accurate information, and the anonymity of the Internet seems to promote scathing, often ill-informed criticisms and personal attacks by people who don't like what they've read, seen, or heard online. Sophisticated image editing software makes it possible to fool viewers. The Internet has also made it more difficult for people to protect their copyrighted intellectual property, whether prose, music, or visual arts.

How Important Is Cultural Context?

Can any aspect of creative expression or recreational activity be fully understood by an outsider to the culture? There is often much going on beneath the surface that only someone with a detailed knowledge of the history and symbolism involved would be able to grasp. It may be the rare observer, or even participant, who is fully aware of all the varied meanings and relationships that affect what is happening. That doesn't mean a person can't enjoy watching or taking part, even if she doesn't understand much of what is going on. But it does mean that the experience is fundamentally different for someone who is in the know, compared to someone who is not.

For example, watching a Texas A&M University football game can be a perplexing experience, as many of the behaviors of the locals are inexplicable to the casual observer. Why are all the A&M students standing up the whole time? Why are there male yell leaders instead of scantily clad female cheerleaders? Why are people chanting "Hullabaloo, caneck, caneck!" and what is the deal with those little white towels? For a similar perspective on the cultural context of extreme high school football in Odessa, Texas, journalist H. G. Bissinger's *Friday Night Lights* (2000) is a fascinating read.

Some scholars, while acknowledging that insiders have a different understanding than outsiders, nevertheless claim that some human creative expressions transcend culture and can be appreciated on their own, without any knowledge of their original cultural context. An example from the museum world may make this notion more concrete.

If you go to the Smithsonian's National Museum of African Art in Washington, D.C., you might see a pair of Bambara *chiwaras* on display. Imagine they are placed side-by-side on a plinth in a darkened room, with a spotlight illuminating their form. The caption might read "Male and female *chiwaras*, from the Bam-

bara people of Mali, West Africa." You will recognize that they represent some type of antelope. You can certainly admire their beauty, noting the graceful arc of the animals' necks, the technical skill of the carvers, the joining together of neck to body or head to neck, and the pleasing proportions of the mother and the baby on her back. You may note the signs of use—shiny areas of patina from the many hands that have grasped the objects, usually in the chest region and below the tail. You may be surprised by the anatomically correct male genitalia. Then you move on to the next piece, perhaps a Senufo fire-spitter mask or a Dogon *kanaga* mask. You marvel at the artistic vision and the technical talents of the makers of such pieces and appreciate them for their style and beauty. After a quick visit to the museum gift shop, you head across the Mall to the Smithsonian's National Museum of Natural History.

You enter the exhibit hall that features cultures of Africa. Immediately, your eyes and attention are drawn to another pair of chiwaras. There may be multiple sets of chiwaras of different styles on display, along with farming implements, examples of the crops that are raised, an interactive map of Mali, and lots of printed information about Bambara horticulture. But the chiwaras that have captured your attention are not static objects artfully posed with dramatic lighting. On the contrary, you are watching a videotape of a group of Bambara men and women dancing in a rural village in Mali. Two of the men are wearing chiwara headdresses, along with costumes that completely disguise their bodies. They carry sticks in their hands that elongate their arms and make them appear more like antelopes.

In addition to the sound track of music and conversation recorded at the dance itself, you can hear the film's narrator explaining the cultural meanings of *chiwara* to the Bambara people. You learn that chiwara is the half-man/half-antelope culture hero who came down from the skies and first taught humans how to grow crops. You learn that the chiwaras dance at the beginning of the farming season as the young men prepare the fields. Chiwaras represent the cooperation between the sun (men) and the Earth (women) in ensuring another successful year of providing food for the village.

You are watching the chiwaras being danced in their cultural context, with all of the accompanying sights and sounds. It's not the same as being there in person, in the 120°F heat, with the sun in your eyes, red dust in your throat, and the smell of cooking fires all around. And it certainly won't have the same meaning to a tourist who is watching as it does to the local villagers who participate. But the type of display offered in the National Museum of Natural History certainly provides a much better situating of the chiwaras in their cultural context than the same pieces viewed as art objects at the Museum of African Art. Learning about the cultural context of the chiwaras gives the observer much more insight into the meanings they hold for the people who make and use them.

Conformity, Style, and Creativity

In every cultural context, people will be limited in terms of what they can create by financial concerns and technical skill, as well as by local shared notions of what is aesthetically pleasing. Individual artists may have a lot of room to express their own creativity, or they may be fairly narrowly constrained to create their artwork in the style that is currently in favor and is expected. If the artwork is created to be sold, then it must have appeal to potential buyers. If it is to be used in a religious ceremony, there may be standards of size, color, and form that must be followed. Artists may be encouraged to come up with new ways of expressing what is important culturally: new styles, new designs, new methods, or new materials. Or, they may be expected to follow the traditions of the elders, recreating famous works from the past before they are allowed to branch out on their own. Of course, artists in any medium are influenced by what they have been exposed to and what others around them are producing. This is why it is often possible to recognize the general area and even the time period of a work of art, a piece of furniture, an item of clothing, and so on.

If you study African art history and contemporary African art, you can quickly learn to distinguish Kente cloth (Ghana) from mud cloth (bògòlanfini, from Mali), from Dutch/Indonesian lost-wax batik cloth (produced commercially and imported to West Africa), from woven raffia fiber cloth (from the Central African rain forest). Indonesian shadow puppets have a readily recognizable form. Australian Aboriginal artwork is very distinctive and dramatically different from that of Northwest Coast Indians, even though both incorporate many stylized representations of animals from the natural world. Such recognizable styles,

however, don't mean that people within the culture cannot express their individual creativity and stylistic improvisations. Expert artists, musicians, and athletes are recognized for their talent in every culture.

We turn now to a more detailed consideration of how anthropologists study music in human cultures.

MUSIC

Music is a human cultural universal. All over the world, people make many different types of music in many ways, including the use of the human voice as well as other parts of their bodies, natural objects, the environment itself, and musical instruments. Music is produced and listened to in a variety of contexts and for many different purposes; thus, the anthropological study of music is complex and far-reaching. In this section, I begin with a look at the different fields that study music and explain a few of the technical aspects of music; this is followed by an overview of contemporary theories about the origins of music and its relationship to language.

Academic Fields and Archives of Music and Culture

Many contemporary scholars view music and language as twin windows into the human brain and mind, and an explosion of research in recent years has revitalized the study of music from both evolutionary and cross-cultural perspectives. One emerging approach is **biomusicology,** the interdisciplinary study of music from a biological point of view. Biomusicology has three main branches. The first is **evolutionary musicology,** which includes music in nonhuman animal species, the origins and evolution of human music, and the search for cross-cultural universals in musical ability and processing in the brain. The second, **neuromusicology,** focuses more narrowly on the neural and cognitive aspects of music production and reception in the brain and the development of musical capacity and skill. The third, **comparative musicology,** is most like traditional ethnomusicology within cultural anthropology, looking at the functions and uses of music and searching for human universals in musical behavior.

Applied musicology is the name given to the study of the therapeutic uses of music in medical and psychological treatment, such as in trance healing in so-called traditional cultures, alternative healing within Western medicine, and the potential of music to influence people's behavior and affect learning.

Within cultural anthropology, the traditional subfield of **ethnomusicology** studies many different technical aspects of music, whether vocal or instrumental, including how it is produced, what types of musical instruments are used, whether the scale is diatonic or pentatonic, the culture of the musicians themselves, and so on. However, the major focus of ethnomusicology is the role of music in human life, including both the social and cultural contexts in which music is found and the symbolic meanings that people attach to the production and hearing of music.

Like other specialties within cultural anthropology, ethnomusicologists use ethnographic research methods such as interviews and participant-observation. They live among the people they are studying for long periods of time and learn the local language. Many often learn to perform music in the local style. There are a number of universities that offer specialized education in ethnomusicology. In addition to cultural anthropologists, the field of ethnomusicology incorporates contributions from archeologists and biological anthropologists, folklorists, historians, linguists, performers (composers, singers, dancers, and instrument-makers), cognitive scientists, and others.

Ethnomusicologists have also been at the forefront of efforts to archive and preserve the world's musical heritage. One of the best known examples is the Archives of Traditional Music at Indiana University, in Bloomington, Indiana. In addition to recordings of music from all over the world, dating back to early recordings on wax cylinders, the archives contain folktales, interviews, oral histories, videotapes, photographs, and manuscripts (Indiana University 2007).

Other significant music and spoken word archives include:

- The Smithsonian Institution's Folkways Recordings, whose mission statement says, in part: "We believe that musical and cultural diversity contributes to the vitality and quality of life throughout the world. Through the dissemination of audio recordings and educational materials we seek to strengthen people's engagement with their own cultural heritage and to enhance their awareness and appreciation of the cultural heritage of others" (Smithsonian Institution 2010).

- The U.S. Library of Congress' Archive of Folk Culture, which includes photographs, manuscripts, audio recordings and moving images. It includes material from all over the world dating back to the 1890s, with many resources on American folk songs and folk life (American Folklife Center 2009).

- The Irish Traditional Music Archive in Dublin; the focus is on Ireland and Irish settlements abroad, but the archives also have material from other regions of the world (ITMA 2010).

- The Archives of Traditional Music in Laos Project, at the Center for Southeast Asian Studies at Northern Illinois University (Lao Language and Culture Learning Resources 1997–2003).

- The Dartmouth Jewish Sound Archive, focusing on Jewish music and culture, dating back to 1904. The archives include Jewish humor, Yiddish folk songs, Israeli folk songs, cantorial performances, radio shows, documentaries, and more (Dartmouth Jewish Sound Archive 2010).

- The Vietnam Veterans Oral History and Folklore Project at Buffalo State College, State University of New York, focusing on the folklore of the Vietnam War, especially the songs written and sung by American troops in Vietnam. The project's founder, anthropologist and folklorist Lydia Fish (1993), writes: "Like all folklore, these songs served as a strategy for survival, as a means of unit bonding and definition, as entertainment. They also provided a means for the expression of protest, fear and frustration, of grief and of longing for home. All of the traditional themes of military folksong can be found in these songs: praise of the great leader, celebration of heroic deeds, laments for the death of comrades, disparagement of other units, and complaints about incompetent officers and vainglorious rear-echelon troops."

Making Music with Voice and Instruments

The human voice itself probably served as the first source of music, long before any musical instruments were created. In addition to speaking, humans can hum, sing in a variety of ways, whistle, and make all manner of sounds using combinations of our lungs, vocal cords, mouth, lips, tongue, teeth, and nose. In addition we can clap our hands, snap our fingers, stamp our feet, and slap our arms against our sides to make sounds.

When you add natural objects and man-made musical instruments to the repertoire, the creative possibilities are virtually infinite. Some music is intended to mimic the sounds of the natural world—running water, ocean waves, rain on the roof, the wind in the trees, and thunder, as well as the calls of different animals, especially birds. The melody or tune of a song can be provided either by voice alone **(a capella),** musical instruments alone, or a combination of voice and instruments. There may be only one person singing, or two, or ten, or a hundred, or even more. When more than one person sings at the same time, you can have harmony as well as multiple melodies, which greatly increases the complexity of the music. Humans can sing without words (vocalizing) or add lyrics to the music.

The Human Voice

The human voice can do more than simply speak, vocalize, or sing in the way most of us typically mean when we think of singing. A few ethnographic examples will illustrate the variety of ways humans use their voices. **Yodeling** is a type of singing in which one extended note is vocalized, but the pitch of the note is rapidly toggled back and forth between a lower register and a higher falsetto one. Yodeling is best known from the Swiss Alps, but it is also found in the musical traditions of foragers in Africa, in some areas of West/Central Asia, and in American country and bluegrass music.

Ululation refers to a specific type of human vocalization, a loud, high-pitched, wavering trill. It is produced by shaping the flow of air, using the uvula in the back of the throat along with rapid side-to-side movements of the tongue. It can express happiness, gratitude, grief, or anger. Ululation is found in many Arab cultures, where it is usually performed by women. It is used in some religious rituals in Ethiopia and India and is found in some eastern and southern African societies as well as in some Native American groups. A form of ululation is found among male Basque sheepherders in Spain, who use it as an expression of joy.

Overtone singing is also known as throat singing or harmonic singing. It involves producing more than one pitch or note (two to four) at the same time by manipulating the shape of the larynx, pharynx, and mouth to produce very resonant and harmonic music that includes both whistling and droning sounds. The most well-known throat singers are the Tuva people of Russia. Tuvan master throat singer, Vladimir Oidoopaa, says of the musical tradition: "Throat singing prevents our nation from dying, spiritually. To me, throat singing means power and philosophy, love for my nation, love for my people, to respect other opinions and to be tolerant of different religions" (*Tuva Throat Singers* 2007). Tuvan throat singing is practiced primarily by male herders, who seek out specific places in the mountains or near water where the best acoustics can be found.

Some scholars think that overtone singing began as an attempt to mimic natural sounds as part of an animistic religion. There are a number of different styles of overtone singing in Tuva, and variations can also be found in other groups in Mongolia, the Altai Republic, Tibet, and the Chukchi peninsula. It is found in a few groups in Europe, including the *canto a tenore* singers of Sardinia, Italy, who have been designated by UNESCO as an Intangible World Heritage creative endeavor. Overtone singing may be a capella or accompanied by instruments from the local tradition.

Eefing is a form of vocalization similar to modern day beat-boxing. It was first developed in rural Tennessee around the end of the nineteenth century as part of a rich tradition of Appalachian music and has been described as "a kind of hiccupping, rhythmic wheeze" that truly must be heard—words cannot do it justice. In 1969, Jimmie Riddle and Jackie Phelps were featured eefing on the first episode of *Hee Haw*, a U.S. country music variety TV show (Riddle and Phelps 1969). Using the vocal tract to mimic various sorts of percussion instruments is also found in India and China, but modern-day beat-boxing is usually associated with American hip-hop music of the 1970s and 1980s. Beat-boxing in its modern form was developed by early hip-hop musicians who used their lips, gums, teeth, and hands to mimic the sounds made by a drum machine, which was itself an electronic instrument intended to imitate the sounds of various percussion instruments. Beat-boxing has spread around the world and gained popularity far beyond the hip-hop music genre. The first world beat-boxing championship was held in 2005 in Leipzig, Germany, and the second in Berlin in 2009. Both drew entrants from many countries around the world.

Musical Instruments

In addition to the human voice and other body parts, people around the world make a variety of musical instruments, including wind instruments, which mimic the human voice in the way they produce sound, through the rush of air through confined spaces. These include goat and sheep horns, sea shells, flutes, recorders, harmonicas, kazoos, whistles, didgeridoos (Australian Aboriginal instruments), reed instruments (e.g., clarinets and saxophones) and brass instruments (e.g., bugles, trombones, and horns), accordions, and bagpipes.

Percussion involves hitting one thing against another and is often used as the main source of rhythm or beat in music. Percussion instruments range from the very simple, such as two stones or pieces of wood banged together, to the very complex, such as drums of all types, including xylophones, balaphones, and the gamelans of Indonesia. There may be one rhythm or multiple overlapping rhythms.

Rattles of various sorts are made by enclosing a number of small objects inside a larger container, and contribute to rhythm when they are shaken or tossed. Some rattles are worn around the ankles, so that they produce sound whenever a dancer stomps or shuffles his feet. Across West Africa, rattles are made out of hollow gourds covered with a loose woven net to which cowrie shells have been attached. These are turned and tossed to create a distinctive sound. Rasps make sounds as a stick or other object is dragged along a corrugated surface. Bells are similar to rattles but depend on the sound made when the outer wood or metal bell is struck by a clapper, producing reverberations.

Some musical instruments make sound through the vibration of strings. The string of a hunting bow can be plucked or strummed to produce sounds, and many different cultures have some version of a stringed instrument, including lyres, koras (in West Africa), harps, guitars, violins, cellos, pianos, and organs, as well as many others. Some musical instruments such as pipe organs or accordions produce sound through a combination of different mechanisms.

Bullroarers are a special example of a noise-maker or musical instrument. They consist of a small rectangular piece of wood, shaped into an aerofoil, and attached to a long cord. The cord is twisted, and the musician then swings the bullroarer in a wide circle above his head, creating a low vibrating tone often described as otherworldly or eerie. The sound of the bullroarer can be changed by varying the size of the circular path as well as the speed, and can be heard at great distances. The earliest archeological evidence of bullroarers comes from Ukraine, from sites dating to 19,000 years ago. Many scholars think bullroarers are much older and were one of the first musical instruments, along with simple flutes and hunting bows. Today, the bullroarer can be found on every continent.

Among traditional Australian Aborigines, the bullroarer often accompanied the didgeridoo and was said to embody the voice of the Rainbow Serpent, a primary Aboriginal religious figure. The Dogon of northern Mali use bullroarers at the start of their Sigui festival, which is held approximately every 60 years. For the Dogon, the sound of the bullroarer is the voice of the original ancestor. Among some Native American tribes, bullroarers were used in religious and healing ceremonies, and miniature ones where made as toys for children. In some cultural contexts, the bullroarer was used mostly for amusement.

Patterns in Music

The continuum of sound that can be produced by the human voice or musical instruments is typically divided into scales. Although in theory scales could have any number of notes, the vast majority of the world's music traditions use either the **diatonic scale,** which has seven notes, or the **pentatonic scale,** which has five notes.

The diatonic scale is also known as the heptatonic or *major scale*. It has seven notes per octave. Some music scholars think that the diatonic scale is a natural musical scale, one that, if not hard-wired into the human brain, is at least the default scale that humans will use if they aren't taught a different scale via their culture. The broadly defined Western musical tradition, including European classical music, is based on the diatonic scale, and modern piano keyboards use this scale. However, many music traditions around the world do not use the diatonic scale, calling into question the notion that it is a natural scale for humans.

Pentatonic scales, which use only five notes per octave, form the foundation of most Asian music and are used in the music of West Africa, African American spirituals, Afro-Caribbean styles, American Blues, jazz, and rock music. Much of the world's traditional folk music is based on the pentatonic scale, including Celtic and Scottish Highland music, some eastern and southern European folk music, and the music of the U.S. Appalachian Mountains region. In the classic science fiction film, *Close Encounters of the Third Kind,* the alien spaceship communicates using the five notes of the pentatonic scale.

All human music makes use of repetition and patterns, as well as modulations in the sound level (from soft to excruciatingly loud), the tempo (from very slow and stately to rapid and playful), and the style (from *legato,* with one note transitioning smoothly into another with no intervals of silence, to *staccato,* where each note is distinct and separate, with an interval of silence), and a number of other variables. Even before the addition of lyrics, these different aspects of music can be combined in an infinite variety of ways, allowing perhaps the fullest expression of human creativity.

Musical instruments range from simple mouth flutes and rattles made out of dried armadillos in Argentina (top left), to accordions, stringed instruments (India), and steam calliopes (bottom right), illustrated by a poster from England in 1874.

Music and Cultural Context

Music and language share many features. Every nonimpaired human has the ability to learn one or more languages. If exposed to one language beginning at birth, children will be fluent in that language by the age of two or three years. They pick it up from their surroundings, listening to and interacting with more competent speakers of the language. Receptive language, the ability to understand what others say, develops first. **Receptive language** refers to the ability to process the sounds that one hears in the environment and transform them into information within your brain ("A train is approaching," or "I've just stepped on the dog," or "Mom wants me to clean up my room"). The ability to speak—to turn one's own thoughts into speech for others to hear—develops more slowly, overlapping with continued growth in receptive language.

Which language a child learns to speak, whether Urdu or Serbo-Croatian or Tagalog or Nahuatl or English, will depend on the language spoken by those around him. There are definitely genetic underpinnings, hard-wiring in the brain if you will, to the ability to learn to understand and speak language. But a child of any biological heritage, if adopted into a family and community that speaks Portuguese, for example, will learn to understand and speak Portuguese, not any of the native languages of his or her biological parents and grandparents. Children can hear before they are born, of course, so newborns are already quite familiar with the sounds and rhythms of their mother's speech. Recent research has discovered that newborns cry with the melody patterns of their mother's native language—French babies cry with falling intonations, while German babies cry with rising intonations, mimicking the sound patterns of their mothers' respective languages (Mampe et al. 2009).

It is not yet clear whether music works in a similar fashion. Most children around the world are exposed to only one or a few types of music as they grow up. Children living in the highlands of Papua New Guinea aren't likely to encounter Mozart or Elton John or other piano music, just as children in Cleveland are seldom exposed to Tibetan chants, Tuvan throat singing, or the music of mariachi bands. But taste in music is not as predictable as which language you will speak, and it is much easier to develop an appreciation for a new and different form of music than it is to learn a new language. In addition, some children grow up literally surrounded by music—someone is always playing a drum or a guitar, or the stereo or radio always plays in the background. Other children grow up rarely hearing music in their homes and communities, or only hearing church music on Sundays. Some children are encouraged from an early age to produce music, either by singing or playing an instrument, while other children experience music primarily as a passive listener.

Which brings us to one of the conundrums of music. Some scholars have suggested that music functions primarily to convey emotion, while language conveys referential information. These scholars claim that all people should respond the same way emotionally to a particular piece of music. For example, they predict that people all over the world should find slow, sonorous music to be sad or depressing, and upbeat music with a lively tempo to be joyous. But this doesn't seem to be the case. Often, unfamiliar music just sounds discordant or disharmonious—like "so much noise or racket, so much screeching"—to the point that one may not even want to recognize it as music. Nor is it possible to translate one type of music into another, the way one can take the same thought or the same packet of information and express it in many different languages or translate it from one language to another. Music cannot be translated in this way. You typically can't take a sound or a tune written in one cultural context and somehow translate it into a different sound or tune that will have the same meaning or evoke the same emotional reaction in a different cultural context.

Music appears to be highly culturally specific, and our ability to recognize and enjoy music is heavily shaped by our cultural surroundings. If one is used to the pentatonic scale, then diatonic music may sound odd, and vice versa. If you grow up listening to classical music, then as an adult you may not find rap or Celtic folk music or West African drumming to fit your taste. Yet, even within a broadly similar culture, you can find many different styles and forms of music, and people can learn to enjoy widely disparate musical styles.

The same piece of music can also be performed in different contexts that evoke different interpretations and arouse different emotions. For example, many

North American Baby Boomers only know Italian composer Rossini's *William Tell Overture* because it was used as the theme song for a popular TV show, *The Lone Ranger*, that aired in the 1940s and 1950s. Likewise, opera fans who speak German and know the lyrics will have a very different reaction to Wagner's *Ride of the Valkyries* than those of us who knew it first from the 1957 cartoon *What's Opera Doc?* (where Elmer Fudd sings "Kill the wabbit! Kill the wabbit! Kill the wabbit!" in reference to Bugs Bunny) or those who associate it with a U.S. helicopter attack on a Vietnamese village from the 1979 film *Apocalypse Now.*

Music lyrics are easier to remember because of the melody, and vice versa, and once melody and lyrics are associated, it can be very difficult to disengage them. What Baby Boomer can hear the theme song to the film and TV show *M*A*S*H* without thinking of the opening words of the song's chorus: "Suicide is painless . . ."? Likewise, hearing the melody of "Happy Birthday" or the theme song to the TV show *Gilligan's Island* calls up the words to the songs for many North Americans. Most people know how long the *S.S. Minnow*'s tour was supposed to last.

The history of the song and its role in your life will affect what emotions it engenders. Music can become closely tied in our memories to specific times and places, and, like scent, can bring back a flood of memories every time a particularly meaningful song is heard. For me, "American Pie" by Don McLean is forever linked to high school art class (1971), while Linda Rondstadt's "Willin'" conjures up a summer archeology field school in the high desert of Nevada (1975). When I hear the sound of the *muezzin* calling the Islamic faithful to prayer, I am transported back to Mali, where I woke every morning before dawn to this beautiful sound. Devout Muslims will experience very different emotions and make different connections when they hear the same sound (perhaps occasionally including resignation that the night is over and it is time to get up and start the day already). For many people, hearing the music of their national anthem will stir certain emotions (whether patriotic or not), while hearing the music of someone else's national anthem will have no emotional impact whatsoever—they may not even recognize it as a national anthem.

Consider a song such as "Taps," played by a lone bugler to honor the death of a U.S. serviceman or woman. To many who hear it, the sound of the bugle is so evocative—sad, haunting, and final—but only because the listener knows the cultural context. It sounds even sadder if one has heard the story of its origin (most likely apocryphal) in which a Union Army captain at a Civil War battle rescued a mortally wounded soldier from the battlefield, only to discover that the soldier was from the Confederate side. In fact, the dead man turns out to be the captain's son, who had been studying music and had enlisted on the side of the Confederacy without his father's knowledge. According to this version of the song's creation myth, the notes to the song were found written on a piece of paper in the dead man's pocket. Many North Americans also know the words to the first verse: "Day is done, gone the sun, from the lake, from the hills, from the sky. All is well, safely rest, God is nigh." To someone unfamiliar with the tune, the lyrics, and the history of the song, would it sound as sad?

It is clear that some sounds evoke similar responses in those who hear them. The sound of a crying baby is upsetting to most people, especially to

It is unlikely that someone completely unfamiliar with the cultural context of the song "Taps" would find it as sad and haunting as any member of the U.S. military does.

women who have children of their own—they want to respond and get the baby to stop crying. This is probably a hard-wired, automatic response with a deep evolutionary history, as crying is the main way that infants of all mammalian species convey distress and elicit maternal care and protection. Many people find the call of peacocks disturbing, and one writer says of peacock music: "[it] resembles a chorus of large, healthy babies being thrown one by one off a cliff" (Conniff 2002:98). The howling of a pack of wolves may elicit fear in some people, while others find it thrilling, romantic, sad, or wistful. Thunder scares some individuals, while others welcome its familiar rumble as evidence that the gods are bowling up in heaven, and still others may be relieved to hear it, knowing that it heralds a much-needed rainstorm.

It is clear that music, like art, can be appreciated by people from outside the culture, but to fully understand the meaning of the music to the people within the culture, one must know the cultural context. At this point, we will shift gears and consider different theories about the origin and evolution of musical abilities in humans, as well as some of the archeological evidence for singing and making musical instruments among early humans.

Theories of the Origins of Music (and Language)

There are three major theories about the origins of music among humans, which can be stated as: (1) music came first, as an evolutionary adaptation, out of which language developed later; (2) language came first, as an evolutionary adaptation, and music developed out of language as a nonadaptive innovation; and (3) music and language both evolved out of a common precursor, *musilanguage.*

Music Came First

Charles Darwin was the first to suggest that human music evolved before language and might be evolutionarily adaptive. In 1871, he wrote:

> When we treat of sexual selection we shall see that primeval man, or rather some early progenitor of man, probably first used his voice in producing true musical cadences, that is in singing, as do some of the gibbon-apes at the present day; and we may conclude from a widely spread analogy, that this power would

have been especially exerted during the courtship of the sexes,—would have expressed various emotions, such as love, jealousy, triumph,—and would have served as a challenge to rivals. It is, therefore, probable that the imitation of musical cries by articulate sounds may have given rise to words expressive of various complex emotions. (Darwin 1871:88)

The view that musical ability came before language, and has been selected for during the course of human evolution, has recently been revived and promoted by Geoffrey Miller (2000). In this view, music comes first, as humans imitate the cries of other animals and birds and expand on the use of vocalizations by apes such as gibbons to identify and defend their territory. There are a number of other animals who produce music for territorial and reproductive purposes, including songbirds, of course, but also whales, gibbons, howler monkeys, and crickets. According to Miller, the ability to produce complex songs requires good health, coordination, and dexterity, as well as some level of intelligence, and may therefore serve as an honest marker of reproductive fitness for both sexes during mate selection, while composing original music requires both mental agility and creativity (Miller 2000). However, although music is used in courting rituals in many societies, this is by no means a culturally universal function of music.

British anthropologist Robin Dunbar points out that, in addition to its role in attracting and evaluating potential mates, music also can function to bind the members of a group together and create solidarity, as well as differentiate one group from another. It is this property of music, he claims, that was the primary selective force shaping musical ability as an evolutionary adaptation. Dunbar thinks that social grooming, found among many higher primates, was gradually replaced by wordless singing as a way of maintaining contact among members of the social group. Eventually, this wordless singing evolved into spoken language (Dunbar 1997).

Language Came First

The second perspective, championed by evolutionary psychologist Steven Pinker, is that language came first and music emerged out of a brain and vocal tract that had evolved to produce spoken language. In this view, music is an accidental by-product of the evolution of language (Pinker 1997). Pinker famously refers to music as *auditory cheesecake*—beautiful to produce and listen to, but hardly necessary for survival (just as cheesecake is wonderful to eat, but wasn't developed until long after humans evolved cravings for fat, sugar, and salt, as well as the cultural capacity to use fire for cooking and transforming food, and to domesticate and milk cows). Once music was accidentally discovered, it could then be endlessly shaped by cultural beliefs and technological innovations for religious, educational, and recreational purposes, as well as be put to use attracting mates and contributing to group solidarity.

Musilanguage / Hmmmmm Came First

The third perspective suggests that both music and language developed out of a common ancestor, referred to as **musilanguage** by Steven Brown (1999) and **Hmmmmm** by Steven Mithen (2006). According to this view, what came first was a system of communication that included both emotional content and referential (informational) meaning. This system then split into music, which emphasizes sound as emotional, and language, which emphasizes sound as referential (although both overlap). This theory accounts for the structural similarities between language and music, while also explaining why some aspects of the two phenomena are controlled by different regions of the brain. An impairment in language (whether due to inherited genetic differences or as a result of brain damage) may not necessarily result in an impairment in musical ability, and vice versa. For example, a person who stutters when speaking may not stutter when they sing; a person who is tone deaf and can't recognize different songs may have no trouble speaking several languages.

We will probably never know for sure whether the biocultural achievements of music and language developed at the same time or if one came first, and if so, which one. Likewise, it may never be clear whether they developed independently or have always been inextricably entwined, both in the mechanics and physiology of the brain/mind/body and in the cultural context of communication among members of a social group. Added to these mysteries is the issue of when musical instruments were first discovered and produced, such that their sounds could be added to the human voice in the production of music.

Archeological Evidence for the Origins of Singing and Musical Instruments

Origins of Singing

Singing, by itself, leaves no lasting impression in the archeological record of early humans. However, in 2008, Iegor Reznikoff put forth an intriguing hypothesis about a possible connection between Upper Paleolithic cave paintings and the use of the human voice. Reznikoff, a specialist in ancient music, studied the placement of Upper Paleolithic paintings on the walls and ceilings of a number of caves in France, as well as the acoustics of different regions of the cave. He found that the areas of the caves with the highest density of paintings were also those with the best acoustics for vocalizing, and that if one hums into some bends of the cave walls, the cave *answers back* with sounds like those of the animals depicted at that spot. Reznikoff believes that sound and music evolved long before spoken language, and carry such deep and fundamental meanings for humans that it is difficult to even talk about them. He thinks that the connections between the paintings and the resonance in the caves were deliberate—that people used their voices as sonar to explore dark caves, and deliberately sited the paintings in chambers with excellent acoustics (Reznikoff 2002, 2005, 2008). Bone flutes and whistles have also been found in some of the painted caves.

An outdoor site in France, Lac des Merveilles, includes a large flat stone, often referred to as an altar, covered with more than a thousand ancient pictures (mostly carved in the rocks). The surrounding area contains more than 36,000 such pictures. Today, when you sing or play musical instruments at the site, the surrounding mountains and lake echo the sounds in a remarkable way. Reznikoff suggests that early humans deliberately sought out spaces such as this for rituals and creative activity based in part on their acoustical properties.

If evidence for early use of the human voice for different purposes is elusive, what about evidence for the manufacture of musical instruments?

Origins of Musical Instruments

Finding early evidence of musical instruments is difficult, because artifacts made of bone, ivory, antler, or wood seldom survive for 40,000 years or longer in the archeological record. Several anthropologists are working on a long-term project to determine if Upper Paleolithic stone artifacts had a musical purpose in addition to their primary function as tools. Modern replicas of Upper Paleolithic blades are capable of producing acoustically pure sounds, including different notes when struck in different places. Retouching the blades through further chipping allows tuning of the tools to different pitches (Cross, Zubrow, and Cowan 2002).

The earliest potential archeological evidence of musical instruments comes in the form of *flutes* recovered from archeological sites in Europe. The oldest potential flute is a piece of a leg bone from a cave bear cub, found in the remains of a Neanderthal fireplace in a cave in Slovenia. The bone itself dates to the end of the Middle Paleolithic, about 43,000 years ago. Some scholars are convinced that it is part of a flute, with holes whose spacing corresponds to the diatonic scale. Others are skeptical, and doubt that the bone is a flute at all.

Clearer evidence comes from archeological sites in Germany dating to the beginning of the Upper Paleolithic, several thousand years later. Two flutes made of bones from swans were discovered in the 1990s. In 2004, anthropologist Nicholas Conard and his colleagues announced the discovery of a third flute, carefully carved from the ivory tusk of a woolly mammoth. The ivory flute is just over 7 inches long and has three finger holes. A variety of notes can be produced even from such a simple musical instrument, and a replica of the ivory flute made of wood produces tones in the pentatonic scale.

In 2009, Conard and his colleagues found a nearly complete bone flute and three fragmentary ivory flutes from nearby archeological sites in Germany dating to the same time period, the beginning of the Upper Paleolithic. The best preserved is the bone flute, made from the radius (lower arm bone) of a griffin vulture. This flute is over 8 inches long, with five carved finger holes. According to Conard and colleagues:

> We can now conclude that music played an important role in Aurignacian life in the Ach and Lone valleys of southwestern Germany. Most of these flutes are from archeological contexts containing an abundance of organic and lithic artefacts, hunted fauna, and burnt bone. This evidence suggests that the inhabitants of the sites played these musical instruments in diverse social and cultural contexts. . . . The flutes . . . demonstrate that a musical tradition existed in the cultural repertoire of the Aurignacian at the time modern humans settled in the Upper Danube region more than 35,000 calendar years ago. (Conard, Malina, and Münzel 2009:740)

We will probably never have a detailed picture of the early development of human music-making capabilities. But the tantalizing archeological evidence, and the fact that music today is a human universal serving a great range of functions, combine to make it clear that music is both an ancient and an essential part of human existence.

Functions of Music

> Be it a song to the child in its mother's womb, sounds made by the woman during the moment of birth, the song to lull the child to sleep, working songs at home or in the fields, music for dance, war songs, trumpet voluntaries for retreat or those for victory, laments for departure or death, healing songs, chants of prayer or praise addressed to the Spirits and to the Invisible World, all these demonstrate that the *power* of sound and also music are used functionally with a precise intention in order to obtain a specific effect. (Reznikoff 2005:2.3)

Music to Calm, Comfort, and Heal

Even before a baby is born, it is surrounded by the sounds of its mother's heartbeat, the blood rushing through her arteries and veins, and the sound of her voice. Newborns, given the choice of their own mother's voice and another woman's voice, will preferentially turn toward their own mother. In most cultures, a special musical speech known as **motherese** is used by mothers and other females to engage babies in social interaction. While not a cultural universal, motherese (known formally as Infant- or Child-Directed Speech) is common enough around the world to suggest that human babies are especially interested in its sounds—a higher pitch, elongated syllables, more emphasis on some words, rhythmic timing, and a cooing intonation that implies affection and caring. For example, research has shown that babies growing up in an all-English-speaking environment will look at and listen longer to a woman when she speaks Japanese motherese than when she speaks Japanese adult-directed language. Motherese is more musical than adult-directed speech, and various researchers have suggested that it helps create affective bonds between mother and baby, helps the child learn to speak, and helps with general cognitive development. Malloch and Trevarthen's edited volume *Communicative Musicality* (2008) suggests that all human communication is based on the musical rhythms and patterns of speech and gesture used by mothers interacting with their children.

Music has the ability to calm and comfort someone who is angry, scared, upset, or lonely and may be used in a number of different contexts, such as at the dentist's office, in commercial businesses, and in structured music therapy sessions. Music is an integral part of many healing traditions around the world, where it is used to promote relaxation and as an aid to entering a trance state, either on the part of the healer, the patient, or both. According to the American Music Therapy Association (1998–2010), "Music therapy interventions can be designed to promote wellness, manage stress, alleviate pain, express feelings, enhance memory, improve communication, and promote physical rehabilitation." Some surgeons play music while they operate, and the use of music in the operating room has been found to reduce pain and decrease the need for sedation in some patients. Many individuals deliberately use music to alter their moods, choosing pieces they know will have the particular desired effect on their emotional state. Some farmers even claim that their cows produce more milk when they pipe pleasant music into the barn.

Music in Religion

Music plays a significant role in many spiritual and religious activities around the world. It is often used as a way to call the faithful to gather together, as a form of worship in and of itself, and as a way to enhance group solidarity based on common religious beliefs. So-called whirling dervishes are members of the Sufi tradition within Islam. Sufi is the inner, mystical dimension of Islam, and dervishes turn counterclockwise (both individually and in a circle) accompanied by music as a form of worship and remembrance of God. Many Western Christian churches are designed specifically to enhance the acoustics of the music, whether that comes in the form of a pipe organ, a large choir, a soloist, or the singing of hymns by everyone in the congregation. In a number of religious traditions, prayers are sung rather than spoken. Anthropologist Luke Lassiter and colleagues have studied the role that Christian hymns, sung in Kiowa, play in the maintenance of tribal identity and culture among the contemporary Kiowa of Oklahoma (Lassiter, Ellis, and Kotay 2002).

Music to Make Work Easier

In a variety of cultural contexts, people use music to make work easier. Music can be used to help organize the rhythm of collaborative work, so that a group of people can more easily coordinate the timing of their movements. Work songs include agrarian songs for working the land, herding songs to help control and move the animals, sea shanties, mining songs, quarrying/rock busting songs, railroad-tie laying songs, and so forth. African American slaves often sang while they worked in the fields, both for entertainment and to help ease the workload. Some African American spirituals were used to transmit coded information about the Underground Railway, including routes to freedom as well as schedules for transport, and to announce secret meetings. In Mali, as in most cultures where women spend several hours a day pounding or grinding grain into flour, there is a rich tradition of work songs that use the sounds of the work itself for percussion. Even in modern postindustrial office contexts, many people find that background music can relieve stress, help concentration, and make the time go by faster, especially if the work is repetitive and otherwise boring.

Music as Political Statement or Protest

Music has long been used as a form of protest by those with less power, aimed at those who oppress them. The lyrics of protest music may be quite explicit, or the rebellious or revolutionary intent may be disguised in language and imagery that only those who are initiated can recognize. Many themes that are too dangerous or unpopular to be expressed openly are tolerated when presented in musical form. Many different political movements around the world have used music to inspire people to join their cause and to express their viewpoint, from "This Land Is Your Land" (Woody Guthrie) and "Get Up, Stand Up" (The Wailers) to "Southern Man" (Neil Young) and "American Idiot" (Green Day). The ethnographic research literature on protest songs is particularly rich, including recent books by Courtney Brown (2007) and Hardeep Phull (2008).

Music as a Marker of Group Membership and Status

One of the most powerful functions of music is as a marker of group membership. Those who know, enjoy, and/or perform the same type of music may be united by their political views, their age, their educational level, their geographic origin, their religion, or their social status. In North American culture, it has long been a pattern for teenagers to rebel against the music of their parents' generation as a way of creating a new and different niche for themselves. Likewise, different groups may adopt certain musical genres as part of their group identity—there is a reason that many National Public Radio stations play mostly classical music, even though not all of their highly educated, middle- and upper-class listeners are fans. In some social circles, to admit that one doesn't *like* classical music is unthinkable. Expressing an appreciation for traditional folk music from exotic locales, or for

world music and *avant-garde* music, is seen by some as a marker of worldly sophistication; some people associate North American country music with rednecks (poorly educated people who make their living performing manual labor outdoors) and poverty.

Music serves as a powerful marker of ethnic identity, especially in circumstances where other aspects of culture, such as religion, may be oppressed by more powerful political forces. Ethnomusicologist Theodore Levin traveled across Central Asia, recording the many different varieties of music, along with musicians' experiences both during and after Soviet domination of the region. His ethnography shows the role of music in maintaining cultural identity, religious practices, and the healing arts (Levin 1999).

Even when people have migrated far from their homelands, or have transferred their primary loyalty from ethnicity to nationalist sentiments, music and

Music often serves as a marker of group membership, whether by nationality or ethnicity, by class, or by age. Left: Swiss Alpenhorns being played at a "National Day of Switzerland" festival in 2008. Bottom left: a Ukrainian ethnic music band performing in a restaurant. Bottom right: a Bedouin bagpiper in Jordan.

dance can serve as markers of ethnic or national heritage. At heritage festivals, in addition to traditional foods and crafts, you can be sure to find traditional music and dance, and the participants often dress in traditional clothing as well. Such links to the past during heritage festivals may persist long after most other aspects of culture have disappeared in daily life.

Music also serves as a marker of the historical times in which one lives. Members of any generation will share many of same songs, from those learned in nursery school or from popular television shows to those that were popular during one's teens and early adulthood. Some songs appear only briefly on the world stage, while others last for centuries. The English nursery rhymes and schoolyard songs "See Saw Marjorie Daw" and "Ring Around the Rosie" date back more than a century. They can still be heard on North American, British, and Irish playgrounds (and probably wherever English-speaking people have migrated).

Music as Mating Ritual

As mentioned earlier, some scholars have suggested that music evolved as a way to advertise reproductive fitness and attract mates. Certainly music and dance play an important role in many activities engaged in by young, unmarried males and females, who may be using these activities as a way to judge the fitness of potential mates. Among the Wodaabe Fulani of Niger, the *gerewol* ritual is a striking example. It is constructed along the same lines as a Miss America pageant, with a focus on beauty, artificial smiles, exaggerated eye movements, face makeup, lining up to perform, and a panel of judges. However, it is young Wodaabe *men* who line up in front of the women of the tribe, trying to seduce the women with the men's beauty, especially the power of their eyes and white teeth. Particularly handsome men will end up with more wives as well as more extramarital opportunities to reproduce.

In a similar vein, Lee Cronk and colleagues' research in Jamaica using motion-capture photography has shown that people asked to judge anonymous dancers rate the dancers with more symmetrical bodies and more coordinated movements as being more attractive (Brown et al. 2005). Public dancing can serve as a way for potential marriage partners to meet and evaluate each other. Explicitly sexualized dancing is frowned upon in some cultures because of the po-

tential for arousing inappropriate passions, and dancing is forbidden altogether in some religious belief systems for the same reason.

Culture and Soundscapes

One of the best known ethnomusicologists is Steven Feld, who has worked extensively with the Kaluli people who live near Mt. Bosavi in Papua New Guinea. Feld describes how the Kaluli use their own voices to interact with the sounds of their rain forest environment to create multiple layers of overlapping sound that fade in and out, overlap, and interlock (Feld 1990). Feld has pioneered the use of **soundscape** recordings and compositions to make people more aware of the auditory background of life in different cultural settings. In addition to producing composite recordings of the Kaluli talking and singing as they work in the forest, in recent years Feld has been studying how people, animals, and bells interact in the acoustic ecology of village and urban life. Jim Cummings writes of Feld's work:

> He's made some interesting discoveries, such as a church in Finland with a large bell that has the same resonant decay time as its ancient organ, and the centuries-old interactions between a flock of birds living in a town square in Norway, and the ringing of the church bells there. He also gives sonic illustration to the ethnographic research of others: on Crete, shepherds know every animal by the sound of its individual bell, and the bells of each flock are tuned by the bellmakers to provide a harmonious timbre. (Cummings 2006)

Feld has also begun work on soundscapes in Ghana and founded a record label, VoxLox, to produce recordings that reflect the acoustic ecology of various regions of the world (Documentary Media Arts 2010).

Music as Timekeeper or Herald

In many cultural contexts, specific music is played to herald the beginning of an activity. Since the music is *always* played in this context, and sometimes *only* played in this context, it serves as a musical announcement to all those listening. It may be a battle cry or trumpet blare to rally the troops and begin the charge, or the organist playing "Here Comes the Bride" to announce the bride as she walks down the aisle in a church wedding. U.S. major league baseball games begin with the playing of the national anthem. The call of the muezzin throughout the Islamic world tells listeners that it is time to pray. The volunteer fire-house sounds the alarm when a call for help comes in, and some communities have loud sirens to announce the approach of dangerous weather. A simple drumroll can also serve the purpose of announcing the imminent beginning of something dramatic and special, and bells and whistles have long been used to mark the beginning and end of the workday.

Music as Entertainment

When you are free to listen to whatever music you enjoy, then music can serve purely as entertainment. Many people enjoy singing or playing musical instruments, either alone or with others, in front of an audience, or just among friends. Music can provide many pleasurable hours of entertainment, in many different formats. Music is often accompanied by dance, and many people enjoy the rhythmic motions of dancing—again, whether alone, with a partner, or in a group, such as traditional circular folk dancing or square dancing or as part of wedding celebrations around the world.

In the introduction, a number of different aspects of recreational activities were introduced, including the distinction between solitary and group experiences, public versus private performance, participant versus observer, and amateur versus skilled. One clear difference distinguishes the cultural experience of music among college students in the United States versus villagers in Mali (Eyre 2000). In the United States, most people are passive listeners, enjoying music that has been professionally produced by experts. People listen via the radio or television, or on music players of various kinds (tape players, CD players, MP3 players such as iPods, etc.). Live music performances are relatively rare. To hear live music you may have to seek it out, and pay to sit in the audience. Many people love music but seldom participate in its production, because they aren't interested, don't have the talent, or don't have the opportunity. Some may rue this lack of opportunity for amateurs to make their own music, but most people in the United States just assume that music production is best left to the professionals and that most of the enjoyment comes from listening.

In Mali, in addition to professional musicians and recorded music, there are scores of people who make music just for themselves, just for the fun of it. Almost every market or rural village will have drummers, singers, and kora players, and many people will be involved in making music for all sorts of occasions, or for no occasion at all. Little children are exposed to music almost continually from before they are born and are welcome to dance, drum, sing, and otherwise participate at most celebratory events. A typical Bambara baby will have spent many hours on his mother's back while she dances, so that the rhythms and the sounds of the culture become part of his very being.

Music Used to Annoy or Harm

Counting on the knowledge that not everyone shares the same musical taste, some people use music deliberately to annoy others. In the United States, a number of businesses have used classical music to drive away urban teenagers from places where they are prone to loiter—whether at the mall, the library parking lot after closing time, or outside a convenience store.

In the classic Woody Allen film *Sleeper* (1973), an historian shows Miles Monroe (who has been cryogenically frozen and then revived 200 years in the future) a videotape of Howard Cosell, a famous twentieth-century sportscaster who had a distinctive voice and style of speaking. The historian says, "We have a theory, that whenever a citizen committed a crime against the state, they were forced to watch this." Miles replies, "Yes, that's exactly what that was." Although played for laughs at the time, the idea of using the human voice and/or music as a means of torture has become a reality.

Several sources trace the U.S. military's use of music for torture to 1989, when U.S. troops in Panama broadcast hard-rock music and *The Howard Stern Show* loudly and continuously for several days outside the Vatican's embassy in Panama, where exiled president Manuel Noriega had taken refuge. They stopped after complaints from the embassy staff, and Noriega eventually surrendered. In Iraq, U.S. military personnel have used exposure to unrelenting loud music as one method of softening *detainees* for interrogation:

> The United States' Psychological Operations Company (Psy Ops) said the aim was to break a prisoner's resistance through sleep deprivation and playing music that was culturally offensive to them. One Psy Ops sergeant told *Newsweek* magazine "These people haven't heard heavy metal. They can't take it. If you

play it for 24 hours, your brain and body functions start to slide, your train of thought slows down, and your will is broken. That's when we come in and talk to them." (BBC News 2003)

The sergeant also reported that music by the metal bands Drowning Pool and Metallica, and the theme songs to the children's TV shows *Barney* and *Sesame Street* were favorites for softening recalcitrant prisoners. Suzanne Cusick has analyzed the use of sound/music as torture on the urban battlefield in Iraq as well as at Abu Ghraib prison and Guantanamo Bay (Cusick 2006). Such uses of music have been criticized by Amnesty International as torture.

Music and Technological Change

In the beginning, people perceived music as it was produced, hearing it via their ears, as well as feeling it bodily through the vibrations of the sound waves. You had to be within shouting distance of the performers in order to hear the music. Once the music stopped, that was it. It might linger on in memory, but if one wanted to hear it again, it had to be produced again. Conditions would be slightly different each time the music was produced, so variations and modifications were continually made, whether intentional or not.

Two technological revolutions altered forever the way humans experience music. The first was the ability to broadcast live music performances to larger audiences through amplifiers and then to even more distant people and places through radio, and eventually through television, video feeds, and the Internet, using satellite technology. With the invention of transmission technology, people far from the source could listen along, and sometimes watch as well, with the local audience. The second technological revolution was the ability to record sound and images in various formats that could be accessed and played again and again by people distant both in space and in time. There isn't room here for even a brief history of the evolution of recording technology, but a few relevant issues relating to music and culture will be explored.

The Cultural Impact of Recording Technology

Recording anything—an interview, a song, a poem, a speech, a play—freezes the performance in time. With every playback, the performance is the same as it was originally (depending on the quality of the recording and playback equipment). Many people, then, can hear exactly the same recording and can hear it many times, making it more difficult for minor variations and changes to creep in. Some people see this as a good thing—and it is amazing to be able to hear music recordings made in the 1890s; or astronaut Neil Armstrong saying, "Houston, *Tranquility Base* here. The *Eagle* has landed," just as he did originally on the lunar surface in 1969; or the Reverend Martin Luther King, Jr., saying, "I have a dream."

However, others see recording as potentially stifling creativity. When people go to a concert of their favorite artists, they want to hear their favorite songs as they sound on the album, which often isn't possible given the use of all sort of technological tricks to produce the sound one hears on a studio recording. For this reason, some bands are never successful at performing in public—they sound awful in live performances, compared to their studio music. The advent of the songwriter-singer has also made it more likely that only one singer or band will record a song. In the early decades of the twentieth century, American songwriters would write songs, and then multiple artists would record them. That meant a variety of different arrangements of a song might be recorded around the same time, as different singers covered the same song. Today, we mostly hear only one version of a song, and people have become less tolerant of different versions.

Portability and Privatization of the Listening Experience

Another major cultural change relates to the portability of broadcast and recorded music. Radios in the United States used to be quite large and cumbersome, as well as relatively expensive, and were found only in the living rooms of families who could afford them. The development of the car radio in the 1920s and the transistor radio in 1947 made radio music much more portable and financially available to many more families. The receiver still broadcast the music into the general environment, so that everyone in the vicinity was able to (or had to) listen to it. Small transistor radios had limited capacity for increasing the volume, however, so only those close to the radio could listen. On a parallel track, home-based systems for playing recorded music began with gramophones, then record players playing 45 and 78 rpm records, and eventually 33 1/3 rpm vinyl albums. Every U.S. teenager had (or wanted) a large, cumbersome stereo system with powerful speakers and stacks of heavy albums.

The development of giant radio/tape cassette *boom boxes* in the 1970s, with larger and more powerful speakers, meant that people could travel around with their musical choices playing at high volume. This was great for a party on the beach, but tended to annoy people in circumstances where it wasn't possible to get away from the sound, especially when others didn't share the boom box owner's taste in music. In such contexts, music could be used as a marker of class, ethnicity, or age, and the foisting of one's music onto others who didn't appreciate it was an overt form of aggression.

A classic scene from the movie *Star Trek IV: The Voyage Home* shows Mr. Spock riding a bus in San Francisco in 1986. A punk rocker is playing a loud, annoying song on his boom box, to the chagrin of other passengers. Mr. Spock walks over and administers a Vulcan nerve pinch, rendering the punk unconscious, and then turns off the music. The other bus passengers (and the movie audience) applaud wildly. This cultural phenomenon of *assault by boom box* faded away with the development of personal music players with earphones that allow each person to listen to music without disturbing those around them.

Personal stereos such as the SONY Walkman, which played cassette tapes, appeared in the late 1970s and by the late 1990s had been replaced by music in compact disk, mini-disk, and DAT formats. The first digital music players using the MP3 format came on the market in the late 1990s, using flash drives. The first iPod was released in the fall of 2001, with continual improvements to song capacity, user interface, battery life, and various other features. Today, iPods corner the MP3 digital music market, and some people now listen to music for many hours a day and easily swap music among friends, but the listening experience remains essentially an individual one.

The evolution of music technology and the Internet have allowed many more people to experience music. Personal stereos are now part of portable devices that combine photography, video, Internet connections, and hundreds of specific applications (apps) that can do everything from work as a carpenter's level to finding the closest pizza parlor. Sites such as YouTube allow anyone to upload and share the music they have written and/or performed, making a much wider array of music available worldwide. At the same time, some people mourn the changing role of music in the world. No longer an activity that many people participate in, either in terms of creating and/or performing, no longer a whole body experience (as the music is piped directly into one's ears), and no longer a shared activity, music is becoming more and more a passive, private, and strictly aural listening experience.

Music in Your Mind

Another change that seems to have accompanied the rise of recorded music and personal music players has been the decline of people relying on their memories to provide a musical sound track for their lives. In her book *Thinking in Pictures*, Temple Grandin discusses human variation in the ability to visualize scenes and replay videos inside one's head (Grandin 1996). This talent exists along a continuum—some people are very good at it, while others can't do it at all, and many who can't do it are not even aware that this talent exists. Some of this variation in the ability to think in pictures may be genetic, but the cultural context of learning how to see and think about the world probably contributes significantly as well. Even people who don't have a genetic predisposition to think this way may be able to learn it.

A similar phenomenon may apply to memory-based audio sound tracks. I grew up listening to music mostly via albums on stereo systems. I listened to the same albums over and over and have memorized the melodies and the lyrics to thousands of songs, as well as the order of songs on albums. To this day, whenever I want, I can listen to John Denver, or the Decemberists, or Willie Nelson, in my head. I don't need a

Opposite page: Listening to music can be a voluntary, group experience, as shown in the top row of the audience at a rock concert (left) and the Decemberists (one of the author's favorite groups) playing at Millennium Park in Chicago in 2007. Middle: anyone walking by will hear the music being played by the busker with his didgeridoo in Barcelona, Spain. Likewise, anyone in the vicinity will hear the music coming from the boom box on the child's shoulder. Bottom: in contrast, listening to music with an MP3 player is essentially a solitary experience. Even when several people gather in the same vicinity, they are likely to be listening to different songs.

radio or an iPod to hear whatever music I want to hear, I just turn on the sound track in my head, and the songs from each album play in order (this talent is known as audiation, the "ability to hear music in one's head, much as he might see a picture in his mind's eye" [Sforza 2006:142]).

Through conversations with students over the years, I have discovered that many people are not able to replay music from memory inside their mind, and some are not even aware that this talent exists. I wonder if the ubiquitous use of radios and portable music players has resulted in people losing, or never developing, the ability to hear music playing in their head from memory. Digitized songs can be played in any order, and songs from one album or artist can be interspersed with songs from other albums and artists— young people don't necessarily listen to an entire album of songs by the same person, in the same order, anymore. Times change, and culture and human experience change along with it.

I turn now to another set of activities and behaviors that humans use to amuse themselves and express their creativity.

SPORTS, GAMES, PLAY, AND OTHER LEISURE-TIME ACTIVITIES

Around the world, in addition to the daily tasks of production and reproduction, people have created an amazing variety of ways to have fun, to enjoy themselves, and to entertain others. In this section, we explore some of the anthropological insights that have come from the study of these aspects of human behavior.

Because recreational activities encompass so many different types of behavior, and because they often have other functions in addition to providing fun, it isn't easy to define exactly what is under study. In many cases, it isn't possible to make distinctions that are valid across all cultural contexts among play, games, leisure, recreation, fun, physical education, arts and crafts, hobbies, and sports. Kendall Blanchard, a sports anthropologist, writes:

> One of the conceptual problems that the anthropology of sport must contend with is the fact that some of

its key terms are without equivalents in many languages. Some groups do not make a clear distinction between work and play, different forms of games, or sport and ritual. Also, physically combative sports are simply nonexistent in some societies (Sipes, 1973:69). (Blanchard 1995:30–31)

One way to grapple with all of the variety is to ask a series of questions about the activity under consideration and how it fits into the broader cultural context.

Different Aspects of Sports and Games

How Organized Is the Activity?

Many scholars distinguish between *child's play* (or adults' *horsing around*) and formal games or sports activities. If there are no specific rules or regulations, no specific goals to achieve or points to score, and no one keeping track of the outcome, then the activity is fundamentally different from an organized, rule-bound recreational activity. Unstructured play is usually voluntary and spontaneous and done purely for the pleasure of engaging in the activity. Structured play can range from simple games that involve only a few rules, with little riding on the outcome, to the incredibly complex world of professional sports, where every aspect of the activity is tightly rule-bound and both status and financial rewards—fame and fortune—hinge on winning. Some scholars try to craft definitions that would break this continuum up into clear conceptual categories, but the same game, such as football, can be found at every point along the continuum from a casual game of touch football among friends to the Super Bowl.

How Competitive Is the Activity?

One theoretical perspective within the anthropology of sports claims that all humans are competitive by nature and that in order to qualify as a game or sport, competition must be an integral part of the activity. However, almost every game, sport, hobby, or other leisure-time activity can be pursued in either a competitive or a noncompetitive fashion. The degree of competitiveness can range from a little friendly competition to fierce, cut-throat striving that leads to cheating and/or sabotage of one's opponent, or the application of pressure to throw the results one way or the other in order to benefit those who have wagered valuable resources on the outcome. Pie-baking contests at the county fair can be highly competitive, and NASCAR racing always is, while working on a model-train set or getting together with friends to knit hats for newborns are fundamentally noncompetitive activities. Some people play Scrabble just for fun and don't bother to keep score, but there are also professional Scrabble players who take tournament play very seriously (Fatsis 2002).

What Skills Are Required to Participate and Excel?

Recreational activities can be classified according to those that require attributes of body size and shape, physical skills, mental skills, attributes of character, elements of chance, or some combination of two or more. Each of these can be further subdivided for analysis.

Different types of sports call for different body types, both in terms of size and shape. Both preselection and training will affect the physical characteristics of athletes, and it isn't always easy to distinguish which aspects are the result of preselection and which are of training. If you want to be a professional jockey and ride racehorses for a living, you must be relatively small but disproportionately strong for your height and weight. If you want to compete in sports involving physical exertion, but aren't tall enough to be a basketball player or big enough to be a football player, you may become a wrestler. Wrestling is a sport in which opponents are matched by weight, and where being short, with relatively long arms and great upper body strength, is the best combination. However, not everyone who excels in a sport will have the stereotypical body size and shape. In 2009, the 6′5″ Jamaican sprinter Usain Bolt demolished the theory that competitive sprinters can't be tall, just as Mugsy Bogues (5′3″) and Spud Webb (5′7″) had earlier shown that short men could become professional basketball players.

Sheer size and bulk can be advantageous in some sports, such as football and sumo wrestling, but detrimental in others, such as ballet dancing or kayak racing. Female gymnasts at the height of their abilities are almost all prepubertal, as once a girl goes through puberty and develops breasts and broader hips, her body shape becomes less suited to gymnastics. However, the strenuous training gymnasts go through reduces a female's body fat to such low levels that puberty may be delayed until the mid- or late teens. Other activities, such as swimming and running, can be continued into old age, and a number of sports have

been modified to accommodate people in wheelchairs, including Murderball, which is a form of full-contact rugby played by people in wheelchairs who have paraplegia (see the documentary of the same name, by Rubin and Shapiro 2005).

A number of recreational activities, whether classified as play, games, sports, or something else, require specific types of strength, instead of, or in addition to, the right body size and shape. Through their training, competitive swimmers develop powerful neck and shoulder muscles, while sprinters are more likely to have strong legs and buttocks. The degree of physical strength required, and which muscle groups are important, vary along a continuum, and some competitive activities require relatively little strength. In addition to strength, per se, some sports involve more physical exertion than others, or in different patterns. Some critics have argued that golf is not a *real sport* because, while it involves strength and skill, little sustained physical exertion is required, compared to sports such as basketball or swimming. There are also differences between sports that require brief but strenuous outputs of strength, such as sprinting, shot-putting, or weight lifting, and those that require more sustained effort, more endurance, such as marathon running, rowing, or decathlons.

For some recreational activities, coordination, dexterity, and/or speed are more important than size, shape, or strength. We can further subdivide coordination into gross motor skills versus fine motor skills. Football and polo on horseback require excellent gross motor skills, including hand-eye coordination. Making fine jewelry, tatting (making lace), or creating miniatures of any kind require very specific fine motor skills. For anyone who pursues recreational activities seriously, *developing* the required strength, speed, and coordination may require much more time than will actually be spent *participating* in the activity.

While most people think of *sports* as primarily involving physical skills, a number of sports, games, and other types of recreational activity require mental skills as well. To be successful in many sports you must be intelligent in a general sense, as well as knowledgeable about specific topics. Knowing the rules is important in any rule-governed activity. Being able to learn, remember, and apply different types of strategies is another specific mental skill that is required for competitive play, whether that means learning complex football plays or classic chess openings. The ability to imagine potential outcomes in the future is another type of mental skill that is useful in a number of activities. Finally, the ability to think outside the box, which we might call *mental dexterity*, may give a person or a team a significant advantage over opponents.

In addition to physical prowess and cognitive skills, many recreational activities rely on specific personality traits for success, most notably courage and character. High-risk sports such as skydiving, ocean surfing, bull riding, and rock climbing require a strong sense of adventure, a willingness to take risks, and both physical and mental courage. Even if a person has the requisite strength and physical skills, if she can't take that final step to put her life at stake, then she can't engage in the activity or compete at a high level of skill.

In addition to their courage, participants may be admired for their powers of concentration—their steely nerves in the face of stiff competition—even if the situation isn't physically risky. Examples might include the focus on the face of a gymnast, diver, or spelling-bee entrant as he prepares to compete. In some situations, the ability to keep a calm external demeanor under stress is an important key to success, such as the expressionless face and bluffing required in poker so as not to give away the value of one's hand. And of course, some sports and recreational activities involve both physical courage and mental control, such as the cliff diving of Acapulco, where divers must time their dives precisely to match the waves crashing on the rocks below.

For many audience members, the enjoyment of watching the sport comes as much from watching the participants face down their fears as from watching them perform athletically. It also gives audience members who have neither the skills nor the courage to participate the opportunity to experience the thrill vicariously, from a place of safety and comfort. Those who actually participate may be admired as much for their courage and focus as for their athletic abilities. For example, in Roman gladiatorial contests, audience members would reward a particularly brave loser by recommending that he be allowed to survive. Ice skaters who fall on the ice, but get back up and continue, without showing any signs of pain or disappointment, are greatly admired by the audience.

Many recreational pastimes involve an element of chance, whether instead of or in addition to physical skills, mental skills, and character traits. The chance factor *levels the playing field* among those of varying skill levels, and adds an element of surprise to whatever endeavor is being pursued. Any games that involve throwing dice, dealing cards, randomly choosing sides or teammates, or the weather during competition, depend on chance. Given that many games and sports activities contain elements of religious ritual, the addition of chance to the mix also allows for supernatural entreaties and interventions in the outcome.

In some games, chance is the only relevant variable affecting the outcome—skill level doesn't matter. The North American children's card game War is an example. Some card games, such as bridge, rely on one part chance—how the cards are dealt—and two parts skill and strategy in bidding and playing the cards. Board games that involve dice are based mostly on chance, although there are also strategies to pursue when playing Monopoly, for example. Many people think they can manipulate the outcome of how the dice land, or which cards are dealt, through magical or supernatural means.

Some types of gambling are based purely on chance, such as simple slot machines. Others are based on a combination of chance and skill or knowledge, such as betting on the outcome of sports games—not just who wins, but what the point spread is, or who is chosen most valuable player.

Potential for Injury or Death

A final aspect of sports behavior that can be studied anthropologically is the potential for injury, especially the spilling of blood, or death. Some sports, even highly competitive ones, do not involve the participants touching one another or pitting their strength directly against that of their opponent and thus have little possibility of leading to violence or injury. **Combative sports,** on the other hand, are specifically defined as involving direct hand-to-hand, body-to-body, or weapon-to-body contact and thus have a very high probability of leading to injury or death. For some members of the audience, this is precisely why they are watching—they are hoping to see someone get hurt, to see blood spilled, even to see someone die. This is a big part of the attraction for spectators at bull fights, sports car races, ice hockey and rugby games, wrestling matches, and cage-fighting contests (also known as ultimate fighting or mixed martial arts).

In some instances, although humans make up the audience, nonhuman animals are the ones doing the fighting—hence the excitement at a cockfight, pit bull fight, scorpion fight, or bear-baiting exhibition. One of the most famous anthropological essays of all time was written by Clifford Geertz about the underlying cultural meanings and values exemplified by a Balinese cockfight. Geertz's *thick description* of a cockfight in Bali is a classic example of how a meticulous ethnographer can make readers halfway around the world, and several decades removed, feel as if they are right in the midst of the action (Geertz 1972).

According to Blanchard (1995), combative sports that involve deliberate physical violence are associated with more complex cultures that engage in warfare, such as chiefdoms and states. Hunters and gatherers, who for the most part do not engage in warfare, likewise seldom have recreational activities that involve one person trying to physically harm or overwhelm another. Even where competitions pit one person against another in terms of strength, such as wrestling, the goal is often simply to pin one's opponent to the ground or push him outside a designated ring, not to draw blood or cause permanent injury. As soon as the criteria are met for declaring one individual the winner, the match is over.

Many physically aggressive sports incorporate various types of protection for the players, such as helmets, face masks, body pads or armor, and so forth. This is an interesting cultural phenomenon—to acknowledge the potential for injury, while at the same time trying to prevent it from being too serious.

Christopher Nowinski's book *Head Games* (2007) provides a detailed analysis of the culture of youth and professional sports in the United States, especially football, lacrosse, and hockey. Nowinski traces the rise of concussions in American sports, focusing particular attention on the cultural beliefs that surround this issue. For example, people disagree on the definition of the term concussion. Some people distinguish between a so-called **true concussion,** where one loses consciousness, and merely *getting one's bell rung.* The latter phrase refers to cases where people are obviously traumatized by a hit to the head—staggering around, mumbling, not knowing where they are or what is going on—but are expected to shake it off and continue to play for the good of the team. The U.S. sports system incorporates a cultural belief that winning is all important, more important, even, than one's health. This leads many players to downplay their symptoms so they can return to the playing field, with coaches, teammates, and parents all doing their part to encourage the player to get up and return to the game.

Nowinski documents the rise in concussion injuries among very young players and notes particularly the long-term cognitive difficulties experienced by professional athletes as well as young children due to multiple concussions. **Second Impact Syndrome** refers to getting a second concussion before the brain has had sufficient time to heal from a first, which can lead to permanent brain damage and even death on the field. Some athletes, unaware of the potentially serious complications of multiple concussions, actually brag about how many concussions they have sustained and are proud of their ability to keep on playing. Even the development of new and improved helmets designed to minimize head injury hasn't reduced the level of injuries. Once new helmets are developed and in use, the players simply increase the level of violence and aggressiveness of their play.

In the United States, some states and local sports' organizations have begun to develop guidelines encouraging or requiring coaches to become certified in assessing head injuries and have mandated specific actions to be taken after a concussion. These may include a mandatory evaluation by a physician and/or designated periods of not being allowed to play following a head injury.

The Origins of Play, Games, and Sports

Little anthropological attention has focused on tracing the origins and early development of recreational and leisure activities, especially compared to that expended on the origins of music, language, and other human behaviors. One reason for this lack of interest has been the view that such activities are extras, tangential to the main business of human survival, even somewhat frivolous. Another reason is that so many of these activities require almost nothing in the way of material culture (artifacts—objects made or modified by humans) and facilities, and so leave an even smaller imprint in the archeological record than religious beliefs or early artistic endeavors. Toys and sports paraphernalia made out of wood or other plant materials likely would not preserve for long, and other items that might have been used as toys or in games or sports might not be recognized as such.

All mammal babies, including human children, **pretend fight,** and wrestling in various forms is found in cultures all over the world. In cultural contexts where wrestling is important and reflects a number of significant cultural values, as among the Nuba of the Sudan or the Mehinaku of Brazil, it may be very simple in terms of technology—essentially just two men pitting their strength against each other. In other situations, such as sumo wrestling in Japan, wrestling may become very formalized, with special uniforms, protective gear, trophies, written records, and so on.

Even fairly complex forms of ball play may leave no evidence if the ball is made of leather, plant material, wood, a goat or sheep's head, or some other material likely to decay quickly once abandoned. Only if the balls are made of stone or dense rubber are they likely to be recovered from archeological sites. Blanchard points out that *chunkey stones* from archeological sites in the American Southeast are only identifiable because the game itself is known from historic contexts. He writes: "Chunkey is a game played among Southeastern tribes (e.g., Choctaws, Creeks) in which a player rolls the large stone along the ground and participants compete by throwing wooden poles in the path of the stone" (Blanchard 1995:97–98).

Of the prehistoric Mesoamerican ball game, Blanchard writes:

> No other prehistoric sporting event has received as much attention or has been the subject of so much controversy, but no other game has been so well represented in the archeological record. With its broad geographic distribution [Middle America and the American Southwest], hundreds of ballcourts, many artistic depictions, stone yokes and other paraphernalia, as well as ethnohistorical references, the classic rubber ball game of Mesoamerica literally demands attention. (Blanchard 1995:103)

There are any number of unusual small objects recovered from archeological sites that may have been part of children's play activities or adult games, but without any cultural context they are impossible to interpret. We know, for example, that children among the Hopi play with small animal bones, pretending that the bones are people, but there would be no way to determine if animal bones from an archeological site were used in the same or similar ways. Children may play with sticks that they float down a stream, or throw rocks to see who can throw the farthest, or catch June bugs and attach a string to them and watch

The two most common sports around the world are wrestling and soccer, probably because they require little equipment, and people of any socioeconomic status and skill level can participate. Left: two Sumo wrestlers are poised to begin the competition. The referee stands between them. Right: a native of Haiti, U.S. Navy Boatswain's Mate Seaman Jean Petitfrere plays soccer in 2010 with West African children as part of a community outreach project from his assigned ship, the *USS Gunston Hall*.

them fly around. Baby animals of various types, often captured when their mothers were killed for food, have provided hours of amusement for children and adults around the world but, again, leave no discernible evidence in archeological sites.

Functions of Play, Games, and Sports

One of the main functions of play, games, and both informal and formal sporting activities is simple enjoyment—the pleasure of participating oneself or observing others participate. Like music, however, such activities may also have religious, political, economic, or other components.

Sports and Games as Status Markers

As pointed out at the beginning of this chapter, some contemporary games and sports are very expensive to participate in. Thus, they serve as a de facto mechanism for making distinctions among people belonging to different socioeconomic levels. People with a wide range of income levels, from rich to poor, can enjoy playing soccer and basketball. Fox hunting, golf, and downhill skiing require rather more money. To participate in the top echelons of horse or camel racing, you need millions of dollars. The Crown Prince of Dubai, Sheikh Hamdan bin Mohammed bin Rashid Al-Maktoum, recently spent $2.72 million for a single camel at an auction in the United Arab Emirates. That amount pales in comparison to the $9.7 million he spent for a horse in 2005, and the $15.5 million he was prepared to spend for another horse in 2006 (he was outbid).

Even to participate in competitive pedigreed dog competitions such as the Westminster Kennel Club's show requires a lot of money. A wealthy family may go on a skiing vacation in Switzerland, while a middle-class family goes to the closest big hill with their sleds and toboggans, and poor inner-city kids slide down a snowy street on a piece of old cardboard. Being a member of the audience can also be expensive. People with disposable income may have season tickets to a professional sports team's games. Middle-class families may go to one professional sports game a year as a special treat, while poorer families only watch the games on TV. Just like houses and cars, leisure activities reflect socioeconomic status and different cultural priorities.

Sports and Games as Reflections of Cultural Values

In many cultures, sporting activities embody a number of beliefs about gender roles and other aspects of importance to the participants, and the same activity can completely change its meaning as it diffuses from one cultural context to another. For example, the contemporary sport of bungee jumping has its origins in a traditional land diving ritual performed by men on Pentecost Island, part of the nation of Vanuatu in the South Pacific.

As part of celebrations marking the end of the yam harvest, local villagers construct towers out of wood and vines, with platforms jutting out at various heights up to 70 feet. The landing area is deliberately placed on a slope, and the ground is tilled and softened to provide some allowance for mistakes in the measuring of the vines. One by one, men climb the tower to different heights, starting with the lowest platform and moving up. They have carefully measured vines, which they tie to the platform and to their ankles. People on the ground sing and dance as each diver prepares to jump. If the vines are too short, the diver will swing back into the tower, too long and the diver will hit the ground head first. The ideal is for one's head to just barely graze the slope. Like cliff diving in Acapulco, Mexico, this is a very dangerous activity, requiring both skill and courage, and not all jumps end safely.

For the people of Pentecost Island, land diving was originally part of an elaborate ritual celebration. The origin myth of land diving says that a cheating wife was chased up a tree by her husband. She leaped to another tree to get away from him, and he leaped after her. Unbeknownst to him, she had tied vines to her ankles in case she missed the jump. They both fell, but only the husband died. Ever since, men have practiced land diving using vines so that if the need ever arises, they will be prepared to chase their wives across the treetops in relative safety.

Land diving is restricted to men, and is viewed primarily as a way for them to demonstrate their courage and manliness. Today, in villages that are easily accessible to tourists, the ceremonies are held more frequently and are staged for the express purpose of bringing in tourist revenues.

The modern-day sport of bungee jumping evolved out of the idea of land diving, but bungee jumpers usually leap from stationary structures such as bridges or

Leisure activities, including participation in sports, reflect socioeconomic status and cultural priorities. Gymnastics, polo, and competitive pedigreed dog competitions all require substantial investments of time and money. In contrast, locals in Mali make fun of *toubabs* (white people), remarking: "Toubabs are so dumb, they'll pay money for a dog!"

towers, often over water. Bungee cords are springy and elastic, allowing for a yo-yo-like experience at the bottom of the dive, which usually ends well above the land or water surface. Bungee jumping is much safer than Vanuatu land diving and doesn't carry the cultural meanings about the treachery of women and the courage of men. In modern bungee jumping, women are allowed to participate, but it is still mostly a male sport. The main point is the adrenaline rush of stepping off, as well as the exhilaration of flying through the air, defying gravity (Soden 2005). Participation may also increase a person's status among his or her peers.

There are many sports activities that provide opportunities for men to demonstrate their strength and courage, including bull fighting, sports car racing, boxing, cliff diving, ultimate fighting, and sumo wrestling. Competitive girls' and women's sports are still rare in many parts of the world, as they were in North America until the 1980s. Even today, most female sports involve strength, speed, and agility, rather than displays of courage in the face of real physical risk. To the extent that sports competitions can be viewed as ritualized combat or warfare, this makes evolutionary sense, as females remain the limiting variable in reproducing the group. Compared to the loss of women, there is less of an impact if some of the men are injured or killed in sports or warfare.

Sports as Politics and Anti-Politics: Buzkashi and Soccer

A number of researchers have noted the warlike nature of some sports competitions, or the sports-like nature of some armed conflicts. Both sports and warfare often involve teams of *us* against *them* and competition over territory. The sport of *buzkashi*, in particular, has been analyzed as a metaphor for, and a microcosm of, struggles for political power among tribal factions in Afghanistan. Buzkashi is a sport, similar to polo, found across the Central Asian steppes. In this region of the world horses were first domesticated for riding, and men take pride both in their horses and in their riding abilities. In the game, men compete to see who can snatch up the carcass of a headless goat or calf, keep it away from other players, and deposit it across a goal line.

Anthropologist Whitney Azoy's (2002) longitudinal study of the sport, beginning in the 1970s, can be found in *Buzkashi: Game and Power in Afghanistan*. Azoy examines both the traditional form of buzkashi as it has been played for centuries, as well as changes in the game during the last few decades as it came to reflect both local and international political struggles. *Buzkashi* represents the first in-depth ethnography focused on a single sport in its cultural and historical contexts.

Soccer (known as football in most of the world) has served both as a powerful force binding together people of different political views, nationalities, languages, religions, occupations, ages, and sexes, as well as an agent of political and cultural change (for example, see Lever 1995). Soccer is the most popular sport worldwide, at least in part because it requires only a ball, which can be home-made, and a relatively flat, open space. Soccer adapts itself to the circumstances, and is played in a range of styles; it can incorporate amateurs as well as experts, young and old, males and females, formal and informal rules. Tara Bahrampour, an Iranian-American journalist who has played soccer on Sunday afternoons in Brooklyn's Prospect Park off and on for years, writes about the power of soccer to unite immigrants of all types: "The only country where a soccer chip does not seem to have been implanted in all infant boys is the United States. Like pasta or borscht, the game was brought over by newcomers." One participant interviewed by Bahrampour says, "It's something that exists that American culture, power, and government has no control over, doesn't really know about. It's one of those places where being part of the dominant culture doesn't buy you anything." The late afternoon Sunday games in Prospect Park have been going on for decades (Bahrampour 2000).

A typical weekend soccer game played by locals in any big city or suburb in the United States constitutes a mini-United Nations, with players from countries all over the world, first-generation immigrants as well as those whose families have been here for generations, including European-Americans of all backgrounds. Bahrampour writes:

> Even as nationalities blend together on the field, cultural variations are not lost. Last December, during Ramadan, the Muslim month of fasting, tempers were short as the afternoon waned; the minute the sun disappeared, several players whipped out bottles of fruit juice, their first nourishment of the day. National origin also affects playing style, dictating who keeps the ball close, who plays it wide, who talks a lot while playing. . . . Political differences, too, must be set aside. Frenchmen play with North Africans, Arabs with Israelis. "All those differences are minor," [a player] said, "compared to whether you hold the ball too long, or never pass it, or know how to run when you don't have the ball." Age varies widely, from teenagers to grandfathers, as does expertise. People who have never kicked a ball play alongside people who played on their national teams. Some novices leave after a season. Others become addicted—to the give of grass beneath their feet, to the steadying arm of a teammate after a fall, to the satisfaction when a perfectly timed touch reverses the ball's course, leaving an opponent running empty. (Bahrampour 2000)

A few females join in these multinational soccer games—mostly younger American women who grew up with more opportunities to play soccer. Not everyone welcomes female players initially:

> A few balk. One player mentioned a devout Muslim man who walked off the field when a woman joined the game. "He told me he wouldn't play if she was there," the player recalled. "I said: 'Listen, she's not here to flirt with you, she's not here to have sex with you, she's not here to marry you. She's here to play soccer.'" Eventually, the man resumed playing. (Bahrampour 2000)

Soccer also has served as way to challenge cultural beliefs and practices. When Awista Ayub began the Afghan Youth Sports Exchange in 2003, her idea was to bring young Afghanis to the United States to develop leadership and sports skills. They would then return to Afghanistan and promote youth sports by teaching soccer to young children. Like buzkashi, soccer in Afghanistan has been a male-dominated activity. In 2004, Ayub brought eight Afghan girls to the United States to teach them to play soccer, with no idea what the long-term implications might be. Simply by returning to Afghanistan and teaching other girls to play soccer, these eight young women challenged traditional views of women and helped expand opportunities for other girls and women both in sports as well as in other aspects of Afghan culture that had traditionally excluded women (Ayub 2009).

Even though games and sports may seem like insignificant leisure activities, unrelated to other cultural institutions, they can be quite important. They both reflect and shape cultural values and teach important lessons to all who participate and watch. They have the power to unite people from vastly different backgrounds in the pursuit of pleasure and camaraderie and can also serve as the agents of cultural change.

Gravity Play, Children's Activities, and Other Pleasurable Pastimes

Defying Gravity

In 1969, Roger Caillois, a scholar of sports and games, classified games into four categories—those based on competition, chance, pretense, and vertigo. He then placed the activities within each of these categories on a continuum from relatively free-form to highly structured by rules and regulations (Caillois 1969). *Vertigo* refers to physical activities that create the effect of defying gravity. These effects may be calming or thrilling, momentary or long-lasting. Stress and anxiety can be alleviated somewhat through repetitive rocking motions, and self-soothing behaviors such as rocking and pacing are often seen in zoo and laboratory animals. Children with cognitive impairments may rock back and forth or use other self-stimulating behaviors such as hand flapping or flicking an object back and forth repeatedly to calm themselves. While in the womb, bipedal walking by the mother

provides this same sort of constant motion, and after birth, many babies are calmed by being rocked, walked, or held in a person's arms while they sway back and forth. Children's swings, teeter-totters, and merry-go-rounds also provide this same type of effect and can provide hours of enjoyment of a relatively calm, passive type.

On the other hand, many people engage in more active behaviors that provide more thrilling movements, longer episodes of feeling unbound by gravity, and even physical risk. Land diving in the South Pacific, discussed earlier, and its high-tech form, bungee jumping, are prime examples of activities that satisfy what Garrett Soden (2005) has called a universal *human obsession with falling*. Other examples range from some types of dancing (waltz or swing), to swimming and gymnastics, which invoke the feeling of weightlessness, as does simply twirling until you are dizzy. Amusement park rides such as roller coasters and elevator drops provide a similar experience. For many people, such rides combine the thrill of knowing intellectually that one is safe, while tricking the body into experiencing the adrenaline rush that accompanies actually taking a risk.

For more dedicated gravity bums, as they are known, the risks need to be real, pitting the individual against the ever-present force of gravity. People looking for this type of exhilaration can find it from downhill skiing and snowboarding, sky diving, base jumping, canoeing or kayaking down wild white-water rivers, and "going vert" or getting air with skateboards, bicycles, and motorcycles.

Soden has studied gravity-defying sports in some detail across a variety of cultural and historical contexts. According to Soden, our evolutionary origins as tree-living primates accounts for our instinctive fear of falling. Gravity is an ever-present force to which our bodies must continually adjust, and falling out of a tree can cause injury or death for any primate. Gravity play involves deliberate approaches to the edge of danger. Soden writes:

> This is the game of gravity that [climbers] speak of: the constant tension between primitive fear and civilized thought. It is so sharp because the fear of falling was hardwired into our basic neurology as a fear that should never be ignored—while our intellect, during gravity play, vigorously attempts to do just that [ignore the fear]. The struggle between what we believe is safe

Humans seem to love defying gravity, as illustrated by these images of a pole-vaulter, a girl performing a jump on a BMX bike, and physicist Stephen Hawking enjoying zero gravity during a flight aboard a modified Boeing 727 aircraft owned by Zero Gravity Corp.

and what feels risky ties thought and emotion into a knot, which surprisingly can create what some describe as a profound revelation. (Soden 2005:268)

In his book *Defying Gravity*, Soden traces the origins of most modern *extreme sports* to surfing on ocean waves—pitting the individual against the power of gravity. Surfing is thought to have originated around AD 400 among Pacific Islanders. It had been practiced across the South Pacific for centuries before it was "discovered" in Hawaii by Captain James Cook in 1778. Soden writes: "The Hawaiians themselves couldn't tell Cook how old surfing was. Everyone had always surfed: men, women, and children; common folk and royalty. Surfing was woven into their oldest myths. . . . There were competitions: in one, the victor won four thousand pigs and sixteen canoes. There were even prayers to bring good waves" (Soden 2005:168).

Over the next century, surfing among South Pacific Islanders was vigorously suppressed by Calvinist Christian missionaries who viewed surfing as being "expressly against the laws of God . . . all who practice [these sports] secure themselves the displeasure of offended heaven" (Soden 2005:169). The sport was reinvigorated in the early 1900s and spread from Hawaii to Australia and to Southern California, where it eventually gave rise not only to modern ocean wave surfing but also to skateboarding and extreme skateboarding.

Skateboarding devotees have a tribal culture all their own:

As a sport that grew outside the mainstream for years because it was considered an outlaw activity by many adults, skateboarding culture developed its own ethics and dialect, especially concerning [names for] tricks. . . . Skateboarders, inline skaters, stunt bike riders, and many of the others don't think of what they do as sports. Their feelings about it run much deeper. "This is the difference between a sport and a lifestyle," Arlo Eisenberg, perhaps the best-known aggressive inline skater, has said in a television interview. "I don't like it being reduced to a science. Because what we do is very unscientific. It's artistic. It's expressionistic. It's about individuals. We're challenging this whole conventional, authoritarian structure," Arlo said. (Soden 2005:238–239)

Ironically, as adult-sanctioned skateboarding parks are built in American cities and suburbs, and rules and restrictions proliferate, the sport loses some of its outlaw status.

Psychological studies of people who are deemed **high sensation seekers**—those who are driven to seek the experiences provided by extreme sports—show that they also tend to be nonconformists and put a greater value than most people on independence, inventiveness, and achievement. They tend to be liberal and permissive in their attitudes and to dislike authority. Soden concludes: "Add to all this the fact that high-sensation seekers know how to use gravity to reach an altered state of consciousness unknown to low-sensation seekers, and you have a recipe for name calling all around. It's no wonder that gravity play creates cultural wars" (Soden 2005:273). It's also no wonder that gravity play and extreme sports thrive in cultural contexts where everyday life is extensively rule-bound, safe, and in many ways boring, at least in terms of physical excitement and risk.

Children's Activities

All over the world, children spend a lot of time interacting with other children, under varying degrees of adult supervision. In some cultures, children's lives are highly age structured, meaning that kids play mostly with others of about the same age, size, and physical capabilities. But in other contexts, all children, regardless of age, are incorporated into whatever game or sport is being played. Children's play may be highly structured, with the same rules, songs, rhymes, or motions remaining fairly consistent for generations, or they may be casual and free-form, like Calvinball, where the rules are constantly evolving. Children may play in the streets, on school playgrounds, at parks, in empty fields, at the local swimming hole or creek, or in abandoned buildings and wastelands, far from the prying eyes of adults.

Cultural anthropologists and folklorists have devoted significant research efforts to understanding **children's culture**—the transmission of beliefs and knowledge about play, games, and sports that occur from child to child, year after year, without input from adults. The most comprehensive studies are Iona and Peter Opie's (1969) work with children in England, Scotland, and Wales, as exemplified by their detailed work *Children's Games in Street and Playground: Chasing, Catching, Seeking, Hunting, Racing, Dueling, Exerting, Daring, Guessing, Acting, and Pretending*. The Opies focused their attention on the games that children between the ages of 6 and 12 years play outdoors when not under adult supervision. For the most part, these games require no equipment at all, not even a ball. The Opies find a number of common themes in this sort of children's play:

> They seldom need an umpire, they rarely trouble to keep scores, little significance is attached to who wins or loses, they do not require the stimulus of prizes, it does not seem to worry if a game is not finished. Indeed, children like games in which there is a sizeable element of luck, so that individual abilities cannot be directly compared. They like games which restart almost automatically, so that everybody is given a new chance. They like games which move in stages, in which each stage, the choosing of leaders, the picking-up of sides, the determining of which side shall start, is almost a game in itself. . . . Adults do not always see, when subjected to lengthy preliminaries, that many of the games, particularly those of the young children, are more akin to ceremonies than competitions. In these games children gain the reassurance that comes with repetition, and the feeling of fellowship that comes from doing the same as everyone else. (Opie and Opie 1969:2–3)

The Opies note that although children's games change and evolve over time, and vary from one region to another, some practices seem to have extraordinary longevity and wide distribution. For example, many chasing games, such as Blind Man's Bluff, involve turning the blindfolded player three times to disorient him—not two, not four, always three, a practice which dates to the seventeenth century in the British Isles, if not earlier, and is still found today among North American children's games. The phrase "You're getting warmer," as a seeker nears a hidden object, was used as early as the mid-1860s by Charles Dickens (1864–1865[2002]) in his novel *Our Mutual Friend*, and is still commonly heard today.

Counting out or dipping refers to the process of choosing who must take on the unpopular role in the game. Dipping rhymes include those still familiar to North American children, such as "One potato, two potato, three potato, four; five potato, six potato, seven potato, more," and the many versions of "Eeny, meenie, miny, mo," such as "Inty, minty, tippety fig" and "Zinti, tinty, tethera, methera" (Opie and Opie 1969).

Elaborate rhyming songs may accompany jump-rope and hand-clapping games, which have always been more popular among girls than boys. Some of the songs I learned as a child can still be heard on playgrounds and in urban streets where children play. Some of the songs gain new lyrics, and the jump-rope tricks have become more elaborate than those I remember.

Just as with other aspects of culture, children's songs and games will vary with the physical environment, the cultural context, and the materials available with which to make toys. Although more difficult to study than adult pastimes, children's play activities and games reflect both the culture of the adults in the society as well as the specific culture of the children. Each generation discovers the games and songs anew.

Other Pleasurable Activities

There are many other activities that people participate in for the pleasure they bring, even though such activities don't exactly qualify as physically active games or sports. As just described, anthropologists and folklorists have studied play, games, and leisure

People around the world indulge in many different types of activities for the physical or emotional pleasure they bring, including walking on the beach, listening to a storyteller, reading a book, playing chess with a friend in the park, or attending a museum exhibit.

activities among children, as these take up a larger proportion of children's time. However, much less attention has been given to such activities among adults, and many researchers view them as peripheral or tangential to adult life. However, the types of leisure activities that people engage in can be just as illuminative of cultural values and beliefs as any other aspects of behavior.

Some of these pleasurable activities are solitary pursuits, such as reading a book, going for a walk, making arts and crafts, or researching one's genealogy on the Internet. Others are group activities, involving a limited number of other individuals who interact through talking and discussion in the course of pursuing some other activity. In the Biological Anthropology Lab at the University of Delaware, faculty members always have a jigsaw puzzle in progress. People come and go, working on the puzzle for just a few minutes or for longer stretches. While puzzling, we talk about our research, writing, classes, and students, or topics not directly related to work, such as movies and restaurants.

In many towns and cities around the world, people go for a stroll around the town square either before or after their evening meal. Such walking is usually leisurely and certainly not competitive. People talk with their walking partner, usually a relative or friend, or with other couples they know. These evening promenades or constitutionals are simple and inexpensive ways to relax and socialize before retiring for the night, and may also serve as venues for young people to meet potential marriage partners in a public, supervised setting. Mall walkers are the closest equivalent in many U.S. suburbs, where town squares seldom exist and/or people prefer to be in climate-controlled environments. Mall walkers participate for the health benefits as well as the social interaction.

The local pub or drinking establishment, where alcoholic beverages are served, has long been a gathering place for working-class men in some cultures. Irish pub culture is probably the best known. Rather than a place to meet members of the opposite sex, or wheel and deal with high-powered business associates, it is a place to go after work and maintain social ties with people you have known all your life. Going "down the pub" or to the *local* is an essential part of a man's daily routine, and his main form of relaxation. In larger towns and cities, the local pub is also a place to hear live traditional Irish music as well as tall tales, and to play darts. In some Irish pubs, the entire family is present, including young children and elderly grandparents.

Coffeehouse culture is alive and well in many regions of the world (Ellis 2004; Jolliffe 2010). Coffeehouses first arose in Turkey in the sixteenth century and spread to Saudi Arabia, Syria and Egypt, before expanding to the rest of Europe and the British Isles in the mid-seventeenth century. They are now found worldwide, although they remain most important around the Mediterranean, including the Middle East and North Africa. Coffeehouses began as a place for men to meet, read newspapers and magazines, and discuss politics and other events of the day. In some areas, coffeehouse culture includes playing games such as chess or backgammon. As alternatives to establishments that serve alcohol, coffeehouses are the site of serious public discussions, especially those of a political bent, as well as places for men to socialize away from their wives and children.

Like Irish pubs, some coffeehouses provide live music, and in some parts of the world, women and children are allowed to frequent these establishments as well. Starbucks is only the latest manifestation of a widespread cultural phenomenon that dates back hundreds of years. Today, however, many coffeehouses in the West are full of people communicating via electronic devices with others who are not physically present, while ignoring the people sitting all around them, thus diminishing the social aspect of going to the coffeehouse.

In societies where men hang out in the coffeehouse or local pub, women have always gathered in small groups for similar purposes, but usually in more private settings and often while also performing work of some sort. For example, Bambara women in many rural Malian villages gather every morning to pound their millet, sorghum, or corn into flour in a social setting; Greek village women gather at the communal ovens to bake bread; farm women hold husking bees to husk corn after harvest, while others have quilting bees to work on producing linens for the household. Modern women gather at playgrounds to talk with other adults while their young children play. Multiple generations of women gather in the kitchen on special occasions to prepare traditional foods such as raviolis, tamales, steamed dumplings, or cinnamon buns (Schenone 2008).

Sidewalk cafes that allow one to eat, drink, and converse with friends while also watching the passing parade of other people have become an important part of many European cities. In cities around the world, but perhaps most famously in Berlin, Germany, families and friends spend hours enjoying Sunday brunch at outdoor restaurants whenever the weather permits.

Many other pleasurable pastimes have one activity as their stated purpose, but serve primarily as acceptable excuses to get together with friends and socialize. The game or activity becomes the central focus around which eating, drinking, and chatting are structured. Some involve a minimum of physical exertion, such as pool (billiards), horseshoes, or video games, while others are played sitting down. There may be groups who get together to play bridge, mah-jongg, Monopoly, or role-playing games like Dungeons and Dragons. Other games have only two participants such as dominoes, checkers, chess, cribbage, or *mancala*. The term mancala refers to a family of strategy-based board games played across Africa and Asia, which are also referred to as sowing or "count and capture" games.

The development of the Internet has allowed even larger groups of people to join together in cyberspace to play competitive or cooperative games online, in which case the sharing of food, drink, and gossip are no longer part of the interaction. The focus is placed on the development of avatars (alternate personas) and the playing of the game itself; players may never interact in person or even know each other's true identities.

In addition to all of these pastimes, women join book clubs or meet and knit together, while men gather for poker games or to watch football on TV. Men's bowling leagues played an important role in American culture for much of the twentieth century, but their popularity has declined in recent years (see Putnam's 2001 book *Bowling Alone*). Men in Western cultures may go duck hunting as an excuse to be out in the natural world, amidst the quiet beauty of wild, unspoiled country, while spending time with their male friends and beloved dogs, away from the multiple demands of a job and family. Publicly, they may feel pressured by their culture to insist that it's "all about the ducks."

Around the world, people devote considerable time and energy to various types of activities that bring them pleasure—it's not all just subsistence, politics, economics, religion, and marriage and family issues. Humans excel at finding and creating ways to amuse themselves and keep their minds and bodies occupied. The focus in this chapter has been on music and sports, defined broadly. In the following chapter, we turn to the visual and performing arts in all of their glorious cross-cultural manifestations, as we continue our exploration of human creative expression.

Key Concepts Review

Humans have a truly breathtaking capacity to learn information, solve problems, and create elaborately structured social worlds; we also seem positively compelled to express ourselves through many creative outlets.

The Upper Paleolithic (40,000 years ago) has been identified as heralding a "Creative Explosion"—with the first unequivocal evidence of human creativity in many realms, from painting to music and sculpture.

Our expressions of creativity and the other things we do for fun reflect underlying cultural beliefs as much as any other aspect of culture and human experience.

Human creativity can be studied from many different angles, including asking: is the activity solitary vs. group, public vs. private, participant vs. observer, amateur vs. expert, competitive or cooperative, just for fun or for serious purposes? are there economic con-

continued

straints? how does changing technology affect creative expression? how important is cultural context? and how much freedom do individual artists have to express themselves?

Music is a human cultural universal; it is produced and listened to in a variety of contexts and for many different purposes; thus, the anthropological study of music is complex and far-reaching.

The major focus of ethnomusicology is the role of music in human life, including the social and cultural contexts and the meanings that people attach to music.

There are a number of specialized archives of music and language around the world, where such resources are preserved for future generations to study and enjoy.

Humans can make music with their voices through whistling, singing, humming, yodeling, ululating, throat singing, eefing, and beat-boxing; people can sing a capella, in four-part harmony, or accompanied by instruments; we can sing alone or in groups.

Musical instruments date to the Upper Paleolithic as well, in the form of percussion using stone tools and flutes made from bones and ivory.

Scholars actively debate which came first, music or language—or did they both evolve from a common musi-language? We'll probably never know, but we do know that while music and language have much in common, they are processed somewhat differently in the brain.

Music has many important functions in every society, including affecting people's emotions (to calm or to stir them to action), to make work easier, to express group membership and status, and to serve as a vehicle for political protests; music can be entertaining or annoying, it can even be used as an instrument of torture.

Changes in recording technology and the portability of music continue to affect the role music plays in daily life.

Sports, games, play, and other leisure activities can be studied from many perspectives, including how formally they are structured; whether they are competitive or not; whether they require physical or cognitive skills, or personal courage; whether they involve the risk of injury or death, as well as whether people participate, or only observe, or both.

Like music, sports and games can serve as status markers, reflect group membership, help establish identity, and reflect many cultural values.

Much human play/sports behavior involves defying gravity in various ways.

Studying children's sports and games provides novel insights into the culture of children, especially those aspects of their lives lived away from adult supervision.

Around the world, people devote considerable time and energy to various types of activities that bring them pleasure—including going to pubs and coffeehouses, playing card games, and many others; it's not all just living and reproducing.

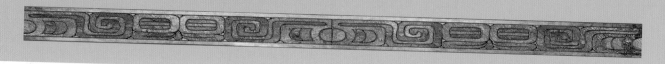

10

HUMAN CREATIVITY

Environments, Bodies, & the Arts

Human cultures offer infinite variety in terms of environmental manipulations, architecture, body modification, and the visual and performing arts. Life provides a veritable feast of opportunities for contributing to and enjoying human creative expression—a fundamental and vital part of the human experience—whether we actively participate or form part of the audience, watching, listening, cheering, and tapping our toes from the sidelines.

In the previous chapter, we explored music and sports as outlets of human creativity and the expression of cultural beliefs and practices. We continue in this chapter, beginning with the ways humans have modified the physical environment to suit our purposes and preferences, rather than merely adapting to it. We can admire the ingenuity of the designers and builders, from Stonehenge to Great Zimbabwe, from the irrigation schemes of the Negev desert to the terraced hillsides of Southeast Asia. We can also ponder the potentially catastrophic human and environmental consequences of such large-scale environmental engineering projects as the Three Gorges Dam in China and artificial islands in Dubai.

We will examine how humans design their communities and living spaces to reflect deeply held cultural beliefs about the proper relationship between humans and the environment, and relationships among groups and within families. Next we will explore the many ways that humans have used their own bodies as the site of creative expression through various types of body adornment and both temporary and permanent physical modifications. The chapter ends with an overview of the visual and performing arts, including the important role that *moving together in time*—through dance, military drill, calisthenics, and marching bands—plays in creating and strengthening group solidarity.

MODIFYING THE ENVIRONMENT

People have been arranging and rearranging the physical environment to suit their purposes for many thousands of years. Perhaps the earliest evidence we have of deliberate shaping of the environment comes from early hominid living sites, where rocks were arranged in a circle or semicircle, perhaps as a windbreak or as part of a structure, the rest of which has long since disappeared.

Evidence for large-scale manipulations of the physical environment date only to the Neolithic, beginning some 10,000 years ago. Daniel Quinn suggests that the origins of agriculture and significant modifications of the environment by humans were accompanied by a profound shift in worldview, from one characterized by the attitude that "humans belong to the world, and must adapt to it just as other living creatures do," to one of "the world belongs to humans, to change, mold, shape, manipulate, use up, and even destroy" (Quinn 1992). This latter belief underlies all human changes to the landscape ranging from the simple rerouting of a stream to water a garden to the dredging of a ship channel, the construction of a hydroelectric dam, or the building of the Panama Canal. Many early human modifications of the environment are hailed as major achievements, signs of progress, and testaments to human ingenuity.

In the highlands of New Guinea and across Southeast Asia, we find ancient evidence of humans terracing steep hillsides and channeling the flow of rainwater down the terraces, allowing for the growing of crops. The prehistoric peoples of Europe moved huge blocks of stone across the landscape and set them upright in circles, most famously at Stonehenge. Pyramids rose from the landscape in Egypt and in North and Central America, built from earth or blocks of stone. Early farmers in Persia built elaborate systems of *qanats* and underground aqueducts to move water across long distances in order to grow crops. Thousands of people in China were put to work over many years building the Great Wall, to keep out enemies.

Want a huge city, such as Los Angeles, where there isn't enough water to provide for people's needs? Divert rivers in other states. Want a reliable source of electricity for factories in a region where there aren't many good sources of power? Build a dam and completely alter the ecology of the region both upstream and downstream. Want to build a relatively flat highway across the mountains? Blast tunnels through solid rock. Want to build a town in an area where there are mountain lions and deer? Go ahead and build, then shoot any deer that forage in your gardens and kill any mountain lions that dare remain behind and prey on humans.

The city of New Orleans, Louisiana, is perhaps the epitome of the hubris of the belief that human technological prowess can triumph over the power of nature. New Orleans is a city built along a coast prone to massive hurricanes, along a major river prone to flooding, and on land that is marshy, with much of it below sea level. When Hurricane Katrina struck the Gulf Coast in 2005, a number of critical le-

Humans routinely alter the physical landscape in a variety of ways to make it more suitable for human needs and wants. Top: water fills intricately carved rice terraces in China, reflecting the sky. Bottom: a NASA satellite image of the coast of Dubai shows the artificial resort islands known as Palm Jumeirah, as well as the grouping of artificial islands known as The World.

vees failed, flooding much of the city. Many experts fully expected the city of almost half a million people to be abandoned, but instead it is being rebuilt, even though there is no way to prevent another massive hurricane from wreaking the same damage or worse. However, for sheer environmental manipulation on a massive scale, the best contemporary examples are the Three Gorges Dam in China and the creation of islands along the coast of Dubai.

Three Gorges Dam, China

A dam across China's mighty Yangtze River has been in the planning process since the early 1930s. The original impetus was flood control, taming the river's periodic floods. However, it wasn't until the 1980s that China's rising energy needs convinced officials to move forward with plans for building the world's largest dam, as well as the world's largest generator of electricity from renewable sources. The dam was built in stages, beginning in 1994. Construction of the dam was largely completed in 2006, and the reservoir reached its maximum levels in 2009. The dam itself is 185 meters tall and 2.3 kilometers long. The reservoir upstream contains almost 40 billion cubic meters of water and is expected to generate 85 billion kilowatt-hours of hydroelectric power per year, replacing the burning of some 50 million tons of coal each year. In addition, some of the Yangtze's flow is being diverted to the arid northern regions of China for agricultural irrigation.

The full environmental consequences of human alteration of the landscape on this scale will not be clear for years. Already, the dam has altered the timing and intensity of changes in river levels downstream, affecting the spawning of the river's four major carp species—a significant food source for millions of people living along the river. Biodiversity is expected to decline precipitously as many species become extinct due to the rapid transformation of the environment. Industrial pollution and raw sewage are dumped into the reservoir and into the river downstream from the dam, and silt builds up behind the dam. Entire communities, including some religious temples, have been submerged by the rising waters of the lake. By 2008, more than 1.4 million people had been relocated to new villages, and authorities estimate another 4 million people will have to be moved in the coming de-

cade. Perhaps of greatest concern to geologists is the likelihood that the rising water, in combination with the area's torrential rains, will destabilize slopes along the river, increasing the risk of landslides. While an earthquake massive enough to destroy the dam is unlikely, the region is already known for strong earthquakes. The sheer weight of the water on seismic faults near the dam and reservoir have raised concerns that the pressure from the water may lead to earthquakes of a magnitude never before seen in the region.

Palm Islands, Emirate of Dubai

Along the Persian (or Arabian) Gulf coastline of the Emirate of Dubai, south of Iran and north of Oman, a series of artificial islands—the Palm Jumeirah, Palm Jebel Ali, Palm Deira, and the 300-island archipelago known as *The World*—are rising up out of the sea to provide a land base for a major series of commercial and residential projects. Construction on the three big islands began in 2001. Each resembles a giant palm tree, with a long trunk connecting the island to the mainland, multiple fronds branching off the top of the trunk providing waterfront building sites, and an arc or crescent of rock-based breakwaters that enclose and protect the fronds. Together the islands are planned to provide marinas, shopping malls, restaurants, sports venues, health spas, more than 100 luxury hotels, and a variety of residential properties for purchase or rent.

The artificial islands are produced from sand dredged from the Persian Gulf. The design of the palm fronds allows for the creation of many kilometers of coastline. On Palm Jumeirah, a monorail provides transportation along the *Golden Mile*—the commercial artery that runs down the center of the trunk. Palm Jebel Ali is even larger than Palm Jumeirah, and its crescent Dubai Waterfront will eventually be home to the *World of Discovery* (four theme parks, built in the shape of an orca whale). In addition, the island is expected to accommodate 1.7 million people by 2020, living in apartments and houses, some of which will be built on stilts over the water. Boardwalks that encircle the fronds of the palms within the crescent spell out a poem in Arabic script. The third and largest island, Palm Deira, is still under construction.

In addition to the three main islands, a man-made archipelago of 300 mini-islands known as The World (together they form a map of the world) is being built between Palm Jebel Ali and Palm Deira. Individuals or corporations can buy one or more islands and then reshape the land base within limits, a process known as **terraforming.** Specific regions of the map include islands designated as primarily residential (with varying levels of population density), resorts, and commercial islands. Some countries have purchased their corresponding islands. The 22 islands that make up Australia and New Zealand were purchased by an investment group from Kuwait. They are being terraformed into a resort known as *OQYANA: World First*, scheduled to begin construction soon (Oqyana 2009) although the recent economic crisis has slowed construction and development of the project.

The environmental consequences of such massive transformations of the world's landscapes to cater to the wealthiest of the wealthy are unpredictable. Since the sea- and boating-focused lifestyle, gorgeous views, and luxurious living and resort experiences are the main selling points of the projects, it is likely that significant efforts will go into preserving the natural beauty of the region and the clarity of the ocean water. At least the region is not prone to earthquakes, tsunamis, flooding, or severe storms.

CREATING THE BUILT ENVIRONMENT

Designing Communities

On a more typical scale, the settlement of people across the landscape and the development of small clusters of houses and families into towns, villages, and cities is the result of many different factors including the physical topography of an area, the technology and natural resources available, and the vagaries of history, as well as deliberate planning according to specific cultural values. Some communities grow organically, by the slow and steady accumulation of people as the population grows across the generations. Other communities spring up almost overnight in response to the discovery of gold or the siting of a new industry that can employ many people. And some communities are deliberately planned and built according to the careful wisdom of urban planners.

However it originated and developed, once the basic infrastructure is in place—the roads, town center, market places, parks, and residential accommodations—newcomers to the region must adapt to what is already in place. Thus, the human built environment both reflects the accumulated cultural beliefs of generations of previous occupants and influences and shapes the cultural beliefs and lifestyles of the current occupants. A few concrete examples will help to clarify this aspect of human community life.

In some regions, security from invaders was a major force in determining where and how towns were constructed. Many towns were originally situated on hilltops, where they could be easily defended, and from which approaching enemies could be seen long before they arrived. Where hills were not available, the town might be encircled by a wall of stone, with only a few gates that could be guarded, controlling who was allowed inside. The modern equivalents of European Medieval walled cities are the suburban gated communities of North America and urban apartment buildings with doormen who control access. In both the prehistoric U.S. Southwest (Mesa Verde) and in northern Mali (the Bandiagara escarpment where the Dogon live), communities were built into the sides of cliffs to make them easier to defend.

In some towns, a central square was an essential part of the design and a focus of daily life. The central square reflected the need for space to set up markets on a weekly basis and served as a public gathering space for all manner of social activities. The town square would logically be the site of municipal buildings, places of religious worship, and often a public fountain where everyone got their water. Eventually, permanent restaurants and shops would be built in the streets adjoining the public square. In many cities, buildings would have commercial shops on the ground floor at pedestrian level and residential spaces above.

Marketplaces often serve as a center of social interaction, whether they are local weekly or monthly markets in West African towns that arise organically out of local need, or large well-planned urban public spaces. The culture of the Eastern Market, a popular weekend produce and flea market in Washington, D.C., is described in Robert Shepherd's ethnography of urban economic and social life, *When Culture Goes to Market* (Shepherd 2007).

The way towns and cities are constructed often reflects important cultural values. Top: almost every town and city in Europe includes an open market square or plaza in the center, where people gather to visit, eat at sidewalk cafes, and shop. In contrast, Dogon villages in Mali are laid out in the shape of a human body, with the smithy and men's meeting house (shown top right) representing the head at one end of the village, and the altars representing the feet at the other end of the village. Bottom left: a typical American suburban housing development, with small front yards and larger back yards laid out along a paved road. Bottom right: the city of Dubrovnik in Croatia is crowded onto a small peninsula that juts out into the Adriatic Sea and is protected from attack, either by land or sea, by massive stone walls.

The development of public transportation such as trolleys, trams, and eventually subways and trains allows people to live farther away from the city center. Many suburban communities sprout up at the end of each trolley line or subway route. People live in outlying parts of the community, but still work and shop in the town or city center, and developments grow up all along the routes of public transportation. As cars become more and more common, residential communities can be built farther and farther away from the town center, and eventually satellite town centers spring up, allowing people to shop and conduct business and leisure activities far from the city center, but closer to their residences.

A recent development in many regions has been the concept of *Kiss & Ride* and *Park & Ride* facilities, where an automobile is used to transport a commuter from a distant suburb or rural area to the nearest form of public transportation—often a light-rail train or subway station—located partway to the city center. At a Kiss & Ride location, someone else drives the car, and the commuter jumps out, kisses the driver goodbye, and gets on the train while the car drives off. At a Park & Ride location, the commuter drives herself to a parking area and leaves the car all day, while she rides the train into work.

Because of the periphery-hub nature of most public transportation, it can be difficult to get around in the suburbs if you don't have a car. In his book about Nuer migrants to Minneapolis, Jon Holtzman writes that public transportation to jobs often takes hours because the Nuer must travel from one suburb into the city center, change buses, and then travel back out to another suburb—there are no suburb-to-suburb bus routes (Holtzman 2008).

In large cities where public transportation is both widely available, affordable, and efficient—such as Vienna, Austria, with its extensive system of subway lines, trolleys, and buses—owning a car is not necessary. Grocery stores, bakeries, and other shops and services can be found within easy walking distance of most residences.

Where land is plentiful, cities may be designed with broad tree-lined boulevards that have central lanes for automobile traffic, but also bike lanes and ample pedestrian sidewalks. Green spaces may be reserved for parks and botanical gardens. Cities can grow out, into the surrounding countryside, rather than up (in the form of skyscrapers), and residential properties can be detached homes with large yards. Where land is at a minimum, such as inside a walled town, along the steep coast of a Mediterranean island, or in the crowded cities of the Northeastern United States, different rules govern the building and growth of towns and cities. For example, in many small towns along the Mediterranean and Aegean Seas, the streets were designed for pedestrians only—they are narrow, steep, and winding, and cannot accommodate cars. Likewise, row houses, which share adjacent walls with other houses and have tiny front- and backyards, are common in big cities in Europe and the Northeastern United States but rare in regions where space is not a limiting factor. Ranch-style houses, built all on one floor, with large front- and backyards, are reflections of cheap land prices as much as design or lifestyle choices.

Examples of Designed Communities

Some communities are deliberately designed to accommodate specific cultural notions of desirable lifestyles. *The Slabs* in the desert of southeastern California, for example, caters to a motley assortment of recreational vehicle owners, campers, squatters, and other transient residents. It has no electricity, no running water, and no source of food or groceries. It does have an outdoor performance area and a library. It is home to about 150 permanent residents, some of whom follow an ethos of living *off the grid*, free from American government control. Every winter, several thousand more residents from northern states and Canada, known as *Snowbirds*, arrive in their recreational vehicles to enjoy the balmy environment. Anthropologists David and Dorothy Counts describe the culture of The Slabs and similar communities in their ethnography *Over the Next Hill: An Ethnography of RVing Seniors in North America* (2001).

Other examples of communities that cater to specific lifestyles include:

- The city of Davis, California, with its focus on bicycle transportation. The University of California campus in Davis is closed to automobile traffic, and the community has designated bike lanes—distinct from sidewalks and car lanes—throughout.

- Plum Creek, a development south of Austin, Texas. It is described as being "designed in accordance with the principles of New Urbanism, including a mix of housing types, homes sited on a variety of lot sizes, garages accessed by rear alleys, and sidewalks and trails that emphasize pedestrian connectivity to open spaces, civic spaces, and neighborhood commercial districts" (Plum Creek 2010).

- *The Farm* in Tennessee, founded in 1971 by Stephen and Ina May Gaskin and a group of followers as a communal work, living, and study center devoted to peace, healthy nutrition, and spirituality (The Farm 2010). It is best known for Ina May Gaskin's work as a midwife, including her influential book *Spiritual Midwifery* (2002).

- Cities constructed to function as centers of scientific and technological research. Such cities include Pardis, Iran, and Tsukuba Science City, Japan.

- Cities constructed to focus on international business and finance. New Songdo City in South Korea and King Abdullah Economic City (also known as KAEC Financial Island) in Saudi Arabia are among the cities designed for this purpose.

Within residential communities, the structure of the living and working spaces themselves reflect important cultural beliefs and practices and, in turn, affect how people experience their lives within such spaces. In the next section, we explore how the design of living spaces varies across cultures.

Designing Living Spaces

In some cultures, people expect to be around, and with, other people all the time (except perhaps when using toilet facilities). They expect everyone to congregate in the same room and live life communally, with conversations always flowing. Tara Bahrampour, in her memoir of a childhood spent partly in Iran, describes a traditional Iranian living room scene:

> Baba and Ali are sitting with their legs under the *korsi*, the table everyone sits around from the first fall frost to the last cold spring night. It is a low, wide square with soft bedrolls and long pillows on all four sides and a heavy quilt laid over the top. Under the table is a big metal plate filled with red-hot embers and covered with gray ash to make sure no one's feet get burned. If I push myself down and stretch my legs I can feel the rim of the plate. . . . [later] We sit with Dadash, Leila-khanoum, Javad, and Roya around their *korsi*, which has a glowing electric heater underneath. It has such thick blankets that even during blackouts the day's heat stays trapped under the table. We drink tea all day. We play backgammon with Dadash and rummy with Leila-khanoum. (Bahrampour 1999:39 and 110)

In other cultures, people expect quiet and privacy even when home at the same time. In many North American households, unless the family is very poor, each person has his own room for sleeping, even very young children and infants. Some Nuer immigrants to the United States express profound loneliness if they are housed with U.S. families and expected to sleep all alone in their own bedroom.

If a family has only one television, everyone must negotiate about what shows to watch, and then watch together, or retreat to another room. In some households, there are multiple television sets. If every child has a television in their own room, and/or a computer, then there may not be very much interaction among family members even when they are all at home.

Such considerations also figure into how much space is considered necessary per person. Some North American municipalities have regulations that specify how many square feet of space are required for each sleeper in a bedroom, and how many square feet of communal living space are required per person for the house overall. In many other regions of the world, such regulations would seem both unnecessary and silly.

My husband and I, along with our daughter, lived in married student housing in graduate school. All of the native-born American families, most with 0–2 children, chafed at the small size of the two-bedroom, one-bath apartments. The kitchen was so small that the refrigerator was in the living room! At the same time, graduate students from other countries, including Africa, Asia, and the Middle East, thought the apartments were quite spacious. They often had two adults and several children, plus one or both sets of grandparents and occasionally unmarried siblings as well. They did not view it as a hardship to share their living space with many close relatives. Indeed, they felt sorry for those of us who didn't have grandparents to help with child care and cooking, which meant we could not dedicate ourselves completely to our studies.

Housing designs change to reflect changing cultural norms as well. For most of the twentieth century, North American houses were built with all of the bedrooms in close proximity. In a two-story house, they were all upstairs; in a ranch-style house, they were all off a common hallway. Only if the house was large enough did the *master* bedroom, designated for the adults/parents, have its own private bathroom. In the last few decades, more and more houses have been built with the master bedroom separate from the other bedrooms. In a two-story house, the master may be on the ground level, with the other bedrooms upstairs. In a ranch, the master bedroom may be on one side of the house, with the other bedrooms on the far side of the communal spaces such as kitchen, dining, and living rooms. This reflects the growing tendency to separate the children of the family from the adults, even when they are infants. In expensive new homes, many builders now provide each bedroom with its own private bath.

Another design change in North America is the size of kitchens, bathrooms, closets, and garages. Over the years, kitchens have gotten larger and more elaborate, even as people cook less and less. Bathrooms have gotten larger, with a separate tub and shower and double sinks. What used to be considered frivolous luxuries are viewed today as standard in all but the smallest houses. Huge walk-in closets and three- or even four-car garages are expected in middle-class homes, compared to the tiny closets and one-car garages of earlier periods. We have to have someplace to keep all our *stuff*, after all. Women, in particular, often require lots of closet space for their clothes and shoes.

A relatively new design concept in North American houses is the **man cave**—a room dedicated to the adult man of the house, where he can have a big-screen TV with surround sound, a wet bar, a pool table, and perhaps a poker table, dart board, or pinball machines. This becomes a space where he and his buddies can gather to watch sports on TV and pursue other manly activities without the women of the household. In this respect, modern North American houses mimic traditional house designs that had **sex-specific spaces,** where only the women gathered, or only the men gathered, or where men and women took turns using the space depending on the time of day. Nuer immigrants living in small apartments in Minnesota have a difficult time coping with the lack of separate spaces for men and women to gather. If they could afford large suburban McMansions, they could easily establish designated areas for the men to congregate (the man cave, back deck, or garage) separate from the women (the kitchen or sewing or scrapbooking rooms).

One of the best places to see Western cultural beliefs about houses in action is on reality TV shows such as the series *House Hunters* and *House Hunters International*. Both feature upper-middle-class and upper-class home buyers and show them touring several homes for sale and making both positive and negative comments about each, before picking one to purchase. Common complaints about older homes include the lack of closet and other storage space, the small size of the bathrooms, and the lack of an updated kitchen. At the turn of the twenty-first century, granite countertops, cherry cabinets, and stainless steel appliances have taken on an almost mythical significance; in the bathroom, pedestal sinks and spa tubs with separate glass-walled showers hold pride of place. One potential buyer complained that the entire kitchen in one house would need to be updated, to which the host of the show responded in disbelief: "This is a brand-new house!"

On *House Hunters International*, people from one country evaluate properties in another country and marvel at the differences in design. "Why is the toilet in the same room as the sink and tub, and where is the bidet?" asks a French couple looking at houses in Vancouver. "Why is there no dishwasher? Where is the garbage disposal?" asks an English couple looking at vacation homes in Italy. "Why is the master bedroom so far from the children's rooms?" asks a couple from Kenya looking at houses in Denver.

The Western version of being a nomad is to take your home with you. Motor homes or recreational vehicles may be very small, in which case they mimic Gypsy wagons in many respects. Or they may be huge, having all the size and amenities of a modest-sized house. As mentioned above, David and Dorothy Counts have studied the culture of Canadian snowbirds who travel with their recreational vehicles to warmer climates in the south during the winter months. Snowbirds share a number of cultural beliefs about what sorts of items are essential to bring along, what sorts of stopping places are appropriate, and what the rules are for interacting with strangers as well as the old friends one meets at campgrounds or RV parks. Like Gypsy and other nomadic peoples, snowbirds value a lifestyle that involves traveling from place to place, seeing different scenery, meeting new people, and encountering new situations on a regular basis (Counts and Counts 2001).

House styles and interior design reflect cultural values, as well as Dettwyler's "stuff theory" of material culture. Top: the tent house of a group of Bakhtiary herders from Iran is contrasted to the interior of a traditional house in Japan. Bottom: the interior of a Mongolian yurt is contrasted to the "man cave" of an American family watching football on TV. The spaces we create in turn help create who we are and how we live our lives.

Houses also differ greatly in terms of their land-scaping, the outside appearance of the house itself, and the decorating style inside. All of these aspects of our living spaces provide blank canvases on which we can inscribe our cultural and individual styles and tastes. Next we turn to the use of the body itself as a canvas for human creativity.

Modifying and Decorating the Body

Across a wide variety of cultural groups, people express their creativity through modifying the appearance of their bodies, either temporarily or permanently, for a variety of purposes. In this section, I begin with a brief discussion of the reasons or functions of such behavior and then explore some specific examples of body modification.

Functions of Body Modification

Body Modification to Increase Attractiveness

There is little evidence for cross-cultural universals in terms of what people find attractive in others. Overall body symmetry, and particularly facial symmetry, may reflect underlying genetic fitness and health, such that people who are considered attractive tend to be those who are more symmetrical. Men in most cultures (but not all) state a preference for women with a specific waist-to-hip ratio of approximately 70 percent (hips broader than waist), which may indicate adequate room for successful childbearing in young adult females. Across a variety of cultures, women claim that men with broad upper faces are more *masculine*, but women seem to prefer more masculine men only when they are ovulating.

All other population differences in what is considered attractive (sexy, beautiful/handsome, desirable, etc.) seem to be the result of powerful cultural forces. In other words, children are enculturated to local notions of what constitutes attractiveness—not only which features are important but also the specific attributes of those features. People learn to respond positively to individuals who exemplify these standards of beauty with longing, love, and even sexual arousal.

To the extent possible, people in many cultures will modify their bodies, either temporarily or permanently, to more closely match local culturally based notions of attractiveness. Such body modifications are aesthetically pleasing to those who share the cultural beliefs but may appear bizarre or off-putting to outsiders. In some cases, the body modifications permanently alter the anatomy and functioning of the body, affecting other aspects of life in deleterious ways.

From the perspective of sexual selection, we would expect more men to engage in such body modifications than women. However, humans seldom mate or choose marriage partners without cultural restrictions. Women in particular often have little say in who fathers their children, but men also may not be free to choose the woman they consider most attractive as the mother of their children. However, in keeping with evolutionary expectations, women in many cultures use their physical features to try to obtain the best quality husband/sperm donor possible, while men use theirs to try to obtain more opportunities to mate, both inside and outside of marriage. In some cultures, the primary participants in body modification are women, and in others, they are men. In many, both men and women participate in different ways, to varying degrees.

Body Modification to Increase the Appearance of Aggression or Power

While not as common as modifications to increase attractiveness, some body modifications are made for the express purpose of causing the person (always male) to appear more frightening, aggressive, and powerful to observers. This may involve actual body modification, such as weight-lifting to increase the size of muscles, even though muscular strength is only partially correlated with size. In many cases, warriors paint or tattoo their bodies and faces to convey their ferocity and psychologically cripple their opponents in hand-to-hand combat.

Body Modification to Reflect Group Identity and Mark Accomplishments

Many different types of body modification and adornment are used as markers of **tribal membership,** whether the tribe is geographically based (national origin, regional, state, or local), or based on any of the many other ways that humans sort themselves into groups including ethnicity, actual kinship-based tribal identity, educational or occupational affiliation, religion, gang membership, military branch and status/rank, sports fans, and so on.

A few religious belief systems require adherents to adopt certain styles of clothing and hairstyle, and/or restrict the use of makeup, the wearing of jewelry, and so on. These modifications may reflect and reinforce aspects of the belief system and often function to identify members of the religion to each other, as well as to distinguish members from nonmembers. Examples include male circumcision among Jewish people, beards without moustaches among the Amish, and the traditional practice among the Dani of highland New Guinea of cutting off the finger joints of little girls as part of the mourning ritual following the death of a relative.

In some cases, the signals and messages presented to the world through body modifications or clothing, hairstyles, makeup, and so forth, are obvious to anyone who sees them, while in other cases only those who are part of the specific local culture will recognize their significance. Outsiders may completely misinterpret the messages that are being sent. They may not even recognize that such aspects of physical appearance have any deeper, symbolic meaning whatsoever, viewing them simply as matters of personal style or preference. People may adopt a particular style of adornment from another group, having no idea what messages they are sending (to those who understand the code) by doing so.

There are a number of instances in which body modification and/or clothing and hairstyles are used to indicate the achievement of certain milestones during one's lifetime. These milestones may be based on chronological age, developmental age, or personal accomplishments. Again, to those who can read the code, the story of a life may be inscribed on the body directly, or be reflected in choices of clothing style, hairstyle, jewelry, medals, and so on. Many people willingly go along with cultural practices that are expected or required of them, while others feel coerced or pressured to conform. The degree to which such practices are obligatory varies from one context to another. Those who rebel and go against the cultural norms may be ridiculed or face other sanctions.

Body Modification as Punishment

At different times in history and in different cultural contexts, body modification has been used to punish people who violated some cultural norm. Thus, in some cultures historically, and still today, a thief may have his or her right hand cut off. This is not only horrifically painful and occasionally fatal due to blood loss and infection, but it also makes it much more difficult to make a living. In addition, in some cultures the left hand is customarily used to clean oneself after toileting and is considered contaminated. If you lose your right hand due to a legal proceeding, then you will have to eat with your left hand. No one will want to shake hands with you or accept anything you offer them.

During the years of legalized slavery in the United States, runaway slaves were often branded on the face or shoulder after being recaptured, so they could be easily identified if they ran away again. In his book *Roots*, Alex Haley describes the experience of his ancestor Kunta Kinte, whose foot was amputated by professional slave catchers after his fourth escape attempt (Haley 1976). Another example of body modification as punishment is the practice of cutting off the nose of a woman who commits adultery, found historically in some Native American cultures and still practiced today in remote villages of Western Asia.

At the end of World War II, a number of people in France were accused of having collaborated with the occupying Germans. More than 20,000 of them, mostly women, had their heads shaved in public. In some cases, their only crime was being sexually involved with German soldiers. Of this practice, known in French as *tondue,* historian Fabrice Virgili writes: "it was the men who wielded the scissors and clippers, [but] the population as a whole—men, women, and children—were present at the event, which was both a spectacle and a demonstration of the punishment to be meted out to traitors" (Virgili 2002:1).

Today, in modern Japan, a member of the *yakuza* (organized crime syndicates who also serve as local keepers of the peace and enforcers of community harmony) may cut off the tip of one of his fingers and present it to his boss as a form of penance or apology for some misstep or mistake on his part or on the part of one of his underlings (Adelstein 2009).

Types of Body Modification

Applying Makeup or Paint to Temporarily Alter One's Appearance

Many examples abound of people changing their appearance through the application of makeup or paint. The earliest evidence we have from the archeological record involves the use of red ochre (an iron-based powdery pigment) applied to small sculptures and also found occasionally applied to the body in early human burials. It is thought that the color red has inherent significance for humans because blood is red, as are the glowing embers of fires. Red is thus a powerful natural symbol of both life and death. In a similar fashion, white is often associated with fertility because both semen and breast milk are white. However, both red and white, as well as all the other colors, may take on different or even multiple meanings depending on local cultural beliefs.

In many cultures, it is the women who wear makeup, usually on their faces, to enhance their features so that they more closely approximate the cultural ideal. This may include drawing attention to positive features, enhancing features that don't quite meet the ideal, and hiding or downplaying negative features. The face is the site of many such cultural modifications, as facial features are important among all primates for individual recognition, for communicating emotional states, and as the focus of judgments about attractiveness. Many of the modifications for women focus specifically on the eyes and mouth, which are the two most mobile and expressive facial features. They are also those most often involved in making or avoiding contact, showing emotion and interest or disinterest, and welcoming or rejecting advances. There may be cultural rules about the use of makeup, including restrictions on age, current styles and fads, and guidelines as to how much makeup is appropriate in different circumstances.

The tribes of the Omo Valley, located at the meeting point of Kenya, Ethiopia, and Sudan, have no architecture or crafts to express their artistic sensibilities. Instead, they use paint and found items—including natural objects such as vegetation and shells—to decorate their bodies, especially their heads and faces, in complex and striking ways. Adolescents of both sexes are particularly devoted to this form of creative expression (Silvester 2009).

In North America, excessive makeup, or makeup considered too heavy for the context—Saturday night at a techno club is different from Sunday morning in church—may be interpreted as an indicator of loose morals. Face makeup on young girls is considered by some to be inappropriate, as it makes them appear that they are trying to attract sexual attention from men even before they reach puberty. Likewise, lack of makeup use may be viewed as an indicator that the person "doesn't care about her appearance" or "is not professional"—actual comments I have received on student evaluations because I don't wear makeup.

Facial makeup is certainly not limited to women. People who appear on camera or on stage usually wear makeup to alter or enhance their appearance. Among the Wodaabe of Niger, the men apply makeup to make themselves more handsome according to local standards (overall yellow complexion on the face; long, thin noses; dark lips; and white teeth) and then compete in the *gerewol* ritual, using movements of their facial features, especially their eyes and mouths, to attract the attention of young women who might become lovers or wives. From an early age, young Wodaabe boys learn to roll and cross their eyes, raise their eyebrows, and smile so that their white teeth are shown to good advantage (Beckwith and Fisher 1993).

Many groups around the world value relatively lighter skin. In such places, there may be a number of commercial or homemade products that people apply in the form of creams to try to lighten their skin, especially on their faces. Some of these products are quite caustic and can cause health problems, while others are more benign, but none of them work particularly well.

Not all makeup serves the purpose of increasing attractiveness. In very different contexts, men heading off to battle may apply makeup to their bodies and faces to make them appear more formidable. Professional football players put dark marks under their eyes, ostensibly to reduce glare, but such marks also make them look fiercer to their opponents.

A number of different marks on the forehead reflect religious beliefs. For example, Ash Wednesday in the Western Christian calendar marks the first day of Lent, 46 days before Easter. In some Christian denominations—but by no means all—Ash Wednesday activities include burning the palm crosses from the previous year's Palm Sunday, mixing the ashes with oil, and then applying the ashes to the foreheads of the faithful as a sign of asking God to forgive their sins. The ashes are left on the skin until they wear off. This often leads to a public acknowledgement of one's religious beliefs, as people who don't understand the significance may point out that the person has dirt on her forehead, prompting an explanation.

In Hinduism, a *tilaka* is a mark on the forehead, usually made with sandalwood paste. Its placement between and just above the eyebrows marks the location of the sixth chakra or focus of energy in the body. This spot is also referred to as the **mind's eye** or Third Eye, and is considered the site of enlightenment, the seat of wisdom. In the past, many Hindus wore a tilaka for religious rituals, but today it is worn mostly by Hindu priests. Bindis are also found in the same location on the forehead. Placing the bindi at this spot is thought to increase mental energy and concentration. Bindis are frequently worn by Hindu women, but their meaning varies and has changed in recent decades. In some regions of India, the wearing of the bindi was limited to married women, while in other regions, any girl past puberty could wear it. Today, bindis are worn throughout South and Southeast Asia, and even by some Western women, as a fashion statement. They no longer *necessarily* convey information about religion, ethnicity or national origin, age, or marital status. Instead of a simple, perfectly round red dot made from vermillion or saffron, many today come in the form of stickers and may be of varying shapes and sizes or even include small jewels or pieces of shiny metal. Traditionally, a new Hindu bride would also have the part in her hair painted with red to signify that she was married. Red was considered a sign of prosperity and fertility.

Mehendi designs, or temporary henna decorations, are traditionally used by women in West and North Africa and across the Middle East and South Asia. The use of mehendi in Western cultures is quite recent and usually serves a purely decorative purpose. Henna comes from a plant, whose leaves are dried, ground, and then mixed with water or oil to form a paste. When applied to the skin, especially the palms of the hands and the soles of the feet, the reddish pigment is absorbed by the skin. The longer one leaves the paste on—from several hours to several days—the darker the red color, even to the point of appearing almost black. Henna applied to the fingernails will stain the nail beds a deep orange-red. Henna designs last until the colored skin cells are replaced, usually within a week, although for nails the process takes several months. Henna marks range from simple dots and lines to incredibly complex and intricate designs.

Hindu brides, even those living in highly Westernized cultural contexts, often view mehendi designs as an essential part of their wedding finery. The bride and her close female friends and relatives will gather a few days before the wedding for the lengthy process of creating the henna designs, and then sitting around visiting while the dye is absorbed. A number of differing beliefs are found with respect to the meaning of mehendi designs, but all point to the wish for a long and successful marriage and the birth of healthy children.

Mehendi is not limited to Hindus. In Mali, for special occasions including weddings and religious holidays, women might dye the soles of their feet and the palms of their hands a solid black. Having dark skin everywhere was viewed as a sign of beauty. While living in Mali, I once dyed my feet black with henna to fulfill a prophecy my husband made to his mother as a child that he was going to "grow up and marry a woman with black feet."

Tattoos

Tattoos are similar to makeup, since they are modifications of the skin, but tattoos consist of designs applied to the deeper layers of the skin using permanent ink and a sharp instrument to inject the ink or dye. Tattooing has an ancient history among humans.

Opposite page: Body modification and decoration runs the gamut from the simple and temporary—hairstyles, clothing, jewelry, and makeup—to the elaborate and permanent—tattoos, scarification, implants, and more. Top left: a Murzi woman from Ethiopia with a large wooden plug in her lower lip, as well as elaborate scarification along her arms and back. Top center: three men from Thailand, known as *kathoey*, who have modified their bodies, hair, clothing, and jewelry to appear to be women. They work as dancers and prostitutes, and some work in the pornographic film industry. Top right: a member of the "modern primitive movement" with subdermal implants, stretched piercings, multiple other piercings, and facial and neck tattoos. Bottom left: champion bodybuilders from the U.S. Army. Bottom right: a Hindu bride having henna designs applied to her hands.

One of the earliest known examples of tattooing comes from Ötzi, the Copper Age Ice-Man, who was found in 1991 melting out of a glacier in the Alps. Ötzi lived about 3,500 years ago and had more than 50 carbon-based tattoos on his body, consisting mostly of simple dots and lines. The placement of the tattoos in regions of the body where he suffered from arthritis—lower back, knees, and ankles—has led some scholars to conclude that Ötzi's tattoos were attempts at pain relief using techniques similar to acupuncture (Fowler 2001). Another early example of tattooing comes from a group of frozen mummies in Greenland dating to AD 1475. Five of the six adult women had facial tattoos on their foreheads and cheeks, and three had tattoos under their chins. Facial tattooing is a cultural practice known from other Arctic populations from historic and early modern times.

Tattoos are found in many cultures around the world and have varied cultural meanings. They most often serve as markers of group identity, ranging from the military to motorcycle gangs to fraternities and sororities on college campuses to the yakuza crime syndicates in Japan, whose colorful whole-body tattoos are one of their trademark identifying features. Tattooing is found across the South Pacific, with the most distinctive designs being those made by the Maori of New Zealand. Men among the Maori had elaborate tattoos carved or chiseled into their faces, buttocks, and legs. Maori women had tattoos on their lips and chins. Maori tattoo designs consist mostly of curvilinear lines and spirals, an artistic motif found throughout all types of Maori artwork. Traditionally, tattooing began at adolescence and continued throughout life as a way to mark significant life events. Although Maori tattooing became less common following the arrival of Europeans, it has experienced something of a revival beginning in the 1990s, as did similar forms of traditional tattooing in the South Pacific (Kuwahara 2005). Today, many Maori people get tattoos as a symbol of ethnic and cultural pride, although most use modern techniques with needles and commercial tattoo inks.

Tattoos in Western cultures had, for many years, an anti-establishment or counterculture vibe. They were sported by rebels, outlaws, outcasts, prison inmates, and others who were happy to be viewed as different from the masses of mainstream, proper citizens. Tattoos were edgy. Over the past few decades, however, tattoos have become more and more popular and mainstream, especially among college students. Many are purely decorative, such as a small heart, bird, butterfly, or cartoon character. Others are sentimental, commemorating one's love for a parent, a sweetheart, or a friend who has died. Others are abstract designs, often incorporating tribal patterns from other regions of the world. Many of these modern tattoos are small and inconspicuous, and placed where they can be easily covered with clothing.

People often get tattooed with symbols or designs that have some special meaning to them. Merely having a tattoo no longer marks one as an outlaw. These days, to be edgy with a tattoo in Western culture you either have to have extensive, brightly colored tattoos that cover large areas of your body, tattoos that are visible even when you are fully clothed, or tattoos that deliberately are designed to offend others.

Hairstyles

Like other primates, all humans are covered with body hair on all skin surfaces except the palms of the hands, the soles of the feet, and mucous membranes such as the gums and inside of the mouth. Human hair usually grows more profusely on the head and, after puberty, in the armpits and pubic region. In addition, males have facial hair that begins growing at puberty. As they get older, some men develop more hair on their chests, backs, arms, and legs. Males have more body hair than females generally, and men in some regions of the world let their facial hair grow into beards, moustaches, and sideburns. Some people have relatively scant body hair, while others have profuse body hair, especially on the face and trunk. Patterns of hair growth vary both within and between populations.

Almost all cultures have customary beliefs and practices about the meaning of different aspects of body hair. In many, males and females are expected to have different hairstyles that immediately identify the sex of the individual to other people. Hair is easily manipulated to reflect group membership, such as religion: tonsures for Christian monks, uncut hair worn covered by a turban among men of the Sikh religion, or ear curls for Orthodox Jewish men. There may be rules about the length of hair, the specific styles of hair, whether the hair can be dyed different colors, whether various jewels or ornaments are placed in the hair, and so on. Across Africa, women (and occasionally men) often devote considerable time and attention to plaiting (braiding) their hair into elaborate styles (Sieber and Herreman 2000). In North America, many older women have relatively short hair, and many dye their hair so it retains its youthful color. Extremely short hair on women may be interpreted by others as an index of sexual orientation, whether or not that is the intent.

Additionally, populations vary in terms of patterns of balding and turning gray with old age. In North America, many men are dismayed to lose the hair on the top of their head as they age and may resort to prescription drugs to promote hair growth, or use hair follicle transplants, comb-overs, or toupees. In cultural contexts where youth is glorified and old age does not bring automatic respect, men may dye their hair once it begins to go gray. But in other societies, gray hair is viewed as a distinguished characteristic, associated with survival and wisdom. Where old age is valued, men (and women) are much less likely to try to disguise their gray hair.

Going against the cultural norms for hairstyles, such as Euro-Americans who wear dread-locks or Mohawks, or middle-aged women who let their hair go gray naturally, is one way to express one's individuality. Like other aspects of style, fads in hairstyles come and go. In North America in the 1960s and 1970s, it was considered radical for men to have long hair, and Afros were common among young African Americans. Unusually colored hair experienced great popularity in the 1990s and 2000s. Women's hair is often considered to be highly sexually charged, especially when it is long and worn down and uncovered. In many different cultural contexts, adult women keep their hair pulled back or up and often cover it with a cap, net, or head scarf to prevent men from being unduly and inappropriately sexually aroused by the sight of their loose locks.

There are many different cultural beliefs and practices concerning men's facial hair. Beards may be required for all adult men, as among some fundamentalist Muslim groups. Anabaptists such as the Amish and Mennonites require men to have beards, but to shave their moustaches. In the Circum-Mediterranean region, a real man is one who has a moustache. Like head hair, facial hair is easily manipulated and styled in many different ways by shaving or not shaving various portions of the face. Styles and fads for men's facial hair come and go, as well as varying across cultures and even occupations. At an anthropology conference, most of the men will have beards, while a gathering of physicists or accountants will be mostly clean shaven. Under Taliban rule in Afghanistan, men were expected to have long beards; many men celebrated the overthrow of the Taliban by shaving off their beards.

Hair on other regions of the body varies more subtly than head and facial hair from person to person and between populations. Such hair is often not visible because of clothing, but that doesn't stop people from sharing different ideas about what is appropriate or aesthetically pleasing. Women in North America, for example, are often expected to shave the hair in their armpits and on their legs, even though most women in Europe do not. The occasional woman who has facial hair often goes to great lengths to disguise it or get rid of it temporarily or permanently.

Excessive body hair on men, especially on the trunk (chest, abdomen, and back) may be viewed as sexy or disgusting, even within the same culture, and some men will resort to laser treatments or other procedures to control the growth of hair on their body. In Japan, one indigenous group, the Ainu, are much more hirsute (hairy) than later immigrants to the island and are referred to, sometimes in a disparaging manner, as "the hairy Ainu." In addition to having more facial and body hair than other Japanese populations, they also have more European facial features. They are thought to be the descendants of the earliest immigrants to the region.

Men involved in some sports, such as swimming and bicycle racing, shave their bodies to reduce the drag of air or water through their hair.

Dental Modifications

Teeth may be modified in various ways. In a few Central African cultures, anterior teeth (the incisors and canines) were traditionally filed to sharp points. Teeth were sometimes etched in lines of cross-hatching. In Mexico and Central America, incisors with gold, silver, and jade inlays have been recovered from archeological sites. Among some tribes in the southern Sudan, young men had their permanent lower central incisors removed—when Nuer youth migrated to Minnesota because of the civil war, they found that this characteristic tribal practice was viewed with dismay in the United States, and some have had replacement teeth made.

A common dental modification in North America is the practice of having adolescents wear orthodontic appliances (braces and traction devices, followed by retainers) for several years to make their teeth line up neatly. Removal of the wisdom teeth is also common among North American young adults. This is a particularly interesting cultural phenomenon for several reasons. Many people assume that all populations have problems with their wisdom teeth and that crowding of the front teeth, and misalignment of the teeth in general, is typical for humans. In fact, the need for braces is both biological and cultural.

Biologically, European populations tend to have small lower faces, tucked underneath their crania, which leaves less room for their teeth to erupt. Many other populations have much larger lower faces that project farther in front of the brain case, leaving plenty of room for the permanent third molars (wisdom teeth) to erupt into the mouth and function perfectly well. In addition, a larger lower face allows the front teeth to fit together in a row, and some people even have a space between their permanent upper central incisors—an indication of more room than needed for the teeth.

Culturally, the growth and development of the face is affected by whether a child was breastfed or bottle-fed. Breastfeeding requires much more effort on the part of the child, resulting in stronger facial muscles and different growth of the facial bones. Where bottle-feeding is common, children's facial structure does not develop normally, so there often isn't enough room for all of the teeth to align side-by-side. The combination of a small European face and bottle-feeding leads to many children in North America having jaws too small to accommodate all their teeth. Dental extractions and braces are quite expensive, however, so having teeth straightened through braces becomes a marker of middle- or upper-class status. Having crooked teeth may then be viewed as an indicator of relative poverty and lower social status.

Scarification

Scarification, like tattooing, is a permanent modification of the body's skin surface. Scarification involves cutting the skin deeply enough that scar tissue forms. People vary with respect to the thickness of their skin, and thin-skinned people often form scars that are amorphous and unsightly. Deliberate scarification for purposes of tribal identification, aesthetics,

or to mark important life stages usually is limited to populations that have relatively thicker skin that forms precise, well-defined scars right along the lines carved into the skin. Sometimes, the cuts in the skin are rubbed with ashes or other pigments so that the result is a combination of a scar and a tattoo, such as the facial tattoos of the Maori.

Among the Nuba of the Sudan, scars are cut into a woman's trunk to reflect her passage through puberty and marriage and to celebrate the birth of each child. Nuba men may have various designs, such as the outline of a bull, carved into their chests. The Nuer traditionally cut six parallel lines across the foreheads of young boys at puberty as part of a ritual of manhood. The boys are expected to remain stoic and not flinch or cry as these deep cuts are made from side to side, down to the bone. These scars, known as *gar*, not only indicate tribal affiliation, but also serve to mark those who are considered adults.

Scars may serve other purposes as well. One of the more elaborate **cultures of scarification** was the dueling scar (*Renommierschmiss*) sported by upper-class Austrians and Germans for a brief time at the end of the nineteenth century. Dueling societies were very popular at universities, and young men would engage in fighting with heavy sabers in an attempt to acquire a dashing scar. The scars indicated that one belonged to the educated upper classes and had the courage to face opponents in one or more duels (McAleer 1994). Women of the time greatly admired and desired men with dramatic facial scars.

In modern North American society, only the details have changed. According to BMEzine Encyclopedia:

> Today, the "chicks dig scars" motivation is expressed in chaotic scarification. Certain activities—be it BMX racing and other extreme sports, or be it fighting and punching out windows—tend to lead to scars because of the injuries they bring. Many view these scars as desirable, and not only seek them out by putting themselves in harm's way, but by rubbing irritants into any wounds to induce them to scar. (Dueling Scar 2010)

Note that such scars are referred to as *chaotic* to distinguish them from deliberate cuts to induce scarring for tribal identification purposes.

In Mali, each tribe traditionally had its own style of facial scars that allowed people to immediately categorize strangers into their specific tribe. These facial scars ranged from very subtle to very obvious. Many Bambara groups carved two short, upright, parallel lines just beyond the outer edge of the eyebrows on both sides of the face. Others, such as the Miniaka, carved deep, wide grooves down both sides of the face, beginning in the mid-forehead, bisecting the eyebrows, and continuing down the cheeks to the level of the mouth.

Piercings

Another form of body modification found in a variety of cultural contexts and having many different meanings is the piercing of various parts of the body. Usually piercings are accompanied by the wearing of jewelry attached through the hole in the skin. The most common location for piercings is through the earlobes, the fleshy part of the ear that contains neither cartilage nor muscle. Earlobe piercing is usually bilateral, and in many societies it differentiates the sexes. In Mali, all newborn females have their ears pierced very early on, so there is never any question of the sex of a baby. Until I figured this out, I was always inquiring after the sex of young infants. People thought I was really dense, as the presence or absence of pierced ears clearly indicated the sex of all Bambara babies to onlookers who understood the cultural code.

In addition to piercing earlobes and the rim of cartilage along the outside of the ear, people also pierce the fleshy tip of the nasal septum that divides the nose into left and right nostrils. Bones, shells, horns, and other decorative items can then be worn through the nasal septum. The outer edge of the nose can be pierced and the varying traditional Hindu customs of women wearing a small nose ring or nose stud on the side of their nose has become trendy in Western cultures as a fashion statement. People also pierce their tongues, lips, cheeks, eyebrows, nipples, navels, genitals, and other regions of the body, for varying reasons.

Piercings can consist of very small holes, through which only a post or ring is slipped to attach a small object, or they can be much larger holes, into which much larger objects can be placed. Both upper and lower lips can be pierced and the hole gradually enlarged until large lip plugs can be inserted. In some cultures, such adornments are found among the women, and the larger the lip plug, the more beautiful the woman is considered. In some regions of East Africa, people realized that slave raiders thought large lip plugs were repugnant. Large lip plugs then became a protection against slavers.

In a few cultural contexts, larger segments of skin and muscle are pierced and then used to support the weight of the body as it hangs in space, or as the person pulls against the piercings while on the ground. According to Fakir Musafar—father of the Modern Primitive Movement and modern-day master of extreme body modification and piercing/hanging rituals—the practice of piercing the body and pulling on or hanging by these piercings arose independently at least twice in human history. The first known example is found among the Tamil people of southern India, who are Savite Hindus (devotees of Lord Siva, Muruga, Murugan, Subramanya, the Great Mother Mari and Kali). Two of their important religious festivals involve piercing the body—usually the chest and/or back—and then hanging suspended from the piercings. Other Hindus, such as those devoted to Vishnu or Krishna, do not practice these body piercing rituals and may even look down on such behaviors (Musafar 2003).

The second example comes from aboriginal North America, where "the practice of piercing the body and ritually pulling or suspending it to achieve some kind of union with divine powers developed quite independently" (Musafar 2003). Traveler, author, and painter George Catlin lived among the Mandan people of North and South Dakota in the 1830s and wrote descriptions and painted images of the O-Kee-Pa ritual. This ritual served as a rite of passage for young men and was also repeated by elder shamans as a way to seek visions and achieve union with supernatural beings. "After many days of fasting and extreme ordeals, Mandan young men who were about to become adults and enter adult life were pierced twice in the chest, and twice in the back" and then "suspended by either set of piercings from the roof of a lodge" (Musafar 2003). Similar rituals were adopted and modified by other Plains Indian groups such as the Arikara, Minitaree, and various Sioux tribes, whose Sun Dance rituals were portrayed in the film *A Man Called Horse* (Silverstein 1970).

Fakir Musafar and Jim Ward, modern-day practitioners of piercing and suspension rituals, participated in similar ceremonies, documented in the film *Dances Sacred & Profane* (Musafar 1985). Clips of both the Sun Dance suspension and the Kavadi ritual from this film are available at Musafar's website (Musafar 2010).

More Elaborate Body Modifications

A variety of more elaborate and complex body modifications are found in different cultural contexts, most of which are applied to women and are designed to make them more physically attractive to men. Examples from around the world include:

- Placing heavy brass rings around a woman's neck, which depress her clavicles (collar bones) resulting in the appearance of a very long neck: Common among the Karen (or Kayan) people of Myanmar, this practice traditionally was a form of tribal identity marking and was thought to make women more attractive as well. Today it continues because tourists will pay money to come and gawk at the elongated necks of the women.

- Cutting open women's breasts to insert bags of silicone or saline to make the woman's breasts appear larger: Found mostly in Western cultures, especially the United States, where breasts are culturally defined as erotic, such implants often impair the biological function of the breast, which is to produce milk for children (lactation). Some types of implant surgery result in loss of sensation in the breasts. Insurance companies in the United States are required by federal law to pay for breast reconstruction surgery following mastectomies due to breast cancer, even though such reconstructed breasts cannot function to produce milk. Cosmetic surgery is not typically covered by insurance companies, but the Women's Health and Cancer Rights Act, passed by Congress in 1998, makes an exception for breasts because of their cultural importance as sex objects in the United States (Department of Labor 2009).

- Various modifications to reduce the apparent size of the waist relative to the hips, including girdles and corsets, but also surgery to remove fat and tighten skin, and remove the lowest pair of ribs: These are found mostly in Western cultures.

- Female circumcision and other genital modifications often justified through religious beliefs or thought to result in cleaner, healthier, or more attractive genitals: These practices are found not only in a variety of African and Asian cultures but also in the modern United States where surgery to expose the clitoris, trim the labia, and tighten the vaginal opening are thought to make orgasm easier for women, improve the appearance of the genitals, and increase pleasure for male partners, respectively (Benson 2010).

- Subincision of the penis: This involves splitting the underside of the penis. It is found in some traditional Australian Aboriginal groups and has become popular as part of the New Tribalism movement in some Western cultures. This movement may include other extreme genital modifications as well as splitting of the tongue, and implanting horns, round metal beads, and other shape-makers under the skin.

- Foot binding, involving bending the four lateral toes underneath the ball of the foot and bending the heel up toward the toes: Eventually the bones of the foot break, resulting in a tiny three- to four-inch-long foot known as a *Golden Lotus* or a *Silver Lotus*. Foot binding was practiced in some regions of China up until the early decades of the twentieth century and was done to make young women more sexually attractive. Having tiny Golden Lotus feet helped a woman improve her own status and that of her children through marriage to a man from a higher-ranking family.

- Deliberately plumping up adolescent girls to make them more attractive to potential husbands: This practice is found in some parts of West and North Africa, including Mauritania. Girls may be secluded for several months and required to sit still while they spend their days eating large quantities of high-fat foods in order to add layers of fat. In Mauritania, girls are encouraged to drink large quantities of camel's milk, which is particularly high in fat and calories.

- Manipulations of height, either to make people taller or shorter: Modifications of height are limited to Western cultures. Short boys may have surgery to break their leg bones and insert steel rods connecting the broken ends some distance apart. The rods are attached to external bolts that can be turned every day to gradually increase the length of the bones and therefore increase final height by a few inches. Girls whose parents worry that they will be too tall may be administered exogenous estrogen to send them through puberty early, artificially ending their growth in height (Cohen and Cosgrove 2009).

- Plastic surgery on the face and other regions of the body, both to correct congenital birth defects and repair the ravages of accidents or diseases: In some cultures, plastic surgery is done on perfectly normal facial features in order to make them more closely match the cultural ideal of beauty, including rhinoplasty (nose jobs) to reduce the size of a woman's nose or even out bumps, chin implants for men with receding chins, and eyelid surgery to make the eyes of Asian women (and some men) appear more European.

Body modifications, both temporary and permanent, both mild and extreme, can reveal many significant cultural beliefs and values, and the body itself serves as the locus of a wide array of creative expressions.

VISUAL ARTS

Some cultures make a distinction between **art,** produced solely for the purpose of being aesthetically pleasing, and **objects of everyday use,** which are quite practical and functional but may be designed and/or decorated to make them more enjoyable to look at, handle, and use. Many people in Western cultures think of *art* as a separate category—*art* is what you hang on the wall to gaze at; *art* is what you go to see at a museum. *Art* may evoke emotions or make a political statement, but it does so primarily through the visual channels of sensory experience. Art is seldom regarded as something necessary for human existence, something that does important work. If you need a comb for your hair, or a fan to alleviate the heat, there is no need for it to be intricately carved or inlaid with ivory and mother-of-pearl, or painted with delicate flowers. Your toaster doesn't need to be aesthetically pleasing. And yet, why not?

Thus, in some cultures, a distinction is made between art and design, or between art and decoration. In others, these categories overlap, and the divisions among them may change over time as fashions change or as new creative individuals come along to shake up established modes of expression. Design elements from one cultural context (or from an earlier time period) may be borrowed in their entirety or modified and adapted to suit new purposes and different tastes.

Cultural beliefs strongly influence both what is depicted in art and decorative objects and how it is presented. For example, depending on the culture, the art may be representational or abstract. In representational art, the images reflect actual people, animals, plants, natural and man-made objects, and specific places. The art may be extremely realistic or it may present its subject in a simplified form, but the subject is clearly identifiable. In some cultural traditions, such as Islamic art, representational images are not allowed, and all design elements must be abstract—lines, dots, curves, spirals, and so forth, but not depictions of people, places, or things. In still other instances, art and decorations may include the fantastical, with depictions of imaginary creatures and places, such as the Star-Bellied Sneetches of Dr. Seuss or the Emerald City of Oz. Some artistic renderings are minimalist and merely hint at their subject, while others are elaborate and crowded with intricate design elements down to the smallest detail.

Visual art can take many forms and serve a variety of purposes. Art from one region of the world, or one specific group of people, may be widely admired and appreciated by others without any special knowledge of its historical and cultural context. However, there are often multiple layers of meaning encoded in art of all kinds, and thus it may evoke different emotions and responses in viewers depending on their level of knowledge of the context in which the art was created. In the following section, we will touch briefly on the major categories of visual art.

Sculpture

Some of the earliest evidence of human artistic creativity comes in the form of small sculptures from the Upper Paleolithic, most depicting either prey animals that people hunted or women with somewhat exaggerated body parts, usually interpreted as icons of female reproductive power. From a contemporary perspective, it is difficult to know exactly what these objects meant to those who made and used them. Were they toys for children to play with, or did they have serious ritual and religious significance? Were they meant to depict specific individuals or more the categories of deer or bird or woman? Some early sculptures are quite expertly carved from bone or ivory or soapstone; others are made from clay. Some look as though they might have been made by or for children, or were practice pieces from artists just developing their skills. Some are stand-alone objects, with three-dimensional depictions of their subject, while others are carved into cave walls in relief, showing only one side.

Some sculptures are small, intended to be kept in a pouch or pocket or worn around the neck, while others are larger and heavier. As we have discussed before, nomadic hunters and gatherers tend to have few material objects to cart around from one place to the next, and thus we see few examples of large or heavy sculptures among such groups. Once people become sedentary, they can decorate their landscape with rock carvings (petroglyphs) and larger sculptures made from a variety of materials. A number of past and contemporary cultures have carved and decorated large wooden sculptures, including the totem poles of Northwest Coast Native American settlements and the funerary carvings of many African and Asian tribal groups. The island of Rapa Nui contains many *moai*—giant stone carvings of people that were erected facing the sea. Sculptural objects can be made of a variety of materials, from stone, wood, and clay to limestone, marble, glass, iron, and steel. Some sculptures have religious significance, while others, such as Calder's giant red mobiles, do not.

Several scholars, including Ellen Dissanayake (1992) and Denis Dutton (2009) have explored the relationship between human evolution and the arts.

Painting

In contrast to sculptures, paintings are usually two-dimensional and use different colors of pigments to depict their subject. Paint (or other pigments) may be applied directly to the walls of caves or rock shelters or to the interior and/or exterior walls of private dwellings or communal gathering places. The pigments may be incorporated into the wall itself, as in frescoes. Paint may be applied to portable material such as boards, cloth, or canvasses stretched on a frame. All sorts of functional objects can be decorated with paint as well.

Once again, the Upper Paleolithic time period provides the earliest evidence of human creative expression through cave paintings, such as those found in Europe, Africa, and Asia. The oldest rock art in Australia is more than 60,000 years old. Typical motifs include animals, plants, natural objects such as the sun and stars, and so-called *shaman* figures. These shamans may be depicted as part human/part animal or may be recognized through standard designs such as skeletal elements (as though the observer were viewing an x-ray) or fringe on the shaman's clothing. Rock art motifs are often grouped together into panels that are thought to tell a story.

Soon after people migrated to the New World, they began painting on the walls of caves and rock shelters (overhangs). Sophisticated cave and rock shelter paintings are known from a number of sites, especially in the arid southwestern United States and northern Mexico. Open-air sites typically deteriorate from the elements, and/or are subject to vandalism by later people. Only remote or well-protected art on the ceilings and walls of caves and rock shelters has survived for thousands of years.

Carolyn Boyd and the Prehistoric Rock Art of the Lower Pecos (Texas/Mexico)

Four thousand years ago bands of hunter-gatherers lived in and traveled through the challenging terrain of what is now southwest Texas and northern Mexico. Today, travelers to the Lower Pecos Canyonlands can view large murals that these early people left behind on canyon walls and cliff overhangs. More than 250 rock shelters in the region are known to contain rock art, and new sites are discovered each year. Based on radiocarbon dates, this artistic tradition emerged around 2000 BC and persisted for almost 1,500 years. The artists who produced these paintings used an array of Earth colors to create elaborate murals that are impressive in the level of skill required to produce them as well as sheer size and complexity. Some of the panels are massive, spanning over 100 feet in length and 30 feet in height—a feat that required significant planning and construction of scaffolding and the use of ladders. Other panels are quite small, tucked away in secluded alcoves high above the canyon floor. These ancient paintings represent some of the most sophisticated and compositionally intricate prehistoric rock art in the world and contain messages from the distant past that are now being studied and interpreted by Dr. Carolyn Boyd.

Boyd, an artist and archeologist by training, has pioneered what she calls an **ethnographic approach** to Lower Pecos rock art interpretation. She argues that many rock art panels represent coherent and highly organized compositions, not random collections of images painted over thousands of years, as other researchers have proposed. Just as detectives look for patterns to solve crimes and cryptologists look for patterns to break secret codes, Boyd looks for patterns to interpret rock art. Patterns are the clues to "making sense" of past human behavior. By identifying patterns or **motifs** in ethnographic, ethnohistoric, and other literary sources that correspond to patterns identified in rock art, Boyd has demonstrated that the rock art murals of the Lower Pecos are pictorial narratives that record histories and detailed prescriptions for ritual, and recount a constellation of myths that are still found today in parts of Mesoamerica and the American Southwest.

This is best exemplified in her analysis of the famous White Shaman rock art panel, which is located in a small rock shelter high on a bluff overlooking the Pecos River near its confluence with the Rio Grande. Dimensions of the pictographic panel are four meters by eight meters. This panel contains over 30 **anthropomorphic** (human-like) figures, deer, and numerous enigmatic figures unidentifiable as human or nonhuman animal. Boyd began her analysis by creating an artistic rendition of the full panel, looking for those elusive code-breaking patterns. A very intriguing pattern emerged. At the White Shaman site, as well as numerous other sites in the region, she found the recurring association of spear-impaled deer, antlered human figures whose antlers are tipped with black dots, and spear-impaled dots. She identified a similar pattern in her analysis of myths and rituals documented among past and present societies in Mesoamerica and the American Southwest. This ethnographic motif is associated with peyotism—the ritual use of *Lophophora williamsii* (peyote cactus). Elements of the motif include the use of peyote and the unification of peyote with deer. Peyote is a small, spineless cactus native to parts of northern and central Mexico and southwest Texas, including the Lower Pecos. It is well-known for its psychoactive properties and has a long history of use by shamans as a religious sacrament, powerful medicine, and a bridge to the otherworld among indigenous Americans.

Can beliefs among historic Native American groups be used to help expand our understanding of this and other patterns in Lower Pecos rock art? Boyd

**This is an artistic rendition of the White Shaman rock art panel by
Carolyn E. Boyd, reprinted from *Rock Art of the Lower Pecos* by
permission of the Texas A&M University Press and the artist.**

maintains that they can. To investigate this train of thought, it is useful to
consider the myths and rituals of one group of Native Americans who once
lived in the Chihuahuan Desert, the Huichol Indians.

Currently, the Huichol live in the states of Jalisco and Nayarit in northwest-
ern Mexico. According to Huichol tradition, their foraging ancestors migrated
into this area from their homeland, Wirikúta, in the Chihuahuan Desert – the
land where the peyote grows. They are one of the few indigenous groups
whose pre-contact religion has remained relatively intact with only minimal
accommodations to Christianity. Huichol myths and rituals have been extensively documented by explorers and scholars over the past 100 years (e.g.,
Preuss, Lumholtz, Zingg, Furst, Myerhoff, Schaefer, and Neurath). In all these
accounts, peyote is at the center of Huichol life and religion. And, in all of
these accounts, deer and peyote are seen as one inseparable sacred symbol.

According to the Huichol Indians, Sacred Deer Person brought peyote to
the ancestors by attaching it to his antler tines. Each year, bands of Huichols
undertake a pilgrimage that reenacts the first pilgrimage that led to the creation of the cosmos and the birth of peyote from the Sacred Deer. They journey to the sacred mountain in Wirikúta to gather peyote from the antlers of
the deer, and to hunt the peyote and the deer so that there will be rain. Each
pilgrim is transformed into one of the original ancestor-deities that participated in the first hunt. The leader of the pilgrims, the *mara'akáme* (shaman),

always becomes Tatewari, Grandfather Fire. Tatewari is believed to have been the first shaman and is said to be the only one with the power to open and close the door that separates the upperworld from the underworld. He carries both the weapon that will be used to slay the deer in Wirikúta and the antler rack of the Sacred Deer. When the pilgrims locate the peyote-deer, they shoot it with an arrow, cut off the top portion of the cactus, and gather it to take back to their people for use as medicine and in ritual.

There is no question that there are serious perils in utilizing present-day ethnographic information as a source for studying rock art from the distant past. Parallels between the past and the present are not necessarily identical. However, the shared patterns, both in the art and the ethnography, beg explanation and provide the basis for developing testable hypotheses regarding the function and meaning of the art. Boyd proposed that patterns consisting of antlered anthropomorphs with dots on their antler tines, found in association with impaled deer and/or impaled dots, portray a metaphorical relationship between deer and peyote. Impaled dots and impaled deer represent the slain peyote-deer. The dots on the tines of antlered anthropomorphs also represent peyote. The anthropomorph represents the bringer of peyote, the first shaman, the anthropomorphized peyote-deer and the ancestral leader of the pilgrims.

The strongest evidence to support Boyd's peyotism hypothesis comes from the archeological record. George Martin recovered three specimens, actual peyote effigies, from the deposits of the Shumla Caves. These effigies contain comparable amounts of alkaloids as peyote and have been radiocarbon dated to around 3500 BC, at least 1,000 years prior to the earliest dates for the Lower Pecos paintings. Additionally, several items of material culture recovered from excavations in the region, including the Shumla Caves, are similar to paraphernalia used in peyote ceremonies by various contemporary aboriginal groups. These include rasping sticks made from either bone or wood, a rattle made from a deer scapula (shoulder blade), a pouch, reed tubes containing cedar incense, and feather plumes.

Identification of the peyotism motif in the rock art of the Lower Pecos provides insight into the possible origins and antiquity of peyotism and the metaphorical association of deer with the sacred peyote cactus, an association that persists in the myths, rituals, and arts of peyote religions into modern times. It also introduces us to other possible identities for anthropomorphic figures presented in Lower Pecos rock art, identities beyond those of shamans. Participants in rituals, such as the peyote pilgrimage, reenact events and actions performed during mythic time by ancestral beings. Participants in the ritual are transformed into ancestor-deities. Anthropomorphic figures, therefore, may represent numerous concepts simultaneously: shaman, ancestor, deity, and mythic character. Boyd argues that to refer to all anthropomorphic figures as shamans fails to acknowledge the extremely rich, highly complex cosmology and worldview of hunter-gatherers.

Exquisite in detail and masterful in execution, the rock art murals of the Lower Pecos are pictorial narratives that recorded histories, detailed prescriptions for ritual, and recounted a constellation of myths that are still enacted today in parts of Mesoamerica and the American Southwest. They represent the oldest known religious narratives in North America. These pictorial narratives reveal social complexities and interactions that today command a sense of awe. How bleak our perspective of the past would be if not for this extraordinarily rich cultural legacy!

Boyd has published her discoveries in several scholarly articles, book chapters, and a book *Rock Art of the Lower Pecos* (2003). She is the Executive Director of the SHUMLA School, a non-profit archeological research and education center located along the Pecos River (www.shumla.org). Today Boyd and her collaborators and students continue to study and document the rock art of the Lower Pecos Canyonlands.

Text by Carolyn E. Boyd and Katherine A. Dettwyler.

Painting styles are constantly changing, as different times and cultures focus on realistic or abstract representations, pleasing and calming, or angry and violent depictions, real people and places versus phantasmagorical imaginary scenes. In many cases, the symbolism of the culture that produced the painter and the painting is very opaque—not easily understood by a viewer from another time period or cultural background. That doesn't mean that one can't like (or dislike) a particular painting, but it does mean that much of the information and meaning the artist intended to convey will be lost on many viewers.

The application of paint to a surface, including the human body, provides virtually limitless opportunities for human creative expression and continues to hold an important place in the artistic expression of many peoples around the world.

Weaving

Spinning fibers into thread, and then making string, twine, cord, or cloth out of the thread through knotting and weaving has an ancient history as a form of human creative expression. Evidence of early weaving comes from fiber remnants discovered at Upper Paleolithic sites in Europe and Israel, dating to 15,000–20,000 years ago. In 2009, researchers reported finding knotted and dyed wild flax fibers from Dzudzuana Cave, an archeological site in the Republic of Georgia, dating to 32,000 years ago. If the dates are confirmed, these flax fibers would be the earliest evidence of human weaving.

String-making is found in all historical cultures around the world. As Elizabeth Barber points out, "string can be used simply to tie things up—to catch, to hold, to carry. From these notions come snares and fishlines, tethers and leashes, carrying nets, handles, and packages, not to mention a way of binding objects together to form more complex tools" (Barber 1994:45). String skirts are depicted as far back as the Upper Paleolithic. A small bone carving of a female figure from Lespugue, France, dated at 22,000 years of age, depicts a woman wearing a string skirt suspended from a hip band (Barber 1994). The remains of similar string skirts have been found on the bodies of young women in Bronze Age coffins. In modern times, string skirts are found across southern and eastern Europe as part of women's traditional costumes.

"Weaving, on the contrary, is much more complicated [than making string] and may have been thought up only once, much too late to spread with humankind. Many cultures were still ignorant of it as the [twentieth] century began" (Barber 1994:70). Weaving is thought to have originated on the steppes of West-

Visual art allows for infinite creativity, as seen in these examples from around the world. Top: a woman in Peru weaves a blanket; and Tibetan monks create an ephemeral sacred sand painting. Middle: graffiti in a tunnel under Hobart, Tasmania (note the ghostly figure standing in the doorway in the center of the image); and a majolica plate from Faenza, Italy, in characteristic blue and white glaze. Bottom: a painting in the style of Australian Aborigines; and adobe designs on the front of a Dogon house in Mali.

ern Asia. Some of the earliest sophisticated woven cloth is found on the mummies preserved in the dry desert region of Ürümchi in western China. These mummies, discovered in 1994, date to about 4,000 years ago, and include men, women, and children, dressed in a variety of clothing, including leggings, boots, and tall pointed hats. Their textiles were brightly colored and looked "astonishingly like the peculiar plaid twill cloths found in the only place in Europe where ancient perishables have survived well, the Bronze Age salt mines [of Austria]. . . . The Austrian plaid twills had been woven by ancestors of the Celts" (Barber 1999:21). It is curious to think that the practice of weaving plaid patterns into twill cloth diffused first from China to Austria and then to Scotland.

In various times and places, people used a variety of raw materials and weaving patterns to create different kinds of cloth. Fibers for weaving can come from plants, including reeds and cotton, or from animal fur or hair (sheep's or goats' wool, llama hair, etc.). By varying the types of dyes, one can make many different colors of string or yarn, and by manipulating multiple aspects of the intertwining of the warp and weft fibers, one can produce a variety of weaves with different characteristics. Today, weaving and clothing design is a major outlet for human creative expression.

Weaving is subject to cultural rules, just as any other human activity. In many societies, women are the weavers, the producers of cloth, baskets, and other woven objects. But in a few cultures, such as the Hopi of Arizona and the Bambara of Mali, it is primarily men who are the weavers. In some cultures, men do certain types of weaving, while women do others. Weaving can be done by hand with hand looms, backstrap looms, or upright looms; mechanized looms were developed and used to make larger quantities of cloth.

Basket-weaving using reeds or other plant fibers is a traditional female art in many cultures and may be passed down in families. Baskets may be used as a way to store items, as aids in processing food, as fish traps, or for many other purposes. Baskets may range in size from incredibly tiny to those large enough to hold one or more people. Some were created for use as burial shrouds. Woven mats may be used for sleeping or as interior walls, room dividers, or window shades. Such weavings may be uniform in color or decorated with a variety of patterns. Particularly skilled weavers may be able to command high prices in the contemporary art market for their work.

The weaving of fishing nets is often a male activity, and fishermen may spend many hours creating and repairing their nets by hand. Among the Dani of highland New Guinea, traditionally it was the men who wove baskets and net bags and made decorative woven bands covered with cowrie shells to be given away at funerals and other important ceremonies. Dani women had often lost many of their fingers to the mourning practices of their culture, and thus were not able to weave as adults, leaving such tasks to the men.

In some regions of the world, the hand-looming of carpets is an ancient and skilled art, and carpets are used as floor coverings, bed coverings, and room dividers. Each region may have it own designs and traditions, with the most expensive rugs having the most hand-tied knots per square inch. In Mali, men use backstrap looms to weave narrow strips of cloth some four to six inches wide, and then hand-stitch the strips together to make larger blankets or rugs that provide warmth during cold desert nights. Fulani wedding blankets are made with a combination of wool and cotton and may be 16 feet long and 8 feet wide. They are usually decorated with abstract geometric designs, with dark blue and maroon as the primary colors other than white. They are used to partition off a corner of the communal family tent to allow newlyweds some privacy.

Pottery

Another major category of visual art is pottery—objects made of clay that are then fired in a kiln at high heat to make them stronger and waterproof. The earliest clay objects recovered from the archeological record are sculptures, rather than containers. However, people quickly figured out that fired clay containers could be use to hold water and other liquids and could also serve as cooking and storage vessels for food. Like baskets, ceramics range in size from miniature to large enough to store grain for an entire year. Pottery may be purely aesthetic—a sculpture designed to sit on a shelf or a table, or rest on a plinth under a spotlight. Much pottery, however, is functional, used for a variety of mundane household as well as ritual purposes.

Because whole pots and pot shards are very durable, they often persist in the archeological record longer than artifacts made of wood or fiber. Stylistic differences in the size, shape, color, and design of pottery make it useful for tracing population migrations and replacements and for examining stylistic changes through time. The source of clay and temper (small grains of harder material mixed into the clay) may provide evidence of trade routes and travel. Pottery often reflects local beliefs and group membership, just as other types of creative expression do.

Clothing and Jewelry

In addition to modifying the body directly, many cultures use specific types and styles of clothing or jewelry to express cultural identity or beliefs, including nationality or ethnic identity, other group or tribal affiliations, power and authority, class, gender, religious affiliation, and lifetime achievements, and/or to increase attractiveness and beauty. The anthropology of clothing is a huge subdiscipline within cultural anthropology, but there is space here to touch on only a few points.

Clothing is practical, as well as decorative. It can provide warmth in cold climates, protect the body from the ultraviolet radiation of intense sunlight near the equator and at high altitudes, and shield the body from other elements of the environment such as blowing sand, sticker bushes, or insect pests. In hot environments, people may wear little or no clothing, and no one considers it immodest or inappropriate. Some groups wear small aprons across the front of their genital regions, either for modesty or simply to protect the area.

Where cultural beliefs say that certain body parts are sexually alluring and should be covered by clothing, people consider it inappropriate to expose those areas unless one is deliberately trying to be provocative. In many Islamic cultures, a woman's hair is an important focus of sexual attraction, and so it should be covered to show that a woman is respectable and modest. Depending on local customs, when out in public, women may be expected to cover not only their hair but also their ankles, hands, and faces, viewing the world through a lace-like panel that covers their eyes. Such coverings go by different names, including chadors and burkas.

The cultural beliefs underlying modest Islamic dress are also found in Western cultures, but with a different part of the body as the focus. In the United States, similar beliefs attach to women's breasts—they should be covered, especially the nipples and areolas, and exposed only for the pleasure of the woman's significant other, in the privacy of the bedroom. Only in a few places in the United States do women have the right—granted everywhere to men—to walk around with their breasts uncovered. Many men in the United States are particularly jealous of other men seeing their girlfriend's or wife's breasts, regardless of the context. Most European countries, though typically considered equally Western and otherwise similar to the United States in many ways, are usually much more relaxed about public nudity and sexuality in general.

Even as some Westerners decry the oppression of Islamic women who are required to be covered from head to toe when out in public, they don't recognize their own oppression at being required to cover their breasts or risk arrest for indecent exposure. Some are also quick to insist that women who are breastfeeding should do so discreetly, either going to the restroom to nurse or covering up with a blanket or a commercial cover-up designed especially for nursing women to ensure that no one is offended by getting a glimpse of their breasts as they feed their children. One popular variety of cover-up is marketed under the name *Hooter Hiders*.

Ironically, even as public breastfeeding remains controversial in the United States, some women in Western cultures deliberately draw attention to their breasts through breast implants, padded or push-up bras, tight-fitting sweaters, and/or low-cut tops. It seems as though acknowledging that breasts are for feeding babies contradicts the strong cultural belief that breasts are mainly for attracting male attention.

Across West Africa, where thighs are erotic, but breasts are ho-hum, women commonly go topless and nurse their children wherever they happen to be without worrying about being discreet. They wouldn't dream of wearing a short skirt or a bikini, however. Foreign visitors and tourists who wear inappropriately short skirts or shorts may be mistaken for prostitutes by the local people.

Clothing differs in color and style and is often used as a clear signal of what sex/gender a person is—pink for girls, blue for boys in the United States. In many cultures, only men wear pants, and this was also typical for the United States until the middle of the twentieth century. In some places, men wear skirts in the form of kilts or sarongs, or long dresses, such as the *boubous* of West Africa. In these circumstances, other aspects of the clothing clearly distinguish men from women. Clothing is also an excellent indicator of group affiliation, whether it involves wearing the clan tartan of your Scottish ancestors, the tie of your preparatory school in England, or a baseball jersey from your favorite team. Clothing can also indicate your level of wealth. Are your clothes custom-tailored, or from expensive designer shops, or are they from Macy's and Nordstrom's, or J.C. Penney's and Sears, or Walmart and Goodwill? Goths, skateboarders, Hare Krishnas, Boy Scouts, chefs, nuns, doctors, policemen, soldiers, urban gang members, and many other occupations have specific uniforms, some of which also carry indicators of rank within the group. Much of the deeper meaning of clothing styles, colors, and patterns is symbolic and accessible or readable only by members of the group—those in the know.

In addition to reflecting group membership, economic status, and religious affiliation, clothing styles may vary by age or stage of the life-span as well. In many Islamic communities, young girls do not have to cover their hair—only when they approach puberty do they become potential objects of male sexual desire and must then don the headscarf.

In some communities, infants and toddlers run around naked and start wearing clothing only once they are toilet trained. When my father was growing up in western Pennsylvania in the early decades of the twentieth century, all infants and toddlers wore dresses, because it was easier to change their diapers. Once toilet-trained, young boys graduated to short pants; only when they got to be 12 or 13 years old were they allowed to wear long pants like adult men.

Because clothing styles can change rapidly from place to place and across time, the type of clothes one wears may also reflect the historical era and local community in which one grew up. Men in most Western cultures in the 1940s and 1950s wore woven or felted hats when out in public; cowboys wore leather, felt, or straw cowboy hats. Today, many men in Texas still wear cowboy hats and boots, even though they never ride horses or round up cattle. Farmers and ranchers may wear *gimme caps*—advertising the local feed store or tractor dealer—to keep the sun out of

their eyes; college students more typically wear such caps backwards or at a jaunty angle, where the bill can no longer serve its purpose as a sun blocker. Contemporary people who participate in historic reenactments, such as Civil War battles, Pony Express rides, and Renaissance fairs, often wear special clothing to match the time period.

The fashioning of jewelry to be worn to decorate the body provides yet another outlet for human creative expression. The earliest jewelry was made of animal teeth, claws, or sea shells that had been perforated in order to string them on a necklace or arm band, or attach them to clothing. Jewelry may reflect the wearer's social status, wealth, power, marital status, religious or tribal affiliation, sexual orientation, age, or other values. Beads made from stone, glass, and ceramic have long served as a medium of exchange across many different parts of the world as well as being incorporated into jewelry and clothing.

Land Art

A final category of visual art is land art (also known as geoglyphs, Earth art, or Earthworks), which refers to large-scale manipulations of the natural landscape to create visually appealing artworks. The Nazca lines created on the desert floor in highland Peru are the most famous example of prehistoric land art; they have been designated by UNESCO as a World Heritage Site. The hundreds of outlines of geometric shapes and huge animals (spiders, monkeys, hummingbirds, orcas, and more) were made by the Nazca people between AD 400 and 650. The construction involved simply removing the red pebbles that covered the desert surface, revealing the lighter colored ground underneath. The designs are best appreciated by modern viewers from the air, but they would not have been visible from that perspective to the people who made them. Although included here in the category of land art, no one really knows what the functions and meanings of the lines might have been, though they were clearly significant to the local community.

Other prehistoric examples of land art are found in England, including the Cerne Abbas giant, the Uffington White Horse (and many other white horses), and the Long Man of Wilmington. From historic times, we have a carving of King George III riding a horse, created in 1808 in the limestone hills of South

Dorset Downs, and the Fovant Badges, regimental badges carved into the chalk hillsides above Fovant, England, during World War I. They were allowed to grow-over during World War II, but have since been restored. The final badge, representing the Royal Corps of Signals, was added in 1970.

The modern land art movement began in the late 1960s and was named Earthworks by one of its earliest and most famous practitioners, Robert Smithson. Smithson's "Spiral Jetty" at the Great Salt Lake in Utah is one of the best known modern Earthworks, although a number of such monumental art projects have been created in recent decades. In 1998, Australian artist Andrew Rogers began construction of a series of land art projects titled "Rhythms of Life." To date, Rogers and more than 6,700 coworkers have created 46 massive geoglyphs and associated structures at sites around the world: Australia, Bolivia, Chile, China, Iceland, India, Israel, Nepal, Slovakia, Sri Lanka, Turkey, and the United States. My favorites are "Ancient Language" in Chile, and "Messenger" from China (Rogers 2010). A number of other land artists have built Earthworks in a variety of formats and places.

Things to Remember

The art of bands of hunters and gatherers, and tribes and chiefdoms of horticulturalists, herders, and fisherfolk qualifies as *art* just as much as any painting by Leonardo da Vinci or Jackson Pollack, any sculpture by Michelangelo or Calder. Art styles that are *foreign* to what we have experienced in childhood—whether from another segment of our own culture and country or from halfway around the world—may take some getting used to. They may be an acquired taste. Sometimes the artist has not been formally trained, or indeed remains unknown, or has created or decorated something that also has a practical purpose. It may be impossible to view a piece of artwork through the eyes of the artist's own culture, if one is not a member. One may fail to see, let alone understand, all of the deeper meanings encoded in a piece of art. Nevertheless, one can still learn to appreciate the beauty and creativity reflected in art from any source and to admire the vision and skill of the artist.

PERFORMING ARTS

A range of performing arts are found in every culture and serve a variety of purposes (Brown 1991). We can define performing arts as those that involve the movements and actions of people and nonhuman animals. Sometimes the performers are quite distinct from the observers (the audience), and other times everyone present participates in the performance in one or more ways. Some performances are mainly for entertainment, while other may be intended to teach or motivate, and still others may have religious significance or celebrate group identity and heritage. In this necessarily brief survey of performing arts from cultures around the world, I try to incorporate a wide variety of examples to show the many ways that people participate in, or watch, artistic performances.

Festivals

A festival can be defined as any gathering of people for a particular celebratory purpose. Festivals may involve the consumption of food and drink, music, dance, and/or commerce. Whether they are religious or secular, restricted to certain groups or open to the general public, one-time occurrences or yearly events, local or international, much of the value of any festival is the social exchange and entertainment that comes from joining together with other like-minded individuals to celebrate and have fun. Examples of festivals from around the world include:

- **Burning Man:** An annual week-long performance-art gathering of more than 48,000 people into a temporary community in Nevada. "These people make the journey to the Black Rock desert for one week out of the year to be part of an experimental community, which challenges its members to express themselves and rely on themselves to a degree that is not normally encountered in one's day-to-day life" (Burning Man 1989–2010).

- **Kanamara Matsuri Festival:** This festival, held every spring in Kawasaki, Japan, originated in the seventeenth century among prostitutes who gathered at the Shinto shrine in Kanamara to pray for protection from sexually transmitted diseases. Today, the festival celebrates the male penis as a sign of strength, power, and fertility and also raises money for HIV/AIDS research. Penis images can be seen everywhere, ranging from giant statues carried by groups of men to penis-shaped lollypops and carved radishes. YouTube has video of recent festivals.

- *Festival in the Desert:* This three-day music festival, held every January in the desert near Timbuktu, in Mali, West Africa, is patterned after the traditional annual gatherings of nomadic Tuareg groups for the purpose of exchanging information, visiting friends and relatives, and dealing with conflicts. The first festival open to the world was held in 2001, and it continues to grow in size every year. During the day, attendees can enjoy traditional Tuareg music, singing, dancing, poetry, ritual swordplay, camel races, and exhibits by craftspeople, artisans, and performance artists. At night, the single music stage is taken over by a variety of mostly Malian and other West African musicians, including the famous Tuareg rock band Tinariwen. Lights and electrical power are provided by generators; otherwise there is no electricity, no running water, and no restrooms. The festival is still "largely a Tuareg event, and it must be the only festival where a large part of the audience arrives in camel caravans. They come from all over the Sahara, some traveling for weeks" (Freston 2007).

Reunions

Gatherings of people who once lived together and shared experiences, or who have common ancestors, are another specific form of social interaction that fits under the umbrella of the performing arts. High school and college reunions, military units from specific times and places who gather to remember their shared experiences and fallen comrades, family reunions that bring together people from around the country or the globe—all serve to establish or re-establish relationships, and to keep memories alive. Reunions may be held on the anniversary of an event that was important to the group. They may involve eating, drinking, music, dancing, storytelling, and lots of catching up on news of family and old friends.

Public Processions and Gatherings

Another type of performing arts is the public procession, where the participants walk, run, or march while dressed in special clothing (costumes) and performing various actions (playing musical instruments; displaying gun handling, baton-twirling, or flag-waving skills; driving around wildly in miniature cars while wearing red hats; etc.). Some public processions are part of a religious pilgrimage, where people come from all over to join the procession, such that the parade becomes a huge swell of people converging on the site of a religious shrine, ritual, or festival. Public parades may celebrate local, national, or international holidays. A number of public processions involve inversion rituals, where people deliberately dress and act in ways contrary to their normal, everyday roles.

Military parades may be designed to show how powerful the rulers are and how numerous, strong, and well-trained their armed forces are. They may be intended to impress the local constituents or foreign observers, or to stir up patriotic feelings when the group is under threat of attack.

Political marches, rallies, and protests may be intended to illustrate the populace's frustration at the state of the economy or the political system, to promote one's viewpoint, or to protest against an opposing view. There is strength in numbers, and people may not be willing to stand alone and object to their government's policies and actions, or lobby for some specific change, but they may be willing to join a large crowd of people who share their viewpoint. Political rallies may be quite influential, depending on the cultural context, how many people participate, the reaction of the government, and the response of outsiders who are watching (cf., Egypt in February 2011).

Theatrical Performances: Dramatic and Comedic Entertainment

Public storytelling and playacting have been part of human culture for many millennia. We can imagine early human ancestors gathering around the campfire, with spectators watching as hunters re-enact a successful hunt, or youngsters listening raptly as an elder relates stories of her youth. There is no archeological evidence of such activities until we find the remains of amphitheaters and arenas, but the performing arts probably began in the Upper Paleolithic, if not earlier (Boyd 2009).

By **theatrical performances** we mean plays, skits, charades, mimes, operas, storytelling, and poetry reci-

Festivals, theater, processions, and dance are part of most, if not all, cultures. In Belgium, the Gilles are the main participants in the Carnival of Binche, held on Shrove Tuesday from 4:00 AM until late in the evening. The Carnival of Binche was proclaimed one of the Masterpieces of the Oral and Intangible Heritage of Humanity by UNESCO in 2003. All the participants are male, including very young boys. They wear traditional masks in the morning procession, along with suits in the colors of the Belgian flag (red, yellow, and black), with large white lace cuffs and collars. They throw blood oranges to the crowd and carry bundles of twigs to ward off evil.

tations, including epic poems that take several days to recount. Whether these performances re-enact actual events or are purely imaginary, they serve educational as well as entertainment purposes. Some are tragic, other comedic, still others satirical or imbued with hidden political messages. Some are designed to frighten, while others take the form of cautionary tales, relating what might happen to someone who doesn't follow the rules or who angers the gods. Some have underlying moral messages, while others are just for fun. Some involve magic tricks, sleight of hand, or other performance tricks such as ventriloquism or off-stage sound effects. Many reflect motifs and themes that are common to other aspects of the culture, reinforcing local beliefs and values.

The development of motion-picture photography and eventually digital recording technology, animation, surround-sound, and sophisticated, computer-generated special effects have greatly expanded the range of stories that can be told while enhancing the sensory experience for the audience. Auditory and visual effects, such as 3-D, have received the most attention, but seats that tremble and move, or blow puffs of air on the audience's feet or necks, even olfactory effects, have been incorporated into some entertainment

venues such as the Disney resorts. The human imagination, though, remains the most powerful source of immersion in a story, however presented.

As students, you may have been frustrated when a professor required you to attend a play or film screening on campus. You may not understand why you can't simply watch the same movie on your computer in your dorm room. But watching a movie on a large screen as part of an audience is a very different experience from watching a videotape of the same performance or movie on a small screen, by yourself. Being part of a larger group allows you to hear and feel the audience's reactions to what is happening on screen—people may laugh, gasp, hide their eyes during scary parts, shudder and moan during gory scenes, or give a standing ovation at the end of the film. People may cry if the story is heartbreaking; they may even yell at the screen as though the screen images were real people (who could hear them). It is much easier to suspend your disbelief and truly enter into the experience when the room is dark, the screen is big, and the sound is coming from all around you. Theater screenings of *Lawrence of Arabia* in 1962 were accompanied by huge increases in the quantity of soda sold, as parched audiences staggered out of the Arabian desert to the refreshment stand during intermission (the movie runs more than three hours).

In some cultural contexts, most movies are viewed outside, so that the weather, moonlight, birds, bats, and insects become part of the experience. It may be difficult to explain to a contemporary college student what the attraction of drive-in theaters was in the United States in the twentieth century. The novelty of sitting in the car to watch a movie; parents with their kids (who were often in their pajamas); the speaker hanging on the slightly opened window; the thrill of trekking across the sea of cars to the refreshment stand to buy popcorn and soda or use the restrooms, then trying to find the car again in the dark—all of these are difficult to explain. As teenagers, seeing a movie at the drive-in meant having a relatively private, but socially acceptable, opportunity to be alone with your boyfriend or girlfriend.

The technology for producing, recording, transmitting, and viewing various sorts of visual images—from professional documentaries to dramatic films to amateur videos and home movies—continues to evolve at an ever-increasing pace. One can only imagine future generations—your children and grandchildren—rolling their eyes and laughing at the old folks' fond reminiscences of watching YouTube, connecting with friends and family through Facebook, using a GPS to navigate, or looking up information on Wikipedia.com.

Moving Together in Time

Humans around the world participate in a variety of activities that involve rhythmic movement, including walking, marching, running, dancing, and communal calisthenics (exercises). Historian William H. McNeill has elaborated on the ability of such communal rhythmic movements to serve as the basis for emotional bonding and community formation. McNeill writes that his own experience of participating in military drill resulted in pervasive feelings of well-being and solidarity with others.

> Obviously, something visceral was at work; something, I later concluded, far older than language and critically important in human history, because the emotion it arouses constitutes an indefinitely expansible basis for social cohesion among any and every group that keeps together in time, moving big muscles together and chanting, singing, or shouting rhythmically. "Muscular bonding" is the most economical label I could find for this phenomenon, and I hope the phrase will be understood to mean the euphoric fellow feeling that prolonged and rhythmic muscular movement arouses among nearly all participants in such exercises. (McNeill 1995:2–3)

He concludes that community dancing is one of the hallmarks of being human and likely arose during the time of *Homo erectus*, prior to the evolution of ana-

Dance is a cultural universal, though it takes many forms and has different meanings in different contexts. Here, Intore dancers from Rwanda perform traditional ballet or "warrior dancing."

Left: young girls learn ballet in England. Right: U.S. Navy Sailors breakdance on the flight deck during a steel beach picnic aboard the Nimitz-class aircraft carrier *USS Abraham Lincoln* in the North Arabian Sea in 2008.

tomically modern *Homo sapiens*. "Extravagant expenditure of muscular energy in dance and song is the most fundamental of all human devices for consolidating community feeling, simply because it arouses a warm sense of togetherness, diminishing personal conflicts and facilitating cooperation" (McNeill 1995:86a). In many cultures, some form of rhythmic movement serves as a portal for entering into the altered states of consciousness associated with religious ecstasy and healing rituals.

Dance

Whether or not one accepts McNeill's claims for the power of rhythmic movement, it is the case that group festivals and celebrations that involve such movements are found in every cultural context. There are many different aspects of the role of dance that can be explored. In some cultures, everyone participates in the dance—the baby on her mother's back, toddlers bobbing and weaving to the beat, children and adults of all ages, and even the elderly, who may only be able to tap their feet or clap along. In other cultural contexts, trained professional dance troupes or solo artists may perform in front of an audience. Dances may be free-form or extremely controlled and stylized. Many community dances involve either holding hands and dancing in a circle, or moving around a fire or other central axis. Curiously, most dances of this kind move in a counter-clockwise direction.

Dancing may serve a variety of specialized purposes in addition to generating community bonding and feelings of well-being among the participants. Dancing may be a way for courtship to take place, with rules about whether and how people can touch while dancing, whether men and women dance together or separately, whether couples dance with the same partner or change partners, and whether the movements of the dance are sexually suggestive, meant to invoke sexual passion, or are very staid and proper. Some dancing is smooth and graceful, such as the waltz in European ballroom dancing. Other styles of dancing are more energetic, such as square-dancing and the tango, and some styles are positively exuberant, such as Russian kick dancing and break dancing. Among many East African cattle-herding societies, the main style of dancing is to stand in place with your arms at your side and jump up as high as you can with both feet off the ground.

Dancing is part of many religious rituals and celebrations, and some types of religious dancing are used to invoke religious ecstasy. Umbanda in Brazil, the Nazaretha Church in South Africa, and many Pentecostal Christian Churches in North America feature dancing as an important part of religious services. McNeill attributes the rapid rise and spread of Islam to the rhythmic movements involved in praying communally five times a day, as well as to dervish orders who use dance to achieve "mystic union with God," writing:

> Westerners called members [of the Mevlevi order] whirling or dancing dervishes because of their custom of dancing in public, whirling round and round and chanting all the while, until [they achieve] the mystic state. . . . Dervish nearness to God made them effective missionaries, and dervish enthusiasm inspired Moslem armies to undertake new conquests across almost every frontier. As a result, between [AD] 1000 and 1700 the realm of Islam expanded enormously—sweeping across India and parts of southeast Asia, across Asia Minor and the Balkans, as well as penetrating east and west Africa, northwest China, and most of the Eurasian steppe . . . it is difficult to exaggerate the impact of dervish forms of piety on Islamic society in the centuries after 900. Everything turned on the emotional conviction aroused by mystical union with God; and that union was achieved through prolonged chanting, with a background of instrumental music and varying levels of rhythmic muscular engagement. (McNeill 1995:92–93)

Military Drill, Calisthenics, and Marching Bands

In addition to dancing, there are several other forms of moving together in time that have been (and still are) used in various cultural contexts to unite groups of people in activities that make them feel good and foster community support and engagement.

In his book, McNeill spends considerable time tracing the development of various forms of military close-order drill, from the warrior classes of the Aztec Empire to the professional soldiers of Gilgamesh in Sumer, followed by the Spartans of Greece and the rowers of Athenian triremes—ships whose three tiers of oarsmen along each side required strength, coordination, cooperation, and precision. Today, learning to move together in time is a standard part of military basic training around the world.

Writing of Maurice of Orange (a Dutch ruler of the sixteenth century), but equally applicable to the all-volunteer U.S. Army of the twenty-first century, McNeill says:

> Prolonged drill allowed soldiers, recruited from the fringes of an increasingly commercialized society—individuals for whom the cunning and constraint of the marketplace were repugnant and unworkable—to create a new, artificial primary community among themselves, where comradeship prevailed in good times and bad and where old-fashioned principles of command and subordination gave meaning and direction to life. Men who had little else to be proud of could share an *esprit de corps* with their fellows and glory in their collective sufferings and prowess. Surrendering personal will to the command of another, while simultaneously merging mindlessly into a group of fellow subordinates, liberates the individual concerned from the burden of making choices. . . . Experience showed that drill quickly made men into soldiers for whom ties beyond the circle of their fellows faded to insignificance. . . . Men born to poverty obeyed their superiors without question, even when, as occasionally happened, this required them to shoot rebellious peasants or rioting city crowds. And as a matter of course, men who had no obvious stake in the outcome, and did have very obvious private reasons for wishing to get out of the path of enemy bullets, nonetheless risked their lives in innumerable battles, deploying and firing their weapons as commanded to do, even when sent to fight in distant, alien lands. (McNeill 1995:131–32)

Calisthenics and less strenuous forms of exercise provide yet another manifestation of the importance of moving together in time. Modern calisthenics developed in Sweden in the 1800s out of German gymnastics. Group calisthenics became part of the school day in most European countries and became especially popular in some Asian countries (McNeill 1995:138). Today, across China, Japan, and other parts of the world, many people start their days with public, communal exercises. For some, this means rigorous calisthenics before starting work in the factory or classes at school. Practitioners of *tai chi* gather in the early mornings to go through a series of stretching and balancing movements that look rather like dancing in slow motion. The purpose of tai chi is to focus the mind, strengthen the body, and relieve stress. Performing the exercises publicly with a group of like-minded people serves as an excellent way to lift one's spirits and create a feeling of camaraderie and goodwill.

Marching bands also take advantage of the collective euphoria generated by moving together in time to coordinate complex routines, even as the members play their musical instruments. At football games and

In addition to community dancing, there are many other ways that people "move together in time." Top left: bagpipers in kilts march in a St. Patrick's Day Parade in London. Top right: men and women in China perform Tai chi chuan exercises outdoors. Middle: the "Fightin' Texas Aggie Band" of Texas A&M University marches in the Lone Star Showdown competition at the University of Texas football field in 2006. Bottom: Iraqi security forces, including military, police, and civil leadership, march in review before Iraqi government officials and U.S. military leaders in Baghdad in 2009.

parades, the sights and sounds of a marching band help establish the mood and often accompany cheers and patterned movements performed by cheer leaders and members of the crowd. The largest military marching band in the world, and one of the most famous, is the Fightin' Texas Aggie Band, of Texas A&M University. Its 350 members, all of whom belong to the Corps of Cadets, practice two to three hours every day. During half-time at football games, the marching band takes the field and executes a series of precise, often visually stunning movements as they play. Their most complex movement is the Four-Way Cross-Through, in which four different contingents approach the center of the field and interweave as they march through each other, emerging unscathed on the other side. Only split-second precision timing allows the band to accomplish such feats, which would otherwise be impossible, as they "require two people to be in the same place at the same time" (Aggie Band 2010).

FINAL THOUGHTS

This whirlwind tour has touched on only a few of the many ways of thinking and behaving that provide outlets for human creative expression. Subsistence strategies and systems of marriage, kinship, economics and politics exhibit a finite range of variation across all the cultures of the world. People are foragers or herders or farmers or office workers. They are, for the most part, either monogamous or polygynous. They are patrilineal or matrilineal or bilateral. They use Eskimo kinship terms or Iroquois or Hawaiian. And so on. But in terms of creative expression through music, sports, leisure activities, architecture, body modification, and the visual and performing arts, we find infinite variety. Life provides a veritable feast of opportunities for contributing to and enjoying human creative expression—a fundamental and vital part of the human experience—whether we actively participate or form part of the audience, watching, listening, cheering, and tapping our toes from the sidelines.

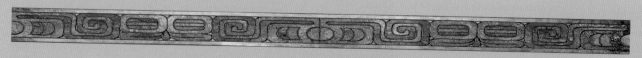

Key Concepts Review

Since the first glimmerings of culture some 2.5 million years ago, humans have modified the physical environment to suit our purposes and preferences, rather than merely adapting to it.

When humans drastically modify the physical environment—damming rivers, tunneling through mountains, digging deep into the Earth, building cities atop seismic fault lines or near coasts prone to flooding and hurricanes—we are placing ourselves at risk of unpredictable, but potentially catastrophic, human and environmental consequences.

The settlement of people across the landscape and the development of small clusters of houses and families into towns, villages, and cities is the result of many different factors including the physical topography of an area, the technology and natural resources available, and the vagaries of history, as well as deliberate planning according to specific cultural values.

The design of living spaces within communities likewise reflects cultural notions of privacy, desired levels of interaction among family members, separation of the sexes, how much room is needed for different activities, how much domestic work is done outside vs. inside, etc.

People modify their bodies, either temporarily or permanently, for four main reasons: (1) to increase attractiveness, (2) to increase the appearance of aggression or power, (3) to reflect group identity and mark accomplishments, and (4) to punish individuals for transgressions.

Types of body modification include: applying makeup or paint to temporarily alter one's appearance, tattoos, hairstyles, dental modifications, scarification, piercings, and more elaborate body modifications.

Body modifications, both temporary and permanent, both mild and extreme, can reveal many interesting cultural beliefs and values, and the body itself serves as the locus of a wide array of creative expressions.

Visual art can take many forms and serve a variety of purposes, from the purely aesthetic to the functional to performing important cultural work.

Art from any community may be widely admired and appreciated by others without any special knowledge of its historical and cultural context.

At the same time, there are often multiple layers of meaning encoded in art of all kinds, and thus it may evoke different emotions and responses in viewers depending on their level of knowledge of the context in which the art was created.

The visual arts all seem to have their origins in the Upper Paleolithic time period, beginning some 40,000 years ago, when anatomically modern humans appear in the fossil and archeological record.

Visual arts include sculpture, painting, weaving, pottery, clothing, and jewelry.

Visual arts include items made purely for aesthetic viewing and pleasure as well as practical items of ev-eryday use that are designed and decorated according to local and individual styles.

The art of foragers, horticulturalists, herders, and fisherfolk qualifies as *art* just as much as any painting by Leonardo da Vinci or Jackson Pollack, or any sculpture by Michelangelo or Calder.

Performing arts are those that involve the movements and actions of people and nonhuman animals and serve the same functions as other forms of human creative expression.

Performing arts include festivals, reunions, public processions and gatherings, theatrical performances, and various forms of *moving together in time* such as dance, military drill, calisthenics, and marching bands, about which William McNeill writes: "Extravagant expenditure of muscular energy in dance and song is the most fundamental of all human devices for consolidating community feeling, simply because it arouses a warm sense of togetherness, diminishing personal conflicts and facilitating cooperation" (1995, p. 86).

In terms of creative expression through music, sports, leisure activities, architecture, body modification, and the visual and performing arts, we find infinite variety across human cultures.

Life provides a veritable feast of opportunities for contributing to and enjoying human creative expression—a fundamental and vital part of the human experience.

Traditional clothing and modern communication, Zhongdian Horse Festival, China.

11

HUMAN COMMUNICATION

Touch Me, See Me, Hear Me, Read Me

*There will never be a dearth of topics for anthropologists to study
when it comes to human communication. We continue to devise
new ways of communicating and miscommunicating,
providing information and misinformation, using language to teach,
to persuade, to inspire, to threaten, to mislead, and to entertain.
Humans without communication—whether in the tactile, visual,
or auditory-vocal channels—are simply unimaginable.*

I love listening to other people talking in a language that I don't understand. Although I am fluent only in American English, I know enough German, Spanish, French, Italian, Arabic, and Bambara to recognize when they are being spoken, and to catch the occasional word or phrase, and sometimes even to figure out what topic is being discussed. I find it even more intriguing to listen in when I can't even tell what language is in use. Sitting in the anthropology lab listening to two of my students from Pakistan speaking Urdu—one in a slower, rural dialect, the other in the rapid patter of urban dwellers—I am reminded of the amazing capabilities and flexibilities of what has been called the **human language instinct.**

How is it possible that I can hear the very same thing my students hear, yet my brain, untrained in Urdu, doesn't respond to the words and phrases? My ears capture the sounds and cadences of their speech, and nerve signals carry the information to the language centers of my brain. But my brain *doesn't* take these sounds and interpret them as ideas and knowledge and opinions and sentiments. My students could be discussing any topic, ranging from world politics to their plans for the afternoon. I have no idea. Yet, these very same sounds, entering their brains, are instantly recognized and understood, and they chat back and forth effortlessly. In addition, they are both fluent in English, and one speaks Japanese as well. It never ceases to amaze me.

In some instances, my brain can't even tell the difference between two sounds. As our brains develop in infancy, if the distinction between two similar sounds is not important in the language(s) we hear, then the neural connections, which would enable us to tell the sounds apart, get pruned away. Later in life, no matter how much we try, we can't distinguish the two sounds, nor can we produce them so that they sound distinct to those who *can* hear the difference. Years ago, when I lived in Mali and was fairly good at discussing the topics of my research in Bambara, I learned to avoid certain other subjects because I couldn't seem to produce the different tones correctly. The words for *dog* and *penis* are almost the same, just ever so slight a difference in tone. Best just not to talk about dogs!

I get frustrated with myself when I can't communicate with others because I don't know the local language or can't pronounce critical words correctly, or because my American Sign Language is rudimentary at best. Even when everyone speaks the same language, miscommunications and misunderstandings often occur. The lack of emotional context provided in e-mail messages, emoticons notwithstanding, often leads to hurt feelings and wrong impressions. In 2001, I was devastated by the seemingly irrational anger of a student who assumed that I had used a term as a racial slur (she was therefore highly offended), when that wasn't my intention at all—the term turns out to have completely different meanings in different regions of the country.

There is so much to say about the role of language and other forms of communication in human culture that it is difficult to know where to begin. In this chapter, I hope to illuminate the wide range of topics studied by anthropological linguists and scholars from related disciplines, as well as the excitement of discovery as ongoing research provides new windows into the workings of the human brain/mind and the role of language in shaping human nature (Bickerton 2009).

CHANNELS OF COMMUNICATION

Without the use of modern technology, there are three main channels for communication between one person and another: the tactile channel, the visual-spatial channel, and the auditory-vocal channel. I begin with a brief exploration of each of these three main channels.

Tactile Channel

The term **tactile** refers to our sense of touch. Tactile communication arose long before the emergence of modern humans. All mammals use their sense of touch to interact with others. Sexual reproduction requires touch, and fighting requires touch of a very different kind, but the vast majority of mammalian tactile communication occurs between a mother and her offspring. The mammalian mother uses physical contact of various sorts immediately after birth to make sure the baby is breathing and to help move it into position for nursing (breastfeeding). Later, she maintains contact with her offspring to keep them safe and warm, to clean them, to pull them out of harm's way, and to teach them appropriate behaviors.

Many mammal species are designated as *carry* species, those whose infants remain in near constant physical contact with their mother's body throughout infancy—the entire time when they are nursing. In the higher primates, the mother first carries the infant on her ventral surface (front), supporting the baby with one arm until it is able to cling to her fur. Eventually, the baby is able to hold on without help and hangs attached below the mother's chest and abdomen as she travels through the trees or across the ground. When the offspring get older, they move around to the mother's dorsal surface (back) and ride like a jockey on a horse.

When a primate mother is at rest, she sits upright, with her arms and hands free and her baby on her lap, where it has access to her mammary glands for nursing and where she can keep it warm and protected, make eye contact, and interact with it socially. Primate infants spend most of their time in a vertical position, with their head up and their spine perpendicular to the ground. All mammals sleep with their young as well. In the higher primates, frequent physical contact between mother and offspring, including nursing and co-sleeping, continues for years. Even fully adult offspring will return to their mother for a reassuring pat on the back, a hug, or just for the comfort of sitting next to her if they are cold, sick, injured, or frightened.

In addition, adult primates spend a lot of time grooming one another, and sitting touching one another, or in close proximity. Adult chimpanzees and bonobos, whether related or not, use touch in the form of pats, hugs, and kisses to reassure and comfort one another and show affection.

In many human cultures, this pattern is still the norm (DeLoache and Gottlieb 2000). Only in a few Western, industrialized nations have people developed cultural rules that separate mothers and children and restrict most physical touch between individuals to contexts involving either sex or violence. In recent years, the adverse consequences of the lack of affectionate tactile interactions between parents and children and among friends in industrialized contexts has become a major focus of study.

Research on the effects of physical contact between human parents and newborns has shown that touch has many beneficial effects (Heller 1997; Montagu 1986; Schön and Silvén 2007); conversely, the absence of touch has negative effects. Much of the research has taken place in hospital neonatal intensive care units using a practice known as Kangaroo Care (although Primate Care would be a better name). Kangaroo Care involves the mother (or other caretaker) holding the baby skin-to-skin, upright, on her chest, for one to many hours a day. Babies provided Kangaroo Care experience many physiological benefits, including:

- More stable heart rates and respiration (breathing)

- Less crying

- More deep sleep

- More time spent in a quiet, alert state
- Greater weight gain (and therefore earlier discharge from the hospital)
- Accelerated maturation of the brain
- Improved function of the immune system
- Greater success at, and longer durations of, breast-feeding
- More intense bonds with their parents, who report more confidence in their roles as caretakers

Tactile stimulation regulates physical growth in the infant through several channels. First, when the mother and infant are separated, growth hormone levels decline while levels of the stress hormone cortisol

rise. Keeping the mother and child together provides the optimal physiological state for normal growth. Mother's touch lowers cortisol levels and increases oxytocin levels. Finally, touch increases parasympathetic vagal nerve activity, which in turns facilitates digestion, and leads to the release of hormones that are responsible for the absorption of nutrients from food (Schön and Silvén 2007).

The tactile channel of communication remains an important one throughout life. People use touch to communicate love, affection, comfort, and sexual interest. Touch can relax muscles, reduce pain, and alleviate worry and stress. We use touch to restrain others, an especially important function when trying to keep infants and toddlers safe from danger. And we use

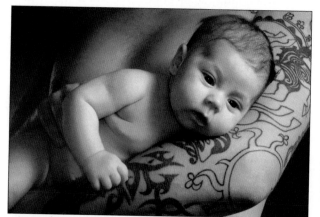

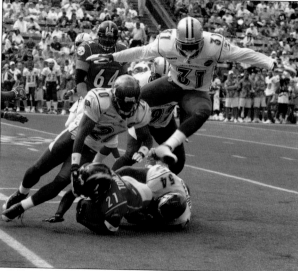

Touch is used by humans to express love and affection, to comfort, to relieve pain or provide physical pleasure, and of course to inflict harm and injury.

touch to get a person's attention, to prod others, to guide their movements, to teach them how to do things, and to propel them forward or pull them back from the brink. Unfortunately, touch also can be used to communicate anger and to inflict pain and violence on others in multiple ways.

Humans may no longer groom one another as intensively as the nonhuman primates do—at least in part because we no longer have thick coats of fur. But we still use the tactile channel of communication to convey information, intent, and emotional states. In cultures where physical contact reflects affection, people touch one another often, hold hands in public, walk with their arms around one another, greet each other with hugs and kisses, and sleep together.

Although written language isn't discussed until a later section, this seems like an appropriate place to mention Braille, the tactile writing and reading communication system for people who are blind or visually impaired. Braille was developed in 1821 by Louis Braille, a blind Frenchman associated with the National Institute for the Blind in Paris, France (Louis Braille Online Museum 2009; Weygand 2009). Braille improved upon a system originally developed by Charles Barbier for military uses, known as night-writing, using a system of 12 raised dots arranged in a rectangular cell. Although Barbier's system turned out to be too complex for soldiers to learn and use to communicate quietly in the dark, Braille was able to adapt it for use for people who were blind. He reduced the number of raised dots to six per cell and then assigned different patterns of raised dots to different letters, different common word endings, contractions, and punctuation marks. Originally, Braille writing was done using a stylus and a slate. Eventually, mechanical devices for producing Braille were developed, including Braille typewriters, an embosser attached to a computer, and a refreshable Braille display. In recent years, the traditional 6-dot code has acquired two additional dots to encode more information.

Most commercially produced Braille documents are written using a system known as Grade 2 Braille, which includes many more contractions and abbreviations in order to fit more on a page and make it faster to read. Grade 3 Braille is a shorthand version used by many individuals for their own personal use.

In recent years, the teaching and learning of Braille in Western contexts has become less common

as sophisticated computer software for scanning books and having the computer read aloud whatever is on the screen has become more widely available. At the same time, a number of countries including Canada, Mexico, and India have added tactile information to their paper currency to enable the visually impaired to distinguished bills of different denominations.

Braille was originally developed for the French language, and was easily adapted to other languages using the Latin (Roman) alphabet. More elaborate modifications were needed for the development of tactile writing and reading systems for Arabic, Chinese, Greek, Hebrew, Japanese, Korean, Russian, and Tibetan.

People who are deaf and blind can neither hear speech nor see sign language, but that doesn't mean they cannot communicate with others. Tactile Sign Language is used to communicate with people who are deaf and blind. Tactile Sign is signed into the deaf-blind receiver's hands. The most common method is hand-over-hand signing. The communicator signs as usual, and the deaf-blind receiver holds the hands of the communicator. The receiver feels the hand movements, reads the signs, and communicates through the hands of the signer.

Visual Channel

As an order of mammals, primates rely on their sense of vision to a much greater degree than do other mammals, which rely more heavily on their sense of smell. All primates have stereoscopic and binocular vision. Like other higher primates, humans have excellent color vision. A large portion of our brains is devoted to processing and interpreting visual information from the environment. The visual channel of communication, by definition, requires being able to see and interpret the messages that others are sending.

When it comes to human-to-human communication, the visual channel makes use of many different spatial modalities—facial expressions, culturally specific body language, movements, and gestures, and fully developed sign languages, including the nonmanual markers that accompany manual signs.

Our nonhuman primate relatives, especially our closest relatives, the chimpanzees and bonobos, use a number of facial expressions and gestures that are still found in all human cultures. Research around the world has revealed that some body postures and facial expressions are cross-cultural universals. People every-where raise their arms in excitement and in anger, and to intimidate others. People everywhere revert to the fetal position (body curled in on itself, hands covering the head or face) when in severe physical or emotional pain. People everywhere use the same facial expressions to show the primary emotional states. People everywhere laugh when they are happy (or nervous), cry when they are sad (or hurt, or emotionally moved), shout with joy, make little happy noises when they eat something wonderful, and scream or moan when in pain (Oatley, Keltner, and Jenkins 2006). Other body postures—such as a woman putting her hands on her hips when she is annoyed, or a teenager rolling his eyes at the sudden onset of stupidity in his parents—have more limited cultural distribution. In Mali, angry children would tuck their fists in their armpits and loudly slap their sides with their elbows, making a very rude-sounding noise.

Cross-cultural research has shown that people everywhere encode emotions on their faces in similar ways, using the same muscles. Likewise, people from many cultures can correctly decode (read and interpret) the emotions expressed on other people's faces with 80–90 percent accuracy, even when working from photographs, and even if the people are from popula-

Facial expressions reflecting the basic emotions are universal across cultures. It isn't difficult to tell that the people in the photos above are angry, interested and content, fearful, and disgusted.

tions with strikingly different facial features (Ekman 2007; Ekman and Friesen 2003). All humans can typically recognize and distinguish among the basic six emotions of happiness, sadness, surprise, fear, anger, and disgust/contempt from looking at facial expressions. Recognizing these facial expressions is part of our mammalian and primate legacy—it is easy to tell when a baboon is angry, a chimpanzee is afraid, or a dog is happy. Research continues on human recognition of facial expressions of the more complex and subtle emotions, such as embarrassment, shame, pride, love, desire, and sympathy.

Of course, it is also the case that people in some cultures or families learn, and may be explicitly taught, to either suppress their emotions or at least not let their faces reflect their internal feelings. Among the Balinese, mothers are advised:

> A very important part of parenting is teaching children how to control their feelings. . . . Encourage your son or daughter to be quiet and polite both at home and in public. Even positive emotions should not be displayed in public. For example, a child who receives an award at school should feel happiness in the heart but not express it overtly. By the same token, if your child is frightened of a stranger or a strange situation, advise your little one not to reveal that fear. . . . In short, you should always encourage calm in the face of trouble, and discourage any display of strong emotions. (DeLoache and Gottlieb 2000:115–116)

In addition, some individuals learn to not reveal any emotions under certain circumstances. Examples include poker players, who must keep a straight face and not give any clues as to the cards they have been dealt, and North American teenagers, whose faces may become a frozen mask when they are being admonished by their mother or father for misbehavior.

There are reports of cultural differences in which part of the face people concentrate their attention for reading emotions. Research by Rachael Jack and her colleagues suggests that some people from eastern Asia focus more on a person's eyes and brows and may miss subtle cues conveyed by the lower face (Jack et al. 2009). This, in turn, may lead to mistakes in interpreting some negative emotions such as fear and disgust. On the other hand, Western experts in detecting deception often pay particular attention to a person's eyes, looking for cues, such as rapid blinking and the direction of the gaze, to tell if a person is lying.

In addition to facial expressions, body postures and specific arm, hand, and mouth gestures are shared in common by humans and chimpanzees. Chimpanzees reach out to others for comfort and hug, kiss, pat each other on the back, bow their bodies and heads in submission, and kiss the hands of those higher in the social ranking. They raise their arms, run about wildly, assume threatening postures, and make loud noises when trying to intimidate others, and they may hit, pinch, slap, and pull the hair of others during fights. They huddle together for comfort when it is cold or raining, and youngsters often retreat to the safety and comfort of their mother's arms when upset.

In addition to these intrinsic visual modes of communication common to many mammalian species, all human groups have developed culturally specific body languages and gestures that individuals must learn to produce and interpret correctly. Given that humans have also developed spoken language, why do we still make extensive use of the visual channel of communication? What are the advantages of gestural modes of communication?

Clearly, the most obvious advantage of gestural language is that it requires neither the ability to hear nor the ability to produce clear speech sounds for others to interpret. People who are not able to hear, or not able to hear clearly—for a variety of reasons—are at a distinct disadvantage if all communication is done through spoken language. Likewise, people who have various cognitive disabilities, or nerve- or muscle-based impairments, may find it difficult to produce speech that can be understood by others. Spoken language relies on a number of complex, coordinated, highly nuanced actions carried out by the brain, the lungs, the vocal cords, the cheeks, the tongue, and the lips.

Long before babies can speak clearly, they can form clear gestures in sign language and communicate with others who know the same sign language (Acredolo, Goodwyn, and Abrams 2009). In the United States, children with Down syndrome are often taught American Sign Language to take advantage of the fact that their minds are capable of receptive and productive language months, or even years, before they have the motor coordination to speak clearly enough to communicate using speech. We will explore the fully developed sign languages of the deaf in detail later. For now, let's contemplate the contexts under which people who can hear and speak might,

Body postures and gestures also convey information to others. Left: his facial expression and outstretched hand express the young man's embarrassment and dismay at being photographed on the toilet with his pants down. Middle: the old man is clearly sad. Top right: when attacked, humans reflexively assume the fetal position, with arms and legs flexed into the body and arms put up to protect the head and face. Bottom right: likewise, raising your arms is a reflexive reaction to freedom, happiness, and accomplishment, as illustrated in this statue of the liberation of slaves from Goree Island, Dakar, Senegal.

nonetheless, find gestural communication more useful than spoken language.

In addition to the primate gestures that continue to be used by all modern humans, people in many regions use a variety of culture-specific gestures to facilitate vocal communication, to add emphasis to their words, and to provide additional information. Typically in North America, if you want someone to approach, you turn your palm up, hold your lateral three fingers flexed into your palm with your thumb, and curl your index finger toward your wrist several times. In Mali, the same meaning of *come here* is conveyed with a similar gesture but made with the palm facing down and all four fingers curling inward repeatedly with the thumb extended. Because of the popularity of soccer worldwide, the gesture for *time out*—one palm held perpendicular to the ground with the other palm placed downward on top of the extended fingers, parallel to the ground, to form a T—is recognized in much of the world.

Any gesture may have different meanings in different cultural contexts, and if you aren't aware of the local subtleties, you may inadvertently offend someone, since many languages include hand gestures that convey insults. In North America, holding up only your middle finger, with your palm facing inward, is widely understood to be rude, especially when exchanged between drivers on the road. The same sentiment is conveyed in other cultural contexts by a variety of different gestures. The *V for victory* sign may change its meaning depending on whether the palm is facing toward the speaker or away; the *OK* sign with thumb and first finger forming a circle refers to sexual intercourse in some cultural contexts. The University of Texas *Hook 'em Horns* sign, to support the football team, with first and last fingers extended and the others held down by the thumb, represents the horns of the devil in some places.

In 2009, U.S. President Barack Obama was criticized for bowing to the Japanese Emperor Akihito on

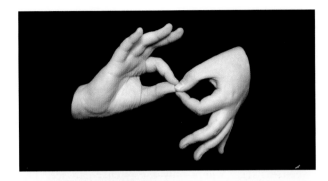

a state visit to Japan. Bowing upon meeting someone is considered a sign of respect in Japanese culture, which is how President Obama meant it. However, some conservative pundits in the United States viewed it as a sign of submission, weakness, or inferiority. International business etiquette courses devote much time to teaching businesspeople the subtleties of body posture, hand gestures, and meeting protocols—including the necessity of sharing food and alcoholic beverages with hosts—in order to minimize the miscommunication and misunderstandings that can occur. As we will see with spoken language, it is a good general rule to assume that someone who is obviously not local did not intend to offend with their gestures. If they did deliberately mean to offend, it will soon become apparent by their other words and actions.

In addition to widely used culturally shaped gestures, humans have invented a variety of gestural communication systems with very specialized, often very localized, use. Any context where others can see you clearly, but not hear you very well, provides an appropriate setting for the use of gestural communication. For example, the deck of an aircraft carrier is too noisy for verbal communication because of the jet engines. Information and instructions about takeoffs and landings are transmitted from the pilots to crew members on the deck through a complex series of hand and body gestures. Communication from boat to boat across an expanse of open ocean is often done through hand, flag, or light signaling systems, as the wind and roar of the waves makes it impossible to hear spoken language. On the floor of the noisy New York Stock Exchange, traders use an extensive system of hand signals to convey orders about what and how much to buy and sell. Even when people are right next to one another but the context is really noisy—during a loud thunder-

There are many different fully developed sign languages around the world, as well as a number of specialized sign systems and visual signal systems used in specific contexts. From top: the ASL sign for "Sign Language Interpreting"; a young toddler mimicking the drawings of the U.S. manual alphabet (finger spelling), which decorate playground equipment in a local park; stock traders signal with their hands on the floor of the stock exchange; and a U.S. Sailor uses signal flags to guide a landing craft air cushion from the amphibious assault ship *USS Bonhomme Richard* onto the beach at Bellows Air Force Station in Hawaii in 2008.

storm, for instance, or at a rock concert or political rally—it may be easier to communicate with gestures.

Visual signals can also be used to communicate over great distances. Paul Revere famously relied on the number of lanterns hung in the bell tower of Christ Church in Boston to know if the British were arriving by land (one lantern) or by sea (two lanterns), so he could then ride through the countryside alerting the troops. Smoke signals have been used by Native Americans and others to communicate from the top of one mountain to the top of another, across great distances. Signal fires lit at night, likewise, were used to send messages along the Great Wall of China to warn of impending attacks.

Another context where gestural communication is advantageous is when silence is required. A group of army scouts advancing on an enemy encampment may coordinate their movements through specialized hand signs. Those in the rear follow the orders of whoever is leading—to advance, halt, retreat, or spread out to the left or right. If a group of hunters is stalking prey, gestures may be used to indicate where the prey animal has been spotted, how far away it is, and who should take the first shot, or move out to the side to

herd the animal in the right direction. The hunters can't speak, even at a whisper, without alerting the prey to their presence and scaring it away.

A final advantage of gestural communication over spoken language is that it is easier to hide gestures from other people's eyes than it is to limit who can hear speech. A great example is the communication that takes place between the catcher and the pitcher during a baseball game. The catcher is crouched down behind the batter and makes signals with one hand between his legs, where only the pitcher can see. The catcher suggests a pitch—fastball, curve ball, slider—and the pitcher either accepts the suggestion and throws the ball, or turns it down by shaking his head from side to side. If the pitcher turns down the first suggestion, the catcher makes a second, and so on, until the pitcher agrees. By using this system of hidden gestures, only the catcher and pitcher know which type of pitch is coming next.

The study of independently created sign languages among populations where many people cannot hear has provided a unique window into both the workings of the human brain/mind and the nature of language itself, as distinct from the ability to hear and decode sounds (language comprehension) and the ability to produce sounds (language production). However, before exploring sign languages of the deaf in more detail, we will consider the development of the auditory-vocal channel of communication in humans. Like tactile and visual communication, human language has its antecedents in the call systems of nonhuman primates. However, humans have elaborated the auditory-vocal channel of communication far beyond the capabilities of any other primate.

Auditory-Vocal Channel

Spoken Words and Sentences

What drove our ancient ancestors to develop spoken language into the complex and infinitely flexible and adaptable system of communication that all humans use today? Theories abound about the many adaptive advantages that spoken language offers, and no doubt each theory contains some kernel of truth, but the specific details of the origins of spoken language will remain lost forever. We don't know exactly when it happened, or where, or how.

William Ellsworth "Dummy" Hoy (1862–1961) was an American center fielder who played Major League Baseball from 1888 to 1902. In addition to being an accomplished deaf ball player, some scholars credit Hoy with creating the signals for safe and out calls.

For example, we don't know if there was once a single, universal language that all members of the genus *Homo* spoke in common across Africa, Asia, and Europe, because such information is not preserved in the fossil or archeological records. We don't know if spoken language developed in fits and starts or in a gradual but continuous fashion. We don't know if spoken language emerged only once in human prehistory or at different times in different places.

We can trace the recent evolution of languages, especially by studying words that constitute the *core vocabulary* (more about this later) and classify languages into families and stocks, but the very first steps along the pathway remain obscured. Some scholars try to extrapolate a date for the origin of language based on such factors as cranial capacity (brain size) and the shape of the bones at the base of the skull and in the throat. Others look at stone tool technology or reconstructed behavior based on archeological remains and argue: "If humans living at this date made complex and beautiful tools, or if they were migrating successfully into new ecological niches, or if they were hunting communally . . . then they *must* have had the cognitive capacity for language." Such hypothetical exercises are certainly fun and can be evaluated based on their internal logic and supporting evidence, or lack thereof. But the truth is, until someone invents a time machine, we will never know for sure.

We can watch as languages continue to change during our lifetimes, with the addition and loss of new words and phrases, new meanings for old terms, the loss of entire languages, and the invention of new ones (Esperanto, Klingon, Na'vi). We also can gain insight into how the human brain processes and produces language by studying inherited genetic variations, developmental issues, and brain injuries, which affect human language capabilities.

The human ability to learn, use, and modify spoken language as a means of communication is often cited as one of the major differences between humans and other animals. However, there is still much we don't know about the communicative abilities of other species. Recent advances in research on whale, dolphin, and elephant communication systems, as well as projects that teach nonhuman primates to communicate with humans, have clearly revealed how little we know about these subjects. Nevertheless, it is widely agreed that humans have a unique ability to use sounds—the auditory-vocal channel of communication—as a means of conveying information of all kinds, as well as more complex activities, including entertainment, persuasion, threats, and so on.

Clearly, there are genetic and anatomical differences between humans and other primates that enable us to speak, and prevent them from speaking. We have specialized brain structures that contribute to our language abilities in a variety of ways. We have specialized vocal cords, with our larynxes farther down in our throats than the other Great Apes. We rely on complex sequences of sounds and generate and express original thoughts—talents that no other animal possesses to the degree that humans do. Clearly, human language abilities have played a major role in our evolution and in the development of a distinct human nature.

As we try to understand why this particular aspect of behavior has been developed so highly in modern humans, we can ask: "What are the advantages of spoken language, as opposed to gestural communication?" When contemplating the evolution of spoken language, we need to remember that our early hominid ancestors lived in a very different sociocultural environment than most of us live in today. They were hunters and gatherers, living in small groups, traveling across the landscape with little in the way of material possessions. We assume that language was adaptive—that it conveyed significant reproductive advantages to those individuals who had the ability to speak and use language.

Assuming that our ancestors began with a system of calls and gestures such as those used by modern chimpanzees and bonobos, what benefits might have come from the addition of spoken language? The most obvious benefit over a system based on gestures is that speaking allows communication among people who can hear, but not see, one another. Life in the dense tropical rain forest canopy would seem an ideal context for communication in the auditory-vocal channel, since lines of sight are often obscured by leaves and branches, and smells are easily dissipated on the wind. Indeed, many nonhuman primates use calls and songs to announce the presence of a food source or a predator, to mark their territorial boundaries, to connect with other members of their troop, to find mates, and so on.

Spoken communication also has obvious advantages in the absence of light for observing visual communication: anywhere after dark or inside a cave or around a campfire at night where flames and shadows disrupt one's view of those on the other side. If you are walking single-file along a trail, even in daylight, you can't see gestural communications from those either in front of or behind you. Spoken language allows communication, at least between adjacent individuals. If you have formed a line to chase animals into a net and everyone is facing the same direction, spoken language allows coordination of activities and movements. If two people are near one another, but not in sight of one another—upstairs/downstairs, around the corner, in different rooms—they can communicate by raising their voices. Certain types of sounds, such as yodeling, can carry much farther across a mountain valley than it would be possible to interpret hand gestures trying to convey the same information.

A final advantage of spoken language over gestural communication is that speech leaves the hands free to engage in other activities. Just as bipedalism frees the hands for other purposes than locomotion while moving about, spoken language frees the hands for other purposes than communication when at rest, allowing people to do all manner of manual work such as carving, flint knapping, grooming, weaving, cooking, child care, and so on, while still communicating freely with anyone within earshot.

It is easy to come up with examples of situations in which the ability to communicate through spoken language provides significant advantages. However, it is clear that humans continue to use both the visual and tactile channels to communicate with others, in addition to the auditory-vocal channel.

The development of writing, plus the ability to transmit a variety of audio and visual communication modes across vast distances—telegraphs, telephones, televisions, cell phones, videoconferences, Skype, mail delivery systems, faxes, e-mail, wireless Internet connections, text-messaging, social networking sites such as Facebook, and most recently Twitter—have utterly transformed how many humans communicate with one another. Beginning with the development of systems of writing (and reading), people no longer had to be in the same place, at the same time, to communicate with others. We will return to a discussion of the advantages and disadvantages of written language later. For now, let us turn to some other interesting aspects of human spoken language.

Other Aspects of Speech

In addition to the words and sentences of each language, there are many other aspects of spoken language that convey factual information and emotional content between speaker and hearer. These include modifications to individual words as well as different styles of speech, which may vary between individuals, between regions, between cultural groups and subgroups, and between languages:

- *Volume and tone of speech:* whether one or more of the words are spoken loudly or quietly, shouted or screamed frantically, whispered lovingly or conspiratorially, said sarcastically or meanly, etc. Some words may be emphasized by raising or lowering the voice. People can speak calmly and quietly even during a crisis (911 operators), or they can speak excitedly, with raised voices, even when discussing the most boring, mundane topics.

- *Tempo of speech:* whether the speaker is speaking slowly and carefully or rushing through his words. Other examples include words spoken smoothly, haltingly, or even clipped (as when your mother calls you by all three of your names in a staccato fashion because she is angry).

- *Clarity of speech:* whether the speaker is articulating each word or slurring her words, running them together, losing track of the point, etc. Clarity may be affected by physical or cognitive impairments, intoxication, illness, and many other factors.

- *Verbosity:* whether using a lot of words where a few will do or using the fewest words possible. People may clearly state what they want to convey, or they may include lots of sidebars and circumlocutions before they get to the point.

Most languages/cultures also include a variety of sounds or noises that aren't technically words but still convey meaning. These include body noises such as crying sounds, yawns, hiccoughs, belches, grunts, and farts (from passing gas). People may also clap their hands, drum their fingers, tap their feet, and make sounds such as *shhhh* when they want silence or are trying to calm someone down, *tsk-tsk-tsk* noises to indicate disapproval, snorts of disbelief or contempt, whistles of admiration, and so on. These extralinguistic sounds and noises will have different meanings, depending on the cultural context. For example, in some cultures, loud farts are considered highly amusing, while in others, they are viewed as shameful and humiliating. In North America, it is acceptable to fart in front of intimate friends and relatives, but would be considered highly inappropriate during a job interview or in a crowded elevator. And who can forget British social anthropologist Raymond Firth's description of the serious consequences of passing gas among the Tikopia of the Solomon Islands? "Tikopia have sometimes chosen odd ways to commit suicide. About the oddest was that chosen by Pu Sao, who, having broken wind in a public gathering, in his shame climbed a coconut palm and sat down on the sharp-pointed hard flower spathe, which pierced his fundament and killed him—a bizarre case of making the punishment fit the crime" (Firth 1967:120–121).

LANGUAGE AS A BOUNDARY MARKER

The most obvious function of language is the *exchange of information* between one individual and one or more others. People give and receive factual information, they entertain one another, they ask for help, they deceive and manipulate others, and so on. However, another critically important social function of language is to serve as a boundary marker—to delineate and emphasize who belongs to a particular group, and who does not. People can indicate their membership in a group not only through the specific language they speak but also through their vocabulary, their accent, their style of speech, and so on. And if you can't speak the language of the group you are interacting with, you are at a distinct disadvantage. Even when everyone is speaking the same mother tongue, there will be numerous subcategories of people who speak in different ways, whether the subcategories are based on ethnicity, age, occupation, region of the country, or other criteria.

Accents

Accents refer to the way words are pronounced. People who speak the same language may have different accents depending on the region where they grew up, their socioeconomic status, and even their ethnic-

ity. Additionally, people who speak English as a second language often have a characteristic way of speaking English that reveals their native tongue. Some accents may be found over a wide area, while others have very restricted ranges, especially if the population is isolated by difficult mountain terrain (as in the Appalachians) or by living on remote islands (Tangier Island, Virginia).

Pronouncing the word *water* as *wooder* indicates an origin in Delaware. Using "you all" (y'all) and the plural form "all you all" (all y'all) marks a person from Texas, while "youse" is found in New Jersey, and "you'uns" in Pittsburgh. Saying you're from "*Loovull*" marks you as a native of Louisville, Kentucky, and people who are from New Orleans pronounce it as "*Noy*-luns." Accents reflect not only general geographic origin but also sometimes the specific section of a city where one grew up, such as South Philly or the Bronx. Some identifiable accents may be associated with income or educational levels, whether such an association reflects reality or is just a stereotype.

Speech Styles

Cockney speech, found in London's East End, provides one example of a speech style. Cockney English includes both a very specific accent and a characteristic style of speaking that historically has been associated with relatively uneducated, working-class people, many of whom were dock workers. Jennifer Worth, describing London Cockney of the 1950s, writes:

> Cockneys love language, and use it continually, with a rich mixture of puns, slang, spoonerisms and rhymes. They carry a verbal library of anecdotes, ditties and yarns in their heads, which can be improvised to suit any occasion. They love long, colorful words. They can throw in description and simile with lightning speed, with a sure instinct for effect. Rhyming is important, and the compelling rhythm of a cockney dialogue is equal to that of a Mozart opera. Cockneys have a verbal mastery second to none in my opinion. The only trouble is, it is so fast and so idiomatic that it goes straight over the heads of most people. (Worth 2002:565–566)

Like Cockneys of the 1950s, modern Texans have a penchant for the use of evocative imagery and similes; they have a saying for every occasion. Among my favorites: "It was so quiet in that room you could hear a mouse pissin' on cotton," and "Now don't get your panty hose in a knot." If someone is not available and no one knows where the person is, a Texan might say, "He's out of pocket." When someone has been injured or is sick, another person might remark, "She's all stove up." In the saying, "That news is really gonna harelip the governor," the word *harelip* is best translated as *upset* or *anger* and bears no connection to anatomical clefts of the upper lip, nor is the person referenced likely to be the governor. It's just one of many colorful sayings that pepper Texas Talk.

In some cultures, people make frequent use of proverbs to comment on the situation. Examples include the Caribbean Creole saying, "If you go to a crab dance, you're gonna get muddy" ("If you sleep around, you'll likely end up pregnant or with a sexually transmitted disease," or, more generally, "If you go someplace you know is dangerous, don't be surprised if you find danger"). The Bambara saying "Late at night is not the time to say you're hungry" means "Always plan ahead." It only makes sense in a cultural context bereft of microwaves, pizza delivery, and all-night Taco Bells.

Specialized Vocabularies

People who belong to various subgroups may use different vocabularies. There are specialized vocabularies for many scholarly disciplines and occupations, for sports activities, for music genres, and so on. Many people working for government agencies speak in acronym-speak on a regular basis, turning initials into words, to the mystification of those not in the know. For example, many Americans in Mali in the 1980s worked for ICRISAT (pronounced just as it looks), which stands for the International Crops Research Institute for the Semi-Arid Tropics. These shorthand methods of referring to lengthy phrases are useful only if everyone is clear about what they mean. In some cases, the words of the original phrase may be forgotten, and the acronym takes over the original meaning. This has happened to *scuba* (self-contained underwater breathing apparatus), radar (radio detecting and ranging), and sonar (sound navigation and ranging). More recently, *jpeg* and *gif* have joined the lexicon. Other acronyms continue to be pronounced by spelling out all the letters, such as PB&J, HIV (but not AIDS, curiously), HTML, RFP, and many others. A few acronyms are pronounced both ways, such as ROTC (R-O-T-C or "rot-see") and NICU, for Neonatal Intensive Care Unit (N-I-C-U or "nick-you").

Learning the specific vocabulary, technical jargon, and styles of speech that go along with membership in any group is an important part of becoming enculturated into that community. Knowing the terms, the abbreviations, the TLAs (three letter acronyms), the code words, and the appropriate conversational and interactional styles marks one as an insider, distinct from those who don't (yet) know the rules.

Reinforcing Status Differentials

Rules of language and interaction styles between people of different status also serve to continually remind those involved of the status differentials, and to reinforce their power and authority. Two examples illustrate how this works.

Bambara Greetings

In Mali and other regions of West Africa, ritualized greetings are very important and must be used appropriately to begin any conversation, whether with a good friend, an acquaintance, or a stranger such as a bank teller. Jumping right into the conversation is considered rude, and people will politely steer you back to the greetings if you forget and just start telling them what you want or asking them for something.

Typically, when two people meet, the lower-ranking person begins the greetings by asking a series of questions. Lower rank can be determined by age, sex, or social status. Generally, if a favor is being asked, the supplicant (asker) is considered to have lower status. The respondent can give actual answers or can use a conventional word—"*M'ba*" for men and "*N'se*" for women—that means, more or less, "I hear you." Once the person who began the greetings has asked enough questions, the respondent takes over and asks many of the same questions back, though usually fewer. The greater the disparity in ranking, and/or the more respect one wants to show, the longer the greetings continue. It is up to the higher-ranking person to move the conversation beyond greetings.

When two men of similar status approach one another on the street, they may begin the greetings simultaneously, and continue them as they meet and pass one another, ending with a volley of repeated "M'bas" until they are out of earshot again. They may compete to see who can sneak in the final "M'ba," which denotes respect for the other person.

The beginning of a typical morning exchange between two Bambara speakers, a younger female (#1), and an older male (#2), is presented at right as an example.

Whipping Out

An example of a similar phenomenon from a North American context would be the tradition of *whipping out* among members of the Corps of Cadets at Texas A&M University. Originally, all members of the student body were men and they were all in the Corps of Cadets (combined ROTC programs for all branches of the armed services). The campus began admitting women in 1964, but women were not admitted to the Corps until 1974. Members of the Corps wear uniforms identifying their branch of service, last name, and rank.

Each fall, a new crop of cadets, known as *fish*, arrive on campus. The males have their heads shaved to mark their status. As fish traverse the campus, going to and from classes, the library, the drill field, and so forth, they are expected to approach higher-ranking Corps members and introduce themselves. They run up to their superior and extend their right hand—whipping it out—for a handshake, while offering greetings and introducing themselves by giving their name. The upperclassman also gives his name. The fish then requests the hometown and academic major of his superior. The higher-ranking Corps member continues to hold and shake hands as long as they are talking, often crushing the fish's hand in a viselike grip. The upperclassman may ask the cadet questions such as, "What's for chow?" or "How many days until Final Review?" or a long list of A&M history trivia questions. The upperclassman gets to decide when to let go, and the lower-ranking person is not supposed to show any indication of discomfort or pain. Cadets are

Speaker	Bambara*	English
#1	"In i sogoma."	You and the morning. (Good morning).
#2	"M'ba. In i sogoma."	I hear you. Good morning.
#1	"I ka kene?"	Are you healthy?
#2	"Toro te."	No problems.
#1	"I muso be di?"	How is your wife?
#2	"A ki'ye kosobe."	She is very well.
#1	"I denw ka kene?"	Are your children healthy?
#2	"Toro tu la."	No problems with them.
#1	"I fa be?"	How is your father?
#2	"A be."	He is (alive still).
#1	"In i fa ma sa."	I haven't seen you for a long time.
#2	"M'ba."	It's true.
#1	"Kan bu fo."	Tell the people of your household I said hello.
#2	"U na me. M'ba."	They shall hear it. Time to say goodbye.
#1	"N'se"	I respect you.

*My written Bambara is based on the work of Charles Bird, John Hutchison, and Mamadou Kanté (1977), as I never learned the official orthography of written Bambara, which was developed after my field research was completed.

often seen around campus in such poses, standing close together facing one another, holding hands.

The most practical result of these exchanges is that the fish get to learn the upperclassmen by name, face, hometown, and major. However, the more significant outcome is that lower-ranking individuals are reminded countless times a day that they are lower ranking and must show respect to their superiors by "whipping out" in a timely manner, using the proper etiquette. These ritualized greetings help reinforce the status quo and emphasize the hierarchical nature of the Corps. In the mid-1990s, two decades after women had integrated the Corps, female upperclassmen still had to contend with male fish who refused to whip out to them because they were women (their official Corps rank was considered less important than their intrinsic, culturally based, inferior status as women). Although such rudeness wasn't officially tolerated, it was commonplace.

THE STUDY OF LANGUAGE AND LESSONS LEARNED

How Scholars Study Language

Because language is such an important and complex part of human nature, it is studied by at least four distinct disciplines, using a variety of methodologies and perspectives: linguistics, anthropology, folklore, and cognitive science. At large universities, there may be separate departments for each of these fields, while at smaller schools, folklore and/or linguistics may be part of the English or Anthropology departments, while cognitive science may be included in the linguistics, philosophy, or biology departments. The lines traditionally separating these varied approaches to the study of language have become blurred in recent years, and cross-disciplinary research has greatly contributed to our understanding of how human language works. The following sections provide a general idea of the topics studied by scholars of human language.

The formal, technical, structural aspects of comparative languages, looking at such features of language as:

- what sounds are used, since no language uses all of the potential sounds humans are capable of making;

- how these sounds are put together to form meaningful parts of speech such as nouns, verbs, adjectives, prepositions, and so on;

- the syntax of the language—how the words are ordered in utterances to indicate meaning, how nouns are inflected for case and gender, how verbs are conjugated for person and number and time, how sentences are formed with multiple subordinate clauses;

- prehistoric and historical aspects of language, including the evolution of language, the study of how languages are related to one another and how long ago they became distinct, how languages change, how new languages form while others become extinct, etc.

The social and cultural aspects of comparative languages, looking at such features as:

- how people use language in everyday life to convey information, status, and group membership, to distinguish males from females, children from adults, younger from older speakers, amateurs from experts, joking relationships between specific relatives, and so on;

- how people use language to persuade, manipulate, or inspire others, for economic, political, or personal purposes;

- how people use language to entertain themselves and others;

- how languages are influenced by population movements and migrations, by demographic forces, and by the invention or introduction of new material goods and new ideas;

- the role of language in shaping issues of class, ethnic, and national identity.

The varieties of narratives, whether for informational, educational, entertainment, or other purposes, and how they fit into other aspects of a culture, such as:

- riddles and jokes;

- insults and curses (it seems to be a cross-cultural universal that insults often involve references to sexual anatomy, inappropriate sexual behavior, or defecation!);

- ritual speech that accomplishes something through its use, such as treaties, magical spells, prayers, and sworn oaths (to tell the truth, to marry someone, to enter into a political office);

- stories of all kinds, whether in the form of short or long (epic) poems, folktales with a moral, folklore about the natural world, stories that recount the founding of a group or settlement or commemorate important historical events, stories of the supernatural (myths), skits, plays, epic dramas, stories that provide information about how to accomplish various tasks, stories that illustrate time-honored truths about the human condition, stories that emphasize particular values, the difference between right and wrong, and what happens to those who behave or misbehave;

- common motifs or stock characters within a culture: the wicked stepmother, the vain queen or king, the trickster, the beautiful princess and the adventurous prince, the poor but courageous commoner, or the dim-witted but amusing sidekick;

- recurring themes within a culture: a quest to fulfill three tasks in order to secure some prize, the triumph of good over evil, men over women, or the powerless over the powerful; the triumph of hard work, perseverance, and a kind heart over intelligence, speed, and trickery; the story, ubiquitous in Western cultures, of how the beautiful but powerless princess is saved by the strong and courageous prince and they live happily ever after; encounters with supernatural beings; encounters with alien beings from a different culture, planet, or galaxy.

The anatomical and cognitive foundations of language within the brain and mind, including:

- which parts of the brain are activated in decoding and encoding language (whether visual or auditory-vocal);

- how children learn one or more languages, including receptive as well as productive language, and why it is so much more difficult to learn to speak another language fluently after early childhood;

- language universals that hint at underlying, genetically based language structures in the brain that are common to all humans;

- how genetic differences among individuals affect language capabilities and development, such as mutations to specific genes, extra chromosomes (Trisomy 21/Down syndrome), missing pieces of chromosomes (Williams' syndrome), Tourette's syndrome, and many others;

- how various brain injuries such as concussions, strokes, dementia, and others affect various language capabilities, such as aphasia;

- speech disorders (the physical inability to speak, or to speak clearly, because of damage to motor nerves or muscles);

- the spontaneous development of indigenous sign languages in isolated settlements where a significant percentage of the population cannot hear.

Lessons Learned: Language in the Auditory-Vocal Channel

Any one of the above bullet-points could be expanded into a book-length treatment of its subject, and indeed, many of them have been. In this brief introductory overview, I will highlight just a few insights that have been gleaned from cross-cultural and laboratory, clinical, and experimental studies of spoken human language.

Word Categories

All known languages, including sign languages, include categories of words that refer to things (nouns), pronouns (people), proper names (specific people), actions (verbs), descriptors of things or people (adjectives), and descriptors of actions (adverbs). In addition, all known languages have some means of indicating the relationships among the various elements in a sentence. The hearer needs to know *who* (subject) is doing *what* (verb) to *whom* (object), and sometimes *with what* (indirect object). Likewise, adjectives must clearly refer to the nouns they modify, and adverbs must clearly refer to the verbs they modify; otherwise, confusion reigns.

Languages make use of varying ways to convey additional information, such as **person,** to indicate who is speaking, with first person referring to oneself, second person referring to the listener, and third person, referring to others. Some languages have **noun classes,** categories of varying types into which nouns are placed, with specific markers on the words to indicate which class they belong to. **Grammatical gender** is a type of noun class, in which nouns may be considered masculine, feminine, or neuter, and the nouns and their associated words, such as adjectives, must match in terms of their form. For example, in Spanish, one would say of a bear, which is a masculine noun, "El oso es bonito" (The bear is beautiful). Of the feminine moon, one would say "La luna es bonita" (The moon is beautiful). Of the neuter *things*, one might say "Lo bello es caro" (That which is beautiful is expensive).

In addition to noun classes that separate words into different grammatical genders, there are a number of languages that have noun classes based on either innate characteristics of the objects being classified, or abstract, perhaps even arbitrary, cultural rules. For example, Swahili, one of the many related Bantu languages spoken by groups across central and southern Africa, has 14 noun classes. Most are distinguished by the form of their initial sounds in both singular and plural forms. Other words that reference the noun, such as verbs and adjectives, are expected to have the same initial sound. One class refers to living creatures, especially people. Words in this class begin with *m-* in the singular, and *wa-* in the plural. Thus, *mtu* means person, while *watu* means people. *Mtoto* means child, and *watoto* means children. The prefix *ba-* refers to an entire group of people, thus the Batutsi (Tutsi people) or the Baganda (Ganda people). Different initial sounds denote classes such as trees and other plants, hand tools, diminutives (smaller versions of other things), things that are dangerous, things that are long and thin, and so forth. The characteristics that the objects in a particular noun class share may be very concrete, or they may be abstract, or derived by extension from a similar type of object. Even linguists who specialize in the study of Swahili disagree about the finer details of the noun classes!

Some Bantu languages may have more noun classes than Swahili, and the basis for noun classes may be very different from one language to another. George Lakoff's book on cognitive semantics—how people from different cultures perceive the world, as revealed in linguistic categories such as noun classes—is titled *Women, Fire, and Dangerous Things* after a noun classification scheme found in Dyirbal, a language spoken by a group of Australian Aborigines (Lakoff 1990).

Color Terms

The world exists in color, and like other higher primates (but unlike most other mammals), humans have eyes capable of distinguishing various colors and shades in the natural world, as well as creating colors and making increasingly fine distinctions between different shades, hues, and tones. One might assume that humans are free to come up with an infinite number of color systems, but there turn out to be specific regularities in the way humans classify and name colors (Berlin and Kay 1999; Fox 2007). First, there are 11 basic color terms: black, white, red, yellow, green, blue, brown, pink, purple, orange, and gray. **Color term** means a word that specifically refers to the property of color. We say that something is *green* rather than "the color of new grass shoots" or *blue* rather than "the color of the sky."

Second, while there are no known languages without any color terms, or with only one color term, there are many languages that have only two color terms. In such languages, all the colors of the visual spectrum are divided into two categories: (1) black/dark, which includes all of the cooler hues, including green, blue, and purple, and (2) white/light, which includes all of the warmer hues, including red, orange, yellow, pink, and so forth.

Third, the older a language is, the more color terms it has, and most of the languages spoken in in-

dustrialized countries use all of the basic 11 color terms. In certain contexts, such as artists' paints or interior house paints, there may be literally hundreds, if not thousands of different terms and phrases used to name slight variations of color in terms of tone, hue, and intensity. For example, the walls in my house are all painted Calming Cream, except for one bedroom, which is painted Acapulco Azure.

Fourth, of those languages that use more than two color terms, additional terms are added in a specific, linear order. Such languages are classified into seven different stages, reflecting the colors they add, in order, as follows.

- *Stage I Languages:* use only the two basic terms, BLACK and WHITE (dark and light)
- *Stage II Languages:* use three color terms, adding RED, to indicate yellowish, reddish, or brownish
- *Stage III Languages:* use four color terms, adding *either* YELLOW *or* GRUE (GREEN/BLUE, not distinguished from one another)
- *Stage IV Languages:* use five color terms, adding whichever color, YELLOW or GRUE, was not added in Stage III
- *Stage V Languages:* use six color terms, splitting GRUE into separate categories of GREEN and BLUE
- *Stage VI Languages:* use seven color terms, adding BROWN as its own color distinct from RED
- *Stage VII Languages:* use eight or more color terms, adding to the above one or more from among: PURPLE, PINK, ORANGE, and GRAY

Quantification Terms

Most languages distinguish different numbers of countable items, and different amounts of volume-measure items. This is referred to in the literature as a count/mass distinction. In terms of enumerating separate objects, not all languages have well-developed counting systems. As with color words, there are no known languages that have no number words. However, there are some languages that have only three basic number words: *one, two,* and *many.* In such cultural contexts, there seems to be no compelling practical need for counting beyond the limits imposed by this three-term system (Menninger 1969; Zaslavsky 1973).

The Pirahã, a small group of hunter-gatherers living in the Brazilian Amazon, provide one example.

Peter Gordon reports that the Pirahã have only three number terms, corresponding to *roughly one* (sometimes one, sometimes a few, or a small amount), *two,* and *many.* Field research with the Pirahã shows that adults fare very poorly on any counting task that requires higher-order number words, such as distinguishing between four and five objects. At the same time, the Pirahã are successful hunter-gatherers, with complex social, spatial, and linguistic skills (Gordon 2004). Another group from the Amazon, the Mundurukú, have number words up to five: one, two, three, four, five, and many (Pica et al. 2004).

Some cultural groups have counting systems that run from one to twenty, based on the fact that humans have 10 fingers and 10 toes. Others count higher than 20 by incorporating additional body landmarks such as facial features (nose, eyes, ears, etc.) and joints (wrists, elbows, shoulders, hips, knees, ankles).

In addition to counting individual objects, all people (including young infants), as well as some monkeys, birds, and rodents, have an ability known as **analog estimation,** whereby the number of items in an array can be estimated with rough accuracy and judged as more or fewer than those in a different array. In addition, most people, even toddlers, can judge which of two items is bigger or contains more individual pieces. It may be that estimating large quantities and judging comparative mass is an innate capability of all humans that does not require language, while counting beyond one or two items necessitates the existence of specific linguistic terms for higher-order numbers.

When referring to singular or plural nouns, there are a number of ways of marking this distinction, and sometimes more than one system is used in a single language. In English, we often add *-s* or *-es* to the end of a word to indicate plural: horse and horses, cup and cups, peach and peaches. Other plurals are made by changing the form of the word in a variety of ways, most often depending on the language from which the word originally came: datum and data, woman and women, mouse and mice, leaf and leaves, cactus and cacti. Still other terms remain the same whether referring to one or more, such as fish and deer. In Bambara, the plural marker is a suffix sound, written as *-w* but pronounced like *-u.* Thus, woman is *muso,* while women is *musow;* child is *den,* and children are *denw.*

When counting money at the market in Mali in the early 1980s, when Malian francs were still used as currency, items were priced according to multiples of five Malian franc pieces, a coin known as a *doromé.* Thus, a pyramid of three tomatoes might be priced at *doromé duuru* (five nickels, essentially). When I hesitated, trying to convert the number of doromés into Malian francs, and thence into U.S. money, to grasp how expensive the item was, the vendor assumed I thought the price was too high and lowered it to *doromé naani* (four nickels)—and I had to begin my calculations again.

Who Is Doing What to Whom with What?

In any language, there must be some way for the speaker to indicate, and the hearer to understand, what role each noun (or pronoun, or person referred to by a proper name) is playing in the sentence. We can talk about the subject of the sentence, *who,* the object of the sentence, *to whom,* and the indirect object, *with what.* If we have no way to tell which term refers to which role, then we can't really know what is going on. For example, if I say "Steven Peter sponge bathing"—it isn't all that clear what is going on. If I had some way to indicate who was giving the bath, who was getting the bath, and what was happening with the sponge, then the hearer could interpret the sentence unambiguously.

Like many languages, English relies primarily on rigid word order and prepositions to tell the listener what is going on—who is doing what to whom, with what object, as well as which adjectives modify which nouns, and which adverbs modify which verbs. If I say "Steven is carefully bathing Peter with a fluffy, blue sponge"—then all is clear to speakers of English, because they know the rules of word order. Steven is the subject, Peter the object, and the sponge is the indirect object. Adjectives come before the noun they modify, so it is clear that fluffy and blue refer to the sponge. In English, adverbs may come at various places in the sentence. The *-ly* suffix makes the word *careful* into an adverb, and since bathing is the only verb, it is clear that it is the bathing that is being done carefully.

Other languages rely on word order as well, but the rules may vary from those found in English. In Romance languages (those derived from Latin, such as French, Spanish, and Italian), adjectives usually come after the noun they modify. Thus, "a fluffy, blue sponge" becomes, in French, "une éponge pelucheuse et bleue," and in Spanish, "una esponja mullida, azul." In German, the adverb follows the verb it modifies, but the adjectives precede the noun they modify, as in English. Thus, the full sentence becomes "Steven badet sorgfältig Peter mit einem flaumigen, blauen Schwamm" (Yahoo! 2010).

Some languages use affixes to indicate the role of the various words in the sentence. An affix is a **morpheme** (meaningful sound) attached to a root word, either before the word as a prefix, or after the word as a suffix. There are many different types of affixes, and in many languages, **inflectional affixes** can be used to alter words to indicate **case**—which word is the subject, which the object, and so on. For example, in Latin, the noun that is the subject is inflected in the *nominative* case, while the noun that is the object is inflected in the *accusative* case. Associated verbs and adjectives may also change their form (be inflected using affixes) to match their respective nouns. The words in a Latin sentence may be in any order yet still convey the same information, as it is the endings of each term that indicate who is doing what to whom, and with what.

Derivational affixes, whether suffixes or prefixes, turn simple words into a set of more complicated words with related meanings. Suffixes come after the root word. Beauty can become beautiful, beautify, or beautification. Wine, nun, and infirm each can gain a suffix to become a place where such a noun might be found: winery, nunnery, infirmary (Fox 2007). Prefixes come before the root word. In English, prefixes such as *non-* or *in-* or *a-* can transform a word into its opposite: sense/nonsense, tolerant/intolerant, moral/amoral. When we learn our first language as infants and toddlers, we seem to absorb it out of the air; we are often not consciously aware of the formal rules that shape it. We know that "red, big ball" and "bathing carefully Peter" sound odd, without knowing why.

Part of the difficulty of learning any new language after early childhood is that one first has to consciously learn and understand the rules of one's native tongue and then find out how the rules differ in the new language. More closely related languages will have similar rules, which is why it is often easier for a native English speaker to learn German than Italian, but learning either of these Indo-European languages is generally easier (for the native English speaker) than learning Dyirbal or Mandarin Chinese or Quechua.

Temporal Terms

Every known language possesses some way to indicate tense, whether something is happening now (present), happened before (past), or will happen later (future). Beyond these basic three, some cultures/languages have developed elaborate systems of carving up the continuum of time into many different categories. Some languages distinguish whether an action occurs often, or only rarely; whether it is ongoing, recently concluded, or happened a long time ago; whether it took only a short time, or continued on for many years; whether it might happen, or will definitely happen, and so forth. Sometimes, temporality or tense is indicated by affixes (either prefixes or suffixes), or by the addition of other words or phrases, the inflection of adverbs or adjectives, and so on. In addition, there may be distinct terms that imply specific notions of time, action, and intention.

Human perceptions of time are grounded in natural phenomenon such as the Earth's rotation around its axis (night and day), the Earth's orbit around the sun (seasons and annual cycles), the waxing and waning of the moon, the movements of the stars and planets in the night sky, and the growth of crops, herds, and children. Beyond these natural cycles, human perceptions of time are highly culturally conditioned, such that some scholars speak of **social/cognitive time,** which can vary widely between cultures (Gell 1996). Understanding such differences is important beyond just an appreciation of cultural diversity. Whenever people from two cultures with disparate notions of time need to interact and cooperate, it is essential that both sides negotiate and agree on what system will be used. Evelyn Wladarsch's ethnographic study of cultural concepts of time in Burkina Faso, West Africa, provides one example of how important different notions of time can be (Wladarsch 2005).

In Texas, the phrase *fixin' to* carries a very specific temporal meaning. If I say "I'm fixin' to go to the store," it means that I am actively getting ready to go, gathering up my keys and shopping list, and asking if there are any special requests. The use of *fixin' to* implies that I'll be leaving shortly, within, say, 10 to 15 minutes, but not right this instant. Likewise, the sentence "She's fixin' to domino" references a woman who is 9+ months pregnant and whose labor is expected to begin very shortly. Once labor begins, a series of further events automatically ensue, just like when you knock over the first in a row of dominoes.

Failure to appreciate cultural notions of time can lead to much frustration and miscommunication. The Spanish term *mañana*, usually misleadingly translated into English as *tomorrow*, is a case in point. After years of living in Texas, I finally understood the concept after seeing a sign that read: "Mañana: It doesn't mean tomorrow, it means *not today*." Suddenly, many previous encounters made sense. Likewise, if an event is supposed to start at 8:00 PM, in some contexts that means precisely at 8:00 PM, not 7:59 or 8:01 PM. Train departures in Switzerland are one example. While traveling in Egypt in 1981, my husband and I were surprised to discover that the trains left precisely on the dot when they were scheduled to depart. All other aspects of Egyptian culture seemed to operate using a more relaxed time frame. Then we found out that the trains were run by a Swiss company.

Across much of West Africa, a starting time of 8:00 PM might mean anywhere from 8:30 to 10:30 PM, or even later—whenever everyone important has arrived and the event is ready to begin. When I visited Cork, Ireland, in 2008, the museum in the park posted an opening time of 10:00 AM, but in actuality, the doors opened whenever the caretaker got there and unlocked them—maybe 10:20, maybe later, and seldom at the same time two days in a row. Many immigrants to the United States from cultures where time is more fluid and flexible have learned to specify if they mean *American time* or *Homeland time*.

Concepts of time and how it should be measured, reckoned, and used are embedded in every culture, and reflected in language. Of the Nuer, Evans-Pritchard had this to say about time:

> The Nuer have no expression equivalent to "time" in our language, and cannot, therefore . . . speak of time as though it were something actual which passes, can be wasted, can be saved and so forth. I do not think that they ever experience the same feeling of fighting against time or having to co-ordinate activities with an abstract passage of time, because their points of reference are mainly the activities themselves, which are generally of a leisurely character. Nuer are fortunate. (Evans-Pritchard 1951:103, cited in Holtzman 2008:55)

In contrast to Evans-Pritchard's description of traditional Nuer conceptions of time in the Sudan of the 1930s and 1940s, Holtzman points out that recent Nuer immigrants in Minnesota are not so fortunate:

> In the United States, the Nuer have found that being on time matters. Appointments may be cancelled if one fails to arrive on time, tardiness at work may lead to dismissal, and classes begin whether students have arrived or not. (Holtzman 2008:55)

Core Vocabulary

Some words in a language typically behave conservatively, changing little over time, even as the language may change in other ways by adding new terms and ideas or new grammatical rules. Conservative words are described by linguists as the **core vocabulary** of a language and include words for mother and father, natural features of the landscape (sun, moon, trees, and water), lower order number terms (one, two, three), basic color terms (black, white, red), and body parts (head, arm, leg, hand). These conservative core terms are especially useful for analyzing the relationships among languages and groups of languages.

A simple comparison of words for mother and father in languages from around the world serves to illustrate this concept (see Table 11.1 on the following page). The words are virtually identical in almost every language. It is easy to imagine that the most important thing in the environment of a newborn human is his mother. It also may be that **phonemes** (sounds) beginning with the consonants *m-*, *b-*, *f-*, *t-*, and *d-*, followed by a short *a* are among the first sounds that human babies can make. Certainly there are no languages where the word for mother begins with an *r-* sound, a *qu-* sound, or a *str-* sound.

The preceding discussion is by no means comprehensive, but hopefully provides a sample of the many intriguing cultural topics that can be explored through the comparative study of spoken languages. In the next section, we will look more closely at sign languages of the deaf as a specific example of how gestural communication in the visual mode has been elaborated by modern humans who cannot, or choose not to, communicate using the auditory-vocal channel.

Lessons Learned: Language in the Visual Channel

For people who cannot hear, the auditory-vocal channel of communication is of limited value. Around the world, whenever and wherever significant numbers of deaf people live in a community, simple gestural

Table 11.1   Words for *mother* and *father*

Language	Word for *Mother*	Word for *Father*
English	Mother	Father
Swahili, E. Africa	Mama	Baba
Mandarin, China	Mama	Baba
Malay, SE Asia	Emak	Bapa
Apalai, Amazon	Aya	Papa
Bengali, India	Ma	Baba
Bambara, Mali	Ba	Fa
Spanish	Madre	Padre
Algonquin, Canada	Mam, ma:ma:	Papam, tatag
Navajo, Arizona	Ma	Ta
Latin, Italy	Mater	Pater
Lingala, Central Africa	Mama	Tata
Sanskrit, India	Matr	Pitr
Yaṇomamö, Amazon	Naya	Haya
Cayapa, Ecuador	Mama	Apa
Turkish, Turkey	Ana	Ata

communications have been elaborated into complex, sophisticated systems of sign language using body postures, facial expressions, movements of the arms and, especially, the hands. "Instead of operating acoustically, sign languages work spatially. Where spoken language transmits information by stringing sounds together into recognizable patterns, sign language does the same thing by manipulating the movement of the hands and body in space" (Fox 2007:18). Language produced and understood via the visual-spatial channel "behaves remarkably like language in the auditory-vocal one; it employs similar grammatical structures; it is acquired in parallel developmental stages; and it is disrupted, as the result of aging or injury, in strikingly similar ways" (Fox 2007:65). It is also processed in the brain using the same regions, which should be thought of as language centers, rather than speech or hearing centers.

Many people think that there is only one, universal signed language based on intuitive similarities between gestures and their meanings. Some signs do start out this way, as iconic or imitative, mimicking the shape or movement patterns of their referents, just as some words in every language are onomatopoeic

(sounding like their referents). As with most words, however, most signs are arbitrary conventions, having no obvious relation to their referents, and varying from one signed language to another.

Today, there are more than 100 separate and distinct signed languages around the world, including the well-developed national or **urban sign languages** found in the United States (American Sign Language), Britain, France, Greece, Israel, China, India, Pakistan, Turkey, and Lebanon, as well as others. More than a dozen village, or rural, sign languages are known from many areas of the world, including Israel (Al-Sayyid Bedouin), Bali (Kata Kolok), Thailand (Bhan Khor), Jamaica (Country Sign), Surinam (Kajana), Ghana (Adamorobe), Mexico (Mayan Sign), and others.

Indigenous village sign languages arise spontaneously under very specific circumstances. They require a traditional, isolated community, the presence of hereditary deafness (usually through autosomal recessive genetic mutations), large families, and intermarriage or in-breeding, which raises the incidence of deafness to a level above that of the surrounding populations. By studying indigenous sign languages as they arise and develop, anthropological linguists gain insight into how the human mind works.

Deafness on Martha's Vineyard, Massachusetts

The most famous example of an indigenous sign language at work is documented in Nora Groce's 1985 ethnography, *Everyone Here Spoke Sign Language: Hereditary Deafness on Martha's Vineyard*. This example is worth describing in some detail. Martha's Vineyard (MV) is an island off the coast of southeastern Massachusetts. The recessive mutation that eventually led to a relatively high frequency of deafness on MV is thought to have originated sometime prior to the 1600s in a remote region of southern England known as the Kentish Weald. A number of related families from the Weald immigrated to the New World in the 1630s and 1640s, settling first in mainland Massachusetts. By the end of the seventeenth century, many of these families and their descendants, including some who were deaf, had moved to Martha's Vineyard.

The first deaf child native to the island was born there in 1704.

There was little immigration to the island after 1700, and most individuals married into neighboring families, including some that were distantly related. By the end of the 1700s, more than 96 percent of the people on the island were married to someone they were related to, increasing the chances that their children might inherit a recessive allele for deafness from each parent. Families were large, and every family might expect to have one or more deaf children. As the generations went by, and inbreeding at different levels continued, more and more people came to have more and more Kentish ancestors in their lineage, so many people were carriers (had one copy of the allele that caused deafness), and more and more marriages were between two carriers. Thus, deaf children were born in ever-increasing numbers, and then as deaf people married carriers or other deaf people, even more deaf children were born.

Deafness on the vineyard peaked in the 1840s, with 45 deaf children being born on the island during that decade. The number of deaf individuals declined slowly thereafter due to two factors. First, the beginning of daily boat service between the island and the mainland in the early 1800s brought an influx of new genetic variation. Second, the departure of deaf children to a dedicated school for the deaf on the mainland beginning in 1820 led to many deaf islanders marrying people who were deaf for other reasons (and whose children, therefore, could hear). At the school for the deaf in Connecticut, Martha's Vineyard students contributed MV Sign to the fledgling American Sign Language (ASL), which was developed from a mix of French and British manual sign languages and the *homesigns* of students from other communities. By 1900, there were only 15 deaf people still living on Martha's Vineyard. By 1925, the number was down to four; the last deaf islander died in the 1950s.

What Groce was able to document, through her research in the 1980s, was that people on Martha's Vineyard had developed their own sign language. Furthermore, because the nonaffected people on the island all learned to sign as well as speak, everyone could communicate with everyone else, deaf or hearing, and no one considered the deaf to be disabled or handicapped. Eventually, almost every family on the island contained deaf members, and people who were not deaf used sign language in addition to speaking whenever they were part of a group that included some deaf members. Deaf individuals were not discriminated against and participated in all community activities. Groce writes that hearing islanders sometimes used sign language among themselves to exclude outsiders, or to tell dirty jokes (Groce 1985).

Unfortunately, there is little evidence of what Martha's Vineyard sign looked like. It is now extinct; it was so commonplace in its day that no one thought it was worthy of being recorded or described. At the time of Groce's research, a few old-timers vaguely remembered a few gestures, but even they could not be sure. However, the lessons of Martha's Vineyard don't rely on knowing precisely what MV sign looked like.

As Nora Ellen Groce so eloquently demonstrated in her ethnography *Everyone Here Spoke Sign Language*, being deaf isn't limiting if everyone can communicate with their hands. Going even further, an architectural and design movement known as *Universal Design* encourages people to consider everyone when designing buildings, signs, and objects. The photograph shows a universally designed map in Otemachi Station in Tokyo, Japan. In addition to written information, the board has a raised map of the layout of the station, Braille labels, and an audio guide system to help blind people.

Groce writes: "The Martha's Vineyard experience suggests strongly that the concept of a handicap is an arbitrary social category. . . . The most important lesson to be learned from Martha's Vineyard is that disabled people can be full and useful members of a community if the community makes an effort to include them" (Groce 1985:108).

Deafness in Al-Sayyid, Israel, and Sign Language Universals

Unlike Martha's Vineyard, the indigenous sign language of the deaf in the small, isolated, Bedouin village of Al-Sayyid in eastern Israel is alive and well, and still developing in complexity. It has been studied since 2000 by a team of four linguists, two from the United States (Carol Padden and Mark Aronoff) and two from Israel (Wendy Sandler and Irit Meir), and their research has been wonderfully chronicled in the book *Talking Hands: What Sign Language Reveals about the Mind*, by journalist and linguist Margalit Fox (2007). The study of Al-Sayyid Bedouin Sign—an indigenous sign language in its early stages of development—has provided a rich resource for scholars interested in how humans can create language "from thin air." As Fox describes it, the village of Al-Sayyid is close to the ideal research situation, one "where everyone spoke a signed language that leapt straight from the brain onto the hands with nothing (no spoken language or other sign languages) to waylay it in between" (Fox 2007:69).

Like Martha's Vineyard Sign, the sign language of Al-Sayyid is spoken by both deaf and hearing villagers. A number of fascinating insights into the nature of the human brain/mind and the early development of language have come out of the linguistic studies of Al-Sayyid and its residents.

The first deaf children were born in Al-Sayyid about 70 years ago—ten children in one generation. These first ten children began by creating homesigns for use within their own family, and as they grew up these homesigns were elaborated into a functional, if rudimentary, sign language. Their children, in the next generation, both deaf and hearing, further developed and expanded Al-Sayyid Bedouin Sign Language. The village of approximately 3,500 residents has about 140 deaf residents today, but many of the hearing villagers know the local sign language as well, and the deaf are not stigmatized. Like the cultural context of Martha's

Vineyard in the 1700s and 1800s, deaf individuals are fully incorporated into all facets of village life.

Although not the case in Al-Sayyid, some signed languages have different styles for male and female signers, especially if men and women lead fairly separate lives, with different spheres of interest. For example, in Dublin, Ireland, from the mid-1800s to about 1950, deaf children attended schools segregated by sex, such that male and female dialects of Irish Sign Language developed. About 70 percent of the signs differed in some way in the two dialects. Women tended to be more adept at decoding men's signs than men were at decoding women's signs. Eventually, both dialects fell into disuse and recent attempts to revive Irish Sign have focused only on the male form (Fox 2007:152).

William Stokoe, a teacher at Gallaudet, a university for the deaf in Washington, D.C., was the first to recognize the *languageness* of sign language. He studied the American Sign Language used by Gallaudet students in the 1950s and 1960s and realized that each sign could be broken down into several components. For Stokoe, these included (1) *hand shape*, (2) *location*, and (3) *movement*. Later researchers added another component, (4) *orientation*, which means whether the palms are facing up, down, left, or right. For ASL, Stokoe identified 19 distinct hand shapes, 12 locations, and 24 types of movements. Combined, they allow users of ASL to converse about an infinite variety of subjects.

Sign languages may use different subsets of all the possible hand shapes, locations, and movements. Hands and fingers can take on many different shapes and perform many motions—they can grasp, clench, push, tap, brush, thrust, slice, and dive; they can point, poke, wiggle, spread, curl, and bend (Fox 2007). While ASL uses 19 hand shapes, some sign languages use fewer, while others have as many as 50. No sign language studied to date uses all of the potential combinations of hand shape, location, and movement.

Just as spoken languages are made up of phonemes (separate sounds) that are combined into morphemes (combinations of sounds that have meaning), so are sign languages made up of gestural phonemes (hand shape, location, and movement) that are combined into gestural morphemes (postures and movements of the hands in space that have meaning).

Signs can be produced in different locations relative to the bodies of the signer and the receiver. Most signs are produced within the quarter-sphere defined horizontally by the front of the signer's body and vertically between the head and the waist. The receiver watches the signer's face for important linguistic information, while their peripheral vision takes in and interprets the movements of the hands and body. Specific word order, so critical in spoken English, is not necessary in most sign languages. Likewise, signs can convey additional information depending on whether they are produced rapidly or slowly, once or repetitively, calmly or excitedly or angrily. Facial expressions and body movements, known as **nonmanual markers** (NMM), serve to augment the information provided by the hands.

All well-developed sign languages share some features in common. One is that *grammar is organized spatially.* Verbs display grammatical agreement with one or more nouns by being linked visually in space. The same technique is used to link adjectives to nouns and adverbs to verbs. For example, the sign for "the boy" may be parked in space at shoulder height to the speaker's right, and then the adjectives "young" and "eager" will be signed at the same location or signed in front and then moved to the location of the parked sign; making it clear that it is the boy who is young and eager. Any sign can be parked in space and referenced later by gesturing toward its physical location.

The linguists studying the relatively young Al-Sayyid Bedouin Sign Language (ABSL) were surprised to find that its speakers had not yet developed spatial grammar to indicate verb-noun agreement. There were lots of verbs, but they were signed without obvious visual reference to their nouns. So how did the villagers know who was doing what to whom? They used rigid word order, specifically SOV—subject, object, verb. As we saw earlier, spoken English also uses rigid word order to convey grammatical information, but in English the order is SVO (subject, verb, object). A number of spoken languages do use SOV word order—indeed, it is the most commonly used word order found around the world—but none of the languages spoken in and around Al-Sayyid use SOV.

It seems that early in the development of any new language, the human mind automatically devises a system for making the meaning of sentences clear. For ABSL, word order served this purpose, as well as others. In ABSL, adjectives come after the noun they modify, and the words for *wh-* questions (who, what, where, when, why, and how) come at the end of the sentence. It is expected that ABSL will eventually develop other means instead of, or in addition to, word order to express grammatical relationships. Currently, ABSL is classified as a Stage I language in the color-term system, with terms only for black and white, but more color terms are expected to develop as well.

A second feature common to all well-developed sign languages is the **symmetry constraint:** in signs where both hands are moving, the hands must move symmetrically, either together as a unit, as mirror images, or in alternating fashion. The hands must have the same shape and be located in the same space in front of the body (both vertically and horizontally). About 60 percent of the signs used in ASL use both hands.

A third feature common to all sign languages is the **dominance constraint.** Some signs involve both hands, but the **base hand** is stationery, while the other hand moves in relation to the base. If the hands use different shapes, then the base hand is constrained to only a few prescribed shapes (six shapes are possible for the base hand in ASL).

Both deaf and hearing speakers of sign language sign in their sleep, and talk to themselves in sign. Babies just learning to sign have been observed babbling with signs, making random or nonsense signs just as babies make random and nonsense sounds when they are learning to speak.

Sign languages change over time just as spoken languages do, with new terms being adopted through diffusion or independent invention. In addition, many signs that began as all or partially iconic evolve over time to be more systematic and standardized, often losing any visual connection to their original referent. As time goes by, younger learners will expand and elaborate on the sign system taught to them by older children and adults, and more and more grammatical features will be added, such as additional color terms, the conjugation of verbs, and inflections for tense and case.

Deaf Culture

During my years as a professor at Texas A&M University, I successfully spearheaded a movement to have American Sign Language accepted to fulfill the university's requirement that all students study a foreign language. One of the objections that some people raised was that foreign language study usually included learning about the culture of the people who spoke the language. These nay-sayers argued that since ASL was just "signed English," its speakers didn't have any corresponding foreign culture for students to study. Of course, as Fox writes:

> ASL is not English. It uses vocabulary and grammatical constructions found nowhere in English. (Some linguists have compared aspects of its grammar to Japanese and Navajo.) It also employs word orders very different from those found in English. Like all signed languages studied to date, ASL displays a grammatical economy that English does not have: with a twist of the wrist or an extra revolution of the arm (for varying the spatial signal gives signed language much of its grammar), a verb can be inflected to convey a nuanced spectrum of meanings that in English requires cloddish circumlocution. (Fox 2007:21)

It is true that in a few cases, such as Martha's Vineyard and Al-Sayyid, deaf individuals have been fully integrated into their communities because the hearing members also learned to sign. However, it has more often been the case that the deaf members of a population have found themselves isolated and discriminated against. In part to help them cope, they have formed many aspects of a culture specific to the deaf community. Fox writes:

> In recent years, the speakers of this rich language [ASL] have come to regard themselves not as disabled—would-be hearing people in need of repair—but, quite simply, as members of a linguistic minority, a signing archipelago in a vast American sea of speech. In the United States and a number of other countries, the deaf view themselves as a cultural minority as well: besides their language, they are vitally connected by shared history and tradition. There are deaf professional and social organizations, and deaf athletic clubs. There is deaf custom: styles of humor, of social interaction, and a deaf folkloric tradition that includes creation stories about the roots of the community itself. (Fox 2007:21)

Today, a number of scholarly books about deaf culture have been published (Bauman 2008; Lindgren, DeLuca, and Napoli 2008; Padden and Humphries

2006). One explores the difficulties of sign language translation at large, multilingual international conferences (McGee and Davis 2010). It is now widely accepted that the deaf, in many circumstances, do indeed develop a distinctive culture, one that requires study in order for outsiders to understand—just as any foreign culture does. The richness of deaf culture has been threatened by the development of new technologies, such as cochlear implants, which allow some deaf people to hear far better. Proponents of cochlear implants, often hearing parents of a deaf child, believe that being deaf is a disability, a problem to be fixed, and are often unfamiliar with, and afraid of, deaf culture. Opponents of cochlear implants, usually deaf adults, view the devices as invasive and unnecessary. These deaf individuals do not consider deafness to be a disability in need of fixing. Two recent documentaries beautifully illustrate the cultural clashes that can occur within the same ethnic, economic, and regional subculture (in this case white, middle-class, New Yorkers) and even within the same family, when people hold vastly different conceptions about what it means to be deaf. These films, by director Josh Aronson, are *Sound and Fury* (2001), and *Sound and Fury: Six Years Later* (2006).

TECHNOLOGY AND HUMAN COMMUNICATION

Transcending Time

The development of writing gave humans, for the first time, the ability to preserve one person's knowledge and ideas for posterity in exactly the terms and phrases he used. Once the communication was written down, it could be preserved for varying lengths of time, depending on the medium, and read by anyone

Opposite page: Tactile communication can be used for more than just one person touching another, and continues to improve as technology evolves. Top left: a child reads a book written in Braille. Top right: an antique telegraph key and sounder—technology of the nineteenth and twentieth centuries for communicating over long distances—are set up at a Civil War reenactment camp in Indiana in 2009. Bottom left: a U.S. Sailor uses a touch screen to operate the missile launch console at his battle station. Bottom right: a communications pay station such as this one in Germany provides pay-for-service telephone and WiFi.

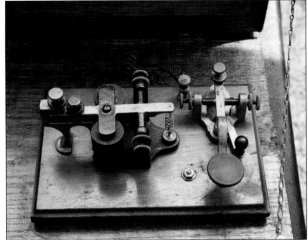

in the future who shared the knowledge of how the information was encoded in letters (representing sounds) or glyphs (representing objects or concepts) and combined into meaningful sentences. Thus, works written in one language could be read days, months, years, or even centuries later, as long as the format by which they were recorded survived, and as long as there were people who knew the code.

If you write something in the sand, it gets washed away with the next wave or high tide. If you write something on paper, it may be destroyed when you spill coffee on it, or the dog eats it. But under the right conditions, writing on paper may survive for centuries. If you write something in stone, it may last for thousands of years. In this way, knowledge, wisdom, beliefs and attitudes, fictional stories, and factual information and data can be preserved for people who haven't even been born yet. All you need is a long-lasting medium on which to record, and an uninterrupted transfer of the knowledge of how to encode (write) and decode (read) the communication. Problems arise when either the medium for recording the information is not long-lasting, or the knowledge of how to encode and decode it is lost.

For example, no one has ever been able to decode Rongorongo, the written language of Rapa Nui (Easter Island). Prior to the 1800s, when it died out, the language was written down by engraving glyphs (small representations that include human and natural figures) onto wooden tablets. Only a few of these wooden tablets have survived to the present, and no one today knows how to read them. A couple of examples from modern times will illustrate the ongoing problems involved in preserving communications for future readers.

Cursive Writing

Before the development of typewriters and computer keyboards, most written communications were either printed in block letters (*manuscript* writing) or written in *cursive* script. Once cursive script was developed, it was taught widely in schools. There are different styles and forms of cursive writing. One of the most popular for writers of English was the Palmer Method, which was taught in schools in the United States beginning in the late 1800s. The Palmer Method involves not only standard forms for upper- and lowercase letters, but movements of the arms and shoulders to form the letters (rather than just the fingers and wrists), and with all the letters connected together. Other methods of cursive handwriting focus more on fine motor control of the fingers and thumb, with the arms and shoulders held relatively stationary.

For many years in the United States, elementary school children were first taught manuscript writing (printing), with all of the letters separate, using a stan-

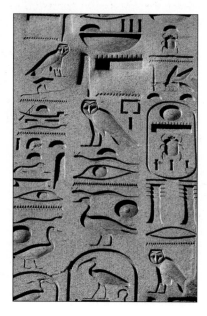

Permanent visual symbols can be encoded in letters (representing sounds) or glyphs (representing objects or concepts) and combined into meaningful communications in a variety of media. Left: Egyptian hieroglyphics carved in stone. Right: *Nsibidi* is the ideographic writing system of the Ejagham (Ekoi) people from the Nigeria–Cameroon border. A number of these ideographs have been identified in old African American quilts made by slaves and their descendants (see Maude Wahlman's 2001 book *Signs and Symbols: African Images in African American Quilts*).

dard form for each upper- and lowercase letter, and all the words printed straight up and down. In this way, any person could read the words printed by any other person. Printing was usually taught in first and second grades, and cursive writing was introduced in third grade.

Cursive writing connected all the letters in one word together, had different standard forms for each upper- and lowercase letter than printing, and the words were slanted slightly to the right (similar to *italics* using a modern word processing program). Children spent several hours a week in school practicing their handwriting. Although idiosyncratic deviations from the standard form were allowed, it was generally understood that you had to stay within certain limits of letter formation if you wanted other people to be able to read your handwriting.

Typing/Keyboarding

For many years, typing was generally not taught until high school, or in special business schools, where young women learned shorthand and touch-typing (typing quickly and accurately using all ten fingers, without looking at the keys) in order to get jobs as secretaries. With shorthand, they could take dictation from their bosses and then type up these communications—letters, memos, reports—on their typewriters. Typing errors had to be fixed laboriously by hand, or else you had to start over at the beginning of the page. Men typically didn't learn either shorthand or typing.

The advent of electric typewriters, then electric typewriters that were self-correcting, and finally personal computers with keyboards and word processing software, meant that more and more people learned to type, at earlier and earlier ages. In recent decades, many people have become quite proficient at typing with two or more fingers, even if they always have to look at the keys. Touch-typing is no longer required, although many people do still learn to type this way. Typing accuracy becomes less important once you can simply back up and retype a word correctly, especially once spell-check, grammar-check, and automatic correction of spelling errors became available as part of commercial word processing programs.

As tape recording technology improved, and more and more people became proficient at using the computer keyboard, shorthand fell out of favor. The boss could record his letters onto a tape, and the secretary could listen to the recording and type directly into the computer. Eventually, most bosses took over composing their own correspondence and did away altogether with the secretary as intermediary. Few people learn shorthand anymore, as there is no need.

Likewise, in recent years, at least in North America, cursive writing has been dropped from most elementary school curriculums in favor of time spent learning to type on computer keyboards. Children are still taught to print, but many are not taught to write in cursive script or are not required to become proficient enough in the standard formation of the letters that someone else can read their handwriting. Each person's handwriting thus becomes a personal code that only she can decipher.

An inability to write quickly and clearly by hand can cause problems for students when teachers don't allow students to take notes on computers, or require hand-written essays for in-class exams. If the teacher can't read the student's answer, it is unlikely to receive a good grade. Research has shown that an essay will be given higher marks if the handwriting is clear and legible, compared to the same essay written in sloppy handwriting that is difficult to decipher. Likewise, many college students today have difficulty deciphering even clearly written cursive writing, because they never learned the conventions for letter formation and connection.

Of even more concern for communicating across the ages than the form of the words—whether printed, written in cursive, or typed—is the medium upon which they are placed. Paper doesn't last forever, but it can last for many hundreds of years under the right conditions. As long as people have functioning vision, and brains that carry the knowledge of how to read the writing, they can read words written many years ago. Newer means of recording information are not so resilient.

Digital Storage of Data and Written Texts

Once machines become involved in storing information, problems of all types arise. When information is digitized—encoded using a string of 0s and 1s—decoding it becomes dependent on having the correct computer software and hardware. However, because the technology for digitizing information changes so rapidly, it becomes a race to keep transferring information from its original format into the newest version.

Just as with music—where you originally bought the Beatles' *The White Album* in LP vinyl, then on 8-track, then cassette tape, then a CD, and finally as an MP3 file on your iPod—the same is true of any written communication or data files. During the middle of the twentieth century, many data sets were recorded on reel-to-reel tapes, which required specific machines to read them. Later, IBM developed punch cards, on which data were stored by punching little rectangular holes into cards using a card-punch machine, which then required another machine, a card-reader, to turn them back into data that a mainframe computer could analyze. Once personal computers were developed in the 1980s, punch cards fell out of use. No one produced punch cards any more, and eventually the card-punch and card-reading machines broke or were thrown away, so even if you had data stored in boxes of cards, there was no way to turn them back into *use-able* information.

In the late 1960s, computer floppy disks were developed for storing data and documents. Eventually, they replaced reel-to-reel and punch cards for storing and exchanging data and written documents. Floppy disks came in 8″, 5¼″, and 3½″ sizes. Many personal computers originally had 5¼″ floppy drives. Soon enough, these were replaced by the smaller, hard-shelled 3½″ disks, and many computers were no longer able to read the larger-format floppies. People had to move their files from 5¼″ to 3½″ disks. By the end of the 1990s, disks were fading in popularity as external hard drives, USB flash drives, or memory cards were developed. Since not all hardware systems are compatible, it can be very difficult to transfer data from one system to another. Today, many universities allow students and faculty to save their files on the university's servers, and there are a number of websites that function the same way for a fee. This means that many people no longer bother to keep digital copies of their work on their personal laptop or desktop computer. Eventually, all manner of portable *physical* data storage (floppy disks, flash drives, external hard drives, etc.) may become obsolete.

Computer software for encoding and decoding files also changes at an ever-increasing pace. Not only do the commercial producers of data and word processing software continually update and improve their products, but open-source software, where anyone can contribute and modify the programs, is now widely available. Problems of incompatibility between different software programs, and between newer and older versions of the same program, continue to make the transfer of information difficult.

Originally, the idea was that you could store massive amounts of data in a very small space and get rid of all the paper cluttering up your office. What we have learned, however, is that tapes and floppies and hard disks can be destroyed by water, heat, humidity, and sunlight. Much of NASA's space flight data from the 1960s and 1970s has been lost because it was recorded on digital tapes that degraded over time; the information can no longer be recovered. In some instances, historic recordings were taped over because no one thought they were important enough to save. If the metal tab gets bent on a 3½″ disk, it can't be inserted into the drive, so all the data it contains are lost. If your CD is scratched or cracked, it no longer works. If the hard drive on your computer crashes, and you have no backups, all your information is gone forever. All your documents, your photos, and your data files can disappear in an instant.

You may find yourself working on a computer that doesn't have USB ports to attach your external hard drive, or has the ports but not the software to recognize the drive. Or you may find yourself in a place that doesn't have wireless (*WiFi*) capability. As I write this, I am working on a computer in Vienna, Austria, and can't figure out how to open a file onto my daughter's laptop from the external hard drive I brought with me. The files are written using Word 2003, and she has the German version of Word 2007. The icons are different—where is the file folder icon?—and of course all the instructions are in German!

Even as we have developed the technology to record more and more information in smaller and smaller spaces—like putting hundreds of books on a digital book reader—at the same time, we keep developing newer and incompatible ways of encoding and decoding the information.

If today we look at a wax cylinder recording of an interview from the early 1900s and wish we knew how to hear it again, imagine our grandchildren looking at a series of MP3 files on an old computer and no longer having iPods to recover that music. Imagine someone from the future finding a floppy disk, a flash drive, a Betamax videotape, or an 8-track tape. Everything that seems new and cutting-edge today will be obsolete in our lifetimes. If information is not transferred or migrated onto each new medium as it comes along, it will be lost to future generations, as it will be virtually impossible to recreate the software and hardware needed to read and decipher older formats. Maybe books aren't such a bad idea after all!

Oral History

Being able to read is a wonderful thing. I can't imagine life without books—I could never be a contestant on the reality TV show *Survivor* because I couldn't live without anything to read for 39 days. Or even one day. At the same time, there are many people in the world who function for their entire lives without being able to read. Indeed, their language may not be a writ-

ten language, as Bambara was not before the work of Bird, Hutchinson, and Kanté in the late 1970s, and then formalized orthography a decade later. There are both advantages and disadvantages to writing, and its companion, reading.

As long as stories are passed down from generation to generation and from friend to friend, the stories are, in some sense, alive. They can be changed to suit the time available, they can be modified to better suit the audience (men, women, mixed groups, children, adults, etc.), new details and alternative endings can be added as the cultural context changes. No two tellings will be exactly the same.

Once a story has been written down, especially if it is formally published and distributed widely, then

Signs in public places are meant to provide information, warn people of danger, or influence people's behavior by encouraging them to uphold cultural rules: no talking on your cell phone while driving, no littering (sign from Mahabalipuram, India), and no graffiti. Someone with a sense of humor has defaced the anti-graffiti sign with graffiti.

this one version becomes *the version*. Later modifications, additions, deletions, and recasting of the story become much more difficult. The story is the same no matter who is reading it, and if they are reading it aloud, no matter who the audience is. It is more difficult to argue or debate the fine points of the tale if one person has the authority to write the official version. The stories become frozen in time. The Grimm brothers collected Germanic folktales during the early 1800s. The many different oral versions tended to be violent and dark. Once published, one particular version prevailed. Over time, translators and editors altered them in places to make them nicer, but they remained pretty much the same until modern cartoon- and filmmakers started adapting them for the screen.

When Disney modified some of these folktales for children's entertainment in the twentieth century, they often drastically modified the story line to make it (supposedly) more appropriate for young children—not just minor details, either, but major plot lines, characters, motivations, and final outcomes. One example is Disney's *Little Mermaid*. In the original 1837 story by Danish writer Hans Christian Andersen, the mermaid indeed trades her tongue/voice to the evil sea witch in exchange for human legs. However, she doesn't marry the handsome prince; he chooses another woman. Heartbroken, the mermaid dies and turns to foam on the waves.

Because Disney versions of stories are so popular and widespread, they take on a life of their own and often supersede the original written version of the story. Many of the folktales put down in writing or transformed into films are shaped by people with a particular perspective to put forward, a particular ax to grind. Even as women made great strides toward achieving equality with men in North America in the twentieth century and beyond, Disney (and other film companies) continue to portray female characters whose identity relies on their association with a man, who values them primarily for their beauty (Cinderella, Snow White, Sleeping Beauty, the Little Mermaid). Some scholars find explicit sexism, homophobia, and racism in Disney films such as *Lion King*: when the good male lions are gone (Mufasa is killed and Simba runs away), the lionesses are helpless to act against the evil Scar (a stereotypically mincing, cowardly homosexual, but a male, nonetheless) and his accomplices, three greedy and stupid hyenas. Additionally, the two hyenas in the film who can speak are voiced by recognizably nonwhite actors (Whoopi Goldberg and Cheech Marin), while other hyenas in the film are depicted as Nazi soldiers. All this, in a children's film! What cultural messages are being taught?

Historical records and accounts are typically written by the victors and tend to focus on the important people and events of the times. Nora Groce, trying to reconstruct the everyday lives of deaf and hearing people on Martha's Vineyard, found that memories extracted through oral history interviews were often more useful than written documents. She notes a number of problems with written records, including that they tend to document the lives of the literate and the wealthier classes—information about the lives of ordinary people is more difficult to obtain. Even demographic information such as births, marriages, and deaths can be incomplete, especially from rural areas. In small communities, everyone knows all the details of each other's lives, and no one sees any reason to write things down. Records involving women often contain only their first name, or sometimes just refer to them as Mrs., followed by their husband's name. Some records are lost over the years through mismanagement, fires, or floods; other records are deliberately lost or destroyed. Some communities include a limited number of first and last names, so it isn't always clear which individual is being referred to. People don't always follow the conventions of using senior, junior, III, IV, and so forth. Sometimes, several children in succession may be given the same name until one survives beyond childhood. According to Groce, an important limitation of written records is that:

> Many things never enter written accounts—the mundane facets of every-day life, neighborhood events and characters, gossip, scandal, and misconduct. Quite often it is only through oral history that one can get full knowledge of an individual or incident, even if it is mentioned in a written record. And in a good number of cases in this study, the written records turned out to be wrong, and the oral information much more accurate. (Groce 1985:117)

When oral histories are used, most people recount their stories to other people who participated, or at least in the presence of others who participated, and the audience serves as a corrective influence. Information is continually exchanged—people add details they remember, and if the storyteller tries to alter the story to cast some person or event in a more favorable light, the audience will object. Oral histories become joint productions of many people's perspectives and memories, while written accounts may be colored by the particular agenda of the author. Wikipedia entries serve as a modern-day analogue of oral histories, because many people can contribute and correct biases or omissions. Not that everything on Wikipedia is accurate!

Another consequence of not having a written language (or not being literate in one's language), and therefore relying on oral histories and memories, is that the brain is expected to learn and remember much more information. Histories, stories, genealogies, scientific knowledge (botanical knowledge, medical knowledge, astronomy, geography, history, etc.) are all expected to be kept in one's head. Vast quantities of information can be stored in the human brain and recalled at will. In addition, in non-literate societies there may be various tricks to help a person remember information—mnemonic devices, the use of rhythms and rhymes in epic poetry, and so forth.

In some cultural contexts, one person or a few people will be charged with remembering all the knowledge about one subject—such as the genealogical history of the village. If you train your brain to memorize things, then they are always available at a moment's notice—you don't have to look them up in a book or on the Internet using Google. As my husband scrolls through his contact list on his phone looking for his mother's phone number, I simply call her, because I have her phone number memorized. Indeed, I have hundreds of phone numbers memorized. It really isn't that hard to do. But people who have come to rely on speed dial or contact lists or the Internet may not know any phone numbers at all—not even important ones. They are dependent on having some device or outside source of the information. If those sources are not available, then they are SOL (to use a TLA).

Multilingualism

In some contexts where people are not literate in any language, many individuals are bi- or multilin-

In societies without written language, ordinary folks memorize vast quantities of historical and genealogical information. Sometimes specialists are charged with this duty and spend years learning their craft. They may also memorize epic poems and create new stories and songs to commemorate important people and events. This *griot* from Burkina Faso in West Africa performs a praise song at a public event in 2009.

gual. The ability to speak more than one language allows a person to communicate with more people than if she speaks only one language. In many parts of the world, children learn two, three, or more languages as they are learning their mother tongue. They are able to communicate not only with those who speak the same native language but also with people who speak one of these other languages, either as their native tongue or as a second or third language.

Our field assistant in Mali, Moussa Diarra, learned to speak Bambara as his native language from his parents. He learned to speak, read, and write French fluently when he went to elementary and high school. He learned a little bit of spoken and written Arabic from the local Koranic school. He learned to speak English fluently when he lived in the United States for several years, mostly from watching cartoons on TV. In addition, because he grew up surrounded by friends, neighbors, and classmates who were from many different ethnic groups, each with their own language, he learned to speak a smattering of Fula, Senufo, Bobo, Bozo, Dogon, Songhrai, and a handful of other West African languages. He could understand Mandinka and Dyula, which are closely related to Bambara. Although Moussa was a particularly well-traveled Malian, with a talent for languages, he was not all that unusual. Most Malians speak Bambara, whether it is their native tongue or not, because it is used as a **lingua franca** (widespread trade language). Many speak at least some French, either from school attendance or just from dealing with government officials and tourists. Many speak at least some English, from movies and music. And many speak one, two, or more of the other languages common in Mali—learned from their parents (who may have been from two different ethnic groups, speaking two different languages to the children), neighbors, and friends.

Across Western Europe, many school children learn English in school, in addition to whatever their native tongue or tongues might be. English is considered by many people to be the main common language of science, and of the Internet. But English is not the language that is most widely spoken across the world. That position belongs to Mandarin Chinese. Mandarin is spoken as the primary language by an estimated 1,100,000,000 people and as a secondary language by an additional 20,000,000 people, for a total of 1,120,000,000 (one billion, one hundred and twenty million) people. English has fewer native speakers, only 330,000,000, but more secondary speakers, with 150,000,000, for a total of 480,000,000 (four hundred and eighty million) people. Spanish ranks third on both lists, in terms of the number of native speakers and secondary speakers. As China becomes more politically and economically powerful, many people in Latin America are learning to speak Mandarin Chinese, instead of English, as a second language, and some wealthy parents in New York City are hiring Chinese nannies to teach their toddlers Mandarin.

In North America, Canada is officially bilingual (English and French). The United States has never legislated English as the official language, but in most regions of the country, English is the only language in which government services are available. However, the state of Hawaii is officially bilingual in English and Hawaiian, while three U.S. territories are bilingual, including Puerto Rico (English and Spanish), American Samoa (English and Samoan), and Guam (English and Chamorro). Several U.S. states with large Spanish-speaking native and immigrant populations, such as Texas, are unofficially bilingual in English and

Spanish, with many government services provided in both languages as a matter of course.

We can't end this discussion without a brief mention of Esperanto, Klingon, Atlantean, and Na'vi. Esperanto is considered an international auxiliary language, meaning that no one speaks it as their native tongue. It was developed in the late nineteenth century by a Russian doctor, Ludovic Zamenhof, in an attempt to create a language that was easy to learn and could be used as a common language for people all over the world. Zamenhof's hope was that by sharing a common language, all people could learn to live together in peace. Today there are an estimated 100,000 to 2,000,000 speakers of Esperanto in more than 100 countries. One university, the International Academy of Sciences in the tiny European country of San Marino, provides its instruction in Esperanto.

Klingon is the language spoken by members of the fictional Klingon species from the *Star Trek* television show, films, and books, as well as an unknown number of earthlings. Klingon was invented by linguist Marc Okrand and is considered a full-fledged language. A number of resources exist for those wishing to learn Klingon, including books such as *The Klingon Dictionary* (Okrand 1985) and audio downloads such as *Star Trek: Conversational Klingon* (2000). Since 1992, the nonprofit Klingon Language Institute has worked to "facilitate the scholarly exploration of the Klingon language and culture" (Klingon 2010) through its website, quarterly journal, correspondence courses, audiocassettes, books, and conferences. In 2004, a documentary film about the Klingon Language Institute, *Earthlings: Ugly Bags of Mostly Water*, was made by Alexandre Philippe (Philippe 2004).

In 2001, Okrand developed the Atlantean language for the Disney film *Atlantis: The Lost Empire*. While Klingon was deliberately constructed to be alien, and to have many unusual features of pronunciation, grammar, and syntax, Atlantean was built on features that are common to many languages around the world, and most of its vocabulary is rooted in Proto-Indo-European.

The most recent language created from scratch is Na'vi, the language of the blue humanoid inhabitants of Pandora, from the 2009 film *Avatar*. It was developed by linguist Paul Frommer. Like Klingon before it, Na'vi has gained an enthusiastic following, aided by websites (Learn Na'vi 2010) as well as Frommer's writings (Frommer 2009).

Literacy

Of course there are advantages to written documents and being literate. A book can connect a reader in one time and place with an author from a distant time and place. If you can read, you have access to all the information and stories available in books, newspapers, journals, diaries, letters, and other written documents, and now the Internet as well. You don't have to have personal, face-to-face, synchronized-in-time contact with another person to get information from him. Being able to read opens many doors of opportunity in cultural contexts where reading and writing are absolutely critical for educational, financial, and social success.

Some organizations use measures of literacy—what percentage of the population can read, especially what percentage of the women can read—as a measure of the level of a country's development. Higher rates of literacy are viewed as reflecting more advanced, more sophisticated, more modern countries. Low rates of literacy are viewed as signs of backwardness, the oppression of women, and the lack of economic potential.

According to the 2009 United Nations Development Report, the top three countries in terms of literacy are Cuba, Estonia, and Latvia, with literacy rates of 99.8 percent. The United States ranks nineteenth on the list, with a literacy rate of 99 percent (United Nations Development Report 2009). But literacy rates are notoriously difficult to measure and have different meanings in different countries. Typical high school graduates in the United States read only at the sixth-grade level, yet they are counted as part of the 99 percent literacy rate. Is it more important to have all members of the population able to read at a basic, functional level, or to have a smaller percentage of the population literate, but at a more fluent level?

There are still many cultural contexts where literacy is not essential. What if we were to use bi- and

Like many other languages, English is written in Roman script, but there are also many languages that use different types of alphabets and scripts. From top: Tibetan script; the language of higher mathematics; Chinese calligraphy written on strips of bamboo; and Arabic script ("No success without God's will").

Written language and the ability to decode it (to read) are important assets in many cultural contexts, but even in literate societies, many people can't read at all, or can't read very well. In other cultural contexts, multilingualism can be just as useful as being able to read. Left: a Medieval illustrated manuscript. Right: the theological hall of the famous baroque Library of Strahov Monastery in Prague, Czech Republic.

multilingualism as our measure of progress and economic potential? By such a measure, the United States would rank very low. In addition to teaching children to read, we should be teaching them to be bilingual in early childhood, when language learning is easiest.

Transcending Space

Technological developments continue to have an impact on how humans communicate across time and space. The invention of writing and audio recording allows people to communicate across time. The development of mail delivery systems (runners, Pony Express, national mail delivery, bicycle couriers, FedEx, UPS, DHL, etc.) has made it much easier to send information and materials to people in all but the most remote regions of the planet. The invention of audio-visual broadcasting and receiving devices allows people to communicate across space and has revolutionized the transfer and exchange of knowledge. Such devices include telegraphs, telexes, radios, televisions, telephones (both landlines and cell phones), faxes, and the Internet.

Recent developments in communication technology have allowed people to communicate indirectly, while allowing time shifting—the participants in the conversation don't have to be available simultaneously. Table 11.2 shows how different modes of communica-

tion compare in terms of whether the participants must be in the same place and/or time and whether there is an audio or written record of the discussion.

One of the great advantages of e-mail over traditional snail mail is that transit time is reduced from days or weeks to minutes or seconds. Still, like letters, the recipient of an e-mail can read and react and ponder his response—unlike a phone call or a face-to-face conversation where your reaction is instantaneous and difficult to disguise. In face-to-face conversations, whether in person or on the phone, each response is expected to follow immediately, so it can't be planned out. You can't wait until you've had time to think something over, or cool down, or ask someone else for advice, before replying.

Although Skype allows you to have a videophone conversation with someone far away, where you can see the other person's face, it has the disadvantage of requiring synchrony in time. Just like face-to-face or phone conversations, the emotional reactions are there for the other person to see as well as hear.

We have gotten used to the convenience of not having to coordinate the timing of our conversations;

Opposite page: Communication technologies continue to evolve, from typewriters, landline telephones, and library card catalogues to cell phones and radio telescopes searching for extraterrestrial communications.

Table 11.2   Time shifting and space constraints in conversations

Mode of Communication	Same Place?	Same Time?	Audio Record	Written Record
Face to face	Yes	Yes	Not usually	Not usually
Telegraph	No	Yes	No	Yes
Telephone/landline	No, but both must be at a phone	Yes, but can leave audio messages	Not usually	Not usually
Cell phone	No, anywhere with a signal will work	Yes, but can leave audio messages	Not usually	Not usually
Fax	No	No	No	Yes
Radio (Shortwave, CB, etc.)	No	Yes	No	No
Letter	No	No	No	Yes
E-mail	No	No	No	Electronic record
Text Messaging	No	No	No	Electronic record
Instant Messaging	No	Yes	No	Yes, in some cases
Skype/video-conferencing	No	Yes	No	No

we don't have to play phone tag, or leave long complicated messages on someone's answering machine. We write her an e-mail or send her a text message and she reads it when she can and responds when she can. One downside is that in some contexts—especially business, government, and health care—people have come to expect that everyone will constantly be wired to the network, constantly checking their e-mail or text messages, and responding right away. For some employees, this means that work no longer ends at a specific time. People are expected to be always available and to respond to communications within minutes of receiving them, regardless of the time, day or night. If someone sends an e-mail or text message and gets no response in a few minutes, he may call the person on the phone to say "Did you get my message? Why aren't you answering?"

E-mail comes with other problems as well. One is *spam*—unsolicited junk e-mail that includes ads for Viagra, requests from Nigerian bankers to collaborate on deals, stupid jokes, political propaganda, and so on. It is easy to forward texts of marginal interest to everyone in your contact list. It is also easy for important messages to become lost in all the clutter. People also tend to be more casual with e-mail. Students send e-mails to professors that begin "Yo!" or "Hey!" and use textese instead of standard English. People often don't sign their names to e-mails, even though their e-mail address may be *dixiechick* or *scrabbleking*—something that gives no clue as to their identity. Although people have the opportunity to sit back and think through their response, with e-mail they often just go ahead and blast off a reply, especially if they are angry. Not always wise.

Cell phones have revolutionized communication in places where there have never been any telephone wires or telegraph lines in place, where even regular mail delivery is sporadic—across much of Africa, for example. Cell phones require functioning orbiting satellites, relay towers, and batteries, but they don't require physical wires that may be difficult to install and maintain and that can easily be cut or destroyed in a storm or during warfare, etc.

An interesting cultural consequence of e-mail, cell phones, and text messaging is their impact on face-to-face communication. The constant exchange of information between people throughout the day means that when they do get together in person, they have less to talk about. I don't need to "tell you about my day" because I've been telling you about it as it happened. This is one reason why you often see several teens or young adults sitting around, but not talking to one another. Instead, they are each talking on their cell phones to someone else, texting someone who is not present, or even texting each other, even though they are sitting side by side.

Likewise, in some cultural contexts, people talk on their cell phones while driving. More than 2,500 people die each year in the United States as a direct result of cell phone use while driving, with 100 times as many injuries. Many municipalities have outlawed cell phone use while driving. Texting while doing something else can be even more dangerous. Emergency room doctors report an alarming rise in the number of serious injuries caused by texting while walking, riding (a bicycle, a horse, or a Segway), and rollerblading. At least two pedestrians have been killed when they stepped in front of cars while texting, and texting while driving a car has been cited as a contributing factor in many traffic accidents, including some that led to fatalities.

FINAL THOUGHTS

The development and growth of the Internet has vastly expanded the human capacity to communicate with multitudes of others who are distant in space. One thing is clear—there will never be a dearth of topics for anthropologists to study when it comes to human communication. We continue to devise new ways of communicating and miscommunicating, providing information and misinformation, using language to teach, to persuade, to inspire, to threaten, to mislead, and to entertain. Humans without communication—whether in the tactile, visual, or auditory-vocal channels—are simply unimaginable.

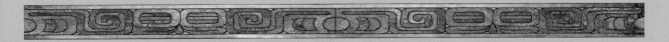

Key Concepts Review

Humans communicate through three distinct channels, the tactile (touch), the visual (body language, facial expressions, gestures, sign languages), and the auditory-vocal (spoken words and sentences and other aspects of speech).

How we speak, including our accents, speech styles, and vocabularies, serve as important boundary markers between groups; language can also be used to reinforce status differentials between individuals and between groups.

Scholars of human communication study:
  The formal, technical, structural aspects of language
  The social and cultural context of language
  The varieties of narratives
  The anatomical and cognitive foundations of language

Studies of human language reveal how culture shapes language, and vice versa.

All languages have concepts of nouns and verbs, adjectives and adverbs, and some have noun classes, which group together similar objects.

Some languages have only two color terms, black and white; when more color terms are added, they come in a specific order, with red as the third.

Some languages only have words for lower order numbers (one, two, many), but all people seem to be able to conceive of quantities and to be able to compare amounts.

Languages employ different strategies to indicate who is doing what to whom, with what—which word is the subject, which the object, which the verb, and which the indirect object.

Rigid word order is the strategy used for this purpose in English, but many languages use other strategies.

Cultural notions of time are encoded into language in different ways.

Core vocabulary refers to basic words that are conservative, and resistant to change, thus providing a basis for analyzing the relationship between related languages; words for *mother* and *father* seem to be the most conservative of all.

The study of the spontaneous development of sign languages among communities with a high proportion of deaf members has provided many insights into how language operates in the brain.

Sign languages of the deaf are fully functioning languages, distinct from the spoken languages of the region.

Sign languages use hand shape, location, movement, and orientation to articulate thoughts, and often use space to organize their grammars.

Communities where all the people—those who are deaf and those who are hearing—speak sign language, such as Martha's Vineyard in the eighteenth to twentieth centuries and the current town of Al-Sayyid, Israel, show us that *disabilities*, like *handicaps*, are culturally constructed.

The development of writing allows humans to transcend the constraints of time. Through encoding (writing) and decoding (reading), the thoughts of one person can be accessed by those who live many years, even centuries, later.

The permanency of written records depends on the survival of the medium by which they were encoded (carved in stone, engraved on wood, or written on paper) as well as the survival of the software within human brains to decode them (the ability to read the language they were written in).

continued

The ability to digitally store data and written texts has resulted in much loss of information, as tapes degrade over time, floppy disks and hard drives are damaged in various ways, and, especially, as rapidly changing technology makes earlier systems obsolete and the data they contain inaccessible.

Oral history and the use of the human brain to maintain important information have several advantages over written records of events.

Multilingualism is widespread outside of the United States; although English may be the most common language of science and the Internet, Mandarin Chinese remains the most widely spoken language in the world (followed by English, then Spanish).

Literacy, the ability to read, is often used as a measure of human development, but many people live in cultural contexts where literacy is not particularly relevant, and where it is more important to be bilingual or multilingual.

Advances in communication technology such as mail delivery systems, telephones, e-mail, the Internet, and text messaging using cell phones have dramatically changed the way people communicate, essentially allowing us to transcend space and freeing us from the constraint of being simultaneously available in order to have a conversation, but advances in communication technology come with disadvantages and risks as well.

12

LIVING IN THE WORLD

One of the great things about learning to think like an anthropologist is that you become more aware of how the world works. There are many right ways to live, many fulfilling ways to be a human being. Life is a feast. *Don't let your assumptions, your fears, or your enculturation during childhood limit you to only* a fraction of the feast.

This final chapter of the text directly addresses multicultural America and the advantages to everyone of being able to understand, appreciate, and partake in the vast panoply of human cultural expression. After an assignment that required a visit to an "ethnic" restaurant, one of my students wrote that he had hitherto been restricted to "a fraction of the feast" by his fear and ignorance of unfamiliar cuisines and appreciated my introducing him to more of the feast. I hope that by the time you reach this part of your introductory anthropology course you have developed more curiosity about the fascinating variety of human experience on this planet—that you are ready to go out and explore and enjoy more of the feast, whether in person through travel and exposure to people from a variety of backgrounds, or through films, books, and restaurants—and that you now understand that *all* cuisines are ethnic.

This chapter begins with a critique of the concept of **cultural competence** that has been making major inroads into U.S. medical, educational, and governmental bureaucratic organizations. The cultural competence movement is based on the idea that *culture* is a real thing (rather than a *heuristic* device for thinking about shared knowledge, beliefs, and practices), that it is uniform across all people of a certain ethnicity or from a certain country, and that in order to properly serve varied constituencies, you must have some knowledge of the beliefs and practices of these uniform "others." This issue deserves substantial consideration in any introductory cultural anthropology class, as many students will be taught this approach in other classes, ranging from nursing to business to early childhood education (and perhaps even in a few cultural anthropology courses). The notion of cultural competence is particularly insidious when "race" or geographic origin is used as the basis for laundry lists of beliefs and practices.

At the end of the chapter, my final message is my hope that you will use what you have learned from your introductory cultural anthropology course to examine and better understand your own beliefs, your own social organization, and your own behavior. I hope that you will have a better understanding of how the world works, and why. I hope that you will be more tolerant of differing viewpoints and that you have come to see cultural diversity as an asset—as what makes life interesting—not as a problem.

THE MYTHS AND DANGERS OF "CULTURAL COMPETENCE"

In 2005, Robert Pool and Wenzel Geissler warned of the dangers of adopting a simplistic approach to culture in their book *Medical Anthropology: Understanding Public Health:*

> During the last few decades medical researchers and public health specialists have shown an increasing interest in anthropology. The main reason for this interest has been the realization that there is more to

health and disease than physical and biological processes. It has become clear that in order to overcome barriers to the uptake of health interventions and develop culturally appropriate, sustainable interventions, it is first necessary to understand the social and cultural context of health and disease. Much of the enthusiasm for including anthropology in medical research has been based on the assumption that anthropology holds the key to target populations' "culture"—that is, their beliefs, attitudes, and practices (and in particular the supposedly wrong beliefs, misconceptions and risk behaviors that contribute to ill health)—and that anthropologists can advise on how to improve adherence in clinical trials or influence and change problematic beliefs, attitudes and behaviors through culturally appropriate interventions. There are two things wrong with this approach:

The approach is based on wrong assumptions about the nature of anthropology and what it has to offer to public health. It tends to define anthropology in methodological terms, as a set of procedures (qualitative methods, in-depth interviews, focus group discussions) for collecting hidden or sensitive data, for discovering "cultural barriers" to change, or for discovering "culturally appropriate" categories for use in survey design.

It is also based on wrong assumptions about the nature of society and social processes; namely, it assumes that they are determinate, that they are explainable in terms of relatively straightforward causal relationships, and that they can be manipulated and engineered in a preplanned manner with anticipated outcomes. (Pool and Geissler 2005:5–6)

Although Pool and Geissler, who are British anthropologists, didn't use the phrase *cultural competence*, they were talking about the same phenomenon. This notion of cultural competence has become more common and widespread in the United States in the past decade, particularly in the context of providing social services and health care to people from a variety of different backgrounds. At first glance, it seems like a good idea—that professionals who are providing services to people who come from a different "culture" should have knowledge of the "cultural beliefs and practices" of those they are serving. Additionally, if the clients (or patients or consumers or students) speak a different language, it helps either to have basic training in the language or to have access to good interpreters. Cynthia Mojab (2004) provides one definition: "Among other things, the development of cul-

tural competence is a life-long process whereby people can learn the information and skills, develop the attitudes and beliefs, and create/modify the structure and processes of institutions so that the culturally-based needs of diverse groups of people can be met effectively and equitably." Georgetown University even has a National Center for Cultural Competence whose mission is to "increase the capacity of health care and mental health care programs to design, implement, and evaluate culturally and linguistically competent service delivery systems to address growing diversity, persistent disparities, and to promote health and mental health equity" (Georgetown University National Center for Cultural Competence 2010). Sounds reasonable. Sounds anthropological.

In many instances, the concept of *cultural competence* has developed into a rapidly growing specialty, by which some consultants are highly paid to provide seminars—lasting from a few hours to a few days—that purport to educate service providers in all they need to know to be certified as culturally competent in a different culture. You can even take online courses for a fee and earn continuing medical education (CME) credits in cultural competency. But is this useful? Or is the notion of cultural competency too often more like "Anthropology Lite"—a superficial laundry list of beliefs and practices supposedly characteristic of all people who are from one country or belong to one ethnic group? Is the cultural competence industry a pseudo-anthropological scam, and are cultural competency training seminars counterproductive disasters in the making?

One problem with the Cultural Competence movement is that in many cases, U.S. Western culture is still presented as the "norm"—as though *we* don't have culture, but *they* do. One wants to reply as Tonto did in response to the question from the Lone Ranger when they were surrounded by hostile Native Americans. The Lone Ranger turned to Tonto and asked, "What are we going to do?" To which Tonto replied, "What do you mean *we*, White Man?" In reality, everyone has multiple overlapping spheres of culture that influence how they view the world, how they view themselves and others, and what they see as their role in helping other people, often with the best of intentions.

As Pool and Geissler pointed out in 2005, another problem with many cultural competence programs is their assumption that as a member of the dominant

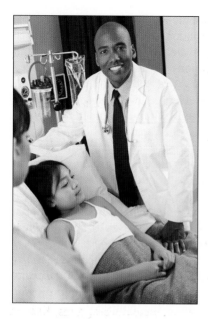
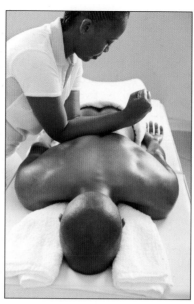

The concept of "cultural competence" has exploded in recent decades, especially in U.S. government agencies and health care settings. Problems with this "Anthro Lite" approach to cultural differences include the assumptions that (1) culture is equivalent to "race," ethnicity, or national origin, and (2) all people of the same "race," ethnicity, or national origin share most aspects of their culture in common. In the image on the left, a typical cultural competence approach would assume that the patient and the health care professional (HCP) come from different *cultures*, that the HCP's way of doing things is better/correct, and that the HCP can learn about the quaint beliefs of their patients either through attending a one-day in-service training seminar or by consulting a handbook, e.g., "If the patient is from Guatemala, see p. 24; if the patient is from Vietnam, see p. 56." In the image on the right, since both patient and chiropractor are African American, a typical cultural competence approach would assume that no such training is necessary—that all African Americans automatically understand all other African Americans.

culture, you need to know about other, so-called "traditional" *beliefs* in order to change them to your own, more correct, more rational, *knowledge*. People are being taught that they can go to a three-hour or three-day training and come away with a ready-reference guide to "Peoples and Cultures of the World." For example, if you are a nurse working on a maternity ward in New York City with Uighur patients (Turkic Muslims from Western China), just turn to page 37 in your Cultural Competency guide, and read the list of "Uighur beliefs about childbirth," since all Uighur are fungible (interchangeable).

Two real-world examples are offered here. In the early 2000s, an employment ad for a social worker in the Philadelphia area read something like this (I'm recreating it from memory):

WANTED: Social Worker to work with immigrant refugees from the civil war in the Sudan. Client population includes men, women, and children who have been through severe physical and emotional trauma, and who have little knowledge of U.S. culture. Job involves coordinating services with various city agencies to provide housing, health care, enrolling children in school, job placement for adults, emergency help

with food and other expenses, and teaching people how to navigate institutional bureaucracies. Requires a Master's Degree in Social Work and five years of experience. Prior work with political refugees preferred. Must speak Dinka.

I remember at the time thinking, "Good luck with that!"—finding someone with the proper education and work experience who just happens to speak Dinka, the language of a small group of agropastoralists who traditionally lived near the Nuer in the southern Sudan. As a graduate student in anthropology, I had read *Divinity and Experience: The Religion of the Dinka* by Godfrey Lienhardt (1961), and more books and articles about the Dinka had been published in the years since, but I didn't expect that (m)any U.S. social workers would be fluent in the Dinka language or have any useful knowledge of traditional Dinka culture or the long and convoluted history of the civil war in the Sudan.

Years later, I read and began assigning to classes one of the best ethnographies of cultural *incompetence* ever written, *The Spirit Catches You and You Fall Down*, by Anne Fadiman (1997). *Spirit* is the story of a Hmong family, the Lees, who were originally from

Laos. In the 1980s, they were political refugees, immigrants to California's Central Valley with a very sick little girl, Lia. The incredible misunderstandings and miscommunications among Lia's parents, health care providers (HCPs) at Merced Community Medical Center, and local child protective services workers would be amusing if they hadn't had such tragic consequences for Lia and her family. Fadiman captures the cultural chasms in her description of Hmong men bringing food to their wives in the hospital after childbirth (since the hospital was either unaware of, or not willing to provide, appropriate food):

> Each day, [her husband] cooked and brought her the diet that is strictly prescribed for Hmong women during the thirty days following childbirth: steamed rice, and chicken boiled in water with five special postpartum herbs. . . . This diet was familiar to the doctors on the Labor and Delivery floor at MCMC, whose assessments of it were fairly accurate gauges of their general opinion of the Hmong. One doctor said of the food: "The Hmong men carried these nice little silver cans to the hospital that always had some kind of chicken soup in them and always smelled great." Another [doctor] said: "They always brought some horrible stinking concoction that smelled like the chicken had been dead for a week." (Fadiman 1997:9)

At first glance, both of these examples might seem like good arguments for training courses in cultural competency. In the first example, a more useful ad might have asked for someone with a good basic background in cultural anthropology, who was sympathetic, caring, understanding, and not prejudiced against Africans (or people with dark skin in general) or people from a different cultural heritage. "Wanted: Someone willing to help strangers in a strange land adjust and cope with their recent (traumatic) past and uncertain future."

In the second example, courses in Hmong language, culture, and history would certainly have been useful. But the truth is that *you don't have to speak Hmong, or know anything about Hmong history and culture, to not be a jerk.* No amount of linguistic training or information about beliefs and practices of the Hmong in a brief seminar is likely to change the second doctor's disdain for the Hmong or cause him to question his automatic assumptions of cultural superiority.

Again, as Pool and Geissler (2005) first mentioned in the context of public health, the perspective being promoted in cultural competency training that focus on foreign immigrants includes:

- These people—these *others*—have some really quaint beliefs, some illogical thought processes, they are uneducated and unsophisticated, and we need to know about their bizarre ideas in order to counteract them.

- We need to know what rubbish they believe in order to better teach them "The Truth" according to our superior vantage point as members of a modern, scientific, rational culture (or as members of the dominant culture).

- We need to overcome culturally based barriers to compliance with Western values and directives.

- We don't need to change anything we believe, or anything that we do, in order to provide care to such people.

In many cultural competence programs, little or no time is devoted to a critical examination of the cultural beliefs and practices of the health care providers themselves. Little or no time is given to examining the types of cultural beliefs and practices that might differ between providers and patients, and what can be done to accommodate such differences. Little or no time is devoted to teaching people to treat others with respect and dignity, as human beings. Little or no time is devoted to developing alternatives to the structures and processes of institutions to better accommodate a variety of belief systems and traditions.

The same concerns apply to cultural competence training aimed at people who are from the United States and are not recent immigrants, but they come from a different ethnic background or their parents or grandparents emigrated from another country. Thus, white middle-class maternity and delivery nurses might be required to attend a training seminar on "African American culture" with a focus on pregnant women who are poor and unmarried, as though all African American women fall in those categories, and as though the common problems of poor people (lack of education, lack of reliable transportation, lack of child care for their older children) are somehow directly a result of having dark skin. At the same time, it is difficult to imagine African American nurses being expected to spend an in-service day learning about "European American" culture with a focus on pregnant women who are upper class and married. All nurses might be expected to obtain certification as culturally competent in "Hispanic culture" or "South Asian culture" or "Japanese culture" depending on the ethnic groups found in a community, but with exemptions if they themselves belong to one of these groups. Obviously, if you are of Japanese descent, you "automatically" know everything about Japanese and Japanese American culture, right?

Such approaches promote the mistaken idea that culture is equivalent to ethnicity or nationality. They promote the mistaken idea that all people who identify as members of one ethnic group, or whose ancestors came from the same country, are equivalent—that they are fungible; that they all believe the same things, to the same extent; and that there are no cultural differences based on any other differences between individuals and groups such as religion, educational level, socioeconomic status, family and individual differences, and so forth. What often results is an approach to culture that I refer to as the "Little Boxes" or "Laundry List" approach. Actual statements from handouts from recent cultural competency training courses include: "If she's Native American, she probably believes . . ."; "Families of Asian origin are likely to think . . ."; and "If your patient is African American, you can safely assume . . ."

This isn't how culture works. Culture is nebulous; it is messy. It is constantly changing, and it is negotiated and emergent depending on the situation. You can't put people in little boxes based on their nationality or ethnicity and then assume that they all believe and practice the same things. At the same time, however, many people who work in health care, teaching, and other service-providing contexts have expressed frustration about the diversity of people they encounter every day. They want a quick and simple-to-use guide to help them deal with those from different backgrounds. "Oh, she's from Guatemala, let me look that up in my handbook of cultural competency. Page 24 . . . OK, here's a list of things people from Guatemala believe, along with suggestions for how to disabuse them of such beliefs." Or, "This patient is of Indian ancestry, and the handbook says most Indians are Hindus. I should mark in his chart that his meals should be vegetarian."

The reality, as you have hopefully learned by now, is that culture consists of many overlapping circles of shared knowledge, beliefs, and practices and is not based solely on nationality or ethnicity. The reality is that each person carries a unique combination of cultural memberships—some things she shares with some other people who also belong to the same group or groups. Should one patient's chart read: "African American, well-educated, upper class, nonobservant Catholic, who is Republican and likes to play golf and listen to classical music" in contrast to another patient, whose chart reads: "Poor white teenager, hasn't finished high school, member of the Holy Ghost church, Libertarian, who likes gigging frogs and listens to country music from the 1950s and 1960s"? Not to mention that these individuals may be very different in a variety of ways from other individuals who belong to all of the same noted groups as these two patients—same ethnicity, same educational and socioeconomic status, same religion, same political leanings, same hobbies and musical tastes. On the other hand, such patients may share many other aspects of culture with the health care provider, even if they are of different ethnicities or national heritages. Perhaps they are both rabid fans of NASCAR racing or the Philadelphia Phillies baseball team. We share much in common with other people because we are all human.

Would it be helpful for providers to be bilingual or multilingual? Indeed, it would be, but that doesn't mean simply speaking the same "language." It may mean understanding the differences in speech between subsets of people who speak the same language—the local argot, the jargon, the idioms. A well-educated, upper-class social worker from Puerto Rico who grew up in New York may speak Spanish fluently, but that doesn't mean she is able to communicate effectively with Guatemalan peasant women in the United States who are workers, or the wives of workers, in the chicken factories in southern Delaware. She may be condescending and clueless about their concerns and find it difficult to believe that some of them don't speak Spanish ("Aren't they from Guatemala?"). She may not be aware that many Central and South Americans speak only their Native American language. Or another example: when my youngest, Alex, was first in preschool, the teacher was concerned that he never urinated at school. She said, "I regularly ask him if he needs to tee-tee, but he always says no." Well . . . that's because "tee-tee" is a local Texas phrase with which our family was not familiar. I suggested she ask him if he needed to *pee*. My daughter just moved from Austria to Wales, and her four-year-old Henry is learning Welsh at school. He will have to learn to "go for wees" or perhaps to "take a slash" (British phrases) or their Welsh equivalents.

Would it be useful for people to know something about the history and culture of other people? Yes, of course. But not at the expense of understanding that every person deserves to be treated with dignity and respect. It is more important to inculcate a culture of tolerance, a culture of understanding, and a culture of flexibility—one that acknowledges that Western medicine isn't necessarily better than traditional beliefs, that one's own religious beliefs aren't necessarily "True," making other people's religious beliefs merely primitive superstitions. Especially in medical contexts, it is important to understand the fact that only in recent years has Western Biomedicine made an attempt to provide treatment that is **evidence based.**

Even today, many practices that have been shown through extensive research to be harmful to mothers and newborns are still routinely carried out in U.S. hospital maternity wards. They continue to be followed because they are more convenient for the staff, or because of fear of liability and lawsuits if "standard practices" are not followed by every hospital, or simply because of tradition: "That's what we've always done here." An incomplete list would include: epidurals; denying the mother food and drink during labor; the use of electronic fetal monitors; keeping the mother on her back; separation of the mother and baby after birth; scheduled feedings; bottles of water, sugar-water, or formula; the use of pacifiers; vigorous scrubbing baths for the baby; failure to use compression boots after C-sections; failure to provide adequate and knowledgeable help with breastfeeding; and many, many more.

Another useful attribute on the part of health care providers would be a sense of humility—that perhaps "we" (however defined) don't know everything and perhaps "they" (however defined) are correct in their beliefs. In Fadiman's book, she describes traditional Hmong beliefs about the purpose and function of a newborn's placenta. She explains that a traditional Hmong belief is that the child's placenta ("jacket") should be buried in the parents' house. The placenta is needed by the child's soul after it dies, in order for it to find its way safely to the afterlife. "If the soul cannot find its jacket, it is condemned to an eternity of wandering, naked and alone" (Fadiman 1997:5).

[Foua's] fourteenth child, Lia, was born in the Merced Community Medical Center . . . Lia's placenta was incinerated. Some Hmong women have asked the doctors at MCMC if they could take their babies' placentas home. Several of the doctors have acquiesced, packing the placentas in plastic bags or take-out containers from the hospital cafeteria; most have refused, in some cases because they have assumed that the women planned to eat the placentas, and have found that idea disgusting. . . . Foua never thought to ask, since she speaks no English, and when she delivered Lia, no one present spoke Hmong. (Fadiman 1997:6)

A well-designed cultural competency program, based on cultural anthropological insights, would have taught all the health care providers at MCMC about Hmong beliefs and provided a way to ask all parents, not just Hmong, if they wanted to take home their child's placenta. If they did, some mechanism would be developed for packaging and identifying the placenta, and storing it properly until the mother was discharged. It shouldn't matter to the HCPs what the parents plan to do with the placenta—whether they plan to bury it under the house for the child's soul to retrieve after death, eat it for dinner, or plant it in the yard with a new tree to commemorate the child's birth. It's really none of their business. A good cultural competency program would have asked the participants to consider the implications *if the Hmong are correct* about the necessity of the placenta. What if those of us who are without access to our placentas are indeed destined to wander naked and alone for all eternity? This is absolutely just as plausible as believing that it doesn't matter, that placentas should be viewed as medical waste and incinerated.

A person can't learn enough useful information about a specific *culture*—in a few hours, or a few days, or even a few weeks—to enable him to provide appropriate care. It isn't about specific cultures and their beliefs and practices. It's about understanding that other people's beliefs and practices are valid and valuable—whether they match your own or not; that other people are worthy of being treated with respect and dignity and should not be discriminated against because they are different from you, no matter in what way; that you must treat people equitably as part and parcel of being a professional in your field, even if you don't like them or harbor deep-seated objections to dealing with them; *and that if you can't set aside your prejudices against certain groups of people or certain individuals, if you can't overcome your ethnocentrism, then perhaps you should be working in a different field—one that doesn't involve interacting with people.*

Can the concept of cultural competency be salvaged? Perhaps. It would be very useful if all people working in the service professions were required to take several classes in general cultural anthropology and perhaps specific classes in the history and culture of people from different parts of the world, if they will be working mostly with one group of immigrants. But only with all the caveats listed above. For example, a useful course in cultural competency would ask students to learn to recognize and understand their own cultural beliefs, to not make assumptions, to treat every individual with respect and dignity, and above all, do no harm.

Additionally, information could be provided about the many axes along which cultural beliefs may be organized and may vary, including:

- Notions of disease and treatment may vary. For example, the "hot/cold" theory is very common around the world.

- Notions of privacy may vary. Issues may include being comfortable with who is present, the sex of the health care provider vis-à-vis the sex of the patient, how much of the body is reasonably exposed, and so forth.

- Power relationships in the family—clan leaders, lineage elders, mother-in-laws, parents, spouses, siblings, and children—may vary. Don't assume that each person acts as an independent agent, regardless of whether they are Dinka or Greek or Chinese or European American.

- Notions of time may vary from one person or one group to another. Does 10:00 AM mean exactly that, or does it mean mid-morning, or whenever the person is available or ready? Can the person read and tell time in the language that instructions are given? If not, what can be arranged to deal with this?

- Any characteristic of the person not relevant to the situation is none of the provider's business—whether she has tattoos, piercings, is a Democrat, or a Wiccan, has 19 children already and is having another, is rich or poor, insured, or homeless and uninsured, young or old, and so forth. I think of this as the "My tattoos are none of your business" lesson.

- People may have different priorities than the service providers. For example, a woman of any cultural background may have different beliefs about whether breastfeeding a baby for the first time is a task to be accomplished (so the nurse can check it off her list) versus a relationship to be developed over time, even if it takes several hours.

- People will have different attitudes toward "experts" and authority figures. Just because you say one course of action is the best doesn't mean that the person has to follow it. Although many U.S. health care providers, especially doctors, are taught to think very highly of themselves and their knowledge, and patients who don't do what they are told are described as "noncompliant," for some individuals—again regardless of their cultural heritage—the doctors, nurses, teachers, or other experts are viewed as being there merely to inform and advise, not to insist on a particular course of action. At the same time, many people are exceedingly deferential to the expert in their presence, considering it rude to disagree publicly, but promptly disregarding everything the expert said once the expert has gone.

- There may be disadvantages or risks for particular courses of action that are accepted as appropriate and commonplace in U.S. health care settings, such as the use of epidurals and electronic fetal monitors. That is, not everything *we* do is logical and based on scientific research.

At the institutional level, planners and administrators can examine their policies and procedures with the goal of making them more inclusive, and more flexible. Then, when people express a preference for something that is not congruent with established policies and procedures, they still can be accommodated. This might include such things as allowing traditional healers to come into the hospital to conduct healing ceremonies, even those that involve the sacrifice of animals or the burning of herbs. Or providing a variety of options to meet food preferences and accommodate food taboos. Or allowing women to choose who will be in the delivery room with them, without any pressure one way or another—husbands if they want, not if they don't want; medical students if the mother doesn't mind, not if she does mind. Or allowing women to choose the position they will assume during labor and delivery. Or allowing extended family members to participate in decision making. And on and on and on. Respect, flexibility, professionalism, and humility are the characteristics to be desired and cultivated through good cultural competency programs.

REMEMBER THESE THINGS

I end this text by reminding you of a number of things I first said at the beginning. As you study cultural anthropology, and learn more about your own culture and the cultures of other groups of people, you will realize that not everyone shares the same beliefs and knowledge or the same ways of doing things. You hopefully will learn not to assume *anything* about what's inside the mind of a person you have just met. You can expect to share some things with everyone—aspects of human nature that we all share by virtue of being cultural animals. You can expect to share some things with some other people—aspects of your biology, through sharing alleles of some genes, and aspects of your beliefs and practices, your culture. Finally, you can expect to be unique, different from all other people in the world—you have a unique combination of genetic information that you inherited from your parents, as well as a unique set of overlapping cultural groups to which you belong. You won't know

what common ground you share, or what differences you have, until you have interacted with another person over at least some period of time and under various circumstances.

Don't Judge a Person Based on His Appearance

You can't judge a person's religious beliefs, or anything else about him, *based on his appearance*. Study the photographs of the people below.

There is nothing at all about the appearance of any of these people to tell you what religion they identify themselves as. The woman from the Balkans is a Muslim, but you can't tell that from her appearance. You can tell she is "Caucasian" in the typical racial classification system used by most Westerners, but you don't know what significance that fact has to her life. Likewise, the Israeli soldier has ancestors from Ethiopia, whose Jewish traditions go back as far as anyone's—they are not recent converts. Based solely on his appearance, he could just as easily be an African American of any religious persuasion. The African American woman isn't Baptist, nor is she a member of the African Methodist Episcopal Church. She is a Zen Buddhist, a well-known and highly respected Buddhist priest who leads the New Dharma Community in Berkeley, California. The last photograph is of Sammy Davis, Jr., who, like individuals from all eth-

You can't judge a person's religious beliefs (or anything else about him/her) by appearance. Left to right: a Muslim woman from the Balkans; a Jewish Israeli soldier of Ethiopian ancestry; an American Buddhist, the Rev. Angel Kyodo Williams, a Zen Buddhist priest; and the late African American singer and entertainer, Sammy Davis, Jr., who was a convert to Judaism.

nic groups and all walks of life, converted to Judaism as an adult. Other converts to Judaism include Connie Chung, a journalist of Chinese ancestry, and the late (and much missed) singer-songwriter Jim Croce, who was of Italian-Catholic heritage. People from many different ethnic backgrounds and religious upbringings have converted to various forms of Judaism, as well as Christianity, Islam, Scientology, Unitarian Universalism, and many other religions.

Don't Judge a Person Based on Her Nationality or Religion

Likewise, you should never assume to know a person's religious beliefs, or anything else about her, based on *where she is from*. Study the photographs below. A person from India—or whose recent ancestors are from India—might be Hindu, or she might be Christian (of many different types) or Muslim or Jewish, or a Scientologist or a Rastafarian (or even a Pastafarian!) or an atheist. A person from Vietnam—or whose recent ancestors are from Vietnam—might be

You should never assume to know a person's religious beliefs based on where he/she is from. Top left: a Christian church in India, founded by St. Thomas the Apostle in AD 52. Top right: the Bahá'í House of Worship, known as the Mother Temple of Africa, in Kampala, Uganda. Bottom left: a Vietnamese Buddhist Temple in Garden Grove, California. Bottom right: the Church of Jesus Christ of Latter-day Saints (Mormons) meetinghouse in Sukhbaatar city, North Mongolia.

Buddhist, but he could also belong to any other religion, or none at all. A person from Utah might be a member of the Church of Jesus Christ of Latter-day Saints (Mormon), but so could a person from Mongolia or Korea or Brazil or South Africa, and there are members of many other religions living in Utah.

Many U.S. citizens are Muslims, including people who were born and raised here as Muslims, people who were born in the U.S. but converted to Islam after being raised in a different religious tradition, and recent immigrants from Muslim countries. The photographs on the right show two famous Muslim Americans, Keith Ellison, a member of the U.S. House of Representatives from Minnesota, and comedian Dave Chappelle.

Likewise, there are Muslims of all nationalities and ethnic identities—there are European ("Caucasian") Muslims, African Muslims, Chinese Muslims, and South American Muslims. Currently, the fastest growing group of converts to Islam in the United States is Hispanic females. For more information on this phenomenon, see the articles on this website: http://www.hispanicmuslims.com/articles/.

As with all religious traditions, there are a number of different types or sects of Islam, including the two largest, Shia and Sunni, as well as Sufi (mystical Islam), Ahmadiyya Islam, and the Wahhabites. As with all religious traditions, some people who identify themselves as Muslim are very devout, while others don't necessarily follow all or any of the teachings of Islam. Most Muslims are not terrorists, and most terrorists acting in the United Sates are not Muslims—*I feel stupid even having to write these words, but some people in the U.S. are confused about this issue.* The vast majority of people who are Muslim, 99.9 percent, are perfectly reasonable, ordinary folks who go about their daily lives not hurting anyone, or even thinking of hurting anyone. Timothy McVeigh, who blew up the Murrah Federal Building in Oklahoma City in 1995, killing 168 people, was raised as a Roman Catholic, as was Adolf Hitler. A number of Roman Catholic priests around the world have been convicted of molesting children, and other Catholics of covering up the crimes. Yet, most Americans don't vilify Roman Catholics in general, as is only fair, since 99.9 percent of Roman Catholics are perfectly reasonable, ordinary folks who go about their daily lives not hurting anyone, or even thinking of hurting anyone.

There are many people around the world, including the United States, who are Muslim. American Muslims include Keith Maurice Ellison (a member of the U.S. House of Representatives, from Minnesota's 5th district) and comedian Dave Chappelle.

Most people in the world are good, hard-working, considerate people trying to lead meaningful lives and provide for themselves and their children. A few people are evil and expend their energy killing and harming others, denying others their rights as humans, and committing heinous atrocities (sometimes under the guise of patriotism or religious fervor). The bad people come from many different nations and belong to many different ethnic groups, religious persuasions, political perspectives, and so on. There is plenty of blame to go around if you want to point the finger at any group. Before detailing the wholesale torture and slaughter of Muslims by Christians in the Balkan Wars between 1821 and 1913, Louis de Bernières points out:

> All war is fratricide, and there is therefore an infinite chain of blame that winds its circuitous route back and forth across the path and under the feet of every people and every nation, so that the people who are the victims of one time become the victimizers a generation later, and newly liberated nations resort immediately to the means of their former oppressors. The triple contagions of nationalism, utopianism and religious absolutism effervesce together into an acid that corrodes the moral metal of a race, and it shamelessly and even proudly performs deeds that it would deem vile if they were done by any other. (de Bernières 2004:257)

It isn't always easy to know whom (if anyone) to fear, and our perceptions are shaped in part by the people who own and control the news media, who are primarily interested in selling advertising time and space. The U.S. Federal Bureau of Investigation publishes reports on terrorism in the United States, which get little coverage in the press. The 2002–2005 report states:

> In keeping with a long-standing trend, *domestic extremists carried out the majority of terrorist incidents during this period. Twenty three of the 24 recorded terrorist incidents were perpetrated by domestic terrorists.* With the exception of a white supremacist's firebombing of a synagogue in Oklahoma City, Oklahoma, all of the domestic terrorist incidents were committed by special interest extremists active in the *animal rights* and *environmental movements.* The acts committed by these extremists typically targeted materials and facilities rather than persons. The sole international terrorist incident in the United States recorded for this period involved an attack at the El Al ticket counter at Los Angeles International Airport, which claimed the lives of two victims.
>
> The *terrorism preventions* for 2002 through 2005 present a more diverse threat picture. *Eight of the 14 recorded terrorism preventions stemmed from right-wing extremism, and included disruptions to plotting by individuals involved with the militia, white supremacist, constitutionalist and tax protestor, and anti-abortion movements.* The remaining preventions included disruptions to plotting by an anarchist in Bellingham, Washington, who sought to bomb a U.S. Coast Guard station; *a plot to attack an Islamic center* in Pinellas Park, Florida; and a plot by [a] prison-originated, Muslim convert group to attack U.S. military, Jewish, and Israeli targets in the greater Los Angeles area. In addition, three preventions involved individuals who sought to provide material support to foreign terrorist organizations, including al-Qa'ida, for attacks within the United States. (Federal Bureau of Investigation 2005, *emphasis added*)

The fact remains that bad people come in all shapes and colors and sizes and ethnicities (including "white" or European, or European American), religious affiliations (including Christian), and cultural heritages (both similar to one's own and others who are very different). Nevertheless, most people of all shapes, colors, sizes, ethnicities, religious affiliations, and cultural heritages are basically good people, trying to live meaningful lives and provide for their families, and not bothering anyone else.

Don't Assume that All People from One Part of the World Look Alike

People from one part of the world, even from one country, may differ drastically in appearance. There are many different genes and gene variants (alleles) that affect skin, hair, and eye color, and facial features such as the shape of the overall face, the eyes, nose, and mouth. People who look similar may be from different regions of the world, while people from one region of the world may vary in appearance. Only someone who had studied human facial variation in some detail, and for this part of the world, or perhaps well-traveled individuals from this part of the world, would be able to recognize where these individuals were most likely from, based on appearance alone. And since humans migrate all over the world, any of these individuals could just as easily be from Los Angeles or Cleveland or Hong Kong or Auckland.

People Share Many Things in Common, No Matter How Different They May Be

People from around the world share many features in common, as best documented in Donald Brown's book *Human Universals* (1991). They all have language, they all have religion, they all have a sense of humor, and they all enjoy eating in the company of others. The images on the facing page show examples of people enjoying commensality—eating together—in vastly differing cultural contexts. Even as we marvel at the differences between individuals and groups, we need to remember all the many things we share in common as human beings.

A list of things to keep in mind as you go out into the world and meet new people and experience different cultures might include:

- The world can't be divided into *us* and *them*.

- People who share skin color (and body shape and facial features, and so on), may belong to many different cultures.

- People who live in one country or nation-state may belong to many different cultures.

- People who share many aspects of culture may end up living in different regions of the world.

People from around the world enjoy food in the company of friends. Left: women eating from a buffet near Ban Dung, Udon Thani province, Thailand. Right: U.S. Army Soldiers eat their Thanksgiving meal on Combat Outpost Cherkatah, Khowst province, Afghanistan, November 26, 2009.

- People who look very different from you may share many aspects of culture with you, especially if they grew up in the same region.
- People who look and act just like you in many ways may, in fact, have very different beliefs and practices concerning some issues.

The World Is Interconnected— What Happens in One Place Has Repercussions Far Away

Globalization is the term used for the widespread dissemination of information, beliefs, and attitudes around the world, or at least everywhere that commercial interests exist. The process of globalization creates a whole new layer of culture that people share all across the globe. Some of this process is driven by scientific research and the accumulating knowledge base of humankind, especially via the Internet. Some is driven by international news, available through a variety of channels (newspapers, news magazines, radio, television, the Internet). Some of this process is driven by the ease with which people can move from one region of the world to another in a matter of hours, thus taking their home cultures and spreading them wherever they go. In the United States, because so many people migrate here for educational, economic, political, or religious freedom reasons, we

have access to a wide array of different perspectives from around the world.

But by far the biggest force in globalization is the economic force of capitalism and the power of multinational companies to import and export raw materials and natural resources as well as the infrastructure to process these resources and then export the finished products. In order to sell their products, they advertise through a variety of media in even the remotest places. Look at the labels in your clothes, and you'll probably find that they were made in one country from cotton or wool from another country, and then imported to wherever you bought them. Look at the foods in your supermarket, and you will find produce from thousands of miles away, as well as all manner of canned and bottled foods from distant regions of the planet.

The photos on the next page show two examples of companies that have extended their reach, through advertising and product availability, to almost every place on Earth. The McDonald's restaurant, with its iconic golden arches, is in Hong Kong. The giant Coca-Cola bottle is in Barat, in central Albania.

For much of the twentieth century, Albania was ruled by a Communist government and dictator, and very limited travel was allowed either into or out of the country. The story of Coca-Cola in Albania is quite illuminating. The following quote comes from a 2007 speech by Muhtar Kent, current Chairman of the Board and Chief Executive Officer, The Coca-Cola Company:

> In 1989, at the age of 36, I was promoted to president of Coca-Cola's East Central European Division to spearhead the entry of Coca-Cola into the former Soviet Union and Eastern Europe after the fall of the Berlin Wall. This was a group of 23 countries where for between 45 and 70 years some 350 million people had lived literally behind a wall. Concepts like basic human rights, freedom of speech, democracy, free enterprise and land ownership were all novelties. There was no Coca-Cola infrastructure to speak of. No bottling plants. No distribution systems. Our challenge was to set up more than 20 bottling plants and a modern distribution system in literally months, across 23 nations.
>
> At one point during this time, I was in Albania in southeastern Europe. Albania at that time was one of the most politically and economically isolated nations in the world. Its economy was in shambles and its people were in great need.
>
> We saw potential there though and we were determined to open a bottling facility. We needed to find the right people to help us. Someone pointed me to a dentist, saying "you should meet this man."
>
> I found the dentist in his office. His practice had no heating and he used wood fruit boxes for his patients to sit on. I developed a relationship with him and would send him copies of Western newspapers and periodicals.
>
> One year later during the first free elections, this dentist—Salih Berisha—became the first elected president of Albania. Coca-Cola became the first foreign investment, and in 1993 we opened the first modern Coca-Cola plant. . . . Today, Coca-Cola directly and

Globalization—and especially capitalism—has spread some aspects of knowledge, beliefs, and practices around the world. Left: a McDonald's in Hong Kong. Right: a giant Coca-Cola bottle obscures the view of Ottoman houses in Barat in central Albania. The houses were designated by UNESCO as a World Heritage Site.

indirectly employs over 2,000 people in this thriving country where we are the undisputed market leader. (Kent 2007)

Did the Coca-Cola Company influence the election? Is that what Kent is implying? Was Coca-Cola the answer to Albania's political and economic troubles? It isn't at all clear. What is clear is that many multinational corporations are making huge profits selling killer commodities to all the peoples of the world (Singer and Baer 2009). Infant formula companies (Nestlé, Abbot Labs, Mead Johnson, and others) and tobacco companies (Philip Morris, the British American Tobacco Company [BAT], RJ Reynolds, and others) are powerful agents of culture change that result in increases in disease and death across the world (Hammond 1998, World Health Organization 1998, World Health Organization 2008). While soft drinks don't have the same serious health consequences as infant formula or tobacco, the availability of Coca-Cola in Albania hardly adds to the Albanians' health or standard of living in any meaningful way.

Globalization ties people and environments together, often in ways that are not immediately apparent. When you buy a cheap hamburger at a fast-food restaurant, the meat may come from cows grazed on tropical pastures that were once rain forest, home to hunters and gatherers. When you consume fruit from Chile during the winter in the northern hemisphere, you contribute to the demand for oil to transport that fruit, and you contribute to poor health for the workers who eventually dismantle retired cargo ships under unsafe conditions. What impact does it have on the world's people and environments when products are made in one place, packaged using nonrenewable resources, and then shipped via cargo ships thousands of miles away to consumers, who then discard the packaging into landfills? Does this way of life make any sense? The makers of the 2005 documentary film *Shipbreakers* summarize the reality this way:

Welcome to Alang, India, the site of a gargantuan scrap yard where ocean-going ships come to die. Forty thousand Indians live and work here, dismembering and scavenging the hulks of 400 vessels every year. This documentary chronicles the daily lives of the people who work here, the barefoot men who take apart giant mountains of steel by hand, piece by piece, as they spend months toiling sun-up to sun-down destroying ship after ship. It is the world's most unreg-

ulated industry. Ship owners rarely bother to abide by the UN Base Convention, which bans shipments of transboundary waste. One worker a day, on average, dies on the job, from gas explosions, falls or from tons of falling steel. Still one in four will contract cancers caused by asbestos, PCBs or other toxic substances. (Kot and Barreveld 2005)

Can one even argue that the products we import and consume are somehow better tasting, of higher quality, or better for us? When you buy drinking water that comes from Fiji (a small island in the South Pacific), you are contributing to a number of global problems, as well as getting an inferior product (Jeffries 2008). In 2007, CNN ranked Fiji Water's ad campaign number 20 in their list of "101 Dumbest Moments in Business" (Horowitz, Jacobson, McNichol, and Thomas 2007). The authors comment:

Crisp. Refreshing. And only ever-so-slightly poisonous. . . . Los Angeles-based Fiji Water runs magazine ads for its bottled water with the headline "The Label Says Fiji Because It's Not Bottled in Cleveland." Cleveland officials retaliate by running tests revealing that Fiji bottled water contains 6.3 micrograms of arsenic per liter, while the city's tap water has none. Fiji counters by saying its own tests found less than 2 micrograms per liter.

Why not drink water out of your tap, assuming it's as safe as Cleveland's water? At least consider the global impact of the choices you make, both short- and long-term, both on yourself and other people, and on the environment. If we are to continue as a species, we must take care of each other, and our planet.

FINAL THOUGHTS

So, how should you approach new people that you meet? Most importantly, *don't make assumptions*. Give people the benefit of the doubt. Learn to appreciate all the many fascinating ways there are of being human. Learn to listen and observe, and try to understand where people are coming from and what their goals are. Try to understand why they do what they do, even if it is very different from what you would do in similar circumstances. Think about the beliefs that underlie your behaviors. Think about the consequences of your actions. Treat everyone with respect, as you would like to be treated. And always . . . enjoy the feast.

References

Abrams, Ira R. and John Bishop. 1994. *Faces of Culture: Patterns of Subsistence.* Ethnographic film. Produced by Ira R. Abrams and John Bishop of the Coast Community College District in cooperation with Harcourt, Brace College Publishers. Distributed by Insight Media.

Acredolo, Linda, Susan Goodwyn, and Doug Abrams. 2009. *Baby Signs: How to Talk to Your Baby Before Your Baby Can Talk,* 3rd. ed. New York: McGraw-Hill.

Adelstein, Jake. 2009. *Tokyo Vice: An American Reporter on the Police Beat in Japan.* New York: Pantheon.

Aggie Band. 2010. Texas A&M Fightin' Texas Aggie Band. http://www.aggieband.org/visitors-about.php (accessed February 25).

Allen, Woody. 1973. *Sleeper.* Commercial release film, written, directed, and starring Woody Allen.

American Academy of Pediatrics. 2005. "Policy statement on breastfeeding and the use of human milk." *Pediatrics* 115(2):496–506. http://pediatrics.aappublications.org/cgi/content/full/115/2/496 (accessed February 6, 2010).

American Academy of Family Physicians. 2010. "Breastfeeding (policy statement)." http://www.aafp.org/online/en/home/policy/policies/b/breastfeedingpolicy.html (accessed February 6).

American Folklife Center. 2009. Collections and Research Services. http://www.loc.gov/folklife/archive.html (accessed February 13, 2010).

American Music Therapy Association. 1998–2010. Music Therapy Makes a Difference. http://www.musictherapy.org (accessed February 13, 2010).

Anonymous, personal communication. The source of this information was a graduate student I knew in the mid-1970s. He had served in the U.S. Navy onboard a diesel submarine in the late 1960s and early 1970s and had participated in these hazing rituals.

Anthony, Carl Sferrazza. 1990. *First Ladies: The Saga of the Presidents' Wives and Their Power 1780–1961.* New York: William Morrow.

Aratow, Paul, Richard Cowan, and Susannah M. Hoffman. 1973. *Kypseli: Men and Women Apart: A Divided Reality.* Ethnographic film. An Aratow-Cowan-Hoffman production in association with the University of San Francisco.

Aronson, Josh. 2001. *Sound and Fury.* Documentary film. Aronson Film Associates and Public Policy Productions in association with Thirteen/WNET and Channel 4. Josh Aronson, Director, Roger Weisberg, Producer, and Jackie Roth, Coordinating Producer.

Aronson, Josh. 2006. *Sound and Fury: Six Years Later.* Documentary film. Aronson Film Associates and Public Policy Productions in association with Thirteen/WNET and Channel 4. Josh Aronson, Director, Roger Weisberg, Producer, and Jackie Roth, Coordinating Producer.

Auel, Jean M. 1984. *Clan of the Cave Bear.* New York: Bantam Books.

Australian Government. 2010. Parks and Reserves: Uluru-Kata Tjuta National Park. http://www.environment.gov.au/parks/uluru/ (accessed February 11).

Ayub, Awista. 2009. *However Tall the Mountains: A Dream, Eight Girls, and a Journey Home.* New York: Hyperion Books.

Azoy, G. Whitney. 2002. *Buzkashi: Game and Power in Afghanistan,* 2nd ed. Long Grove, IL: Waveland Press.

Backyard Chickens. 2010. http://www.backyardchickens.com (accessed January 28).

Bahrampour, Tara. 1999. *To See and See Again: A Life in Tehran and America.* Berkeley: University of California Press.

Bahrampour, Tara. 2000. "Years pass. The game endures." *New York Times,* July 16. http://www.nytimes.com/2000/07/16/nyregion/years-pass-the-game-endures.html (accessed February 13, 2010).

Bailey, Ronald. 1997. "Kids as status symbols." http://www.slate.com/id/2451/ (accessed February 9, 2010).

Barber, Elizabeth Wayland. 1994. *Women's Work, the First 20,000 Years: Women, Cloth, and Society in Early Times.* New York: W. W. Norton.

Barber, Elizabeth Wayland. 1999. *The Mummies of Ürümchi.* New York: W. W. Norton.

Bartick, Melissa and Arnold Reinhold. 2010. "The burden of suboptimal breastfeeding in the United States: A pediatric cost analysis." *Pediatrics* 125:1048–1056. http://pediatrics.aappublications.org/cgi/content/abstract/125/5/e1048 (accessed April 28).

Bauman, H-Dirksen L. (ed.). 2008. *Open Your Eyes: Deaf Studies Talking.* Minneapolis: University of Minnesota Press.

Baumeister, Roy F. 2005. *The Cultural Animal: Human Nature, Meaning, and Social Life.* Oxford: Oxford University Press.

BBC News. 2003. "*Sesame Street* breaks Iraqi POWs." http://news.bbc.co.uk/2/hi/middle_east/3042907.stm (accessed February 13, 2010).

BBC News. 2004. "'Virgin Mary' toast fetches $28,000." http://news.bbc.co.uk/2/hi/americas/4034787.stm (accessed February 11, 2010).

BBC News. 2007. "Van Gogh work 'by another artist.'" http://news.bbc.co.uk/2/hi/entertainment/6929086.stm (accessed February 11, 2010).

Beckwith, Carol and Angela Fisher. 1993. *Nomads of Niger.* New York: Abradale Press, Harry N. Abrams.

Bennett, John W. 2007. *Northern Plainsmen: Adaptive Strategy and Agrarian Life.* New Brunswick, NJ: AldineTransaction. Reprint of 1969 Aldine Publishers edition.

Benson, Royal H., III. 2010. http://www.clitoralunhooding.com/dr-benson.html; see also http://www.labiaplastysurgeon.com/dr-benson.html (accessed February 5).

Berlin, Brent and Paul Kay. 1999. *Basic Color Terms: Their Universality and Evolution.* Stanford, CA: Center for the Study of Language and Information Publications.

Bickerton, Derek. 2009. *Adam's Tongue: How Humans Made Language, How Language Made Humans.* New York: Hill and Wang.

Biesele, Megan. 1997. "An ideal of unassisted birth: Hunting, healing, and transformation among the Kalahari Ju/'hoansi." In Robbie E. David-Floyd and Carolyn F. Sargent (eds.), *Childbirth and Authoritative Knowledge: Cross-Cultural Perspectives,* pp. 474–492. Berkeley: University of California Press.

Bird, Charles, John Hutchison, and Mamadou Kanté. 1977. *An Ka Bamanankan Kalan: Beginning Bambara.* Bloomington: Indiana University Linguistics Club.

Bissinger, H. G. 2000. *Friday Night Lights: A Town, a Team, and a Dream.* New York: Da Capo Press.

Blanchard, Kendall. 1995. *The Anthropology of Sport: An Introduction,* revised edition. Westport, CT: Bergin & Garvey.

Blank, Les. 1980. *Garlic Is as Good as Ten Mothers.* Documentary film. Produced by Les Blank. El Cerrito, CA: Flower Films.

Borghi, Penny. 2006. "Surprise field office receives visitors from Australia's western desert." *News.bytes Extra,* Issue 241. US Department of the Interior, Bureau of Land Management, California. http://www.blm.gov/ca/news/newsbytes/xtra-06/241-xtra_martu.html (accessed January 28, 2010).

Boyd, Brian. 2009. *On the Origin of Stories: Evolution, Cognition, and Fiction.* Cambridge, MA: Belknap Press.

Boyd, Carolyn E. 2003. *Rock Art of the Rio Grande Valley.* College Station: Texas A&M University Press.

Brenneman, Robert L. 2007. *As Strong as the Mountains: A Kurdish Journey.* Long Grove, IL: Waveland Press.

Brokaw, Tom 2004. *The Greatest Generation.* New York: Random House.

Brown, Courtney. 2007. *Politics in Music: Music and Political Transformation from Beethoven to Hip-Hop.* Decatur, GA: Farsight Press.

Brown, Donald E. 1991. *Human Universals.* New York: McGraw-Hill.

Brown, Steven. 1999. "The 'Musilanguage' model of music evolution," in N. L. Wallin, B. Merker, and S. Brown (eds.), *The Origins of Music,* pp. 271–301. Cambridge, MA: MIT Press.

Brown, William M., Lee Cronk, Keith Grochow, Amy Jacobson, C. Karen Liu, Zoran Popovic, and Robert Trivers. 2005. "Dance reveals symmetry, especially in young men." *Nature* 438(22/29):1148–1150.

Buckley, Thomas and Alma Gottlieb (eds.). 1988. *Blood Magic: The Anthropology of Menstruation.* Berkeley: University of California Press.

Burning Man. 1989–2010. http://www.burningman.com/whatisburningman/ (accessed February 25, 2010).

Caillois, Roger. 1969. "The structure and classification of games." In John Loy and Gerald Kenyon (eds.), *Sport, Culture, and Society,* pp. 44–55. New York: Macmillan.

Coalition for Improving Maternity Services. 1996. Making Mother-Friendly Care a Reality. http://www.motherfriendly.org/mfci.php (accessed February 6, 2010).

Cohen, Susan and Christine Cosgrove. 2009. *Normal at Any Cost: Tall Girls, Short Boys, and the Medical Industry's Quest to Manipulate Height.* New York: Tarcher/Penguin.

Colapinto, John. 2001. *As Nature Made Him: The Boy Who Was Raised as a Girl.* New York: Harper Perennial.

Conard, Nicholas J., Maria Malina, and Susanne C. Münzel. 2009. "New flutes document the earliest musical tradition in southwestern Germany." *Nature* 460(6):737–740. DOI: 10.1038/nature08169.

Conniff, Richard. 2002. *The Natural History of the Rich: A Field Guide.* New York: W. W. Norton.

Cooper, Merian C. and Ernest B. Schoedsack (directors). 1925. *Grass: A Nation's Battle for Life.* Documentary film. Paramount Pictures.

Counts, Dorothy Ayers and David R. Counts. 2001. *Over the Next Hill: An Ethnography of RVing Seniors in North America.* Toronto: Broadview Press.

Crampton, Hazel. 2006. *The Sunburnt Queen: A True Story.* London: SAQI.

Cross, I., E. Zubrow, and F. Cowan. 2002. "Musical behavior and the archaeological record: A preliminary study." In J. Mathieu (ed.), *Experimental Archaeology.* British Archaeological Reports International Series 1035:25–34.

Cultural Survival. 2010. http://www.culturalsurvival.org/ (accessed January 28).

Cummings, Jim. 2006. *Research Reports for the Ears: Soundscape Art in Scientific Presentations.* As presented at Sound, Environment, and Connective Technologies Conference, University of California, Riverside, May 12, 2006. http://www.acousticecology.org/presentation/intro.html [includes sound clips] (accessed February 13, 2010).

Cusick, Suzanne G. 2006. "Music as torture/music as weapon." *Transcultural Music Review,* #10. http://www.sibetrans.com/trans/trans10/cusick_eng.htm (accessed February 13, 2010).

Daily Mail. 2008, October. "Chocolate sex spread taken off shelves over chemical fears." http://www.dailymail.co.uk/news/article-1078699/Chocolate-sex-spread-taken-shelves-chemical-fears.html (accessed February 1, 2010).

Dartmouth Jewish Sound Archive. 2010. http://www.dartmouth.edu/~djsa/ (accessed February 13).

Darwin, Charles. 1871. *The Descent of Man and Selection in Relation to Sex.* London: John Murray.

Davidson, Jean. 1996. *Voices from Mutira: Changes in the Lives of Rural Gikuyu Women, 1910–1995,* 2nd ed. Boulder, CO: Lynne Rienner.

Davie, Michael. 2001. *Honor among Men: The Killing of Women in Pakistan.* Documentary film, produced for National Geographic.

Davis-Floyd, Robbie E. 1992. *Birth as an American Rite of Passage.* Berkeley: University of California Press.

Davis-Floyd, Robbie E. and Carolyn F. Sargent (eds.). 1997. *Childbirth and Authoritative Knowledge: Cross-Cultural Perspectives.* Berkeley: University of California Press.

Davis-Floyd, Robbie E., Lesley Barclay, Betty-Anne Daviss, and Jan Tritten (eds.). 2009. *Birth Models that Work.* Berkeley: University of California Press.

de Bernières, Louis. 2004. *Birds Without Wings.* New York: Alfred A. Knopf.

Delaney, Carol. 2000. "Making babies in a Turkish village." In Judy S. DeLoache and Alma Gottlieb (eds.), *A World of Babies: Imagined Childcare Guides for Seven Societies,* pp. 117–144. Cambridge, UK: Cambridge University Press.

DeLoache, Judy S. and Alma Gottlieb. 2000. *A World of Babies: Imagined Childcare Guides for Seven Societies.* Cambridge, UK: Cambridge University Press.

Department of Labor. October 2009. Your Rights After a Mastectomy: The Women's Health and Cancer Rights Act of 1998. http://www.dol.gov/ebsa/publications/whcra.html (accessed February 27, 2010).

Dettwyler, Katherine A. 1995a. "A time to wean: The hominid blueprint for the natural age of weaning in modern human populations." In Patricia Stuart-Macadam and Katherine A. Dettwyler (eds.), *Breastfeeding: Biocultural Perspectives,* pp. 39–73. New York: Aldine de Gruyter.

Dettwyler, Katherine A. 1995b. "Beauty and the breast: The cultural context of breastfeeding in the United States." In Patricia Stuart-Macadam and Katherine A. Dettwyler (eds.), *Breastfeeding: Biocultural Perspectives,* pp. 167–208. New York: Aldine de Gruyter.

Dettwyler, Katherine A. 2004a. "When to wean: Biological versus cultural perspectives." *Clinical Obstetrics and Gynecology* 47(3): 712–723.

Dettwyler, Katherine A. 2004b. "Culture and breastfeeding." In Katherine A. Dettwyler and Vaughn M. Bryant (eds.), *Reflections on Anthropology: A Four-Field Reader,* pp. 21–27. New York: McGraw-Hill.

Diamond, Jared. 2005. *Guns, Germs, and Steel: The Fates of Human Societies.* New York: W. W. Norton

Dickens, Charles. 1864–1865[2002]. *Our Mutual Friend.* New York: Modern Library Classics.

Diener, Marissa. 2000. "Gift from the Gods: A Balinese guide to early child rearing." In Judy S. DeLoache and Alma Gottlieb (eds.), *A World of Babies: Imagined Childcare Guides for Seven Societies,* pp. 91–116. Cambridge, UK: Cambridge University Press.

Dissanayake, Ellen. 1992. Homo aestheticus: *Where Art Comes From and Why.* New York: The Free Press.

Dixson, Alan F. 1999. *Primate Sexuality: Comparative Studies of the Prosimians, Monkeys, Apes, and Human Beings.* Oxford: Oxford University Press.

Documentary Media Arts. 2010. VoxLox. Steven Feld. http://www.voxlox.net (accessed February 13).

Douglas, Mary. 1966. *Purity and Danger: An Analysis of Concepts of Pollution and Taboo.* London: Routledge & Kegan Paul.

Douglas, Mary. 2003. *Natural Symbols: Explorations in Cosmology,* 3rd. ed. London: Routledge.

Dueling Scar. *BMEzine Encyclopedia.* 2010. http://wiki.bmezine.com/index.php/Dueling_Scar (accessed February 17).

Dunbar, Robin. 1997. *Grooming, Gossip, and the Evolution of Language.* Cambridge, MA: Harvard University Press.

Dutton, Denis. 2009. *The Art Instinct: Beauty, Pleasure, & Human Evolution.* New York: Bloomsbury Press.

Ekman, Paul. 2007. *Emotions Revealed: Recognizing Faces and Feelings to Improve Communication and Emotional Life,* 2nd ed. New York: Henry Holt.

Ekman, Paul and Wallace V. Friesen. 2003. *Unmasking the Face: A Guide to Recognizing Emotions from Facial Expressions.* Los Altos, CA: Malor Books.

Elder, Sarah and Leonard Kamerling. 1988. *The Drums of Winter (Uksuum Cauyai).* Ethnographic film. Directed by Sarah Elder and Leonard Kamerling. Watertown, MA: Documentary Educational Resources.

Ellis, Markman. 2004. *The Coffee-House: A Cultural History.* London: Weidenfeld & Nicholson.

Ellison, Peter. 2001. *On Fertile Ground: A Natural History of Human Reproduction.* Cambridge, MA: Harvard University Press.

Ethical Culture Movement. 2010. American Ethical Union. http://www.aeu.org (accessed February 11).

Evans-Pritchard, E. E. 1940. *The Nuer: A Description of the Modes of Livelihood and Political Institutions of a Nilotic People.* Oxford: Clarendon Press.

Evans-Pritchard, E. E. 1951. *Kinship and Marriage among the Nuer.* Oxford: Oxford University Press.

Evans-Pritchard, E. E. 1956. *Nuer Religion.* Oxford: Oxford University Press.

Evans-Pritchard, E. E. 1976. *Witchcraft, Oracles, and Magic among the Azande.* Oxford: Clarendon Press.

Eyre, Banning. 2000. *In Griot Time: An American Guitarist in Mali.* Philadelphia: Temple University Press.

Fadiman, Anne. 1997. *The Spirit Catches You and You Fall Down: A Hmong Child, Her American Doctors, and the Collision of Two Cultures.* New York: Farrar, Strauss & Giroux.

Farmer, Paul. 2004. *Pathologies of Power: Health, Human Rights, and the New War on the Poor.* Berkeley: University of California Press.

Farrer, Claire R. 2011. *Thunder Rides a Black Horse: Mescalero Apaches and the Mythic Present*, 3rd ed. Long Grove, IL: Waveland Press.

Fatsis, Stefan. 2002. *Word Freak: Heartbreak, Triumph, Genius, and Obsession in the World of Competitive Scrabble Players.* New York: Penguin.

Fausto-Sterling, Anne. 2002. "The five sexes, revisited." *The Sciences* 40(4):19–23.

Federal Bureau of Investigation. 2005. *Terrorism 2002–2005.* Washington, DC: US Department of Justice, Federal Bureau of Investigation, Counterterrorism Division. http://www.fbi.gov/publications/terror/terrorism2002_2005.htm (accessed September 15, 2010).

Feld, Steven. 1990. *Sound and Sentiment: Birds, Weeping, Poetics, and Song in Kaluli Expression.* Philadelphia: University of Pennsylvania Press.

FFPS. 2010. Fun-Fair-Positive Soccer. http://www.ffps.org (accessed February 13).

Firth, Raymond. 1967. *Tikopia Ritual and Belief.* Boston: Beacon Press.

Fish, Lydia. 1993. "Songs of Americans in the Vietnam War." http://faculty.buffalostate.edu/fishlm/folksongs/americansongs.htm (accessed February 13, 2010).

Ford, Clellan S. and Frank A. Beach. 1951. *Patterns of Sexual Behavior.* New York: Harper.

Fowler, Brenda. 2001. *Iceman: Uncovering the Life and Times of a Prehistoric Man Found in an Alpine Glacier.* Chicago: University of Chicago Press.

Fox, Margalit. 2007. *Talking Hands: What Sign Language Reveals About the Mind.* New York: Simon & Schuster.

Freegans. 2010. "Strategies for sustainable living beyond capitalism." www.freegan.info/?page_id=2 (accessed January 28).

Freston, Tom. 2007. "Desert blues: Showtime in the Sahara." *Vanity Fair*, July. www.vanityfair.com/culture/features/2007/07/malifestival200707; the festival's website is http://www.festival-au-desert.org/ (accessed February 25, 2010)

Frommer, Paul. 2009, December 19. "Some highlights of Na'vi." *Language Log*, Institute for Research in Cognitive Science at the University of Pennsylvania. http://languagelog.ldc.upenn.edu/nll/?p=1977 (accessed February 28, 2010).

Fry, Douglas P. 2000. *The Human Potential for Peace: An Anthropological Challenge to Assumptions about War and Violence.* Oxford: Oxford University Press.

Fry, Douglas P. 2007. *Beyond War: The Human Potential for Peace.* Oxford: Oxford University Press.

Gaskin, Ina May. 2002. *Spiritual Midwifery*, 4th ed. Summertown, TN: Book Publishing Co.

Geertz, Clifford. 1972. "Deep play: Notes on the Balinese cockfight." *Daedalus* 101:1–37.

Gell, Alfred. 1996. *The Anthropology of Time: Cultural Constructions of Temporal Maps and Images.* Oxford: Berg.

Georgetown University National Center for Cultural Competence. 2010. http://www11.georgetown.edu/research/gucchd/nccc (accessed September 11).

Gilmore, David D. 1991. *Manhood in the Making: Cultural Concepts of Masculinity.* New Haven: Yale University Press.

Glass, Matthew. 2005. "Devils Tower, *Mato Tipi*, or Bear's Lodge (Wyoming)." In Bron Taylor (ed.), *Encyclopedia of Religion and Nature*, pp. 477–479. London and New York: Continuum.

Glass-Coffin, Bonnie. 1998. *The Gift of Life: Female Spirituality and Healing in Northern Peru.* Albuquerque: University of New Mexico Press.

Gmelch, George. 1992. "Superstition and ritual in American baseball." *Elysian Fields Quarterly* 11(3):25–36.

Goodall, Jane. 2000. *Through a Window: My Thirty Years with the Chimpanzees of Gombe.* New York: Mariner Books.

Goodman, Roger. 2000. *Children of the Japanese State: The Changing Role of Child Protection Institutions in Contemporary Japan.* Oxford: Oxford University Press.

GORDIE. 2010. The Gordie Foundation. http://www.gordie.org (accessed February 11).

Gordon, Peter. 2004. "Numerical cognition without words: Evidence from Amazonia." *Science* 306(5695):496–499. DOI 10.1126/science.1094492.

Grandin, Temple. 1996. *Thinking in Pictures and Other Reports from My Life with Autism.* New York: Vintage.

Granstrom, Chris. 1998. "They live and breathe letterboxing." *Smithsonian* 29(1):82–91.

Gribble, Karleen. 2008. "Long-term breastfeeding: Changing attitudes and overcoming challenges." *Breastfeeding Rev.* 16(1):5–15.

Grinker, Roy Richard. 2007. *Unstrange Minds: Remapping the World of Autism.* New York: Basic Books.

Groce, Nora Ellen. 1985. *Everyone Here Spoke Sign Language: Hereditary Deafness on Martha's Vineyard.* Cambridge, MA: Harvard University Press.

Haley, Alex. 1976. *Roots.* New York: Doubleday & Company.

Hammond, Ross. 1998. "Big tobacco's global expansion." In *Addicted To Profit: Big Tobacco's Expanding Global Reach.* Washington, DC: Essential Action. http://www.takingontobacco.org/addicted/main.html (accessed September 15, 2010).

Hardin, Garrett. 1968. "The tragedy of the commons." *Science* 162(3859):1243–1248. Also available at http://www.garretthardinsociety.org/articles/art_tragedy_of_the_commons.html

Heider, Karl G. 1976. "Dani sexuality: A low energy system." *Man* 11(2):188–201.

Heider, Karl G. 2002. "Postscript: Revisiting *Dani sexuality.*" In Suzanne LaFont (ed.), *Constructing Sexualities: Readings in Sexuality, Gender, and Culture,* pp. 94–95. Upper Saddle River, NJ: Prentice-Hall.

Heller, Sharon. 1997. *The Vital Touch: How Intimate Contact with Your Baby Leads to Happier, Healthier Development.* New York: Henry Holt.

Herdt, Gilbert. 2005. *The Sambia: Ritual, Sexuality, and Change in Papua New Guinea,* 2nd ed. Belmont, CA: Wadsworth.

Hewlett, Barry S. 1992. *Father-Child Relations: Cultural and Biosocial Contexts.* Edison, NJ: Aldine Transaction.

Hewlett, Barry S. 1993. *Intimate Fathers: The Nature and Context of Aka Pygmy Paternal Infant Care.* Ann Arbor: University of Michigan Press.

Hirsch, Jennifer S. and Holly Wardlow (eds.). 2006. *Modern Loves: The Anthropology of Romantic Courtship and Companionate Marriage.* Ann Arbor: University of Michigan Press.

Hobbes, Thomas. 1651[2009]. *Leviathan.* Oxford: Oxford University Press.

Hoebel, E. A. 1967. *The Law of Primitive Man: A Study in Comparative Legal Dynamics.* Cambridge, MA: Harvard University Press.

Holtzman, Jon D. 2008. *Nuer Journeys, Nuer Lives: Sudanese Refugees in Minnesota,* 2nd ed. New York: Allyn & Bacon.

Home of the Makah People. 2010. www.makah.com (accessed January 28).

Homewood, Katherine, Patti Kristianson, and Pippa Chenevix Trench (eds.). 2009. *Staying Maasai?: Livelihoods, Conservation and Development in East African Rangelands.* New York: Springer.

Horowitz, Adam, David Jacobson, Tom McNichol, and Owen Thomas. 2007, July 1. "101 dumbest moments in business: The year's biggest boors, buffoons, and blunderers." *CNNMoney.com.* http://money.cnn.com/galleries/2007/biz2/0701/gallery.101dumbest_2007/20.html (accessed September 9, 2010).

Horrigan, Leo, Robert S. Lawrence, and Polly Walker. 2002. "How sustainable agriculture can address the environmental and human health harms of industrial agriculture." *Environmental Health Perspectives* 110(5):445–456. http://www.ncbi.nlm.nih.gov/pmc/articles/pmc1240832/pdf/ehp0110-000445.pdf (accessed February 1, 2010).

Huffman, Alan. 2005. *Mississippi in Africa: The Saga of the Slaves of the Prospect Hill Plantation and Their Legacy in Liberia Today.* New York: Gotham.

ICONS, A Portrait of England. 2010. www.icons.org.uk/theicons/collection/bowler-hat/biography/bowler-hat-finished (accessed January 27).

Indiana University. 2007. Archives of Traditional Music. http://www.indiana.edu/~libarchm/ (accessed February 13, 2010).

Internet Sacred Text Archive. 2010. Bahá'í Faith. http://www.sacred-texts.com/bhi/index.htm (accessed February 11).

ITMA. 2010. Irish Traditional Music Archive. http://www.itma.ie/ (accessed February 13).

Jack, Rachael E., Caroline Blais, Philippe G. Schyns, and Roberto Caldara. 2009. "Cultural confusions show facial expressions are not universal." *Current Biology* 19(18):1543–1548.

Jacoby, Annice (ed.). 2009. *Street Art San Francisco: Mission Muralismo.* New York: Abrams.

James, Brett, Hillary Lindsey, and Gordie Sampson. 2005. "Jesus take the wheel," recorded by Carrie Underwood on the album *Some Hearts.* www.cowboylyrics.com/lyrics/underwood-carrie/jesus-take-the-wheel-16549.html (accessed February 11, 2010).

Janszen, Karen. 1980. "Meat of life." *Science Digest* Nov/Dec:78–81.

Jeffries, Adrianne. 2008, September 25. "Is it green?: FIJI Bottled Water." http://www.inhabitat.com/2008/09/25/is-it-green-fiji-water/#more-14571 (accessed September 9, 2010).

Jerardo, Andy. 2008. "What share of U.S. consumed food is imported?" *Amber Waves: The Economics of Food, Farming, Natural Resources, and Rural America.* A publication of the United States Department of Agriculture, Economic Research Service, February. http://www.ers.usda.gov/AmberWaves/February08/DataFeature/ (accessed January 31, 2010).

Jolliffe, Lee (ed.). 2010. *Coffee Culture, Destinations and Tourism.* Buffalo, NY: Channel View.

Jordan, Brigitte and Robbie Davis-Floyd. 1993. *Birth in Four Cultures: A Crosscultural Investigation of Childbirth in Yu-*

catan, Holland, Sweden, and the United States. Long Grove, IL: Waveland Press.

Katz, Richard, Megan Biesele, and Verna St. Denis. 1997. *Healing Makes Our Hearts Happy: Spirituality and Cultural Transformation among the Kalahari Ju | 'hoansi.* Rochester, VT: Inner Traditions Press.

Katz, Solomon H. and Mary M. Voight. 1986. "Bread and beer: The early use of cereals in the human diet." *Expedition* 28(2):23–34.

Kay, Margarita (ed.). 1982. *Anthropology of Human Birth.* Philadelphia: F. A. Davis.

Kent, Muhtar. 2007, April 12. "Remarks at the Coca-Cola Scholars Banquet, 4/12/07, Atlanta, Georgia." http://www.thecoca-colacompany.com/presscenter/viewpoints_kent_scholars.html (accessed September 9, 2010).

Kettlewell, Caroline. 2002. "Thinking inside the box." *Washington Post*, July 12, WE28. http://www.washingtonpost.com/ac2/wp-dyn?pagename=article&node=&contentId=A55308-2002July11 (accessed February 13, 2010).

Khan, Tahira S. 2006. *Beyond Honour: A Historical Materialist Explanation of Honour Related Violence.* Oxford: Oxford University Press.

Kimbrell, Andrew (ed.). 2002. *The Fatal Harvest Reader: The Tragedy of Industrial Agriculture.* Washington, DC: Island Press.

Kingsolver, Barbara. 2007a. "The blessings of dirty work." *Washington Post*, September 30, B1. http://www.washingtonpost.com/wp-dyn/content/article/2007/09/28/AR2007092801324.html (accessed January 28, 2010).

Kingsolver, Barbara. 2007b. *Animal, Vegetable, Miracle: A Year of Food Life.* New York: Harper Perennial.

Kinsey, Alfred C., Wardell B. Pomeroy, and Clyde E. Martin. 1998a. *Sexual Behavior in the Human Male.* Bloomington: Indiana University Press. Originally published by W. B. Saunders in 1948.

Kinsey, Alfred C., Wardell B. Pomeroy, Clyde E. Martin, and Paul H. Gebhard. 1998b. *Sexual Behavior in the Human Female.* Bloomington: Indiana University Press. Originally published by W. B. Saunders in 1953.

Klingon Language Institute. 2010. Website maintained by Paramount Pictures. http://www.kli.org/ (accessed February 28).

Kot, Michael and Ed Barreveld. 2004. *Shipbreakers.* Documentary film produced by Storyline Entertainment Inc., The National Film Board of Canada, the Canadian Broadcasting Corporation, and National Geographic Channel International. New York: Cinema Guild

Kraybill, Donald B. 1989. *The Riddle of Amish Culture.* Baltimore: Johns Hopkins University Press.

Kurutz, Steven. 2007. "Not buying it." *New York Times*, June 21. http://www.nytimes.com/2007/06/21/garden/21freegan.html?_r=1 (accessed January 28, 2010).

Kuwahara, Makiko. 2005. *Tattoo: An Anthropology.* New York: Berg Publishers.

Lakoff, George. 1990. *Women, Fire, and Dangerous Things: What Categories Reveal About the Mind.* Chicago: University of Chicago Press.

Lao Language and Culture Learning Resources. 1997–2003. Center for Southeast Asian Studies, Northern Illinois University. http://www.seasite.niu.edu/lao/ (accessed February 13, 2010).

Lassiter, Luke, Clyde Ellis, and Ralph Kotay. 2002. *The Jesus Road: Kiowas, Christianity, and Indian Hymns.* Lincoln: University of Nebraska Press.

Lawson, Graeme and Chris Scarre (eds.). 2006. *Archaeoacoustics.* Cambridge, UK: McDonald Institute Monographs, McDonald Institute for Archaeological Research.

Laurgaard, Rachel K. 1981. *Patty Reed's Doll: The Story of the Donner Party.* Provo, UT: McCurdy Historical Doll Museum.

Learn Na'vi. 2010. http://www.learnnavi.org/ (accessed February 28).

Lever, Janet. 1995. *Soccer Madness: Brazil's Passion for the World's Most Popular Sport.* Long Grove, IL: Waveland Press.

Lévi-Strauss, Claude. 1968. *The Savage Mind.* Chicago: University of Chicago Press.

Lévi-Strauss, Claude. 1995. *Myth and Meaning: Cracking the Code of Culture.* New York: Schocken.

Levin, Theodore. 1999. *The Hundred Thousand Fools of God: Musical Travels in Central Asia (and Queens, New York).* Bloomington: Indiana University Press.

Lienhardt, Godfrey. 1961. *Divinity and Experience: The Religion of the Dinka.* Oxford: Oxford at the Clarendon Press.

Lindgren, Kristin A., Doreen DeLuca, and Donna Jo Napoli (eds.). 2008. *Signs and Voices: Deaf Culture, Identity, Language, and Arts.* Washington, DC: Gallaudet University Press.

Louis Braille Online Museum. 2009. http://www.afb.org/louisbraillemuseum (accessed October 25, 2010).

Lourdes-France. 2010. Lourdes, France. www.lourdes-france.org/index.php?contexts=en&id=405 (accessed February 11).

Malloch, Stephen and Colwyn Trevarthen. 2008. *Communicative Musicality: Exploring the Basis of Human Companionship.* Oxford: Oxford University Press.

Mampe, Birgit, Angela D. Friederici, Anne Christophe, and Kathleen Wermke. 2009. "Newborns' cry melody is shaped by their native language." *Current Biology* 19(23):1994–1997.

Manchester, William. 1983. *The Last Lion, Winston Spencer Churchill, Visions of Glory 1874–1932.* Boston: Little, Brown.

Mayell, Hillary. 2002. "Thousands of women killed for family 'honor.'" *National Geographic News*, February 12.

McAleer, Kevin. 1994. *Dueling: The Cult of Honor in Fin-de-Siecle Germany*. Princeton, NJ: Princeton University Press.

McGee, Rachel Locker and Jeffery Davis (eds.). 2010. *Interpreting in Multilingual, Multicultural Contexts*. Washington, DC: Gallaudet University Press.

McIntosh, Peggy. 1988[1990]. "White privilege: Unpacking the invisible knapsack." http://www.amptoons.com/blog/files/mcintosh.html (accessed February 10, 2010).

McKiernan, Kevin. 2006. *The Kurds: A People in Search of Their Homeland*. New York: St. Martin's Press.

McLeod, Christopher. 1983. *Four Corners: A National Sacrifice Area?* Documentary film. Produced by Christopher McLeod, Glenn Switkes, and Randy Hayes. Written and directed by Christopher McLeod.

McNeill, William H. 1976. *Plagues and Peoples*. New York: Anchor Press/Doubleday.

McNeill, William H. 1995. *Keeping Together in Time: Dance and Drill in Human History*. Cambridge, MA: Harvard University Press.

McWilliams, James E. 2007. "Food that travels well." *New York Times*, August 6. www.nytimes.com/2007/08/06/opinion/06mcwilliams.html (accessed February 1, 2010).

Mead, Margaret. 1935[2001]. *Sex and Temperament in Three Primitive Societies*. New York: Harper Perennial.

Mead, Margaret. 1949[2001]. *Male and Female*. New York: Harper Perennial.

Mennella, Julie A. 2009. "Flavour programming during breastfeeding." In Gail Goldberg, Andrew Prentice, Ann Prentice, Suzanne Filteau, and Kirsten Simondon (eds.), *Breastfeeding: Early Influences on Later Health*, pp. 113–120. Advances in Experimental Medicine and Biology, Vol. 639. Dordrecht, Netherlands: Springer.

Menninger, K. 1969. *Number Words and Number Symbols: A Cultural History of Numbers*. Cambridge, MA: MIT Press.

Millennium Park, Chicago. 2010. *Cloud Gate* on the AT&T Plaza. http://www.millenniumpark.org/artandarchitecture/cloud_gate.html (accessed February 13).

Miller, Barbara D. 2009. *Cultural Anthropology*, 5th ed. Upper Saddle River, NJ: Prentice-Hall.

Miller, Geoffrey F. 2000. "Evolution of human music through sexual selection." In N. L. Wallin, B. Merker, and S. Brown (eds.), *The Origins of Music*, pp. 329–360. Cambridge, MA: MIT Press.

Mithen, Steven. 1998. *Creativity in Human Evolution and Prehistory*. London: Routledge.

Mithen, Steven. 2006. *The Singing Neanderthals: The Origins of Music, Language, Mind, and Body*. Cambridge, MA: Harvard University Press.

Mojab, Cynthia Good. 2004. "Guilt, research on populations, and cultural competence." http://home.comcast.net/~ammawell/guilt_populations_culture.html (accessed September 13, 2010).

Montagu, Ashley. 1986. *Touching: The Human Significance of the Skin*, 3rd ed. New York: Harper.

Montgomery, Heather. 2008. *An Introduction to Childhood: Anthropological Perspectives on Children's Lives*. New York: Wiley-Blackwell.

Mudcloth. 2010. "Create your own virtual *bògòlanfini*." http://www.mnh.si.edu/africanvoices/mudcloth/html/index_text?showhtml#bogolanfini (accessed February 17).

Muecke, Marjorie A. 1984. "Make money not babies: Changing status markers of northern Thai women." *Asian Survey* 24(4):459–470. http://www.jstor.org/stable/2644338 (accessed February 10, 2010).

Murdock, George Peter. 1980. *Theories of Illness: A World Survey*. Pittsburgh: University of Pittsburgh Press.

Musafar, Fakir. 1985. Documentary film. *Dances Sacred and Profane*.

Musafar, Fakir. 2003. "Suspensions & tensions: Yesterday." *BME News,* November 15. http://news.bmezine.com/2003/11/15/suspensions-tensions-yesterday-fakir-rants-raves/ (accessed February 27, 2010).

Musafar, Fakir. 2010. http://www.fakir.org and www.bodyplay.com (accessed February 27).

Mylan, Megan and Jon Shenk. 2004. *Lost Boys of Sudan*. Documentary film. Produced and directed by Megan Mylan and Jon Shenk for Actual Films. http://www.lostboysfilm.com/ (accessed February 5, 2010).

Nanda, Serena. 2000. *Gender Diversity: Crosscultural Variations*. Long Grove, IL: Waveland Press.

National Diabetes Information Clearinghouse. 2009. Part of the National Institutes of Health. http://diabetes.niddk.nih.gov/DM/pubs/pima/index.htm (accessed February 6, 2010).

National Park Service. 2010. Devils Tower. http://www.nps.gov/deto (accessed February 11).

National Park Service. 2010. Vietnam Veterans Memorial. http://www.nps.gov/vive/index.htm (accessed February 11).

Neel, James V. 1962. "Diabetes mellitus: A 'thrifty' genotype rendered detrimental by 'progress'?" *American Journal of Human Genetics* 14:353–362. www.ncbi.nlm.nih.gov/pmc/articles/PMC2557712/ (accessed February 6, 2010).

Newberg, Andrew and Mark Robert Waldman. 2006. *Why We Believe What We Believe: Uncovering Our Biological Need for Meaning, Spirituality, and Truth*. New York: Free Press.

NORS: CDC National Outbreak Reporting System. 2010. http://www.cdc.gov/healthywater/statistics/wbdoss/nors (accessed February 1).

Nowinski, Christopher. 2007. *Head Games: Football's Concussion Crisis from the NFL to Youth Leagues*. East Bridgewater, MA: The Drummond Publishing Group.

Nuer, The. 1970. Ethnographic film. Produced by Robert Gardner and Hilary Harris for the Film Study Center of the Peabody Museum, Harvard.

Oatley, Keith, Dacher Keltner, and Jennifer M. Jenkins. 2006. *Understanding Emotions,* 2nd ed. Malden, MA: Wiley-Blackwell.

Okrand, Marc. 1985. *The Klingon Dictionary (Star Trek).* New York: Pocket Books.

Okrand, Marc. 2000. *Star Trek: Conversational Klingon.* New York: Simon & Schuster Audio.

Opie, Iona and Peter Opie. 1969. *Children's Games in Street and Playground: Chasing, Catching, Seeking, Hunting, Racing, Dueling, Exerting, Daring, Guessing, Acting, and Pretending.* Oxford: Oxford University Press. Reprinted by Floris Books of Edinburgh in 2009.

Oqyana. 2009. Website for Oqyana Resort. http://www.oqyana.com (accessed February 25, 2010).

Orr, Julian E. 1996. *Talking About Machines: The Ethnography of a Modern Job.* Ithaca, New York: Cornell University Press.

Oths, Kathryn S. and Servando Z. Hinojosa (eds.). 2004. *Healing by Hand: Manual Medicine and Bonesetting in Global Perspective.* Walnut Creek, CA: Altamira Press.

Padden, Carol A. and Tom L. Humphries. 2006. *Inside Deaf Culture.* Cambridge, MA: Harvard University Press.

Petryna, Adriana. 2002. *Life Exposed: Biological Citizens after Chernobyl.* Princeton, NJ: Princeton University Press.

Pfeiffer, John E. 1982. *The Creative Explosion: An Inquiry into the Origins of Art and Religion.* New York: Harper & Row.

Philippe, Alexandre. 2004. *Earthlings: Ugly Bags of Mostly Water.* Documentary film. Denver, CO: SONEW Productions and Mostly Water Productions.

Phull, Hardeep. 2008. *Story Behind the Protest Song: A Reference Guide to the 50 Songs that Changed the 20th Century.* Santa Barbara, CA: Greenwood.

Pica, Pierre, Cathy Lemer, Véronique Izard, and Stanislas Dehaene. 2004. "Exact and approximate arithmetic in an Amazonian indigene group." *Science* 306(5695):499–503. DOI 10.1126/science.1102085.

Pinker, Steven. 1997. *How the Mind Works.* New York: W. W. Norton.

Pirog, Rich and Andrew Benjamin. 2003. "Checking the food odometer: Comparing food miles for local versus conventional produce sales to Iowa institutions." A publication of the Leopold Center for Sustainable Agriculture, Iowa State University, July. http://www.leopold.iastate.edu/pubs/staff/files/food_travel072103.pdf (accessed January 30, 2010).

Plum Creek. 2010. http://www.plumcreektx.com (accessed February 17).

Pollan, Michael. 2008. *In Defense of Food: An Eater's Manifesto.* New York: Penguin Press.

Pool, Robert and Wenzel Geissler. 2005. *Medical Anthropology: Understanding Public Health.* New York: Open University Press.

Popenoe, David. 2005. "Marriage and family: What does the Scandinavian experience tell us?" In Barbara Dafoe Whitehead and David Popenoe (eds.), *The State of Our Unions: The Social Health of Marriage in America*, pp. 6–14. National Marriage Project. http://www.virginia.edu/marriageproject/pdfs/SOOU2005.pdf (accessed February 7, 2010).

Prosterman, Roy. 1972. *Surviving to 3000: An Introduction to the Study of Lethal Conflict.* Belmont, CA: Duxbury Press.

Putnam, Robert D. 2001. *Bowling Alone: The Collapse and Revival of American Community.* New York: Simon & Schuster.

Quinn, Daniel. 1992. *Ishmael: An Adventure of the Mind and Spirit.* New York: Bantam Books.

Raphael, Dana. 1979. "Margaret Mead—a tribute." *The Lactation Review* 4(1):1–3.

Rapp, Rayna. 2000. *Testing Women, Testing the Fetus: The Social Impact of Amniocentesis in America.* New York: Routledge.

Reese, Debbie. 2000. "A parenting manual, with words of advice for Puritan mothers." In Judy S. DeLoache and Alma Gottlieb (eds.), *A World of Babies: Imagined Childcare Guides for Seven Societies,* pp. 29–54. Cambridge, MA: Cambridge University Press.

Research Council of Norway and World Science Staff. 2006. "Oldest known ritual: Python worship, archaeologist says." http://www.world-science.net/othernews/061130_python.htm (accessed January 19, 2009).

Reznikoff, Iegor. 2002. "Prehistoric paintings, sound and rocks." In E. Hickmann et al. (eds.), *Studien zur Musikarchäologie*, vol. 3, pp. 39–56. Papers from the 2nd Symposium of the International Study Group on Music Archaeology, Monastery Michaelstein, Rahden, Germany, September 2000.

Reznikoff, Iegor. 2005. "On primitive elements of musical meaning." *Journal of Music and Meaning* 3(Fall 2004/Winter 2005), sec. 2.

Reznikoff, Iegor. 2008. "Sound resonance in prehistoric times: A study of Paleolithic painted caves and rocks." Paper presented at Acoustics 08 Paris. *Journal of the Acoustical Society of America.* http://intellagence.eu.com/acoustics2008/cd1/data/articles/000892.pdf (accessed February 13, 2010).

Riddle, Jimmie and Jackie Phelps. 1969. "Eephing and hamboning on *Hee Haw.*" http://www.youtube.com/watch?v=OVe6ZKKi3qk (accessed February 13, 2010).

Ridington, Robin. 1995. "Braided stories: Encounters with 'The Real Omaha.'" In Bruce Grindal and Frank Salamone (eds.), *Bridges to Humanity: Narratives on Anthropology and Friendship*, pp. 131–145. Long Grove, IL: Waveland Press.

Ro, Hee-Kyung and K. A. Dettwyler. 1995. "Comparisons of infant feeding patterns of Koreans living in Texas, USA and local populations." *Korean Journal of Nutrition* 28(7):636–643.

Rogers, Andrew. 2010. *Rhythms of Life.* http://www.andrewrogers.org/.

Rosenberg, Karen R. and Wenda R. Trevathan. 2003. "The evolution of human birth." *Scientific American* 13:80–85.

Rosenberg, Karen R. and Wenda Trevathan. 1995. "Bipedalism and human birth: The obstetrical dilemma revisited." *Evolutionary Anthropology* 4(5):161–168.

Rothman, Barbara Katz. 1986. *The Tentative Pregnancy.* New York: Viking Press.

Rozin, Elizabeth. 1992. *Ethnic Cuisine: How to Create the Authentic Flavors of Over 30 International Cuisines.* New York: Penguin.

Rubin, Henry Alex and Dana Adam Shapiro. 2005. *Murderball.* Documentary film. Produced by Paramount Pictures.

Rush, Ed and George Cromarty. 1962. "Plastic Jesus," on the album *Here They Are! The Goldcoast Singers.* Additional lyrics added later by Ernie Marrs. www.guntheranderson.com/v/data/plastic0.htm (accessed February 11, 2010).

Schenone, Laura. 2008. *The Lost Ravioli Recipes of Hoboken: A Search for Food and Family.* New York: W. W. Norton.

Scheper-Hughes, Nancy. 1993. *Death without Weeping: The Violence of Everyday Life in Brazil.* Berkeley: University of California Press.

Schneider, Harold K. 1979. *Livestock and Equality in East Africa: The Economic Basis for Social Structure.* Bloomington: Indiana University Press.

Schön, Regine A. and Maarit Silvén. 2007. "Natural parenting—back to basics in infant care." *Evolutionary Psychology* 5(1):102–183. http://www.epjournal.net (accessed February 27, 2010).

Sforza, Teri. 2006. *The {Strangest} Song: One Father's Quest to Help His Daughter Find Her Voice.* Amherst, NY: Prometheus.

Sharma, Devinder. 2005. "Patently unfair: Rice in a private grip." Share the World's Resources (STWR) www.stwr.org/food-security-agriculture/patently-unfair-rice-in-private-grip.html (accessed February 6, 2010).

Shepherd, Robert J. 2007. *When Culture Goes to Market: Space, Place, and Identity in an Urban Marketplace.* New York: Peter Lang.

Sieber, Roy and Frank Herreman (eds.). 2000. *Hair in African Art and Culture.* Munich and New York: Prestel.

Silverstein, Elliot (director). 1970. *A Man Called Horse.* Cinema Center Films.

Silvester, Hans. 2009. *Natural Fashion: Tribal Decoration in Africa.* London: Thames & Hudson.

Simopoulos, Artemis P., J. E. Dutra de Oliveira, and I. D. Desai (eds.). 1995. *Behavioral and Metabolic Aspects of Breastfeeding: International Trends.* Basel, Switzerland: S. Karger.

Singer, Merrill and Hans A. Baer (eds.). 2009. *Killer Commodities: Public Health and the Corporate Production of Harm.* Lanham, MD: Altamira Press.

Slab City. 2010. http://www.slabcity.org (accessed January 28).

Smith, Alison, Paul Watkiss, Geoff Tweddle, et al. 2005. *The Validity of Food Miles as an Indicator of Sustainable Development: Final Report produced for DEFRA.* ED50254, Issue 7, July. http://www.wildchicken.com/grow/defra%20foodmiles%20execsumm.pdf (accessed July 8, 2010).

Smithsonian Institution. 2010. Smithsonian Folkways. "Our mission and history." http://www.folkways.si.edu/about/_us/mission_history.aspx (accessed July 8).

Soden, Garrett. 2005. *Defying Gravity: Land Divers, Roller Coasters, Gravity Bums, and the Human Obsession with Falling.* New York: W. W. Norton. Originally published in 2003 as *Falling: How Our Greatest Fear Became Our Greatest Thrill: A History.*

Steward, Julian H. 1938[1970]. *Basin-Plateau Aboriginal Sociopolitical Groups.* Smithsonian Institution, Bureau of American Ethnology, Bulletin 120, 1938. Reprinted in 1970 by University of Utah Press, Salt Lake City.

Stoller, Paul and Cheryl Olkes. 1989. *In Sorcery's Shadow: A Memoir of Apprenticeship among the Songhay of Niger.* Chicago: University of Chicago Press.

Strassman, Beverly I. 1997. "The biology of menstruation in *Homo sapiens*: Total lifetime menses, fecundity, and nonsynchrony in a natural-fertility population." *Current Anthropology* 38(1):123–129.

Sustainable Urban Gardens. 2007–2008. http://www.sacgardens.org/ (accessed January 28, 2010).

Swidey, Neil. 2005. "What makes people gay?" *The Boston Globe*, August 14. http://www.boston.com/news/globe/magazine/articles/2005/08/14/what_makes_people_gay/ (accessed July 9, 2010).

The Farm. 2010. http://www.thefarm.org (accessed February 17).

Trei, Lisa. 2006. "Martu art exhibit reveals relationship with ancestral lands." *Stanford University News.* July 12, 2006. http://news-service.stanford.edu/news/2006/july12/aborigine-071206.html (accessed January 28, 2010).

Trevathan, Wenda R. 1987. *Human Birth: An Evolutionary Perspective.* New York: Aldine de Gruyter.

Tri-State Bird Rescue and Research. http://www.tristatebird.org (accessed October 25, 2010).

Turner, Edith, with William Blodgett, Singleton Kahona, and Fideli Benwa. 1992. *Experiencing Ritual: A New Interpretation of African Healing.* Philadelphia: University of Pennsylvania Press.

Tuva Throat Singers. 2007. Documentary film. Produced by Journeyman Pictures in October 2007. www.YouTube.com/watch?v=xw9hizi5heM (accessed February 13, 2010).

Tylor, Edward Burnett. 1920[1871]. *Primitive Culture: Researches into the Development of Mythology, Philosophy, Religion, Language, Art, and Custom,* 6th edition. New York: G. P. Putnam's Sons.

UCSC. 2008. "Campus mascot: How the Banana Slugs became UCSC's official mascot." http://www.ucsc.edu/about/campus_mascot.asp (accessed February 11, 2010).

Unitarian Universalist Association of Congregations. 1996–2010. http://www.uua.org (accessed February 11, 2010).

United Nations Development Report. 2009. http://www.undp.org (accessed February 27, 2010).

Usborne, David. 2004. "Tragic end of the boy who was brought up as a girl." *The Independent,* May 12. http://www.independent.co.uk/news/world/americas/tragic-end-of-the-boy-who-was-brought-up-as-a-girl-563086.html (accessed February 13, 2010).

Vaillant, John. 2005. *The Golden Spruce: A True Story of Myth, Madness, and Greed.* New York: W. W. Norton.

van Gennep, Arnold. 1960. *The Rites of Passage.* Chicago: University of Chicago Press.

van Voorst, Arno. 2006. "On scaffolds and sweet potatoes." www.in-mind.org/issue-1/on-scaffolds-and-sweet-potatoes-39.html (accessed January 27, 2010).

Vietnam Veterans Memorial, The. 2010. The Wall-USA. http://thewall-usa.com/ (accessed February 11).

Virgili, Fabrice. 2002. *Shorn Women: Gender and Punishment in Liberation France.* New York: Berg.

Wahlman, Maude Southwell. 2001. *Signs and Symbols: African Images in African American Quilts.* Atlanta, GA: Tinwood Books.

Walker, Marsha. 2007. *Still Selling Out Mothers and Babies: Marketing of Breast Milk Substitutes in the USA.* Weston, MA: National Alliance for Breastfeeding Advocacy.

Weygand, Zina. 2009. *The Blind in French Society from the Middle Ages to the Century of Louis Braille.* Stanford, CA: Stanford University Press.

"What is modern slavery?" 2010. Anti-Slavery International, London. http://www.antislavery.org/english/slavery_today/what_is_modern_slavery.aspx (accessed February 9).

Whitehead, Barbara Dafoe and David Popenoe (eds.). 2005. *The State of Our Unions: The Social Health of Marriage in America.* National Marriage Project. http://www.virginia.edu/marriageproject/pdfs/SOOU2005.pdf (accessed February 7, 2010).

Williamson, Ray A. 1984. *Living the Sky: The Cosmos of the American Indian.* Boston: Houghton Mifflin.

Wladarsch, Evelyn. 2005. *Time–Health–Culture: Cultural Time Concepts and Health-related Time Preferences in Burkina Faso.* Berlin: Reimer.

World Health Organization. 1980. *International Classification of Impairments, Disabilities, and Handicaps (ICIDH): A Manual of Classifications Relating to the Consequences of Disease.* Geneva, Switzerland: WHO.

World Health Organization. 1998. *The Tobacco Epidemic: A Crisis of Startling Dimensions.* Geneva, Switzerland: WHO.

World Health Organization. 2003. "Global strategy for infant and young child feeding." http://www.who.int/nutrition/topics/global_strategy/en/index.html (accessed July 9, 2010).

World Health Organization. 2008. *Report on the Global Tobacco Epidemic, 2008—Fresh and Alive. The MPOWER Package.* Geneva, Switzerland: WHO.

World Health Organization. 2009. "Baby-friendly hospital initiative." http://www.who.int/nutrition/topics/bfhi/en/index.html (accessed February 6, 2010).

World POP Clock Projection. 2010. www.census.gov/ipc/www/popclockworld.html (accessed February 27).

Worth, Jennifer. 2002. *The Midwife: A Memoir of Birth, Joy, and Hard Times.* New York: Thorndike Press.

Yahoo! 2010. http://babelfish.yahoo.com/translate_txt (accessed July 12).

Yuan, Lu. 2000. "Land of the walking marriage." *Natural History* 109(9):58–65. http://findarticles.com/p/articles/mi_m1134/is_9_109/ai_67410989 (accessed February 5, 2010).

Zaslavsky, C. 1973. *Africa Counts: Number and Pattern in African Culture.* Boston: Prindle, Weber, and Schmidt.

Index

437

Photo Credits

p. 59 (top left) Tanya Thomas, US Army; p. 109 (left) Steve Evans; p. 126 (top left) Bartholomew Dean, 1988; p. 126 (top right) Tabea Huth; p. 126 (bottom left) Hans Hillewaert; p. 127 (left) Joe Mabel; p. 133 (top right) C. H. Graves; p. 133 (bottom) Mila Zinkova; p. 141 Frank and Frances Carpenter Collection, Library of Congress; call no. Lot 11453-3, no. 7; p. 150 Salim Fadhley from London UK; p. 161 (top) Dorothy Voorhees; p. 163 (left) David Shankbone; p. 171 (left) Thomas & Joanna Ainscough; p. 178 Karen Dettwyler; p. 187 (right) Martin Dürrschnabel; p. 202 (right) Rick Drdul; p. 214 (left) 710928003; p. 214 (right) Paul; p. 217 Alexander Stübner; p. 218 (left) © European Union, 2004–2011; p. 218 (right) Loozrboy; p. 220 (bottom right) April Sikorski; p. 224 (right) Gerard Barrau; p. 231 (top center) Aimaimyi; p. 231 (middle right) Nehrams2020; p. 232 Starol; p. 237 (center) Tom Maisey; p. 232 (bottom) Library of Congress National Child Labor Committee Collection; p. 248 (left) Frank C. Miller; p. 248 (right) Túrelio; p. 252 (top) Photo generously provided by Mark Hamilton; p. 255 Tomascastelazo; p. 261 (top center) Ben Schumin; p. 261 (top right) Hmm. . . ; p. 262 jankie; p. 263 Philipp Salzgeber; p. 266 (top right) Matthew Logelin; p. 270 (middle center) Marco Schmidt; p. 270 (bottom right) Dbu; p. 276 Franz Luthi; p. 277 (left) Yurgan Vishujoyshe; p. 277 (right) Bantosh; p. 277 (bottom) FishOil at en.wikipedia; p. 287 (top) Paul M. Walsh; p. 287 (bottom) Joe Mabel; p. 290 Mizu basyo at ja.wikipedia; p. 293 (top right) Thomas Schoch; p. 293 (bottom left) Matthias Kabel; p. 294 (top) Figuura; p. 294 (bottom) Fred Jala; p. 303 (top left) revolution cycle; p. 303 (bottom left) haabet2003; p. 310 (top) Wouter Hagens; p. 315 (top right) Jeremy Farmer; p. 315 (middle left) Lalupa; p. 322 (bottom right) John Leslie; p. 325 (bottom) NASA; p. 327 (top left) Pasteur; p. 333 (bottom) NASA; p. 336 (top left) Böhringer Friedrich; p. 336 (top right) Taguelmoust; p. 340 (top left) Hamed Saber; p. 345 (top left) Mauritsv; p. 345 (top right) Nicor; p. 357 (middle left) Noodle snacks; p. 357 (middle right) Rosco; p. 363 Marie-Claire Lefébure; p. 365 (left) Dan Hughes; p. 367 (top right) SONGMY; p. 367 (middle) Johntex; p. 370 © Gil Azouri; p. 380 Library of Congress Prints and Photographs Division. Benjamin K. Edwards Baseball Card Collection. No. bbc.0383f; p. 393 Mariko GODA; p. 397 (top right) John Schanlaub; p. 397 (bottom right) Davidmoerike; p. 398 (right) Maude Wahlman; p. 403 Roman Bonnefox; p. 405 (top) Smbdh; p. 419 (middle left) David Bicchetti; p. 419 (middle right) Bethanie Hines, courtesy of Angel Kyodo Williams; p. 419 (right) Alan Light; p. 420 (top left) Tim Schapker; p. 420 (top right) NicholasJB; p. 420 (bottom left) Toksave; p. 420 (bottom right) Bogomolov.PL; p. 421 (right) A: Tim Schapker; B: NicholasJB; C: Toksave; D: Bogomo12.4.BDavej1006; p. 424 (left) Ian Mutto; p. 424 (right) Gert Holmertz.